Visual Basic

Annotated Archives

ABOUT THE AUTHORS ...

David Jung has been programming on personal computers since the early 1980s. A graduate of California State Polytechnic University, Pomona, David has a bachelor of science degree in business administration emphasizing computer information systems. His development expertise is in architecting and constructing cross-platform client/server and distributed database solutions using Visual Basic, Java, Access, SQL Server, Oracle, DB2, and Internet technology.

He is a member of the Pasadena IBM Users Group's technical staff and leads its Visual Basic Special Interest Group. He is also a frequent speaker at seminars and users groups showing how Visual Basic, Java, and Internet technology can be integrated into business solutions.

David has co-authored a number of books on Visual Basic from introductory and reference titles to client/server titles. He also currently writes for Sys-Con Publications' *Java Developers Journal* and Advisor Publications' *e-Business Advisor*.

When he's not programming, writing, and presenting, David can be found on bike trails and golf courses in Southern California, and spending time with his wife, Joanne, and their two dogs (that he pretends he likes).

Jeff Kent is an assistant professor of computer science at Los Angeles Valley College in Valley Glen, California. He teaches a number of programming languages, including C, C++, Java, and Assembler, but his favorite is Visual Basic.

Jeff has had a varied career, or careers. He graduated from UCLA with a bachelor of science degree in economics, then obtained a juris doctor degree from Loyola (Los Angeles) School of Law, and went on to practice law. During this time, when personal computers still were a gleam in Bill Gates' eye, Jeff also was a professional chess master, earning a third place finish in the United States Under-21 Championship, and later, an international title. These days, however, Jeff's focus is on computers. In addition to teaching and other college duties, he also manages a Windows NT network for a Los Angeles law firm and, of course, writes. His current interest is the integration of programming languages, applications such as the Microsoft Office suite, and the Internet technologies, to provide solutions for businesses, particularly professional services firms.

Jeff, like his co-author, belongs to the Pasadena IBM Users Group and its Visual Basic Special Interest Group, at which he speaks when they get desperate for speakers.

Jeff does find time to spend with his wife, Devvie, which is not difficult since she also is a computer science professor at Valley College. He also bikes and roller-blades with his daughters, Elise and Emily, who describe him as a stork on skates. His goal is to resume running marathons, since he feels the ability to run fast and far can be important to a programmer, particularly when the program does not work.

Visual Basic

Annotated Archives

David Jung and Jeff Kent

Osborne/**McGraw-Hill**

Berkeley   New York   St. Louis   San Francisco   Auckland   Bogotá
Hamburg   London   Madrid   Mexico City   Milan   Montreal   New Delhi
Panama City   Paris   São Paulo   Singapore   Sydney   Tokyo   Toronto

Osborne/**McGraw-Hill**
2600 Tenth Street
Berkeley, California 94710
U.S.A.

For information on translations or book distributors outside the U.S.A., or to arrange bulk purchase discounts for sales promotions, premiums, or fund-raisers, please contact Osborne/**McGraw-Hill** at the above address.

Visual Basic Annotated Archives

1234567890 DOC DOC 90198765432109

ISBN 0-07-882502-4

Publisher	**Proofreader**
Brandon A. Nordin	Paul Tyler
Associate Publisher and	**Indexer**
Editor-in-Chief	Jack Lewis
Scott Rogers	**Computer Designers**
Acquisitions Editor	Roberta Steele
Wendy Rinaldi	Ann Sellers
Project Editor	**Illustrators**
Madhu Prasher	Beth Young
Editorial Assistant	Bob Hansen
Monika Faltiss	**Series Design**
Technical Editor	Roberta Steele
Bob Noble	Peter Hancik
Copy Editor	**Cover Design**
Claire Splan	Regan Honda

I would like to dedicate this book to my wife, Joanne. Without her love and support, I couldn't accomplish all that I have.
—David Jung

I would like to dedicate this book to my family: my wife Devvie, my daughters Elise and Emily, my brother Brian, my mom Beatrice Kent, and my dad Arnold Kent, who, while no longer with us, lives in our minds and thoughts every day.
—Jeff Kent

Contents at a Glance

PART 3
The Internet and Distributed Computing

Contents

PART 1

User Interface

PART 2

Business Objects

PART 3

The Internet and Distributed Computing

Acknowledgments

Our heartfelt thanks to Wendy Rinaldi, without whose help, guidance, and patience this book in the Annotated Archives series would not exist. We especially appreciate her understanding when we said, "We just need one more day." Monika Faltiss and Madhu Prasher also played an important part in getting this book into print.

Thanks to Claire Splan and Bob Noble for wading through mounds of pages of our manuscript and keeping our writing as honest as it could possibly be.

There are a lot of other talented people behind the scenes who also helped to get this book out the door, and like in an Academy Awards speech, we're bound to forget to mention them. That doesn't mean we don't appreciate all their hard work, because we do.

Many thanks to Sean Alexander and David Mendlen, as well as the entire Microsoft Visual Basic division for continually enhancing this amazing product.

David would like to personally give thanks to his co-author, Jeff Kent, for his constant encouragement. He would also like to give thanks to his friends and family for putting up with him during the writing of this book and understanding that he "couldn't come out and play." As strange as it may sound, he'd like to thank his dogs for always showing up with toys to provide a good distraction from coding. But most importantly, he would like to thank his wife, Joanne, for her enduring love and support. As crazy as it has gotten, she was always there with positive encouragement and support (and understood when I couldn't take the dogs for their walk).

Jeff would like to personally give thanks to his co-author, David Jung, without whom Jeff never would have become involved with this book. He also would like to thank his family for putting up with his highs and lows during the trials and tribulations of this book, and for not having him committed when he talks about writing his "next" book.

Introduction

We did not write this book as a road to riches or fame. We are misguided, but not that misguided. We wrote this book because we believe it fills a need. There already are many good "how to" and reference books, and unfortunately also many bad rehashes of Microsoft Visual Basic manuals. However, there are relatively few books that focus on advanced Visual Basic topics such as the Windows API, subclassing, ActiveX and Internet programming, and transaction processing development. Perhaps the reason is a belief that the market for an "advanced" Visual Basic book is too small. However, these topics, advanced or not, are integral to the arsenal of a professional Visual Basic programmer, and also someone who aspires to be one.

This book is part of Osborne/McGraw-Hill's "Annotated Archives" series. A hallmark of this series is thorough annotations of code. Textbooks often comprehensively annotate code to assist the student's learning of new concepts. Unfortunately, few "trade" books adopt this approach, though many readers, such as students, are reading the book to learn something new. Additionally, most of us have had the frustrating experience of being stymied by an unexplained line of code. Comprehensive annotations may not eliminate this possibility, but they certainly lessen it.

Another hallmark of Osborne/McGraw-Hill's "Annotated Archives" series is that the code examples can be put to practical use; therefore, many of the examples demonstrate the use of Visual Basic in real-world situations. However, the examples do not purport to exemplify the one "right" way. To the contrary, in Visual Basic, as in most programming languages, there is more than one way to do something. Which of the alternatives is the best will vary depending on the situation. Indeed, the annotations often explain why the programmer followed a particular alternative, and the circumstances under which another alternative would be preferable.

The combination of the subject matter covered by the book and the approach of thoroughly annotated code intrigued us enough to risk the anger of neglected spouses and other dangers and write this book for you, the Visual Basic programmer. Which leads to the next subject.

WHO THIS BOOK IS FOR

This book is for anyone who will pay for it! Just kidding, though no buyers will be turned away. Actually, we wrote this book so it will be useful to all Visual Basic programmers.

Given the advanced nature of the book's topics, it is easy to envision how this book would benefit advanced-level programmers. This book also will help intermediate-level programmers bring their skills up to an advanced level. But how can a book that discusses advanced topics also benefit beginning-level programmers?

The answer is twofold. First, studying code which is well-written (if we do say so ourselves) and object-oriented will teach a beginning-level programmer to write well-written, object-oriented code. By learning good habits, bad habits need not be unlearned. Second, the programming concepts that are discussed are equally applicable to simple projects as they are to complex ones.

To put it simply, if you program in Visual Basic, then you will find this book useful.

HOW TO USE THIS BOOK

This book is divided into three parts, "User Interface" (Chapters 1-7), "Business Objects" (Chapters 8-13), and "The Internet and Distributed Computing" (Chapters 14-15). While there is a progression from one chapter to another in a given part, each chapter is self-contained. Therefore, you are able to go straight to any chapter without having to read a previous one. Within a chapter, some exercises build on previous ones, so it may be a good idea to go through a given chapter from the start rather than attempting to jump into the middle.

All of the projects can be copied from the CD-ROM (see the section "Using the CD-ROM"). In many cases, the code can be used as is, but there will be some cases where you will have to make some modifications to suit your situation or system configuration. Regardless, be sure to read the annotations, not only to understand how the code works, but also because where applicable, the annotations include possible procedure modifications and updates.

CONVENTIONS IN THIS BOOK

The code for each example appears twice. First, the code appears in its entirety. Next, the code is annotated, one logical section at a time.

Because of the line-length limit within the book's printed page, the display of the code is limited to 69 characters per line. This limit may affect the look of the code on the page, but we can assure you that the code still runs. Any splitting of a line of code lines follows the Visual Basic line continuation convention. The line continuation convention is a space and an underscore at the end of one code line to be concatenated with the following code line. The code found in the project on the CD-ROM also follows the same line breaks and conventions, so the code you see on the printed page should be identical to the code on the CD-ROM.

All Visual Basic keywords are highlighted in **bold**. Variables, function parameters, control names, and so on are formatted in different ways, such as by being italicized.

USING THE CD-ROM

In the CD-ROM directory structure, each directory contains all of the code and support files relevant to that chapter.

All of the projects assume the following:

- ◆ You are running Windows 95, 98, or NT.

- ◆ You are running Visual Basic 6.0 Professional or Enterprise Editions. Some of the projects were tested using version 5.0 of Visual Basic, but we make no guarantees that the projects are compatible with version 5.0.

- ◆ For some examples, you will need Personal Web Server (Windows 95/98 systems) or Internet Information Server (Windows NT system) installed with the Microsoft Transaction Server and Microsoft Message Queue.

- ◆ All the database examples are stored in Microsoft Access 97 data files.

The latest version of all projects, examples, and support files can be found on the Web site **http://www.vb2java.com**.

CONTACTING THE AUTHORS

We enthusiastically welcome gushing praise. We also are receptive to comments, suggestions, and yes, even criticism. The best way to contact us is via e-mail; you can use books@vb2java.com. Alternatively, visit our Web site, **http://www.vb2java.com**, which contains resources and updated information about the scripts and contents of this book.

We hope you enjoy this book as much as we enjoyed writing it.

User Interface

Getting Control of Your Form

Centering a Form (CenterForm.vbp)

Controlling the Resizing of a Form
   (Resize.vbp)

Controlling the Movement of a Form
   (LimitMove.vbp)

Forms are the most common user interface element in Visual Basic. Indeed, new Visual Basic projects by default start with a Form1. While Version 6 of Visual Basic support windowless UserControls, it is difficult even to conceptualize an application that does not use a form. Forms literally are the window through which application users view information and interact with the application.

Visual Basic provides numerous built-in properties, methods, and events for forms. Often these properties, methods, and events are sufficient for the purposes of your application. However, the built-in functionality of Visual Basic forms has limitations. If the demands of the application require you to go beyond those limitations, then you have to go beyond Visual Basic and plunge into the wonderful world of dynamic link libraries, the Windows 32 API, and subclassing. While the degree of difficulty is increased, so are the rewards. Besides, if programming powerful Visual Basic applications were easy, everyone would be doing it.

This chapter will demonstrate how to control the position, movement, and resizing of forms far more precisely than possible with the built-in functionality of Visual Basic. It also will be the starting point for the techniques demonstrated in the subsequent chapters. Let the adventure begin!

Centering a Form

CenterForm.vbp

Centering a form at run-time is a typical application task. While this task is not difficult to do correctly, the code suggested in texts and other sources often is inadequate.

Visual Basic forms do have a **StartUpPosition** property. The available settings and corresponding constants and values are set forth in Table 1-1.

While the **StartUpPosition** property is easy to use, the options it makes available are limited. It can only be used to specify the position of the form when it *first* appears. It cannot be used for any subsequent change in the form's position. Additionally, the values of the **StartUpPosition** property are limited to those stated in Table 1-1. The **StartUpPosition** property cannot be used, for example, to center the form on the desktop, which is the portion of the screen not including the taskbar. Furthermore, if you are running Visual Basic 5.0 in SDI Development Environment

Constant	Value	Description
VbStartUpManual	0	No initial setting specified.
VbStartUpOwner	1	Center on the item to which the UserForm belongs.
VbStartUpScreen	2	Center on the whole screen.
VbStartUpWindowsDefault	3	Position in upper-left corner of screen.

TABLE 1-1.   **StartUpPosition** Settings

mode and have a form with a menu, a known bug in Visual Basic will change **StartUpPosition** to manual when the form is run regardless of its previous setting.

Visual Basic forms have, in addition to a **StartUpPosition** property, **Left**, **Top**, **Width,** and **Height** properties which may be used in centering. The form's position is determined by its **Left** and **Top** properties. The **Left** property is the distance between the internal left edge of the form and the left edge of its container. In our first examples, the container will be the screen. Usually (though not always), the value of the x coordinate of the left edge of the screen is 0, so the value of the **Left** property typically would be the x coordinate of the internal left edge of the form.

The **Top** property is the distance between the internal top edge of the form and the top edge of its container. Therefore, in our first examples in which the screen is the container, the value of the **Top** property is the y coordinate of the internal top edge of the form.

The form's size is determined by its **Width** and **Height** properties. These properties define, respectively, the form's external width and height (including its borders and title bar).

These properties appear straightforward and they are, but there is a trap for the unwary. In Windows screen coordinates and measurements are expressed in pixels. The word *pixel* is short for "picture element," a dot that represents the smallest graphic unit of measurement on a screen. In Visual Basic, by contrast, screen coordinates and measurements are expressed in twips. A *twip* is a unit of screen measurement equal to 1/20 of a printer's point. There are approximately 1,440 twips to a logical inch or 567 twips to a logical centimeter (the length of a screen item measuring one inch or one centimeter when printed). Care must be taken not to provide a value in twips to a function which is expecting the value in pixels, or vice versa. This issue will arise and be handled in the code for this example.

CENTERING ON THE SCREEN

Centering a form on the screen is the simplest of the centering scenarios and therefore best illustrates the basic logic. To center a form horizontally on a screen, the form's left edge would be positioned at one-half the difference between the width of the screen and the width of the form. This would automatically position the right edge of the form at the same distance (that is, 50% of the difference between the width of the screen and the width of the form) from the right side of the screen, thereby centering the form horizontally. Determining the width of the screen is easy because, in Visual Basic, the screen is an object (called **Screen**, of course) which, like a form, has a **Width** (and a **Height**) property.

Putting this logic into code terms, a form is centered horizontally by setting its **Left** property to one-half the difference between the **Width** property of the **Screen** and the **Width** property of the variable representing the form being centered. Similarly, a form is centered vertically by setting its **Top** property to one-half the

difference between the **Height** property of the **Screen** and the **Height** property of
the form variable. This logic suggests the following often-used subroutine:

```
Public Sub CenterForm(frm As Form)
   frm.Left = (Screen.Width - frm.Width) / 2
   frm.Top = (Screen.Height - frm.Height) / 2
End Sub
```

This subroutine then could be called from any form with the statement:

```
CenterForm Me
```

However, this subroutine, while it will center a form on the screen, is not the best.
Since its execution involves two steps, on a system with a slow processor or video
the user might see the form shift position first horizontally (as the ".**Left** =" code is
executed), then vertically (as the ".**Top** =" code is executed).

The subroutine can be improved by using the **Move** method. This method takes
four parameters, *left*, *top*, *width*, and *height*, respectively. These parameters
correspond to the properties of the same name. Only the first parameter is required,
the others being optional and, if not specified, remaining unchanged from their
prior values. If an optional parameter is to be specified, then, as with use of the
Optional keyword, all optional parameters appearing before the specified optional
parameter also must be specified. For example, if *width* is to be specified, then *left*
and *top* also must be specified, but *height* does not need to be specified.

With the **Move** method, both horizontal and vertical repositioning may be
performed in one statement:

```
frm.Move = (Screen.Width - frm.Width)/2,
   (Screen.Height - frm.Height)/2
```

Using the **Move** method eliminates the problem of the user seeing two form
movements instead of one and also executes faster. However, once again there are
traps for the unwary. First, when executing a **Move** method on a form, Visual Basic
expects the values of the parameters to relate to twips. If the values instead relate to
pixels, the result probably will not be what was intended.

Additionally, executing the **Move** method on a form which is minimized will
cause an error. Whether a form is minimized, maximized, or normal can be
determined by the form's **WindowState** property (see Table 1-2).

Using the **Move** method and checking the **WindowState** property results in the
following improved code:

```
Public Sub CenterForm(frm As Form)
   If Me.WindowState = vbNormal Then _
      frm.Move = (Screen.Width - frm.Width)/2, _
          (Screen.Height - frm.Height)/2
End Sub
```

Value	Constant	Description
0	VbNormal	Normal window
1	VbMimimized	Minimized window
2	VbMaximized	Maximized window

TABLE 1-2. Values of **WindowState** Property

The **Move** method usually would be used only if the form's **WindowState** property is **vbNormal**, since you normally would not be concerned about centering a maximized form. If you had this concern, then the test would be **Me.WindowState <> vbMinimized**.

OTHER CENTERING SCENARIOS

The previous subroutines assume the container is the screen. However, the task may be to center a dialog box on its containing form or a MDI (multiple document interface) child form on the parent form. The logic used above when the container was the screen also will work for these scenarios. The width and height of the containing form simply is substituted for that of the screen.

A more complicated scenario involves, once again, centering on the screen. However, this time the task is to center the form on the portion of the screen which does not include the taskbar that may be present in a Windows 95, 98, or NT environment. This task, while more complex (and discussed in detail below), nevertheless uses the same logic as the other scenarios. The code first determines the width and height of the container area (here the desktop area other than the taskbar). The code then invokes the **Move** method to reposition the form so that its **Left** property is one-half the difference between the container area's **Width** property and the form's **Width** property and its **Top** property is one-half the difference between the container area's **Height** property and the form's **Height** property.

Different procedures could be written for each scenario. However, this not only makes your code less reusable by fragmenting it among different procedures, but also introduces the potential complication of the logic of one procedure being affected by the logic of another procedure. That the code for these scenarios shares the same logic suggests writing the code in a single module which addresses the various scenarios in a consistent manner. To enhance the reusability of this code component, it will be written as a class module, which will be called clsCenterForm.

SYNOPSIS OF CODE

The CenterForm class concludes by using the **Move** method to reposition the form with the logic discussed above of using one-half the difference between the container area's width and height and the form's width and height. The work done by the code is to determine the width and height of the container area. The first step in doing so is to determine the type of container area involved.

The code first checks if the form is a MDI child. If it is, then the container area is the MDI parent, the assumption being that the parent form already has been centered properly in the manner next discussed.

If the form is not a MDI child (that is, a MDI parent, a stand-alone form, or a dialog box), then the container area is that portion of the desktop area which is not used by the taskbar. The taskbar area is disregarded since, even though it is technically part of the desktop, most users would not consider it part of the "work area."

The code first checks if there is a taskbar. If there is no taskbar, then the container area is the desktop. However, if there is a taskbar, and there usually is in computers running Windows 95, 98, or NT 4, then the code has to determine the dimensions of the taskbar in order to adjust for them in determining the dimensions of the desktop without the taskbar. Of course, there is no certainty that the taskbar is located at the bottom of the desktop, so the code must determine whether the taskbar is located at the top, bottom, left, or right of the screen before performing the adjustment.

Knowing how to determine the visibility and dimensions of the taskbar will become increasingly important in properly centering a form. A taskbar is an appbar. An *appbar* is a shortened term for an application desktop toolbar—a window that attaches itself to an edge of your screen. The taskbar is a window that contains several child windows: the Start button, a notification window (which contains a clock), and a SysTabControl32 common control. The feature that distinguishes an appbar from other windows is that it can always be accessible to the user.

The taskbar is the most common example of an appbar, but it is not the only one. An application can have more than one appbar. An example of an application appbar is the Office shortcut bar (msoffice.exe) in Microsoft Office 95 and 97.

Appbars could be very useful in an application. An appbar could be used to display system information, to launch applications (like the Office shortcut bar), or to start utilities such as a calculator or a phone dialer. As appbars proliferate, it will become increasingly important to determine their visibility and dimensions in order to properly center a form. The following code, while focusing on taskbars, could be adapted to situations involving multiple appbars.

NEED FOR THE WINDOWS API

While the logic of checking for the existence, location, and dimensions of the taskbar is impeccable (if we do say so ourselves), there is one minor problem: Visual Basic has no built-in way of doing this. Visual Basic 5 does include a SysInfo control which can be used to obtain this information. However, this means having to include the control when distributing your application, with all the attendant problems of size, versioning, etc.

There is a better alternative: the Windows API. API stands for "Application Programmer's Interface." In plain English, this means a collection of functions which may be used in programming an application. Both operating systems and applications may have an API. The Windows API simply is a collection of functions that are part of Windows and may be accessed by any Windows application. Since the Windows API functions are guaranteed to exist on every Windows operating system, there is no need to worry about distribution and related issues which arise with custom ActiveX controls.

There is a downside to using the Windows API. It is not easy to use correctly. Additionally, if you do make a mistake, the application may crash, and you, like Ratbert, the computer consultant in Dilbert, may end up explaining to the application user whose unsaved work just got lost, "It's not my fault, it's General Protection's." However, with care, you can tame the Windows API and use its power to go well beyond the limits of Visual Basic.

Two Windows APIs

Actually there are two Windows APIs. One, used by 16-bit operating systems (Windows 3.0, 3.1, 3.11), is referred to as Win16. The other, used by 32-bit operating systems (Windows 95, 98 and NT 3.5x, 4), is referred to as Win32. Since 16-bit operating systems are phasing out, this book will concern itself exclusively with the Win32 API. However, Appendix A will discuss how, with conditional compilation, your code may include the Win16 API as well so your application also may run on 16-bit operating systems.

CODE

```
Private Type RECT
      Left As Long
      Top As Long
      Right As Long
      Bottom As Long
End Type

Private Type APPBARDATA
    cbSize As Long
    hwnd As Long
    uCallbackMessage As Long
    uEdge As Long
    rc As RECT
    lParam As Long
    End Type

    Private Const ABS_AUTOHIDE = &H1
    Private Const ABM_GETSTATE = &H4
    Private Const ABM_GETTASKBARPOS = &H5

Private Declare Function GetDesktopWindow Lib "user32" _
    () As Long

Private Declare Function GetParent Lib "user32" _
    (ByVal hWnd As Long) As Long

Private Declare Function GetClientRect Lib "user32" _
    (ByVal hWnd As Long, lpRect AS RECT) As Long

Private Declare Function SHAppBarMessage Lib "shell32.dll" _
    (ByVal dwMessage As Long, pData As APPBARDATA) As Long

Public Sub CenterForm(Frm As Form)
      Dim ClientRect As RECT
      Dim BarData As APPBARDATA
      Dim X As Variant
      Dim Y As Variant
    If Frm.MDIChild Then
      GetClientRect GetParent(Frm.hWnd), ClientRect
    Else
```

```
      Call GetClientRect(GetDesktopWindow(), ClientRect)
      BarData.cbSize = Len(BarData)
      BarData.hwnd = Frm.hwnd
   If Not SHAppBarMessage(ABM_GETSTATE, BarData) = _
      ABS_AUTOHIDE Then
        Call SHAppBarMessage(ABM_GETTASKBARPOS, BarData)
          If (BarData.rc.Right - BarData.rc.Left) > _
          (BarData.rc.Bottom - BarData.rc.Top) Then
            If BarData.rc.Top <= 0 Then
                ClientRect.Top = ClientRect.Top + _
                    BarData.rc.Bottom
            Else
                ClientRect.Bottom = ClientRect.Bottom - _
                    (BarData.rc.Bottom - BarData.rc.Top)
            End If
     Else
            If BarData.rc.Left <= 0 Then
                ClientRect.Left = ClientRect.Left + _
                 BarData.rc.Right
            Else
                ClientRect.Right = ClientRect.Right - _
                   (BarData.rc.Right - BarData.rc.Left)
            End If
        End If
     End If
   End If
With Frm
     X = (((ClientRect.Right + ClientRect.Left) * _
          Screen.TwipsPerPixelX) - .Width) / 2
     Y = (((ClientRect.Bottom + ClientRect.Top) * _
          Screen.TwipsPerPixelY) - .Height) / 2
     .Move X, Y
End With
End Sub
```

ANNOTATIONS

```
Private Type RECT
      Left As Long
      Top As Long
      Right As Long
      Bottom As Long
End Type
```

The user-defined type RECT holds the x and y coordinates that define the top-left and lower-right corners of a rectangular area. A user-defined type is the Visual Basic equivalent of a structure in C, the language of the Windows API. Indeed, the user-defined type RECT is declared to correspond to a RECT structure which is used by Windows API functions in this program. The use of a Visual Basic user-defined type which corresponds to a C structure used in a Windows API function will be a recurring theme in this and upcoming examples.

User-defined types in class modules must be private. This is just as well, for generally it is good programming practice for variables in a class module to be private.

```
Private Type APPBARDATA
    cbSize As Long
    hwnd As Long
    uCallbackMessage As Long
    uEdge As Long
    rc As RECT
    lParam As Long
End Type
```

This user-defined type corresponds to the APPBARDATA structure used by the API function **SHAppBarMessage** discussed below to obtain information about the existence and dimensions of the taskbar. The APPBARDATA structure contains information about a system appbar message.

The information contained in the APPBARDATA structure will be discussed below when it is used in the code.

```
    Private Const ABS_AUTOHIDE = &H1
    Private Const ABM_GETSTATE = &H4
    Private Const ABM_GETTASKBARPOS = &H5
```

These constants will be used by the API function **SHAppBarMessage**. These values may be obtained by the API Viewer tool, an add-in which comes with Visual Basic. Their meanings and usage will be discussed below when they are used in the code.

```
Private Declare Function GetDesktopWindow Lib "user32" _
    () As Long
Private Declare Function GetParent Lib "user32" _
    (ByVal hWnd As Long) As Long
Private Declare Function GetClientRect Lib "user32" _
    (ByVal hWnd As Long, lpRect As RECT) As Long
Private Declare Function SHAppBarMessage Lib "shell32.dll" _
    (ByVal dwMessage As Long, pData As APPBARDATA) As Long
```

These are the declarations for the Windows API functions used in the class module. Windows API functions must be declared before they are used. The syntax for declaring Windows API functions and the tools Visual Basic provides for creating these declarations are discussed in Appendix A. The purpose of these particular Windows API functions is discussed below.

```
Public Sub CenterForm(Frm As Form)
```

This subroutine will be called to center the form. The subroutine must be public because it will be called outside of the class.

```
Dim ClientRect As RECT
Dim BarData As APPBARDATA
Dim X As Variant
Dim Y As Variant
```

ClientRect is a variable of the RECT user-defined type previously defined in the class. *ClientRect* will hold the left, right, top, and bottom coordinates of the container in which the form will be centered. *BarData* is a variable of the APPBARDATA user-defined type also previously defined in the class. It will be used to process messages concerning the existence and dimensions of the taskbar. X and Y are temporary variables which ultimately will hold the **Left** and **Top** properties to which the form will be moved.

```
If      Frm.MDIChild Then
        GetClientRect GetParent(Frm.hWnd), ClientRect
```

The **MDIChild** property returns true if the form is an MDI child form and is displayed inside the parent MDI form. Otherwise, the property returns false. This test is made because, as discussed in the introductory comments to the code, the code first checks if the form is a MDI child, and if it is, then the container area is the MDI parent, the assumption being that the parent form already has been centered properly.

GetClientRect is a Windows API function which retrieves the upper-left and lower-right coordinates of the window's client area. This function takes two parameters: a handle to the window whose coordinates are being retrieved and the address of the structure to hold the coordinates. A *handle* is a 32-bit integer (long data type in Visual Basic) assigned by the operating system to windows and a number of other objects (for example, bitmaps, fonts, menus) for the purpose of identifying the object.

Since the form being centered is a MDI child, the form whose coordinates are desired, and therefore the form whose handle is needed by the first parameter of **GetClientRect**, is the MDI parent. The trick to obtaining a handle to the MDI parent is first to obtain a handle to the MDI child. Forms, among other Visual Basic objects, have a **hWnd** property which returns a handle to the form. Since the variable *Frm* is the MDI child, the statement **Frm.hWnd** returns the handle to the MDI child. The Windows API function **GetParent** then is used. **GetParent** takes one parameter—the handle to the window whose parent is being sought; that is, the MDI child—and returns the handle of the parent window. Thus, the statement **GetParent(Frm.hWnd)** uses the handle to the MDI child to return a handle to the MDI parent as the first parameter to **GetClientRect**.

The second parameter of **GetClientRect** hold the address of a structure into which the coordinates being retrieved (in this case of the MDI parent) are stored. That structure, which is the second parameter, is *ClientRect*, a variable of the user-defined type RECT. RECT was declared as containing four members, each of the data type long. Thus, RECT has the correct number of members of the correct data type to store the coordinates being retrieved by GetClientRect. This is the first of many examples of the use of a user-defined type which corresponds to a C structure used in a Windows API function.

ClientRect is passed "by address." **ByVal** is the Visual Basic equivalent to passing by value in C, and **ByRef** is the Visual Basic equivalent to passing by address in C. For most Visual Basic data types, **ByRef** is the default, so unless **ByVal** explicitly precedes the variable, the variable is being passed by address. *ClientRect* is passed by address simply by the omission of **ByVal** in front of the *lpRect* variable in the declaration of **GetClientRect**:

```
Private Declare Function GetClientRect Lib "user32" _
    (ByVal hWnd As Long, lpRect As RECT) As Long
```

There are two reasons why *ClientRect* is passed by address. The first reason is a practical one: A user-defined type cannot be passed by value as a single argument. The second reason why *ClientRect* must be passed by address is so the values of its internal variables (Left, Top, Right, and Bottom) may be modified, in this case by the coordinates of the MDI parent.

In summary, if the form being centered is a MDI child, then the *ClientRect* variable will hold the coordinates of its MDI parent.

```
Else
 Call GetClientRect(GetDesktopWindow(), ClientRect)
```

If the form being centered is not a MDI child, then the window whose handle is sought as the first parameter to **GetClientRect** no longer is the MDI parent, but instead the desktop window, in other words, the entire screen. The handle to the desktop window is returned by the aptly named API function **GetDesktopWindow**, which takes no parameters. Thus, at this point *ClientRect* holds the coordinates of the entire desktop, including any taskbar.

```
BarData.cbSize = Len(BarData)
BarData.hwnd = Frm.hwnd
If Not SHAppBarMessage(ABM_GETSTATE, BarData) = ABS_AUTOHIDE Then
    Call SHAppBarMessage(ABM_GETTASKBARPOS, BarData)
```

SHAppBarMessage is an API function which sends a message to Windows to retrieve or set information concerning an appbar. **SHAppBarMessage** has two parameters. The first parameter is the message being sent. These messages are summarized in Table 1-3.

Message	Description
ABM_ACTIVATE	Notifies the system that an appbar has been activated.
ABM_GETAUTOHIDEBAR	Retrieves the handle to the autohide appbar associated with a particular edge of the screen.
ABM_GETSTATE	Retrieves the autohide and always-on-top states of the Windows taskbar.
ABM_GETTASKBARPOS	Retrieves the bounding rectangle of the Windows taskbar.
ABM_NEW	Registers a new appbar and specifies the message identifier that the system should use to send notification messages to the appbar.
ABM_QUERYPOS	Requests a size and screen position for an appbar.
ABM_REMOVE	Unregisters an appbar, removing the bar from the system's internal list.
ABM_SETAUTOHIDEBAR	Registers or unregisters an autohide appbar for an edge of the screen.
ABM_SETPOS	Sets the size and screen position of an appbar.
ABM_WINDOWPOSCHANGED	Notifies the system when an appbar's position has changed.

TABLE 1-3.   Messages Which May Be Sent with **SHAppBarMessage**

The second parameter is the address of the APPBARDATA structure. The return value of **SHAppBarMessage** depends on the message being sent.

The message ABM_GETSTATE retrieves the "Auto hide" and "Always on top" states of the Windows taskbar. The settings for these properties are shown by the dialog box which appears by right-clicking an open area of the taskbar and selecting properties (see Figure 1-1).

If the **Auto hide** property is true (in other words, checked in the dialog box), then the taskbar will not take up any discernible space on the desktop, and therefore its dimensions need not be considered in centering the form. Otherwise, **SHAppBarMessage** again is called, this time with the ABM_GETTASKBARPOS message. This message retrieves the bounds of the rectangle of the Windows taskbar and stores this information in the **rc** member of the APPBARDATA structure passed in the second parameter, *BarData*. The **rc** member is a RECT structure which contains the bounding rectangle, in screen coordinates, of the Windows taskbar.

When **SHAppBarMessage** is called with either the ABM_GETSTATE or the ABM_GETTASKBARPOS message, it is necessary first to initialize two other members of the APPBARDATA structure. The first member to initialize is **cbSize**, which contains the size of the structure in bytes. This is done by using the **Len** function, which when used with a user-defined type will return the number of bytes to store it. The second member to initialize is **hWnd**, which contains the handle to

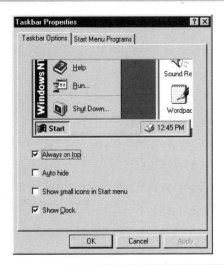

FIGURE 1-1. The Taskbar Properties dialog box

the appbar's window. That window in this case is the test form, which was passed as a parameter (*Frm*) to CenterForm, so the **hwnd** property of that parameter is assigned to the **hWnd** member of the APPBARDATA structure. The members of the APPBARDATA structure are summarized in Table 1-4.

Member	Description
cbSize	Contains the size of the structure, in bytes. Discussed in this example.
hWnd	Contains the handle to the appbar's window. Discussed in this example.
lParam	Used with the ABM_SETAUTOHIDEBAR message. Not discussed in this example.
rc	RECT structure to contain the bounding rectangle, in screen coordinates, of an appbar or the Windows taskbar. Discussed in this example with the ABM_GETTASKBARPOS message.
uCallbackMessage	Application-defined message identifier used when sending the ABM_NEW message. Not discussed in this example.
uEdge	Value that specifies the top, bottom, left, or right edge of the screen. Used when setting or retrieving the taskbar's size and position or a handle to an autohide taskbar. Not discussed in this example.

TABLE 1-4. Members of APPBARDATA Structure

It is not always necessary to initialize members of the APPBARDATA structure before calling **SHAppBarMessage**. Whether this is necessary depends on the message being passed as the first parameter.

The remaining task is to determine whether the taskbar is at the top, bottom, left, or right of the screen.

```
If (BarData.rc.Right - BarData.rc.Left) > _
   (BarData.rc.Bottom - BarData.rc.Top) Then
```

If this condition is true, then the taskbar's width is greater than its height. This means that the taskbar is either at the top or bottom of the screen.

```
If BarData.rc.Top <= 0 Then
   ClientRect.Top = ClientRect.Top + _
      (BarData.rc.Bottom - BarData.rc.Top)
Else
   ClientRect.Bottom = ClientRect.Bottom - _
      (BarData.rc.Bottom - BarData.rc.Top)
End If
```

If the *Top* variable of the taskbar (represented by **BarData.rc.Top**) is equal to or less than zero, then the taskbar is at the top of the screen. It is important to test for **BarData.rc.Top <= 0** and not **BarData.rc.Top = 0**. The y coordinate of the top of the taskbar may have a small negative value.

If the taskbar is at the top of the screen, then the y coordinate of the top of the desktop needs to be increased to just below the y coordinate of the bottom of the taskbar. This means that the value of the height of the taskbar (**BarData.rc.Bottom – BarData.rc.Top**) needs to be added to the top of the desktop (**ClientRect.Top**). If the *Top* variable of the taskbar is greater than zero, then the taskbar is at the bottom of the screen. In this case, the height of the taskbar needs to be subtracted from the value of the bottom of the desktop. In either case, *ClientRect* now represents the coordinates of the desktop not including the taskbar.

```
Else
   If BarData.rc.Left <= 0 Then
      ClientRect.Left = ClientRect.Left + _
         (BarData.rc.Right - BarData.rc.Left)
   Else
      ClientRect.Right = ClientRect.Right - _
         (BarData.rc.Right - BarData.rc.Left)
   End If
End If
```

If this block of code executes, then the taskbar is either at the left or right of the screen. The logic of the code is similar to that of the preceding block. If the *Left* variable of the taskbar is equal to (or less than) zero, then the taskbar is at the left of the screen. If the taskbar is at the left of the screen, then the x coordinate of the top of the desktop needs to be increased to just to the right of the x coordinate of the right

of the taskbar. This means that the value of the width of the taskbar
(**BarData.rc.Right** – **BarData.rc.Left**) needs to be added to the left of the desktop
(**ClientRect.Left**). If instead the taskbar is at the right of the screen, then the width of
the taskbar needs to be subtracted from the right of the desktop.

```
With Frm
  X = (((ClientRect.Right + ClientRect.Left) * _
        Screen.TwipsPerPixelX) - .Width) / 2
  Y = (((ClientRect.Bottom + ClientRect.Top) * _
        Screen.TwipsPerPixelY) - .Height) / 2
      .Move X, Y
End With
```

The **Move** method should look familiar, but there are several nuances in the code
which precedes it. The values returned by the API functions were in pixels, whereas
the coordinates used by the **Move** method are in twips. Therefore, a conversion
from pixels to twips is necessary before the **Move** method is invoked. The property
TwipsPerPixelX returns the number of twips per pixel for an object (in this case the
screen) measured horizontally. Similarly, the property **TwipsPerPixelY** returns the
number of twips per pixel for the object measured vertically. The conversion is
necessary only for the members of *ClientRect*, which were assigned values by the
API functions, and not for the **Width** and **Height** properties of the *Frm* variable,
which already are in twips.

Another nuance is that with RECT structures the point specified by the right and
bottom fields usually is *not* part of the rectangle. Thus, if the values of left and top
were 0 and the values of right and bottom were 1, then there would not be 4 pixels
(0,0; 0,1; 1,0; 1,1) but instead only 1 pixel (0,0). This means that subtracting left from
right will result in the width and subtracting bottom from top will result in the height.

The final nuance is that the code requires the sum, not the difference,
between the **Right** and **Left** (and **Top** and **Bottom**) members of *ClientRect*; that
is, **ClientRect.Right + ClientRect.Left**, not **ClientRect.Right - ClientRect.Left**.
Otherwise, the code will only work if the taskbar is at the bottom or right of the
screen, and not when the taskbar is at the top or left. This is not an unusual error.
Subtraction works as well as addition if the taskbar is at the bottom or right of the
screen since the **Top** (or **Left**) property of *ClientRect* remains 0. However, if the
taskbar is at the top or left, the *x* (or *y*) parameter of the **Move** method needs to be
increased, not decreased.

TEST THE CODE

1. Start a new project, Standard Exe. The default form may be the startup form.
   Accept the name Form1 and the other default properties.

2. Place a command button on the form, name it **cmdCenter**, and give it the
   caption "Center Me!" Your form should look like Figure 1-2.

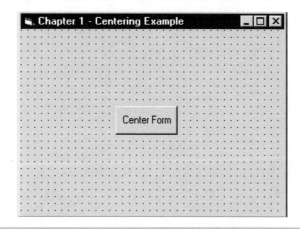

FIGURE 1-2.   The Centering Example form

3. Insert a new class module named clsCenterForm and paste in it the above CenterForm code (also on the CD-ROM).

4. Place the following code in the **Click** event of cmdCenter:

```
Private Sub cmdCenter_Click()
    Dim ctr As clsCenterForm
    Set ctr = New clsCenterForm
    ctr.CenterForm Me
    Set ctr = Nothing
End Sub
```

The CenterForm cannot be called directly since it is in a class module, not a standard module. Instead, it must be called from an object of the type clsCenterForm using the Object.Method syntax. A clsCenterForm object is created first by declaring it with the **Dim** statement and then instantiating it with the **New** keyword. The **Set** statement is necessary because **ctr** is an object, not a primitive data type such as an integer. An alternative syntax is

```
Dim ctr As New clsCenterForm
```

The object variable **ctr** then is instantiated when it first invokes a property or method, here by calling the CenterForm method in the statement **ctr.CenterForm Me**. This method is less preferable because it provides less certainty or control over when the object variable is instantiated.

Enough theory! Have fun! Try moving around the form and also resizing and moving the taskbar. The form stays centered (see Figure 1-3).

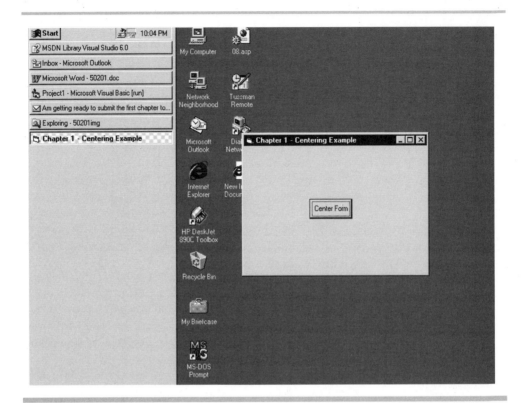

FIGURE 1-3. You can't fool clsCenterForm!

Resize.vbp

Controlling the Resizing of a Form

As a Visual Basic developer, you may wish to restrict the user's ability to resize a form during run-time. For example, you may want to prevent the form from being resized so small that some of its controls near the edge being removed disappear. You may wish to prevent the form from being resized so large as to distort the appearance of its controls or to cover other forms. You may also wish to preserve a ratio of the form's width to its height. Still another example of restricting resizing is in the Find Files or Folders program in Windows 95, 98, and NT. This program permits horizontal resizing but prohibits vertical resizing of the form until a search is initiated, presumably because until there is a search there are no results for the user to view.

Unfortunately, Visual Basic does not provide an effective built-in method to restrict but not prohibit the user's ability to resize a form. The form's border can be made nonsizable, but this eliminates any ability of the user to resize the form, a more drastic limitation than you may wish to impose. Another alternative is to test the form's width and height properties in the form's **Resize** event and, if size or ratio limitations are "violated," move the form back to the desired size or ratio. However, moving the form back in range from the **Resize** event may cause an annoying flicker because the **Resize** event occurs after the form has already moved.

Windows sends a WM_GETMINMAXINFO message when the size or position of the window is about to change. For example, the message is sent when the user clicks Move or Size from the window menu or clicks the sizing border or title bar.

The WM_GETMINMAXINFO message includes a pointer to a MINMAXINFO structure which has as members points, that is, each specify an x,y coordinate. These members are set forth in Table 1-5.

Since the MINMAXINFO structure contains all the information necessary to control the size of the form, the indicated solution is to set the members of a MINMAXINFO structure pointed to by a WM_GETMINMAXINFO message to the desired values. However, Visual Basic does not provide a way of doing this. It simply passes the WM_GETMINMAXINFO message (and the MINMAXINFO structure which goes with it) unchanged to your application.

SUBCLASSING

The Windows API does provide a method of intercepting the WM_GETMINMAXINFO message before Visual Basic receives it for the purpose of setting the MINMAXINFO structure members to the values to which the resizing of the form is to be restricted. The message is then sent on to Visual Basic with the modified values.

Each window has a default window function which handles messages associated with that window. However, a window does not have to use the default function. Instead, the window may call a user-defined function. The user-defined function

Members	Description
ptReserved	Reserved for internal use.
ptMaxSize	Specifies the maximized width (point.x) and the maximized height (point.y) of the window.
ptMaxPosition	Specifies the position of the left side of the maximized window (point.x) and the position of the top of the maximized window (point.y).
ptMinTrackSize	Specifies the system-defined default minimum tracking width (point.x) and the minimum tracking height (point.y) of the window. The minimum tracking size is the smallest window size that can be produced by using the borders to size the window.
ptMaxTrackSize	Specifies the system-defined default maximum tracking width (point.x) and the maximum tracking height (point.y) of the window. The maximum tracking size is the largest window size that can be produced by using the borders to size the window.

TABLE 1-5. Members of MINMAXINFO Structure

may process the messages it was designed to intercept and then pass the other messages to the default window function. This technique is called *subclassing*.

There are different subclassing techniques, depending on what needs to be accomplished. The methodology followed here is typical:

1. The API function **SetWindowLong** is used to redirect messages from the default window procedure to your substitute window message procedure.

2. The return value of **SetWindowLong**, the address of the default window procedure, is saved in a variable. This is *critical* so that the default procedure can be restored before the application terminates. If this restoration does not occur, an illegal exception will be the rule, not the exception!

3. Your substitute window message procedure handles the messages in which you are interested and passes the others to the default window procedure.

4. The API function **SetWindowLong** is used once again, this time to restore the default window procedure as the window procedure for the window.

This sounds simple, but subclassing can be as safe as juggling chainsaws. The message often heard on shows for children, "Don't try this at home kids, we're trained professionals," applies here. However, as readers of this book, you are trained professionals. Nevertheless, it is strongly suggested that you read the "Subclassing" section of Appendix A before trying it.

SYNOPSIS OF CODE

The technique for intercepting the WM_GETMINMAXINFO message and then changing the values of the members of the MINMAXINFO structure is typical for subclassing. The parameters of the subclassing function include the handle of the window being resized and the message being passed. If the handle is to the form and the message is WM_GETMINMAXINFO, then:

1. The members of the MINMAXINFO structure pointed to by the message are copied into a local MINMAXINFO structure using the **CopyMemory** function.

2. The members of the local MINMAXINFO structure are changed to the desired values.

3. In the reverse of step 1, the members of the local MINMAXINFO structure are copied into the MINMAXINFO structure pointed to by the message, again using the **CopyMemory** function.

4. The MINMAXINFO structure pointed to by the message, with the values of its members modified, then is passed to your application.

CODE

```
Option Explicit

Public defWindowProc As Long

Public minX As Long
Public minY As Long
Public maxX As Long
Public maxY As Long

Public Const GWL_WNDPROC As Long = (-4)
Public Const WM_GETMINMAXINFO As Long = &H24

Public Type POINTAPI
 x As Long
 y As Long
End Type

Type MINMAXINFO
 ptReserved As POINTAPI
 ptMaxSize As POINTAPI
 ptMaxPosition As POINTAPI
 ptMinTrackSize As POINTAPI
 ptMaxTrackSize As POINTAPI
End Type

Public Declare Function SetWindowLong Lib "user32" _
    Alias "SetWindowLongA" _
    (ByVal hwnd As Long, ByVal nIndex As Long, _
     ByVal dwNewLong As Long) As Long

Public Declare Function CallWindowProc Lib "user32" _
    Alias "CallWindowProcA" _
    (ByVal lpPrevWndFunc As Long, ByVal hwnd As Long, _
     ByVal uMsg As Long, _
     ByVal wParam As Long, ByVal lParam As Long) As Long

Public Declare Sub CopyMemory Lib "kernel32" _
    Alias "RtlMoveMemory" _
    (hpvDest As  Any, hpvSource As Any, ByVal cbCopy As Long)
```

```
Public Sub SubClass(hwnd As Long)
 On Error Resume Next
 defWindowProc = SetWindowLong _
     (hwnd, GWL_WNDPROC, AddressOf WindowProc)
 End Sub

Public Sub UnSubClass(hwnd As Long)
 If defWindowProc Then
SetWindowLong hwnd, GWL_WNDPROC, defWindowProc
defWindowProc = 0
 End If
End Sub

Public Function WindowProc(ByVal hwnd As Long, _
   ByVal uMsg As Long, _
   ByVal wParam As Long, ByVal lParam As Long) As Long
On Error Resume Next
Select Case hwnd
Case Form1.hwnd
 On Error Resume Next
 Select Case uMsg
Case WM_GETMINMAXINFO
 Dim MMI As MINMAXINFO
 CopyMemory MMI, ByVal lParam, LenB(MMI)
  With MMI
 .ptMinTrackSize.x = minX
 .ptMinTrackSize.y = minY
 .ptMaxTrackSize.x = maxX
 .ptMaxTrackSize.y = maxY
End With
 CopyMemory ByVal lParam, MMI, LenB(MMI)
 WindowProc = 0
Case Else
WindowProc = CallWindowProc _
    (defWindowProc, hwnd, uMsg, wParam, lParam)
End Select
End Select
 End Function
```

ANNOTATIONS

```
Public defWindowProc As Long
```

This variable will store the address of the default window procedure and therefore has a Long data type. That address must be stored because the default window procedure must be restored before the application ends.

```
Public minX As Long
Public minY As Long
Public maxX As Long
Public maxY As Long
```

These variables will be used to store the desired values of the members of the MINMAXINFO structure. These variables are assigned values in the **Click** event of an option button control array on the test form. The creation of this form and the code for the **Click** event are discussed in the following "Test the Code" section.

```
Public Const GWL_WNDPROC As Long = (-4)
Public Const WM_GETMINMAXINFO As Long = &H24
```

These constants will be used by the API functions. How their values can be obtained is discussed in Appendix A.

```
Public Type POINTAPI
 x As Long
 y As Long
End Type
```

The POINTAPI structure is used to store x,y coordinates. These coordinates correspond to the data type of the members of the MINMAXINFO structure passed by the WM_GETMINMAXINFO message.

```
Type MINMAXINFO
 ptReserved As POINTAPI
 ptMaxSize As POINTAPI
 ptMaxPosition As POINTAPI
 ptMinTrackSize As POINTAPI
 ptMaxTrackSize As POINTAPI
End Type
```

This is another example of the use of a Visual Basic user-defined type which corresponds to a C structure used in a Windows API. A Visual Basic user-defined type parallel to the MINMAXINFO structure next is declared to hold and change the values of the members of the MINMAXINFO structure passed by the WM_GETMINMAXINFO message.

Next the API functions are declared. This already was discussed in the previous example on centering a form. The purpose of these API functions is discussed below when they are called. However, one of the declarations deserves some comment:

```
Public Declare Sub CopyMemory Lib "kernel32" Alias "RtlMoveMemory" _
    (hpvDest As Any, hpvSource As Any, ByVal cbCopy As Long)
```

This appears to be a normal declaration of an API function. However, there is no function called **CopyMemory** in the Windows API. To make a long story short, **CopyMemory's** alias is **RtlMoveMemory**. **RtlMoveMemory** in turn is an alias for the C **memcpy** function. While neither **memcpy** nor any other C library function can be called from Visual Basic, kernel32.dll does contain an entry for **RtlMoveMemory**. In other words, the API function really being called is **RtlMoveMemory**. However, "everybody" calls it **CopyMemory**, so we will too.

```
Public Sub SubClass(hwnd As Long)
 On Error Resume Next
 defWindowProc = SetWindowLong(hwnd, GWL_WNDPROC, _
     AddressOf WindowProc)
End Sub
```

The purpose of **SubClass** is to have Windows call your substitute window procedure in place of the default procedure. **SetWindowLong** is an API function which is used to redirect messages to your substitute window message procedure. It takes three parameters. The first parameter is a handle to the window involved, **hwnd** being passed by the form as a handle to itself when **SubClass** is called during the **Form_Load** event (see the next section, "Test the Code").

The second parameter is a constant which refers to the information to be returned by the function. As discussed above, it is critical to store the address of the default window procedure so that the default procedure can be restored before the application terminates. Therefore, the constant in this case calls for the address of the window function for this window, that is, the default window function. Similarly, the variable *defWindowProc* is used to store the address of the default window procedure.

The third parameter is the new value for the information specified by the second parameter. Since we want to substitute our window function for the default one, the third parameter is the address of the new window procedure. That new window procedure is **WindowProc**, and the **AddressOf** operator obtains its address.

The **AddressOf** operator was introduced with Version 5 of Visual Basic. It is used to pass the address of a procedure to an API procedure that expects a function pointer as a parameter. It is used extensively in callbacks, which will be discussed later. One limitation of **AddressOf** is that the procedure whose address it passes must be declared in a standard module, and not a class module, which does impact on code reuse.

```
Public Sub UnSubClass(hwnd As Long)
 If defWindowProc Then
SetWindowLong hwnd, GWL_WNDPROC, defWindowProc
 defWindowProc = 0
 End If
End Sub
```

UnSubClass, as its name suggests, undoes that which **SubClass** did. **UnSubClass** restores the default window function by using, as a third parameter, the *defWindowProc* variable. That variable stored the return value of **SetWindowLong**—the address of the default window function—when **SetWindowLong** was called in the subroutine **SubClass**. **UnSubClass** is called in the **Form_Unload** event as discussed in the "Test the Code" section below.

```
Public Function WindowProc(ByVal hwnd As Long, _
    ByVal uMsg As Long, _ ByVal wParam As Long, _
    ByVal lParam As Long) As Long
```

WindowProc, despite the API-sounding name, is the user-defined substitute window procedure designed to handle the messages needing special treatment, in this case the WM_GETMINMAXINFO message. Its first parameter is a handle to the window. The second is a constant which is the numeric value of the message being passed. The third and fourth parameters, by tradition named *wParam* and *lParam*, carry additional information needed by the message. When more than two values are needed, they usually are placed in a structure the address of which is contained in the *lParam* argument.

```
Select Case hwnd
   Case Form1.hwnd
```

We only are concerned about messages relating specifically to the window. General system messages will be passed to the default window procedure.

```
Select Case uMsg Case WM_GETMINMAXINFO
```

WM_GETMINMAXINFO is the only message in which we are interested. Other messages will be passed to the default window procedure. Note that the data type of **uMsg** is a long because Windows messages are passed by their numeric value. Similarly, at the start of this module WM_GETMINMAXINFO was defined as a constant of a long data type with the numeric value of that message:

```
Dim MMI As MINMAXINFO
```

MMI is the local variable into which the values of the members of the MINMAXINFO structure passed by the WM_GETMINMAXINFO message will be copied.

```
CopyMemory MMI, ByVal lParam, LenB(MMI)
```

As discussed above, purists will tell you, correctly, that **CopyMemory**, at least by that name, is not really an API function, but for our practical purposes we will treat it as an API function. Its first parameter is the address of the destination to which the copy is being sent, the second parameter is the address of the source being copied, and the third parameter is number of bytes to be copied. With the WM_GETMINMAXINFO message, *lParam* is the address of the structure passed by the message, so *lParam* as the second parameter in **CopyMemory** passes the address of the MINMAXINFO structure which accompanied the WM_GETMINMAXINFO message.

```
With MMI
 .ptMinTrackSize.x = minX
 .ptMinTrackSize.y = minY
 .ptMaxTrackSize.x = maxX
 .ptMaxTrackSize.y = maxY
End With
```

This simply assigns to the members of the MMI structure the values to which resizing will be restricted. These values are assigned in the **Click** event of an option button control array on the test form. The creation of this form and the code for the **Click** event are discussed in the following "Test the Code" section.

```
CopyMemory ByVal lParam, MMI, LenB(MMI)
```

This now reverses the process of the prior call to **CopyMemory** and copies into the MINMAXINFO structure passed by the message the desired values which were just copied into the MMI structure.

```
WindowProc = 0
```

Microsoft documentation suggests that if the message is processed the function should return 0.

```
Case Else
WindowProc = CallWindowProc(defWindowProc, hwnd, uMsg, _
    wParam, lParam)
```

CallWindowProc is an API function. It passes the window messages to the function whose address is specified in the first parameter. That function is the default window procedure whose address was saved in **SubClass**. This default procedure will handle all messages other than the WM_GETMINMAXINFO message passed to the window. However, **CallWindowProc** only passes a particular message to the default window function. It does not redirect future messages back from your user-defined function to the default window procedure. That task—which must be performed before the application terminates—requires the API function **SetWindowLong** which is called in **UnSubClass**.

TEST THE CODE

1. Start a new project, Standard Exe. The default form may be the startup form. Accept the name Form1 and the other default properties. In particular, the **BorderStyle** property should be 2 – Sizable, the **WindowsState** property should be 0 – Normal, and the **StartUpPosition** property should be 3 – Windows Default.

2. Place on the form three option buttons in a control array (optResize(0) – optResize(2)) and a command button named cmdEnd. Your form in design view should look like Figure 1-4.

3. Place the code above in a standard module.

4. Place the following statements in the declarations of the form:

```
Option Explicit

Private StartupHeight As Long
Private StartupWidth As Long
```

These variables will hold the height and width of the form at startup.

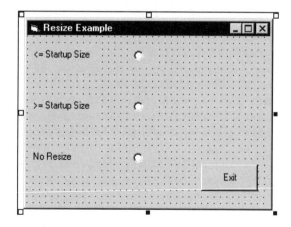

FIGURE 1-4.   Design view of the Resize Example form

5. Place the following code in the **Load** event of Form1:

```
Private Sub Form_Load()
    StartupWidth = Me.Width \ Screen.TwipsPerPixelY
    StartupHeight = Me.Height \ Screen.TwipsPerPixelY

    optResize(0).Value = True
    Call SubClass(Me.hwnd)
End Sub
```

The width and height of the form at startup are stored in the variables *StartupWidth* and *StartupHeight*. The **TwipsPerPixelX** and **TwipsPerPixelY** properties are used because these measurements will be passed to an API function which uses pixels instead of twips. The \ operator is used instead of the / operator because an integer result, not a floating point result, is desired. Finally, **SubClass** is called so that the window procedure for Form1 will be your user-defined procedure. Note that **SubClass** is passed a handle to Form1 as a parameter.

6. Place the following code in the **Click** event of the option button control array. The comments indicate the behavior caused by each option button:

```
Private Sub optResize_Click(Index As Integer)
    Select Case Index
        Case 0   'Don't Allow Resizing Larger than Startup Size
            minX = 0
            minY = 0
            maxX = StartupWidth
            maxY = StartupHeight
        Case 1   'Don't Allow Resizing Smaller than Startup Size
            minX = StartupWidth
            minY = StartupHeight
            maxX = Screen.Width \ Screen.TwipsPerPixelX
            maxY = Screen.Height \ Screen.TwipsPerPixelY

        Case 2   'Don't Allow any Resizing
            minX = Me.Width \ Screen.TwipsPerPixelX
            minY = Me.Height \ Screen.TwipsPerPixelY
            maxX = Me.Width \ Screen.TwipsPerPixelX
            maxY = Me.Height \ Screen.TwipsPerPixelY
    End Select
End Sub
```

7. Place the following code in the **Click** event of the command button:

```
Private Sub cndEnd_Click()
    Unload Me
End Sub
```

This code will trigger the **Unload** event of the form. This event also will be triggered by the user closing the form by the close button in the title bar or the close item of the system menu.

8. Place the following code in the **Unload** event of Form1:

```
Private Sub Form_Unload(Cancel As Integer)
    Call UnSubClass(Me.hwnd)
End Sub
```

This will call **UnSubClass** to restore the default window procedure as the window procedure for the window.

This restoration will not occur if you simply execute an End statement or, in the VB IDE, you execute the Run-End command from the menu or the toolbar button. *The result may well be an illegal exception or worse.*

Run the code. Try the different options of not allowing resizing larger than startup size, smaller than startup size, or any resizing at all.

LimitMove.vbp

Controlling the Movement of a Form

This is another topic on "controlling." Nothing psychological should be read into this (please). Rather, the purpose of this book is to provide you, the developer, with the tools to have your application do what you want rather than be limited to that which Visual Basic gives you.

This topic is related to the preceding one and, in fact, is a superset of it. A window's position changes when it is being resized. However, a window's position may change without it being resized, that is, when it is being moved.

This section will show you how to control the positioning of the form. Controlling the positioning of the form may be important not only to the aesthetics but also the functionality of your application. A form may appear distorted if the ratio of its height to its width strays outside of certain parameters, and a form which is permitted to wander into another part of the screen may block input or the display of information.

Windows sends a WM_WINDOWPOSCHANGING message as well as a WM_GETMINMAXINFO message when the size or position of the window is about to change. Just as the WM_GETMINMAXINFO message includes a pointer to a MINMAXINFO structure, the WM_WINDOWPOSCHANGING message includes a pointer to a WINDOWPOS structure.

The members of the WINDOWPOS structure are similar but not identical to those of the MINMAXINFO structure, and are set forth in Table 1-6.

Member	Description
hwnd	Identifies the window.
hwndInsertAfter	Identifies the window behind which this window is placed.
x	Specifies the position of the left edge of the window.
y	Specifies the position of the right edge of the window.
cx	Specifies the window width, in pixels.
cy	Specifies the window height, in pixels.
flags	Specifies window-positioning options.

TABLE 1-6.   Members of WINDOWPOS Structure

The **flags** member contains the flags set forth in Table 1-7. The flags SWP_NOSIZE and SWP_NOMOVE used in this example respectively prevent any sizing or moving at all.

Flags	Description
SWP_HIDEWINDOW	Hides the window.
SWP_NOACTIVATE	Does not activate the window.
SWP_NOCOPYBITS	Discards the entire contents of the client area. If this flag is not specified, the valid contents of the client area are saved and copied back into the client area after the window is sized or repositioned.
SWP_NOMOVE	Retains current position (ignores the **x** and **y** members).
SWP_NOOWNERZORDER or SWP_NOREPOSITION	Does not change the owner window's position in the Z-order.
SWP_NOSIZE	Retains current size (ignores the **cx** and **cy** members).
SWP_NOREDRAW	Does not redraw changes.
SWP_NOSENDCHANGING	Prevents the window from receiving the WM_WINDOWPOSCHANGING message.

TABLE 1-7.   Flags in WINDOWPOS Structure

SYNOPSIS OF CODE

Having just read about WM_GETMINMAXINFO, the following, at least up to a point, will seem, in the famous words of Yogi Berra, like "déjà vu all over again." The WM_WINDOWPOSCHANGING message which Visual Basic otherwise simply would pass unchanged to your application is intercepted and the members of the WINDOWPOS structure are modified to the values to which the positioning of the form is to be restricted. Inspecting the parameters of the subclassing function, if the handle is to the form and the message is WM_ WINDOWPOSCHANGING, then:

1. The members of the WINDOWPOS structure pointed to by the message are copied into a local WINDOWPOS structure using the **CopyMemory** function.

2. The members of the local WINDOWPOS structure are changed to the desired values.

3. In the reverse of step 1, the members of the local WINDOWPOS structure are copied into the WINDOWPOS structure pointed to by the message, again using the **CopyMemory** function.

4. The WINDOWPOS structure pointed to by the message, with the values of its members modified, then is passed to your application.

CODE

```
Option Explicit
Public x As Long
Public y As Long


Public defWindowProc As Long

Private Type WINDOWPOS
    hWnd As Long
    hWndInsertAfter As Long
    x As Long
    y As Long
    cx As Long
    cy As Long
    flags As Long
End Type


Public Const LIMITMOVEMENT as single = .1
Public Const GWL_WNDPROC As Long = (-4)
```

```
Private Const WM_WINDOWPOSCHANGING = &H46
Private Const SWP_NOSIZE = &H1
Private Const SWP_NOMOVE = &H2

Public Declare Function SetWindowLong Lib "user32" _
    Alias "SetWindowLongA" _
   (ByVal hwnd As Long, ByVal nIndex As Long, _
    ByVal dwNewLong As Long) As Long

Public Declare Function CallWindowProc Lib "user32" _
    Alias "CallWindowProcA" _
   (ByVal lpPrevWndFunc As Long, ByVal hwnd As Long, _
    ByVal uMsg As Long, _
    ByVal wParam As Long, ByVal lParam As Long) As Long

Private Declare Sub CopyMemory Lib "Kernel32" _
    Alias "RtlMoveMemory" _
   (lpDest As Any, lpSource As Any, ByVal nCount As Long)

Public Sub SubClass(hwnd As Long)
 On Error Resume Next
 defWindowProc = SetWindowLong(hwnd, GWL_WNDPROC, _
  AddressOf WindowProc)
End Sub

Public Sub UnSubClass(hwnd As Long)
 If defWindowProc Then
   SetWindowLong hwnd, GWL_WNDPROC, defWindowProc
   defWindowProc = 0
 End If
End Sub

Public Function WindowProc(ByVal hwnd As Long, _
    ByVal uMsg As Long, _
    ByVal wParam As Long, ByVal lParam As Long) As Long
On Error Resume Next
Select Case hwnd
Case Form1.hwnd
 On Error Resume Next
 Select Case uMsg
 Case WM_WINDOWPOSCHANGING
 Dim WINPOS As WINDOWPOS
 CopyMemory WINPOS, ByVal lParam, LenB(WINPOS)
```

```
If Form1.chkNoMove Or Form1.chkNoSize Then
   If Form1.chkNoMove = False Then
      WINPOS.flags = WINPOS.flags Or SWP_NOSIZE
   ElseIf Form1.chkNoSize = False Then
      WINPOS.flags = WINPOS.flags Or SWP_NOMOVE
   Else
      WINPOS.flags = WINPOS.flags Or SWP_NOMOVE Or SWP_NOSIZE
   End If
End If
If Form1.chkLimitMove Then
   If WINPOS.x > x Then WINPOS.x = x
   If WINPOS.y > y Then WINPOS.y = y
End If
If Form1.chkKeepSquare Then
   If WINPOS.cx <> WINPOS.cy Then WINPOS.cx = WINPOS.cy
End If
CopyMemory ByVal lParam, WINPOS, LenB(WINPOS)
WindowProc = 0
Case Else
WindowProc = CallWindowProc _
   (defWindowProc, hwnd, uMsg, wParam, lParam)
End Select
End Select
End Function
```

ANNOTATIONS

Most of the code is the same as the prior resizing example because the logic is quite similar and keeping the examples consistent is easier on you, the reader, and only coincidentally also on the author. Therefore, only the differences are analyzed.

```
Public x As Long
Public y As Long
```

These variables will be used to store the x,y coordinates which define the left and top limits of the form. In this case, if the application user chooses the Limit Movement checkbox on the test form (see the following section, "Test the Code"), then the left border can never be less than 1/10 across the screen and the top border will can never be less than 1/10 down the screen.

```
Public flags As Long
```

This variable will be used to store a preference of the user that the form may not be moved or resized.

```
Private Type WINDOWPOS
    hWnd As Long
    hWndInsertAfter As Long
    x As Long
    y As Long
    cx As Long
    cy As Long
    flags As Long
End Type
```

This user-defined type is the local WINDOWPOS structure to be used by **CopyMemory** to modify the values of the members of the WINDOWPOS, which is pointed to by the WM_ WINDOWPOSCHANGING message. This is another example of the use of a Visual Basic user-defined type which corresponds to a C structure used in a Windows API.

```
Public Const LIMITMOVEMENT as integer = .1
```

This constant relates to the user option to limit movement so the left border will be no more than 1/10 across the screen and the top border will be no more than 1/10 down the screen. The denominator is stored as a constant so this limitation may be modified by changing only one place in the code.

```
Public Const GWL_WNDPROC As Long = (-4)
Private Const WM_WINDOWPOSCHANGING = &H46
Private Const SWP_NOSIZE = &H1
Private Const SWP_NOMOVE = &H2
```

GWL_WNDPROC was discussed in the resizing example. The purpose of the constant declaration for WM_WINDOWPOSCHANGING is the same as that for WM_GETMINMAXINFO in the resizing example. The constants SWP_NOSIZE and SWP_NOMOVE (which respectively prevent resizing or moving) are flags in the **flag** member of the WINDOWPOS structure and, like the messages, have a corresponding value.

The code continues as in the resizing example until in **WndProc**, the user-defined window function, the message being looked for is WM_WINDOWPOSCHANGING instead of WM_GETMINMAXINFO:

```
Select Case uMsg Case WM_WINDOWPOSCHANGING
```

A local variable WINPOS (instead of MINMAXINFO) then is declared, and **CopyMemory** is used to copy the values of the WINDOWPOS structure passed by the WM_WINDOWPOSCHANGING message into the local WINDOWPOS variable:

```
Dim WINPOS As WINDOWPOS
CopyMemory WINPOS, ByVal lParam, LenB(WINPOS)
```

At this point the logic of the user-defined Windows procedure departs from the previous example. In the resizing example the only concern was resizing. This time there are other concerns, such as position and whether the user has chosen to prohibit movement or resizing altogether.

```
If Form1.chkNoMove Or Form1.chkNoSize Then
    If Form1.chkNoMove = False Then
      WINPOS.flags = WINPOS.flags Or SWP_NOSIZE
    ElseIf Form1.chkNoSize = False Then
      WINPOS.flags = WINPOS.flags Or SWP_NOMOVE
    Else
      WINPOS.flags = WINPOS.flags Or SWP_NOMOVE Or SWP_NOSIZE
    End If
End If
```

This simply checks to see if the user has chosen to prohibit movement, resizing, or both. If so, the appropriate flags are set in the WINPOS structure. The **Or** operator is used to set more than one flag, that is, **SWP_NOMOVE Or SWP_NOSIZE** sets the flags to prohibit movement *and* resizing. Additionally, the flags selected by the application user are combined with **WINPOS.flags** using the **Or** operator to avoid overwriting any other flags that the WINDOWPOS structure passed by the WM_WINDOWPOSCHANGING message.

```
If Form1.chkLimitMove Then
    If WINPOS.x > x Then WINPOS.x = x
    If WINPOS.y > y Then WINPOS.y = y
End If
```

This checks to see if the user chose to limit movement so the left border will be no more than 1/10 across the screen and the top border will be no more than 1/10 down the screen. If the user has chosen this option, then both the left and top coordinates are checked, and if the left coordinate is too far to the left, or the top coordinate is too far down (or both), the offending coordinate is adjusted to the maximum restriction.

```
If Form1.chkKeepSquare Then
    If WINPOS.cx <> WINPOS.cy Then WINPOS.cx = WINPOS.cy
End If
```

This checks to see if the user has chosen to keep the form the shape of a square. If so, then the height and are checked. If they do not equal each other, the width is adjusted to equal the height.

```
Case Else
 WindowProc = CallWindowProc _
    (defWindowProc, hwnd, uMsg, wParam, lParam)
End Select
```

This branch of the control structure will apply only if the user selected no control. In this case the WINDOWPOS message simply passes through to your application, which is what would have happened if you hadn't written all this code in the first place!

TEST THE CODE

1. Start a new project, Standard Exe. The default form may be the startup form. Accept the name Form1 and the other default properties.

2. Place on the form four checkboxes within a frame and a command button named cmdEnd. The names and purposes of the checkboxes are as follows:

Name	Purpose
chkKeepSquare	Keeps the form square in shape.
chkLimitMove	Prevents the left border from being more than 1/10 across the screen or the top border from being more than 1/10 down the screen.
chkNoMove	Prevents any movement.
chkNoSize	Prevents any resizing.

Your form should look like Figure 1-5.

3. Place the code above in a standard module.

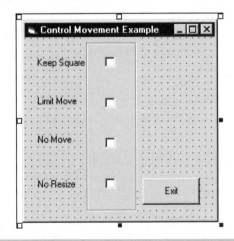

FIGURE 1-5.   The Control Movement Example form

4. Place the following code in the **Load** event of the form:

```
Private Sub Form_Load()
  x = (Screen.Width * LIMITMOVEMENT) \ Screen.TwipsPerPixelX
  y = (Screen.Height * LIMITMOVEMENT) \ Screen.TwipsPerPixelY
  If Me.Height < Me.Width Then
    Me.Height = Me.Width
  Else
  Me.Width = Me.Height
  End If
  Form1.Show
  Call SubClass(Form1.hwnd)
End Sub
```

This code starts the form in a default startup size. The *x* variable is assigned the value of 1/10 across the screen and the *y* variable is assigned the value of 1/10 down the screen. These variables will be used later if the user chooses to limit movement so the left border will be no more than 1/10 across the screen and the top border will be no more than 1/10 down the screen. These values are converted from twips to pixels using the **TwipsPerPixelX** and **TwipsPerPixelY** properties because these values will be passed to an API function which uses pixels instead of twips. As in the resize example, the \ operator is used instead of the / operator because an integer result, not a floating point result, is desired. The form is then shown before checking for the WM_WINDOWPOSCHANGING message, otherwise, the initial display of the form could cause unintended and undesirable side effects in your user-defined windows procedure. Finally, **SubClass** is called so that the window procedure for Form1 will be your user-defined procedure. Once again, **SubClass** is passed a handle to Form1 as a parameter.

5. Place the following code in the **Click** event of the command button:

```
Private Sub cndEnd_Click()
   Unload Me
End Sub
```

This code is the same as the corresponding code in the preceding section.

6. Place the following code in the **Unload** event of Form1:

```
Private Sub Form_Unload(Cancel As Integer)
   Call UnSubClass(Me.hwnd)
End Sub
```

This code also is the same as the corresponding code in the preceding section.

Try out all the alternatives!

Mouse Magic With Your Form

Like most people, you probably most often use the mouse as the input device, unless, like the authors, you sometimes find yourself in the middle seat of a cramped airplane between two sumo wrestlers and the passenger in front of you has his or her seat tilted all the way back. Perhaps because the mouse is almost always the way in which the user interacts with Windows applications, most applications give free rein to the mouse. For example, while command buttons and menu items often are disabled, the mouse generally is permitted to travel anywhere on the screen. Additionally, the default behavior of the mouse is unaltered. For example, double-clicking on an application shortcut does the expected: The application opens. The consistency of the default behavior of the mouse furthers the goal of a consistent Windows application user interface.

Indeed, the examples in Chapter 1, which controlled the resizing and movement of forms by intercepting the messages Windows sends when a window's size or position is about to be changed, did not tinker with the default behavior of the mouse. Moving the mouse cursor over a border or corner of the window and then dragging the border (or corner) while holding down the left mouse button remained the method of resizing the window with the mouse. Left-clicking on the title bar and then dragging the mouse would move the form. By contrast, left-clicking on the client area and then dragging the mouse would not move the form.

It is possible to change the default behavior of the mouse. Just as Windows sends messages to a window when its size or position is about to be changed, Windows also sends messages to a window when a mouse is moved over it or a mouse button is pressed or released on it. These mouse input messages, like the messages Windows sends when a window's size or position is about to be changed, can be inspected and changed before the message is sent on to your application.

Of course, as your parents may have told you, just because you can do something does not mean you should. However, though the virtues of consistent mouse behavior have just been extolled, there are times when it is desirable to change the default behavior of the mouse. This chapter will provide several examples.

hittest.vbp

Subclassing Mouse Messages to Control the Resizing and Moving of a Form

The examples in Chapter 1 controlled the resizing and movement of forms by intercepting the messages Windows sends when a window's size or position is about to be changed. This example will control the resizing and movement of forms in a different way, by intercepting the messages Windows sends on mouse input. Windows sends numerous messages to a window when a mouse is moved over it or a mouse button is pressed or released on it. These messages, like the messages Windows sends when a window's size or position is about to be changed, have parameters which, through subclassing, can be changed before the message is sent on to your application.

There are practical reasons why you may want to control the resizing and movement of forms by subclassing mouse input messages rather than window resizing and repositioning messages. One reason is to increase the functionality of your application. For example, while a form may be moved by left-clicking on the title bar and then dragging the mouse, your application may include a form without a title bar. Under these circumstances—or even if the form has a title bar—it may be desirable to permit the user to move the form by left-clicking *anywhere* on the form (for example, the client area) and dragging.

Another reason for controlling the resizing and movement of forms by subclassing mouse input messages rather than window resizing and repositioning messages is to avoid giving false cues to your application's users. In the examples in Chapter 1, even when the user selected the option to prohibit resizing, pressing the left mouse button and then moving the mouse cursor over the border of the window nevertheless would create the double-arrow cursor. This is because the mouse input message is passed to Windows before the windows resizing and repositioning messages (since the mouse is placed over the border before it is dragged). The presence of this cursor would give the application user the justifiable (though incorrect) expectation that the window would resize. When no resizing occurred, the user quite legitimately may believe there is something wrong with your application.

Using the Windows API to control mouse input messages as well as window resizing and repositioning messages gives you another tool in your arsenal for enhancing your Visual Basic applications.

MOUSE INPUT MESSAGES

There are a number of mouse input messages. The more important ones are listed in Table 2-1.

Mouse Message Constant	Mouse Event
WM_LBUTTONDBLCLK	User double-clicks the left mouse button while the cursor is in the client area of a window.
WM_LBUTTONDOWN	User presses the left mouse button while the cursor is in the client area of a window.
WM_LBUTTONUP	User releases the left mouse button while the cursor is in the client area of a window.
WM_MOUSEMOVE	Message is posted to a window when the cursor moves.
WM_NCHITTEST	Message is sent to a window when the cursor moves, or when a mouse button is pressed or released.

TABLE 2-1.   Mouse Input Messages

Mouse Message Constant	Mouse Event
WM_NCLBUTTONDBLCLK	User double-clicks the left mouse button while the cursor is within the nonclient area of a window.
WM_NCLBUTTONDOWN	User presses the left mouse button while the cursor is within the nonclient area of a window.
WM_NCLBUTTONUP	User releases the left mouse button while the cursor is within the nonclient area of a window.
WM_NCRBUTTONDBLCLK	User double-clicks the right mouse button while the cursor is within the nonclient area of a window.
WM_NCRBUTTONDOWN	User presses the right mouse button while the cursor is within the nonclient area of a window.
WM_NCRBUTTONUP	User releases the right mouse button while the cursor is within the nonclient area of a window.
WM_RBUTTONDBLCLK	User double-clicks the right mouse button while the cursor is in the client area of a window.
WM_RBUTTONDOWN	User presses the right mouse button while the cursor is in the client area of a window.
WM_RBUTTONUP	User releases the right mouse button while the cursor is in the client area of a window.

TABLE 2-1.   Mouse Input Messages *(continued)*

HOT SPOTS AND HIT CODES

When the user moves the mouse, the system moves a bitmap on the screen which the user sees as the mouse cursor. The mouse cursor contains a single-pixel point called the *hot spot*, a point that the system tracks and recognizes as the position of the cursor. When a mouse event occurs, the system posts a mouse message to the window that contains the cursor hot spot at the time the mouse event occurs unless another window has captured the mouse (a situation not addressed in this example).

One of the important mouse input messages is WM_NCHITTEST, which usually is sent to the window when a mouse event occurs over the window. The message sends the applicable window the mouse coordinates of the mouse event.

While the WM_NCHITTEST message reports the coordinates of the mouse event, the information you really need to know is the part of the window (for example, the title bar, the border, the client area) where the mouse event occurred. Unfortunately, the coordinates do not provide Windows (or you) with that information. However, when the message is WM_NCHITTEST, then the return value of the API function **CallWindowProc** is a constant, known as a *hit code*, which represents the part of the window in which the hot spot is located. The hit codes used in this example are listed in Table 2-2.

Constant	Window Area
HTBOTTOM	In the lower, horizontal border of a window
HTLEFT	In the left border of a window
HTBOTTOMLEFT	In the lower-left corner of a window border
HTBOTTOMRIGHT	In the lower-right corner of a window border
HTCAPTION	In a title bar
HTCLIENT	In a client area
HTNOWHERE	On the screen background or on a dividing line between windows
HTRIGHT	In the right border of a window
HTTOP	In the upper, horizontal border of a window
HTTOPLEFT	In the upper-left corner of a window border
HTTOPRIGHT	In the upper-right corner of a window border

TABLE 2-2.   Hit Codes Used in Code Example

SYNOPSIS OF CODE

By subclassing, the code will intercept a WM_NCHITTEST message. The API function **CallWindowProc** then will be called to obtain the hit code. To enable movement by left-clicking and dragging on the client area, if the hit code is HTCLIENT, representing the client area, that value will be changed to HTCAPTION, which represents the title bar, and then returned to Windows. In other words, the function "fibs" to Windows that a click on the client area is a click on the caption. Dragging the mouse then will move the form as though the title bar had been clicked and dragged.

Similarly, to prevent resizing, if the hit code is one of the borders (for example, HTTOP or HTRIGHT) or corners (for example, HTTOPRIGHT or HTBOTTOMLEFT), then the hit code will be changed to HTNOWHERE, which then will be returned to Windows. Since Windows thinks that the mouse cursor is outside the window, dragging the mouse will not resize the window even though in reality the mouse was over a border or corner.

CODE

```
Option Explicit
Public defWindowProc As Long

Public Const GWL_WNDPROC As Long = (-4)
Public Const WM_NCHITTEST As Long = &H84
Public Const HTCAPTION As Long = 2
Public Const HTCLIENT As Long = 1
Public Const HTBOTTOM As Long = 15
Public Const HTBOTTOMLEFT As Long = 16
Public Const HTBOTTOMRIGHT As Long = 17
Public Const HTNOWHERE As Long = 0
Public Const HTRIGHT As Long = 11
Public Const HTLEFT As Long = 10
Public Const HTTOP As Long = 12
Public Const HTTOPLEFT As Long = 13
Public Const HTTOPRIGHT As Long = 14

Declare Function GetWindowLong Lib "user32" _
   Alias "GetWindowLongA" _
 (ByVal hwnd As Long, ByVal nIndex As Long) _
   As Long

Declare Function SetWindowLong Lib "user32" _
  Alias "SetWindowLongA" _
 (ByVal hwnd As Long, ByVal nIndex As Long, _
  ByVal dwNewLong As Long) As Long

Declare Function CallWindowProc Lib "user32" _
   Alias "CallWindowProcA" _
 (ByVal lpPrevWndFunc As Long, ByVal hwnd As Long, _
  ByVal Msg As Long, _
 ByVal wParam As Long, ByVal lParam As Long) As Long

Public Sub SubClass(hwnd As Long)
 On Error Resume Next
 defWindowProc = SetWindowLong(hwnd,
   GWL_WNDPROC, AddressOf WindowProc)
End Sub

Public Sub UnSubClass(hwnd As Long)
 If defWindowProc Then
```

```
    SetWindowLong hwnd, GWL_WNDPROC, defWindowProc
    defWindowProc = 0
    End If
End Sub

Public Function WindowProc(ByVal hwnd As Long, _
   ByVal uMsg As Long, _
  ByVal wParam As Long, ByVal lParam As Long) As Long
  On Error Resume Next
  Dim retVal As Long
  retVal = CallWindowProc(defWindowProc,
    _ hwnd,
    _ uMsg,
    _ wParam,
    _ lParam)
Select Case uMsg
Case WM_NCHITTEST
If retVal = HTCLIENT Then
    retVal = HTCAPTION
ElseIf retVal = HTTOP Or HTTOPLEFT _
    Or HTLEFT Or HTBOTTOMLEFT Or HTBOTTOM Or _
    HTBOTTOMRIGHT Or HTRIGHT Or HTTOPRIGHT Then
    retVal = HTNOWHERE
End If
Case Else
End Select
WindowProc = retVal
End Function
```

ANNOTATIONS

The structure of this code should look familiar by now. The first new concept is the use of **CallWindowProc** in the user-defined window function **WindowProc**. As discussed in the first chapter, **CallWindowProc** is an API function which processes the message specified in the third parameter (which is whichever message is being passed) to the window whose handle is specified in the second parameter function (the test form in our examples) with the function whose address is specified in the first parameter (the default window procedure).

In prior examples, **CallWindowProc** was called as follows:

```
WindowProc = CallWindowProc(defWindowProc, hwnd, Msg, wParam, lParam)
```

The effect of assigning the return value of **CallWindowProc** to the return value of the user-defined Windows procedure **WindowProc** is to process the message in the default manner. The value returned by the user-defined Windows procedure **WindowProc** to Windows determines how the message is processed. Here, that return value is the value returned by the default Windows procedure from the call to **CallWindowProc**.

In this example, the call to **CallWindowProc** is different:

```
retVal = CallWindowProc(defWindowProc, hwnd, Msg, wParam, lParam)
```

The difference is that the return value of **CallWindowProc** is not assigned to the return value of the user-defined Windows procedure **WindowProc**, but instead stored in the variable *retVal*. Therefore, at this point the value being returned by the default Windows procedure is *not* being passed on to Windows. Additionally, if in the further code the value of *retVal* is changed before it is assigned to the return value of **WindowProc**, then the message will be processed by Windows differently than in the default manner. Of course, if in the further code the value of *retVal* is *not* changed before it is assigned to the return value of **WindowProc**, then the message will be processed by Windows in the default manner.

Assigning the return value of **CallWindowProc** to *retVal* instead of the return value of **WindowProc** permits the opportunity first to inspect the value returned by **CallWindowProc** and, depending on the value, to decide whether to change that value before assigning *retVal* to the return value of **WindowProc**.

Specifically, if the message is WM_NCHITTEST, then the value returned by the default window function as a result of the call to **CallWindowProc** will be the constant (for example, HTCLIENT) representing the hit code of the hot spot. The value of that constant will be stored in *retVal*.

```
Select Case uMsg
Case WM_NCHITTEST
If retVal = HTCLIENT Then
   retVal = HTCAPTION
```

The only message which requires inspection of the value returned by **CallWindowProc** is WM_NCHITTEST. If the message is WM_NCHITTEST, then the value assigned to *retVal* from the return value of **CallWindowProc** is the hit code of the hot spot.

The variable *retVal* is inspected to determine if its value is the client area constant HTCLIENT. If it is, then the value of *retVal* is changed to the hit code of the caption (title bar) hot spot, HTCAPTION. This new hot spot then is returned to Windows with the statement

```
WindowProc = retVal
```

Now if the application user drags the mouse over the client area, Windows thinks the title bar is being dragged, and moves the window.

```
ElseIf retVal = HTTOP Or HTTOPLEFT Or HTLEFT _
    Or HTBOTTOMLEFT Or HTBOTTOM Or _
    HTBOTTOMRIGHT Or HTRIGHT Or HTTOPRIGHT Then
    retVal = HTNOWHERE
End If
```

If the value of the variable *retVal* is not the client area hit code, then it is inspected to determine if its value is the hit code for any of the sides or corners. If so, then *retVal* is changed to the hit code for outside of the window, HTNOWHERE, and once again the new hot spot is returned to Windows with the statement:

```
WindowProc = retVal
```

Finally, this statement also handles those messages which are not specifically addressed **WindowProc** by passing on to Windows the unchanged value of *retVal*. In other words, if the message was the one for which **WindowProc** was designed, the value of *retVal* already has been changed and is ready to be passed to Windows. Otherwise, *retVal* already contains the correct value as a result of the invocation of the default Windows procedure by **CallWindowProc** and is ready to be passed to Windows.

TEST THE CODE

1. Start a new project, Standard Exe. The default form may be the startup form. Accept the name Form1 and the other default properties.

2. Place on the form a command button named **cmdEnd** and captioned "Exit." Your form should look like Figure 2-1.

3. Place the code above in a standard module.

4. Place the following code in the **Load** event of the form procedure:

```
Private Sub Form_Load()
 Call SubClass(Me.hwnd)
End Sub
```

5. Place the following code in the **Click** event of the command button:

```
Private Sub cndEnd_Click()
    Unload Me
End Sub
```

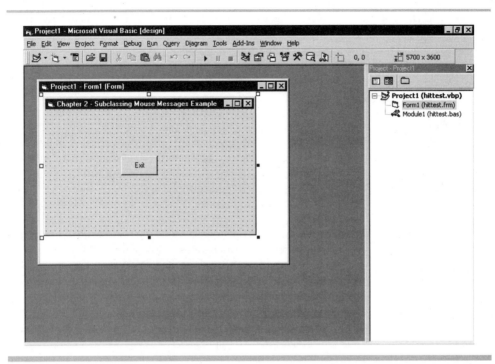

FIGURE 2-1. Subclassing Mouse Messages Form in Design view

6. Place the following code in the **Unload** event of Form1:

```
Private Sub Form_Unload(Cancel As Integer)
    Call UnSubClass(Me.hwnd)
End Sub
```

Steps 4 through 6 have been covered in the preceding two examples.

Test the code! Clicking on the client area of the form with the left mouse button and then dragging the mouse will move the form. Moving the mouse over the border and then dragging it while holding down the left mouse button will not resize the window.

sendmsg.vbp

Using a Mouse to Move a Form With SendMessage

This example, like the preceding one, will enable to the user to move a form by clicking *anywhere* on the form (for example, the client area) and dragging. This time we won't fib to Windows that the user clicked on the title bar when the user really clicked in the client area. Instead, we simply will send Windows a message to act as if the user clicked on the title bar if the user clicks anywhere on the form.

SENDMESSAGE

SendMessage is an API function by which you can send a message to a window or control. **SendMessage** sends a message by immediately calling the Windows function (usually the default) for the specified window. The function does not return until the Windows function completes its execution. Therefore, **SendMessage** returns a value. However, unless the message being sent returns a value which is meaningful, the return value of **SendMessage** usually is ignored.

A related API function is **PostMessage**, which sends a message by posting the message to the message queue for the window to be processed in due course by the Windows function. The queue is simply a line of messages waiting to be processed by the window. The **PostMessage** function returns immediately, before the Windows function executes the message, so **PostMessage** does not return a value.

SendMessage has four parameters: the window, the message, and the *wParam* and *lParam* accompanying the message. The *wParam* and *lParam* parameters carry additional information about the message. The nature of that information depends on the specific message being sent.

The data type of *wParam* is long. The data type of *lParam* is … well, it depends. This issue is discussed in the annotations.

SYNOPSIS OF CODE

Windows sends a WM_NCLBUTTONDOWN message when the user presses the left mouse button while the cursor is within the nonclient area of a window, for example, the title bar, menu bar, or window frame. The message carries with it two long values, a *wParam* and a *lParam*. Here it is *wParam* in which we are interested because, in the case of a WM_NCLBUTTONDOWN message, it contains the hit code for the hot spot.

If the user left-clicks the form, then **SendMessage** is called. Its parameters are the handle to the form, the WM_NCLBUTTONDOWN message, the hit code HTCAPTION, and 0& since the value of the *lParam* is of no interest. The return value of **SendMessage** is ignored because it is not meaningful in the case of a WM_NCLBUTTONDOWN message.

SendMessage tells Windows to act as if the user clicked on the title bar with the left mouse button. Dragging the mouse then will move the form.

The code is entirely in the form. There are no standard or class modules or any controls on the form. There is only one form procedure, in the **MouseDown** event. The remainder of the code is in declarations.

CODE

```
Private Declare Function SendMessage Lib "User32" _
   Alias "SendMessageA" _
   (ByVal hWnd As Long, ByVal wMsg As Long, _
   ByVal wParam As Long, _
  lParam As Any) As Long

Private Declare Sub ReleaseCapture Lib "User32" ()

Const WM_NCLBUTTONDOWN As Long = &HA1
Const HTCAPTION As Long = 2

Private Sub Form_MouseDown(Button As Integer, Shift As Integer, _
   X As Single, Y As Single)
Dim lngReturnValue As Long
 If Button = vbLeftButton Then
 Call ReleaseCapture
 lngReturnValue = SendMessage(Me.hWnd, _
   WM_NCLBUTTONDOWN, _ HTCAPTION, 0&)
 End If
End Sub
```

ANNOTATIONS

This code is quite different from the preceding examples. The main difference is that there is no subclassing. Only the default window procedure is used.

```
Private Declare Function SendMessage Lib "User32" _
   Alias "SendMessageA" _
   (ByVal hWnd As Long, ByVal wMsg As Long, _
   ByVal wParam As Long, _
  lParam As Any) As Long
```

Note that *lParam* is declared "As Any." The reason is that *lParam* can be a number (passed **ByVal** and *Long*), a string (passed either **ByRef** or **ByVal**, and declared as either String or Any), or can contain an array or a user-defined Type (passed **ByRef** as Any). In addition, *lParam* can, again depending on the message passed, return a value from the call in the parameter passed (usually a user-defined type) where the call fills in certain members, like a RECT structure. In this case the *lParam* is always passed **ByRef** as Any.

Since *lParam* can be different data types, and may be passed either **ByVal** or **ByRef**, it is prudent to use the **Alias** keyword in Visual Basic to define new **SendMessage** declarations named to reflect the type of data being passed. This can reduce the possibility of mismatched variable types and other errors. Thus, for passing numbers in *lParam*, the function could be declared:

```
Private Declare Function SendMessageNum Lib "user32" _
   Alias "SendMessageA" _
   (ByVal hwnd As Long, ByVal wMsg As Long, _
   ByVal wParam As Long, _
   ByVal lParam As Long) As Long
```

By constrast, for passing strings in *lParam*, the function could be declared:

```
Private Declare Function SendMessageStr Lib "user32" _
   Alias "SendMessageA" _
   (ByVal hwnd As As Long, ByVal wMsg As Long,
   ByVal wParam As Long, _
   ByVal lParam As String) As Long
```

Finally, to pass arrays and user-defined types:

```
Private Declare Function SendMessage& Lib "user32" _
   Alias "SendMessageA" _
   (ByVal hwnd As Long, ByVal wMsg As Long,  _
   ByVal wParam As Long, _
   lParam As Any) As Long
```

Otherwise, the declarations of the API functions and constants should be second nature by now, though what **ReleaseCapture** does and why it is necessary is not so obvious (but will be explained shortly).

```
Private Sub Form_MouseDown(Button As Integer, Shift As Integer, _
   X As Single, Y As Single)
If Button = vbLeftButton Then
```

Our code is only interested in a mouse click on the form if the left mouse button is pressed. The constant **vbLeftButton**, as its name suggests, indicates the left button is pressed. The code is placed in the **MouseDown** event, but it also could be placed in the form's **MouseMove** event instead.

```
Call ReleaseCapture
```

The **ReleaseCapture** API function releases the mouse capture from a window in the current thread and restores normal mouse input processing. This function is necessary because if a mouse event occurs while the pointer is over a form or control, that object "captures" the mouse and receives all mouse events. We need to free the mouse for the **SendMessage** call.

```
lngReturnValue = SendMessage(Me.hWnd, WM_NCLBUTTONDOWN, HTCAPTION, 0&)
```

Here we send Windows the WM_NCLBUTTONDOWN message with the *wParam* indicating that the hot spot is the title bar. Now if the mouse is dragging while continuing to depress the left button, Windows acts as if the title bar is being dragged.

TEST THE CODE

1. Start a new project, Standard Exe. The default form may be the startup form. Accept the name Form1 and the other default properties.

2. Place the code above in the form, the declarations in general declarations, and the procedure in the **MouseDown** event of the form.

The form can be moved by left-clicking and dragging anywhere on the form.

SENDMESSAGE VS. SUBCLASSING

Permitting moving of the form by left-clicking and dragging anywhere on the form certainly is easier to accomplish using **SendMessage** than subclassing. So why use subclassing?

There are circumstances, such as the one just shown, where you can accomplish the same task with **SendMessage** as you could with subclassing. Under these circumstances, **SendMessage** is preferable as it is both easier and less dangerous than subclassing. However, **SendMessage** is more limited than subclassing. **SendMessage** only can send a message to Windows. **SendMessage** cannot change a message which has been sent by Windows.

SendMessage, like subclassing, is a tool. No programming tool is the best choice for all your tasks in writing an application program any more than one construction tool can be used for all construction operations involved in building a house. The more programming tools you master, the better able you will be to solve effectively the task at hand.

closefrm.vbp

Disabling the Close Button Without Affecting the System Menu

The saving of data, the prevention of memory leaks, or other application integrity issues may require the execution of code upon the termination of your application. Often this termination code is located in the **Click** event of your "Exit" command button, menu item, or toolbar button. However, this code is bypassed if the application user clicks the Close button ("X") on the title bar of the window.

One solution is to use the **QueryUnload** and **Unload** events. However, under certain circumstances these events are not guaranteed to occur before your application terminates, and even if they do, they may not provide you with the control you need to perform your application termination code.

The safest solution is to make the Close button on the title bar disappear. This cannot be accomplished satisfactorily by Visual Basic's built-in properties. The Close button on the title bar can be removed by setting the **ControlBox** property to False. However, this has the side effect of also removing the Minimize and Maximize buttons and the system menu (also called the *control menu*), which may not be what you want to do.

However, by subclassing you can disable the Close button on the title bar while leaving intact the Minimize and Maximize buttons and the system menu (in the next chapter we will remove the application user's ability to use the Close item on the system menu). This is a good example of the power of subclassing and the Windows API, which solves easily an issue for which Visual Basic has no satisfactory solution.

SYNOPSIS OF CODE

As in the first example of this chapter, the user-defined Windows function will call **CallWindowProc** to obtain the message, and then look for the WM_NCHITTEST message. If that is the message, then the hit code is checked. If the hit code is the Close button on the title bar (HTCLOSE), then the hit code is changed to HTNOWHERE. Otherwise, the hit code is passed through without change.

There is one other detail which will be discussed in the analysis of the code.

CODE

```
Option Explicit

Public defWindowProc As Long

Public Const GWL_WNDPROC As Long = (-4)
Public Const WM_NCHITTEST As Long = &H84
Public Const HTNOWHERE As Long = 0
Public Const HTCLOSE As Long = 20

Declare Function GetWindowLong Lib "User32" _
    Alias "GetWindowLongA" _
    (ByVal hWnd As Long, ByVal nIndex As Long) As Long

Declare Function SetWindowLong Lib "User32" _
    Alias "SetWindowLongA" _
    (ByVal hWnd As Long, ByVal nIndex As Long, _
    ByVal dwNewLong As Long) As Long
```

```
Declare Function CallWindowProc Lib "User32" _
   Alias "CallWindowProcA" _
   (ByVal lpPrevWndFunc As Long, ByVal hWnd As Long, _
   ByVal Msg As Long, _
   ByVal wParam As Long, ByVal lParam As Long) As Long

Public Sub SubClass(hWnd As Long)
 On Error Resume Next
 defWindowProc = SetWindowLong(hWnd, _
    GWL_WNDPROC, AddressOf WindowProc)
End Sub

Public Sub UnSubClass(hWnd As Long)
 If defWindowProc Then
    SetWindowLong hWnd, GWL_WNDPROC, defWindowProc
    defWindowProc = 0
 End If
End Sub

Public Function WindowProc(ByVal hWnd As Long, _
    ByVal uMsg As Long, _
    ByVal wParam As Long, ByVal lParam As Long) As Long

On Error Resume Next
 Dim retVal As Long

 retVal = CallWindowProc(defWindowProc, _
   hWnd, uMsg, wParam, lParam)
If uMsg = WM_NCHITTEST Then
 If retVal = HTCLOSE Then retVal = HTNOWHERE
End If
WindowProc = retVal
End Function
```

ANNOTATIONS

```
Public Const HTNOWHERE As Long = 0
Public Const HTCLOSE As Long = 20
```

These are the usual declarations of constants—in this case, for hit codes. However, the value for HTCLOSE is not in Visual Basic's API Viewer tool. Yet this hit code does have a value. How that value can be determined is discussed next.

```
If uMsg = WM_NCHITTEST Then
 If retVal = HTCLOSE Then retVal = HTNOWHERE
End If
WindowProc = retVal
```

This code is at the heart of the user-defined code **WindowProc**. If the message is WM_NCHITTEST, then the hit code is examined. If the hit code is HTCLOSE, then it is changed to HTNOWHERE. Otherwise the hit code is unchanged.

Now for how the value of HTCLOSE is determined: The simplest among several methods is to place the following statement just below the If statement testing if the message parameter (*uMsg*) is WM_NCHITTEST:

```
Debug.Print retVal
```

Open the immediate window and run the program. When the cursor goes over the Close button, the value in the immediate window changes to 20.

TEST THE CODE

1. Start a new project, Standard Exe. The default form may be the startup form. Accept the name Form1 and the other default properties.

2. Place on the form a command button named **cmdEnd** and captioned "Exit." Your form should look like Figure 2-2.

3. Place the code above in a standard module.

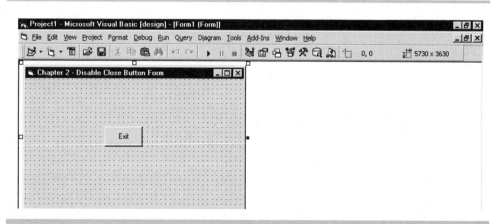

FIGURE 2-2. The Disable Close Button Form in Design view

4. Place the following code in the **Load** event of the form procedure:

```
Private Sub Form_Load()
 Call SubClass(Me.hwnd)
End Sub
```

5. Place the following code in the **Click** event of the command button:

```
Private Sub cndEnd_Click()
    Unload Me
End Sub
```

6. Place the following code in the **Unload** event of Form1:

```
Private Sub Form_Unload(Cancel As Integer)
    Call UnSubClass(Me.hwnd)
End Sub
```

Steps 4 through 6 have been covered in the preceding two examples.

The form should now behave as a normal form with the exception that the Close button on the title bar is disabled.

CursorTest.vbp

Confining the Mouse to the Form

Thus far we have had examples in which the mouse controlled the form. Turnabout is fair play. In this example, the form will control the mouse. Specifically, the movement of the mouse will be confined to the form.

As discussed at the start of this chapter, the mouse usually is given free rein to go to wherever on the screen the application user moves it. However, this may not always be desirable. There are circumstances, particularly with modal forms and dialog boxes, in which you may want to confine the mouse to the form until the form has been dismissed.

Additionally, there are circumstances in which you may want to direct the precise location of the mouse cursor. The **SetFocus** method can direct the mouse to a control, but you may want greater precision than that method permits, such as to direct the mouse to a particular location within the control.

The following example shows how to accomplish both tasks.

SYNOPSIS OF CODE

Confining a mouse to a form is accomplished with the **ClipCursor** API function. This function takes one parameter, the rectangular area to which the mouse will be confined. The rectangular coordinates of the form are obtained from the form's **Left**, **Top**, **Height**, and **Width** properties, discussed in the "Centering a Form" example in Chapter 1. The values of these properties must be converted from the unit of screen coordinate measurement used in Visual Basic, twips, to the unit of screen coordinate measurement used in API functions, pixels. This is accomplished using the **TwipsPerPixelX** or **TwipsPerPixelY** property of the **Screen** object, also discussed in the "Centering a Form" example in Chapter 1.

Moving the mouse cursor to a precise location within a control is more difficult because the control's **Left** and **Top** properties, unlike the form, are not relative to the screen, but relative to the containing form. However, the **ClientToScreen** API function may be used to convert a given location within the control (0,0 being the top-left corner of the control) to the corresponding screen coordinates.

CODE

```
Option Explicit

Private Type POINTAPI
        X As Long
        Y As Long
End Type

Private Type RECT
    Left As Long
    Top As Long
    Right As Long
    Bottom As Long
End Type

Private Declare Function GetCursorPos Lib _
    "user32" (lpPoint As POINTAPI) As Long
Private Declare Function SetCursorPos Lib _
    "user32" (ByVal X As Long, ByVal Y As Long) As Long
Private Declare Function ClientToScreen Lib _
    "user32" _
    (ByVal hwnd As Long, lpPoint As POINTAPI) As Long
Private Declare Function ClipCursor Lib "user32" _
    (lpRect As RECT) As Long
Private Declare Sub ClipCursorClear Lib "user32" _
    Alias "ClipCursor" (ByVal lpRect As Long)

Private Property Get X() As Long
    Dim tmpPoint As POINTAPI
    Call GetCursorPos(tmpPoint)
    X = tmpPoint.X
End Property
```

```
Private Property Let X(ByVal vNewValue As Long)
   Call SetCursorPos(vNewValue, Y)
End Property

Private Property Get Y() As Long
   Dim tmpPoint As POINTAPI
   Call GetCursorPos(tmpPoint)
   Y = tmpPoint.Y
End Property

Private Property Let Y(ByVal vNewValue As Long)
   Call SetCursorPos(X, vNewValue)
End Property

Public Sub SnapTo(ctl As Control)
   Dim pnt As POINTAPI
   Dim xx As Long
   Dim yy As Long
   pnt.X = pnt.Y = 0
   Call ClientToScreen(ctl.hwnd, pnt)
   xx = pnt.X + (ctl.Width \ 2)
   yy = pnt.Y + (ctl.Height \ 2)
   Call SetCursorPos(xx, yy)
End Sub

Public Sub ClipTo(Frm As Form)
   On Error Resume Next
   Dim tmpRect As RECT
   With Frm
      tmpRect.Left = (.Left \ Screen.TwipsPerPixelX)
      tmpRect.Top = (.Top \ Screen.TwipsPerPixelY)
      tmpRect.Right = (.Left + .Width) \ _
         Screen.TwipsPerPixelX
      tmpRect.Bottom = (.Top + .Height) \ _
         Screen.TwipsPerPixelY
      Call ClipCursor(tmpRect)
   End With
End Sub

Private Sub Class_Terminate()
   Call ClipCursorClear(0&)
End Sub
```

ANNOTATIONS

```
Private Type POINTAPI
        X As Long
        Y As Long
End Type

Private Property Get X() As Long
    Dim tmpPoint As POINTAPI
    Call GetCursorPos(tmpPoint)
    X = tmpPoint.X
End Property

Private Property Let X(ByVal vNewValue As Long)
    Call SetCursorPos(vNewValue, Y)
End Property

Private Property Get Y() As Long
    Dim tmpPoint As POINTAPI
    Call GetCursorPos(tmpPoint)
    Y = tmpPoint.Y
End Property

Private Property Let Y(ByVal vNewValue As Long)
    Call SetCursorPos(X, vNewValue)
End Property
```

The **GetCursorPos** API function retrieves the cursor's position, in screen coordinates. It has one parameter, a pointer to a POINT structure that receives the screen coordinates of the cursor.

The POINT structure has two members that hold the x and y coordinates respectively of a point. As in preceding examples, a user-defined type, POINTAPI, is declared to parallel the structure used by the API function.

The data type of the members of the POINT structure is Long. Reference materials are conflicting on whether POINT's members are Longs of Integers. Many examples define the members of POINT as having integer values. The data type of the members of the POINT structure *was* Integer in 16-bit Windows. However, this no longer is the case in 32-bit Windows. Indeed, at the risk of violating the rule "Never Generalize," data types which were Integer in 16-bit Windows are Long in 32-bit Windows.

Property procedures are used to read and write to the members of POINTAPI. **Property Get** procedures are used to retrieve the value of a member variable, and **Property Let** procedures are used to assign a value to a member variable. If the member variable is an object instead of a primitive data type such as an integer, then a **Property Set** procedure is used instead of a **Property Let** procedure.

The **Property Get X** and **Property Get Y** procedures retrieve the X and Y coordinates respectively of the POINTAPI structure. Each procedure calls **GetCursorPos** to obtain a POINTAPI structure containing the screen coordinates of the cursor, and accesses the X or Y member to retrieve the value of the desired coordinate. The syntax for calling a **Property Get** procedure is discussed below in the code.

The **Property Let X** and **Property Let Y** procedures assign values to the X and Y coordinates respectively of the POINTAPI structure. The assignment is accomplished with the **SetCursorPos** API function. **SetCursorPos** is the converse of **GetCursorPos**; **SetCursorPos** moves the cursor to the screen coordinates specified by its two parameters, which are the new x and y coordinates respectively. The syntax for calling a **Property Let** procedure also is discussed below in the code.

Usually **Property** procedures are used to *encapsulate* the data (that is, variables) of the class. The variables are declared as Private so they cannot be accessed directly from outside of the class. Instead, the variables may be accessed only through **Property** procedures, which contain the logic for error checking (for example, confirming that the assigned value of the correct data type) and data validation (for example, confirming that the data within the correct range). In these circumstances the **Property** procedures must be declared as Public so they can be accessed from outside of the class.

In this example, the **Property** procedures are being accessed only from inside of the class. Therefore, they are declared as Private. However, here the **Property** procedures are useful even though they are not being used to encapsulate data. If the **clsCursor** class was developed further, there may be many occasions within the class to read from or write to the X or Y coordinates of a POINTAPI structure. Without the **Property** procedures, the logic would have to be repeated throughout the class. If the logic ever were changed, those changes would have to be propagated in numerous places throughout the class. By contrast, with the **Property** procedures, any need for a member function of the class to read from or write to the X or Y coordinates of a POINTAPI structure would be accomplished with a call to the **Property** procedures, and any change in the read or write logic need only be made in one place, the **Property** procedures. This is an advantage of object-oriented programming.

These **Property** procedures are declared after the declarations of the API functions. The reason is that the **Property** procedures use two of the API functions, **GetCursorPos** and **SetCursorPos**. The API functions have to be declared before they can be used.

```
Private Type RECT
    Left As Long
    Top As Long
    Right As Long
    Bottom As Long
End Type
```

The **ClipCursor** function, discussed further below, confines the cursor to a rectangular area on the screen. That function takes one parameter, a pointer to a RECT structure that contains the screen coordinates of the top-left and bottom-right corners of the confining rectangle. This RECT structure **ClipCursor** function has four members, the x coordinate of the top-left corner of the form, the y coordinate of the top-left corner of the form, the x coordinate of the bottom-right corner of the form, and the y coordinate of the bottom-right corner of the form. As in preceding examples, a user-defined type, RECT, is declared to parallel the structure used by the API function.

```
Private Declare Function GetCursorPos Lib "user32" _
    (lpPoint As POINTAPI) As Long
Private Declare Function SetCursorPos Lib "user32" _
    (ByVal X As Long, ByVal Y As Long) As Long
Private Declare Function ClientToScreen Lib "user32" _
    (ByVal hwnd As Long, lpPoint As POINTAPI) As Long
Private Declare Function ClipCursor Lib "user32" _
    (lpRect As RECT) As Long
Private Declare Sub ClipCursorClear Lib "user32" _
    Alias "ClipCursor" (ByVal lpRect As Long)
```

As discussed above, the **ClipCursor** function confines the cursor to a rectangular area on the screen. Its converse, the **ClipCursorClear** function, releases the cursor to a rectangular area on the screen. The difference between the two API functions is the data type of their one parameter. The data type of the parameter of the **ClipCursor** function is the RECT structure to which the mouse will be confined. By contrast, the data type of the parameter of the **ClipCursorClear** function is a long value, specifically 0. Therefore, the **Alias** keyword is used to differentiate between the two API calls. The concept of using the **Alias** keyword to differentiate between two API calls which differ only in the data type of a parameter was discussed in the preceding example, "Using a Mouse to Move a Form With SendMessage."

```
Public Sub ClipTo(Frm As Form)
    On Error Resume Next
    Dim tmpRect As RECT
    With Frm
        tmpRect.Left = (.Left \ Screen.TwipsPerPixelX)
        tmpRect.Top = (.Top \ Screen.TwipsPerPixelY)
        tmpRect.Right = (.Left + .Width) \ Screen.TwipsPerPixelX
        tmpRect.Bottom = (.Top + .Height) \ Screen.TwipsPerPixelY
        Call ClipCursor(tmpRect)
    End With
End Sub
```

This function confines the mouse cursor to the form. It takes one parameter, a reference of the form to which the mouse will be confined. The **Left**, **Top**, **Height**, **and Width** properties, discussed in the "Centering a Form" example in Chapter 1, are used to assign values to the members of the RECT structure, the x and y coordinates of the top-left and bottom-right corners of the form. The **TwipsPerPixelX** and **TwipsPerPixelY** properties of the **Screen** object, also discussed in the "Centering a Form" example in Chapter 1, are necessary because the unit of measurement of screen coordinates in Visual Basic is twips whereas in API functions it is pixels.

Once values are assigned to the RECT structure, the structure is passed as a parameter to **ClipCursor** to confine the mouse cursor within the coordinates of that rectangle.

```
Public Sub SnapTo(ctl As Control)
    Dim pnt As POINTAPI
    Dim xx As Long
    Dim yy As Long
    pnt.X = pnt.Y = 0
    Call ClientToScreen(ctl.hwnd, pnt)
    xx = pnt.X + (ctl.Width \ 2)
    yy = pnt.Y + (ctl.Height \ 2)
    Call SetCursorPos(xx, yy)
End Sub
```

This function "snaps" the cursor to the center of the control whose reference is passed as a parameter to the function. In this example the control is the Close command button. Once the screen coordinates of the center of the Close command button are obtained, then those coordinates are passed as parameters to the **SetCursorPos** API function to move the cursor to those coordinates.

The logic of obtaining the screen coordinates of the center of the Close command button is first to obtain the x and y coordinates of the top-left corner of the command button. Adding to the x coordinate of the control one-half of the width of the control, using the **Width** property of the control (ctl.Width), provides the x coordinate of the center of the control. Similarly, adding to the y coordinate of the control one-half of the height of the control, using the **Height** property of the control (ctl. Height), provides the y coordinate of the center of the control.

The difficulty is obtaining the x and y screen coordinates of the top-left corner of the command button. The problem is that, unlike the form's **Left** and **Top** properties, the control's **Left** and **Top** properties are not relative to the screen but rather relative to the form.

The solution is the **ClientToScreen** API function. This function converts the client coordinates of a specified point to screen coordinates. *Screen coordinates* are used to express the position of a window. The point of origin is the upper-left corner of the screen. By contrast, the position of points in a window is expressed in *client coordinates*. The point of origin in this case is the upper-left corner of the window or client area. The purpose of client coordinates is consistent coordinate values while drawing in the window, regardless of the position of the window on the screen. For example, client coordinates are used to retain the position of controls relative to their containing form.

The **ClientToScreen** function takes two parameters. The first is the handle to the source of the client coordinates, in this example the Close command button (which itself is a window). The second parameter is a pointer to a POINTAPI structure which will hold the screen coordinates. The client coordinates are the top-left corner of the control, 0,0. The corresponding screen coordinates are assigned to the members of the POINTAPI structure **pnt**, which then are passed as parameters to the **SetCursorPos** API function to move the cursor to those coordinates.

The assignment of the values to the members of the POINTAPI structure is not a direct assignment, but rather through the **Property Let** procedures. For example, the statement

```
pnt.X = pnt.Y = 0
```

uses the **Property Let Y** procedure to assign to the Y member variable of **pnt** the value on the right side of the assignment operator, 0.

Similarly, the statement

```
xx = pnt.X + (ctl.Width \ 2)
```

does not directly access the X member variable of **pnt**. Rather, it uses the **Property Get X** procedure to access that value.

```
Private Sub Class_Terminate()
    Call ClipCursorClear(0&)
End Sub
```

The call to **ClipCursorClear** is necessary to release the confinement of the cursor caused by **ClipCursor**. Otherwise the cursor remains confined in the Visual Basic IDE after the application terminates. **ClipCursorClear** takes one parameter, 0.

The call to **ClipCursorClear** is made in the **Terminate** event of the class. This event occurs when all references to an instance of a class are removed from memory by setting all the variables that refer to the object to Nothing or when the last reference to the object falls out of scope. When the form unloads, the one reference to the **clsCursor** class goes out of scope, triggering the **Terminate** event.

TEST FORM

1. Start a new project, Standard Exe. The default form may be the startup form. Accept the name Form1 and the other default properties.

2. Place the following controls on the form:

Control	Name	Caption
Command Button	cmdClose	Close
Label	Label1	Whatsamatter U Advanced VB Class

Your form should look like Figure 2-3.

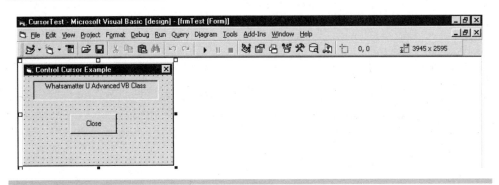

FIGURE 2-3. Control Cursor Form in Design view

3. Place the code above in a class module called **clsCursor**.

4. Place the following code in the general declarations of the test form:

```
Option Explicit
Dim Cursor As cCursor
```

Cursor is the instance of the class **clsCursor** used in this example.

5. Place the following code as indicated:

```
Private Sub Form_Load()
    Set Cursor = New cCursor
End Sub
```

This is necessary to instantiate **Cursor** as a **clsCursor** object.

```
Private Sub Form_MouseMove(Button As Integer, _
    Shift As Integer, X As Single, Y As Single)
    Cursor.ClipTo Me
End Sub
```

The **ClipTo** method of **clsCursor** should not be called in the **Load** event of the test form because at startup the mouse pointer may be outside the coordinates of the test form. The **MouseMove** event is a safe place to call the **ClipTo** method.

```
Private Sub Label1_Click()
    Cursor.SnapTo cmdClose
End Sub
```

```
Private Sub Form_MouseUp(Button As Integer, _
    Shift As Integer, X As Single, Y As Single)
    Label1_Click
End Sub
```

When the mouse is released on the form or the label is clicked, the mouse pointer snaps to the center of the **cmdClose** command button.

```
Private Sub cmdClose_Click()
    Unload Me
End Sub
```

Test the code! The mouse remains confined to the form, and snaps to the center of the Close command button when the mouse is released on the form or the label is clicked. This behavior remains true even when the form is moved to different places on the screen.

AnimCursor.vbp

Animating Your Cursor

Animated cursors not only make your application more interesting and fun to use, the animation may provide your application's user with visual cues. For example, an animation of a lengthy sorting procedure may be more helpful than an hourglass while your application is sorting, and an animation of a pair of scissors may be helpful to cue your application's user that a portion of a bitmap is being "cut" to the clipboard.

A customized cursor may be assigned to a form using the form's **MouseIcon** property. However, an animated cursor cannot be assigned to the **MouseIcon** property. If you try to do so, you will receive the error message "Invalid picture (Error 481)." Help will tell you that assigning an unsupported graphics format caused the error.

Once again, the Windows API will help you transcend a limitation of Visual Basic.

SYNOPSIS OF CODE

This code uses subclassing, but in a different manner than the prior examples. This time there is no user-defined Windows function that substitutes for the default Windows function. Rather, the handle of the animated mouse cursor is substituted for the handle of the default mouse cursor. However, as before, care must be taken to restore the default mouse cursor when the application terminates.

CODE

```vb
Option Explicit

Private hOldCursor As Long
Private hNewCursor As Long

Private Const GCL_HCURSOR As Long = (-12)
Private Const CURSORDIR As String = "Cursors\"
Private Const CURSORFILE As String = "cut.ani"

Private Declare Function LoadCursorFromFile Lib "user32" _
    Alias "LoadCursorFromFileA" _
    (ByVal lpFileName As String) As Long

Private Declare Function SetClassLong Lib "user32" _
    Alias "SetClassLongA" _
    (ByVal hwnd As Long, ByVal nIndex As Long, _
    ByVal dwNewLong As Long) As Long

Private Declare Function GetWindowsDirectory _
    Lib "kernel32" Alias _
    "GetWindowsDirectoryA" _
    (ByVal lpBuffer As String, _
    ByVal nSize As Long) As Long

Public Sub SubClass(hwnd As Long)
    hNewCursor = LoadCursorFromFile(GetCursorFile)
    hOldCursor = SetClassLong _
      (hwnd, GCL_HCURSOR, hNewCursor)
End Sub

Public Sub UnSubClass(hwnd As Long)
    hOldCursor = SetClassLong _
      (hwnd, GCL_HCURSOR, hOldCursor)
End Sub

Private Function GetCursorFile() As String
    Dim Temp As String
    Dim Ret As Long
```

```
    Const MAX_LENGTH = 145
    Temp = String$(MAX_LENGTH, 0)
    Ret = GetWindowsDirectory(Temp, MAX_LENGTH)
    Temp = Left$(Temp, Ret)
    If Temp <> "" And Right$(Temp, 1) <> "\" Then
        GetCursorFile = Temp & "\" & CURSORDIR & CURSORFILE
    Else
        GetCursorFile = Temp & CURSORDIR & CURSORFILE
    End If
End Function
```

ANNOTATIONS

```
Private hOldCursor As Long
Private hNewCursor As Long
```

The variables *hOldCursor* and *hNewCursor* will hold the handles to the default and animated cursors respectively.

```
Private Const GCL_HCURSOR As Long = (-12)

Private Declare Function SetClassLong _
   Lib "user32" Alias "SetClassLongA" _
   (ByVal hwnd As Long, ByVal nIndex As Long, _
   ByVal dwNewLong As Long) As Long
```

The constant GCL_HCURSOR is used in conjunction with the API function **SetClassLong**. The constant is passed as the second parameter to **SetClassLong** to indicate that the handle of the cursor associated with the window class should be replaced with the cursor handle specified.

In prior subclassing examples the constant GCL_WNDPROC was used in conjunction with the API function **SetWindowLong** to indicate that a user-defined Windows procedure should be substituted for the default Windows procedure. Some of the constants used with **SetWindowLong** are set forth in Table 2- 3.

SetClassLong and **SetWindowLong** are similar. The difference is that **SetWindowLong** is used for *instance subclassing*, which is changing the window procedure for a particular window instance. **SetClassLong** is used for *global subclassing*, which is changing the window procedure for all windows of that class. Since **SetClassLong** is used for global subclassing, it should not be used to subclass standard Windows controls.

```
Private Const CURSORDIR As String = "Cursors\"
Private Const CURSORFILE As String = "cut.ani"
```

Constant	Description
GCL_HBRBACKGROUND	Replaces the handle of the background brush associated with the class.
GCL_HCURSOR	Replaces the handle of the cursor associated with the class.
GCL_HICON	Replaces the handle of the icon associated with the class.
GCL_MENUNAME	Replaces the address of the menu name string. The string identifies the menu resource associated with the class.
GCL_STYLE	Replaces the window-class style bits.
GCL_WNDPROC	Replaces the address of the window procedure associated with the class.

TABLE 2-3.   Constants Used with SetWindowLong

The animated cursors are in the Cursors subdirectory of the Windows directory. The file Cut.ani is one of the animated cursors. Animated cursors generally have the extension .ani.

```
Private Declare Function LoadCursorFromFile Lib "user32" _
    Alias "LoadCursorFromFileA" (ByVal lpFileName As String) As Long
```

The **LoadCursorFromFile** function creates a cursor based on the file specified in the first parameter. Files containing cursor data may be in either cursor (.cur) or animated cursor (.ani) format. The function returns a handle to the newly created cursor.

```
Private Declare Function GetWindowsDirectory _
    Lib "kernel32" Alias _
    "GetWindowsDirectoryA" _
    (ByVal lpBuffer As String, _
    ByVal nSize As Long) As Long
```

The **GetWindowsDirectory** function retrieves the path of the Windows directory. This function is used in place of hard-coding the path to the Windows directory, which may be different on Windows 95/98 workstations (c:\windows) than on Window NT workstations (c:\winnt).

```
Public Sub SubClass(hwnd As Long)
    hNewCursor = LoadCursorFromFile(GetCursorFile)
    hOldCursor = SetClassLong(hwnd, GCL_HCURSOR, hNewCursor)
End Sub
```

As discussed above, the return value of **LoadCursorFromFile** is the handle to the cursor whose file is specified in its parameter. This handle is then used as the third parameter to **SetClassLong** to indicate the replacement handle of the cursor for the window class. The constant GCL_HCURSOR is passed as the second parameter to **SetClassLong** to indicate that the handle of the cursor associated with the window class should be replaced with the cursor handle specified. The first parameter is the handle to the window, in this case the test form. The return value is the previous handle to previous default cursor. As in the other subclassing examples, it is critical to preserve this value so that the default cursor can be restored when the application terminates.

```
Public Sub UnSubClass(hwnd As Long)
    hOldCursor = SetClassLong(hwnd, GCL_HCURSOR, hOldCursor)
End Sub
```

This subroutine is called when the test form unloads and restores the default cursor, the handle of which, preserved in the variable *hOldCursor*, is the third parameter. The return value here is not used.

```
Private Function GetCursorFile() As String
    Dim Temp As String
    Dim Ret As Long
    Const MAX_LENGTH = 145
    Temp = String$(MAX_LENGTH, 0)
    Ret = GetWindowsDirectory(Temp, MAX_LENGTH)
    Temp = Left$(Temp, Ret)
    If Temp <> "" And Right$(Temp, 1) <> "\" Then
        GetCursorFile = Temp & "\" & CURSORDIR & CURSORFILE
    Else
        GetCursorFile = Temp & CURSORDIR & CURSORFILE
    End If
End Function
```

This function concatenates the Windows directory returned by the API function **GetWindowsDirectory** with the Cursors subdirectory and the specified animated cursor.

TEST THE CODE

1. Start a new project, Standard Exe. The default form may be the startup form. Accept the name Form1 and the other default properties.

2. Place the code above in a class module named **clsAnimCursor**.

3. Place the following code in the general declarations of the form:

```
Option Explicit
Dim cAnim As clsAnimCursor
```

4. Place the following code in the **Load** event of Form1:

```
Private Sub Form_Load(Cancel As Integer)
    Set cAnim = New clsAnimCursor
    SubClass Me.hwnd
End Sub
```

5. Place the following code in the **Unload** event of Form1:

```
Private Sub Form_Unload(Cancel As Integer)
    UnSubClass Me.hwnd
End Sub
```

Test the code! The cursor turns into a pair of scissors that has a cutting motion.

Customizing the System Menu

V isual Basic forms by default have a system menu, often also referred to as a *control menu* (see Figure 3-1). The items on the system menu, by default, are Restore, Move, Size, Minimize, Maximize, and Close. These items also relate to the title bar buttons. Disabling the Restore, Minimize, Maximize, or Close items will disable their counterpart buttons on the title bar and the corresponding **Click** event on the title bar (for example, double-clicking on the title bar by default restores a maximized window and maximizes a normal window and double-clicking the control box by default closes the window). Similarly, disabling the Move item will disable the ability to move the form by clicking on and dragging the title bar, and disabling the Size item will disable the ability to resize the window by its borders and corners.

The requirements of your application may warrant deleting or disabling existing system menu items or adding new items. The examples below discuss several reasons why you may wish to do this. However, Visual Basic offers only a limited ability to customize the system menu. Fortunately, the Windows API enables you to go beyond Visual Basic's limitations and customize the system menu to your heart's content.

Deleting an Item on the System Menu

KillClose.vbp

As discussed in the Close Form example in Chapter 2, the saving of data, the prevention of memory leaks, or other application integrity issues may require the execution of code upon the termination of your application. The problem was that this termination code, generally located in the **Click** event of your Exit command button, menu item, or toolbar button, could be bypassed if the application user simply clicked the Close button (X) on the title bar of the window.

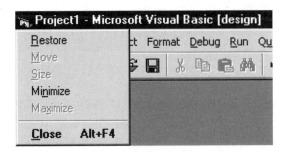

FIGURE 3-1. The system menu

The code in the Close Form example attempted to prevent bypassing of the termination code by disabling the Close button on the title bar (by changing the hit code from **HTCLOSE** to **HTNOWHERE**) while otherwise leaving intact the default functionality of the form. However, this meant that the application user still could bypass the termination code by using the system menu (see Figure 3-1), either by clicking the Close menu item or double-clicking the control box.

The indicated solution is to delete the Close item on the system menu. Visual Basic permits the easy removal of certain menu items from the system menu box by use of a form's **MaxButton**, **MinButton**, and **BorderStyle** properties (see Table 3-1). However, the Close item is not one of the system menu items which can be removed simply by setting a property of the form. The Close item can be deleted only by the overkill of deleting the system menu itself (as well as the Minimize, Maximize, and Close buttons on the title bar) by setting the form's **ControlBox** property to False.

SYNOPSIS OF CODE

The Windows API provides you with the flexibility Visual Basic lacks to manipulate the system menu and makes it possible to delete the Close item on the system menu.

The first step in removing a system menu item is to obtain a handle to the system menu. This is done with the API function **GetSystemMenu**. Next, the menu item is removed by the API function **RemoveMenu**. An item is removed by referring either to the item's "command ID" or to its position on the menu. The command ID is a long number, usually represented by a constant, which is used by Windows to refer to a specific menu item. The position is zero-based, so the position of the second item is 1.

Several helper functions are available. The number of menu items is obtained with the API function **GetMenuItemCount**. This function is especially helpful in

Property	Setting	Eliminates from System Menu	Eliminates from Title Bar	Other
MaxButton	False	Maximize	Maximize	Double-click on title bar does not maximize form.
MinButton	False	Minimize	Minimize	
BorderStyle	1 or 3	Restore, Size, Minimize, Maximize	Minimize, Maximize	Dragging borders and corners does not resize form.

TABLE 3-1. Form Property Settings Which Affect System Menu Items and Title Bar Buttons

removing the last item by reference to its position. The command ID of a menu item at a given position may be determined by the API function **GetMenuItemID**. This function is helpful in removing an item by reference to its command ID.

CODE

```
'clsKillClose
Option Explicit

Public Const MF_BYPOSITION = &H400
Private Const MF_BYCOMMAND = &H0&
Public Const MF_REMOVE = &H1000
Private Const SC_CLOSE = &HF060&

Private Declare Function GetSystemMenu Lib "user32" _
    (ByVal hwnd As Long, _
        ByVal bRevert As Long) As Long

Private Declare Function GetMenuItemCount Lib "user32" _
    (ByVal hMenu As Long) As Long

Private Declare Function GetMenuItemID Lib "user32" _
    (ByVal hMenu As Long, _
        ByVal nPos As Long) As Long

Private Declare Function RemoveMenu Lib "user32" _
    (ByVal hMenu As Long, _
        ByVal nPosition As Long, ByVal wFlags As Long) As Long

Public Sub cmdKillClose KillClose(frm As Form)

Dim hMenu As Long
Dim menuItemCount As Long
  hMenu = GetSystemMenu(frm.hwnd, 0)
    If hMenu Then
      If RemoveMenu(hMenu, SC_CLOSE, MF_BYCOMMAND)
        menuItemCount = GetMenuItemCount(hMenu)
        If Not GetMenuItemID(hMenu, menuItemCount - 1) Then _
          Call RemoveMenu(hMenu, menuItemCount - 1, _
              MF_BYPOSITION)
      End If
    End If
End Sub
```

ANNOTATIONS

`'clsKillClose`

This code is being placed in a class module. This is permitted because the code does not use the **AddressOf** operator, which must be in a standard module. A class module is preferred over a standard module because it can be compiled as an ActiveX DLL (or EXE) for code reusability.

```
Public Const MF_BYPOSITION As Long = &H400
Private Const MF_BYCOMMAND As Long = &H0&
Private Const SC_CLOSE As Long = &HF060&
```

The first two constants are menu flags, the abbreviation for which is their MF prefix. These flags are used in a number of the API menu manipulation functions. The flag MF_BYPOSITION is used when the function is referring to a menu item by its position. The flag MF_BYCOMMAND is used when the function is referring to a menu item by its command ID. There are a number of other flags which are used by the API menu manipulation functions and several of them will be used in the following examples (see Table 3-2).

The other constant is a system command, hence its SC prefix. SC_CLOSE is the system command for closing the window, and therefore is associated with the Close item on the system menu. SC_CLOSE also is the command ID for the Close item.

Constant	Description
MF_BITMAP	Uses a bitmap as the menu item.
MF_BYPOSITION	Indicates that the second parameter specifies the zero-based relative position of the new menu item.
MF_CHECKED	Places a checkmark next to the item.
MF_DISABLED	Disables the menu item so that it cannot be selected, but this flag does not gray it.
MF_ENABLED	Enables the menu item so that it can be selected and restores it from its grayed state.
MF_GRAYED	Disables the menu item and grays it so that it cannot be selected.
MF_POPUP	Specifies that the menu item opens a drop-down menu or submenu.
MF_SEPARATOR	Draws a horizontal dividing line.
MF_STRING	Specifies that the menu item is a text string.
MF_UNCHECKED	Does not place a checkmark next to the item (the default).

TABLE 3-2.   Common Menu Flags

There are a number of other system commands which are used by the API menu manipulation functions, including ones for the other default system menu items, for example, SC_MOVE for the Move item, SC_SIZE for the Size item, SC_MAXIMIZE for the Maximize item, and so on (see Table 3-3).

The values of these constants can be obtained from Visual Basic's API Viewer tool. However, that tool leaves out the ampersand (&) at the end of the constant declaration. This makes a difference. The value of &HF060& (the hex value F060) is 61,536, whereas the value of &HF060 is –4,000. Obviously this could (and does) make a difference in whether your code works. The reason for the –4,000 value is that, without the ampersand (&) at the end of the constant declaration, &HF060 is interpreted as an integer. Since the range for integers is -32,768 to –32,767, a value of 61,536 "overflows" the range and results in an unexpected value. Placing the ampersand (&) at the end of the constant declaration results in the constant being interpreted as a long, and 61,536 is well within the range of that data type. This is just one of the quirks of Visual Basic that can keep you up at night wondering why your code is not working as expected.

```
Private Declare Function GetSystemMenu Lib "user32" _
    (ByVal hwnd As Long, _
        ByVal bRevert As Long) As Long

Private Declare Function GetMenuItemCount Lib "user32" _
    (ByVal hMenu As Long) As Long

Private Declare Function GetMenuItemID Lib "user32" _
    (ByVal hMenu As Long, _
        ByVal nPos As Long) As Long

Private Declare Function RemoveMenu Lib "user32" _
    (ByVal hMenu As Long, _
        ByVal nPosition As Long, ByVal wFlags As Long) As Long
```

These are the declarations of the API menu manipulation functions. In a class module, they must be declared as private. They will be discussed in detail when they are called, but their purposes are evident from their names. **GetSystemMenu** returns a handle to the system menu, **GetMenuItemCount** returns the number of menu items, **GetMenuItemID** returns the menu item's ID, and **RemoveMenu** removes a menu item.

```
Public Sub cmdKillClose KillClose(frm As Form)
```

Constant	Description
SC_CLOSE	Closes the window.
SC_DEFAULT	Selects the default item when the user double-clicks the system menu.
SC_HSCROLL	Scrolls horizontally.
SC_KEYMENU	Retrieves the system menu as a result of a keystroke.
SC_MAXIMIZE	Maximizes the window.
SC_MINIMIZE	Minimizes the window.
SC_MOUSEMENU	Retrieves the system menu as a result of a mouse click.
SC_MOVE	Moves the window.
SC_RESTORE	Restores the window to its normal position and size.
SC_SIZE	Sizes the window.
SC_VSCROLL	Scrolls vertically.

TABLE 3-3. Common System Commands

This is the method which will be called to remove the menu item. It must be declared as public so it can be invoked outside of the class.

```
Dim menuItemCount As Long
  hMenu = GetSystemMenu(frm.hwnd, 0)
    If hMenu Then
```

GetSystemMenu returns a handle to the system menu, assuming there is a system menu. There may not be one, depending on the properties of the window. For example, if the **ControlBox** property of the form is set to False, then there is no system menu. If there is no system menu, then **GetSystemMenu** returns zero. In that event, the statements following **If hMenu** do not execute. In our example there is a system menu so the following statements do execute.

```
If RemoveMenu(hMenu, SC_CLOSE, MF_BYCOMMAND)
```

RemoveMenu deletes a menu item. It has a return value—non-zero on success, zero on failure. The If statement checks for a true (non-zero) return value. If the return value is zero, the remaining code will not execute.

RemoveMenu takes three parameters. The first parameter is a handle to the system menu. This handle was obtained by the invocation of **GetSystemMenu**. The second parameter is *either* the position *or* the command ID of the menu item. Whether the second parameter refers to the position or the command ID depends on the third parameter. That parameter is a flag, either MF_BYPOSITION or MF_BYCOMMAND. If the flag is MF_BYPOSITION, then the second parameter refers to position. If the flag is MF_BYCOMMAND, then the second parameter refers to command ID.

In this case the flag is MF_BYCOMMAND, so the second parameter refers to the command ID of the menu item to be removed. In the next call to **RemoveMenu**, discussed below, the second parameter will refer instead to position.

As mentioned in the discussion of the constant declarations, the command ID of a default menu item in the system menu is a constant with the prefix SC. The constant SC_CLOSE is the command ID for the Close menu item, which is the item to be removed.

```
menuItemCount = GetMenuItemCount(hMenu)
If Not GetMenuItemID(hMenu, menuItemCount - 1) Then _
    Call RemoveMenu(hMenu, menuItemCount - 1, MF_BYPOSITION)
```

The Close item has been removed. However, above the Close item there likely is a separator bar. Having it remain may make your application look less professional. If it is there, then the above code will get rid of it.

GetMenuItemCount returns the number of entries in the menu whose handle is passed as the first paramenter. The numbering of the entries is zero-based.

GetMenuItemID returns the menu ID of the entry at the position specified in the second parameter (the first parameter is the handle to the system menu). Since the number of entries is zero-based, to obtain the position of the last entry the second parameter must be *menuItemCount – 1*, not *menuItemCount*.

If the last entry (now that the Close item has been removed) is the separator bar, then the value returned by **GetMenuItemID** is zero. Thus, the **NOT** operator in front of **GetMenuItemID** tests for the separator bar being the last item. If and only if it is, then the remainder of the code executes.

RemoveMenu is called with the third parameter, this time being the MF_BYPOSITION flag. Using this flag means the second parameter refers to the position (instead of the command ID) of the menu item to be removed. In this case, the last entry, the separator bar, is removed. This time, for simplicity's sake, the return value of **RemoveMenu** is ignored by use of the Call statement. In a commercial quality application there would be error-checking here.

The logic employed in removing the separator bar also could have been used in the first invocation of **RemoveMenu** which removed the Close item. However, the Close item is a default item that appears only once, so it could be safely assumed that the direct approach of referring to its command ID would work without the necessity of determining the menu count, and so on.

Similarly, the logic employed in removing the Close item also could have been used in the second invocation of **RemoveMenu** which removed the separator bar. However, it is possible that there is more than one separator bar, and we only wanted to remove the separator bar if it was the last item. Therefore, the approach of referring to the item's position was preferable to referring to its command ID.

This is another example of the advantage of knowing different methods of accomplishing the same task.

A final note is that no call was necessary to the API function **DrawMenuBar**, which redraws (that is, refreshes) the menu bar. Sometimes a call to this function, which takes as its one parameter the handle to the window (not the menu), may be necessary. In the next example it will be necessary to call **DrawMenuBar**.

TEST THE CODE

1. Start a new project, Standard Exe. The default form may be the startup form. Accept the name Form1. The StartUpPosition should be 2 – Center Screen.

2. Place on the form a command button named **cmdEnd**. You will need this command button because otherwise you will have no way to close your form from your application. Your form should look like Figure 3-2.

3. Insert a new class module named clsKillClose and paste in it the above code (which is also on the CD-ROM).

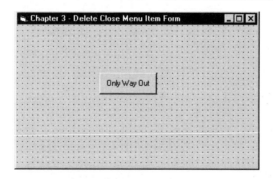

FIGURE 3-2. The Delete Close Menu Item form

4. Place the following code in the **Click** event of **cmdEnd**:

```
Private Sub cmdEnd_Click()
 End
End Sub
```

5. Place the following code in the **Load** event of the form:

```
Private Sub Form_Load()
  Dim kClose As clsKillClose
  Set kClose = New clsKillClose
  kClose.KillClose Me
  Set kClose = Nothing
End Sub
```

As discussed in the Center Form example in Chapter 1, the **KillClose** method cannot be called directly since it is in a class module, not a standard module. Instead, it must be called from an object of the type clsKillClose using the **Object.Method** syntax. Therefore, a clsKillClose object **kClose** first is created. This is done by declaring it with the Dim statement and then instantiating it with the **New** keyword. The Set statement is necessary because **kClose** is an object, not a primitive data type such as an integer.

Run the project. The Close menu item and the separator bar above it have been removed from the system menu. Additionally, double-clicking on the control box will not close the form. Finally, the close button on the title bar has been grayed out and clicking on it will not close the form. (See Figure 3-3.)

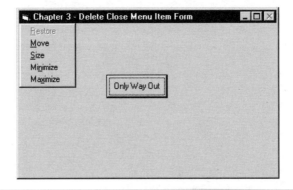

FIGURE 3-3. The Delete Close Menu Item Form in operation

Disable.vbp

Disabling an Item on the System Menu

Removing the Close item in the system menu may be more drastic than necessary. It may be sufficient simply to disable the Close item, which has the side effect of also disabling both the title bar Close button and the usual closing effect of double-clicking on the control box. Indeed, you may want to disable the Close item only in certain situations and otherwise leave it enabled. For example, you may want to disable the Close item and button while your application is processing data.

The same logic could be applied to the other items on the system menu. For example, SC_SIZE could be disabled in certain situations to prevent resizing of the window, SC_MOVE could be disabled in certain situations to prevent moving of the window, and so on.

SYNOPSIS OF CODE

The form will have a checkbox for the user to decide whether or not to disable the Close item. Clicking the checkbox calls the **DisableClose** method of the class clsDisableClose. The **DisableClose** method calls the API function **ModifyMenu**. If the checkbox is checked, the code disables the Close item using the flag MF_GRAYED. If the checkbox is unchecked, then the code enables the Close item using the flag MF_ENABLED. There are several other nuances which will be covered in the annotations.

CODE

```
'clsDisableClose
Option Explicit

Private Const MF_BYCOMMAND As Long = &H0&
Private Const MF_GRAYED As Long = &H1&
Private Const SC_CLOSE As Long = &HF060&
Private Const MF_ENABLED As Long = &H0&
Private Const FOOLVB As Long = -10

Private Declare Function DrawMenuBar Lib "user32" _
    (ByVal hwnd As Long) As Long

Public Declare Function GetSystemMenu Lib "user32" _
    (ByVal hwnd As Long, _
        ByVal bRevert As Long) As Long
```

```
Private Declare Function ModifyMenu Lib "user32" _
   Alias "ModifyMenuA" _
       (ByVal hMenu As Long, ByVal nPosition As Long, _
       ByVal wFlags As Long, _
       ByVal wIDNewItem As Long, ByVal lpString As Any) As Long

Public Sub DisableClose(frm As Form)

Dim hMenu As Long
Dim menuItemCount As Long
  hMenu = GetSystemMenu(frm.hwnd, 0)
  If hMenu Then
    If Form1.chkDisableClose Then
     Call ModifyMenu(hMenu, SC_CLOSE, _
    MF_BYCOMMAND Or MF_GRAYED, FOOLVB, "Close")
    Else
     Call ModifyMenu(hMenu, FOOLVB, _
        MF_BYCOMMAND Or MF_ENABLED, SC_CLOSE, "Close")
    End If
    Call DrawMenuBar(Form1.hwnd)
 End If
End Sub
```

ANNOTATIONS

```
Private Const MF_BYCOMMAND As Long = &H0&
Private Const MF_GRAYED As Long = &H1&
Private Const SC_CLOSE As Long = &HF060&
Private Const MF_ENABLED As Long = &H0&
```

Two of these constants are new. MF_GRAYED disables a menu item and also draws it in light gray to give the application user a visual cue that the menu item is disabled. MF_ENABLED, as its name suggests, enables the menu item. These two flags will be used to toggle the Close item between an enabled and disabled state.

```
Private Const FOOLVB As Long = -10
```

The FOOLVB constant will be discussed below. Its name may be indicative of its purpose.

```
Private Declare Function DrawMenuBar Lib "user32" _
   (ByVal hwnd As Long) As Long
```

```
Public Declare Function GetSystemMenu Lib "user32" _
    (ByVal hwnd As Long, _
        ByVal bRevert As Long) As Long

Private Declare Function ModifyMenu Lib "user32" _
    Alias "ModifyMenuA" _
        (ByVal hMenu As Long, ByVal nPosition As Long, _
        ByVal wFlags As Long, _
        ByVal wIDNewItem As Long, ByVal lpString As Any) As Long
```

Two of these API functions are new. **ModifyMenu** will be used to modify the system menu to enable or disable the Close item. **DrawMenuBar**, mentioned briefly in the last example, will be used to redraw (refresh) the menu each time the enabled state of the Close item is changed.

```
Public Sub DisableClose(frm As Form)
```

As in the previous example, this class method must be declared as public so it can be accessed outside the class. In this example it will be accessed in the **Click** event of the checkbox control on the test form.

```
Dim hMenu As Long
Dim menuItemCount As Long
  hMenu = GetSystemMenu(frm.hwnd, 0)
  If hMenu Then
```

As in the previous example, it first is necessary to ensure that there is, in fact, a system menu.

```
    If Form1.chkDisableClose Then
     Call ModifyMenu(hMenu, SC_CLOSE, _
    MF_BYCOMMAND Or MF_GRAYED, FOOLVB, "Close")
    Else
     Call ModifyMenu(hMenu, FOOLVB, _
        MF_BYCOMMAND Or MF_ENABLED, SC_CLOSE, "Close")
    End If
```

ModifyMenu takes five parameters. The first is a handle to the menu. The second is either the position or command ID of the menu item, depending on whether the flag in the third parameter is MF_BYPOSITION or MF_BYCOMMAND. The third parameter may, and in this example does, also include other flags using the **Or** operator. The fourth parameter is the new command ID for the menu item. The fifth and final parameter is the string to set into the menu.

The difference in the third parameter between the If and Else blocks is the flag MF_GRAYED or MF_ENABLED. This simply reflects the toggling of the enabled status of the Close menu item based on whether the checkbox is checked.

Far less intuitive is why both the second and fourth parameters of **ModifyMenu** are different between the call in the If block and the call in the Else block. The expected call to **ModifyMenu** to disable the Close menu item would be:

```
Call ModifyMenu(hMenu, SC_CLOSE, _
MF_BYCOMMAND Or MF_GRAYED, SC_CLOSE, "Close")
```

However, what happens is that Visual Basic re-enables the menu item whose command ID is SC_CLOSE. To avoid this, the fourth parameter, the new command ID, is set to –10, represented by the constant FOOLVB. When Visual Basic looks for a menu item with the command ID of SC_CLOSE (61,536), it cannot find one because the Close menu item has been changed to a command ID of –10.

As so often happens in programming, solving one problem creates another. When we want to re-enable the Close menu item, the expected call would be:

```
Call ModifyMenu(hMenu, SC_CLOSE, _
MF_BYCOMMAND Or MF_ENABLED, SC_CLOSE, "Close")
```

However, this will not work because Visual Basic cannot find the Close menu item because we have changed it to –10. Therefore, the second parameter needs to be changed to –10, again represented by the constant FOOLVB. However, the fourth parameter now has gone back to SC_CLOSE instead of remaining –10. The reason is similar to why, in the prior call to **ModifyMenu**, the fourth parameter was changed from SC_CLOSE to –10. If the fourth parameter remains –10 instead of being changed to SC_CLOSE, Visual Basic will disable the menu item whose command ID is –10.

The reason –10 is used is that this value is unlikely to be the command ID of any other menu item. The value 0 is not a good alternative as menu separators have that command ID.

This workaround using the –10 value for the command ID is one of those instances in which the programmer needs to fool Visual Basic to get around its default behaviors. Hence the name of the constant, FOOLVB.

```
Call DrawMenuBar(Form1.hwnd)
```

This is necessary to redraw the Close button on the title bar in light gray to indicate its disabled state. **DrawMenuBar** is not necessary to redraw the Close item on the system menu.

In the previous example in which the Close item was deleted, **DrawMenuBar** did not need to be called to draw the Close button in light gray. The reason was that the Close item on the system menu was removed during the **Load** event of the form. Therefore the Close button was disabled when the form was first drawn. Here, however, the Close item and therefore the Close button are enabled when the form is first drawn. Therefore, each time the enabled state of the button is toggled by a click of the checkbox, **DrawMenuBar** needs to be invoked to refresh the Close button to display its new status. By contrast, **DrawMenuBar** does not need to be invoked to refresh the Close menu item, the reason being that it is not the top-level menu item.

TEST THE CODE

1. Start a new project, Standard Exe. The default form may be the startup form. Accept the name Form1. The StartUpPosition should be 2 – Center Screen.

2. Place on the form a checkbox named chkDisableClose, for which the caption will be "Disable Close?" There will be no command button to end the application because when the checkbox is not checked you will be able to close the form from the system menu item or the Close button on the title bar. Your form should look like Figure 3-4.

3. Insert a new class module named clsDisableClose and paste in it the above code (which is also on the CD-ROM).

4. Place the following code in the **Click** event of chkDisableClose:

```
Private Sub chkDisableClose_Click()
    Dim disClose As clsDisableClose
    Set disClose = New clsDisableClose
    disClose.DisableClose Me
    Set disClose = Nothing
End Sub
```

This step is essentially the same as in the prior example except that here it is not in the **Load** event of the form.

Run the project. If the checkbox is unchecked, the form works normally. However, if the checkbox is checked, the Close item on the system menu has been disabled, double-clicking on the control box will not close the form, and the Close button on the title bar has been grayed out. This time the separator bar above the Close item has not been removed since the Close item was only disabled, not removed (see Figure 3-5).

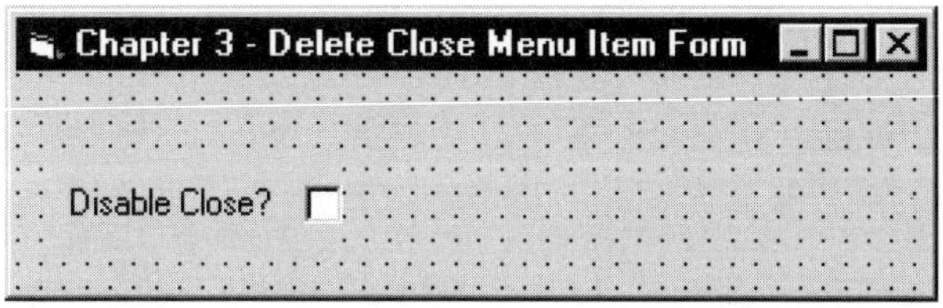

FIGURE 3-4. The Form in Design view

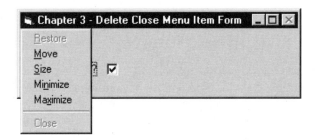

FIGURE 3-5. The Disable Item example—Form in operation

Prompting Before Executing Close Item of System Menu

DisablePrompt.vbp Instead of disabling the Close menu item, your application may require the execution of code or other actions when the user chooses the Close item or button.

This example will accomplish the common application task of asking the user to confirm whether he or she really wants to close. If the answer is yes, then the application proceeds to close. However, if the answer is no, then the user's action in choosing the Close item or button is cancelled, and the application remains open.

However, the concept illustrated by this example could be expanded to implement far more complex scenarios when the user chooses the Close item or button.

SYNOPSIS OF CODE

Subclassing is required because, when the message is sent by Windows upon the selection of the Close item or button, it is not known if the user will answer yes or no to the request to confirm that he or she wants to close the application. Subclassing was not required in the previous example of disabling the Close item because when the Windows message was sent, the state of the checkbox already was known.

The technique for subclassing follows the previous examples. This time the message being intercepted is WM_SYSCOMMAND. A window receives the WM_SYSCOMMAND message when the user chooses a command from the system menu or when the user clicks on the Close, Minimize, Maximize, or Restore buttons on the title bar. The **MsgBox** function asks the user to confirm that he or she wants to close the application. If the answer is no, then action is taken to cancel the WM_SYSCOMMAND message. If the answer is yes, or if other system menu items, title bar buttons, or messages are involved, then the message is routinely processed.

CODE

```
Option Explicit

Public defWindowProc As Long

Public Const GWL_WNDPROC As Long = (-4)
Public Const WM_SYSCOMMAND As Long = &H112&
Public Const SC_CLOSE = &HF060&

Declare Function GetWindowLong Lib "User32" _
    Alias "GetWindowLongA" _
    (ByVal hWnd As Long, _
    ByVal nIndex As Long) As Long

Declare Function SetWindowLong Lib "User32" _
    Alias "SetWindowLongA" _
    (ByVal hWnd As Long, ByVal nIndex As Long, _
    ByVal dwNewLong As Long) As Long

Declare Function CallWindowProc Lib "User32" _
    Alias "CallWindowProcA" _
    (ByVal lpPrevWndFunc As Long, ByVal hWnd As Long, _
    ByVal Msg As Long, _
    ByVal wParam As Long, ByVal lParam As Long) As Long

Public Sub SubClass(hWnd As Long)
 On Error Resume Next
 defWindowProc = SetWindowLong _
    (hWnd, GWL_WNDPROC, AddressOf WindowProc)
 End Sub

Public Sub UnSubClass(hWnd As Long)
 If defWindowProc Then
 SetWindowLong hWnd, GWL_WNDPROC, defWindowProc
 defWindowProc = 0
 End If
End Sub

Public Function WindowProc(ByVal hWnd As Long, _
    ByVal uMsg As Long, ByVal wParam As Long, _
    ByVal lParam As Long) As Long
```

```
On Error Resume Next
 Dim retVal As Long
Select Case uMsg
Case WM_SYSCOMMAND
If (wParam And &HFFF0&) = SC_CLOSE Then
Dim str As String
str = "Do you want to close?"
If MsgBox(str, vbYesNo, "Are You Sure?") = vbNo Then
retVal = 0
Else
retVal = CallWindowProc _
    (defWindowProc, hWnd, uMsg, wParam, lParam)
End If
Else
retVal = CallWindowProc _
    (defWindowProc, hWnd, uMsg, wParam, lParam)
End If
Case Else
retVal = CallWindowProc _
    (defWindowProc, hWnd, uMsg, wParam, lParam)
End Select
WindowProc = retVal
End Function
```

ANNOTATIONS

```
Public Const WM_SYSCOMMAND As Long = &H112&
```

This constant is new. A window receives the WM_SYSCOMMAND message when the user chooses a command from the system menu or when the user clicks on the Close, Minimize, Maximize, or Restore buttons on the title bar.

The code which follows is typical of the previous subclassing examples until we reach the user-defined Window function **WindowProc**.

```
Select Case uMsg
Case WM_SYSCOMMAND
```

The message we are looking for is WM_SYSCOMMAND. The intent of the application is to prompt the user if he or she clicks the Close item or button, and WM_SYSCOMMAND is the message which will be sent by Windows when this user action occurs.

```
If (wParam And &HFFF0&) = SC_CLOSE Then
```

The WM_SYSCOMMAND message, like other messages, has a *wParam* and a *lParam*. In the case of a WM_SYSCOMMAND message, the *lParam* holds the screen coordinates of the mouse event and is of no interest here. The *wParam* specifies the system command. As discussed in the previous examples, SC_CLOSE is the system command when the user clicks the Close item or button.

The comparison is not directly between the *wParam* and SC_CLOSE. Instead, *wParam* first is combined with the value &HFFF0& using the bitwise **And** operator. The reason is that, in WM_SYSCOMMAND messages, the four low-order bits of the *wParam* parameter are used internally by the system. A straight comparison between *wParam* and the commandID may or may not work correctly, depending on which command ID (which represents a long number) is chosen. A bitwise comparison of *wParam* and &HFFF0& using the **And** operator is necessary to assure a correct comparison of the value of *wParam* with the command ID.

```
Dim str As String
str = "Do you want to close?"
If MsgBox(str, vbYesNo, "Are You Sure?") = vbNo Then
retVal = 0
Else
retVal = CallWindowProc(defWindowProc, hWnd, uMsg, wParam, lParam)
End If
```

This block of code is executed only if the user selected the Close item or button. The user is prompted to confirm whether the application should be closed. If the user says yes, then the Else block of code executes with a call to **CallWindowProc**. The message then is handled by the default window function and the return value (which will be to carry out the command and close the window) is stored in *retVal*. However, if the user says no, the If block of code executes, and *retVal* is set to 0.

```
Else
retVal = CallWindowProc(defWindowProc, hWnd, uMsg, wParam, lParam)
End If
Case Else
retVal = CallWindowProc(defWindowProc, hWnd, uMsg, wParam, lParam)
End Select
```

In all other instances the message is handled by the default window function and the return value is stored in **retVal**.

```
WindowProc = retVal
```

This statement passes **retVal** to Windows. Passing 0 to Windows (that is, the user clicked the Close item or button but then chose not to proceed with closing the window) results in the user's action of clicking the Close item or button being ignored. Otherwise, the value of **retVal** that is normal for the user's action is passed to Windows.

TEST THE CODE

1. Start a new project, Standard Exe. The default form may be the startup form. Accept the name Form1 and the other default properties, except the StartUpPosition should be 2 – Center Screen.

2. Place the code above in a standard module. As discussed, a class module cannot be used because the procedure whose address is passed by the **AddressOf** operator, **WindowProc**, must be in a standard module.

3. Place the following code in the **Load** event of the form procedure:

```
Private Sub Form_Load()
 Call SubClass(Me.hwnd)
End Sub
```

4. Place the following code in the **Unload** event of Form1:

```
Private Sub Form_Unload(Cancel As Integer)
 Call UnSubClass(Me.hwnd)
End Sub
```

Steps 3 through 4 have been covered in the preceding examples.

Run the code. When you attempt to close the form via the Close button on the title bar or the Close item on the system menu, a message box with Yes and No buttons will prompt you to confirm that you really want to close (see Figure 3-6). If you do, then the form will close. Otherwise, it will not.

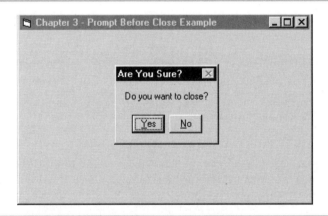

FIGURE 3-6. The Disable Prompt Form in operation

Add.vbp

Adding an Item to the System Menu

Thus far we have removed, disabled, and subclassed existing items on the system menu. Now we will add a new item to the system menu. The new item could be very useful, like a command to switch between different MDI child forms, analogous to the Switch to item on the system menu in Windows 3.1.

The new item in this example will be a Tip of the Day. Choosing this new item will bring up a Tip of the Day form. Some find these tips obnoxious. Perhaps you will find this tip humorous.

SYNOPSIS OF CODE

Adding an item is relatively simple. The **GetSystemMenu** API function returns the handle to the system menu, and the **AppendMenu** API function then inserts the new menu item.

The problem is having your application respond to the new item. Visual Basic responds to WM_COMMAND messages, which Windows sends when a menu item is clicked. However, when the menu is a system menu, Windows does not send a WM_COMMAND message, but instead a WM_SYSCOMMAND message. Visual Basic does not have a problem with the WM_SYSCOMMAND messages generated by clicking on the default system menu items. However, Visual Basic does not know what to do with the WM_SYSCOMMAND message generated by the clicking of your custom item on the system menu.

The solution, as you may have guessed by now, is subclassing. The WM_SYSCOMMAND message is intercepted, a parameter of the message is tested for the new item, and if there is a match, the code executes the desired action.

CODE

```
Option Explicit

Public defWindowProc As Long

Public Const GWL_WNDPROC As Long = (-4)
Public Const WM_SYSCOMMAND As Long = &H112&
Public Const SC_CLOSE As Long = &HF060&
Private Const MF_STRING As Long = &H0
Private Const MF_SEPARATOR As Long = &H800
Private Const IDM_TIP As Long = 10
```

```vb
Declare Function GetWindowLong Lib "user32" _
   Alias "GetWindowLongA" _
  (ByVal hwnd As Long, ByVal nIndex As Long) As Long

Declare Function SetWindowLong Lib "user32" _
   Alias "SetWindowLongA" _
  (ByVal hwnd As Long, ByVal nIndex As Long, _
   ByVal dwNewLong As Long) As Long

Private Declare Function AppendMenu Lib "user32" _
   Alias "AppendMenuA" _
  (ByVal hMenu As Long, ByVal wFlags As Long, _
   ByVal wIDNewItem As Long, _
   ByVal lpNewItem As String) As Long

Private Declare Function GetSystemMenu Lib "user32" _
  (ByVal hwnd As Long, ByVal bRevert As Long) As Long

Declare Function CallWindowProc Lib "user32" _
   Alias "CallWindowProcA" _
  (ByVal lpPrevWndFunc As Long, ByVal hwnd As Long, _
   ByVal Msg As Long, _
   ByVal wParam As Long, ByVal lParam As Long) As Long

Public Sub CenterForm(frm As Form)
If frm.WindowState <> vbMinimized Then _
   frm.Move (Screen.Width - frm.Width) / 2, _
   (Screen.Height - frm.Height) / 2
End Sub

Public Sub AddTiptoMenu(frm As Form)
    Dim i As Long, hMenu As Long
    hMenu = GetSystemMenu(frm.hwnd, False)
    i = AppendMenu(hMenu, MF_SEPARATOR, 0, 0&)
    i = AppendMenu(hMenu, MF_STRING, IDM_TIP, "&Tip of the Day")
End Sub

Public Sub SubClass(hwnd As Long)
 On Error Resume Next
 defWindowProc = SetWindowLong _
   (hwnd, GWL_WNDPROC, AddressOf WindowProc)
End Sub
```

```
Public Sub UnSubClass(hwnd As Long)
 If defWindowProc Then
    SetWindowLong hwnd, GWL_WNDPROC, defWindowProc
    defWindowProc = 0
 End If
End Sub


Public Function WindowProc(ByVal hwnd As Long, ByVal uMsg As Long, _
    ByVal wParam As Long, ByVal lParam As Long) As Long

On Error Resume Next
 Dim retVal As Long
Select Case uMsg
Case WM_SYSCOMMAND
If wParam = IDM_TIP Then frmLousyTip.Show
WindowProc = CallWindowProc _
    (defWindowProc, hwnd, uMsg, wParam, lParam)
Case Else
WindowProc = CallWindowProc(defWindowProc, _
    hwnd, uMsg, wParam, lParam)
End Select
End Function
```

ANNOTATIONS

```
Private Const MF_STRING As Long = &H0
Private Const MF_SEPARATOR As Long = &H800
Private Const IDM_TIP As Long = 10
```

These constants are new. All are menu flags as their MF prefix suggests. MF_STRING is a flag to place a specified string for the new item. MF_SEPARATOR is a flag to place a separator bar at the new entry. IDM_TIP will be the new command ID for the new item. Its value must be less than &HF000& (61,440), which is the lowest value for a default system menu item (SC_SIZE). The value 0 is avoided because this is the value of the separator bar.

```
Private Declare Function AppendMenu Lib "user32" _
    Alias "AppendMenuA" _
    (ByVal hMenu As Long, ByVal wFlags As Long, _
    ByVal wIDNewItem As Long, _
    ByVal lpNewItem As String) As Long
```

This API function adds a menu item to the menu whose handle is the first parameter. The second parameter is a flag or flags to determine if the new menu item will be a separator bar, be described by a string, and so on. The third parameter is the command ID of the new menu item. The fourth parameter generally is the string of the menu entry.

There is another API function, **InsertMenuItem**, which permits the insertion of a menu item at any location in the menu, not just the end, and permits additional customization of the menu item. In this example, however, the less complex **AppendMenu** is sufficient. Additionally, **InsertMenuItem** is not supported in Windows NT 3.5*x*, whereas **AppendMenu** is.

```
Public Sub CenterForm(frm As Form)
If frm.WindowState <> vbMinimized Then _
    frm.Move (Screen.Width - frm.Width) / 2, _
    (Screen.Height - frm.Height) / 2
End Sub
```

This code should look familiar from the Center Form example in Chapter 1. Both forms will use this method to center this form on the screen. If we wanted to take the taskbar into account, the clsCenterForm class module instead would be incorporated into this project.

```
Public Sub AddTiptoMenu(frm As Form)
    Dim i As Long, hMenu As Long
    hMenu = GetSystemMenu(frm.hwnd, False)
    i = AppendMenu(hMenu, MF_SEPARATOR, 0, 0&)
    i = AppendMenu(hMenu, MF_STRING, IDM_TIP, "&Tip of the Day")
End Sub
```

This method will be called from the **Load** event of the main form to add the menu items. The first invocation of **AppendMenu** adds a separator bar. The second parameter accordingly has the MF_SEPARATOR flag. The third parameter is 0 since that is the command ID of the separator bar. The fourth parameter also is 0, since the separator bar has no string or bitmap. The type-declaration character & is added to the 0 because **AppendMenu** expects the data type of the third parameter to be long.

The second invocation of **AppendMenu** adds the Tip of the Day menu item. The second parameter has a MF_STRING flag since this menu item will have a string associated with it. The third parameter is the command ID of 10 represented by the previously declared constant IDM_TIP. The fourth parameter is the string which will appear for the menu item, "Tip of the Day."

The code which follows once again is typical of the previous subclassing examples until we reach the user-defined Window function **WindowProc**.

```
Select Case uMsg
Case WM_SYSCOMMAND
If wParam = IDM_TIP Then frmLousyTip.Show
WindowProc = CallWindowProc _
```

```
    (defWindowProc, hwnd, uMsg, wParam, lParam)
Case Else
WindowProc = CallWindowProc _
    (defWindowProc, hwnd, uMsg, wParam, lParam)
End Select
```

Once again the message we are looking for is WM_SYSCOMMAND. This time we are checking to see if the user chose the Tip of the Day menu item. If so, the Tip of the Day form first is shown, and then the message is passed on for default processing with the now-familiar call to **CallWindowProc**. If the user chose another system menu item, or if the message is other than WM_SYSCOMMAND, the message simply is passed directly for default processing by the invocation of **CallWindowProc**.

TEST THE CODE

1. Start a new project, Standard Exe. The default form may be the startup form. Accept the name Form1 and the other default properties. Your form should look like Figure 3-7.

2. Create another form. It is referred to in the code as frmLousyTip. It too may have the standard default properties. Add to it a command button named **cmdOK**.

3. Place the code above in a standard module. As discussed, a class module cannot be used because the procedure whose address is passed by the **AddressOf** operator, **WindowProc**, must be in a standard module.

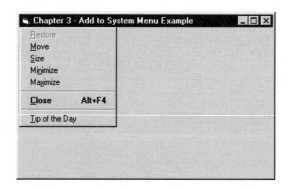

FIGURE 3-7. Add to System Menu form

4. Place the following code in the **Load** event of Form1:

```
Private Sub Form_Load()
 CenterForm Me
 AddTiptoMenu Me
 Call SubClass(Me.hwnd)
End Sub
```

5. Place the following code in the **Unload** event of Form1:

```
Private Sub Form_Unload(Cancel As Integer)
 Call UnSubClass(Me.hwnd)
End Sub
```

Steps 4 and 5 have been covered in the preceding examples.

6. Place the following code in the **Load** event of frmLousyTip:

```
Private Sub Form_Load()
 CenterForm Me
End Sub
```

7. Place the following code in the **Click** event of the command button on frmLousyTip:

```
Private Sub cmdOK_Click()
 Unload Me
End Sub
```

Run the code. The system menu now has an additional item, Tip of the Day, separated from the other items with a separator bar. When you select Tip of the Day, the tip form will appear with insightful advice (see Figure 3-8).

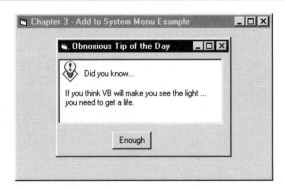

FIGURE 3-8.   Advice like this is priceless!

Menu Magic

This chapter, like the last one, concerns menus. However, this time the focus is not on the system menu, but rather on the Windows menu that you see in most applications you use, that is, the menu bar with top-level items such as File, Edit, Window, and Help.

There are two types of menus: top-level and pop-up. A top-level menu appears on the menu bar. File, Edit, Window, and Help are examples of top-level menu items. A pop-up menu often appears as dropping down from a top-level menu item, usually after the top-level menu item is clicked. For example, pop-up menu items Open, Save, and Exit appear when the user clicks the top-level File menu item. However, a pop-up menu item may appear upon the mouse clicking or moving over another pop-up menu item. For example, moving the mouse over the pop-up Toolbar menu item under the top-level View menu item displays another pop-up menu listing the available toolbars. Still another pop-up menu is displayed when an object is clicked with the right mouse button. This type of pop-up menu often is called a *context menu*.

As the previous chapter shows, Visual Basic gives you precious little assistance in modifying the appearance or functionality of the system menu. By contrast, Visual Basic provides an easy-to-use Menu Editor tool for creating a Windows menu. With the Menu Editor, a professional-looking menu with the pop-up menu items properly associated with the corresponding top-level menu items can be created almost as quickly as you can type and click.

Associating code with menu items is no more difficult than associating code with command buttons and other objects. A menu item has one event, **Click**, and writing code for that event is no different than writing code for the **Click** event of a command button.

While it is relatively easy to create and write code for a menu, relying exclusively on Visual Basic has its limitations. If the width of a menu item changes dynamically—such as a menu item reflecting the path of the last-closed file—there is no built-in Visual Basic event which enables the width of the menu to follow the change. This will result in a menu which either cuts off the menu item or is far too wide. However, as discussed in the first example, "Dynamically Resizing a Menu," through subclassing the message Windows sends when you click on the top-level menu item you can resize the width of the menu to accommodate the revised widths of the pop-up menu items.

You may also want to enhance the professional appearance of your application by having bitmaps next to the text of the menu item as in Office 97 applications and, indeed, Visual Basic 5 and 6. This cannot be done with the Menu Editor. However, it can be done, as the second example, "Putting Pictures on Your Menu," shows.

Finally, you may not be content with modifying the appearance of the menu by the insertion of bitmaps, but instead may want to design your own menu. For example, a color picker, instead of listing colors by name, could display color bars with widths and offsets of your choosing. The Menu Editor certainly cannot do this. However, you can, as the last example in this chapter, "Creating Designer Menus," shows.

Using the Windows 32 API and subclassing, you can overcome and go beyond Visual Basic's limitations in menu design.

Dynamically Resizing a Menu

BadInitMenu.vbp
GoodInitMenu.vbp

The top-level File menu item in applications such as Microsoft Word often contain a pop-up menu item, just above the Exit command, which displays the relative path to one or more of the most recently used files (see Figure 4-1).

The property of the recently used files pop-up menu item which displays the file's path is the **Caption** property. The **Caption** property is the string displayed in the menu item. For example, the value of the **Caption** property of the top-level File menu item is "&File", the "&" being used so that the "F" in "File" is the accelerator key, as indicated by the letter being underlined.

This example will involve a pop-up menu item named **mnuFileLastClosed**, which will display the path of the file most recently closed. This pop-up menu item is accessed by clicking on the top-level File menu item, which in this example will be named **mnuFile**.

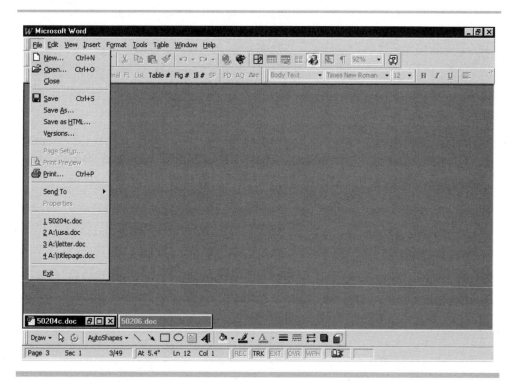

FIGURE 4-1.   The recently used menu item in Microsoft Word

The **Caption** property is read/write, so it may be used to set as well as get the text of the menu item. Therefore, if we want **mnuFileLastClosed** to display the path of the file most recently closed, the indicated solution would be:

1. When a file, which in these examples will be displayed in a Rich TextBox control named **RichTextBox1**, is closed, the filename (including the path) will be assigned to a string variable, which in these examples will be named **strLastClosed**, such as:

```
strLastClosed = RichTextBox1.filename
```

2. When **mnuFile**, is clicked, the **Caption** property of **mnuFileLastClosed** will be set to **strLastClosed**:

```
Private Sub mnuFile_Click()
 mnuFileLastClosed.Caption = strLastClosed
End Sub
```

Needless to say, this implementation is imperfect, for otherwise a solution so simple would not merit extended treatment in this book. However, identifying and analyzing the problems with this implementation is instructive, and the test form used for this implementation also will be used for the "new and improved" solution. Therefore, the test form and its code first will be analyzed.

TEST FORM

The test form should be set up as follows:

1. Start a new Standard Exe project. Accept for the default form the name Form1 and the other default properties.

2. Add to the form the controls described here:

Control	Name	Caption
Common Dialog	Common Dialog1	Not Applicable
RichTextBox	RichTextBox1	Not Applicable
Command Button	cmdOpen	Open
Command Button	cmdClose	Close

3. Using Menu Editor, create the menu described here where File and Help are the top-level menu items and the others are first-level submenu items of File:

Name	Caption	Level
mnuFile	&File	First
mnuFileOpen	&Open	Second
mnuFileClose	&Close	Second
mnuFileSeparator1	-	Second
mnuFileLastClosed	<--->	Second
mnuFileSeparator2	-	Second
mnuFileExit	E&xit	Second
mnuHelp	&Help	First

4. The completed form should look like Figure 4-2 in Design view.

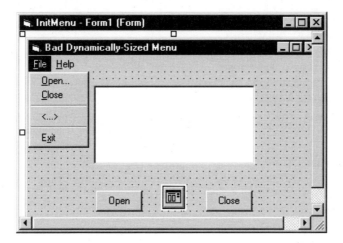

FIGURE 4-2. Test form in Design view

CODE FOR TEST FORM

```
Option Explicit

Private blnFileOpen As Boolean
Private strLastClosed As String

Public Sub EnableOpenClose()
    cmdOpen.Enabled = Not blnFileOpen
    mnuFileOpen.Enabled = Not blnFileOpen
    mnuFileLastClosed.Enabled = Not blnFileOpen
    cmdClose.Enabled = blnFileOpen
    mnuFileClose.Enabled = blnFileOpen
End Sub

Private Sub Form_Load()
    ChDir App.Path
    ChDrive App.Path
    blnFileOpen = False
    EnableOpenClose
End Sub

Private Sub cmdOpen_Click()
    CommonDialog1.Filter = "Text files|*.txt"
    CommonDialog1.ShowOpen
    RichTextBox1.LoadFile CommonDialog1.filename, rtfText
    blnFileOpen = True
    EnableOpenClose
End Sub

Private Sub cmdClose_Click()
    CommonDialog1.ShowSave
    strLastClosed = RichTextBox1.filename
    RichTextBox1.SaveFile strLastClosed, rtfText
    blnFileOpen = False
    RichTextBox1.Text = ""
    EnableOpenClose
End Sub

Private Sub mnuFileOpen_Click()
    cmdOpen_Click
End Sub
```

```
Private Sub mnuFileClose_Click()
    cmdClose_Click
End Sub


Private Sub mnuFileExit_Click()
    Unload Me
End Sub


Private Sub mnuFile_Click()
    mnuFileLastClosed.Caption = strLastClosed
End Sub


Private Sub mnuFileLastClosed_Click()
    RichTextBox1.LoadFile strLastClosed, rtfText
    blnFileOpen = True
    EnableOpenClose
End Sub
```

ANNOTATIONS TO TEST FORM CODE

```
Private blnFileOpen As Boolean
```

The variable **blnFileOpen** will reflect whether a file has been loaded in the Rich TextBox control. Testing for whether the **FileName** property of the RichTextBox control is an empty string does not work. Even once a file is closed, the **FileName** property will continue to hold the name of that file until another file is opened in the RichTextBox control. Setting the **FileName** property to an empty string also will not work because that property only can be set to a valid filename.

```
Private strLastClosed As String
```

The variable **strLastClosed** is a string containing the filename, including path, of the last closed file.

```
Public Sub EnableOpenClose()
    cmdOpen.Enabled = Not blnFileOpen
    mnuFileOpen.Enabled = Not blnFileOpen
    mnuFileLastClosed.Enabled = Not blnFileOpen
    cmdClose.Enabled = blnFileOpen
    mnuFileClose.Enabled = blnFileOpen
End Sub
```

The **EnableOpenClose** subroutine toggles the enabled status of the Open and Close command buttons and menu items in accordance with the value of **blnFileOpen**, which, as discussed above, reflects whether a file is loaded in the

Rich TextBox control. This prevents the user from attempting to load a second file into a RichTextBox control in which a file already has been loaded, or from attempting to close a file when no file is loaded in the RichTextBox control.

```
Private Sub Form_Load()
    ChDir App.Path
    ChDrive App.Path
    blnFileOpen = False
    EnableOpenClose
End Sub
```

The first two statements change the current drive and directory to the one in which the Visual Basic application is located. This enables the application to use the relative path to components residing in other files, such as a database or help file. As a general rule, these statements should be incorporated into the code of the **Startup** object, generally either **Sub Main()** or the **Load** event of the main form. The third statement explicitly sets the value of **blnFileOpen** to False since no file has yet been loaded in the Rich TextBox control. The default value of **blnFileOpen** is False but usually it is prudent not to rely on default values. Finally, the subroutine **EnableOpenClose** is called to set the enabled status of the Open and Close command buttons and menu items.

```
Private Sub cmdOpen_Click()
    CommonDialog1.Filter = "Text files|*.txt"
    CommonDialog1.ShowOpen
    RichTextBox1.LoadFile CommonDialog1.FileName, rtfText
    blnFileOpen = True
    EnableOpenClose
End Sub
```

This subroutine, called by clicking the Open command button, shows the CommonDialog control for opening a file. The **Filter** property of the control is set to text files so only text files appear in the list of files which may be opened. The **ShowOpen** method displays the control's Open dialog box. This is the dialog box which appears when you click the Open pop-up menu item under the top-level File menu item.

The **LoadFile** method of the RichTextBox control loads a file into the control. The first argument is the path and filename of the file to load into the control. This information is obtained from the **FileName** property of the Common Dialog control. The **FileName** property includes the path as well as the filename. The second argument is the type of file to be loaded. The rtfText constant permits any text file to be loaded.

Finally, the value of **blnFileOpen** is set to True because a file has been opened, and the subroutine **EnableOpenClose** is called to set the enabled status of the Open and Close command buttons and menu items.

```
Private Sub cmdClose_Click()
    CommonDialog1.ShowSave
    strLastClosed = RichTextBox1.filename
    RichTextBox1.SaveFile strLastClosed, rtfText
    RichTextBox1.Text = ""
    blnFileOpen = False
    EnableOpenClose
End Sub
```

This subroutine, called by clicking the Close command button, shows the CommonDialog control for saving a file. The **SaveFile** method displays the control's Save As dialog box. This is the dialog box which appears when you click the Save As pop-up menu item under the top-level File menu item. The RichTextBox control's **FileName** property, which contains the path and filename of the file which is displayed in the control, is assigned to the variable *strLastClosed* so that value later can be retrieved to display in the **mnuFileLastClosed** item.

The **SaveFile** method of the RichTextBox control saves the contents of the control to a file. The first argument is the path and filename of the file to receive the contents of the control. The effect of using *strLastClosed* for this argument is that the contents of the control are saved to the file from which those contents originated. This information is obtained from the **FileName** property of the Common Dialog control. The second argument is the type of file to be saved. As before, the *rtfText* constant is used, this time to permit the contents to be saved as a text file. The **Text** property of the RichTextBox control then is set to an empty string so the display of the control is blank.

Finally, the value of **blnFileOpen** is set to False because there is no open file, and the subroutine **EnableOpenClose** is called to set the enabled status of the Open and Close command buttons and menu items.

```
Private Sub mnuFileOpen_Click()
    cmdOpen_Click
End Sub


Private Sub mnuFileClose_Click()
    cmdClose_Click
End Sub
```

These subroutines simply connect the Open and Close menu items to the corresponding command buttons.

```
Private Sub mnuFile_Click()
    mnuFileLastClosed.Caption = strLastClosed
End Sub
```

This subroutine, called when the top-level File menu item (**mnuFile**) is clicked, assigns to the **Caption** property of **mnuFileLastClosed** the value of the variable *strLastClosed*, which contains the path and filename of the file last closed.

```
Private Sub mnuFileLastClosed_Click()
    RichTextBox1.LoadFile strLastClosed, rtfText
    blnFileOpen = True
    EnableOpenClose
End Sub
```

Clicking on the **mnuFileLastClosed** first causes the file displayed in that menu item's caption to be loaded into the RichTextBox control using the **LoadFile** method discussed above. The value of **blnFileOpen** is set to True because a file has been opened, and the subroutine **EnableOpenClose** is called to set the enabled status of the Open and Close command buttons and menu items.

It would not be desirable for the statements in this subroutine to execute if either no file is displayed in the menu item (which would be the case when the application starts) or if a file already is loaded in the RichTextBox control. However, when the application starts, the menu item is disabled by the call to **EnableOpenClose** in the form's **Load** event, and after a file is loaded the menu item is disabled by a call to **EnableOpenClose** in the **Click** event of **cmdClose**.

```
Private Sub mnuFileExit_Click()
    Unload Me
End Sub
```

Finally, this menu item causes the **Unload** event of the form to occur. This becomes important in the next example where subclassing is used, since it is in the **Unload** event that the default window procedure is restored.

TEST THE TEST FORM

1. Run the project. The **mnuFileLastClosed** item is blank and the width of the menu is normal. (See Figure 4-3.)

2. Open a file, preferably one with a long path, close the file, and then click on the File menu. The width of the menu is unchanged. As a result, the path displayed in **mnuFileLastClosed** is cut off on the right. (See Figure 4-4.)

3. Open a file, preferably one with a short path, close the file, and then click on the File menu. The width of the menu now is wide enough to include the long path of the previous file, and is far too wide for the smaller path of the file last closed. (See Figure 4-5.)

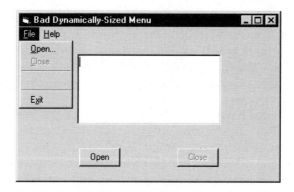

FIGURE 4-3. **mnuFileLastClosed** at startup

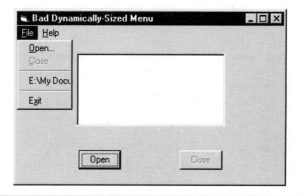

FIGURE 4-4. **mnuFileLastClosed** is not wide enough

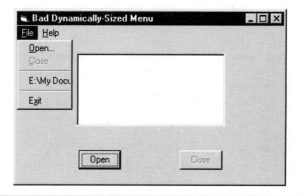

FIGURE 4-5. **mnuFileLastClosed** is too wide

WHAT WENT WRONG?

The File menu's **Click** event did occur before the menu was displayed. Therefore, the **Caption** property of **mnuFileLastClosed** could be changed in the **Click** event so that **mnuFileLastClosed** always accurately displayed the path and filename of the file last closed. However, once a file was closed, the width of the menu was always "one behind." The reason is that, before the **Click** event of the File menu, Windows already had calculated the width of the menu based on the then-existing entries. The changing in the **Click** event of the **Caption** property of **mnuFileLastClosed** did not cause a recalculation of the menu's width. If the new text for the caption was longer than the width of the menu, then the text was cut off. Conversely, if the new text for the caption was shorter than the previous text, then the menu was too wide.

SYNOPSIS OF CODE

Windows sends the WM_INITMENUPOPUP message to your application when a drop-down menu or submenu is *about* to become active. Thus, this message is sent when **mnuFile** is clicked but *before* the submenu items, including **mnuFileLastClosed**, are displayed. Intercepting the WM_INITMENUPOPUP message in the user-defined Windows function permits modification of the **Caption** property of **mnuFileLastClosed** before the drop-down menu is displayed and, more important for our purposes, before the width of the menu has been calculated.

Given all the subclassing examples we have gone through, this seems to be routine subclassing that could be written in your sleep. However, there is one aspect of the code that could turn your code-writing sleep into a nightmare.

The test form has two top-level menus, File and Help. Windows sends the WM_INITMENUPOPUP message if either the File menu or the Help menu is clicked. We are interested in modification of the **Caption** property of **mnuFileLastClosed** only if the File menu is clicked.

The WM_INITMENUPOPUP message, like other messages, has *wParam* and *lParam* parameters. In the context of the WM_INITMENUPOPUP message, the low-order word of *lParam* specifies the zero-based relative position of the menu item that opens the drop-down menu or submenu. Thus, if the low-order word of *lParam* is 0, then the user clicked on the File menu, whereas if the low-order word of lParam is 1, then the user clicked on the Help menu.

The concept of the low-order word of *lParam* (there also is a high-order word, as you may have guessed) may be new to those of you who may not have previously dealt with terms like **DWord** and **Word**, or used bitwise operations to cram **Words** into **DWords** or rip **Words** out of **DWords**. From a practical standpoint, even more important than understanding exactly what is a low-order word, is how to extract it from *lParam*. In C, this is easy: You just use the LOWORD macro. However, we are not using C, but instead Visual Basic, which has no built-in utility for determining low-order or high-order words.

Not to worry. All these tasks are very doable, as the "Annotations" section following the code explains.

CODE

```
Option Explicit

Private defWindowProc As Long
Public strLastClosed As String

Public Type HILOWORD
    loWord As Long
    hiWord As Long
End Type

Private Const GWL_WNDPROC As Long = (-4)
Private Const WM_INITMENUPOPUP = &H117

Declare Function SetWindowLong Lib "User32" Alias "SetWindowLongA" _
   (ByVal hWnd As Long, ByVal nIndex As Long, _
    ByVal dwNewLong As Long) As Long

Declare Function CallWindowProc Lib "User32" Alias "CallWindowProcA" _
   (ByVal lpPrevWndFunc As Long, ByVal hWnd As Long, ByVal Msg As Long, _
    ByVal wParam As Long, ByVal lParam As Long) As Long

Public Sub SubClass(hWnd As Long)
 On Error Resume Next
 defWindowProc = SetWindowLong(hWnd, GWL_WNDPROC, _
    AddressOf WindowProc)
End Sub
```

```
Public Sub UnSubClass(hWnd As Long)
 If defWindowProc Then
   SetWindowLong hWnd, GWL_WNDPROC, defWindowProc
   defWindowProc = 0
 End If
End Sub

Function getHiLoWord(ByVal lngParam As Integer) As HILOWORD
     Dim hilo As HILOWORD
     hilo.loWord = lngParam And &HFFFF&
     hilo.hiWord = lngParam \ &H10000 And &HFFFF&
     getHiLoWord = hilo
End Function

Public Function WindowProc(ByVal hWnd As Long, ByVal uMsg As Long, _
  ByVal wParam As Long, ByVal lParam As Long) As Long

  On Error Resume Next
  Dim retVal As Long

  Select Case uMsg
    Case WM_INITMENUPOPUP
      Dim hilo As HILOWORD
      hilo = getHiLoWord(lParam)
      If hilo.loWord = 0 Then
        Form1.mnuFileLastClosed.Caption = strLastClosed
        retVal = 0
      Else
        retVal = CallWindowProc(defWindowProc, hWnd, _
          uMsg, wparam, lParam)
      End If
      Case Else
      retVal = CallWindowProc(defWindowProc, hWnd, _
        uMsg, wParam, lParam)
  End Select
  WindowProc = retVal
End Function
```

Additionally, there are four small changes to be made in the form's code:

1. In the **Load** event of the form add the following statement so the window procedure for the form will be the user-defined window procedure:

   ```
   Call SubClass (Me.hwnd)
   ```

2. In the **Unload** event of the form add the following statement so the default window procedure will be restored when the form unloads:

   ```
   Call UnSubClass (Me.hwnd)
   ```

3. Comment out the statement in the **Click** event of **mnuFile** because the changing of the value of the **Caption** property of **mnuFileLastClosed** is being handled in the user-defined window function:

   ```
   Private Sub mnuFile_Click()
       'mnuFileLastClosed.Caption = strLastClosed
   End Sub
   ```

4. Comment out the declaration of the variable *strLastClosed* in the form.

   ```
   'Public strLastClosed As String
   ```

This variable now is being declared at the module level rather than at the form level. It is declared here as Public because it is being accessed by form procedures. In a commercial-quality application this variable would be declared as Private, and read and write access would be handled by functions with appropriate error-checking and validation. This step is omitted here to keep the code as short as possible and focused on the task of properly sizing the width of the menu.

ANNOTATIONS

```
Private Const WM_INITMENUPOPUP = &H117
```

The value of the WM_INITMENUPOPUP message is declared. As discussed above, Windows sends the WM_INITMENUPOPUP message to your application when a drop-down menu or submenu is *about* to become active, so this message is sent when **mnuFile** is clicked but *before* the submenu items, including **mnuFileLastClosed**, are displayed. The use of this message in the user-defined Windows function is discussed below.

```
Public Type HILOWORD
    loWord As Long
    hiWord As Long
End Type
```

The parameters of Windows messages include two long integers which, for historical reasons, are named *wParam* and *lParam*. In the case of the message involved in this example, WM_INITMENUPOPUP, the *lParam*, a **DWord**, has a low word and a high word.

Some of you must be wondering why we are talking about words when just a minute ago we were talking about numbers. The reason is a matter of terminology. A **DWord** is another name for a long (or 32-bit) number, and a **Word** is another name for a 16-bit integer. A **DWord** is made up of a low-order word and a high-order word. A common bitwise operation in C is ripping **Words** out of a **DWord**.

You now may be wondering why you ever would want to rip **Words** out of a **DWord**. The reason is that often the low- or high-order words of a *lParam* (or *wParam*) may contain a value quite significant to your application. For example, the low-order word of the *lParam* parameter of the message WM_INITMENUPOPUP contains the value of the menu item that opens a drop-down menu or submenu. Thus, the low-order word will tell you if the user clicked on the File menu or the Help menu.

The user-defined type **HILOWORD** is declared to contain the values of the low- and high-order words of a *wParam* or *lParam* passed to it.

```
Function getHiLoWord(ByVal lngParam As Integer) As HILOWORD
      Dim hilo As HILOWORD
      hilo.loWord = lngParam And &HFFFF&
      hilo.hiWord = lngParam \ &H100 And &HFF&
      getHiLoWord = hilo
End Function
```

C has the HIWORD and LOWORD macros to separate parts of long integers into its low-order word and high-order word. Visual Basic does not provide any bitwise functions for ripping apart long integers into its low-word and high-word components, so it is necessary to write a function to accomplish this task. The **getHiLoWord** function rips the low- and high-order **Words** out of a **DWord** and stores the low- and high-order words in the appropriate members of the **HILOWORD** user-defined type.

The code continues the same as many of the other subclassing examples. In the user-defined Windows function **WindowProc**, the familiar Select Case structure is used to give special treatment to the message WM_INITMENUPOPUP.

```
Select Case uMsg
  Case WM_INITMENUPOPUP
    Dim hilo As HILOWORD
    hilo = getHiLoWord(lParam)
```

```
    If hilo.loWord = 0 Then
      Form1.mnuFileLastClosed.Caption = strLastClosed
      retVal = 0
    Else
      retVal = CallWindowProc(defWindowProc, hWnd, _
          uMsg, wparam, lParam)
    End If
    Case Else
    retVal = CallWindowProc(defWindowProc, hWnd, _
        uMsg, wParam, lParam)
  End Select
  WindowProc = retVal
End Function
```

The message, unless it is WM_INITMENUPOPUP, is sent by **CallWindowProc** to be processed by the default Windows function, and the return value of **CallWindowProc** in turn becomes the return value of **WindowProc**. The result is that the message is handled as if there were no subclassing.

If the message is WM_INITMENUPOPUP, then the **getHiLoWord** function is called to extract the low-order word from the *lParam* variable. The low-order word contains the value of the zero-based relative position of the menu item that opens the drop-down menu or submenu. Here there are two menu items: the File menu, its value being zero, and the Help menu, its value being one.

If the low-order word equals one, then the menu item clicked was the Help menu. Since we are not interested in the WM_INITMENUPOPUP message if the Help menu is clicked, the message is sent to **CallWindowProc** to be processed by the default Windows function, as was the case with messages other than WM_INITMENUPOPUP.

However, if the low-order word equals zero, then the menu item clicked was the File menu. The **Caption** property of **mnuFileLastClosed** is assigned the value of *strLastClosed*. The variable *retVal*, which contains the value to be returned by **WindowProc**, is then set to zero so the WM_INITMENUPOPUP message is not processed further by Windows. No further processing of the WM_INITMENUPOPUP message is necessary or desirable since the **Caption** property of **mnuFileLastClosed** already has been modified. When Windows next displays the menu, the width of the menu will be sized appropriately to the number of characters in the path and filename of the last-closed file.

TEST THE CODE

1. Run the project. The **mnuFileLastClosed** item is blank and the width of the menu is normal as shown in Figure 4-3 earlier.

2. Open a file, preferably one with a long path, close the file, and then click on the File menu. This time the width of the menu is wide enough to accommodate the long path. (See Figure 4-6.)

3. Open a file, preferably one with a short path, close the file, and then click on the File menu. The width of the menu now has decreased to accommodate the shorter path of the file last closed. (See Figure 4-7.)

Once again, success through subclassing!

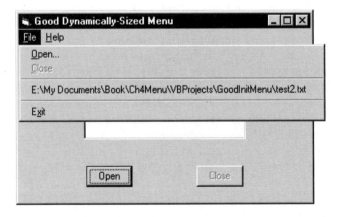

FIGURE 4-6.   The width of the menu has grown to fit the long path of the last-closed file

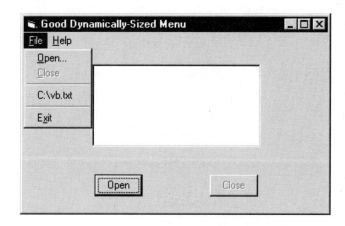

FIGURE 4-7. The width of the menu has shrunk to fit the shorter path of the last-closed file

Bmp+Text.vbp

Putting Pictures on Your Menu

Office 97 applications and, indeed, Visual Basic 5 and 6 sport menus in which a number of the submenu items (such as those under the Project menu in Visual Basic) have bitmaps next to the text of the menu item. (See Figure 4-8.) Being able to do this in your applications would enhance the professional appearance of your application.

Unfortunately, Visual Basic does not provide the ability to add bitmaps next to the text of a menu item. Visual Basic does allow the display of a checkmark next to the menu item. This is accomplished by setting the **Checked** property of a menu item to True. However, all that can be displayed next to the menu item is a checkmark.

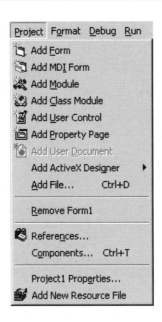

FIGURE 4-8.   Menu items with associated bitmaps in Visual Basic 5

SYNOPSIS OF CODE

Since a checkmark can be placed next to the menu item text, the ideal solution would be simply to replace the checkmark with a bitmap. The solution is achievable with the Windows 32 API.

One problem is that the size of the bitmap may be different than the size of the checkmark and therefore may look too small or have a portion cut off when displayed next to the menu item text. Indeed, the size of the bitmap usually is larger than the checkmark.

The first task is to find out the height and width of the checkmark. As discussed in the "Annotations" section, this is easier said than done, but it is doable. In fact, two different methods can be used to accomplish this task.

The next task is to resize the bitmap to the dimensions of the checkmark. This is done with the help of the **PictureClip** control.

Finally, the checkmark is replaced by the bitmap using the API function **SetMenuItemBitmaps**.

TEST FORM

The test form should be set up as follows:

1. Start a new Standard Exe project. Accept for the default form the name Form1 and the other default properties.

2. Add to the form the controls described here:

Control	Name	ActiveX Control	Component
PictureClip	PictureClip1	PicClp32.ocx	Microsoft PictureClip Control 5.0 (SP2)
ImageList	ImageList1	comctl32.ocx	Microsoft Windows Common Controls 5.0 (SP2)

3. Using Menu Editor, create the menu described in the following table where File and Edit are the top-level menu items, the others first-level submenu items of File:

Name	Caption	Level
mnuFile	&File	First
mnuFileNew	&New	Second
mnuFileOpen	&Open	Second
mnuFileSave	&Save	Second
mnuFileSeparator1	-	Second
mnuFileExit	E&xit	Second
mnuEdit	&Edit	First
mnuEditCut	Cu&t	Second
MnuEditCopy	&Copy	Second
MnuEditPaste	&Paste	Second

4. The completed form should look like Figure 4-9 in Design view.

5. Add to the subdirectory in which your application is located the following bitmaps: new.bmp, open.bmp, save.bmp, cut.bmp, copy.bmp, and paste.bmp. These can be found in your Visual Basic directory under \Graphics\Bitmaps\Tlbr_w95.

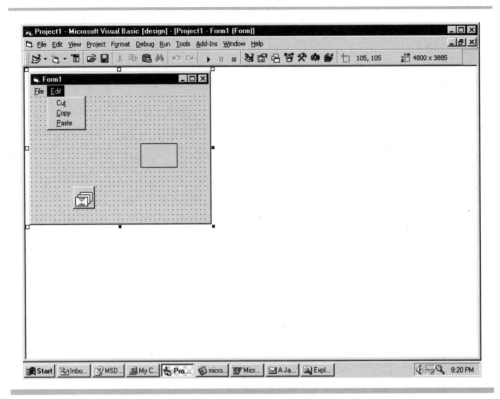

FIGURE 4-9.   Test form in Design view

CODE

The code for the test form is very brief. The current drive and directory are pointed to the subdirectory of the application, and then the module-level procedure **SetMenuBmp** is called, passing a reference to the form as a parameter.

```
Private Sub Form_Load()
    ChDir App.Path
    ChDrive App.Path
    SetMenuBmp Me
End Sub
```

The following is the code for the module-level procedure **SetMenuBmp**:

```
Option Explicit

Private nHeight As Integer
Private nWidth As Integer
```

```
Private Const MF_BYPOSITION = &H400&
Private Const SM_CXMENUCHECK = 71
Private Const SM_CYMENUCHECK = 72

Declare Function GetSystemMetrics Lib "user32" _
   (ByVal nIndex As Long) As Long

Declare Function GetMenu Lib "user32" (ByVal hwnd As Long) As Long

Declare Function GetSubMenu Lib "user32" _
   (ByVal hmenu As Long, ByVal nPos As Long) As Long

Declare Function SetMenuItemBitmaps Lib "user32" _
   (ByVal hmenu As Long, ByVal nPosition As Long, _
  ByVal wFlags As Long, ByVal hBitmapUnchecked As Long, _
  ByVal hBitmapChecked As Long) As Long

Public Sub SetMenuBmp(frm As Form)

    Dim hmenu As Long
    Dim hsubmnuFile As Long
    Dim hsubmnuEdit As Long
    Dim hresult As Long
    Dim imgX As ListImage

    hmenu = GetMenu(frm.hwnd)
    hsubmnuFile = GetSubMenu(hmenu, 0)
    hsubmnuEdit = GetSubMenu(hmenu, 1)
    nWidth = GetSystemMetrics(SM_CXMENUCHECK)
    nHeight = GetSystemMetrics(SM_CYMENUCHECK)

 Dim colFiles As New Collection
    With colFiles
      .Add ("new.bmp")
      .Add ("open.bmp")
      .Add ("save.bmp")
      .Add ("cut.bmp")
      .Add ("copy.bmp")
      .Add ("paste.bmp")
End With
```

```
Dim img As ListImage
Dim x As Integer
For x = 1 To colFiles.Count
    With Form1.PictureClip1
        Set .Picture = LoadPicture(colFiles.Item(x))
        .ClipHeight = .Height
        .ClipWidth = .Width
        .StretchX = nWidth
        .StretchY = nHeight
        .Picture = .Clip
        Set img = Form1.ImageList1.ListImages.Add(, , .Picture)
    End With

    With Form1.ImageList1
        If x <= 3 Then
        Call SetMenuItemBitmaps(hsubmnuFile, x - 1, MF_BYPOSITION, _
            .ListImages(x).Picture, 0)
        Else
        Call SetMenuItemBitmaps(hsubmnuEdit, x - 4, MF_BYPOSITION, _
            .ListImages(x).Picture, 0)
        End If
    End With
Next x
End Sub
```

ANNOTATIONS

```
Private nHeight As Integer
Private nWidth As Integer
```

These variables will hold the width and height of the dimensions (in pixels) of the default menu checkmark bitmap. These values will be retrieved by an API function.

```
Private Const SM_CXMENUCHECK = 71
Private Const SM_CYMENUCHECK = 72

Declare Function GetSystemMetrics Lib "user32" _
  (ByVal nIndex As Long) As Long
```

The API function **GetSystemMetrics** function retrieves various system metrics, that is, the widths and heights of display elements. This function takes one parameter, a constant which specifies the system metric setting to retrieve. Constants prefixed with "SM_CX" or "SM_CY" refer to the width (SM_CX*) or height (SM_CY*) of numerous user interface elements such as the screen, a maximized or minimized window, menu bar buttons, or thumb boxes in a scroll bar, just to name a few. The constants SM_CXMENUCHECK and SM_CYMENUCHECK call for the retrieval of the width and height respectively of the default menu checkmark bitmap.

These constants have to be assigned values. Normally this task is accomplished with the API viewer tool. However, these constants are nowhere to be found in the API viewer tool. Additionally, while these constants are mentioned in other documentation, their values are not.

The solution may be instructive, as the problem of locating values for constants is not unusual. The constants SM_CXMENUCHECK and SM_CYMENUCHECK are defined in the header (.h) file winuser.h, used by C and C++ programs. The values of these constants are 71 and 72 respectively.

An alternative to using **GetSystemMetrics** is the API function **GetMenuCheckMarkDimensions**. This function, which takes no parameters, returns the dimensions of the default checkmark bitmap. The return value specifies the height and width, in pixels, of the default checkmark bitmap. The high-order word contains the height; the low-order word contains the width. Extracting the high- and low-order words out of a long integer was covered in the preceding example. However, Microsoft cautions regarding **GetMenuCheckMarkDimensions**: "This function is obsolete. Use the **GetSystemMetrics** function with the CXMENUCHECK and CYMENUCHECK values to retrieve the bitmap dimensions."

```
Declare Function GetMenu Lib "user32" (ByVal hwnd As Long) As Long
```

The API function **GetMenu** retrieves the handle to the menu assigned to the window whose handle is passed as a parameter. This handle is used to obtain the handle to the submenus.

```
Declare Function GetSubMenu Lib "user32" _
    (ByVal hmenu As Long, ByVal nPos As Long) As Long
```

The API function **GetSubMenu** retrieves the handle to one of the submenus of the menu whose handle was obtained by **GetMenu** and here is passed as the first parameter. The second parameter specifies the zero-based relative position in the given menu of an item that activates a drop-down menu or submenu. For example, in our menu, to retrieve the handle of the File menu, the second parameter would be 0, whereas to retrieve the handle of the Edit menu, the second paramenter would be 1.

```
Declare Function SetMenuItemBitmaps Lib "user32" _
   (ByVal hmenu As Long, ByVal nPosition As Long, _
  ByVal wFlags As Long, ByVal hBitmapUnchecked As Long, _
  ByVal hBitmapChecked As Long) As Long
```

The **SetMenuItemBitmaps** function associates the specified bitmap with a menu item. Whether the menu item is checked or unchecked, the system displays the appropriate bitmap next to the menu item.

The first parameter is the handle to the menu, or here the submenu. This value is the handle to the File menu returned by **GetSubMenu**.

The second parameter specifies the menu item to receive the new bitmap, either by its zero-based position, if the third parameter is MF_BYPOSITION, or by command ID, if the third parameter is MF_BYCOMMAND. In this example the third parameter is MF_BYPOSITION. In the File menu, whose handle will be specified by the first parameter, the position of the New menu item is 0, the position of the Open menu item is 1, and the position of the Save menu item is 2.

The fourth and fifth parameters are the handles to the bitmap to be displayed when the menu item is not checked or checked respectively. In this example we will only be concerned about the bitmap when the menu item is not checked, but the **SetMenuItemBitmaps** API function permits different bitmaps for each case.

```
Public Sub SetMenuBmp(frm As Form)

    Dim hmenu As Long
    Dim hsubmnuFile As Long
    Dim hsubmnuEdit As Long

    hmenu = GetMenu(frm.hwnd)
    hsubmnuFile = GetSubMenu(hmenu, 0)
    hsubmnuEdit = GetSubMenu(hmenu, 1)
```

The above code obtains handles to the File and Edit menus respectively. The call to **GetMenu** returns the handle to the menu of the form whose handle is passed as a parameter. That menu handle is then passed as the first parameter of the next two calls to **GetSubMenu**. Those two calls differ only in their second parameter, which is the zero-based position of the menu. Therefore, the first call to **GetSubMenu** returns to **hsubmnufile** the handle to the File menu, and the second call to **GetSubMenu** returns to **hsubmnuEdit** the handle to the Edit menu.

```
    nWidth = GetSystemMetrics(SM_CXMENUCHECK)
    nHeight = GetSystemMetrics(SM_CYMENUCHECK)
```

These two calls to **GetSystemMetrics** return the width (specified by SM_CXMENUCHECK) and the height (specified by SM_CYMENUCHECK) of the default dimensions of the default menu checkmark bitmap and store these values in *nWidth* and *nHeight* respectively.

```
Dim colFiles As New Collection
  With colFiles
    .Add ("new.bmp")
    .Add ("open.bmp")
    .Add ("save.bmp")
    .Add ("cut.bmp")
    .Add ("copy.bmp")
    .Add ("paste.bmp")
  End With
```

This code creates a collection and adds to it the strings which specify the filenames of the bitmaps to be used. No path is necessary because these bitmaps are stored in the same subdirectory as the application and the **ChDrive** and **ChDir** statements in the **Load** event of the form point the current directory to the application's subdirectory.

```
Dim img As ListImage
Dim x As Integer
For x = 1 To colFiles.Count
    With Form1.PictureClip1
        Set .Picture = LoadPicture(colFiles.Item(x))
        .ClipHeight = .Height
        .ClipWidth = .Width
        .StretchX = nWidth
        .StretchY = nHeight
        .Picture = .Clip
        Set img = Form1.ImageList1.ListImages.Add(, , .Picture)
    End With
```

The **ClipHeight** and **ClipWidth** properties specify the height and width respectively of the bitmap section to be copied by the **Clip** property. These properties are assigned the values contained in the **Height** and **Width** properties, which contain the height and width (in pixels) of the bitmap contained in the control. The **StretchX** and **StretchY** properties specify the target size for the bitmap created with the **Clip** property. These properties are assigned the values contained in the variables *nWidth* and *nHeight*, which contain the default height and width of the default menu checkmark bitmap. Next, the **Picture** property is assigned the return value of the **Clip** property, which returns a bitmap of the area in the **PictureClip** control specified by the values contained in *nWidth* and *nHeight*. Finally, the properly sized bitmap is added to the ImageList.

```
With Form1.ImageList1
    If x <= 3 Then
    Call SetMenuItemBitmaps(hsubmnuFile, x - 1, MF_BYPOSITION, _
        .ListImages(x).Picture, 0)
    Else
    Call SetMenuItemBitmaps(hsubmnuEdit, x - 4, MF_BYPOSITION, _
        .ListImages(x).Picture, 0)
    End If
End With
Next x
```

This code takes the images in the ImageList and associates them with the appropriate submenu items.

TEST THE CODE

Run the application. The File menu should look like Figure 4-10 and the Edit menu should look like Figure 4-11.

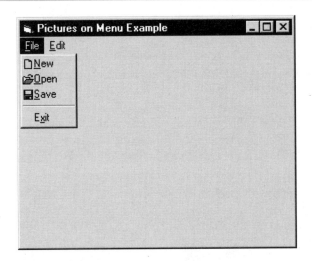

FIGURE 4-10. The File menu with bitmaps

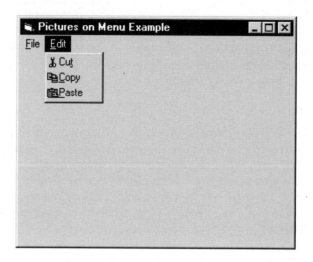

FIGURE 4-11. The Edit menu with bitmaps

OwnrDraw.vbp

Creating Designer Menus

Thus far we have enhanced the standard Visual Basic menu. We have dynamically resized the width of the menu to meet changes in the width of the text of the menu items, and have replaced the default checkmark with a properly sized bitmap. However, in each case we relied on Visual Basic to redraw the menu with our changes. This reliance was possible because the basic structure of the menu item, space for a checkmark followed by space for text, was unchanged.

There are circumstances in which you may not want to be constrained by the menu structure used by Visual Basic and instead wish to design your own menu structure. The example used here will be a color picker. Clicking on the color menu of the form will display bars of color. Clicking on one of those bars would set the color of an object. In this case, so the code is no more complex than necessary, the color being changed is the color of text in a textbox, but it would not be difficult to utilize the value of the color selected in other ways useful to your application.

These designed menus are referred to as "owner-drawn" because the owner (that's you) has to draw the menu rather than having Visual Basic do it. This means good news and bad news. The good news is that you have far more flexibility in the menu's appearance. The bad news is that you have to do the work normally done by Visual Basic to properly size and draw the menu.

SYNOPSIS OF CODE

The Windows operating system is responsible for drawing menus, but it is not responsible for drawing owner-drawn menus. As the term "owner-drawn" indicates, the window that owns a menu is responsible for drawing owner-drawn menus.

When a menu item needs to be drawn, such as when it is first displayed or when the user selects it, the menu sends a WM_MEASUREITEM message and a WM_DRAWITEM message to the window procedure of the menu's owner window. Through subclassing, our user-defined Windows function will intercept these messages.

The WM_MEASUREITEM and WM_DRAWITEM messages point to MEASUREITEMSTRUCT and DRAWITEMSTRUCT structures respectively. A MEASUREITEMSTRUCT structure contains information about the dimensions of an owner-drawn control or menu item. A DRAWITEMSTRUCT structure provides information the owner window must have to determine how to paint an owner-drawn control or menu item.

The **CopyMemory** function, first discussed in the "Controlling the Resizing of a Form" example in Chapter 1, is used to change the value of the members of the MEASUREITEMSTRUCT structure to the desired dimensions of the menu item. Members of the DRAWITEMSTRUCT structure are used to properly paint the menu control. The painting will be done with "brushes." More on this in the "Annotations" section.

TEST FORM

The test form should be set up as follows:

1. Start a new Standard Exe project. Accept for the default form the name Form1 and the other default properties.

2. Add to the form the controls described here:

Control	Name	Comments
TextBox	Text1	Text property = "Change text color"
PictureBox	picColor	None
Label	Label1	Caption property = Text Color

3. Using Menu Editor, create the menu described in the following table where File and Color are the top-level menu items, the others first-level submenu items of File:

Name	Caption	Index
MnuFile	&File	N/A
MnuFileExit	....E&xit	Second
mnuColor	&Color	N/A
mnuColors	....<black>	0
mnuColors	....<blue>	1
mnuColors	....<green>	2
mnuColors	....<cyan>	3
mnuColors	....<red>	4
mnuColors	....<magenta>	5
mnuColors	....<yellow>	6
mnuColors	....<white>	7
mnuColorSep10	....-	N/A
mnuColorDefault	....&Default	N/A

4. The completed form should look like Figure 4-12 in Design view.

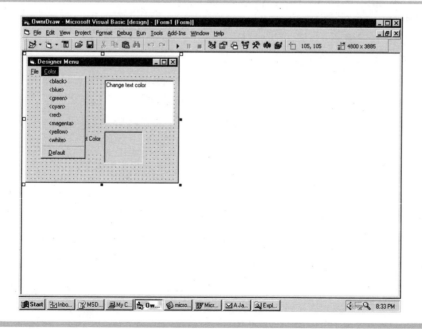

FIGURE 4-12. Test form in Design view

CODE

The code for the test form is brief. The form's **Load** event calls the **SetMenu** subroutine in the module which redraws the Color menu, and then calls the **Subclass** subroutine as in the preceding subclassing examples so that messages will be handled first by the user-defined Windows function. The form's **Unload** event restores the default Windows function by calling the **UnSubClass** subroutine. The **BackColor** property of the form and PictureBox, and the **ForeColor** property of the textbox, are set to the color of the submenu item clicked under the Color menu unless the user clicks on the Default submenu item, in which case the default backcolor and forecolor are restored.

```
Option Explicit

Private Sub Form_Load()
    SetUpMenu Me
    Call SubClass(Me.hWnd)
End Sub

Private Sub Form_Unload(Cancel As Integer)
    Call UnSubClass(Me.hWnd)
End Sub

Private Sub mnuColorDefault_Click()
    picColor.BackColor = BackColor
    Text1.ForeColor = vbBlack
End Sub

Private Sub mnuColors_Click(Index As Integer)
    picColor.BackColor = QBColor(8 + Index)
    Text1.ForeColor = QBColor(8 + Index)
End Sub

Private Sub mnuFileExit_Click()
    Unload Me
End Sub
```

The following is the code for the module-level procedure. Unlike the form's code, it is lengthy, but there is much to be learned!

```
Option Explicit

Public defWindowProc As Long

Private Type RECT
    left As Long
    top As Long
    right As Long
    bottom As Long
End Type

Private Type DRAWITEMSTRUCT
    CtlType As Long
    CtlID As Long
    itemID As Long
    itemAction As Long
    itemState As Long
    hwndItem As Long
    hdc As Long
    rcItem As RECT
    itemData As Long
End Type

Private Type MEASUREITEMSTRUCT
    CtlType As Long
    CtlID As Long
    itemID As Long
    itemWidth As Long
    itemHeight As Long
    itemData As Long
End Type

Private Const ODS_SELECTED = &H1
Private Const COLOR_MENU = 4
Private Const COLOR_WINDOW = 5
Private Const COLOR_HIGHLIGHT = 13
Private Const MF_OWNERDRAW = &H100
Private Const MF_BYCOMMAND = &H0
Public Const MF_BYPOSITION = &H400&
Private Const SM_CYMENU = 15
```

```vb
Private Const WM_DRAWITEM = &H2B
Private Const WM_MEASUREITEM = &H2C
Public Const GWL_WNDPROC As Long = (-4)

Private Declare Function GetMenu Lib "User32" _
    (ByVal hWnd As Long) As Long

Private Declare Function GetSubMenu Lib "User32" _
    (ByVal hMenu As Long, ByVal nPos As Long) As Long

Private Declare Function ModifyMenu Lib "User32" _
    Alias "ModifyMenuA" _
    (ByVal hMenu As Long, ByVal nPosition As Long, _
    ByVal wFlags As Long, _
    ByVal wIDNewItem As Long, _
    ByVal nValue As Any) As Long

Private Declare Function GetMenuItemID Lib "User32" _
    (ByVal hMenu As Long, ByVal nPos As Long) As Long

Private Declare Function CreateSolidBrush Lib "gdi32" _
    (ByVal crColor As Long) As Long

Private Declare Function SelectObject Lib "gdi32" _
    (ByVal hdc As Long, ByVal hObject As Long) As Long

Private Declare Function DeleteObject Lib "gdi32" _
    (ByVal hObject As Long) As Long

Private Declare Function Rectangle Lib "gdi32" _
    (ByVal hdc As Long, ByVal X1 As Long, _
    ByVal Y1 As Long, _
    ByVal X2 As Long, ByVal Y2 As Long) As Long

Private Declare Function InflateRect Lib "User32" _
    (lpRect As RECT, ByVal x As Long, _
    ByVal y As Long) As Long

Private Declare Function FillRect Lib "User32" _
    (ByVal hdc As Long, lpRect As RECT, _
    ByVal hBrush As Long) As Long
```

```
Private Declare Function GetSysColor Lib "User32" _
   (ByVal nIndex As Long) As Long

Private Declare Function GetSystemMetrics Lib "User32" _
   (ByVal nIndex As Long) As Long

Private Declare Sub CopyMemory Lib "Kernel32" _
   Alias "RtlMoveMemory" _
   (lpDest As Any, lpSource As Any, ByVal nCount As Long)

Declare Function GetWindowLong Lib "User32" _
   Alias "GetWindowLongA" _
   (ByVal hWnd As Long, ByVal nIndex As Long) As Long

Declare Function SetWindowLong Lib "User32" _
   Alias "SetWindowLongA" _
   (ByVal hWnd As Long, ByVal nIndex As Long, _
   ByVal dwNewLong As Long) As Long

Declare Function CallWindowProc Lib "User32" _
   Alias "CallWindowProcA" _
   (ByVal lpPrevWndFunc As Long, ByVal hWnd As Long, _
   ByVal Msg As Long, ByVal wParam As Long, _
   ByVal lParam As Long) As Long

Public Sub SubClass(hWnd As Long)
 On Error Resume Next
 defWindowProc = SetWindowLong(hWnd, _
   GWL_WNDPROC, AddressOf WindowProc)
 End Sub

Public Sub UnSubClass(hWnd As Long)
 If defWindowProc Then
   SetWindowLong hWnd, GWL_WNDPROC, defWindowProc
   defWindowProc = 0
 End If
End Sub

Public Sub SetUpMenu(frm As Form)
  Dim hMenu As Long
    Dim i As Long
    Dim j As Long
    hMenu = GetMenu(frm.hWnd)
```

```
    hMenu = GetSubMenu(hMenu, 1)
    For i = 0 To 7
      j = GetMenuItemID(hMenu, i)
      j = ModifyMenu(hMenu, j, MF_BYCOMMAND _
          Or MF_OWNERDRAW, j, _
          QBColor(8 + i))
    Next I
End Sub

Public Function WindowProc(ByVal hWnd As Long, _
   ByVal uMsg As Long, _
   ByVal wParam As Long, _
   ByVal lParam As Long) As Long


On Error Resume Next
 Dim retVal As Long
 Dim tmp As Long, rc As RECT
 Dim hBrush As Long, hOldBrush As Long
 Dim DrawInfo As DRAWITEMSTRUCT
 Dim MeasureInfo As MEASUREITEMSTRUCT
    Select Case uMsg
        Case WM_DRAWITEM
            If wParam = 0 Then
                CopyMemory DrawInfo, _
                    ByVal lParam, Len(DrawInfo)
                If DrawInfo.itemState And _
                    ODS_SELECTED Then
                  hBrush = CreateSolidBrush _
                      (GetSysColor(COLOR_HIGHLIGHT))
                Else
                  hBrush = CreateSolidBrush _
                      (GetSysColor(COLOR_MENU))
                End If

                rc = DrawInfo.rcItem
                FillRect DrawInfo.hdc, rc, hBrush
                DeleteObject hBrush
                tmp = (rc.bottom - rc.top) / 5
                InflateRect rc, -tmp, -tmp
                hBrush = CreateSolidBrush _
                    (DrawInfo.itemData)
                hOldBrush = SelectObject _
                    (DrawInfo.hdc, hBrush)
```

```
                    Rectangle DrawInfo.hdc, rc.left, _
                        rc.top, rc.right, rc.bottom
                    SelectObject DrawInfo.hdc, hOldBrush
                    DeleteObject hBrush
                End If
                retVal = 0
            Case WM_MEASUREITEM
                CopyMemory MeasureInfo, ByVal lParam, _
                    Len(MeasureInfo)
                MeasureInfo.itemWidth = 70
                MeasureInfo.itemHeight = _
                    GetSystemMetrics(SM_CYMENU)
                CopyMemory ByVal lParam, _
                    MeasureInfo, Len(MeasureInfo)
                retVal = 0
            Case Else
                retVal = CallWindowProc _
                    (defWindowProc, hWnd, _
                    uMsg, wParam, lParam)
        End Select
WindowProc = retVal
End Function
```

ANNOTATIONS

```
Private Type RECT
    left As Long
    top As Long
    right As Long
    bottom As Long
End Type
```

This and the next two user-defined types mimic corresponding Windows structures which are used in the Windows API functions to be called. This technique was first introduced in Chapter 1 in the "Controlling the Resizing of a Form" example. The RECT structure will be used to contain the dimensions of the menu control.

```
Private Type DRAWITEMSTRUCT
    CtlType As Long
    CtlID As Long
    itemID As Long
    itemAction As Long
```

```
    itemState As Long
    hwndItem As Long
    hdc As Long
    rcItem As RECT
    itemData As Long
End Type
```

```
Private Const WM_DRAWITEM = &H2B
```

When a menu item must be drawn, such as when it is first displayed or when the user selects it, Windows sends the WM_DRAWITEM message to the window procedure of the menu's owner window. The *wParam* of this message specifies the identifier of the control that sent the message. If the message was sent by a menu, the value of this parameter is zero. Thus the test in the user-defined Window procedure **WindowProc**:

```
If wParam = 0 Then
```

The *lParam* of the WM_DRAWITEM message is a pointer to a DRAWITEMSTRUCT structure containing information about the item to be drawn and the type of drawing required. Therefore, a user-defined type corresponding to a DRAWITEMSTRUCT structure is declared.

A DRAWITEMSTRUCT structure has a number of members. The meanings and uses of several of them are discussed below when they are used. In essence, the members of DRAWITEMSTRUCT provide information the owner window must have to determine how to paint an owner-drawn control or menu item.

```
Private Type MEASUREITEMSTRUCT
    CtlType As Long
    CtlID As Long
    itemID As Long
    itemWidth As Long
    itemHeight As Long
    itemData As Long
End Type
```

```
Private Const WM_MEASUREITEM = &H2C
```

When a menu item must be drawn, such as when it is first displayed or when the user selects it, Windows sends a WM_MEASUREITEM message as well as a WM_DRAWITEM message to the window procedure of the menu's owner window. As with the WM_DRAWITEM message, the *wParam* of a WM_MEASUREITEM message specifies the identifier of the control that sent the message, and has a value of zero if the message was sent by a menu.

The *lParam* of the WM_MEASUREITEM message is a pointer to a MEASUREITEMSTRUCT structure containing information about the dimensions of an owner-drawn control or menu item. Therefore, a user-defined type corresponding to a MEASUREITEMSTRUCT structure is declared.

A number of new constants and API declarations are next declared. Given the large number of them, they will be discussed below when they are used.

```
Public Sub SetUpMenu(frm As Form)
  Dim hMenu As Long
    Dim i As Long
    Dim j As Long
    hMenu = GetMenu(frm.hWnd)
    hMenu = GetSubMenu(hMenu, 1)
    For i = 0 To 7
      j = GetMenuItemID(hMenu, i)
      j = ModifyMenu(hMenu, j, MF_BYCOMMAND Or MF_OWNERDRAW, j, _
          QBColor(8 + i))
    Next I
End Sub
```

This subroutine is called in the **Load** event of the test form with the parameter being the **Me** keyword to reference the form. The variable *hMenu* first is assigned the handle to the form's menu through the call to **GetMenu**. The variable next is assigned the handle to the second submenu (the second parameter is 1 and the relative positions of the submenu items are zero-based), which in this case is the Color menu, through the call to **GetSubMenu**.

There are nine submenu items, but the interest here is only in the first eight, which correspond to colors. The ninth submenu item, labeled "Default," will be treated differently. Since the relative positions of the submenu items are zero-based, the for loop starts at 0 and goes through 7.

The API function **GetMenuItemID** retrieves the menu item identifier of a menu item located at the specified position in a menu. The first parameter is the handle to the menu that contains the item whose identifier is to be retrieved. That parameter is the return value of **GetSubMenu**. The second parameter is the zero-based relative position of the menu item whose identifier is to be retrieved. The return value, assigned to the variable *j*, specifies the identifier of the given menu item. In each iteration of the for loop, *j* will hold the command ID of one of the first eight submenu items under the Color menu which correspond to colors.

The API function **ModifyMenu** changes an existing menu item. Microsoft tells us that the **ModifyMenu** function has been superseded by **SetMenuItemInfo**. The **SetMenuItemInfo** function has parameters not present in **ModifyMenu** and therefore supports menu features not possible with **ModifyMenu**. Microsoft allows that **ModifyMenu** still may be used if there is no need for any of the extended features of **SetMenuItemInfo**. Another reason to use **ModifyMenu** is that it, unlike **SetMenuItemInfo**, is supported in Windows NT 3.51, and there still are a number of NT 3.51 workstations.

ModifyMenu has five parameters. The first parameter once again is the handle to the menu that contains the item whose identifier is to be retrieved. That parameter is the return value of **GetSubMenu**. The second parameter specifies the menu item to be changed, either by position if the third parameter is MF_BYPOSITION, or by command ID if the third parameter is MF_BYCOMMAND. Here MF_BYCOMMAND is the third parameter (the MF_OWNERDRAW parameter is discussed below), so the second parameter refers to the command ID, which is stored in the variable *j* as a result of the call to **GetMenuItemID**.

The fourth parameter specifies the identifier of the modified menu item, which again is stored in the variable *j*. Coincidentally, *j* also holds the zero-based position of the submenu item because the first eight submenu items are part of a control array.

The fifth parameter is a pointer to the content of the changed menu item. The interpretation of this parameter depends on whether the third parameter includes the MF_BITMAP, MF_OWNERDRAW, or MF_STRING flag. MF_BITMAP contains a bitmap handle, and MF_STRING contains a pointer to a null-terminated string (the default). Since MF_OWNERDRAW is part of the third parameter, the fifth parameter contains a 32-bit value supplied by an application that is used to maintain additional data related to the menu item.

In this example, the fifth parameter is the return value of the **QBColor** function. This function returns a long integer representing the RGB (Red-Blue-Green) color code corresponding to the number in its one parameter. The numbers used here (the value of the counter **i** plus 8) and their corresponding colors are set forth in Table 4-1.

Thus, each of the first eight submenu items under the Color menu have as related data the long integer representing the RGB color code of its particular color.

The value of the fifth parameter also will be the value in the **itemData** member of the structure pointed to by the *lParam* parameter of the WM_MEASUREITEM or

Color Code	Color
9	Light Blue
10	Light Green
11	Light Cyan
12	Light Red
13	Light Magenta
14	Light Yellow
15	Bright White

TABLE 4-1.   Color Codes and Colors of **QBColor** Function Used in Example

WM_DRAWITEM messages sent when the menu item is created or its appearance is updated. The importance of this will become apparent below.

```
Public Function WindowProc(ByVal hWnd As Long, ByVal uMsg As Long, _
    ByVal wParam As Long, ByVal lParam As Long) As Long


On Error Resume Next
 Dim retVal As Long
 Dim tmp As Long, rc As RECT
 Dim hBrush As Long
 Dim hOldBrush As Long
 Dim DrawInfo As DRAWITEMSTRUCT
 Dim MeasureInfo As MEASUREITEMSTRUCT
    Select Case uMsg
        Case WM_DRAWITEM
            If wParam = 0 Then
                CopyMemory DrawInfo, ByVal lParam, Len(DrawInfo)
                If DrawInfo.itemState And ODS_SELECTED Then _
                  hBrush = _CreateSolidBrush _
                      (GetSysColor(COLOR_HIGHLIGHT))
                Else
                  hBrush = CreateSolidBrush(GetSysColor(COLOR_MENU))
                End If
```

The *wParam* of the WM_DRAWITEM message is zero if the control is a menu. The members of the DRAWITEMSTRUCT structure pointed to by the message are copied into a local DRAWITEMSTRUCT structure, DrawInfo, using the **CopyMemory** function. As discussed in the "Controlling the Resizing of a Form" example in Chapter 1, the **CopyMemory** function has three parameters. The first parameter is the address of the destination to which the copy is being sent, the second parameter is the address of the source being copied, and the third parameter is number of bytes to be copied. With the WM_DRAWITEM message, *lParam* is the address of the structure passed by the message, so *lParam* as the second parameter in **CopyMemory** passes the address of the DRAWITEMSTRUCT structure which accompanied the WM_DRAWITEM message.

The statement

```
If DrawInfo.itemState And ODS_SELECTED Then
```

tests if the user selected one of the eight Color items, in which case the statement

```
hBrush = CreateSolidBrush(GetSysColor(COLOR_HIGHLIGHT))
```

executes. Otherwise, if the user selected the Default submenu item, the execution is of the statement

```
hBrush = CreateSolidBrush(GetSysColor(COLOR_MENU))
```

The API function **GetSysColor** retrieves the current color of the display element specified in the first parameter. The constant COLOR_HIGHLIGHT refers to the item selected in a control. Thus, if the submenu item concerns the color Magenta, then that color will be returned by **GetSysColor**. The constant COLOR_MENU refers to the menu background. Accordingly, if the user selected the Default submenu item, then the color returned by **GetSysColor** would be the default, in this case Gray.

The API function **CreateSolidBrush** creates a logical brush that has the specified solid color. A *brush* is a graphics tool that a Win32-based application uses to paint the interior of shapes. There are two types of brushes: logical and physical.

A *logical brush* is a description of the ideal bitmap that an application would use to paint shapes. There are four types of logical brushes: *solid*, *stock*, *hatch*, and *pattern*. A *solid brush* is a logical brush that contains 64 pixels of the same color. This example will use a solid brush since the colors in the submenu items are solid, and therefore will use the **CreateSolidBrush** function.

A *physical brush* is the actual bitmap that a device driver creates based on an application's logical-brush definition. When an application calls one of the functions that create a brush, it retrieves a handle that identifies a logical brush. In this example, that handle is the return value of **CreateSolidBrush** and is assigned to the variable *hBrush*.

```
rc = DrawInfo.rcItem
```

The **rcItem** member of DRAWITEMSTRUCT specifies a rectangle that defines the boundaries of the control to be drawn. That value is stored in *rc*, which is a variable of the user-defined RECT type.

```
FillRect DrawInfo.hdc, rc, hBrush
```

The **FillRect** function fills a rectangle by using the specified brush. The first parameter is the **hdc** member of DRAWITEMSTRUCT. This member is a handle to a device context; this device context must be used when performing drawing operations on the control. The second parameter, *rc*, is the RECT variable that defines the boundaries of the control to be drawn. The third parameter, *hBrush*, holds the value of the handle that identifies a logical brush.

```
DeleteObject hBrush
```

The **DeleteObject** function deletes the logical brush. This is necessary to free the system resources associated with the brush. After the brush is deleted, the handle *hBrush* no longer is valid.

```
tmp = (rc.bottom - rc.top) / 5
InflateRect rc, -tmp, -tmp
```

The **InflateRect** function increases or decreases the width and height of the specified rectangle. The **InflateRect** function has two parameters. The number of units specified in the first parameter is added (or subtracted in the case of a negative number) to the left and right ends of the rectangle. The number of units specified in the second parameter is added (or subtracted in the case of a negative number) to the top and bottom of the rectangle. In this case, the width and height of the Color submenu items are cropped so they are not flush against each other.

```
hBrush = CreateSolidBrush(DrawInfo.itemData)
```

Thus, each of the first eight submenu items under the Color menu have as related data the long integer representing the RGB color code of its particular color.

As you may recall, the value of the fifth parameter of **ModifyMenu** was the return value of the **QBColor** function, a long interger representing the RGB (Red-Blue-Green) color code corresponding to the color of the Color submenu item. As you may also recall, this value also became the value in the **itemData** member of the structure pointed to by the *lParam* parameter of the WM_DRAWITEM messages sent when the menu item is created or its appearance is updated. Here that color is retrieved so **CreateSolidBrush** creates a logical brush with that color. As before, the return value of **CreateSolidBrush** is a handle that identifies that logical brush, and that handle is assigned to the variable *hBrush*.

```
hOldBrush = SelectObject(DrawInfo.hdc, hBrush)
```

The **SelectObject** function selects an object into the specified device context. The new object replaces the previous object of the same type. The first parameter, the **hdc** member of DRAWITEMSTRUCT, is a handle to a device context which must be used when performing drawing operations on the control. The second parameter is the handle to the object to be selected. That handle is to the newly created logical brush. The return value is the handle of the object being replaced. This function returns the previously selected object of the specified type. An application should always replace a new object with the original, default object after it has finished drawing with the new object. This should sound familiar. In subclassing, when we diverted messages to our user-defined Windows function, we saved a reference to the default Windows function so that the default function could be restored before the application terminated.

```
Rectangle DrawInfo.hdc, rc.left, rc.top, rc.right, rc.bottom
```

The API function **Rectangle** draws, you guessed it, a rectangle. The dimensions of the rectangle previously were assigned from the **rcItem** member of DRAWITEMSTRUCT, which specifies a rectangle that defines the boundaries of the control to be drawn, to *rc*, which is a variable of the user-defined RECT type.

```
        SelectObject DrawInfo.hdc, hOldBrush
        DeleteObject hBrush
    End If
retVal = 0
```

The **SelectObject** function restores the default brush, and the **DeleteObject** function restores the system resources used by the brush. The value returned by the user-defined Windows function to the default Windows function is zero as all processing of the message has been done.

```
Case WM_MEASUREITEM
   CopyMemory MeasureInfo, ByVal lParam, Len(MeasureInfo)
   MeasureInfo.itemWidth = 70
   MeasureInfo.itemHeight = GetSystemMetrics(SM_CYMENU)
   CopyMemory ByVal lParam, MeasureInfo, Len(MeasureInfo)
   retVal = 0
```

This code does the following:

1. The members of the MINMAXINFO structure pointed to by the message are copied into the local MEASUREITEMSTRUCT structure, **MeasureInfo,** using the **CopyMemory** function.

2. The members of the local MEASUREITEMSTRUCT structure, **MeasureInfo,** are changed to the desired values. The width of the menu control is specified at 70 pixels. The height is determined using the API function **GetSystemMetrics** discussed earlier in this chapter. The paramenter SM_CYMENU causes the function to return the standard system height of a menu.

3. In the reverse of step 1, the members of the local MEASUREITEMSTRUCT structure, **MeasureInfo,** are copied into the MEASUREITEMSTRUCT structure pointed to by the message, again using the **CopyMemory** function.

4. The MEASUREITEMSTRUCT structure pointed to by the message, with the values of its members modified, then is passed to the application.

```
Case Else
  retVal = CallWindowProc _
    (defWindowProc, hWnd, uMsg, wParam, lParam)
End Select
```

If the message is not one of the two in which we are interested, it is passed to the default Windows function.

```
WindowProc = retVal
```

As in the preceding subclassing examples, the value returned by the user-defined Windows function is zero if the message was processed by our code, and otherwise is unchanged from that which it would have been if there had been no user-defined Windows function.

TEST THE CODE

Run the project, click on the Color menu, and choose both Color and Default submenu items. (See Figure 4-13.)

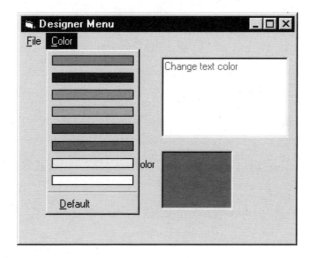

FIGURE 4-13. The color purple (trust me)

Toolbars

T his chapter is about bars, but not the kind which inspired the song "Looking for Love in All the Wrong Places." While the uninformed may deem single bars more interesting (as computer programmers you are not supposed to be interested in such places anyway), the bar which is the subject of this chapter not only is safer, but also enables you to enhance your application both functionally and visually.

One bar which is part of a computer programmer's life is the toolbar. Toolbars are an important part of an application's graphical user interface. The functionality of the toolbar button generally duplicates the functionality of menu items. However, the toolbar buttons have two advantages over the menu items. First, the toolbar buttons are immediately visible and accessible. By contrast, menu items may be nested several levels deep and can be accessed only by several mouse clicks or keystrokes. Second, the toolbars are visual, whereas the menu items are text, and generally visual items are more attractive and apparent than text items to the application user. This is *Visual* Basic, after all.

Both Versions 5 and 6 of Visual Basic include controls for toolbars. The built-in functionality of these controls is quite adequate for building standard toolbars.

However, the theme of this book is to go where no VB programmer has gone before (hoping, of course, there is not a good reason why others haven't gone where we are going). If you want your application's toolbar to be floating and docking, as in the following examples, the built-in functionality of the toolbar is not sufficient. You will need to use, as you probably have guessed, the Windows 32 API and, usually, subclassing.

The good news is that you can use Windows 32 API and subclassing examples from the preceding chapters to help implement the enhanced functionality. Indeed, this chapter ties together concepts discussed in the preceding chapters and extends the application of those concepts beyond forms to include controls as well.

This chapter also illustrates the advantage of modular, object-oriented programming techniques. Once the code is written for a floating toolbar, only a few lines of code need to be changed to add docking behavior. Finally, to enhance the toolbar with the new flat, coolbar style, all that is necessary, once a class providing this functionality is added to the project, is to add three lines to the existing code.

Floatbar.vbp

Creating a Floating Toolbar

Toolbars traditionally have been at the top of a window, in the non-client area, just below the menu bar. However, fashion changes and now "floating" toolbars are common. These toolbars "float" in the sense that they can be moved around a window. Examples of floating toolbars in the Visual Basic IDE are the Toolbox and the Debug toolbar.

The ability of a toolbar to float in the window is quite desirable. It enables the application user to move the toolbar to a location where it can be accessed conveniently without blocking a portion of the window which needs to be viewed or accessed.

Enabling a toolbar to float in the window, while desirable, does require the resolution of programming issues which are not present with the traditional stationary toolbar. The primary problem is keeping the toolbar inside of the application window. This problem has two different aspects. The first is to prevent the toolbar from leaving the application window altogether. (See Figure 5-1.) The second is to prevent the toolbar from disappearing under the application window's border. (See Figure 5-2.)

The method of preventing the toolbar from leaving the application window altogether is to make the toolbar a "child" window and the application window the "parent" window.

A window either may have one parent window or not have a parent window. A window cannot have more than one parent window.

A window without a parent window is a top-level window. The main window of an application typically does not have a parent window. Visual Basic stand-alone forms in a Single Document Interface (SDI) application and the MDI form in a Multiple Document Interface (MDI) application (more on MDI shortly) also are top-level windows.

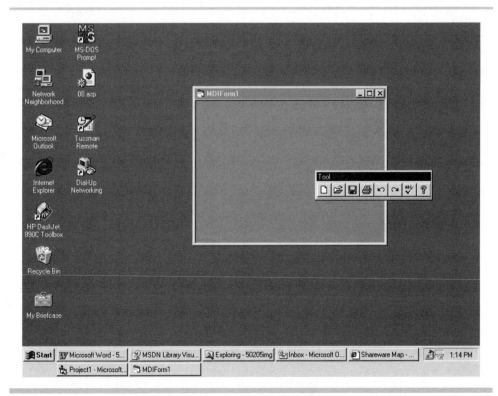

FIGURE 5-1.   Toolbar leaving the application window

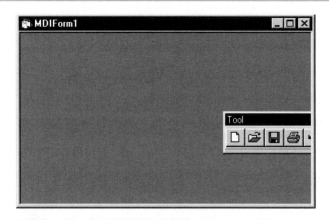

FIGURE 5-2.   Toolbar disappearing under the application window's border

Two types of windows have parent windows. *Owned windows* may appear anywhere on the screen. A pop-up window, usually used for dialog boxes, is an example of an owned window. (See Figure 5-3.) *Child windows*, by contrast, are confined to the client area of their parent. For example, Figure 5-4 shows a child window in Microsoft Word, bearing the caption "Document20," and its parent (and top-level window), bearing the caption "Microsoft Word." While a child window can have only one parent, a parent window may have many owned and child windows.

Table 5-1 describes how methods or events of the parent window can affect its owned and child windows.

Thus, making the toolbar the child of the main application window will prevent the toolbar from straying outside of the borders of the main application window. Making the toolbar the child of the main application window can be accomplished simply by making the toolbar a control of the main form. A control is a window, and the child of the form which is its container. In fact, this is the standard method of including a toolbar in the application.

Parent Window Action	Effect on Child Window	Effect on Owned Window
Shown	Shown after parent (if visible)	Shown after parent (if visible)
Hidden	All hidden	All hidden
Moved	Move with parent	None
Destroyed	Automatically destroyed before parent	Automatically destroyed before parent

TABLE 5-1.   Effect of Methods or Events of the Parent Window on Owned and Child Windows

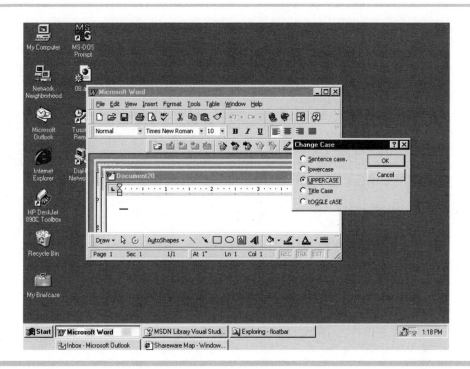

FIGURE 5-3. An owned window, which is not confined to its parent window

The approach does not work, however, if the toolbar is to be able to float in the window. The reason is that Visual Basic has no built-in method for moving a toolbar. As a general rule, absent special programming, at run-time forms can be moved, but controls cannot. This suggests the solution: Put the toolbar in a form just large enough to contain the toolbar and make that form the child of the main application window.

Making a form a child window of another form can be accomplished programmatically via the Windows 32 API. This is not difficult and works well enough if there are only two forms, the main application form and the toolbar form. However, if the application involves a number of forms, each of which is to use the toolbar, then shifting the parentage of the toolbar form becomes quite difficult.

Visual Basic has a built-in solution. The main application window is an MDI form, adding the Project | Add MDI Form command. The toolbar form, as well as any other forms in the application, are MDI child forms. They are added as standard forms, and their **MDIChild** property is set to True. As a result, the toolbar form is the child of the main application window and therefore cannot float outside of it. Additionally, the other child forms can have access to the toolbar form since they all have the same parent.

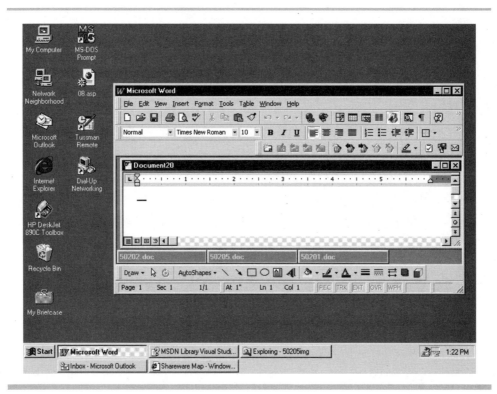

FIGURE 5-4.   A child window, which is confined to its parent window

While making the toolbar a "child" window and the application window the "parent" window will prevent the toolbar from leaving the application window altogether, it will not prevent the toolbar from disappearing under the application window's border. This cannot be prevented by Visual Basic, but it can be prevented with the Windows API.

As discussed in Chapter 1 in the "Controlling the Movement of a Form" example, by subclassing the WM_WINDOWPOSCHANGING message, the location of the form can be checked whenever the position of the form is about to change. If a border of the toolbar form is about to go beyond the corresponding border of the parent window, then, using the same methodology as in the "Controlling the Movement of a Form" example, the new position of the toolbar form can be changed by using the **CopyMemory** API function so the toolbar form will not disappear under the parent window's border.

Another feature of this example is the ability to "flip" the toolbar so that its orientation is vertical rather than horizontal (as you will see later in Figure 5-8). This feature is useful to position the toolbar so it is accessible but not in the way. However, this feature also creates additional programming issues.

First, while the width of the horizontally oriented toolbar becomes the height of the vertically oriented taskbar, the height of the horizontally oriented toolbar cannot be used as the width of the vertically oriented taskbar. The width of the vertically oriented taskbar is the width of the toolbar button (which is the same regardless of the orientation of the toolbar) plus the width of the two side borders of the vertically oriented toolbar. Since the height of the toolbar button is not necessarily the same as the width (and usually is not), the height of the horizontally oriented toolbar cannot be used to compute the width of the vertically oriented taskbar. Therefore, it is necessary to restate the toolbar dimensions when flipping the toolbar.

Second, flipping the toolbar may result in a portion of the toolbar being outside the borders of the parent window. However, this undesirable side effect of flipping the toolbar also can be prevented by Windows API functions.

⎣ CODE

The code is divided among a class module, **clsRect;** a standard module, with the highly original name Module1.bas; and the code behind the MDI and toolbar forms.

The purpose of the class module is to provide utility functions to determine the dimensions of the MDI parent and toolbar forms. This code could have been placed in the standard or form modules. However, placing the code in the class module enhances the reusability of the code.

⎣ CLASS MODULE CODE

```
Private Type Rect
    left As Long
    top As Long
    right As Long
    bottom As Long
End Type


Private Declare Function GetWindowRect Lib "user32" _
    (ByVal hwnd As Long, lpRect As Rect) As Long


Private Declare Function GetClientRect Lib "user32" _
    (ByVal hwnd As Long, lpRect As Rect) As Long


Public Function GetWinHeight(ByVal hwnd As Long) As Long
    Dim temp As Rect
    Call GetWindowRect(hwnd, temp)
    GetWinHeight = temp.bottom - temp.top
End Function
```

```
Public Function GetWinWidth(ByVal hwnd As Long) As Long
    Dim temp As Rect
    Call GetWindowRect(hwnd, temp)
    GetWinWidth = (temp.right - temp.left)
End Function

Public Function GetWinTop(ByVal hwnd As Long) As Long
    Dim temp As Rect
    Call GetWindowRect(hwnd, temp)
    GetWinTop = temp.top
End Function

Public Function GetWinLeft(ByVal hwnd As Long) As Long
    Dim temp As Rect
    Call GetWindowRect(hwnd, temp)
    GetWinLeft = temp.left
End Function

Public Function GetCliHeight(ByVal hwnd As Long) As Long
    Dim temp As Rect
    Call GetClientRect(hwnd, temp)
    GetCliHeight = temp.bottom - temp.top
End Function

Public Function GetCliWidth(ByVal hwnd As Long) As Long
    Dim temp As Rect
    Call GetClientRect(hwnd, temp)
    GetCliWidth = temp.right - temp.left
End Function
```

STANDARD MODULE CODE

```
Option Explicit

Private tBarWidth As Long
Private tBarHeight As Long
Private cRec As clsRect
Private newWidth As Long
Private defWindowProc As Long


Private Type WINDOWPOS
```

```
    hwnd As Long
    hWndInsertAfter As Long
    X As Long
    Y As Long
    cx As Long
    cy As Long
    flags As Long
End Type

Private Type POINTAPI
    X As Long
    Y As Long
End Type

Private Const GWL_WNDPROC As Long = (-4)
Private Const WM_WINDOWPOSCHANGING As Long = &H46

Declare Function MoveWindow Lib "user32" _
    (ByVal hwnd As Long, ByVal X As Long, _
    ByVal Y As Long, ByVal nWidth As Long, _
    ByVal nHeight As Long, ByVal bRepaint As Long) As Long

Private Declare Function SetWindowLong Lib "user32" _
    Alias "SetWindowLongA" (ByVal hwnd As Long, _
    ByVal nIndex As Long, ByVal dwNewLong As Long) As Long

Private Declare Function GetParent Lib "user32" _
    (ByVal hwnd As Long) As Long

Private Declare Sub CopyMemory Lib "kernel32" Alias "RtlMoveMemory" _
    (hpvDest As Any, hpvSource As Any, ByVal cbCopy As Long)

Private Declare Function CallWindowProc Lib "user32" Alias _
    "CallWindowProcA" (ByVal lpPrevWndFunc As Long, _
    ByVal hwnd As Long, ByVal uMsg As Long, ByVal wParam As Long, _
    ByVal lParam As Long) As Long

Private Declare Function ClientToScreen Lib "user32" _
    (ByVal hwnd As Long, lpPoint As POINTAPI) As Long

Public Sub CalculateTBar(frm As Form, tBarName As String)
    Set cRec = New clsRect
```

```
        tBarWidth = cRec.GetWinWidth(frm.hwnd)
        tBarHeight = cRec.GetWinHeight(frm.hwnd)

    Dim btnWidth As Long
    Dim I As Integer
    For I = 0 To frm.Controls.Count - 1
      If frm.Controls(I).Name = tBarName Then
          btnWidth = frm.Controls(I).ButtonWidth \ _
          Screen.TwipsPerPixelX
          newWidth = btnWidth + (tBarWidth - _
          (btnWidth * frm.Controls(I).Buttons.Count))
          Exit For
      End If
Next I
End Sub

Public Sub Flip(hChild As Long, hParent As Long)
    Dim tempRect As New clsRect
    Dim pnt As POINTAPI
    pnt.X = 0
    pnt.Y = 0

    Call ClientToScreen(hParent, pnt)
    Dim top As Long, left As Long, height As Long, width As Long
    top = tempRect.GetWinTop(hChild)
    left = tempRect.GetWinLeft(hChild)
    width = tempRect.GetWinWidth(hChild)
    height = tempRect.GetWinHeight(hChild)

    If width > height Then
        Call MoveWindow(hChild, left - pnt.X, _
            top - pnt.Y, newWidth, tBarWidth, True)
    Else
        Call MoveWindow(hChild, left - pnt.X, _
            top - pnt.Y, tBarWidth, tBarHeight, True)
    End If

End Sub

Public Sub SubClass(hwnd As Long)
 On Error Resume Next
 defWindowProc = SetWindowLong(hwnd, GWL_WNDPROC, AddressOf _
```

```
    WindowProc)
End Sub

Public Sub UnSubClass(hwnd As Long)
 If defWindowProc Then
   SetWindowLong hwnd, GWL_WNDPROC, defWindowProc
   defWindowProc = 0
 End If
End Sub

Public Function WindowProc(ByVal hwnd As Long, _
   ByVal uMsg As Long, ByVal wParam As Long, _
   ByVal lParam As Long) As Long

On Error Resume Next
Select Case uMsg
    Case WM_WINDOWPOSCHANGING
    Dim WINPOS As WINDOWPOS
    CopyMemory WINPOS, ByVal lParam, LenB(WINPOS)

    Dim retval As Long
    retval = GetParent(hwnd)

        If WINPOS.X < 0 Then WINPOS.X = 0

        ElseIf WINPOS.Y < 0 Then WINPOS.Y = 0

        ElseIf WINPOS.X > cRec.GetCliWidth(retval) - WINPOS.cx _
            Then WINPOS.X = cRec.GetCliWidth(retval) - WINPOS.cx

        ElseIf WINPOS.Y > cRec.GetCliHeight(retval) - WINPOS.cy _
            Then WINPOS.Y = cRec.GetCliHeight(retval) - WINPOS.cy

        Else 'do nothing

        End If

    CopyMemory ByVal lParam, WINPOS, LenB(WINPOS)
    End Select
WindowProc = CallWindowProc(defWindowProc, hwnd, uMsg, wParam, _
                        lParam)
End Function
```

ANNOTATIONS

CLASS MODULE

```
Private Type Rect
    left As Long
    top As Long
    right As Long
    bottom As Long
End Type
```

Once again a user-defined type is declared to correspond to the RECT structure used by the API functions. The RECT structure will hold the four points of the rectangles of either the entire window or the client area of the window, depending on the API function used.

Care should be taken to declare the member variables of the user-defined type in the exact order as they are declared in the corresponding structure. For example, the first member variable of the structure used by the API functions, *left*, is the *x* coordinate of the left-top corner of the rectangle. If the member variables of the user-defined type are all present, but the first one listed is *top* (*y* coordinate of the top-left corner) rather than *left*, then the value of the *x* coordinate returned by the API function will be stored in a variable which represents the value of the *y* coordinate. The result will be a logical error which is not obvious from a review of the code but quite obvious from the display of the window.

```
Private Declare Function GetWindowRect Lib "user32" _
    (ByVal hwnd As Long, lpRect As Rect) As Long

Private Declare Function GetClientRect Lib "user32" _
    (ByVal hwnd As Long, lpRect As Rect) As Long
```

GetClientRect was discussed in the "Centering a Form" example in Chapter 1. This API function assigns to its second parameter, a RECT structure, the position of the rectangle of the client area of the window whose handle is passed as the first parameter. **GetWindowRect** is similar, but the values assigned to the RECT structure are from the rectangle of the *entire* window (not just the client area) whose handle is passed as the first parameter. The RECT structure used by these functions will be stored in a variable of the **Rect** user-defined type.

Both functions are used in this example because information on both the client area and the entire window area are necessary. **GetWindowRect** is used to obtain the dimensions of the toolbar form. **GetClientRect** is used to obtain the dimensions of the client area of the MDI parent form, as this client area is the container for the toolbar form.

```
Public Function GetWinHeight(ByVal hwnd As Long) As Long
    Dim temp As Rect
    Call GetWindowRect(hwnd, temp)
    GetWinHeight = temp.bottom - temp.top
End Function
```

This function "wraps" the functionality of **GetWindowRect** to return the height of a window. "Wrapping" API functions is common in advanced programming. Indeed, Microsoft Foundation Classes (MFC), used extensively in Microsoft Visual C++, in essence wrap Windows API functions in classes for more object-oriented access to the API functions.

The reason for wrapping API functions goes to one of the philosophies underlying object-oriented programming (OOP), which is for your object to show "what it does" without having to show "how it does it." This way, the complexity of accessing the API functions can be hidden from someone accessing the public methods of your application. This makes your application easier and more understandable for other programmers to use and therefore more attractive and presumably more successful commercially.

The wrapper functions used in this example do make life easier for anyone using this code. For example, the API functions do not return the height, width, etc. of the window. Rather, they change values in a structure that is one of their parameters, and that structure has to be mirrored by a user-defined type. By contrast, the wrapper functions and the class which contains them have done all the hard work, and all that is necessary is to obtain their return value.

Additionally, wrapping the API functions in functions that address specific practical problems (such as determining a window's height) also save the user the trouble of figuring out a solution to those practical problems. For example, if there is a need to determine a window's height, there is no need to determine the algorithm. All that is necessary is to make a call to **GetWinHeight**.

```
Public Function GetWinWidth(ByVal hwnd As Long) As Long
    Dim temp As Rect
    Call GetWindowRect(hwnd, temp)
    GetWinWidth = (temp.right - temp.left)
End Function


Public Function GetWinLeft(ByVal hwnd As Long) As Long
    Dim temp As Rect
    Call GetWindowRect(hwnd, temp)
    GetWinLeft = temp.left
End Function
```

```
Public Function GetWinTop(ByVal hwnd As Long) As Long
    Dim temp As Rect
    Call GetWindowRect(hwnd, temp)
    GetWinTop = temp.top
End Function
```

These functions, similar to **GetWinHeight**, return the width, x coordinate of the top-left corner, and y coordinate of the top-left corner of the window whose handle is passed as a parameter.

```
Public Function GetCliHeight(ByVal hwnd As Long) As Long
    Dim temp As Rect
    Call GetClientRect(hwnd, temp)
    GetCliHeight = temp.bottom - temp.top
End Function

Public Function GetCliWidth(ByVal hwnd As Long) As Long
    Dim temp As Rect
    Call GetClientRect(hwnd, temp)
    GetCliWidth = temp.right - temp.left
End Function
```

These functions are similar to **GetWinHeight** and **GetWinWidth** except that they return the height and width of the client area whose handle is passed as a parameter.

The functionality of these functions is described in Table 5-2.

Function Name	Window Area Involved	Return Value
GetWinHeight	Entire Window	Height
GetWinWidth	Entire Window	Width
GetWinLeft	Entire Window	X coordinate of left border
GetWinTop	Entire Window	Y coordinate of top border
GetCliHeight	Client Area	Height
GetCliWidth	Client Area	Width

TABLE 5-2. Summary of Functions "Wrapping" **GetWindowRect** and **GetClientRect**

STANDARD MODULE

```
Private tBarWidth As Long
Private tBarHeight As Long
```

These variables will hold the values of the toolbar form's width and height, respectively, when that form is oriented horizontally, which would be the usual orientation.

```
Private newWidth As Long
```

This variable will hold the width of a toolbar button plus the sum of the width of the left and right borders of the toolbar form when the form is oriented horizontally. The resulting sum will be the width of the toolbar form when it is oriented vertically.

```
Private cRec As clsRect
```

This variable will represent an instance of the **clsRect** class discussed above and will be used to hold the return values of the member functions of that class which wrap the API functions **GetWindowRect** and **GetClientRect**.

```
Private defWindowProc As Long
```

As in prior examples, this variable will hold the address of the default Windows procedure so it can be restored when subclassing is finished.

```
Private Const WM_WINDOWPOSCHANGING As Long = &H46
```

Windows sends a WM_WINDOWPOSCHANGING message when the size or position of the window is about to change. This constant represents the value of that message. This constant was discussed in the "Controlling the Movement of a Form" example in Chapter 1.

```
Private Type WINDOWPOS
    hwnd As Long
    hWndInsertAfter As Long
    X As Long
    Y As Long
    cx As Long
    cy As Long
    flags As Long
End Type
```

This user-defined type parallels the WINDOWPOS structure to which the WM_WINDOWPOSCHANGING points. The WINDOWPOS structure also is discussed in the "Controlling the Movement of a Form" example in Chapter 1, and its members are described in Tables 1-6 and 1-7 of that chapter.

```
Private Type POINTAPI
    X As Long
    Y As Long
End Type
```

The POINTAPI structure is used to store x,y coordinates. These coordinates correspond to the data type of members of various structures used by the API functions, including the X and Y members of the WINDOWPOS structure passed by the WM_WINDOWPOSCHANGING message.

```
Private Const GWL_WNDPROC As Long = (-4)
```

This constant is used in subclassing, in the call to the API function **SetWindowLong**, to indicate that the function is being called to set a new address for the window procedure.

```
Private Declare Function SetWindowLong Lib "user32" _
    Alias "SetWindowLongA" (ByVal hwnd As Long, _
    ByVal nIndex As Long, ByVal dwNewLong As Long) As Long
```

SetWindowLong is an API function which is used to redirect messages to your substitute window message procedure. This API function was discussed in the "Controlling the Resizing of a Form" example in Chapter 1.

```
Private Declare Function CallWindowProc Lib "user32" Alias _
    "CallWindowProcA" (ByVal lpPrevWndFunc As Long, _
    ByVal hwnd As Long, ByVal uMsg As Long, ByVal wParam As Long, _
    ByVal lParam As Long) As Long
```

CallWindowProc is an API function which also was discussed in the "Controlling the Resizing of a Form" example in Chapter 1. It passes the window messages to the function whose address is specified in the first parameter. That function will be the default window. This default procedure will handle all messages other than the messages being subclassed. However, **CallWindowProc** only passes a particular message to the default window function. It does not redirect future messages back from your user-defined function to the default window procedure. That task—which must be performed before the application terminates—requires the API function **SetWindowLong.**

```
Private Declare Sub CopyMemory Lib "kernel32" Alias "RtlMoveMemory" _
    (hpvDest As Any, hpvSource As Any, ByVal cbCopy As Long)
```

CopyMemory is yet another function which was discussed in the "Controlling the Resizing of a Form" example in Chapter 1. As discussed there, **CopyMemory**, at least by that name, is not really an API function, but for our practical purposes we will treat it as an API function. Basically, it copies values of the members of the structure passed by a message into a corresponding user-defined type, in which those values can be changed and then passed back to the structure before the structure is sent on to the application.

```
Private Declare Function ClientToScreen Lib "user32" _
   (ByVal hwnd As Long, lpPoint As POINTAPI) As Long
```

This API function was discussed in the "Confining the Mouse to the Form" example in Chapter 2. The solution is the **ClientToScreen** API function. This function converts the client coordinates of a specified point to screen coordinates. *Screen coordinates* are used to express the position of a window. The point of origin is the upper-left corner of the screen. By contrast, the position of points in a window is expressed in *client coordinates*. The point of origin in this case is the upper-left corner of the window or client area. The purpose of client coordinates is consistent coordinate values while drawing in the window, regardless of the position of the window on the screen. For example, client coordinates are used to retain the position of controls relative to their containing form.

The **ClientToScreen** function takes two parameters. The first is the handle to the source of the client coordinates—in this example, the Close command button (which itself is a window). The second parameter is a pointer to a POINTAPI structure which will hold the screen coordinates. The client coordinates are the top-left corner of the control, 0,0. The corresponding screen coordinates are assigned to the members of the POINTAPI structure **pnt**, which then are passed as parameters to the **SetCursorPos** API function to move the cursor to those coordinates.

```
Declare Function MoveWindow Lib "user32" _
   (ByVal hwnd As Long, ByVal X As Long, _
   ByVal Y As Long, ByVal nWidth As Long, _
   ByVal nHeight As Long, ByVal bRepaint As Long) As Long
```

The **MoveWindow** function changes the position and dimensions of the specified window. For a top-level window, the position and dimensions are relative to the upper-left corner of the screen. For a child window, they are relative to the upper-left corner of the parent window's client area.

```
Private Declare Function GetParent Lib "user32" _
   (ByVal hwnd As Long) As Long
```

The **GetParent** function retrieves a handle to the specified child window's parent window. If the function succeeds, the return value is a handle to the parent window.

```
Public Sub CalculateTBar(frm As Form, tBarName As String)
   Set cRec = New clsRect
   tBarWidth = cRec.GetWinWidth(frm.hwnd)
   tBarHeight = cRec.GetWinHeight(frm.hwnd)

   Dim btnWidth As Long
   Dim I As Integer
   For I = 0 To frm.Controls.Count - 1
    If frm.Controls(I).Name = tBarName Then
       btnWidth = frm.Controls(I).ButtonWidth \
```

```
Screen.TwipsPerPixelX
        newWidth = btnWidth + (tBarWidth - _
          (btnWidth * frm.Controls(I).Buttons.Count))
        Exit For
    End If
  Next I
End Sub
```

CalculateTBar calculates the height and width of the toolbar form for both its horizontal and vertical orientations. It is called only once, at the start of the application, because the dimensions of the toolbar form in its two orientations should not change during the running of the application. Indeed, calling this function repeatedly (such as each time the orientation of the toolbar form is changed) runs the risk of unintentionally shrinking the size of the toolbar form due to the dropping of remainders during division.

The function first calculates the width and height of the toolbar form in its default orientation, horizontal. A variable of the **clsRect** class, *cRec*, is used to access the member functions of **clsRect** which calculate the width and height of a window using the API function **GetWindowRect**. The member functions, **GetWinWidth** and **GetWinHeight**, are discussed above. The return value of **GetWinWidth**, the width of the toolbar form in pixels, is saved in the variable *tBarWidth*, and the return value of **GetWinHeight**, the height of the toolbar form in pixels, is saved in the variable *tBarHeight*.

The next step is to calculate the width and height of the toolbar form in its vertical orientation. The height of the toolbar form in its vertical orientation simply is the width of the toolbar form in its horizontal orientation. That value already has been calculated and then stored in the variable *tBarWidth*.

The width of the toolbar form in its vertical orientation is more difficult to calculate because it is not the same as the height of the toolbar form in its horizontal orientation. Rather, the width of the vertically oriented taskbar is the width of the toolbar button (which is the same regardless of the orientation of the toolbar) plus the width of the two side borders of the vertically oriented toolbar. Since the height of the toolbar button is not necessarily the same as the width (and usually is not), the height of the horizontally oriented toolbar cannot be used to compute the width of the vertically oriented taskbar.

In order to determine the width of a button in or borders of a toolbar control, it is necessary to identify the toolbar control on the form. The second parameter of **CalculateTBar** is the name of the toolbar control. This parameter is passed when the form containing the toolbar calls the function. This avoids hard-coding the toolbar name. However, since the name of the toolbar control is not hard-coded, it is necessary to find the toolbar control among the controls contained in the form which calls the function. This is done by looping through the collection of controls in the form until a control whose name matches the second parameter is found.

Once the toolbar control is identified (by its index in the collection of controls contained in the form calling the function), the width of a toolbar button is determined using the **ButtonWidth** property of the toolbar control. However, since the **ButtonWidth** property returns the width in twips, it is necessary to convert that value to pixels, the unit of measurement used by Windows API functions. This conversion uses the **TwipsPerPixelX** property of the **Screen** object. This property was first explained in the "Centering a Form" example in Chapter 1. The resulting value, the width of a toolbar button in pixels, is stored in the variable *btnWidth*.

The width of the toolbar form in its vertical orientation includes, in addition to the width of the toolbar button, the width of the borders on the left and right of the toolbar button. The collective width of these borders is the difference between the width of the vertically oriented toolbar form and the collective width of all the toolbar buttons. The width of the vertically oriented toolbar form already has been determined and stored in the variable *tBarWidth*. The number of buttons is determined by the **Count** property of the **Buttons** collection of the toolbar. That number is multiplied by *btnWidth*, the width of a toolbar button, and the result is subtracted from *tBarWidth* to obtain the width of the borders on the left and right of the toolbar button. The result, which will be the width of the toolbar form in its vertical orientation, is stored in the variable *newWidth*.

```
Public Sub Flip(hChild As Long, hParent As Long)
    Dim tempRect As New clsRect
    Dim pnt As POINTAPI
    pnt.X = 0
    pnt.Y = 0

    Call ClientToScreen(hParent, pnt)
    Dim top As Long, left As Long, height As Long, width As Long
    top = tempRect.GetWinTop(hChild)
    left = tempRect.GetWinLeft(hChild)
    width = tempRect.GetWinWidth(hChild)
    height = tempRect.GetWinHeight(hChild)

    If width > height Then
        Call MoveWindow(hChild, left - pnt.X, _
            top - pnt.Y, newWidth, tBarWidth, True)
    Else
        Call MoveWindow(hChild, left - pnt.X, _
            top - pnt.Y, tBarWidth, tBarHeight, True)
    End If
End Sub
```

The **Flip** function toggles the orientation of the toolbar form between horizontal and vertical. The toolbar form, when it changes orientation, keeps the same x, y coordinates for its top-left corner. However, the dimensions of the toolbar form change.

As discussed above, the **MoveWindow** API function is used to change the position or the dimensions of a window. Its first argument is the handle to the window. That handle was passed in the first parameter of **Flip**. The fourth and fifth arguments are the new width and height respectively.

The first step in flipping the toolbar form is to determine whether to flip it from horizontal to vertical or from vertical to horizontal. This requires determining the present orientation of the form. If the form's width is greater than its height, its orientation is horizontal; otherwise, its orientation is vertical. The toolbar form's width and height are determined using the **GetWinWidth** and **GetWinHeight** member functions of the *cRect* instance of the **clsRect** class. The return values of these functions are stored in the local variables *width* and *height* respectively.

If the orientation of the form before **Flip** was called was horizontal, then the condition following the **If** keyword (width > height) is True. In that case, the width of the toolbar form, vertically oriented, and therefore the fourth argument of **MoveWindow**, is *newWidth*. This variable, as discussed above, is the width of the toolbar button plus the sum of the width of the borders on the left and right of the toolbar button. The new height of the vertically oriented toolbar form, and therefore the fifth argument of **MoveWindow**, is *tBarWidth*, which is the width of the toolbar form in its vertical orientation.

If the orientation of the form before **Flip** was called was vertical, then the statements following the **Else** keyword execute. In that case, the width of the toolbar form, horizontally oriented, and therefore the fourth argument of **MoveWindow**, is *tBarWidth*, and the height of the horizontally oriented toolbar form, and therefore the fifth argument of **MoveWindow**, is *tBarHeight*.

The second and third arguments of **MoveWindow** are the x and y coordinates respectively of the top-left corner of the window. Even these coordinates remain the same regardless of the toolbar form's orientation; paradoxically, calculating these coordinates is more difficult than setting the toolbar form's new width and height, which do change with the toolbar form's orientation.

Under **MoveWindow**, the x and y coordinates of the window's top-left corner are determined differently depending on whether the window is a top-level window or a child window. For a top-level window, these coordinates are relative to the upper-left corner of the screen. However, for a child window, these coordinates are relative to the upper-left corner of the parent window's client area.

The toolbar form is a child window. Therefore, the coordinates of its upper-left corner are relative to the upper-left corner of the parent MDI form's client area. This requires subtracting the coordinates of the upper-left corner of the client area of the parent form from the corresponding coordinates of the upper-left corner of the toolbar form. For example, if the coordinates of the toolbar form's upper-left corner relative to the screen are 300, 300, but the coordinates of the client area of the parent form's upper-left corner relative to the screen are 100, 100, the second and third arguments to **MoveWindow** would be 200, 200, not 300, 300.

The **GetWinTop** and **GetWinLeft** member functions of **clsRect** determine the upper-left coordinates of the toolbar form and store the results in the local variables *top* and *left* respectively. The **GetWinTop** and **GetWinLeft** member functions wrap the **GetWindowRect** API function. The coordinates given by **GetWindowRect** are relative to the upper-left corner of the screen. Therefore, the second argument of **MoveWindow** requires subtracting from *left* the *x* coordinate of the upper-left corner of the client area of the parent window. Similarly, the third argument of **MoveWindow** requires subtracting from *top* the *y* coordinate of the upper-left corner of the client area of the parent window.

Determining the screen coordinates of the upper-left corner of the client area of the parent window is done with the API function **ClientToScreen**. As discussed in the "Confining the Mouse to the Form" example in Chapter 2, this function converts the client coordinates of a specified point to screen coordinates. *Screen coordinates* are used to express the position of a window. The point of origin is the upper-left corner of the screen. By contrast, the position of points in a window are expressed in *client coordinates*. The point of origin in this case is the upper-left corner of the window or client area.

The **ClientToScreen** function takes two parameters. The first is the handle to the source of the client coordinates, in this example the MDI parent. The second parameter is a pointer to a POINTAPI structure. The client coordinates, 0, 0, which represent the upper-left corner of the client area, are passed to **ClientToScreen**. This is accomplished by declaring a local variable *pnt* of the **POINT** user-defined type and assigning 0 to its *X* and *Y* members, and passing *pnt* as the second argument. **ClientToScreen** then assigns the corresponding screen coordinates to the *X* and *Y* members of *pnt*. The second argument of **MoveWindow** then is *left – pnt.X*. Similarly, the third argument of **MoveWindow** is *top – pnt.Y*.

The final parameter of **MoveWindow** specifies whether the window is to be repainted. To make life simple, this parameter is *TRUE*. If the parameter is *FALSE*, no repainting of any kind occurs, and the application must explicitly invalidate or redraw any parts of the window and parent window that need redrawing.

The flipping of the toolbar form could cause it, depending on its location in the client area, to go outside the client area. What does the **Flip** subroutine do to prevent this? The answer is absolutely nothing, because it does not have to. Why is discussed below.

```
Public Sub SubClass(hwnd As Long)
 On Error Resume Next
 defWindowProc = SetWindowLong(hwnd, GWL_WNDPROC, AddressOf _
 WindowProc)
End Sub
```

```
Public Sub UnSubClass(hwnd As Long)
 If defWindowProc Then
   SetWindowLong hwnd, GWL_WNDPROC, defWindowProc
   defWindowProc = 0
 End If
End Sub
```

These functions are the same as in the previous examples. **SubClass** will be called in the **Load** event of the toolbar form. Similarly, **UnSubClass** will be called in the **Unload** event of the toolbar form.

```
Public Function WindowProc(ByVal hwnd As Long, _
   ByVal uMsg As Long, ByVal wParam As Long, _
   ByVal lParam As Long) As Long


On Error Resume Next
Select Case uMsg
    Case WM_WINDOWPOSCHANGING
    Dim WINPOS As WINDOWPOS
    CopyMemory WINPOS, ByVal lParam, LenB(WINPOS)
```

Windows sends a WM_WINDOWPOSCHANGING message when the size or position of the window is about to change. Therefore, this message would be sent when the toolbar form either is moved or flipped. The second parameter of the user-defined Windows function **WindowProc** is the message being sent by Windows. Unless the message is WM_WINDOWPOSCHANGING, the message simply is sent on to the application. However, if the message is WM_WINDOWPOSCHANGING, then the **CopyMemory** function is called.

As discussed in Chapter 1, **CopyMemory** copies the values of a structure to a user-defined type, or vice versa. The WM_ WINDOWPOSCHANGING message includes a pointer to a WINDOWPOS structure. That structure contains, among other member variables, the variables X and Y, which reflect the x and y coordinates of the upper-left corner of the new position of the window. **CopyMemory** is used to copy that WINDOWPOS structure to a local variable of the **WINDOWPOS** user-defined type, which parallels the WINDOWPOS structure. The X and Y values of a local variable of the **WINDOWPOS** user-defined type then are checked to see if either goes beyond the borders of the client area of the parent form. If so, the value of the offending x or y coordinate is changed so it does not go beyond the borders of the client area of the parent form. Finally, **CopyMemory** is called again to copy the values of the local variable of the **WINDOWPOS** user-defined type back to the WINDOWPOS structure. The WINDOWPOS structure, with its values being modified as necessary to prevent the toolbar form from going beyond the borders of the client area of the parent MDI form, then is passed on to the application.

The first step is to copy, using **CopyMemory**, the WINDOWPOS structure to a local variable of the **WINDOWPOS** user-defined type. That local variable, *WINPOS*, is the first parameter of **CopyMemory**. As discussed in Chapter 1, the first parameter of **CopyMemory** is the address of the destination to which the copy is being sent.

The second parameter of **CopyMemory** is the address of the source being copied. That parameter is the WINDOWPOS structure pointed to by the WM_ WINDOWPOSCHANGING message. With the WM_ WINDOWPOSCHANGING message, *lParam*, the fourth parameter of the user-defined Windows function, **WindowProc**, is the address of the structure passed by the message. Therefore, the second parameter of **CopyMemory** is *lParam*.

The third parameter of **CopyMemory** is the number of bytes to be copied. The **LenB** function, which is a Visual Basic function, not an API function, returns the in-memory size of the user-defined type in its one argument. Therefore, the third parameter of **CopyMemory** is the **LenB** function with *WINPOS* as its argument.

```
Dim retval As Long
retval = GetParent(hwnd)
```

The next step is to obtain a handle to the MDI parent. The **GetParent** function retrieves a handle to the parent window of the child window whose handle is the argument to **GetParent**. In this case, the handle to the toolbar form, *hwnd*, is the first argument of **WindowProc**. The handle to the parent form is stored in the local variable *retval*.

It is necessary to obtain a handle to the parent window in order to determine whether one of the borders of the toolbar form has gone beyond the borders of the client area of the parent form.

```
If WINPOS.X < 0 Then WINPOS.X = 0
ElseIf WINPOS.Y < 0 Then WINPOS.Y = 0
ElseIf WINPOS.X > cRec.GetCliWidth(retval) - WINPOS.cx Then _
    WINPOS.X = cRec.GetCliWidth(retval) - WINPOS.cx
ElseIf WINPOS.Y > cRec.GetCliHeight(retval) - WINPOS.cy _
    Then WINPOS.Y = cRec.GetCliHeight(retval) - WINPOS.cy
Else 'do nothing
End If
```

The next step is to check the X and Y values of *WINPOS* to see if either goes beyond the borders of the client area of the parent form. If so, the value of the offending x or y coordinate is changed so it does not go beyond the borders of the client area of the parent form.

The X and Y values of *WINPOS* are relative to the client area of the parent form, and not to the screen. This simplifies checking to see if the left border of the toolbar form goes beyond the left border of the client area of the parent form. The value of the X coordinate of the left border of the parent form's client area is zero, and the X coordinate of the toolbar form is relative to the left border of the parent form's client area. Thus, if the *X* value of *WINPOS* is less than zero, it is changed to zero.

Checking to see if the top border of the toolbar form goes beyond the top border of the client area of the parent form is similarly straightforward. If the *Y* value of *WINPOS* is less than zero, it is changed to zero.

Checking to see if the right border of the toolbar form goes beyond the right border of the client area of the parent form is more complicated. This is determined by checking if the *X* coordinate of the left border of the toolbar form is greater than the difference between the width of the parent form's client area and the width of the toolbar form. If it is, then *WINPOS.x* is assigned the difference between the width of the parent form's client area and the width of the toolbar form.

The value of the *X* coordinate of the left border of the toolbar form is, once again, the *X* value of *WINPOS*.

The width of the client area of the parent form is determined by the **GetCliWidth** member function of **clsRect**. This function, given the handle to the parent form (*retval*), wraps and uses the API function **GetClientRect** to return the width of the client area in pixels.

Determining the remaining item of information, the width of the toolbar form does not require first determining whether the orientation of the toolbar form is horizontal or vertical. The *cx* member of the WINDOWPOS structure (and user-defined type) is the width of the window in its current orientation. Therefore, *WINPOS.cx* supplies the width of the toolbar form.

If *WINPOS.x* is greater than the difference between the width of the parent form's client area and the width of the toolbar form, then it is assigned the difference between the width of the parent form's client area and the width of the toolbar form.

Checking to see if the bottom border of the toolbar form goes beyond the bottom border of the client area of the parent form involves essentially the same process. Of course *WINPOS.y* and *WINPOS.cy* take the place of *WINPOS.x* and *WINPOS.cx*, and **GetCliHeight** takes the place of **GetCliWidth**.

The **Else** case is important. It covers the situation when the WM_WINDOWPOSCHANGING message will be sent but no action should be taken. In that situation the toolbar form remains within the borders of the parent form's client area.

As mentioned in the annotations to the **Flip** subroutine, the flipping of the toolbar form could cause it, depending on its location in the client area, to go outside the client area. Also as mentioned above, the **Flip** subroutine did nothing to prevent this because it does not have to. The reason is that Windows sends a WM_WINDOWPOSCHANGING message when the toolbar form is flipped as well as when the toolbar form is moved by dragging its title bar with the mouse. The code discussed above then readjusts the position of the flipped toolbar form, just as it readjusts the position of a dragged toolbar form, so its borders do not stray outside the borders of the parent MDI form.

```
        CopyMemory ByVal lParam, WINPOS, LenB(WINPOS)
    End Select
WindowProc = CallWindowProc(defWindowProc, hwnd, uMsg, wParam, _
    lParam)
End Function
```

The final step is again to call **CopyMemory**, this time to copy the values of the local variable of the **WINDOWPOS** user-defined type back to the WINDOWPOS structure. The WINDOWPOS structure, with its values being modified as necessary to prevent the toolbar form from going beyond the borders of the client area of the parent MDI form, then is passed on to the application.

TEST THE CODE

1. Start a new project, Standard Exe.

2. Add a MDI form. Accept the name MDIForm1 and the other default properties.

3. Add a pop-up menu to the MDIForm1 as described in Table 5-3. The visible checkbox for the top-level menu item, **mnuDock**, is unchecked, so the menu will not appear until the application user right-clicks and releases the mouse on the form, as discussed below. This is typical for a pop-up menu.

    Figure 5-5 shows the MDI form with the pop-up menu displayed.

4. Add a form to the project. Table 5-4 shows the following changes to its default properties.

5. Place on the toolbar form a toolbar. Accept the default name Toolbar1. The number of toolbar buttons and the text or pictures on those buttons is up to you as the buttons are not functional in this example. Your toolbar form should look something like Figure 5-6.

6. Place the code above in the class and standard modules as indicated.

Caption	Name	Index	Visible
mnuDock	mnuDock	NA	False
Show	DockMenu	0	True
Hide	DockMenu	1	True
-	DockMenu	2	True
Flip	DockMenu	3	True

TABLE 5-3.   Pop-up Menu for the MDI Form

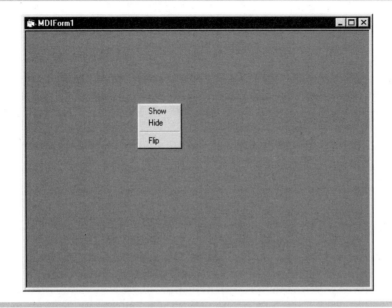

FIGURE 5-5.   MDI form with the pop-up menu displayed

7. Place the following code in the **Load** event of the MDIForm1:

```
Private Sub MDIForm_Load()
    Me.Show
    VBControlWin.Show
End Sub
```

This code simply shows the MDI parent and toolbar forms.

Property	Setting
Name	VBControlWin
BorderStyle	4-Fixed ToolWindow
Caption	Tool
ControlBox	False
MaxButton	False
MDIChild	True
MinButton	False

TABLE 5-4.   Changes to Default Properties in Toolbar Form

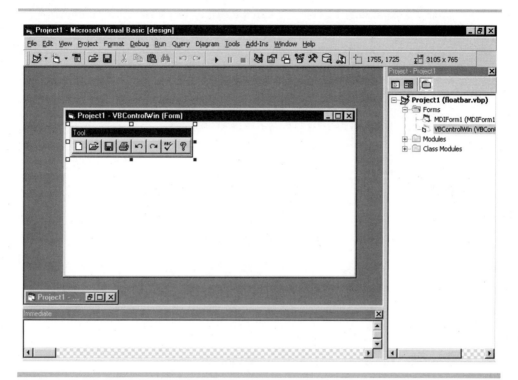

FIGURE 5-6.   The toolbar form in Design view

8. Place the following code in the **MouseUp** event of MDIForm1:

```
Private Sub MDIForm_MouseUp(Button As Integer, _
    Shift As Integer, X As Single, Y As Single)
    If Button = vbRightButton Then
        PopupMenu mnuDock
    End If
End Sub
```

This code shows the pop-up menu **mnuDock** if the user right-clicks the form
and then releases the mouse. The **PopupMenu** method displays a pop-up
menu on an **MDIForm** or **Form** object at specified coordinates, or if, as here,
none are specified, at the current mouse location. The only argument of the
PopupMenu method is the name of the pop-up menu to be displayed.

9. Place the following code in the **Click** event of **DockMenu** in MDIForm1:

```
Public Sub DockMenu_Click(Index As Integer)
   Select Case Index
     Case 0 'show
         VBControlWin.Visible = True
     Case 1 'hide
         VBControlWin.Visible = False
     Case 3 'flip
         Flip VBControlWin.hwnd, MDIForm1.hwnd
     End Select
End Sub
```

There is no Case 2 because 2 is the index of the separator bar.

10. Place the following code in the **Load** and **Unload** events, respectively, of the toolbar form:

```
Private Sub Form_Load()
   CalculateTBar Me, "Toolbar1"
   SubClass Me.hwnd
End Sub
```

```
Private Sub Form_Unload(Cancel As Integer)
    UnSubClass Me.hwnd
End Sub
```

The function **CalculateTBar** is called to pass the handle to the toolbar form and the name of the toolbar control. The latter parameter avoids the necessity of hard-coding the name of the toolbar control. The **CalculateTBar** function was discussed above in the annotations to the standard module.

The calls to the **Subclass** and **UnSubClass** subroutines are the same as in the previous examples. The only difference is that the calls are made from a child form rather than the main form. This difference does create an issue. The issue is what happens if the MDIForm is unloaded first. The following code in the **QueryUnload** event of MDIForm1 ensures that the toolbar form is first unloaded.

```
Private Sub MDIForm_QueryUnload(Cancel As Integer, UnloadMode As Integer)
    VBControlWin.Hide
    UnSubClass (VBControlWin.hwnd)
    Unload VBControlWin
End Sub
```

Test the code. The toolbar should float within the window but not go outside or under its borders. Additionally, the toolbar can be flipped, by clicking on Flip on the pop-up menu, again without straying outside (or under) the borders.

Dockbar.vbp

Creating a Docking Toolbar

Docking is the trait of toolbars "snapping" to one of the four sides of a window. The taskbar in Windows 95, 98, and NT 4.0, though not a toolbar, exhibits this behavior. The Office Shortcut Bar in Microsoft Office 95 and 97 also exhibits this behavior.

Enabling toolbars to dock adds a desirable feature to your application. The presumption is that when the application user positions a floating toolbar to the side of the application window, the application user wishes to move the toolbar out of the way. Docking the toolbar to the side of the application window fulfills the application user's presumed wish.

In this example, if the top of the toolbar form is positioned at the top of the parent form's client area, then the toolbar form will be docked, in a horizontal orientation, at the top of the parent form's client area. (See Figure 5-7.) The orientation of the toolbar form will be horizontal even if that orientation had been vertical when its top touched the top of the parent form's client area. Similarly, if the bottom of the toolbar form is positioned at the bottom of the parent form's client area, then the toolbar form will be docked, in a horizontal orientation, at the bottom of the parent form's client area.

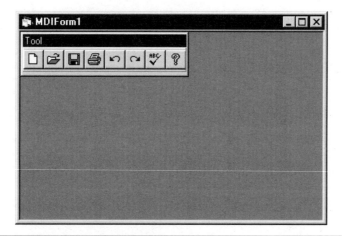

FIGURE 5-7.   The toolbar form docked at the top

The docking behavior is similar if docking occurs on the left or right. If the left border of the toolbar form is positioned at the left border of the parent form's client area, then the toolbar form will be docked, this time in a vertical orientation, at the top of the parent form's client area. (See Figure 5-8.) The orientation of the toolbar form will be vertical even if that orientation had been horizontal when its left border touched the left border of the parent form's client area. Similarly, if the right border of the toolbar form is positioned at the right border of the parent form's client area, then the toolbar form will be docked, again in a vertical orientation, at the right border of the parent form's client area.

SYNOPSIS OF CODE

This example illustrates the advantage of code which is object-oriented and modular. Only a few lines of code in the previous example need to be changed in order to implement the docking behavior.

The code that is changed is in the user-defined Windows function **WindowProc**. Once again, this function subclasses the WM_WINDOWPOSCHANGING message, and uses the **CopyMemory** function to check and, if necessary, change the values of the WINDOWPOS structure pointed to by that message before sending the message on to the application.

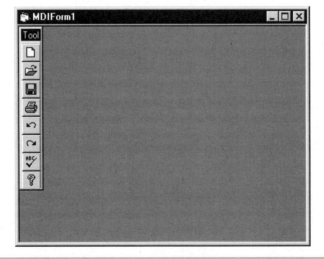

FIGURE 5-8.   The toolbar form docked at the left

The difference between this example and the previous one is how the values of the WINDOWPOS structure are modified. For example, if the left border of the toolbar form is going to move beyond the left border of the parent form's client area, then the toolbar form first is oriented horizontally (using the **Flip** subroutine) if it is not already oriented that way. By contrast, in the prior example the toolbar form's orientation only was changed if the application user clicked **Flip** on the pop-up menu. Second, the X and Y members of the WINPOS structure then are set to zero so the upper-left corner of the toolbar form is at the upper-left corner of the parent form's client area. By contrast, in the prior example only the X *or* the Y member of the WINPOS structure was changed, depending on which border of the parent form's client area was involved, with the other member remaining unchanged.

REVISED CODE OF USER-DEFINED WINDOWS FUNCTION

```
Public Function WindowProc(ByVal hwnd As Long, _
    ByVal uMsg As Long, ByVal wParam As Long, _
    ByVal lParam As Long) As Long

On Error Resume Next

Select Case uMsg

    Case WM_WINDOWPOSCHANGING
    Dim WINPOS As WINDOWPOS
    CopyMemory WINPOS, ByVal lParam, LenB(WINPOS)

    Dim retval As Long
    retval = GetParent(hwnd)

        If WINPOS.X < 0 Then
            If cRec.GetWinWidth(hwnd) > cRec.GetWinHeight(hwnd) _
                Then Flip hwnd, retval
            WINPOS.X = 0
            WINPOS.Y = 0

        ElseIf WINPOS.Y < 0 Then
            If cRec.GetWinWidth(hwnd) < cRec.GetWinHeight(hwnd) _
                Then Flip hwnd, retval
            WINPOS.X = 0
            WINPOS.Y = 0
```

```
            ElseIf WINPOS.X > cRec.GetCliWidth(retval) - WINPOS.cx Then
                If cRec.GetWinWidth(hwnd) > cRec.GetWinHeight(hwnd) _
                    Then Flip hwnd, retval
                WINPOS.X = cRec.GetCliWidth(retval) - newWidth
                WINPOS.Y = 0

            ElseIf WINPOS.Y > cRec.GetCliHeight(retval) - WINPOS.cy Then
                If cRec.GetWinWidth(hwnd) < cRec.GetWinHeight(hwnd) _
                    Then Flip hwnd, retval
                WINPOS.Y = cRec.GetCliHeight(retval) - tBarHeight
                WINPOS.X = 0

            Else 'do nothing

            End If

        CopyMemory ByVal lParam, WINPOS, LenB(WINPOS)
        End Select

WindowProc = CallWindowProc(defWindowProc, hwnd, uMsg, wParam, _
        lParam)

End Function
```

The only difference between this and the prior example lies in the statements in the If-ElseIf-Else control structure.

ANNOTATIONS

```
If WINPOS.X < 0 Then
    If cRec.GetWinWidth(hwnd) > cRec.GetWinHeight(hwnd) Then _
        Flip hwnd, retval
    WINPOS.X = 0
    WINPOS.Y = 0
```

This tests to see if the left border of the toolbar form is going to move beyond the left border of the parent form's client area. If so, then, using the **GetWinWidth** and

GetWinHeight member functions of the **clsRect** class, there is a test to see if the toolbar form's width is greater than its height. If so, then the toolbar form is oriented horizontally. Since the goal is that the toolbar form docked on the left is to be vertically oriented, the **Flip** subroutine is called to change the orientation of the toolbar form. Of course, if the toolbar form already is oriented vertically, the **Flip** subroutine is not called.

Once the proper orientation of the toolbar form is assured, both the *X* and *Y* members of the WINPOS structure are set to zero so the upper-left corner of the toolbar form is at the upper-left corner of the parent form's client area.

```
Else If WINPOS.Y < 0 Then
    If cRec.GetWinWidth(hwnd) < cRec.GetWinHeight(hwnd) Then _
        Flip hwnd, retval
    WINPOS.X = 0
    WINPOS.Y = 0
```

This code is similar to the one just annotated concerning the left border. The first test is whether the top border of the toolbar form is going to move beyond the top border of the parent form's client area. If so, then, using the **GetWinWidth** and **GetWinHeight** member functions of the **clsRect** class, there is a test to see if the toolbar form's width is less than its height. If so, then the toolbar form is oriented vertically. Since the goal is that the toolbar form docked on the top is to be horizontally oriented, the **Flip** subroutine is called to change the orientation of the toolbar form. Of course, if the toolbar form already is oriented horizontally, the **Flip** subroutine is not called.

As above, once the proper orientation of the toolbar form is assured, both the *X* and *Y* members of the WINPOS structure are set to zero so the upper-left corner of the toolbar form is at the upper-left corner of the parent form's client area.

```
        ElseIf WINPOS.X > cRec.GetCliWidth(retval) - WINPOS.cx Then
        If cRec.GetWinWidth(hwnd) > cRec.GetWinHeight(hwnd) Then _
            Flip hwnd, retval
        WINPOS.X = cRec.GetCliWidth(retval) - newWidth
        WINPOS.Y = 0
```

The first test is whether the right border of the toolbar form is going to move beyond the right border of the parent form's client area. This is determined by checking if the *X* coordinate of the left border of the toolbar form is greater than the difference between the width of the parent form's client area and the width of the toolbar form. The methodology for making this determination is the same as in the prior example. *WINPOS.x* represents the left border of the toolbar form, the width of the client area of the parent form is determined by the **GetCliWidth** member function of **clsRect**, and *WINPOS.cx* supplies the width of the toolbar form.

If *WINPOS.x* is greater than the difference between the width of the parent form's client area and the width of the toolbar form, then the code follows the concept used when the toolbar form is docking on the left side of the parent form's client area. Using the **GetWinWidth** and **GetWinHeight** member functions of the **clsRect** class, there is a test to see if the toolbar form's width is greater than its height. If so, then the toolbar form is oriented horizontally. Since the goal is that the toolbar form docked on the right is to be vertically oriented, the **Flip** subroutine is called to change the orientation of the toolbar form. Of course, if the toolbar form already is oriented vertically, the **Flip** subroutine is not called.

Once the proper orientation of the toolbar form is assured, the next step is to position the toolbar form so its upper-right corner is at the upper-right corner of the parent form's client area. The *Y* member of the WINPOS structure is set to zero, but the *X* member of the WINDOWPOS structure is set to the difference between the width of the parent form's client area and the width of the toolbar form in its vertical orientation, stored in the variable *newWidth*.

```
ElseIf WINPOS.Y > cRec.GetCliHeight(retval) - WINPOS.cy Then
    If cRec.GetWinWidth(hwnd) < cRec.GetWinHeight(hwnd) _
        Then Flip hwnd, retval
    WINPOS.Y = cRec.GetCliHeight(retval) - tBarHeight
    WINPOS.X = 0
```

Checking to see if the bottom border of the toolbar form goes beyond the bottom border of the client area of the parent form involves essentially the same process. Of course *WINPOS.y* and *WINPOS.cy* take the place of *WINPOSxy* and *WINPOS.cx*, **GetCliHeight** takes the place of **GetCliWidth**, and *tBarHeight* takes the place of *newWidth*.

```
Else 'do nothing
```

Once again, the **Else** case covers the situation when the WM_WINDOWPOSCHANGING message will be sent but no action should be taken because the toolbar form remains within the borders of the parent form's client area.

Also once again, the **Flip** subroutine does not need to address the possibility that the flipping of the toolbar form could cause it, depending on its location in the client area, to go outside the client area. When the toolbar form is flipped, Windows sends a WM_WINDOWPOSCHANGING message which is subclassed by **WindowProc**. The code discussed above readjusts, if necessary, the position of the flipped toolbar form so its borders do not stray outside the borders of the parent MDI form.

TEST THE CODE

The remainder of the code, including the test form, is identical to the prior example.

Flatbar.vbp

Creating a Flat Toolbar

Starting with Internet Explorer 3.0, toolbars took on a new appearance. Instead of the toolbar buttons looking like, well, buttons, the toolbar buttons were flat, with no borders around a button or between buttons. (See Figure 5-9.) However, when the mouse moved over a button, the button then raised, with borders appearing around the button.

This appearance has now become common to many applications, including Microsoft Office 97. Indeed, the toolbars in the Visual Basic 5 and 6 IDE have this appearance. Therefore, flat toolbars may help to make your application look up-to-date.

The control used to create the appearance of a flat toolbar is the Rebar control, also commonly known as the *Coolbar* control. A Coolbar control contains child windows, such as toolbars and bitmaps, and manages the size and position of the child windows it contains. Once you create the child windows and assign them to the Coolbar control, the child windows are displayed in it.

Visual Basic 6 has a Coolbar control. However, having the Coolbar control host a toolbar is not particularly easy. As of this writing, the Coolbar control doesn't automatically support flat-style buttons. Microsoft does offer a TransTBWrapper control. This control must be added as a private ActiveX control and made a child of the Coolbar control; then the toolbar is assigned to the toolbar property of the TransTBWrapper control. Additionally, before the parent form unloads, the toolbar

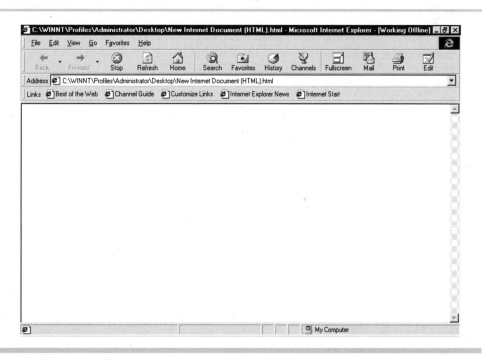

FIGURE 5-9. Flat toolbar in Internet Explorer 4

property of the TransTBWrapper control must be set to nothing to avoid a General Protection Fault. If this appears somewhat complicated, it is. Additionally, distributing your application now involves yet more controls.

Fortunately, the Windows API provides an easy way of converting your toolbar to a "coolbar" with just a few lines of code.

SYNOPSIS OF CODE

This example further illustrates the advantage of code which is object-oriented and modular. Once a class which converts the toolbar to the coolbar is added to the project, only three lines of code need to be added to the **Load** event of the toolbar form to make the toolbar flat.

The code which converts the toolbar into a coolbar is in a class module named **clsFlatBar**. The class has one member function, descriptively named **MakeFlat**. The form which contains the toolbar calls **MakeFlat** and passes the form's handle as a parameter. **MakeFlat** then passes the form's handle and other information to the **FindWindowEx** API function to determine the handle to the toolbar control. **MakeFlat** next uses the **SendMessage** API function to determine the existing style of the toolbar, and again uses **SendMessage** to combine the existing style with the flat toolbar style.

CODE

```
Option Explicit

Private style As Long
Private hToolbar As Long

Private Const WM_USER As Long = &H400
Private Const TB_SETSTYLE As Long = WM_USER + 56
Private Const TB_GETSTYLE As Long = WM_USER + 57
Private Const TBSTYLE_FLAT As Long = &H800

Private Declare Function SendMessageLong Lib "user32" _
    Alias "SendMessageA" (ByVal hwnd As Long, ByVal wMsg As Long, _
    ByVal wParam As Long, ByVal lParam As Long) As Long

Private Declare Function FindWindowEx Lib "user32" _
    Alias "FindWindowExA" (ByVal hWnd1 As Long, _
    ByVal hWnd2 As Long, ByVal lpsz1 As String, _
    ByVal lpsz2 As String) As Long
```

```
Public Sub MakeFlat(hwnd As Long)
   hToolbar = FindWindowEx(hwnd, 0&, "ToolbarWindow32", _
      vbNullString)
   style = SendMessageLong(hToolbar, TB_GETSTYLE, 0&, 0&)
  Call SendMessageLong(hToolbar, TB_SETSTYLE, 0, style Or _
      TBSTYLE_FLAT)
End Sub
```

ANNOTATIONS

`Private style As Long`

This variable will hold the style of the toolbar. Toolbar styles are discussed below.

`Private hToolbar As Long`

This variable will hold the handle to the toolbar control.

`Private Const WM_USER As Long = &H400`

There are two types of messages: system-defined and application-defined. The system sends or posts a *system-defined message* when it communicates with an application. It uses these messages to control the operations of applications and to provide input and other information for applications to process. An application can also send or post system-defined messages.

An application also can create *application-defined messages* to be used by its own windows or to communicate with windows in other processes. If an application creates its own messages, the window procedure that receives them must interpret the messages and provide appropriate processing.

The WM_USER constant is used by applications to help define private messages, usually of the form WM_USER+X, where X is an integer value. There is a possibility that the first few values above the value of the WM_USER constant may be used by the application, so it is prudent to start at an integer value of no less than 5.

`Private Const TB_SETSTYLE As Long = WM_USER + 56`
`Private Const TB_GETSTYLE As Long = WM_USER + 57`

TB_GETSTYLE and TB_SETSTYLE are messages associated with the toolbar control. TB_GETSTYLE retrieves the styles currently in use for a toolbar control, whereas TB_SETSTYLE sets the style for a toolbar control. Neither message has a pre-defined value, so each is defined as a private message with a WM_USER+X value.

`Private Const TBSTYLE_FLAT As Long = &H800`

TBSTYLE_FLAT is one of the toolbar styles. It creates a flat toolbar, in which both the toolbar and the buttons are transparent, and button text appears under button bitmaps.

There are other toolbar styles. Table 5-5 summarizes often-used styles, which can be combined:

```
Private Declare Function SendMessageLong Lib "user32" _
    Alias "SendMessageA" (ByVal hwnd As Long, ByVal wMsg As Long, _
    ByVal wParam As Long, ByVal lParam As Long) As Long
```

As discussed in the "Using a Mouse to Move a Form with SendMessage" example in Chapter 2, **SendMessage** is an API function by which you can send a message to a window or control. Also as discussed in Chapter 2, the *lParam* parameter may be a number, a string, an array, or a user-defined type. This not only affects the data type of *lParam*, but also whether it is passed *ByVal* or *ByRef*. Additionally, *lParam* may, again depending on the message passed, return a value from the call in the parameter passed (usually a user-defined type) where the call fills in certain members, like a RECT structure.

Since *lParam* can be different data types, and may be passed either *ByVal* or *ByRef*, it was recommended in Chapter 2 that the programmer use the **Alias** keyword in Visual Basic to define new **SendMessage** declarations named to reflect the type of data being passed. **SendMessageLong** is an example of the implementation of this recommendation. The *lParam* parameter is explicitly declared as **Long** and is passed *ByVal*.

```
Private Declare Function FindWindowEx Lib "user32" _
    Alias "FindWindowExA" (ByVal hWnd1 As Long, _
    ByVal hWnd2 As Long, ByVal lpsz1 As String, _
    ByVal lpsz2 As String) As Long
```

Toolbar Style	Description
TBSTYLE_ALTDRAG	Allows users to change a toolbar button's position by dragging it while holding down ALT.
TBSTYLE_FLAT	Creates a flat toolbar. Both the toolbar and the buttons are transparent, with button text appearing under button bitmaps.
TBSTYLE_LIST	Places button text to the right of button bitmaps.
TBSTYLE_TOOLTIPS	Creates a tooltip control that an application can use to display descriptive text for the buttons in the toolbar.
TBSTYLE_TRANSPARENT	Creates a transparent toolbar. The toolbar is transparent but the buttons are not, and button text appears under button bitmaps.

TABLE 5-5.   Toolbar Control Styles

This Windows API function is discussed below in connection with the class member function **MakeFlat**.

```
Public Sub MakeFlat(hwnd As Long)
```

The subroutine **MakeFlat** will be called from the toolbar form, which passes its handle as a parameter.

```
hToolbar = FindWindowEx(hwnd, 0&, "ToolbarWindow32", vbNullString)
```

The **FindWindowEx** function retrieves a handle to a window whose class name and window name match the specified strings. The function searches child windows, beginning with the one following the given child window. This function does not perform a case-sensitive search.

The first parameter of **FindWindowEx** is the handle to the parent window whose child windows are to be searched. In this example the parent window is the toolbar form which contains the toolbar control. The handle to the toolbar form was passed as a parameter to **MakeFlat**.

The second parameter of **FindWindowEx** is the handle to a child window. If, as in this example, the second parameter is null (that is, 0&), then the search begins with the first child window of the parent window whose handle was specified in the first parameter.

The third parameter of **FindWindowEx** is a string that specifies the class name of the child window being searched for. The class name of the toolbar control is "ToolbarWindow32."

The fourth parameter of **FindWindowEx** is a string that specifies the window name (also described as the window's *title*). If, as in this example, the parameter is null (that is, 0&), then all window names match.

The return value of **FindWindowEx** is a handle to the window that has the specified class and window names. That return value, which is the handle to the toolbar control, is stored in the class variable *hToolbar*.

```
style = SendMessageLong(hToolbar, TB_GETSTYLE, 0&, 0&)
```

As discussed in Chapter 2, **SendMessage** (or here **SendMessageLong**) returns a value because it sends a message by immediately calling the Windows function for the specified window, and does not return until the Windows function completes its execution. However, generally the message being sent does not return a value which is meaningful, so consequently the return value of **SendMessage** usually is ignored.

This is one of those exceptions where the return value is meaningful. When the second parameter is TB_GETSTYLE, **SendMessage** returns a **Long** value that is a combination of the current styles of the toolbar control.

```
Call SendMessageLong(hToolbar, TB_SETSTYLE, 0, style Or _
                TBSTYLE_FLAT)

End Sub
```

When the second parameter is TB_SETSTYLE, **SendMessage** sends to the toolbar control whose handle is specified in the first parameter the value in the fourth parameter specifying the styles to be set for the control. Again, this value can be a combination of toolbar control styles. Here the value is the existing style combined with the flat toolbar style of TBSTYLE_FLAT.

TEST THE CODE

The only other change to the code in the prior example is to add the italicized code to the **Load** event in the toolbar form:

```
Private Sub Form_Load()
    CalculateTBar Me, "Toolbar1"
    Dim cFlatBar As New clsFlatBar
    cFlatBar.MakeFlat (Toolbar1.hwnd)
    Toolbar1.Refresh
    SubClass Me.hwnd
End Sub
```

The first italicized line declares a new instance of **clsFlatBar**. That new instance calls the **MakeFlat** member function of **clsFlatBar**, passing as a parameter the toolbar form's handle. The **Refresh** method of the toolbar then is called so the appearance of the toolbar can reflect the changes made by the **MakeFlat** member function.

Test the code. The toolbar now has a flat appearance. (See Figure 5-10.) Additionally, moving the mouse over a toolbar button raises the button.

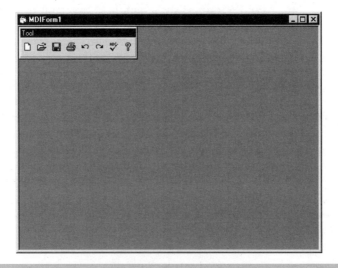

FIGURE 5-10. The floating, docking, and now flat toolbar

Combo and List Boxes

Combo Box and List Box controls are the workhorses of Visual Basic applications. These controls list items for viewing by the application user. The listed items usually are related, such as names in a database or, as in the upcoming examples, screen fonts. These controls also permit the application user to interact with the listed items, either by selecting an item with mouse clicks or keystrokes, or by editing the item. These display, selection, and editing capabilities no doubt contribute to the prevalence of Combo Box and List Box controls in Visual Basic applications.

Combo Box and List Box controls have a rich set of properties and methods. However, the searching capability of these controls is inefficient. In essence, finding, selecting, or deselecting an item or items requires a loop through *all* of the items in the combo or list box. This linear search can be time-consuming when, as often happens, the control contains hundreds of items. If searches are frequent, the performance degradation is magnified.

Additionally, the vertical and horizontal sizing of combo box controls are rigid. The display of the drop-down list box portion of a combo box is limited to eight items. The width of a combo box can be set to different values. However, if the application user enters an item whose length is longer than the width of the combo box, there is no efficient way of determining this or resizing the width of the combo box to avoid cutting off the display of the lengthy item.

The solution, as you may have guessed, is the Windows API. This is not to suggest that the Windows API will solve all of your difficulties. If you are having problems with your spouse, the opposite sex or, still worse, both, the Windows API will do you little good, except perhaps to speed up your application so that you can get out of town sooner. However, if your concern is speeding up and enhancing your List Box and Combo Box controls, then the Windows API is the answer.

cboSearch.vbp

Creating a Combo Box Smart Search Feature

It is time-consuming for the application user to scroll through a large number of items to look for a particular item. Therefore, many applications have a search feature to help the application user more quickly locate an item. The application user enters a search string, and an item matching the search criteria is displayed.

Unfortunately, neither the List Box nor Combo Box control has any property or method that permits the direct look-up of the index of an item from its name. Your code can loop through the items until the item searched for is found or all of the items have been checked. However, this linear search is relatively slow and, in a list with numerous items, can degrade the performance of your application, especially if searches are frequent.

The solution involves the API function **SendMessage**. This function allows you to send a specific message to a window. With the message used in the first example, **SendMessage** will return the zero-based index number of the first item in the combo box with a prefix that matches the search text. That index then is used to retrieve the text of the found item to display to the application user. This logic will be encapsulated in a class module to facilitate reuse. Further examples will extend this class module to also include searches of list boxes, finding multiple matches, and much, much more.

SYNOPSIS OF CODE

The message CB_FINDSTRING is sent by **SendMessage** to determine the index of the first string in the combo box whose prefix matches the search string typed by the application user in the edit area of the combo box. The edit area then displays the found item. The edit area visually differentiates the search string from the characters added to display the found item. It does so by selecting the added characters.

The ease of use of the combo box also is enhanced. The list box portion of the combo box drops down when the application user clicks the arrow on the right side of the edit area. However, this requires the application user to switch from the keyboard to the mouse. The application user would not have to switch from the keyboard to the mouse to drop down the list box if he or she could drop down the list box simply by pressing the ENTER key in the edit area. This is accomplished by sending the combo box a CB_SHOWDROPDOWN message.

CODE

Create a new class module, named **clsBoxSearch**, with the following code:

```
Private Const CB_ERR As Long = (-1)
Private Const CB_FINDSTRING As Long = &H14C
Private Const CB_SHOWDROPDOWN As Long = &H14F

Private Declare Function SendMessageStr Lib _
    "user32" Alias "SendMessageA" _
    (ByVal hwnd As Long, _
    ByVal wMsg As Long, _
    ByVal wParam As Long, _
    ByVal lParam As String) As Long

Public Sub FindIndexStr(ctlSource As Control, _
    ByVal str As String, intKey As Integer, _
    Optional ctlTarget As Variant)

Dim lngIdx As Long
Dim FindString As String

If (intKey < 32 Or intKey > 127) And _
```

```
        (Not (intKey = 13 Or intKey = 8)) Then Exit Sub
If Not intKey = 13 Or intKey = 8 Then
    If Len(ctlSource.Text) = 0 Then
        FindString = str & Chr$(intKey)
    Else
        FindString = Left$(str, ctlSource.SelStart) & Chr$(intKey)
    End If
End If


If intKey = 8 Then
    If Len(ctlSource.Text) = 0 Then Exit Sub
    Dim numChars As Integer
    numChars = ctlSource.SelStart - 1

  If numChars > 0 Then FindString = Left(str, numChars)

End If

If IsMissing(ctlTarget) And TypeName(ctlSource) = "ComboBox" Then
    Set ctlTarget = ctlSource
    If intKey = 13 Then
        Call SendMessageStr(ctlTarget.hwnd, _
            CB_SHOWDROPDOWN, True, 0&)
        Exit Sub
    End If

    lngIdx = SendMessageStr(ctlTarget.hwnd, _
        CB_FINDSTRING, -1, FindString)
    If lngIdx <> -1 Then
            ctlTarget.ListIndex = lngIdx
            ctlSource.SelStart = Len(FindString)
            ctlSource.SelLength = Len(ctlSource.Text) - _
                ctlSource.SelStart
    End If
    intKey = 0
Else
    Exit Sub
End If
End Sub
```

ANNOTATIONS

```
Private Const CB_ERR As Long = (-1)
```

This constant reflects the value of the **ListIndex** property of the combo box if no item in the combo box matches the search criteria. The **ListIndex** property returns or sets the index of the currently selected item in the control. The indices of items in a combo box are zero-based positive numbers. Therefore, the value –1 indicates that no item is currently selected. For a Combo Box control, the **ListIndex** property also will have a value of –1 if the user has entered new text into the edit area of the combo box.

```
Private Const CB_FINDSTRING As Long = &H14C
```

CB_FINDSTRING is one of the many messages that an application may send, using **SendMessage**, to a combo box. When used with **SendMessage**, CB_FINDSTRING returns the index of the first string in the combo box that matches a given prefix. This is a wildcard search. For example, if the letter "M" is typed is the edit area of the Combo Box control, **SendMessage** will return the index of the first item that begins with "M" or –1 if no item begins with "M."

An alternative to CB_FINDSTRING is CB_ SELECTSTRING. This message appears to perform the same task as CB_FINDSTRING. If CB_ SELECTSTRING is used, it needs to be declared as follows:

```
Private Const CB_SELECTSTRING As Long = &H14D
```

If the search is for an exact match instead of a matching prefix, then the message, instead of being a CB_FINDSTRING or CB_ SELECTSTRING message, should be CB_FINDSTRINGEXACT. This and the further examples do not utilize the CB_FINDSTRINGEXACT message. However, it would be relatively easy to extend the example to ask the application user, with a set of two option buttons, whether the search should be a wildcard or exact match, and then send the appropriate message based on the user's choice.

```
Private Const CB_SHOWDROPDOWN As Long = &H14F
```

A CB_SHOWDROPDOWN message is sent to show or hide the list box portion of a combo box. Whether the list box portion is shown or hidden depends on a flag sent with the message. This is discussed below in the annotation to the **SendMessage** call using the CB_SHOWDROPDOWN message.

The CB_SHOWDROPDOWN message applies to combo boxes with either the Drop Down or Drop Down List style. The message does not apply if the Simple Combo style is chosen because in that style the list box is never shown. These styles are described in Table 6-1.

Constant	Value	Description
vbComboDropDown	0	(Default) Dropdown Combo. Includes a drop-down list and a text box. The user can select from the list or type in the text box.
vbComboSimple	1	Simple Combo. Includes a text box and a list, which doesn't drop down. The user can select from the list or type in the text box. The size of a Simple combo box includes both the edit and list portions. By default, a Simple combo box is sized so that none of the list is displayed. The list can be displayed by increasing the **Height** property.
vbComboDropDownList	2	Dropdown List. This style allows selection only from the drop-down list.

TABLE 6-1.   Style Settings for the Combo Box control

```
Private Declare Function SendMessageStr Lib _
    "user32" Alias "SendMessageA" _
    (ByVal hwnd As Long, _
     ByVal wMsg As Long, _
     ByVal wParam As Long, _
     ByVal lParam As String) As Long
```

SendMessage, as has been discussed in previous chapters, is an API function by which you can send a message to a window or control. Also as discussed in Chapter 2, the *lParam* parameter may be a number, a string, an array, or a user-defined type, which not only affects the data type of *lParam*, but also whether it is passed *ByVal* or *ByRef*. Since *lParam* can be different data types, and may be passed either *ByVal* or *ByRef*, it is recommended that the programmer use the **Alias** keyword in Visual Basic to define new **SendMessage** declares, which are named to reflect the type of data being passed. **SendMessageStr** is an example of the implementation of this recommendation, just as **SendMessageLong** was in the last chapter. The *lParam* parameter is explicitly declared as a *String* and is passed *ByVal*.

```
Public Sub FindIndexStr(ctlSource As Control, _
    ByVal str As String, intKey As Integer, _
    Optional ctlTarget As Variant)
```

This user-defined function does most of the work in this class. It takes the parameters described in Table 6-2.

The fourth and final parameter, *ctlTarget*, is declared as **Optional**. The **Optional** keyword is used for a parameter which may be, but is not required to be, an argument when the function is called. This parameter is the last one because an **Optional** parameter may only be followed by other **Optional** parameters. This parameter is declared as a **Variant** because, as explained below in the annotation to the **IsMissing** function, **Variants** have a "missing" flag bit which can be checked to see if the **Optional** parameter in fact was passed.

In this example, the *ctlTarget* parameter is not used. The reason is that, when a combo box is involved, the control supplying the search string, which is the first parameter *ctlSource*, is the same as the control represented by *ctlTarget*, which contains the items to be searched. This is true because a combo box contains both the edit area that supplies the search string (*ctlSource*) and the list box that contains the items to be searched (*ctlTarget*).

By contrast, if a list box is being searched, the control that is supplying the search string, a Text Box control, is not the same control as the one that contains the items to be searched, the List Box control. In that circumstance, while the *ctlSource* parameter would be used to specify the Text Box control, the *ctlTarget* parameter would be used to specify the List Box control.

Parameter Name	Description
ctlSource	This is the control which contains the search string. In this example, this control will be the Combo Box. In the next example, it instead may be a Text Box control, depending on whether the application user is searching a combo box or a list box.
str	This is the search string. It will be taken from the edit area of the Combo Box control. In the next example, it instead may be taken from the Text property of the Text Box control, depending on whether the application user is searching a combo box or a list box.
intKey	This is the ASCII value of the key which was just pressed. As discussed below in "Test the Code," the **FindIndexStr** function is called from the **KeyPress** event of the control which contains the search string.
ctlTarget	This is the control which contains the items to be searched. In this example, this control will be the Combo Box. In the next example, it instead may be the List Box control, depending on whether the application user is searching a combo box or a list box.

TABLE 6-2.　　Parameters of **FindIndexStr**

Using an **Optional** parameter enables this class module to be used for both combo box and list box searches. It makes sense to have one class handle both searches, since the two searches are far more alike than they are different.

```
Dim lngIdx As Long
```

This variable will hold the index returned. That index will be the one corresponding with the item which meets the search criteria, unless no item meets the search criteria, in which case the value will be –1. This is explained above in the discussion of CB_ERR.

```
Dim FindString As String
```

This variable will hold the search string. The item which was found by the search string is the second parameter of **FindIndexStr**, *str*.

```
If (intKey < 32 Or intKey > 127) And _
    (Not (intKey = 13 Or intKey = 8)) Then Exit Sub
```

The third parameter, *intKey*, is the ASCII value of the key that was just pressed. Keystrokes having an ASCII value of less than 33 are nonprinting ASCII characters, such as the carriage return or the bell. Keystrokes from 33 through 127 include alpha characters, numeric characters, and punctuation marks. Keystrokes having an ASCII value of more than 127 are part of the extended ASCII characterset, mostly involving non-English language characters. Therefore, with two exceptions, characters outside of the range of 33 through 127 are ignored. One exception is 13, the ASCII value of the character that corresponds to the ENTER key. That keystroke, though not generating a printable character, is, as discussed below, used to "drop down" the list box portion of the combo box. The other exception is 8, the ASCII value of the character that corresponds to the BACKSPACE key. That character can be used to change the search string (by deleting the last character of the search string) and therefore also is enabled, as discussed below.

```
If Not intKey = 13 Or intKey = 8 Then
    If Len(ctlSource.Text) = 0 Then
        FindString = str & Chr$(intKey)
    Else
        FindString = Left$(str, ctlSource.SelStart) & Chr$(intKey)
    End If
End If
```

These statements build a string unless the keystroke was pressing the ENTER key or the BACKSPACE key. The **If** branch of the control structure tests if any text *previously* has been entered in the edit area of the combo box. The word "previously" is emphasized because the *current* keystroke is not *yet* in the edit area of the combo box. This is because the **FindIndexStr** function is called from the **KeyPress** event of the combo box. Since the key has only been pressed, and not yet released, the keystroke has not yet been completed and therefore does not yet appear in the edit area.

If the text portion of the combo box is empty, such as if the keystroke is the first in the text portion, then *str* is a blank string (that is, ""). In this event, *FindString* simply will be the character which corresponds to the key that just was pressed.

If the text portion of the combo box is not empty, then the content of the edit area is the first item in the combo box whose prefix matches the search criteria, and *not* the aggregation of the previously entered keystrokes. For example, if the letter "M" was typed in the edit area, then the text in the edit area would not be the search string "M," but instead the found item "MS Sans Serif."

Since the content of the edit area is not the search string but instead the first item in the combo box which matches the search criteria, the parameter which passes the content of the edit area, *str, is not* the search string, but instead *contains* the search string. Therefore, it is necessary to extract from *str* the portion which is the search string. In other words, it is necessary to distinguish between the keystrokes which have been entered and the characters which have been added to the search string in order to display in the edit area the first item in the combo box that matches the search criteria.

The edit area of the combo box distinguishes between the keystrokes which have been entered and the characters which have been added to complete the found item by "selecting" the added characters. For example, if the letter "M" is typed and the first match is "MS Sans Serif," then the text portion of the combo box would appear: MS Sans Serif. The mouse insertion point would be after the "M," that is, at the end of the unselected portion. (See Figure 6-1.) This break between the unselected and selected portion of the string in the edit area not only distinguishes between the keystrokes which have been entered and the characters that have been added to complete the found item, but also has the valuable side effect of giving the application user a visual cue of both the search string and the item found by the search string.

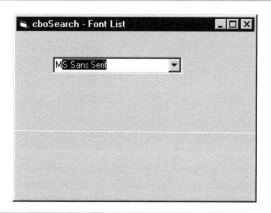

FIGURE 6-1. The "M" search string

Since the mouse insertion point would be after the "M," that is, at the end of the unselected portion, further character keystrokes are added to the end of the unselected portion of the text. A new search is made upon each keystroke. For example, if both "MS Sans Serif" and "MS Serif" are in the combo box, then, as Figure 6-1 shows, typing "M" would bring up "MS Sans Serif," not "MS Serif," because "MS Sans Serif" comes first alphabetically. However, if the application user types the search string "MS Se" in the edit area, then "MS Serif" would be found. Again, the found item would appear in the edit area as "MS Serif." (See Figure 6-2.)

```
If intKey = 8 Then
    If Len(ctlSource.Text) = 0 Then Exit Sub
    Dim numChars As Integer
    numChars = ctlSource.SelStart - 1

    If numChars > 0 Then FindString = Left(str, numChars)

End If
```

A new search also would be made if the keystroke deleted instead of added characters. For example, if the search string was "MS Se" and then the application user pressed the BACKSPACE key, the search string would change from "MS Se" to "MS S," resulting in the found item changing from "MS Serif " to "MS Sans Serif." The selected and unselected portions would adjust accordingly to "MS Sans Serif." (See Figure 6-3.)

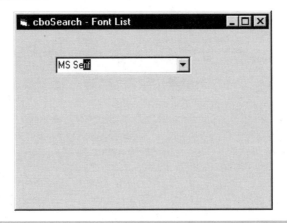

FIGURE 6-2.   The "MS Se" search string

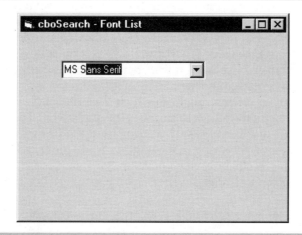

FIGURE 6-3. Using the BACKSPACE key to change the search string

The first **If** statement tests if the ASCII value of the pressed key is 8, which corresponds to the BACKSPACE key. If so, the next **If** statement tests to see if the length of the text in the edit area is zero. If so, then the BACKSPACE keypress is ignored.

If there is text in the edit area, then, as explained below, the **SelStart** property reflects the number of characters in the search string. The value of the **SelStart** property is decreased by one because the pressing of the BACKSPACE key deleted one character of the search string. The value of the **SelStart** property, minus one, is stored in the variable *numChars*. The **Left** function, which takes the *x* leftmost characters from a string, is used to take the leftmost, minus one (*numChars*), characters of the search string. In effect, the new value of *FindString* is the prior search string with the rightmost character deleted to reflect the pressing of the BACKSPACE key.

The test for whether *numChars* > 0 is made because of the possibility that the application user, while the cursor is in the edit box, presses the HOME key, then the SHIFT-END combination to highlight the contents of the box, and finally the BACKSPACE key in an attempt to clear the contents of the edit box. Without the test for whether *numChars* > 0, there would be an error. The reason is that *ctlSource.Text* is > 0 but *ctlSource.SelStart* is = 0. Therefore, when the *ctlSource.SelStart – 1* is assigned to *numChars*, the value of *numChars* is –1. Passing this value as the second parameter of the **Left** function will cause an error because the second parameter is the zero-based position of where the **Left** function is supposed to start. The test for whether *numChars* > 0 prevents this possibility.

```
Left$(str, ctlSource.SelStart) & Chr$(intKey)
```

The **Left** function returns either a **Variant** or a **String** containing a specified number of characters from the left side of a string. The return value is a **Variant** unless, as here, the type declaration character $ follows the function name (**Left$**), indicating that the return value is a **String**. If the return value always will be a **String**, it is preferable to use **Left$** rather than **Left** since a **String** requires less storage space than a **Variant**.

The first parameter is the string from which the leftmost characters will be returned. The string in the edit area supplies this parameter. The purpose of using the **Left** function is to extract the search string from the string in the edit area.

As discussed above, the string in the edit box is not the search string but instead the first item in the combo box which matches the search criteria. Therefore, the second parameter of **FindIndexStr**, *str*, *is not* the search string, but instead *contains* the search string.

The second parameter of the **Left** function is the number of leftmost characters to return. As discussed above, the edit box distinguishes between the keystrokes which have been entered (that is, the search string) and the characters which have been added to complete the found item by "selecting" the added characters. Therefore, to extract the search string from the string in the edit area, the number of leftmost characters to return will be the number of characters that are *not* selected. This number can be determined by the **SelStart** property. This property either sets or, as here, returns the starting point of text selected. The range of values of **SelStart** is from 0, which means no text has been selected, to the text length, which means all the text in the edit area has been selected. In this case, the value of the **SelStart** property will be the same as the number of characters that are not selected. Thus, the second parameter is *ctlSource.SelStart*.

Finally, to update the search string, the current keystroke, *intKey*, is added to the previous search string.

```
If IsMissing(ctlTarget) And TypeName(ctlSource) = "ComboBox" Then
```

The function **IsMissing** returns a Boolean value indicating whether an **Optional Variant** argument has been passed to a procedure. Its one parameter contains the name of the **Optional Variant** procedure argument, which here is *ctlTarget*. **IsMissing** returns True if no value has been passed for the specified argument; otherwise, it returns False. **IsMissing** is used to check if an argument is missing because use of the missing argument in other code likely will cause an error.

The reason *ctlTarget* is declared as a **Variant** in **FindIndexStr** is that **Variants** have a "missing" flag bit. By contrast, simple data types such as **Integer** do not provide for a "missing" flag bit and therefore cannot be used as the data type of an **Optional** argument.

The function **TypeName** returns a **String** that states the data type of the variable in its one parameter. If the variable is a simple data type, the return value could be, for example, "Integer" or "Boolean." The variable also may be an object, in which case the return value would be, as in this and the following examples, "ComboBox,"

"ListBox," or "TextBox." The one limitation is that the variable passed as a parameter to **TypeName** cannot be a user-defined type.

As a practical matter, in this example, using both **IsMissing** and **TypeName** is overkill. Either test alone would suffice to determine if the control being searched was a Combo Box or a List Box. However, both functions are useful and are analytically distinct, so both are used for illustration purposes.

```
Set ctlTarget = ctlSource
```

The parameter *ctlTarget* is used in later code since this class module is designed to cover both combo box and list box searches. However, if the **Optional** parameter *ctlTarget* is missing, as it would be if the search is of a combo box instead of a list box, then use of the *ctlTarget* parameter could cause an error because that parameter has not been assigned a value. Since, in the case of a combo box search, the target control is the same as the source control, the *ctlTarget* parameter is assigned the value of the *ctlSource* parameter, which is the combo box. The **Set** statement is used because both *ctlSource* and *ctlTarget* refer to an object rather than a simple data type.

```
If intKey = 13 Then
    Call SendMessageStr(ctlTarget.hwnd, _
        CB_SHOWDROPDOWN, True, 0&)
    Exit Sub
End If
```

The ENTER key has an ASCII value of 13. If that key is pressed, then a CB_SHOWDROPDOWN message is sent. As discussed above, this message shows or hides the list box portion of a combo box, depending on the *wParam* parameter of the message. This parameter is either True or False. A value of True shows the list box; a value of False hides it. In this case, the value is True, to show (drop down) the list box portion of the combo box. The *lParam* parameter is not used, so it must be zero.

```
lngIdx = SendMessageStr(ctlTarget.hwnd, _
    CB_FINDSTRING, -1, FindString)
```

SendMessage has four parameters. The first parameter is the handle of the control which will be searched. That parameter is *ctlTarget*, not *ctlSource*. The reason is that in a list box search *ctlSource* is the text box which contains the search string, not the list box which contains the items to be searched.

The second parameter is the message to be sent. CB_FINDSTRING returns the index of the first string in the combo box which matches a given prefix. As discussed above, this is a wildcard search which will return the index of the first item whose prefix matches the search string. If there is no match, then the value –1 is returned.

The third parameter of **SendMessageStr**, which is the *wParam* parameter of the CB_FINDSTRING message, specifies the zero-based index of the item before the first item to be searched. When the search reaches the bottom of the combo box, the search continues from the top of the combo box back to the item specified by *wParam*. If *wParam* is −1, as in this example, the entire combo box is searched from the beginning.

The fourth and final parameter CB_FINDSTRING, which is the *lParam* parameter of the CB_FINDSTRING message, is the search string. The search string is **FindString**, which is discussed above. The search is not case-sensitive, so this string can contain any combination of uppercase and lowercase letters.

```
If lngIdx <> CB_ERR Then
        ctlTarget.ListIndex = lngIdx
        ctlSource.SelStart = Len(FindString)
        ctlSource.SelLength = Len(ctlSource.Text) - _
            ctlSource.SelStart
    End If
```

The **If** control structure tests to see if an item was found. CB_ERR has the value of −1, which is returned if no item was found.

If a search item was found, then the index of the search item is assigned to the **ListIndex** property of *ctlTarget*, here the combo box. This assignment has the same effect as clicking that item in the combo box. This means that the item found by the search will appear in the edit area of the combo box.

As discussed above, this code distinguishes between the search string and those characters in the edit area which were added to the search string to complete the found item by selecting the added characters. The selection is done first by determining the length of the search string *FindString*. The length of the search string is determined by the **Len** function, which returns the number of characters in a string. The return value then is assigned to the **SelStart** property. The **SelStart** property was used above to return the starting point of the text selected. Here that property is used to set the starting point. This setting has the effect of making the selection point in the edit area just after the search string and just before the characters which were added to the search string to complete the found item.

Now that the start of the selection is in the correct place, the remaining task is to have the length of the selection cover all of the added characters. The **SelLength** property returns or, as here, sets the number of characters selected. The number of characters to be selected is the difference between the length of the entire text in the edit area and the length of the search string since the search string is not to be selected.

```
        intKey = 0
```

The keystroke should be suppressed. Changing the ASCII value of the keystroke to 0 cancels the keystroke so the object receives no character. This is necessary because the keystroke already has been added to the edit area.

```
Else
    Exit Sub
End If
End Sub
```

The **Else** statement takes care of other controls which are not supported by this class module.

TEST THE CODE

1. Start a new project, Standard Exe.

2. Add a combo box, named **cboFonts**. The style should be the default, 0 **(vbComboDropDown).** The **Style** property settings for the Combo Box control are described in Table 6-1.

    In this case we want the application user to be able to type in the combo box. This eliminates the last option, **vbComboDropDownList**. The other remaining option, **vbComboSimple**, is not used because it takes up space on the screen with the list box, whereas with the **vbComboDropDown** style the list does not appear until the drop-down arrow on the text box is clicked. In this example we will extend this drop-down functionality so the combo box also will drop down when the user presses the ENTER key.

    The form should look like Figure 6-4.

3. In the general declarations of the form module place the following code:

```
Option Explicit
Dim cBox As New clsBoxSearch
```

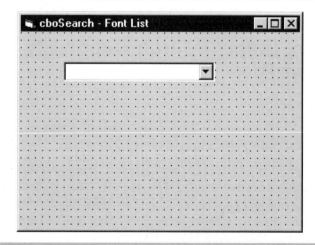

FIGURE 6-4. The cboSearch form in Design view

An instance of **clsBoxSearch**, *cBox*, is instantiated to use the **FindIndexStr** subroutine in **clsBoxSearch**.

4. Place this code in the **Load** event of the form:

```
Private Sub Form_Load()
   Dim i As Integer
   Dim max As Integer
   max = Screen.FontCount
   If max > 35 Then max = 35
   For i = 1 To max
      cboFonts.AddItem Screen.Fonts(i)
      Next I
End Sub
```

This code loads the combo box with up to 35 screen fonts.

5. Add this code to the **KeyPress** event of **cboFonts**:

```
Private Sub cboFonts_KeyPress(KeyAscii As Integer)
 cBox.FindIndexStr cboFonts, cboFonts.Text, KeyAscii
End Sub
```

The **KeyPress** event of the combo box is the logical place to call the **FindIndexStr** function since the search starts when the application user types a search string in the edit area.

Test the code! Type **M**. The text in the edit area will appear as shown in Figure 6-1. Next, type additional characters so the search string is **MS Se**. The text in the edit area will appear as shown in Figure 6-2. Finally, press the BACKSPACE key so the search string is **MS S**. The text in the edit area will appear as shown in Figure 6-3.

Extending Smart Search Capability to the List Box

cbo+ListSearch.vbp

This example will again illustrate the advantage of modular, object-oriented code. Only a few additional statements need to be added to extend the class module to include searches of list boxes as well as combo boxes.

SYNOPSIS OF CODE

The class module uses the **TypeName** function to determine if the control containing the items to be searched is a Combo Box or a List Box. If the control is a List Box, then **SendMessage** sends a LB_FINDSTRING message. The LB_FINDSTRING message is similar to the CB_FINDSTRING message except it applies to a list box instead of a combo box.

CODE

The code which is added to the class module is italicized.

```
Private Const LB_FINDSTRING As Long = &H18F
Private Const LB_ERR As Long = (-1)
Private Const CB_ERR As Long = (-1)
Private Const CB_FINDSTRING As Long = &H14C
Private Const CB_SHOWDROPDOWN As Long = &H14F

Private Declare Function SendMessageStr Lib _
    "user32" Alias "SendMessageA" _
    (ByVal hwnd As Long, _
     ByVal wMsg As Long, _
     ByVal wParam As Long, _
     ByVal lParam As String) As Long

Public Sub FindIndexStr(ctlSource As Control, _
    ByVal str As String, intKey As Integer, _
    Optional ctlTarget As Variant)

Dim lngIdx As Long
Dim FindString As String

If (intKey < 32 Or intKey > 127) And _
    (Not (intKey = 13 Or intKey = 8)) Then Exit Sub

If Not intKey = 13 Or intKey = 8 Then
    If Len(ctlSource.Text) = 0 Then
        FindString = str & Chr$(intKey)
    Else
        FindString = Left$(str, ctlSource.SelStart) & Chr$(intKey)
    End If
End If

If intKey = 8 Then
    If Len(ctlSource.Text) = 0 Then Exit Sub
    Dim numChars As Integer
    numChars = ctlSource.SelStart - 1
    FindString = Left(str, numChars)
End If
```

```vb
If IsMissing(ctlTarget) And TypeName(ctlSource) = "ComboBox" Then
    Set ctlTarget = ctlSource
        If intKey = 13 Then
          Call SendMessageStr(ctlTarget.hwnd, _
            CB_SHOWDROPDOWN, True, 0&)
          Exit Sub
        End If


    lngIdx = SendMessageStr(ctlTarget.hwnd, _
        CB_FINDSTRING, -1, FindString)
ElseIf TypeName(ctlTarget) = "ListBox" Then
    If intKey = 13 Then Exit Sub
    lngIdx = SendMessageStr(ctlTarget.hwnd, _
        LB_FINDSTRING, -1, FindString)
Else
    Exit Sub
End If

If lngIdx <> -1 Then
        ctlTarget.ListIndex = lngIdx
        If TypeName(ctlSource) = "TextBox" Then _
          ctlSource.Text = ctlTarget.List(lngIdx)
        ctlSource.SelStart = Len(FindString)
        ctlSource.SelLength = Len(ctlSource.Text) - _
          ctlSource.SelStart
End If
intKey = 0
End Sub
```

ANNOTATIONS

The code is quite similar to the previous example. Only two constants and an additional branch to the control structure are added. These additional statements are annotated.

```vb
Private Const LB_FINDSTRING As Long = &H18F
Private Const LB_ERR As Long = (-1)
```

The constants LB_FINDSTRING and LB_ERR are the list box equivalents of CB_FINDSTRING and CB_ERR respectively.

```vb
ElseIf TypeName(ctlTarget) = "ListBox" Then
    If intKey = 13 Then Exit Sub
    lngIdx = SendMessageStr(ctlTarget.hwnd, _
        LB_FINDSTRING, -1, FindString)
```

This **ElseIf** branch is added to **FindIndexStr**. The **TypeName** function checks if the **Optional** *ctlTarget* parameter is a list box. If it is, then the ENTER key is ignored, as there is no drop-down as with the combo box. Additionally, the message to be passed by **SendMessageStr** is LB_FINDSTRING, not CB_FINDSTRING.

TEST THE CODE

1. Make a copy of the previous project and rename it cbo+ListSearch.vbp.

2. Add a list box, named **lstFonts**. The style should be the default, 0 (Standard).

3. Add a text box called **txtFillBox**.

Your form should look like Figure 6-5.

4. Add the italicized line of code below to the **Load** event of the form:

```
Private Sub Form_Load()
    Dim i As Integer
    Dim max As Integer
    max = Screen.FontCount
    If max > 35 Then max = 35
    For i = 1 To max
        lstFonts.AddItem Screen.Fonts(i)
        cboFonts.AddItem Screen.Fonts(i)
        Next I
End Sub
```

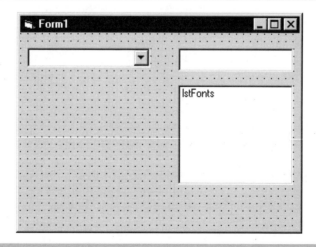

FIGURE 6-5. The cbo+ListSearch form in Design view

This additional statement adds the screen fonts to the list box.

5. Add this code to the **KeyPress** event of **txtFillBox**:

```
Private Sub txtFillBox_KeyPress(KeyAscii As Integer)
    cBox.FindIndexStr txtFillBox, txtFillBox.Text, KeyAscii, _
        lstFonts
End Sub
```

This code is similar to that in the **KeyPress** event of **cboFonts**. The parameters are different, however. The first parameter is the text box instead of the combo box since the text box is the source of the search string. Similarly, the second parameter is the **Text** property of the text box instead of the combo box. The third parameter is the same, the ASCII value of the key which was pressed. The fourth parameter, which is **Optional**, here is present, the list box which contains the items to be searched.

Test the code! Type **M** in the text box. The text in the text box will appear as shown in Figure 6-6. Next, type additional characters in the text box so the search string is **MS Se**. The text in the edit area will appear as shown in Figure 6-7. Finally, press the BACKSPACE key so the search string is **MS S**. The text in the text box will appear as shown in Figure 6-8.

Finding Multiple Matches in a List Box with Smart Search

MultiSearch.vbp The two previous examples found the first match in the combo box or list box. However, often it is desirable to find not just the first match, but all matches.

This example will extend that capability to list all matches in the list box. This example also easily can be modified to add this capability to combo box searches as well.

This example will further illustrate the advantage of modular, object-oriented code. Once again, only a few additional statements need to be added to extend the class module to list all matches in the list box.

SYNOPSIS OF CODE

As in the previous example, **SendMessage** sends a LB_FINDSTRING message to find the first item in the list box with a prefix that matches the search string. If there is a match, then a loop continues to call **SendMessage** to send a LB_FINDSTRING message to find the next item in the list box with a prefix that matches the search string. The loop continues until it again reaches the first found item. Each found item is added to another list box which lists all found items.

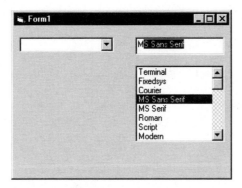

FIGURE 6-6. The "M" search string

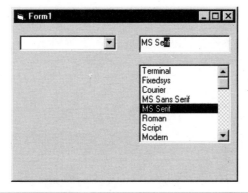

FIGURE 6-7. The "MS Se" search string

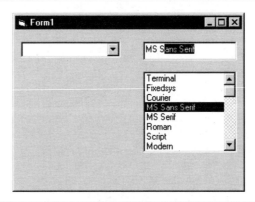

FIGURE 6-8. The effect of BACKSPACE on the search string

CODE

The code which is added to the class module is italicized.

```
Private Const LB_FINDSTRING As Long = &H18F
Private Const LB_ERR As Long = (-1)
Private Const CB_ERR As Long = (-1)
Private Const CB_FINDSTRING As Long = &H14C
Private Const CB_SHOWDROPDOWN As Long = &H14F

Private Declare Function SendMessageStr Lib _
    "user32" Alias "SendMessageA" _
    (ByVal hwnd As Long, _
     ByVal wMsg As Long, _
     ByVal wParam As Long, _
     ByVal lParam As String) As Long

Public Sub FindIndexStr(ctlSource As Control, _
    ByVal str As String, intKey As Integer, _
    Optional ctlTarget As Variant, _
    Optional ctlOutput As Variant)

Dim lngIdx As Long
Dim FindString As String

If (intKey < 32 Or intKey > 127) And _
    (Not (intKey = 13 Or intKey = 8)) Then Exit Sub

If Not intKey = 13 Or intKey = 8 Then
    If Len(ctlSource.Text) = 0 Then
        FindString = str & Chr$(intKey)
    Else
        FindString = Left$(str, ctlSource.SelStart) & Chr$(intKey)
    End If
End If

If intKey = 8 Then
    If Len(ctlSource.Text) = 0 Then Exit Sub
    Dim numChars As Integer
    numChars = ctlSource.SelStart - 1
    FindString = Left(str, numChars)
End If
```

```
If IsMissing(ctlTarget) And _
      TypeName(ctlSource) = "ComboBox" Then
    Set ctlTarget = ctlSource
        If intKey = 13 Then
          Call SendMessageStr(ctlTarget.hwnd, _
            CB_SHOWDROPDOWN, True, 0&)
          Exit Sub
        End If


    lngIdx = SendMessageStr(ctlTarget.hwnd, _
        CB_FINDSTRING, -1, FindString)

ElseIf TypeName(ctlTarget) = "ListBox" Then
    ctlOutput.Clear
    If intKey = 13 Then Exit Sub
    lngIdx = SendMessageStr(ctlTarget.hwnd, _
          LB_FINDSTRING, -1, FindString)
    Dim i As Integer
    i = -1
    If lngIdx <> -1 Then
        i = lngIdx
        Do
            ctlOutput.AddItem ctlTarget.List(i)
            i = SendMessageStr(ctlTarget.hwnd, _
              LB_FINDSTRING, i, FindString)
        Loop While i > lngIdx
    End If
Else
    Exit Sub
End If


If lngIdx <> -1 Then
        ctlTarget.ListIndex = lngIdx
        If TypeName(ctlSource) = "TextBox" Then _
          ctlSource.Text = ctlTarget.List(lngIdx)
        ctlSource.SelStart = Len(FindString)
        ctlSource.SelLength = _
          Len(ctlSource.Text) - ctlSource.SelStart
End If

intKey = 0
End Sub
```

ANNOTATIONS

```
Public Sub FindIndexStr(ctlSource As Control, _
   ByVal str As String, intKey As Integer, _
   Optional ctlTarget As Variant, _
   Optional ctlOutput As Variant)
```

An additional **Optional** parameter is added for the control (another List Box) which will display the matching strings. This parameter is **Optional** because other implementations of this class module in later examples will not use the output list box. If this parameter were not **Optional** it could not be listed after *ctlTarget* because an **Optional** parameter may only be followed in a parameter list by another **Optional** parameter.

```
ElseIf TypeName(ctlTarget) = "ListBox" Then
    ctlOutput.Clear
    If intKey = 13 Then Exit Sub
    lngIdx = SendMessageStr(ctlTarget.hwnd, _
        LB_FINDSTRING, -1, FindString)
    Dim i As Integer
    i = -1
    If lngIdx <> -1 Then
        i = lngIdx
        Do
            ctlOutput.AddItem ctlTarget.List(i)
            i = SendMessageStr(ctlTarget.hwnd, _
              LB_FINDSTRING, i, FindString)
        Loop While i > lngIdx
    End If
```

If *lngIdx* is–1, that is, no item was found, then there is no reason to look further. Otherwise, a loop is started, and the first found item is added to the list. A search then is made for the *next* matching item.

The third parameter of **SendMessageStr**, which is the starting index for the loop, is not –1 as in the previous examples. If it were, then the first found item would be found over and over again. Instead, the third parameter of **SendMessageStr** is the index of the last found item. That index will be held by the variable *i*.

Initially, *i* is set to *lngIdx*, the index of the first found item. The variable *i* then is assigned the return value of **SendMessageStr**, which is the next found item, so during the next iteration the loop will start at the newly found item.

As the loop continues, it is guaranteed that further matches will be found. The reason is that with an LB_FINDSTRING message, when the search reaches the bottom of the list box, it continues from the top of the list box back to the item specified by the starting index. Therefore, sooner or later the loop will "find" the first found item. However, all good things, including the loop, must end.

Accordingly, when the starting index for the search, the variable *i*, again equals *lngIdx* as it did when the loop started, then the loop has come full circle and stops.

TEST THE CODE

1. Make a copy of the previous project and rename it Multicbo+ListSearch.vbp.

2. Add a list box named **lstOutput**.

   Your form should look like Figure 6-9.

3. Add the code shown without boldface to the **KeyPress** event of **cboFonts**:

```
Private Sub txtFillBox_KeyPress(KeyAscii As Integer)
  cBox.FindIndexStr txtFillBox, txtFillBox.Text, _
    KeyAscii, lstFonts, lstOutput
End Sub
```

   This code is essentially the same as that in the **KeyPress** event of **txtFillBox** in the previous example. The only difference is the addition of the parameter for the output list box.

   Test the code! Type **M** in the text box. The output list will list all fonts in the list box which begin with the letter "M." (See Figure 6-10.)

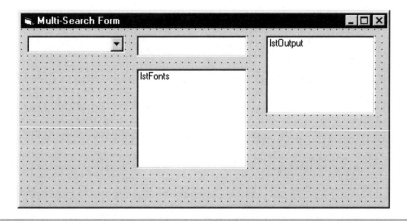

FIGURE 6-9.   Multicbo+ListSearch form in Design view

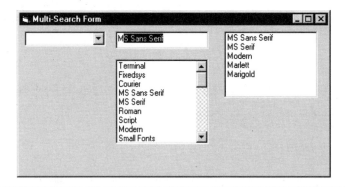

FIGURE 6-10.   Output of all matches in the list box

Retrieving Multiple List Selections Using SendMessage

SelectMultiSearch.vbp

List boxes can permit more than one item to be selected at one time. Combo boxes do not have this capability. The reason probably is that the text portion of the combo box is supposed to show the item selected in the combo box, and it would not be feasible for the text box to show multiple items.

The ability to make multiple selections can be quite useful. For example, in Windows Explorer, you can, with the SHIFT or CTRL key, choose multiple files to be moved, copied, or deleted. It would be quite tedious to have to repeat the same operation for each file.

This capability of making multiple selections is enabled simply by setting the **MultiSelect** property to one of the two multiple selection values described in Table 6-3.

Value	Constant	Description
0	vbMultiSelectNone	(Default) Multiple selection isn't allowed.
1	vbMultiSelectSimple	Simple multiple selection. A mouse click or pressing the SPACEBAR selects or deselects an item in the list. Arrow keys move the focus.
2	vbMultiSelectExtended	Extended multiple selection. Pressing SHIFT and clicking the mouse or pressing SHIFT and one of the arrow keys extends the selection from the previously selected item to the current item. Pressing the CTRL key and clicking the mouse selects or deselects an item in the list.

TABLE 6-3.   MultiSelect Styles for the List Box Control

Once the application user has made his or her multiple selections, those selections need to be retrieved. The List Box control has a **Selected** property. This property is an array of Boolean values. The number of values in the array, and their order, correspond with the number and order of the items in the list box. For example, if a list box contains four items, and the first and third are selected, but the second and fourth are not, the array would be True, False, True, False. Whether an item at index *i* was selected could be determined by whether **List.Selected(i)** was True or False.

Unfortunately, the List Box control has no property or method which permits the direct look-up of the selected indexes in the **Selected** array. Your code can loop through the **Selected** array to retrieve the items selected. However, as discussed in the previous example, this linear search is relatively slow. If the list box, and consequently the **Selected** array, contains hundreds of items, this linear search can degrade the performance of your application. If searches are frequent, the performance degradation is magnified.

Many applications permit the user to make multiple selections or deselections by Select All and Deselect All buttons. For example, by choosing the Custom option when installing an application, the application user may, in lieu of checking or unchecking the options which are checked or unchecked by default, select or deselect all of the options. However, the List Box control has no property or method which permits the direct selection or deselection of all items in a list box. As before, your code can loop through the **Selected** array and change all True items to False. However, this is a linear search and therefore will, as previously discussed, degrade the performance of your application.

Once again, the Windows API rides to the rescue.

SYNOPSIS OF CODE

The API function **SendMessage** is used to speed the look-up of the items which were selected by the application user. **SendMessage** first sends a LB_GETSELCOUNT message to retrieve the total number of selected items in a multiple-selection list box. That value is used to set the upper bound of an array. **SendMessage** next sends a LB_GETSELITEMS message to fill that array with an array of integers that specify the item numbers of selected items in a multiple-selection list box. Looping through this array is much faster than looping through the **Selected** array. For example, if a list box contains 1,000 items, but only 20 are selected, using the Windows API requires only 20 iterations instead of 1,000.

SendMessage also is used to quickly select or deselect all items. **SendMessage** simply sends a LB_SETSEL message to the list box to select or deselect, as the case may be, all items in the list box.

CODE

The code which is added is italicized.

```
Private Const LB_FINDSTRING As Long = &H18F
Private Const LB_ERR As Long = (-1)
Private Const CB_ERR As Long = (-1)
Private Const LB_GETSELCOUNT As Long = &H190
Private Const LB_GETSELITEMS As Long = &H191
Private Const LB_SETSEL As Long = &H185
Private Const CB_FINDSTRING As Long = &H14C
Private Const CB_SHOWDROPDOWN As Long = &H14F

Private Declare Function SendMessageStr Lib _
    "user32" Alias "SendMessageA" _
    (ByVal hwnd As Long, _
     ByVal wMsg As Long, _
     ByVal wParam As Long, _
     ByVal lParam As String) As Long

Private Declare Function SendMessageLong Lib _
    "user32" Alias "SendMessageA" _
    (ByVal hwnd As Long, _
     ByVal wMsg As Long, _
     ByVal wParam As Long, _
     ByVal lParam As Long) As Long

Private Declare Function SendMessageArray Lib _
    "user32" Alias "SendMessageA" _
    (ByVal hwnd As Long, _
     ByVal wMsg As Long, _
     ByVal wParam As Long, _
     lParam As Any) As Long

Public Sub FindIndexStr(ctlSource As Control, _
   ByVal str As String, intKey As Integer, _
   Optional ctlTarget As Variant, Optional ctlOutput As Variant)

Dim lngIdx As Long
Dim FindString As String

If (intKey < 32 Or intKey > 127) And _
   (Not (intKey = 13 Or intKey = 8)) Then Exit Sub
```

```
If Not intKey = 13 Or intKey = 8 Then
    If Len(ctlSource.Text) = 0 Then
        FindString = str & Chr$(intKey)
    Else
        FindString = Left$(str, ctlSource.SelStart) & Chr$(intKey)
    End If
End If


If intKey = 8 Then
    If Len(ctlSource.Text) = 0 Then Exit Sub
    Dim numChars As Integer
    numChars = ctlSource.SelStart - 1
    FindString = Left(str, numChars)
End If


If IsMissing(ctlTarget) And TypeName(ctlSource) = "ComboBox" Then
    Set ctlTarget = ctlSource
        If intKey = 13 Then
            Call SendMessageStr(ctlTarget.hwnd, _
                CB_SHOWDROPDOWN, True, 0&)
            Exit Sub
        End If
    lngIdx = SendMessageStr(ctlTarget.hwnd, _
        CB_FINDSTRING, -1, FindString)
ElseIf TypeName(ctlTarget) = "ListBox" Then
    If intKey = 13 Then Exit Sub
    lngIdx = SendMessageStr(ctlTarget.hwnd, _
            LB_FINDSTRING, -1, FindString)
    Dim i As Integer
    i = -1
    If lngIdx <> -1 Then
        i = lngIdx
If IsMissing(ctlOutput) Then
            Do
                i = SendMessageStr(ctlTarget.hwnd, _
                    LB_FINDSTRING, i, FindString)
                ToggleSelect ctlTarget, True, i
            Loop While i > lngIdx
        Else
            ctlOutput.Clear
            Do
                ctlOutput.AddItem ctlTarget.List(i)
```

```
                    i = SendMessageStr(ctlTarget.hwnd, _
                  LB_FINDSTRING, i, FindString)
              Loop While i > lngIdx
          End If
    End If

Else
    Exit Sub
End If
If lngIdx <> -1 Then
        ctlTarget.ListIndex = lngIdx
        If TypeName(ctlSource) = "TextBox" Then _
           ctlSource.Text = ctlTarget.List(lngIdx)
        ctlSource.SelStart = Len(FindString)
        ctlSource.SelLength = Len(ctlSource.Text) - _
             ctlSource.SelStart
End If
intKey = 0
End Sub


Public Sub FindMultiSelect(ctlSource As Control, _
   ctlTarget As Control, Optional fMove As Boolean)
Dim lngIdx As Long
Dim FindString As String
    If TypeName(ctlTarget) <> "ListBox" Then Exit Sub
    If ctlSource.MultiSelect = 0 Then Exit Sub
    Dim numSelected As Long
    Dim i As Integer
    numSelected = SendMessageLong(ctlSource.hwnd, _
       LB_GETSELCOUNT, 0&, 0&)
    If numSelected > 0 Then
       If IsMissing(fMove) Or fMove = False Then ctlTarget.Clear
       ReDim sselected(1 To numSelected) As Long
       lngIdx = SendMessageArray(ctlSource.hwnd, _
          LB_GETSELITEMS, numSelected, sselected(1))
       For i = 1 To numSelected
          ctlTarget.AddItem ctlSource.List(sselected(i))
       Next I

       If Not IsMissing(fMove) And fMove = True Then
          For i = 1 To numSelected
```

```
            ctlSource.RemoveItem (sselected(i) - (i - 1))
        Next I
      End If
    End If
End Sub


Public Sub ToggleSelect(ByVal ctlSource As Control, _
    flag As Boolean, idx As Integer)
    Call SendMessageLong(ctlSource.hwnd, LB_SETSEL, flag, idx)
End Sub
```

ANNOTATIONS

```
Private Const LB_GETSELCOUNT As Long = &H190
Private Const LB_GETSELITEMS As Long = &H191
```

The LB_GETSELCOUNT message retrieves the total number of selected items in a multiple-selection list box. Its return value is the count of selected items in the list box.

The LB_GETSELITEMS message fills a buffer with an array of integers that specify the index numbers of selected items in a multiple-selection list box. In other words, if the first, third and fourth of five items are selected, the integer array would be 0, 2, 3. The upper bound of the array is the value returned from the LB_GETSELCOUNT message.

```
Private Const LB_SETSEL As Long = &H185
```

The LB_SETSEL message selects or unselects, depending on whether a flag is set to True or False, either the item whose index is specified or all items if –1 is specified.

```
Private Declare Function SendMessageLong Lib _
    "user32" Alias "SendMessageA" _
    (ByVal hwnd As Long, _
    ByVal wMsg As Long, _
    ByVal wParam As Long, _
    ByVal lParam As Long) As Long


Private Declare Function SendMessageArray Lib _
    "user32" Alias "SendMessageA" _
    (ByVal hwnd As Long, _
    ByVal wMsg As Long, _
    ByVal wParam As Long, _
    lParam As Any) As Long
```

SendMessage, as has been discussed, is an API function by which you can send a message to a window or control. The *lParam* parameter may be a number, a string, an array, or a user-defined type, which not only affects the data type of *lParam*, but also whether it is passed *ByVal* or *ByRef*. Since *lParam* can be different data types, and may be passed either *ByVal* or *ByRef*, it has been recommended that the programmer use the **Alias** keyword in Visual Basic to define new **SendMessage** declares which are named to reflect the type of data being passed.

SendMessageStr, used in the previous examples, implemented this recommendation, just as **SendMessageLong** did in Chapter 5. These two implementations of **SendMessage** are used in this example, as well as a new implementation, **SendMessageArray**.

The *lParam* parameter in **SendMessageStr** is declared as a **String** and the *lParam* parameter in **SendMessageLong** is declared as a **Long** since these implementations of **SendMessage** concern **String** and **Long** parameters respectively. In both implementations the *lParam* parameter is passed *ByVal*.

The *lParam* parameter in **SendMessageArray** is declared as **Any** and is passed *ByRef*. The *lParam* is declared as **Any** and is passed *ByRef* if it passes an array or a user-defined type. Here it is passing an array. In addition, the sending of the message (by **SendMessageArray**) can assign values to the members of the array (or user-defined type) passed in the *lParam* parameter. In this example, the LB_GETSELITEMS message will be sent by **SendMessageArray** to fill an array of integers with the item numbers of selected items in a multiple-selection list box.

```
ElseIf TypeName(ctlTarget) = "ListBox" Then
    If intKey = 13 Then Exit Sub
    lngIdx = SendMessageStr(ctlTarget.hwnd, _
            LB_FINDSTRING, -1, FindString)
    Dim i As Integer
    i = -1
    If lngIdx <> -1 Then
        i = lngIdx
    If IsMissing(ctlOutput) Then
        Do
            i = SendMessageStr(ctlTarget.hwnd, _
                LB_FINDSTRING, i, FindString)
            ToggleSelect ctlTarget, True, i
        Loop While i > lngIdx
    Else
        ctlOutput.Clear
        Do
            ctlOutput.AddItem ctlTarget.List(i)
            i = SendMessageStr(ctlTarget.hwnd, _
                LB_FINDSTRING, i, FindString)
        Loop While i > lngIdx
    End If
```

The italicized code has been added. The code which precedes it was discussed in the preceding example. Briefly, that code calls **SendMessageStr** with the LB_FINDSTRING message to find the first item in the list box (*ctlTarget*) whose prefix matches the search string. **SendMessageStr**, with the LB_FINDSTRING message, will return the index of the found item, unless no item is found, in which case it will return –1.

Unless the return value is –1, the added code determines, in both the **If** and **Else** branches of the control structure, if there are any other items in the list box whose prefix matches the search string. This is done by calling **SendMessageStr** with the LB_FINDSTRING message inside of a Do While loop. However, the third parameter, the index after which the search starts, no longer is –1. Rather, that index is the index of the previously found item so the search will start after the previously found item. Otherwise the first item will be found again and again in an endless loop. The loop ends when the search comes full circle and the index of the previously found item becomes equal to the first found item. This is essentially the logic used in the previous example.

The **If Else** control structure branches depending on whether the *ctlOutput* parameter is missing. The *ctlOutput* parameter is passed if the intent is that the found items are to appear in **lstOutput**. The *ctlOutput* parameter is not passed if the found items will not appear in **lstOutput** until the MoveSelectLeft button is clicked. The difference in code is that if the *ctlOutput* parameter is not passed, then the statement is:

```
ToggleSelect ctlTarget, True, I
```

This statement calls the **ToggleSelect** function, discussed below, to select the found item. On the other hand, if the *ctlOutput* parameter is not passed, then the statement is:

```
ctlOutput.AddItem ctlTarget.List(i)
```

This statement simply adds the found item to **lstOutput**.

Since the two Do While loops are identical except for one line of code, they could be replaced with one Do While loop which, in each loop, tests by an **If** statement whether the *ctlOutput* parameter is missing, and depending on the result, either selects the found item in *ctlTarget* or adds the found item to **lstOutput**. The code could read:

```
If IsMissing(ctlOutput) Then ctlOutput.Clear
Do
    i = SendMessageStr(ctlTarget.hwnd, _
      LB_FINDSTRING, i, FindString)

  If IsMissing(ctlOutput) Then
     ToggleSelect ctlTarget, True, I
  Else
     ctlOutput.AddItem ctlTarget.List(i)
  End if
Loop While i > lngIdx
```

This alternative does have the virtue of making the *text* of your code *shorter* by replacing two Do While loops with one. However, it also has the vice of making the *running* of your code *longer*. The reason is that, in the code actually used, whether the *ctlOutput* parameter is missing is evaluated once, and then one of the two Do While loops executes depending on whether the parameter is missing. However, in the alternative above, whether the *ctlOutput* parameter is missing is evaluated during each iteration of the loop. This will slow down the running of your code because an evaluation is made many times rather than just once. The evaluation during each loop iteration of whether the *ctlOutput* parameter is missing also is unnecessary because the answer will not change as the loop is executing. If the *ctlOutput* parameter is missing at the start of the loop, then it is guaranteed to be missing at the end of the loop. Conversely, if the *ctlOutput* parameter is present at the start of the loop, then it is guaranteed to be present at the end of the loop.

```
Public Sub FindMultiSelect(ctlSource As Control, _
    ctlTarget As Control, Optional fMove As Boolean)
```

This function builds an array of the selected items in the list box.

```
Dim lngIdx As Long
Dim FindString As String
    If TypeName(ctlTarget) <> "ListBox" Then Exit Sub
```

This function only is implemented for list boxes. Accordingly, the **TypeName** function is used to check if *ctlTarget* is a list box. If it is not, then the subroutine ends. If *ctlTarget* is a list box, then the subroutine continues.

```
    If ctlSource.MultiSelect = 0 Then Exit Sub
```

This function only is implemented for list boxes which permit multiple selections. If multiple selections are not permitted then the subroutine ends. Otherwise, it continues.

```
    Dim numSelected As Long
    Dim i As Integer
    numSelected = SendMessageLong(ctlSource.hwnd, _
        LB_GETSELCOUNT, 0&, 0&)
```

An application sends an LB_GETSELCOUNT message to retrieve the total number of selected items in a multiple-selection list box. With this message, neither *wParam* nor *lParam* is used, so their values must be zero. Therefore, the third and fourth parameters of **SendMessageLong** are 0&. The & is a type declaration character to indicate a **Long** value. The return value, which is stored in the variable *numSelected*, is the count of selected items in the list box.

```
    If numSelected > 0 Then
        If IsMissing(fMove) Or fMove = False Then ctlTarget.Clear
```

If the *fMove* parameter is missing, then the intent is to display the search results in the output list. Therefore, the output list needs to be cleared to accurately show the results of the search. Otherwise the previous search results also would be in the output list.

On the other hand, if selected items are to be moved into the output list, the items which previously were selected should remain, since the intent is for the output list to display all items which have been selected, not only the items which just were selected.

```
ReDim sselected(1 To numSelected) As Long
```

An array is declared. Its upper bound is the number of items selected, as determined by the LB_GETSELCOUNT message.

```
lngIdx = SendMessageArray(ctlSource.hwnd, _
    LB_GETSELITEMS, numSelected, sselected(1))
```

The LB_GETSELITEMS message fills a buffer with an array of integers that specify the item numbers of selected items in a multiple-selection list box. In other words, if the first, third and fourth of five items are selected, the integer array would be 0, 2, 3. The upper bound of the array is the value returned from the LB_GETSELCOUNT message.

An application sends an LB_GETSELITEMS message to fill a buffer with an array of integers that specify the item numbers of selected items in a multiple-selection list box. With this message, *wParam* specifies the maximum number of selected items whose item numbers are to be placed in the buffer. This value is taken from the value returned from the LB_GETSELCOUNT message. *lParam* is a pointer to a buffer large enough for the number of items selected. This is the array whose upper bound is the value returned from the LB_GETSELCOUNT message.

```
For i = 1 To numSelected
    ctlTarget.AddItem ctlSource.List(sselected(i))
Next I
```

The selected items are added to the output list.

```
If Not IsMissing(fMove) And fMove = True Then
    For i = 1 To numSelected
        ctlSource.RemoveItem (sselected(i) - (i - 1))
    Next I
    End If
    End If
End Sub
```

If the *fMove* parameter is not missing, that means that the selected items are to be moved into the output list. Therefore, the items in the source list need to be removed so they cannot be chosen again. Otherwise, duplicates could appear in the output list.

The parameter of the **RemoveItem** method is the **ListIndex** of the item to be removed. However, the removal of items changes the index of those items below. Therefore, the index parameter for the **RemoveItem** method is adjusted by $i - 1$.

```
Public Sub ToggleSelect(ByVal ctlSource As Control, _
    flag As Boolean, idx As Integer)
    Call SendMessageLong(ctlSource.hwnd, LB_SETSEL, flag, idx)
End Sub
```

The LB_SETSEL message selects or unselects, depending on whether a flag is set to True or False, either the item whose index is specified or all items if an index of –1 is specified.

The LB_SETSEL message, like most messages, has two parameters, *wParam* and *lParam*. The *wParam* parameter, the *flag* parameter in **SendMessageLong**, specifies how to set the selection. If *wParam* is True, the string is selected and highlighted; if *wParam* is False, the highlight is removed and the string is no longer selected.

The *lParam* parameter, the *idx* parameter in **SendMessageLong**, specifies the zero-based index of the string to set. If *lParam* is –1, the selection is added to or removed from all strings, depending on whether *wParam* is True or False.

TEST THE CODE

1. Make a copy of the previous project and rename it SelectMultiSearch.vbp.

2. Add the controls described in Table 6-4.

Control Type	Control Name	Comments
List Box	lstOutput	
Command Button	cmdMoveSelectLeft	Caption is >. Purpose is to move items selected in list box on left to list box on right.
Command Button	cmdMoveAllLeft	Caption is >>. Purpose is to move all items in list box on left to list box on right.
Command Button	cmdMoveSelectRight	Caption is <. Purpose is to move items selected in list box on right to list box on left.
Command Button	cmdMoveAllRight	Caption is <<. Purpose is to move all items in list box on right to list box on left.
Command Button	cmdDeselect	Caption is Deselect All. Purpose is to deselect all selected items in list box on left.

TABLE 6-4.   Additional Controls for the Form in SelectMultiSearch.vbp

Your form should look like Figure 6-11.

3. Modify the code to the **KeyPress** event of **txtFillBox** to read as follows:

```
Private Sub txtFillBox_KeyPress(KeyAscii As Integer)
    cBox.FindIndexStr txtFillBox, txtFillBox.Text, _
      KeyAscii, lstFonts
End Sub
```

This is the same code as in the previous example except that the last parameter has been omitted. The reason is simply to show the new functionality, which is to select, rather than immediately list in the output box, the matching items. The command button **MoveSelectLeft** is used to move the selected items into the output list.

4. Add the following code to the **Click** event of **cmdMoveSelectLeft**:

```
Private Sub cmdMoveSelectLeft_Click()
  cBox.FindMultiSelect lstFonts, lstOutput, True
End Sub
```

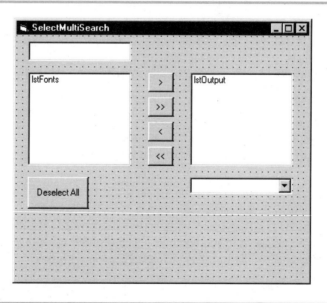

FIGURE 6-11. Form in SelectMultiSearch.vbp in Design view

This subroutine uses the **FindMultiSelect** method of **clsBoxSearch** to move the selected items in the list box in the first parameter to the list box in the second parameter.

5. Add the following code to the **Click** event of **cmdMoveAllLeft**:

```
Private Sub cmdMoveAllLeft_Click()
cBox.ToggleSelect lstFonts, True, -1
cBox.FindMultiSelect lstFonts, lstOutput, True
End Sub
```

This subroutine uses the **ToggleSelect** method of **clsBoxSearch** to select all of the items in the list box in the first parameter. It then uses the **FindMultiSelect** method of **clsBoxSearch** to move the selected items in the list box in the first parameter to the list box in the second parameter.

6. Add the following code to the **Click** event of **cmdMoveSelectRight**:

```
Private Sub cmdMoveSelectRight_Click()
 cBox.FindMultiSelect lstOutput, lstFonts, True
End Sub
```

This code is the converse of that in the **Click** event of **cmdMoveSelectLeft**.

7. Add the following code to the **Click** event of **cmdMoveAllRight**:

```
Private Sub cmdMoveAllRight_Click()
cBox.ToggleSelect lstOutput, True, -1
cBox.FindMultiSelect lstOutput, lstFonts, True
End Sub
```

This code is the converse of that in the **Click** event of **cmdMoveAllLeft**.

8. Add the following code to the **Click** event of **cmdDeselect**:

```
Private Sub cmdDeselect_Click()
cBox.ToggleSelect lstFonts, False, -1
cBox.ToggleSelect lstOutput, False, -1
End Sub
```

This subroutine uses the **ToggleSelect** method of **clsBoxSearch** to deselect all of the items in both list boxes.

Test the code! Typing **M** in the text box lists all fonts beginning with the letter "M." (See Figure 6-12.) Clicking the command button with the ">" caption then moves these items into the output box. (See Figure 6-13.)

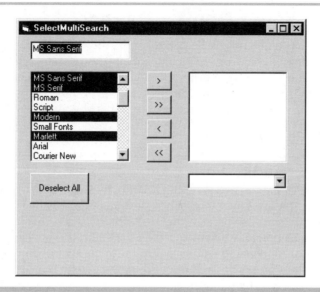

FIGURE 6-12. Selecting all fonts matching the search prefix

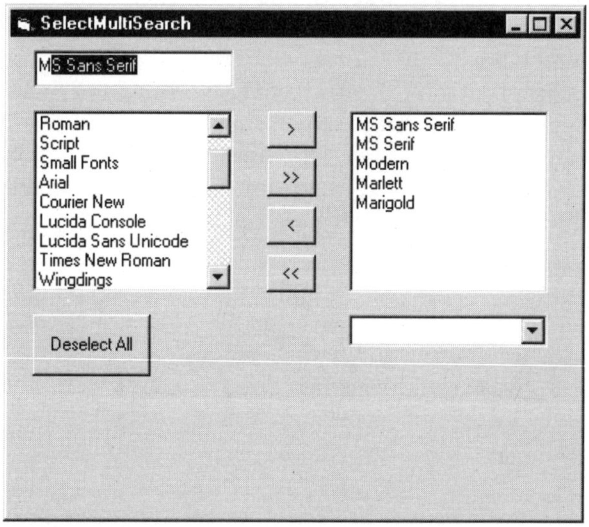

FIGURE 6-13. Moving selected fonts into the output list

cboHeight.vbp

Creating Taller Combo Boxes

The list box of the combo box, in its default style, the **vbComboDropDown** mode (see Table 6-1), includes a drop-down list and a text box. In that default style, the list box drops down when the application user clicks on the arrow on the right side of the text box (also referred to as the *edit area*). However, this means that, in order for the application user to drop down the list box, he or she must take his or her hands off the keyboard to click the mouse. Accordingly, previous examples in this chapter improved the functionality of the combo box by using the CB_SHOWDROPDOWN message to enable the application user to drop down the list box by pressing the ENTER key in the edit area.

While the use of the CB_SHOWDROPDOWN message makes it easier for the application user to drop down the list box portion of the combo box, it does not change the fact that, in Visual Basic, the drop-down list box displays only eight items. Your application may be enhanced by the ability to show a greater number of items (Visual Basic appears to enforce a minimum number of eight items). However, there are no built-in properties and methods of the combo box by which the number of items to be displayed by the drop-down list box may be increased.

SYNOPSIS OF CODE

Once again the Windows API permits you to go beyond the limitations of Visual Basic. The CB_GETITEMHEIGHT message determines the height of an item in the combo box. That height is multiplied by the number of items to be displayed. The **MoveWindow** API function, discussed in Chapter 5, then is used to resize and reposition the combo box.

If this sounds simple, it isn't. Twips have to be converted to pixels, client coordinates have to be converted to screen coordinates, and screen coordinates have to be converted to client coordinates. However, these conversions have been done before in prior chapters. Besides, if programming were easy, everyone could do it. That's why we programmers make the big bucks!

CODE

Add the following declarations to the class module:

```
Private Const CB_GETITEMHEIGHT As Long = &H154
```

Add the following subroutine to the class module:

```
Public Sub BoxHeight(frm As Form, cbo As ComboBox, num As Long)
    Dim pt As POINTAPI
    Dim rc As RECT
    Dim cWidth As Long
    Dim newHeight As Long
    Dim editHeight As Long
    Dim oldScaleMode As Long
    Dim numItemsToDisplay As Long
    Dim itemHeight As Long
    cWidth = cbo.Width \ Screen.TwipsPerPixelX
    itemHeight = SendMessageLong(cbo.hWnd, CB_GETITEMHEIGHT, 0, 0)
    editHeight = SendMessageLong(cbo.hWnd, CB_GETITEMHEIGHT, -1, 0)
    newHeight = (itemHeight * num) + (editHeight * 2)
    Call GetWindowRect(cbo.hWnd, rc)
    pt.x = rc.Left
    pt.y = rc.Top
    Call ScreenToClient(frm.hWnd, pt)
    Call MoveWindow(cbo.hWnd, pt.x, pt.y, cWidth, newHeight, True)
End Sub
```

ANNOTATIONS

```
Private Const CB_GETITEMHEIGHT As Long = &H154
```

A CB_GETITEMHEIGHT message is sent by **SendMessage** to determine the height of items in a combo box.

```
Public Sub BoxHeight(frm As Form, cbo As ComboBox, num As Long)
```

This subroutine has three parameters. The first parameter is the form that contains the combo box. The second parameter is the combo box. The third parameter is the number of items to be displayed.

```
Dim pt As POINTAPI
```

A number of Windows API functions, including two used in this example, have as a parameter a POINT structure. This structure, which has been discussed in examples in previous chapters, has two members which hold the x and y

coordinates, respectively, of a point. Also as in preceding examples, a user-defined type, **POINTAPI**, is declared to parallel the structure used by the API function.

```
Dim rc As RECT
```

A RECT structure also is a parameter to a number of Windows API functions, including one used in this example. This structure, which has been discussed in examples in previous chapters, has four members. These members specify, respectively, the x coordinate of the upper-left corner of the rectangle (left), the y coordinate of the upper-left corner of the rectangle (top), the x coordinate of the lower-right corner of the rectangle (right), and the y coordinate of the lower-right corner of the rectangle (bottom). Also as in preceding examples, a user-defined type, also named **RECT**, is declared to parallel the structure used by the API function. It does bear repetition, as this issue often causes errors which are hard to identify, that the members of the user-defined type must be declared in the same order as in the structure, that is, left, top, right, and bottom.

```
Dim cWidth As Long
```

This variable will hold the width of the combo box.

```
Dim newHeight As Long
```

This variable will hold the height of the combo box required to display the desired number of items—in this example, ten.

```
Dim editHeight As Long
Dim itemHeight As Long
```

The *editHeight* variable will hold the height of the edit area in the combo box. The *itemHeight* variable will hold the height of a list item in the list box portion of the combo box.

```
cWidth = cbo.Width \ Screen.TwipsPerPixelX
```

The variable *cWidth*, which is to hold the width of the combo box, is assigned the value of the **Width** property of the combo box divided by the number of twips per pixel in the screen's width. This division is necessary because the **Width** property of the combo box is measured in twips while API functions use pixels. The number of twips per pixel in the screen's width is determined by the **Screen** object's **TwipsPerPixelX** property.

```
itemHeight = SendMessageLong(cbo.hWnd, CB_GETITEMHEIGHT, 0, 0)
editHeight = SendMessageLong(cbo.hWnd, CB_GETITEMHEIGHT, -1, 0)
```

A CB_GETITEMHEIGHT message is sent by **SendMessage** to determine the height of items in a combo box. The *wParam* parameter specifies the combo box component whose height is to be retrieved. This parameter is –1 to retrieve the height of the selection field and 0 to retrieve the height of list items. Here, a parameter of 0 is passed to assign to *itemHeight* the height of list items and then the parameter –1 is passed to assign to *editHeight* the height of the edit area.

With a CB_GETITEMHEIGHT message, the *lParam* parameter always is 0.

```
newHeight = (itemHeight * num) + (editHeight * 2)
```

The *newHeight* variable holds the height of the combo box required to display the desired number of items—in this example, ten. The *itemHeight* variable, as a result of the CB_GETITEMHEIGHT message sent by **SendMessage**, holds the height of list items. However, simply multiplying *itemHeight* by the desired number of items to display (the *num* parameter) will result in an insufficient height to display this number of items. The height of the edit area (*editHeight*) needs to be added to take into account the size of the edit area as it relates to the height of a list item. The height of the edit area is multiplied by two to compensate for borders and rounding off.

```
Call GetWindowRect(cbo.hWnd, rc)
```

GetWindowRect is an API function which was discussed in Chapter 5. It assigns to its second parameter a variable (*rc*) of the **RECT** user-defined type, the position of the rectangle of the window whose handle is passed as the first parameter.

```
pt.x = rc.Left
pt.y = rc.Top
```

As a result of the **GetWindowRect** call just discussed, the *rc* variable of the **RECT** user-defined type holds the left-top and right-bottom coordinates of the combo box. The coordinates retrieved by **GetWindowRect** are screen coordinates, that is, they are relative to the upper-left corner of the screen.

The left and top coordinates are assigned to the *x* and *y* members of a variable (*pt*) of a **POINTAPI** user-defined type.

```
Call ScreenToClient(frm.hWnd, pt)
```

Previous chapters have discussed the API function **ClientToScreen**. That function converts the client coordinates of a specified point to screen coordinates. The API function **ScreenToClient** does the converse. It converts the screen coordinates of a specified point on the screen to client coordinates.

In this example, the *pt* variable holds the screen coordinates of the top-left corner of the combo box. These coordinates need to be converted to the client coordinates relative to the position of the form. Why this is necessary is explained next in the annotation to the call to **MoveWindow**.

The first parameter of **ScreenToClient** is the handle to the window whose client area will be used for the conversion. That window is the form, because the screen coordinates of the top-left corner of the combo box need to be converted to the client coordinates relative to the position of the form. The second parameter is a variable (*pt*) of the **POINTAPI** user-defined type in which the client coordinates will be stored.

```
    Call MoveWindow(cbo.hWnd, pt.x, pt.y, cWidth, newHeight, True)
End Sub
```

The **MoveWindow** function changes the position and dimensions of the window whose handle is passed as the first parameter. For a top-level window, the position and dimensions are relative to the upper-left corner of the screen. For a child window, they are relative to the upper-left corner of the parent window's client area.

In this example, the window whose handle is passed as the first parameter is the combo box, which is a child window of the form which contains it. Therefore, the second and third arguments of **MoveWindow** are the *x* and *y* coordinates respectively of the top-left corner of the combo box *relative* to the upper-left corner of the form's client area.

Since the combo box is a child window of the form that contains it, its coordinates must be relative to the upper-left corner of the form. However, the coordinates of the upper-left corner of the combo box retrieved by the call to **GetWindowRect** were screen coordinates. Therefore, these screen coordinates had to be converted to client coordinates by the call **ScreenToClient** so those coordinates could be passed as parameters to **MoveWindow**.

TEST THE CODE

Add the line of code shown unbolded to the **Load** event of the form:

```
Private Sub Form_Load()
    Dim i As Integer
    Dim max As Integer
    max = Screen.FontCount
    If max > 35 Then max = 35
    For i = 1 To max
       lstFonts.AddItem Screen.Fonts(i)
       cboFonts.AddItem Screen.Fonts(i)
       Next I
    cBox.BoxHeight Me, cboFonts, 10
End Sub
```

The last parameter is the number of items to show. In this example it is hard-coded. In an actual application the number of items would not be hard-coded. Instead, it could be set as a preference of the application user, saved to the registry, and then read in from the registry when the application is loaded.

Test the code! When the ENTER key is pressed, ten items, not eight, are shown. (See Figure 6-14.)

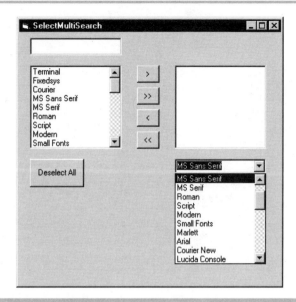

FIGURE 6-14. Ten items displayed by the combo box

cboWidth.vbp

Auto-Resizing the Combo Box Width

One of the features of a combo box is that the application user can add items to it during the running of the application. However, if the width of the item is longer than the width of the combo box, the combo box will not resize its width. Instead, part of the item is cut off. (See Figure 6-15.)

One solution is to size the combo box to be wide enough to accommodate a very long string. However, this takes up space on the form and also makes your application look less than professional.

The solution (as usual) is the Windows API.

SYNOPSIS OF CODE

The Windows API function **GetTextExtentPoint32** is used to calculate the width of the longest item in the list box. The longest width then is stored in a variable in the class module. A CB_SETDROPPEDWIDTH message then is sent by **SendMessage** to resize the width of the combo box in accordance with the value of that variable. When an item is added, the width of the new item is calculated, again by

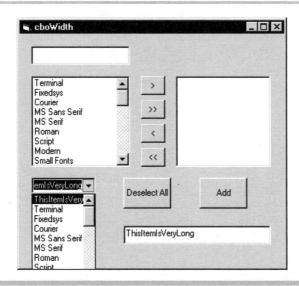

FIGURE 6-15.   The combo box does not resize the width for a long added item

GetTextExtentPoint32. If the new item is wider than the previous ones, then its width is stored in the variable, and the combo box is resized, again by **SendMessage** sending a CB_SETDROPPEDWIDTH message.

Again, there are complexities, this time new ones, concerning device contexts, stock fonts, and other new concepts. However, these complexities are easily surmountable.

CODE

The following constants should be added to the class module:

```
Private Const CB_SETDROPPEDWIDTH As Long = &H160
Private Const SYSTEM_FONT As Long = 13
```

The following variable needs to be added:

```
Private lngStringWidth As Long
```

The following additional user-defined type needs to be added to the class module:

```
Private Type SIZE
   cx As Long
   cy As Long
End Type
```

The following API functions need to be declared:

```
Private Declare Function GetStockObject Lib "gdi32" _
   (ByVal nIndex As Long) As Long

Private Declare Function DeleteObject Lib "gdi32" _
   (ByVal hObject As Long) As Long

Private Declare Function ReleaseDC Lib "user32" _
   (ByVal hwnd As Long, ByVal hDc As Long) As Long

Private Declare Function GetDC Lib "user32" _
   (ByVal hwnd As Long) As Long

Private Declare Function SelectObject Lib "gdi32" _
   (ByVal hDc As Long, ByVal hObject As Long) As Long

Private Declare Function GetTextExtentPoint32 _
      Lib "gdi32" Alias "GetTextExtentPoint32A" _
      (ByVal hDc As Long, _
      ByVal lpsz As String, _
      ByVal cbString As Long, _
      lpSize As SIZE) As Long
```

Add the following code to the **Initialize** event of the class module:

```
Private Sub Class_Initialize()
   lngStringWidth = 0
End Sub
```

Add the following subroutine to the class module:

```
Public Sub SetBoxWidth(frm As Form, cbo As ComboBox)
   Call SendMessageLong(cbo.hwnd, CB_SETDROPPEDWIDTH, _
               lngStringWidth, 0)
End Sub
```

Finally, add the following function to the class module:

```
Public Function SetMaxWidth(frm As Form, str As String) As Long

Dim hFont As Long
   Dim hFontOld As Long
   Dim hDc As Long
```

```
   Dim sz As SIZE
   hDc = GetDC(frm.hwnd)
   hFont = GetStockObject(SYSTEM_FONT)
   hFontOld = SelectObject(hDc, hFont&)
   Call GetTextExtentPoint32(hDc, str, Len(str), sz)
   If sz.cx > lngStringWidth Then lngStringWidth = sz.cx
   Call SelectObject(hDc, hFontOld)
   Call DeleteObject(hFont)
   Call ReleaseDC(frm.hwnd, hDc)
   SetMaxWidth = lngStringWidth
End Function
```

ANNOTATIONS

```
Private Const CB_SETDROPPEDWIDTH As Long = &H160
```

The CB_SETDROPPEDWIDTH message, sent by **SendMessage**, sets the maximum allowable width, in pixels, of the list box portion of a combo box with the **vbComboDropDown** or **vbComboDropDownList** style (see Table 6-1). This message will be used to resize the width of the list box portion of the combo box.

```
Private Const SYSTEM_FONT As Long = 13
```

This constant specifies the System font. This is a proportional font based on the Windows character set, and is used by the operating system to display window titles, menu names, and text in dialog boxes. It will be used as the font to determine the length in pixels of an item.

An advantage of using the System font is that it is always available. Other fonts are available only if they are installed.

```
Private lngStringWidth As Long
```

This variable will hold the length in pixels of the longest item in the combo box. The **SetMaxWidth** function discussed below will set its value.

```
Private Sub Class_Initialize()
   lngStringWidth = 0
End Sub
```

The **Initialize** event occurs when a variable of a class is instantiated. This event occurs when a class variable is explicitly instantiated, such as:

```
Dim var as ClassSomething
Set var = New ClassSomething
```

The **Initialize** event also occurs when a variable of a class is instantiated. This event occurs when a class variable is implicitly instantiated, such as when the variable, already declared with the **New** statement, first uses a property or method:

```
Dim var as New Class Something
var.SomeMethod
```

The **Initialize** event is a good place to initialize variables. In this case, the initial value of *lngStringWidth*, which will hold the length in pixels of the longest item in the combo box, is set to zero.

```
Private Type SIZE
    cx As Long
    cy As Long
End Type
```

The SIZE structure is used by API functions. It specifies the width and height of a rectangle. Its members, **cx** and **cy**, specify the *x* and *y* extent, respectively, of the rectangle. As in many other previous examples, a user-defined type is declared to parallel the structure used by the API function involved.

```
Private Declare Function GetDC Lib "user32" _
    (ByVal hwnd As Long) As Long
```

The **GetDC** function retrieves a handle to display a device context for the specified window. A *device context* is a Windows data structure containing information about the drawing attributes of a device such as a display or a printer. The handle returned by **GetDC** is used by other GDI (graphics device interface) functions. The use of **GetDC** is discussed in the annotation that follows where it is called.

```
Private Declare Function GetStockObject Lib "gdi32" _
    (ByVal nIndex As Long) As Long
```

The **GetStockObject** function retrieves a handle to one of the predefined stock pens, brushes, fonts, or palettes. In this example it will be used to retrieve a handle to the System font.

```
Private Declare Function SelectObject Lib "gdi32" _
    (ByVal hDc As Long, ByVal hObject As Long) As Long
```

The **SelectObject** function selects an object into the specified device context. The new object replaces the previous object of the same type. In this example, the **SelectObject** function will be used to select the System font into the device context.

```
Private Declare Function DeleteObject Lib "gdi32" _
    (ByVal hObject As Long) As Long
```

The **DeleteObject** function deletes a logical pen, brush, font, bitmap, region, or palette, freeing all system resources associated with the object. In this example, it will be used to delete the System font from the device context.

```
Private Declare Function ReleaseDC Lib "user32" _
    (ByVal hwnd As Long, ByVal hDc As Long) As Long
```

The **ReleaseDC** function releases a device context (DC), freeing it for use by other applications.

```
Private Declare Function GetTextExtentPoint32 _
    Lib "gdi32" Alias "GetTextExtentPoint32A" _
    (ByVal hDc As Long, _
    ByVal lpsz As String, _
    ByVal cbString As Long, _
    lpSize As SIZE) As Long
```

The **GetTextExtentPoint32** function computes the width and height of the specified string of text, and stores this information in a **SIZE** object.

```
Public Sub SetBoxWidth(frm As Form, cbo As ComboBox)
    Call SendMessageLong(cbo.hwnd, CB_SETDROPPEDWIDTH, _
lngStringWidth, 0)
End Sub
```

The CB_SETDROPPEDWIDTH message, sent by **SendMessage**, sets the maximum allowable width, in pixels, of the list box portion of a combo box with the **vbComboDropDown** or **vbComboDropDownList** style (see Table 6-1). This message will be used to resize the width of the list box portion of the combo box.

The *wParam* parameter is the width of the list box portion in pixels. This value is held by *lngStringWidth*. The method by which *lngStringWidth* is assigned a value is discussed below in the annotation to **SetMaxWidth**. The *lParam* parameter is not used, and must be zero.

```
Public Function SetMaxWidth(frm As Form, str As String) As Long
```

This function will be used to assign a value to *lngStringWidth*, which holds the number of pixels of the longest string in the combo box.

```
Dim hFont As Long
    Dim hFontOld As Long
```

These variables will be used to hold a handle to the fonts which are "selected in" and "selected out." What this means is discussed below in the annotation to **SelectObject**.

```
    Dim hDc As Long
```

This variable will hold the handle to the device context.

```
    Dim sz As SIZE
```

This variable will hold an instance of a **SIZE** user-defined type. It will be used in the API function **GetTextExtentPoint32**.

```
hDc = GetDC(frm.hwnd)
```

The **GetDC** function retrieves a handle to display a device context for the specified window or the entire screen. It has one parameter, which is either a handle to the window whose device context is to be retrieved, or **NULL** if the screen device context is to be retrieved. This handle is stored in the variable *hDc*, whose use in discussed in the following annotations.

```
hFont = GetStockObject(SYSTEM_FONT)
```

The **GetStockObject** function retrieves a handle to one of the predefined stock pens, brushes, fonts, or palettes. The system provides six stock fonts. A *stock font* is a logical font that an application can obtain by calling the **GetStockObject** function and passing a value that identifies the requested font. Table 6-5 lists the six values that you can specify to obtain a stock font.

Value	Meaning
ANSI_FIXED_FONT	Specifies a monospace font based on the Windows character set. A Courier font is typically used.
ANSI_VAR_FONT	Specifies a proportional font based on the Windows character set. MS Sans Serif is typically used.
DEVICE_DEFAULT_FONT	Specifies the preferred font for the given device. This is typically the System font for display devices; however, for some dot-matrix printers this is a font that is resident on the device. (Printing with this font is usually faster than printing with a downloaded, bitmapped font.)
OEM_FIXED_FONT	Specifies a monospace font based on an OEM character set. For IBM® computers and compatibles, the OEM font is based on the IBM PC character set.
SYSTEM_FONT	Specifies the System font. This is a proportional font based on the Windows character set, and is used by the operating system to display window titles, menu names, and text in dialog boxes. The System font is always available. Other fonts are available only if they have been installed.
SYSTEM_FIXED_FONT	Specifies a monospace font compatible with the System font in Windows versions earlier than 3.0.

TABLE 6-5.   Stock Fonts

In this case the variable *hFont* will hold the handle to the System font.

```
hFontOld = SelectObject(hDc, hFont&)
```

The **SelectObject** function selects an object into the specified device context. The new object replaces the previous object of the same type. In this example, the **SelectObject** function will be used to select the System font into the device context. The first parameter is the handle to the device context. That handle, stored in the variable *hDc*, was obtained by the previous call to **GetDC**. The second parameter is the handle to the font that is being selected into the device context. Here, the second parameter is *hFont*, which is the handle to the System font obtained by the prior call to **GetStockObject**.

The return value of **SelectObject** is the handle of the object being replaced. That handle is stored in the variable *hOldFont*. The return value is saved so the font being used by the application can be restored when this function finishes.

```
Call GetTextExtentPoint32(hDc, str, Len(str), sz)
```

The **GetTextExtentPoint32** function computes the width and height of the specified string of text. The first parameter is the handle to the device context. That handle, stored in the variable *hDc*, was obtained by the previous call to **GetDC**. Its second parameter is a pointer to a string of text. In this example, that string was the second parameter to **SetMaxWidth** and is the item being added to the combo box. The third parameter is the number of characters in the string. That value is obtained by the **Len** function, which takes as a parameter the string whose length needs to be determined. The fourth and final parameter of **GetTextExtentPoint32** is a SIZE object in which the dimensions of the string are to be returned. In this example, only the width and not the height of the string is of interest.

```
If sz.cx > lngStringWidth Then lngStringWidth = sz.cx
```

If the width of the newly added item, represented by *sz.cx*, is greater than the previously longest width, represented by *lngStringWidth*, then *sz.cx* is assigned to the *lngStringWidth* variable.

```
Call SelectObject(hDc, hFontOld)
```

The handle of the font which was used by the application before this function started executing, represented by *hFontOld*, was saved when **SelectObject** was called before to select the System font. Now the former font is selected back in. There is no reason to save the handle to the System font, so the return value of **SelectObject** is ignored by use of the **Call** statement.

```
Call DeleteObject(hFont)
```

The **DeleteObject** function deletes a logical pen, brush, font, bitmap, region, or palette, freeing all system resources associated with the object. In this example, it will be used to delete the System font from the device context.

```
Call ReleaseDC(frm.hwnd, hDc)
```

The **ReleaseDC** function releases the device context, freeing system resources.

```
SetMaxWidth = lngStringWidth
End Function
```

The value lngStringWidth is returned by the function. In this example, that return value is not used, but it could be useful in other situations.

TEST THE CODE

1. Add to the previous project a Text Box control named **txtCombo** and a command button named **cmdAddCombo**. The purpose of these controls is that the text in **txtCombo** is added to the combo box **cboFonts** when **cmdAddCombo** is clicked. The form should look like Figure 6-16.

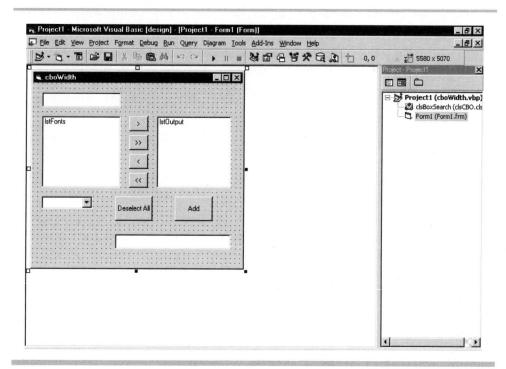

FIGURE 6-16. The cboWidth form in Design view

2. Add the lines of code shown unbolded to the **Load** event of the form:

```
Private Sub Form_Load()
   Dim i As Integer
   Dim max As Integer
   max = Screen.FontCount
   If max > 35 Then max = 35
   For i = 1 To max
      lstFonts.AddItem Screen.Fonts(i)
      cboFonts.AddItem Screen.Fonts(i)
      Call cBox.SetMaxWidth(Me, Screen.Fonts(i))
      Next I
   cBox.BoxHeight Me, cboFonts, 10
   cBox.SetBoxWidth Me, cboFonts
End Sub
```

There is a call to the **SetMaxWidth** method of the class module each time an item is added to the combo box. The width of the new item is compared to the previously widest item and the larger of the two widths is stored as the widest width of the combo box.

The call to the **SetBoxWidth** method of the class module resizes the combo box in accordance with the widest item.

3. Add the following code to the **Click** event of **cmdAddCombo**:

```
Private Sub cmdAddCombo_Click()
If Len(txtAddCombo.Text) > 0 Then _
   cboFonts.AddItem txtAddCombo.Text, 0
   Call cBox.SetMaxWidth(Me, txtAddCombo.Text)
   cBox.BoxWidth Me, cboFonts
End Sub
```

If there is text in **txtAddCombo**, then it is added as the first item to **cboFonts**. Next, the newly added string is passed to the **SetMaxWidth** method of the class module. The reason is that, if the newly added string is wider than the previously widest item in the combo box, the variable holding that information will be updated. The **BoxWidth** method of the class module then is called to resize the combo box.

Test the code! Enter a long string. The combo box will resize to accommodate the length of the new string. (See Figure 6-17.)

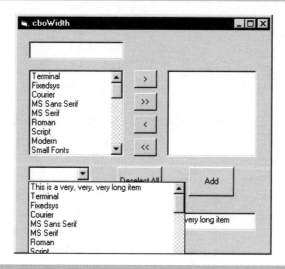

FIGURE 6-17. Auto-resizing the combo box width

ActiveX Controls

In the beginning—O.K., in 1991, Microsoft created Visual Basic. Programming Windows applications would never be the same. Previously, Windows applications were written in C. Writing even the "Hello World" Windows program in C was no trivial task. Indeed, many would-be C Windows programmers ended up writing "Goodbye Cruel World."

Visual Basic was different. An application window (the form) could be created without having to write one line of code. Controls could be added to the form also without code, simply by dropping them onto the form. Further, the properties of the controls (and the form also) easily could be set at design time through a graphical user interface.

Few controls came with Version 1.0 of Visual Basic. However, custom controls could be added to the Visual Basic toolbox. Some of these custom controls improved on existing Visual Basic controls (such as a "better" Text Box control). Other custom controls had no parallel, even in a simplified form, among the standard Visual Basic controls. In either case, the custom controls, once added, became as much a part of the Visual Basic integrated development environment (IDE) as the built-in controls.

These custom controls, which extended the Visual Basic IDE, not surprisingly were called VBX (Visual Basic eXtension) controls. There were two ways (at least *legal* ways) for Visual Basic developers to obtain these controls. One alternative, harkening back to the pioneer spirit that built this country, was for Visual Basic developers to write the controls themselves. However, writing VBX controls required a sophisticated knowledge of C or C++ and the Windows Software Developers Kit (SDK), and avoiding the complexity of C Windows programming was, after all, the initial reason for Visual Basic's existence.

Another alternative was suggested by the words of a famous but not-to-be named athlete: "I don't read or write real good, but I have the money to hire people who read and write real good." Developers who lacked the knowledge of C and the Windows SDK to write their own controls could buy them instead.

The demand for VBXs created a new breed of third-party independent software vendors (ISVs) who made these custom controls. In turn, the variety of relatively inexpensive custom controls created by the ISVs made Visual Basic even more popular, which led to more Visual Basic developers, which led to more demand for custom controls, and so on.

VBX controls have gone the way of dinosaurs and 16-bit Windows. They were succeeded in 32-bit Windows by OLE custom controls, initially referred to as OCXs and later, through the magic of marketing, as ActiveX controls (more on this later). However, VBXs were the first step towards building applications with "reusable software components."

"Reusable software components" is the computer programming equivalent of motherhood and apple pie. It is a positive concept but too often remains just that—a concept, untranslated to reality. Perhaps this is because the concept, while simply worded, rarely is explained.

Software is "reusable" when it can be used in many different applications. For example, a Visual Basic Combo Box control can be reused in application after application simply by adding it to a form.

However, a Combo Box control would be of little use, reusable or not, if you, as the programmer, could not control its features (properties), actions (methods), and reactions (events). For example, a Combo Box control includes a **ListIndex** property by which the index of the selected item can be accessed, an **AddItem** method by which an item can be added to the **ListBox** combo box, and a **Click** event which fires when a mouse clicks on the combo box or an item in it. Having properties, methods, and events is the hallmark of a software "component."

Reusable software components held out great promise. A programmer could write a control that either improved on or added to the Visual Basic toolbox and then leverage the development time by using the control in many different applications.

For example, the "smart search" combo box discussed in Chapter 6 could be used effectively in many different types of applications. The project in Chapter 6 is a standard Combo Box control accompanied by a class module. To enable a standard Combo Box control to have smart-search capability, the class module would have to be added to every application that uses the "smart search" combo box.

Life is much easier if the standard Combo Box control is converted into an ActiveX control. Once converted, the control need only be dropped onto the application form. No class module or other code would need to be added.

While the concept of "reusable software components" held out great promise, turning that concept into reality was easier said than done. Rather large books have been written on how to write code components so that their properties, methods, and events may be accessed using the Component Object Model (COM). The 32-bit Windows successors of VBX controls, OCX controls, are based on COM. OCXs, like the VBXs before them, were written in C or C++, and also required a thorough knowledge of COM. Needless to say, OCXs were difficult to write.

Version 5 of Visual Basic was a breakthrough in OCX development. Visual Basic developers now could write their own OCXs (a.k.a. ActiveX controls) without having to know C/C++ or COM. The ActiveX control could be created in the Visual Basic IDE with only Visual Basic code. This is consistent with Visual Basic's promise of enabling Windows programming without the complexity of C or C++.

Buy vs. Build

Now that ActiveX controls can be created in the Visual Basic IDE with only Visual Basic code, building your own control is a viable alternative to buying one. Indeed, the subject of this chapter is how to build your own ActiveX control. Nevertheless, with so many well-written, reasonably priced and royalty-free controls available, you may be asked by an interested party (such as your boss) why the company should invest thousands of dollars in development time when it could spend a few hundred dollars and have a professionally written control.

The response you should give your boss is an explanation of the advantages of building your own control. First, the control can be customized to meet your needs. The ISV-built controls normally are quite good. However, since these controls have to meet the needs of a wide range of customers, they necessarily are "one size fits all" and therefore somewhat generic.

Even if the ISV-built control currently meets your needs, business needs change. If changes in the business require changes in or additions to the control, you can make these changes without having to put them on the vendor's "wish list" and hope they are adopted in the "next release."

Second, another consequence of the ISV-built controls being "one size fits all" is that the control contains more features than you can possibly use. A control may offer over 200 methods, properties, and events, but you may only need to use 20. These additional features might be desirable to someone else with different needs, but for you they are only flab that makes the control unnecessarily large and slow.

Third, by writing your own control, you will be able to limit the number of resources that need to be shipped with the control. Yet another consequence of the ISV-built controls being "one size fits all" is their reliance on a plethora of DLLs which would need to be shipped with your application. Alternatively, by tailoring your control to your needs, you can limit the number of DLLs.

The fourth and final reason is the most important: What if something goes wrong? For example, it is not unusual for OCXs to have memory leaks. Since you have access to and control over the source code, you can fix the problem. Your boss, of course, has access to and control over the employees who have access to and control over the source code, and can give them the "S" speech. For those of you unfamiliar with that motivational tool, it goes, "Salary begins with 'S' and sweat begins with 'S'; get the message?" Needless to say, the same speech given to an ISV would fall on deaf ears.

Clearly, there are circumstances when a control should be built rather than bought. However, before turning to how to build an ActiveX control, it is worthwhile to discuss what an ActiveX control is. For that matter, what is ActiveX?

ActiveX—What's In a Name?

As discussed above, when 32-bit Windows replaced 16-bit Windows, OCX controls replaced VBX controls. Windows is still 32-bit, but the controls no longer are referred to as OCX. Instead, the controls are referred to as ActiveX.

What happened to OCX controls? The answer is: nothing. Indeed, ActiveX controls often have the extension .ocx. Microsoft just changed the name of OCX controls to ActiveX controls. Why? Not being on a first-name (or even last-name) basis with Bill Gates, we do not know for certain. However, an educated guess is that changing the name to ActiveX was a marketing move. Certainly "ActiveX" sounds sexier than "OCX." Of course, it probably is a sad commentary on the life of certain computer programmers (like these authors maybe) that we would use the word "sexier" in the context of a code component.

Since this book is for computer programmers and not advertising agency executives, the more interesting question is: What is an ActiveX (or OCX) control?

A technical answer is that ActiveX controls—and also ActiveX Servers, which are the subject of Chapter 12—comply with COM. Several thick books have been written on COM. However, you do not need to worry about COM's nuances. Your ActiveX control will comply with COM if you create it using (correctly, of course) the Visual Basic IDE. This is just another example of how Visual Basic makes your life easier.

Trying to describe ActiveX controls is no easy task. ActiveX controls are a hybrid. They have code. However, unlike other code components, they also have a visual component. The visual component is like a form, but it is not a form; rather, it is a "UserControl." Unlike forms, ActiveX controls cannot exist outside of a container. The container itself usually is a Visual Basic form. In addition, developers do not create controls, but rather use them as consumers. If you find this a bit confusing, you are not alone.

An approach that is superior to attempting to define an ActiveX control was suggested by a Justice of the United States Supreme Court. This learned judge, while unable to define obscenity, nevertheless confidently asserted: "I know it when I see it." Of course, we all have seen code that would fit the definition of obscenity. At the risk of a bad analogy, you'll know an ActiveX control when you create one.

xcbo.vbg

Converting a "Smart Search" Combo Box into an ActiveX Control

The combo box in the cboHeight.vbp project in Chapter 6 enhanced the standard Combo Box control in three respects. First, the Combo Box control had a "smart search" capability. Second, it was capable of showing more than eight items in its drop-down list. Third, it resized the width of its drop-down list to accommodate the widest item.

This project will turn the enhanced combo box into an ActiveX control which can be reused in many applications. Since the code is essentially unchanged from that in the cboHeight.vbp project in Chapter 6, the format of this chapter will be different from the previous chapters. Instead of starting with code, followed by annotations of the code, here we will give step-by-step instructions to convert the existing code into an ActiveX control.

SYNOPSIS OF CODE

There are three stages to converting the existing code into an ActiveX control. First, an ActiveX control project is created. Next, a Standard Exe project is created to test the ActiveX control. Finally, once we are satisfied that the ActiveX control works properly, it is compiled into an .ocx file.

While the code for the ActiveX control already has been written, converting the code into an ActiveX control is no simple task, and involves a number of nuances. However, the ability to perform intellectually difficult tasks is why we programmers are admired for our intelligence, make good money, and are irresistible to the opposite sex (well, two out of three ain't bad).

CONVERTING THE CODE

1. Create a new project. However, this time the project is not Standard Exe. Rather, it is ActiveX Control. Save the project under the name cboctl.vbp.

   Our ActiveX Control must be *public* to be used by other applications. Public controls can only exist in ActiveX Control projects.

   An ActiveX Control project, unlike a Standard Exe project, does not start with a form. Rather, it starts with a UserControl object with the default name UserControl1. (See Figure 7-1.)

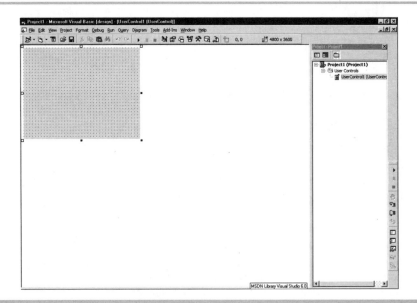

FIGURE 7-1.   Default UserControl object in ActiveX Control project

2. In Project Explorer, right-click on cboctl.vbp and choose Properties from the context menu. This will bring up the Project Properties dialog box. (See Figure 7-2.)

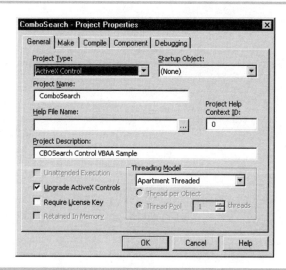

FIGURE 7-2. ActiveX Control Project Properties dialog box

Most of the entries discussed are under the General tab. The project type is ActiveX Control. This entry was made by the IDE when you chose ActiveX Control in step 1.

The Startup Object should be None. In a Standard Exe project, either a startup form or Sub Main must be selected. Here, however, the startup object will be in another project. The other project, which will be used to test the ActiveX control, will be built in the later steps of this example.

The project name identifies the ActiveX control in the Windows Registry and the Object Browser. Therefore, the name must be a legal identifier.

Most descriptions are, well, merely descriptive and therefore optional. However, the Project Description is very important. The Project Description for an ActiveX control is the text that appears in the Components dialog box. This also will be important when we build the test project.

3. Add a Combo Box control to the UserControl object just as you would add a Combo Box control to a form. Name the Combo Box control *cboFonts*. When prompted, save the UserControl as cboSearch.ctl.

The UserControl object is similar to a Visual Basic form. One similarity is that the UserControl object, like a form, has a visual designer on which controls may be added by dragging and dropping, as was the Combo Box control *cboFonts* in this example.

All ActiveX controls created in Visual Basic have a UserControl plus one or more controls placed on the UserControl.

The source code and property values of the UserControl and its constituent controls are stored in plain text files, with the extension .ctl. This is equivalent to the .frm file for forms.

Additionally, a UserControl which includes bitmaps or other graphical elements stores this information in a .ctx file having the same name as the UserControl's .ctl file. This is analogous to the .frx files for forms.

The UserControl also has an "interface." In fact, it has two of them, a user interface and a code interface.

The control's user interface is that which the user sees and interacts with. In this example, the user interface is the Combo Box control *cboFonts*. The application user sees the Combo Box control and interacts with it as with any other combo box, by typing in the edit area, clicking the arrow for the drop-down list, and so on.

The control's code *interface* is its public properties, methods, and events. At least some of the methods must be public in order for the developer to write code so his or her application may use your ActiveX control. The public properties, methods, and events can be seen from the Object Browser. (See Figure 7-3.)

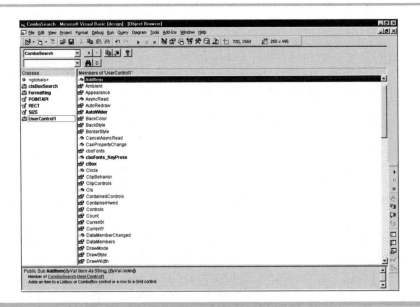

FIGURE 7-3.   UserControl1 in the Object Browser

4. Add the class module clsCBO.cls from the cboHeight.vbp project in Chapter 6 to the ActiveX project cboctl.vbp.

   An ActiveX project, like a Standard Exe, may have a class module. The advantage of storing the code for the ActiveX control in a class module is the same as for using a class module in a Standard Exe project. Your code is more modular and object-oriented.

5. Make the following changes to the class module. The first parameter in each of the procedures **SetBoxWidth**, **SetMaxWidth**, and **BoxHeight** is "frm As Form." Change the word "Form" to "UserControl1." Thus, the header for the procedure **SetMaxWidth** now is:

```
Public Function SetMaxWidth(frm As UserControl1, str As String) As Long
```

   The change from "Form" to "UserControl1" is because the Combo Box control is located in a UserControl instead of a form. The parameter type is "UserControl1" since that is the name of the UserControl.

6. Add the following Property Procedure to the UserControl:

```
Public Property Get hWnd() As Long
    hWnd = UserControl.hWnd
End Property
```

   The first parameter in the procedures **SetMaxWidth** and **BoxHeight** was "frm As Form" because that code in these procedures needed to access the handle of the form. The form's handle was accessed using the form's **hWnd** property, the code therefore being *frm.hwnd*.

   The *frm* parameter now refers to the UserControl instead of the form. UserControls also have handles, and that handle also may be accessed with the **hWnd** property. Therefore, it would appear that the code *frm.hwnd* still works. However, the statement *frm.hwnd* does not work without adding a **Property Get** procedure to the UserControl to access the UserControl's **hWnd** property. Otherwise, the statement *frm.hwnd* in the class module will cause the compile error "Method or Data member not found."

   In the cboHeight.vbp project in Chapter 6, the form did not need a **Property Get** procedure in order for the class module to access the form's handle with the statement *frm.hwnd*. The reason is that, if the needed **Property** procedure was not supplied by the programmer, Visual Basic calls default **Property Get** and **Let** (or **Set**) procedures to read from or write to the form's properties. The same does not appear to be true of UserControls. Accordingly, an attempt to access a private property from outside of the UserControl (such as the class module) will result in an error because the private property is not visible outside of the UserControl. The **Property Get** procedure, being public, makes the UserControl's **hWnd** property accessible from outside of the UserControl.

The **Property Get** procedure can be added "manually" by typing in the General Declarations portion of the UserControl's code module. It also can be added by using the Tools | Add Procedure menu command. However, another alternative, which often is useful when working with ActiveX controls, is the ActiveX Control Interface Wizard.

The ActiveX Control Interface Wizard is an add-in and is loaded and accessed like any other Visual Basic IDE add-in. Once started, it, like other wizards, uses a series of screens to guide you. The first screen is an introduction. Your work starts with the second screen, titled "Select Interface Members." The left pane lists "available" (that is, intrinsic) properties, methods, and events of the UserControl. The right pane lists the properties, methods, and events that have been selected. Use the command button captioned ">" to select the **hWnd** property. (See Figure 7-4.)

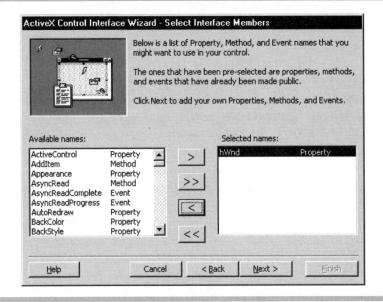

FIGURE 7-4.   ActiveX Control Interface Wizard – Select Interface Members screen

The next screen is titled "Create Custom Interface Members." This screen will be skipped for now. We will use it later.

The next screen is titled "Set Mapping." The left pane is a list box of the properties, methods, and events that were selected in the previous screens. There are two drop-down boxes on the right listing the controls and members respectively. We will map the **hWnd** property to the **hWnd** member of the UserControl. (See Figure 7-5.)

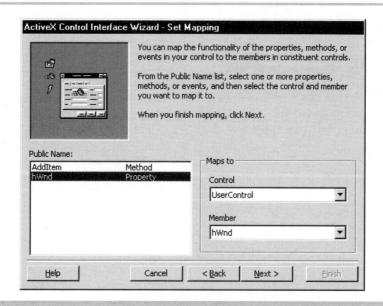

FIGURE 7-5. ActiveX Control Interface Wizard - Set Mapping screen

The next screen is titled "Set Attributes." This screen also will be skipped for now. We will use it later. The next and final screen is appropriately titled "Finished."

If the ActiveX Control Interface Wizard is used to add the **Property Get** procedure, the code includes comments:

```
'WARNING! DO NOT REMOVE OR MODIFY THE FOLLOWING COMMENTED LINES!
'MappingInfo=UserControl,UserControl,-1,hWnd
Public Property Get hWnd() As Long
    hWnd = UserControl.hWnd
End Property
```

The penalty for ignoring the warning and removing the comments is the same as for removing the tag on your mattress; a long, free stay at "Club Fed." Actually, the comments are used by the ActiveX Control Interface Wizard to know what it has already done if you need to use the wizard again to add or modify properties, methods, or events. The comments are not necessary for your code to work.

7. Insert the following code in the General Declarations of the UserControl:

```
Dim cBox As New clsBoxSearch
```

A UserControl has a code module similar to a form. The Object Box, which is the drop-down box shown in Figure 7-6, shows General, the object (here UserControl instead of Form), and the constituent controls, here *cboFonts*.

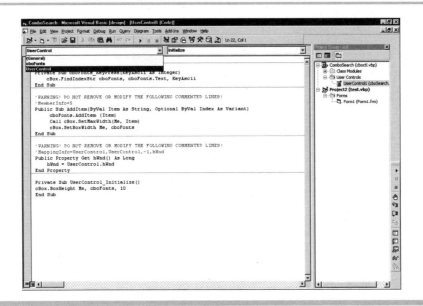

FIGURE 7-6.   Object Box for UserControl code module

In the cboHeight.vbp example in Chapter 6, *cBox* was declared in the General Declarations of the form as a reference by which the form accessed the class module. Similarly, here *cBox* is the reference by which the UserControl will access the class module.

8. Add the following code to the **Intitialize** event of the UserControl:

```
Private Sub UserControl_Initialize()
    cBox.BoxHeight Me, cboFonts, 10
End Sub
```

The **Initialize** event occurs every time an instance of your control is created or re-created. It is always the first event in a control instance's lifetime.

9. Insert the following code in the **KeyPress** event of *cboFonts*:

```
Private Sub cboFonts_KeyPress(KeyAscii As Integer)
    cBox.FindIndexStr cboFonts, cboFonts.Text, KeyAscii
End Sub
```

This also is similar to the cboHeight.vbp example in Chapter 6. The UserControl's code module, like a form's code module, has a Procedures/

Events Box that lists the procedures and events of each object in the Object Box. As in Chapter 6, this code triggers the smart search logic in the class module.

10. Add a Project, Standard Exe. Save the project as test.vbp. When prompted, save the project group as xctl.vbg.

    It is important to *add* a project. Choosing New Project or Open Project under the File menu will *close* the existing ActiveX Control project. The goal is to keep the ActiveX project open and start another project to test the ActiveX project.

    The two open projects are part of a Visual Basic *group*. The group file is represented by a .vbg extension. A .vbg file is to the constituent projects in the group what a .vbp file is to the constituent forms and modules of a single project.

11. While selecting test.vbp, choose Components under the Project menu, find CBOSearch Control VBAA Sample, and check the box next to it. (See Figure 7-7.)

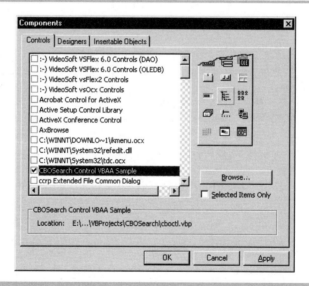

FIGURE 7-7.   CBOSearch Control VBAA sample in Components

The name "CBOSearch Control VBAA Sample" is the Project Description given in the ActiveX Control project. Note that the location shown in Figure 7-7 is the cboctl.vbp file.

12. While still selecting test.vbp, open the toolbox. The new Active X control is the last one in the toolbox. (See Figure 7-8.) Add the ActiveX control by dragging and dropping it onto the form.

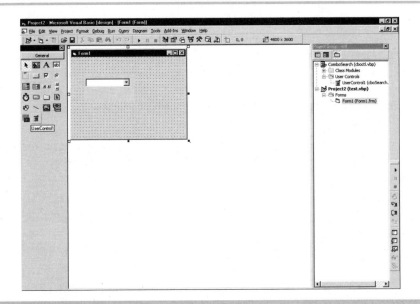

FIGURE 7-8.   ActiveX control in the toolbox

The ActiveX control developed in the ActiveX Control project cboctl.vbp is a *control class*. It is a template from which instances of the controls will be created.

A control instance cannot exist by itself. It must be placed in a container object. A Visual Basic form is a container object. Placing, also called *siting*, the control on a form or other container object creates an instance of the ActiveX control class.

The control instance created by placing the control on a form at design time is a *design-time instance*. The closing of the form, by clicking its Close button, by closing the project, or by running the project, destroys the design-time instance of the control. If the project is placed in Run mode, a *run-time instance* of the control is created when the form is loaded. This run-time instance is destroyed when the form is unloaded. When the form once again appears in design mode, a new design-time instance of the control is created.

13. Add the following code to the **Load** event of the form:

```
Private Sub Form_Load()
    Dim i As Integer
    Dim max As Integer
    max = Screen.FontCount
    If max > 35 Then max = 35
    For i = 1 To max
        usrCBO.AddItem Screen.Fonts(i)
    Next I
End Sub
```

As in the Chapter 6 example, this code simply fills the Combo Box control, in this case with up to 35 screen fonts. However, the form cannot directly access the Combo Box *cboFonts* in the UserControl. Accordingly, it accesses an **AddItem** method in the UserControl. The UserControl can directly access *cboFonts* and therefore may call *cboFonts'* **AddItem** method.

There is one minor problem with this logic. The UserControl has no **AddItem** method. However, the problem is truly minor. We can give the UserControl a custom **AddItem** method.

14. Add the following code to the UserControl:

```
Public Sub AddItem(ByVal Item As String, _
    Optional ByVal Index As Variant)
        cboFonts.AddItem (Item)
        Call cBox.SetMaxWidth(Me, Item)
        cBox.SetBoxWidth Me, cboFonts
End Sub
```

This method also can be added using the ActiveX Control Interface Wizard. In the second screen, titled "Select Interface Members," use the command button captioned ">" to choose from the left pane the **AddItem** method. Skip the next screen titled "Create Custom Interface Members." In the next screen, titled "Set Mapping," you do not need to map the **AddItem** method. In the next screen titled "Set Attributes," accept the defaults, including the argument "ByVal Item As String, Optional ByVal Index as Variant." (See Figure 7-9.) The next screen is the final one, titled "Finished."

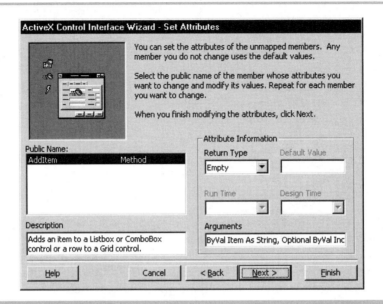

FIGURE 7-9. ActiveX Control Interface Wizard – Set Attributes screen

The following comments to the **AddItem** procedure are added by the ActiveX Control Interface Wizard:

```
'WARNING! DO NOT REMOVE OR MODIFY THE FOLLOWING COMMENTED LINES!
'MemberInfo=5
```

15. In Project Explorer, right-click test.vbp and select "Set as Startup."

16. Also in Project Explorer, again right-click test.vbp, choose Properties from the context menu, and choose the form as the startup object.

    The purpose of the last two steps is simply to make sure that the application starts from the Standard Exe project and its startup object (in this case its one form) rather than from the ActiveX Control project, which has no startup object.

    Run the project! The combo box has a smart search capability. Additionally, it drops down to show ten items and resizes to accommodate the widest item.

    Now that we know the ActiveX control works, it is time to compile it into an OCX.

17. In Project Explorer, select cboctl.vbp, and under the File menu click Make cboctl.ocx. (See Figure 7-10.)

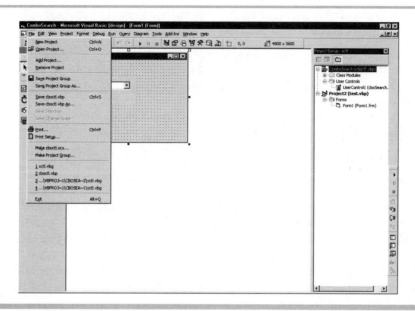

FIGURE 7-10. Making an OCX file

18. In Project Explorer, select test.vbp and then choose Project | Components.
    Using the Browse button, select the file cboctl.ocx. This will replace the .vbp
    file as the component. (See Figure 7-11.)

FIGURE 7-11. Substituting the OCX file as the component

19. In Project Explorer, right-click cboctl.vbp and select Remove from Project from the context menu. Run the project again.

The ActiveX Control project no longer is needed. We now are running a Standard Exe project with an ActiveX control added to a form. This ActiveX control can be added to any form simply by checking the .ocx file as a component and adding it, by drag and drop, to the form.

xcboppg.vbg

Adding Property Pages

While we now have a working ActiveX control, there still is room for improvement. The number of items shown in the drop-down list is hard-coded at ten. The customer who purchased our control may want a larger number. Alternatively, if a small dialog box is involved, the customer may want to stay with the minimum of eight. In either case, our customer is stuck with ten.

Additionally, the ability of the control to resize its width to accommodate the widest item is enabled whether or not our control's customer wants that functionality. The width-resizing functionality may slow down an application if a large number of items were involved. The code checks each item as it is added and compares its width to the width of the previously widest item. If a large number of items were added at one time, the performance of the application might suffer.

Since there is nothing magic about ten being the number of items shown in the drop-down list, our customer should be given a choice on the number of items. Similarly, since there is a performance downside to the control's ability to resize its width to accommodate its widest item, our customer should be given a choice as to whether that ability should be enabled.

The word "customer" has been used repeatedly in the preceding paragraphs. Normally that word means the end user of the application. This is not usually the case with ActiveX controls.

In the case of ActiveX controls, there are three roles: the author, the developer, and the user. The author of a control (that's us) creates an ActiveX control that is compiled as an .ocx file. The developer purchases the control and incorporates it into the developer's application, the .ocx file being included in the application's setup program. The user installs and uses the application.

In this scenario, it is the developer, not the end user, who is your customer. Similarly, it is normally the developer, not the end user, who will decide the property settings for the control. However, this is not always the case. For example, end users can change property settings for ActiveX controls used in a Microsoft Office application project.

Now that we know who our customers are (hopefully we will have some), the next issue is how the customers will be able to change the property settings for the ActiveX control.

Usually a control's property settings are changed through the Properties window. This window can be brought up by right-clicking the control and choosing Properties from the context menu or by selecting the control and using the F4 hotkey. (See Figure 7-12.)

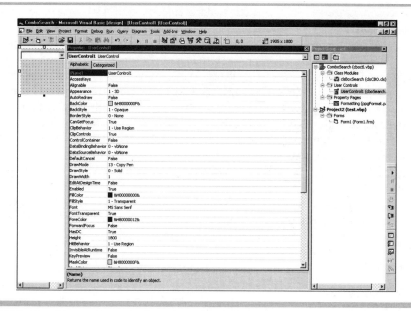

FIGURE 7-12. Properties window for a control

However, for custom controls, right-clicking the control and choosing Properties from the context menu instead will bring up a tabbed dialog box called Property Pages. (See Figure 7-13.) Choosing Custom from the Properties window also can bring up a custom control's property pages.

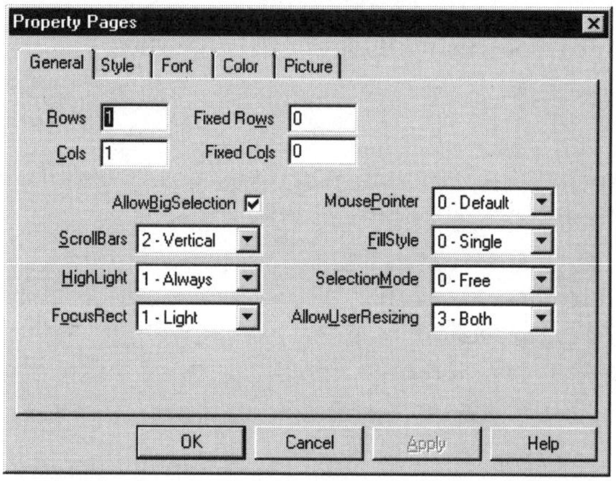

FIGURE 7-13. The Property Pages dialog box for the MSFlexGrid control

The reason for the property pages is that the custom control has properties in addition to those that are included among the properties listed in the Properties window. These additional properties sometimes are referred to as "custom" properties, which perhaps is why they can be chosen by selecting Custom from the Properties window.

Of course, the property pages, like the Properties window, can be accessed only during design time, and not run-time. Therefore, developers, not end users, usually use them. However, as mentioned above, end users of Microsoft Office suite applications can access the properties of ActiveX controls that they may incorporate in their projects.

The number of items displayed by the drop-down list, and whether or not the Combo Box control will resize its width to accommodate its widest item, are not properties listed in the Properties window. Accordingly, we will be using property pages to access these custom properties.

Creating property pages is relatively simple. Connecting properties to your control, and the creating the code to make these properties have the desired functionality, is not so simple. This task is the focus of the next example.

SYNOPSIS OF CODE

There are four steps:

1. Add the properties to the UserControl.

2. Add property procedures corresponding to the added properties to the UserControl.

3. Create a property page as a user interface for the developer to change the values of these properties.

4. Add procedures to the property page to read and write the properties when the control is initialized and to write the properties when the control is terminated.

Once these steps are completed, the custom properties are part of the project. All that remains is to add code using the custom properties.

BUILD THE PROJECT

1. Add the following additional code (italicized below) to the General Declarations of the UserControl:

```
Dim cBox As New clsBoxSearch
Const m_def_NumShow = 8
Const m_def_AutoWider = 0
Dim m_NumShow As Long
Dim m_AutoWider As Boolean
```

The variable *m_NumShow* will represent the number of items to show in the drop-down list. The constant *m_def_NumShow* has the value 8, which is the default number of items to show.

The variable *m_AutoWider* is Boolean. It will have the value True if the developer enables the control's ability to resize the width of the combo box to the width of the widest item, and False if the developer chooses not to enable this functionality, presumably for performance reasons. The constant *m_def_AutoWider* has the default value False.

The reason for this correspondence between the custom property and a default value will become evident in the code below for the **ReadProperties** and **WriteProperties** events of the UserControl.

2. Add the following property procedures to the UserControl corresponding to the properties which we added in step 1:

```
Public Property Get NumShow() As Integer
    NumShow = m_NumShow
End Property

Public Property Let NumShow(ByVal New_NumShow As Integer)
    m_NumShow = New_NumShow
    PropertyChanged "NumShow"
End Property

Public Property Get AutoWider() As Boolean
    AutoWider = m_AutoWider
End Property

Public Property Let AutoWider(ByVal New_AutoWider As Boolean)
    m_AutoWider = New_AutoWider
    PropertyChanged "AutoWider"
End Property
```

The paired **Property Get** and **Property Let** procedures are conceptually the same as in prior chapters except for the **PropertyChanged** method, which is new.

The **PropertyChanged** method notifies the UserControl of a change in the value of the property whose name is the argument of the method. This notification is necessary because the container would not know if an instance of the object needed to be saved (through raising a **WriteProperties** event) unless the container was notified that a property's value had changed.

The **PropertyChanged** method needs to be called, for example, when a user changes a property value on a property page, or the object itself changes a property value.

The code for the Property procedures, as well as the properties themselves, can be generated by the ActiveX Control Interface Wizard. At the third screen, titled "Create Custom Interface Members," add two properties, **NumShow** and **AutoWider**. (See Figure 7-14.)

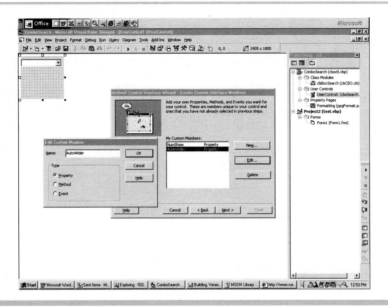

FIGURE 7-14.   Creating properties **NumShow** and **AutoWider** with the wizard

The next screen is titled "Set Mapping." Neither property needs to be mapped to a control. (See Figure 7-15.)

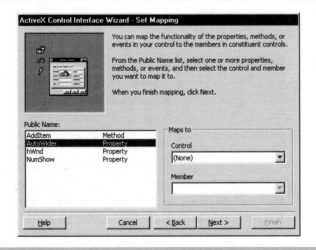

FIGURE 7-15.   No mapping of custom properties in Set Mapping screen

The next screen is titled "Set Attributes." **AutoWider** will be a Boolean variable whose default value is 0. (See Figure 7-16.) **NumShow** will be a Long whose default value is 8. (See Figure 7-17.)

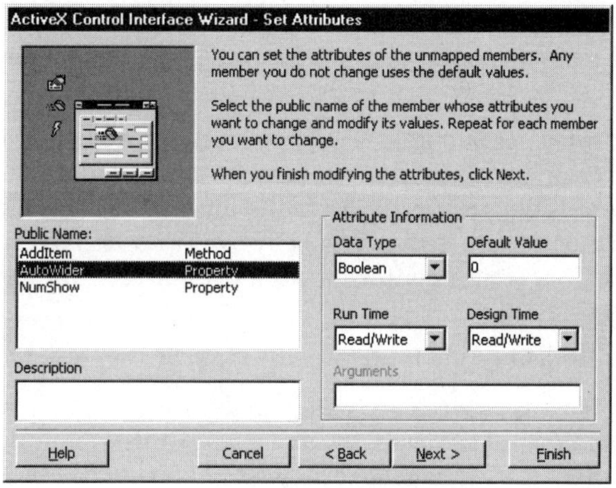

FIGURE 7-16. Set Attributes of **AutoWider** property

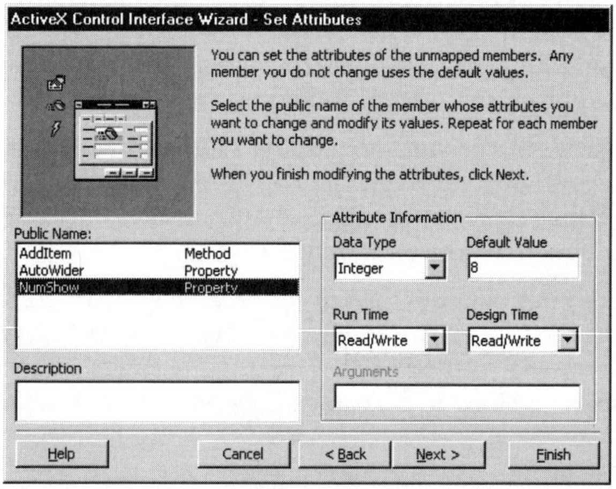

FIGURE 7-17. Set Attributes of **NumShow** property

3. Add the following code for the **InitProperties** event:

```
Private Sub UserControl_InitProperties()
    m_NumShow = m_def_NumShow
    m_AutoWider = m_def_AutoWider
End Sub
```

The **InitProperties** event occurs when a new instance of an object is created. The code assigns to the properties their respective default values.

The **InitProperties** event does not occur when an existing instance of the object is being loaded. In that circumstance, we would not want to assign to the properties their respective default values. Instead, we would want to assign to the properties their respective values when the control was last unloaded. That assignment will be done in the code for the **ReadProperties** event discussed next.

4. Add the following code for the **ReadProperties** event:

```
Private Sub UserControl_ReadProperties(PropBag As PropertyBag)
    m_NumShow = PropBag.ReadProperty("NumShow", m_def_NumShow)
m_AutoWider = PropBag.ReadProperty("AutoWider", m_def_Auto _
    Wider)
    If m_NumShow > m_def_NumShow Then _
        cBox.BoxHeight Me, cboFonts, m_NumShow
End Sub
```

The **ReadProperties** event occurs when loading an existing instance of an object. The **ReadProperties** event occurs immediately after a control's **Initialize** event, usually when its parent form is loaded within the run-time or the design-time environment. This is the appropriate time to retrieve all of your stored property settings and apply them to the ActiveX control.

The property settings are stored in the **PropertyBag** object. The **PropertyBag** object was introduced in Version 5 of Visual Basic. As its name suggests, its purpose is the storage of properties. Absent such storage, the control's properties would not be persistent.

The **PropertyBag** object is passed as a parameter to the control during the **ReadProperties** event. The saved state of each property is retrieved by calling the **ReadProperty** method of the **PropertyBag** object. The first argument of the **ReadProperty** method is the name of the property to be read. The second argument, which is optional, is the default value of that property. The reason for the default value is to supply a value to return if no value had been stored.

After the properties have been retrieved, the number of items to be displayed by the drop-down list is set with the statement:

```
If m_NumShow > m_def_NumShow Then _
        cBox.BoxHeight Me, cboFonts, m_NumShow
```

In the previous example, the **BoxHeight** method of the class module was called (with the hard-coded value of 10 rather than the variable *m_NumShow*) in the **Initialize** event of the UserControl. Now that the number of items to be displayed by the drop-down list is a variable whose value is retrieved from the **PropertyBag** object, the **BoxHeight** method of the class module no longer can be called from the **Initialize** event. The reason is that the property's value is not retrieved until after the **Initialize** event, during the **ReadProperties** event.

5.   Delete the code in the **Initialize** event of the UserControl:

```
Private Sub UserControl_Initialize()
    cBox.BoxHeight Me, cboFonts, 10
End Sub
```

As just discussed, the **BoxHeight** method now has to be called in the **ReadProperties** event.

6.   Add the following code for the **WriteProperties** event of the UserControl:

```
Private Sub UserControl_WriteProperties _
    (PropBag As PropertyBag)
    Call PropBag.WriteProperty("NumShow", _
        m_NumShow, m_def_NumShow)
    Call PropBag.WriteProperty("AutoWider", _
        m_AutoWider, m_def_AutoWider)
End Sub
```

The **WriteProperties** event is used to store, and thereby make persistent, design-time changes to properties. It occurs when the client form is unloaded or after a property has been changed within the Visual Basic IDE.

The **WriteProperties** event, like the **ReadProperties** event, has one argument, a **PropertyBag** object. This time the **PropertyBag** object is used to store rather than to retrieve property values.

The saving of the state of each property is done by calling the **WriteProperty** method of the **PropertyBag** object. The **WriteProperty** method has three arguments. The first argument of the **WriteProperty** method is the name of the property to be stored. The second argument is the data value to be stored. The third argument, which is optional, is the default value of that property.

The reason for the default value is to avoid unnecessary storage of a value. The **WriteProperty** method will store the specified data unless the data value matches the default value. If the specified data value matches the default value, there is no need to store the value, since the **ReadProperty** method will supply the default value. However, if no default value is specified in the call to the **WriteProperty** method, then the data value will have to be stored.

7. Add the following italicized code to the **AddItem** method of the UserControl:

```
Public Sub AddItem(ByVal Item As String, _
    Optional ByVal Index As Variant)
    cboFonts.AddItem (Item)
    If m_AutoWider Then
    Call cBox.SetMaxWidth(Me, Item)
    cBox.SetBoxWidth Me, cboFonts
    End If
End Sub
```

This code executes the width-resizing functionality of the combo box if the developer has enabled that functionality by setting *m_AutoWider* to True.

8. Add a Property Page by selecting Project | Add Property Page.

The Property Page will be used to permit the developer to change the values of setting *m_AutoWider* and *m_NumShow*.

9. Add the following controls to the property page:

Control Type	Name	Comments
Check Box	chkAutoWider	Caption is "AutoWider."
Text Box	txtNumShow	Set Enabled property to False.
Vertical Scroll Bar	VScroll1	Max is 16. Min is 8.

The property page in Design view appears like Figure 7-18.

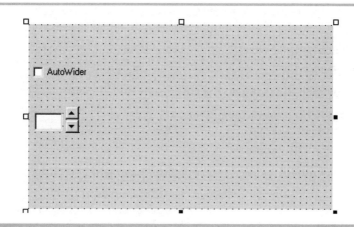

FIGURE 7-18.   PropertyPage in Design view

Usually an UpDown control would be used instead of a vertical scrollbar. However, UpDown controls do not appear to work in property pages.

10.   Add the following code to the **Click** event of chkAutoWider:

```
Private Sub chkAutoWider_Click()
    Changed = True
End Sub
```

The **Changed** property is a Boolean flag that indicates whether the value of a property on a property page has changed. This flag is used to enable the **ApplyChanges** event, annotated below, to fire when the developer presses the OK button or the Apply button on the property page, or when property pages are switched by selecting tabs.

11. Add the following code to the **Change** event of the vertical scrollbar:

```
Private Sub VScroll1_Change()
    txtNumShow.Text = VScroll1.Value
End Sub
```

12. Add the following code to the **Change** event of txtNumShow:

```
Private Sub txtNumShow_Change()
    Changed = True
End Sub
```

13. Add the following code to the **SelectionChanged** event of the PropertyPage:

```
Private Sub PropertyPage_SelectionChanged()
    chkAutoWider.Value = (SelectedControls(0).AutoWider And _
        vbChecked)
    txtNumShow.Text = SelectedControls(0).NumShow
End Sub
```

The **SelectionChanged** event of a property page occurs when the property page is first brought up for a control and then each time the selection of controls on the form has changed. The firing of this event notifies the property page that the selection of controls has changed, and therefore the display of current property values may need to be updated. The **SelectedControls** property should be read to find out the new set of selected controls.

The **SelectedControls** property returns a collection that contains all the currently selected controls on the form. The **SelectedControls** property is not available at the property page's authoring time, and is available in read-only form at the property page's run-time. This collection is useful to a property page in determining which controls are currently selected, and therefore which controls might need properties changed. Some containers only allow one control to be selected at once; in that case **SelectedControls** will only contain one control. Other containers allow more than one control to be selected at once; in that case there may be more than one control selected, and the property page must iterate through the controls in the **SelectedControls** collection and attempt to set the changed properties.

14. Add the following code to the **ApplyChanges** event of the PropertyPage:

```
Private Sub PropertyPage_ApplyChanges()
    SelectedControls(0).AutoWider = (chkAutoWider.Value = vbChecked)
    SelectedControls(0).NumShow = txtNumShow.Text
End Sub
```

The **ApplyChanges** event of a property page occurs when the developer presses the OK button or the Apply button on the property page, or when property pages are switched by selecting tabs. As its name suggests, the **ApplyChanges** event is where changes made to property values in the property page are applied.

The **ApplyChanges** event will be raised only if the **Changed** property is set to True. This is the reason for the Changed = True statement in the **Change** or **Click** event of the controls on the property page.

Now it's time to test the project! View the form in design mode. If the ActiveX control is cross-hatched as in Figure 7-19, you first need to close the UserControl design window.

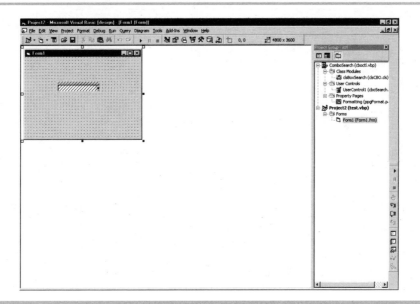

FIGURE 7-19. Cross-hatching of the ActiveX control indicates that you need to close the UserControl design window

While viewing the form in design mode, right-click on the ActiveX control and choose Properties from the context menu. This will bring up the property page. (See Figure 7-20.)

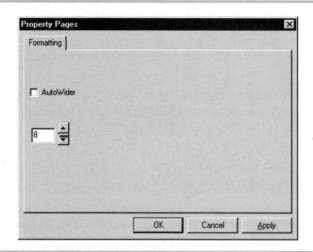

FIGURE 7-20. The property page

If the AutoWider checkbox is checked, the drop-down list will resize to accommodate the widest item as in the example in Chapter 6. If the checkbox is not checked, the drop-down list will not resize, and some of the items will be cut off.

The vertical scrollbar also can be used to change the number shown in the text box (typing directly in the text box is prevented by setting its Enabled property to False). While it is somewhat counterintuitive, the number in the text box is increased by clicking the down arrow of the vertical scrollbar. The drop-down list will show the number in the text box, the minimum being 8 and the maximum being 16.

Business Objects

The Windows Registry
Database Connectivity
Manipulating Strings

Manipulating Drives and Files
ActiveX Servers
Automation Using VBA-Compliant
Applications

The Windows Registry

Viewing the Registry (RegViewer.vbp)   Writing to the Registry (RegWrite.vbp)

A t the risk of violating the maxim "Never generalize," all professional applications save certain information about themselves upon exiting. This information may include the window size and position upon exiting, so that the next time the application literally "will start up where it left off." The saved information also may include user preferences. For example, if the application user wants the File menu in Microsoft Word to show the last eight most recently used (MRU) files instead of the default four, the user chooses Tools | Options, goes to the General tab, and selects the value. The next time Microsoft Word is started, the last eight most recently used files will show up at the bottom of the File menu.

Sometimes the saved information is quite important. For example, a data entry application whose data source is a database should save the name and path of the database.

It's helpful to understand the history of how the Registry came about. While this is a programming book, not a history book, in the words of the Spanish-American philosopher George Santayana, "Those who do not learn history are condemned to repeat its mistakes." As cutting-edge programmers, we are bound to make new mistakes on our own. There is no reason also to make old ones.

Brief (We Promise) History of the Registry

History lessons usually start with the words "Long ago," so this one will too. Long ago (which in the context of computer programming is a few years ago) in the dark old days of Microsoft Windows 3.*x*, applications stored configuration data in the win.ini file. Similarly, the operating system stored its configuration data in the system.ini file.

Since these .ini files were ASCII files, the application user could view and edit the files using any text editor, such as the DOS editor or Notepad. This was both good news and bad news. The good news was that the application user easily could add, edit, or delete entries in the .ini files. The bad news was that the application user easily could add, edit, or delete entries in the .ini files. As the saying goes, "You can make something foolproof, but you can't make it damn-foolproof." As ASCII text, the .ini files lacked the structure of, for example, a database; it was all too easy for an unsophisticated application user to make a mistake. Unfortunately, the consequences of a mistake, particularly with the ystem.ini file, could be severe, such as the computer failing to boot.

Additionally, as applications proliferated, more and more applications stored their configuration information to the win.ini file. This resulted in a very long file which for that reason alone was difficult to view or edit. Even worse, there were no rules for the order or location of the added information. Thus, it not only was difficult to find an item, it was difficult to determine which portions of the application information needed to be changed or to identify all of the entries which should be changed.

Furthermore, win.ini files were limited in size to 64KB. This size could be exceeded if the computer had many applications, and there was no way to increase the size of the file.

Even if all the applications could fit in the one win.ini file, there was a greater problem. If an entry for even one application became corrupted, then potentially all of the other applications could be affected.

The solution became for each application to have its own private .ini file. Thus, Visual Basic had a Vb.ini file. Having application-specific .ini files did avoid the problems inherent in all applications sharing one win.ini file. There also were Windows API functions, including **GetPrivateProfileString** and **WritePrivateProfileString**, which could be used by the programmer to create, modify, or delete entries in a private .ini file.

However, application-specific .ini files were not a cure-all. First, they were no more secure than the win.ini file. Since the application-specific .ini files, like the win.ini file, were plain text files, they still could be edited easily by the application user. Additionally, since the application-specific .ini files, like the win.ini file, lacked the internal structure of a database, it was all too easy for the application user to make changes incorrectly, sometimes with disastrous results.

Additionally, since each application had its own separate .ini file, there was no reliable means for them to share configuration information and other data. This became a problem for applications that used dynamic data exchange (DDE) or object linking and embedding (OLE).

Windows 3.1 included, in addition to the .ini files, a Registration Database. The Registration Database was used by the operating system to store OLE-specific information. Now, applications that used OLE (or DDE) could share configuration information and other data.

However, the Registration Database could not be accessed by API functions. It could be accessed only by the operating system. Therefore, the Registration Database was of little use to programmers. Nevertheless, the Registration Database is the direct ancestor of the Registry in Microsoft Windows 95/98 and Windows NT.

The Registry in Microsoft Windows 95/98 is similar to the Registry in Windows NT. However, because of the differences between the two operating systems, the two implementations of the Registry also differ. For example, the Windows 95/98 Registry has no security attributes. However, for the most part the two implementations are quite similar. The differences will be discussed where they are germane to the following discussion and examples.

Structure of the Registry

The Registry is a centralized database for information specific to the operating system, the machine, users, and applications. The database structure of the Registry eases the task of locating information and reduces the likelihood of redundant information stored in different locations.

The Registry can be edited by an application user, but not as easily as plain text .ini files. The tool used to view and edit the Registry is the Registry Editor, which can be started by running "regedit" (without the quotes) by clicking Start and selecting Run. (See Figure 8-1.)

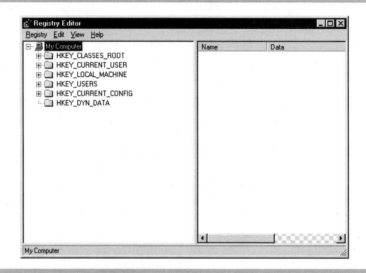

FIGURE 8-1.   The Registry Editor

The Registry stores data in a tree with a hierarchical structure. Therefore, the Registry Editor displays this hierarchically structured tree in, not surprisingly, a tree view control.

Each node in the tree is called a key. Each key has a name. A key name consists of one or more printable ANSI characters (values in the range 32 through 127) and cannot include spaces, backslashes, or wildcard characters (* and ?). In the HKEY_CLASSES_ROOT key discussed below, names may not begin with a period (.)—that is reserved for filename extensions—but may include a period within its name.

Each key can have one or more child keys, which are known as *subkeys*. A subkey simply is a key that is subordinate in the hierarchy to another key. Subkeys also have names. The name of a subkey must be unique with respect to the key immediately above it in the hierarchy, that is, its parent key. A subkey is delimited by a backslash (\) from the key to which it is subordinate.

A key does not necessarily have any subkeys. Indeed, the lowest key in a given hierarchy has no subkeys.

A key (or subkey) may also have a *value*. A value is a data entry that is associated with a key or subkey. A value has a name, which is its identifier, and its data, which is the value of, well, the value. The data may be one of several data types, such as a long, a Unicode string, an ANSI string, or an array of strings. These data types are discussed later in this chapter.

Values are at the bottom of the hierarchy. Values do not have subsidiary values or subkeys. A key or subkey may have many values, but a value has only one associated key or subkey.

While a value must have one and only one associated key, a key does not necessarily have any values. A key may have only a default value or no value at all.

Nevertheless, while a key need not have either a subkey or a value, it must have at least one subkey *or* at least one value.

Figure 8-2 uses the Registry Editor to show keys, subkeys, and values. HK_CURRENT_USER is a key. Control Panel is one of several subkeys. The Control Panel subkey has a number of subkeys, including Desktop. The Desktop subkey has its own subkey named "WindowMetrics" (which has no subkeys) and also a number of values. One of the values has the name "CursorBlinkRate" and the value "530."

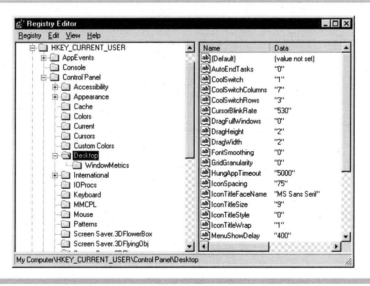

FIGURE 8-2.   Registry Editor showing keys, subkeys, and values

All Win32 operating systems have predefined keys at the root of the Registry. These top-level root keys also are referred to as *hives*. They are shown in Figure 8-1 and described in Table 8-1.

Key	Purpose
HKEY_CLASSES_ROOT	Registry entries subordinate to this key define types (or classes) of documents and the properties associated with those types. An example would be the association of a file extension (for example, .doc) with an application (Microsoft Word). Data stored under this key is used by shell applications and by object linking and embedding (OLE) applications. This key also provides backward compatibility with the Windows 3.1 Registration Database by storing information for DDE and OLE support.
HKEY_USERS	Registry entries subordinate to this key define the default user configuration for new users on the local computer and the user configuration for the current user and other users of the computer.
HKEY_CURRENT_USER	Registry entries subordinate to this key define the preferences of the current user. These preferences include the settings of environment variables, data about program groups, colors, printers, network connections, and application preferences. This key maps to the current user's branch in HKEY_USERS. Software vendors use this key to store the current user-specific preferences to be used within their applications. Microsoft, for example, creates the HKEY_CURRENT_USER\Software\Microsoft key for its applications to use, with each application creating its own subkey under the Microsoft key.
HKEY_DYN_DATA	Windows 95 and Windows 98: Registry entries subordinate to this key allow you to access performance data. This key is used to store dynamic Registry data, that is, data which changes frequently, such as performance statistics shown by the system monitor.
HKEY_PERFORMANCE_DATA	Windows NT: Registry entries subordinate to this key allow you to access performance data. This key used in the Windows NT operating system corresponds to the HKEY_DYN_DATA data key used in the Windows 95 and Windows 98 operating systems.
HKEY_LOCAL_MACHINE	Registry entries subordinate to this key define the physical state of the computer, including data about the bus type, system memory, and installed hardware and software; Plug and Play information; network logon preferences and security information; and server names and location.

TABLE 8-1.   Root Registry Keys

Key	Purpose
HKEY_CURRENT_CONFIG	Registry entries subordinate to this key store nonuser-specific configuration information that pertains to hardware. For example, an application can store a different server name for its data depending on whether the system is attached to a network. The HKEY_CURRENT_CONFIG key is mapped to a subkey within HKEY_LOCAL_MACHINE.

TABLE 8-1. Root Registry Keys *(continued)*

A key must be opened or, if it does not already exist, created before data can be added to the Registry. A key is opened or created by reference to a key that is its immediate or direct ancestor (that is, a parent, grandparent, great-grandparent, and so on) *and is already open*. This presents a conundrum. If an already opened key is required to open a key, how does the already opened key get opened?

The answer is that the predefined, top-level keys in the root of the Registry are always open. Further, the handles to these keys are constants so there is no need to obtain the value of these handles. Thus, the handles to the root keys are the entry points to the Registry. Additionally, since these top-level keys are predefined, the programmer can rely on their presence in any Win32 operating system.

Visual Basic Registry Functions

Visual Basic includes four functions to read or write to the Registry, **SaveSetting**, **GetSetting**, **GetAllSettings**, and **DeleteSetting.** These functions are described in Table 8-2.

Function Name	Purpose
SaveSetting	Saves an application's existing Registry entry or, if the entry did not previously exist, creates a new Registry entry for the application.
GetSetting	Returns the value data from an application's Registry entry.
GetAllSettings	Returns an array of value names and corresponding value datas from an application's Registry entry.
DeleteSetting	Deletes a value or key setting from an application's Registry entry.

TABLE 8-2. Visual Basic Registry Functions

This chapter is not about how to use these Visual Basic Registry functions, but instead how to go beyond their limitations by using Windows API Registry functions. Nevertheless, an understanding of the Visual Basic Registry functions is helpful to understanding how the Windows API Registry functions work.

The four Visual Basic Registry functions only manipulate keys inside one specific section of the Registry. This section is under the HKEY_CURRENT_USER key, Software first-level subkey, VB and VBA Program Settings section second-level subkey. The path of this section is HKEY_CURRENT_USER\Software\VB and VBA Program Settings. In Figure 8-3, in the VB and VBA Program Settings section, there is a third-level subkey, "StudentTracker"; a fourth-level subkey, "Directories"; and three values with corresponding names and data.

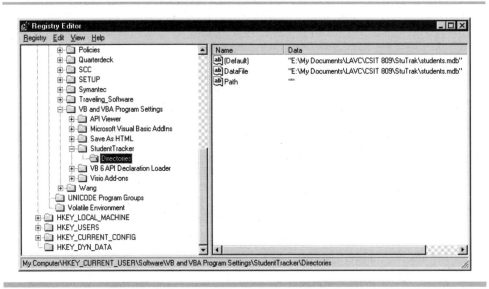

FIGURE 8-3.   Registry Entry for StudentTracker application

The following code excerpts will show how the Visual Basic Registry functions could be used to manipulate the Registry entries for the StudentTracker application.

SAVESETTING   **SaveSetting** could be used to change the path associated with the value name "DataFile" to the "D:\VBAA" directory. The syntax of **SaveSetting** is

```
SaveSetting appname, key, valuename, valuedata
```

These parameters are explained in Table 8-3.

Parameter Name	Data Type	Required	Description
appname	String	Yes	The name of the application key. This key is immediately under the VBA and VBA Settings key in the hierarchy.
key	String	Yes	The name of the key under the application key.
valuename	String	Yes	The name of the value to be changed.
valuedata	String	Yes	The new or modified data.

TABLE 8-3. Parameters of **SaveSetting**

Thus, the syntax of the call to **SaveSetting** would be:

```
SaveSetting "StudentTracker", "Directories", "DataFile", _
    "D:\VBAA\students.mdb"
```

As mentioned above, **SaveSetting** may be used not only to save changes to existing entries but also to create a new value, key, or even application under VBA and VBA Settings. For example, to create Registry entries for a new application called "WaterTorture" with a key "UserPreferences" that itself has a subkey "Directories" with a value name of "Data" and data of "C:\VBAA\example.mdb," the call to **SaveSetting** would be

```
SaveSetting "WaterTorture", "Directories", "Data", _
    "C:\VBAA\example.mdb"
```

GETSETTING   **GetSetting** would be used to retrieve the value of the path associated with the value name "DataFile." The syntax of **GetSetting** is

```
GetSetting appname, key, valuename, [Optional]default
```

These parameters are explained in Table 8-4.

The call to **GetSetting** to retrieve the value of the path associated with the value name "DataFile" is

```
GetSetting "StudentTracker", "Directories", "DataFile", ""
```

The value of an empty string ("") will be returned if, for example, there was no "Directories" key or value with the name "DataFile."

GETALLSETTINGS   **GetAllSettings** is used to return all the value names and data under a key. This return value is a **Variant**. The content of this **Variant** is a two-

Parameter Name	Data Type	Required	Description
appname	String	Yes	Same as with **SaveSetting**, the name of the application key. As before, this key is immediately under the VBA and VBA Settings key in the hierarchy.
key	String	Yes	Same as with **SaveSetting**, the name of the key under the application key.
value name	String	Yes	Same as with **SaveSetting**, the name of the value, except here the value's data is to be retrieved, not changed.
default	Variant	No. Optional.	Contains the value to return if no data is set in the key setting. If omitted, default is assumed to be a zero-length string ("").

TABLE 8-4.   Parameters of **GetSetting**

dimensional array of strings containing all of the value names and data under the key. The syntax of **GetAllSettings** is

```
GetAllSettings appname, key
```

These parameters are explained in Table 8-5.

The call to **GetAllSettings** to retrieve the value names and data under the key "Directories" is

```
GetAllSettings "StudentTracker", "Directories"
```

Parameter Name	Data Type	Required	Description
appname	String	Yes	Same as with **SaveSetting**, the name of the application key. As before, this key is immediately under the VBA and VBA Settings key in the hierarchy.
key	String	Yes	Same as with **SaveSetting**, the name of the key under the application key.

TABLE 8-5.   Parameters of **GetAllSettings**

The return value would be a two-dimensional array with the three value names and corresponding data. If either *appname* or *key* did not exist, then **GetAllSettings** would return an uninitialized **Variant**.

DELETESETTING **DeleteSetting** deletes a specified value, or a subkey and all of its values if no value is specified. The syntax of **DeleteSetting** is

```
DeleteSetting appname, key, [Optional] valuename
```

These parameters are explained in Table 8-6.
The call to **DeleteSetting** to delete the value named "DataFile" is

```
DeleteSetting "StudentTracker", "Directories", "DataFile"
```

The call to **DeleteSetting** to delete the key "Directories" and all of its values is

```
DeleteSetting "StudentTracker", "Directories"
```

The value of an empty string ("") will be returned if, for example, there was no "Directories" key or value with the name "DataFile."
DeleteSetting must be used with caution. A run-time error occurs if the key or optional value passed to **DeleteSetting** does not exist.

Limitations of Visual Basic Registry Functions

The Visual Basic Registry functions have two important limitations. First, they only manipulate keys inside one specific section of the Registry: HKEY_CURRENT_USER\ Software\VB and VBA Program Settings. Thus, they cannot be used to access keys

Parameter Name	Data Type	Required	Description
appname	String	Yes	Same as with **SaveSetting**, the name of the application key. As before, this key is immediately under the VBA and VBA Settings key in the hierarchy.
key	String	Yes	Same as with **SaveSetting**, the name of the key under the application key.
value name	String	No. Optional.	Same as with **SaveSetting**, the name of the value. If omitted, the key, and all of the values, will be deleted.

TABLE 8-6. Parameters of **DeleteSetting**

outside of this Registry section if any other information is required. Second, they only can be used to read or write value data of the **String** data type. Often value data may be binary or another non-string data type.

Overview of Windows API Registry Functions

Windows API Registry functions permit the programmer to go beyond the limitations of the Visual Basic Registry functions. The Windows API Registry functions are not limited to one section of the Registry and they can read or write data types other than **String**.

There are both Win16 and Win32 Registry functions. The name of a Win32 version of a Registry function usually is the same as the corresponding Win16 Registry function plus the letters "Ex" appended. For example, **RegOpenKey** is a Win16 function, and **RegOpenKeyEx** is the corresponding Win32 function.

The Win16 functions work in Windows 95/98 and Windows NT as well as in Windows 3.1. However, using the Win32 function is preferable to using the corresponding Win16 function. The Win32 functions often have more parameters than the corresponding Win16 functions and therefore permit more information to be obtained.

Additionally, some of the Win16 functions are more limited than the corresponding Win32 functions. For example, **RegQueryValue** only retrieves the data of the default value of a specified Registry key, and the data type of the value is limited to a null-terminated string. By contrast, **RegQueryValueEx** retrieves the data for any value of a specified Registry key, and the data type may be any of the ones allowable in the Registry.

Finally, there are certain Win32 functions, such as **RegEnumValue**, that have no corresponding Win16 function.

There are Registry functions for creating a key, opening a key, reading the value of a key, writing to the key, enumerating through keys, closing a key, and deleting a key. There also are miscellaneous Registry functions such as reading from or writing to the security attributes of a key.

A key is created or opened by referring to the key as a subkey of a currently open key. As discussed above, the predefined keys at the root of the Registry are always open. **RegOpenKey** or **RegOpenKeyEx** is used to open a key. **RegCreateKey** or **RegCreateKeyEx** is used to create a key.

Data is retrieved from the Registry typically by enumerating the subkeys of a key until the desired subkey is found and then by retrieving the data from the value or values associated with that subkey. **RegEnumKey** or **RegEnumKeyEx** will enumerate the subkeys of a given key. **RegEnumKeyEx** returns a subkey and its class, but **RegEnumKey** returns only the subkey, not the class.

Once the subkey is located, the **RegQueryInfoKey** function will obtain information about the key. The **RegGetKeySecurity** function retrieves a copy of the security descriptor protecting a key.

The **RegQueryValue** or **RegQueryValueEx** function will retrieve a particular value for a key. An application typically calls **RegEnumValue** to determine the value names and then **RegQueryValueEx** to retrieve the data for the names.

RegQueryValue and **RegQueryValueEx** differ in how they treat unexpanded references to environment variables. If an unnamed value contains an unexpanded environment variable (for example, %PATH%), **RegQueryValue** expands the variable into the storage buffer provided as one of its parameters. **RegQueryValueEx**, however, does not expand these references, though these references can be expanded with the **ExpandEnvironmentStrings** function.

An application can use either the **RegSetValue** or **RegSetValueEx** function to associate a value and its data with a key. **RegSetValue** works only with strings (values having the REG_SZ type). **RegSetValueEx**, however, can write values with any type of data. Either of these functions can create a key and its value at the same time.

An application can use the **RegDeleteValue** to delete the value from a key. The **RegDeleteKey** function deletes a key. A deleted key is not removed until the last handle to it has been closed. Subkeys and values cannot be created under a deleted key.

To change a key's security information, an application can use the **RegSetKeySecurity** function.

An application can use the **RegCloseKey** function to close a key and write the data it contains into the Registry. **RegCloseKey** does not necessarily write the data to the Registry before returning; it can take as long as several seconds for the cache to be flushed to the hard disk. If an application must explicitly write Registry data to the hard disk, it can use the **RegFlushKey** function. **RegFlushKey**, however, uses many system resources and should be called only when absolutely necessary.

These keys are summarized in Table 8-7.

The following examples will use most of these functions. The first example, a Registry Viewer, will view keys and enumerate their subkeys and values, but make no changes to the Registry. The second example will add and edit Registry entries.

RegViewer.vbp

Viewing the Registry

The Registry Viewer reads a key and enumerates the names of all subkeys and the names and data of all values of that key. It permits the user both to "drill down" into the Registry, level by level, or to move up the Registry hierarchy, again level by level.

Win16 and Win32	Win32 only	Description
RegCloseKey	None additional	Closes the specified key.
RegCreateKey	RegCreateKeyEx	Creates the specified key or, if the key already exists, opens it.
None	RegDeleteKey	Windows 95: Deletes the specified subkey and all its descendants. Windows NT: Deletes the specified subkey only. The subkey to be deleted must not have subkeys. To delete a key and all of its subkeys in Windows NT, a recursive delete function should be implemented using **RegEnumKeyEx** and **RegDeleteKey**.
None	RegDeleteValue	Deletes a value associated with the specified subkey.
RegEnumKey	RegEnumKeyEx	Enumerates subkeys of the specified open key. The subkeys are enumerated one at a time each time the function is called, so the function usually is called in a loop.
None	RegEnumValue	Enumerates the values of the specified open key. The subkeys are enumerated one at a time each time the function is called, so the function usually is called in a loop.
None	RegFlushKey	Writes all the attributes of the specified open key to the Registry.
RegOpenKey	RegOpenKeyEx	Opens the specified key.
None	RegQueryInfoKey	Returns information about the specified key.
RegQueryValue	RegQueryValueEx	**RegQueryValue**: Retrieves the data associated with the default or unnamed value of a specified Registry key. The data must be a null-terminated string. **RegQueryValueEx**: Retrieves the data for a specified value name associated with a specified open key.
RegSetValue	RegSetValueEx	**RegSetValue**: Sets the data for the default or unnamed value of the specified open key. The data must be a text string. **RegSetValueEx**: Sets the data and data type of a specified value associated with a specified open key.

TABLE 8-7.   Windows API Registry Functions

The Registry Viewer only reads; it does not write—that is, it does not add keys or values. That functionality will be implemented in the next example.

SYNOPSIS OF CODE

The Registry Viewer uses **RegQueryInfoKey** to determine the number of subkeys of the key currently being manipulated. If there are any subkeys, the Registry Viewer loops through those subkeys, using **RegEnumKey** to obtain the names of the keys.

The Registry Viewer uses **RegQueryInfoKey** once again, this time to determine the number and data types of the values of the key currently being manipulated. If there are any values, the Registry Viewer loops through those values, using an implementation of **RegEnumValue** specific to the data type involved to obtain the name and data pairs of the values.

The Registry Viewer also uses **RegOpenKeyEx** to open keys and **RegCloseKey** to close keys.

The functionality of the Registry Viewer is contained in a class module which "wraps" the API functions in user-defined Visual Basic functions. The class module also contains variables which contain the value of the key currently being manipulated, and property procedures and functions to validate any attempt to change the value of the key.

CODE

```
Option Explicit

Private m_key As String
Private m_root As Long

Public Enum RegRoot
  HKEY_CLASSES_ROOT = &H80000000
  HKEY_CURRENT_USER = &H80000001
  HKEY_LOCAL_MACHINE = &H80000002
  HKEY_USERS = &H80000003
  HKEY_PERFORMANCE_DATA = &H80000004
  HKEY_CURRENT_CONFIG = &H80000005
  HKEY_DYN_DATA = &H80000006
End Enum
```

```
Public Enum RegData
 REG_NONE = 0&
 REG_EXPAND_SZ = 2&
 REG_SZ = 1&
 REG_BINARY = 3&
 REG_DWORD = 4&
 REG_DWORD_BIG_ENDIAN = 5&
 REG_LINK = 6&
 REG_MULTI_SZ = 7&
 REG_RESOURCE_LIST = 8&
 REG_FULL_RESOURCE_DESCRIPTOR = 9&
End Enum

Public Enum ErrorList
 ERROR_SUCCESS = 0&
 ERROR_FILE_NOT_FOUND = 2&
 ERROR_ACCESS_DENIED = 5&
 ERROR_INVALID_HANDLE = 6&
 ERROR_OUTOFMEMORY = 14&
 ERROR_INVALID_PARAMETER = 87&
 ERROR_BAD_PATHNAME = 161&
 ERROR_MORE_DATA = 234&
 ERROR_NO_MORE_ITEMS = 259&
 ERROR_BADKEY = 1010&
 ERROR_CANTOPEN = 1011&
 ERROR_CANTREAD = 1012&
 ERROR_CANTWRITE = 1013&
 ERROR_KEYDELETED = 1018&
 ERROR_EMPTY_ARRAY = vbObjectError + 512 + 5
End Enum

Private Const SYNCHRONIZE = &H100000
Private Const STANDARD_RIGHTS_ALL As Long = &H1F0000
Private Const READ_CONTROL As Long = &H20000
Private Const STANDARD_RIGHTS_READ As Long = (READ_CONTROL)
Private Const STANDARD_RIGHTS_WRITE As Long = (READ_CONTROL)

Private Const KEY_QUERY_VALUE As Long = &H1
Private Const KEY_SET_VALUE As Long = &H2
Private Const KEY_CREATE_SUB_KEY As Long = &H4
Private Const KEY_ENUMERATE_SUB_KEYS As Long = &H8
Private Const KEY_NOTIFY As Long = &H10
Private Const KEY_CREATE_LINK As Long = &H20
Private Const KEY_READ As Long = _
```

```
 ((STANDARD_RIGHTS_READ Or KEY_QUERY_VALUE Or _
 KEY_ENUMERATE_SUB_KEYS Or KEY_NOTIFY) _
 And (Not SYNCHRONIZE))
Private Const KEY_EXECUTE As Long = _
 ((KEY_READ) And (Not SYNCHRONIZE))
Private Const KEY_WRITE As Long = _
 ((STANDARD_RIGHTS_WRITE Or KEY_SET_VALUE _
 Or KEY_CREATE_SUB_KEY) And (Not SYNCHRONIZE))
Private Const KEY_ALL_ACCESS As Long = _
 ((STANDARD_RIGHTS_ALL Or KEY_QUERY_VALUE Or _
 KEY_SET_VALUE Or KEY_CREATE_SUB_KEY Or _
 KEY_ENUMERATE_SUB_KEYS Or KEY_NOTIFY Or _
 KEY_CREATE_LINK) And (Not SYNCHRONIZE))

Private Const REG_OPTION_NON_VOLATILE As Long = 0

Private Type FILETIME
 dwLowDateTime As Long
 dwHighDateTime As Long
End Type

Private Declare Function RegOpenKeyEx Lib _
 "advapi32.dll" Alias "RegOpenKeyExA" _
 (ByVal hkey As Long, ByVal lpSubKey As String, _
 ByVal ulOptions As Long, ByVal samDesired As Long, _
 phkResult As Long) As Long

Private Declare Function RegCloseKey Lib _
 "advapi32.dll" (ByVal hkey As Long) As Long

Private Declare Function RegQueryInfoKey Lib _
 "advapi32.dll" Alias "RegQueryInfoKeyA" _
 (ByVal hkey As Long, ByVal lpClass As String, _
 lpcbClass As Long, ByVal lpReserved As Long, _
 lpcSubKeys As Long, lpcbMaxSubKeyLen As Long, _
 lpcbMaxClassLen As Long, lpcValues As Long, _
 lpcbMaxValueNameLen As Long, lpcbMaxValueLen As Long, _
 ByVal lpcbSecurityDescriptor As Long, _
 lftLastWriteTime As FILETIME) As Long

Private Declare Function RegEnumKeyEx Lib _
 "advapi32.dll" Alias "RegEnumKeyExA" _
 (ByVal hkey As Long, ByVal dwIndex As Long, _
```

```
      ByVal lpName As String, lpcbName As Long, _
      ByVal lpReserved As Long, ByVal lpClass As String, _
      lpcbClass As Long, lpftLastWriteTime As FILETIME) As Long

Private Declare Function RegEnumValueNull Lib _
 "advapi32.dll" Alias "RegEnumValueA" _
 (ByVal hkey As Long, ByVal dwIndex As Long, _
 ByVal lpValueName As String, lpcbValueName As Long, _
 ByVal lpReserved As Long, lpType As Long, _
 lpData As Byte, lpcbData As Long) As Long

Private Declare Function RegEnumValueString Lib _
 "advapi32.dll" Alias "RegEnumValueA" _
 (ByVal hkey As Long, ByVal dwIndex As Long, _
 ByVal lpValueName As String, lpcbValueName As Long, _
 ByVal lpReserved As Long, lpType As Long, _
 ByVal lpValue As String, lpcbData As Long) As Long

Private Declare Function RegEnumValueLong Lib _
 "advapi32.dll" Alias "RegEnumValueA" _
 (ByVal hkey As Long, ByVal dwIndex As Long, _
 ByVal lpValueName As String, lpcbValueName As Long, _
 ByVal lpReserved As Long, lpType As Long, _
 lpValue As Long, lpcbData As Long) As Long

Private Declare Function RegEnumValueBinary Lib _
 "advapi32.dll" Alias "RegEnumValueA" _
 (ByVal hkey As Long, ByVal dwIndex As Long, _
 ByVal lpValueName As String, lpcbValueName As Long, _
 ByVal lpReserved As Long, lpType As Long, _
 lpValue As Byte, lpcbData As Long) As Long

Private Sub Class_Initialize()
 m_root = HKEY_CURRENT_USER
 m_key= "Software\VB and VBA Program Settings"
End Sub

Public Property Get Root() As RegRoot
 Root = m_root
End Property

Public Property Let Root(ByVal idx As RegRoot)
 If idx < HKEY_CLASSES_ROOT Or idx > HKEY_DYN_DATA _
```

```
  Then Exit Property
 m_root = idx
End Property


Public Property Get Key() As String
 Key = m_key
End Property


Public Function ModifyKey(strKeySuffix As String, _
 flag As Boolean) As ErrorList
Dim strOldKey As String
strOldKey = m_key


If flag Then
 If Len(m_key) = 0 And Len(strKeySuffix) = 0 Then
  m_key = ""
 ElseIf Len(m_key) = 0 Then
  m_key = strKeySuffix
 ElseIf Len(strKeySuffix) = 0 Then
  m_key = m_key
 ElseIf Right(strKeySuffix, 1) = "\" Then
  m_key = m_key & strKeySuffix
 Else
  m_key = m_key & "\" & strKeySuffix
 End If
Else


If Len(m_key) >= Len(strKeySuffix) Then _
        m_key = Left(m_key, Len(m_key) - Len(strKeySuffix))


End If


Dim hKey As Long, lRetVal As Long
lRetVal = RegOpenKeyEx(m_root, m_key, 0, KEY_ALL_ACCESS, hKey)


If OpenKey(hKey) = ERROR_SUCCESS Then
 RegCloseKey (hKey)
Else
 m_key = strOldKey
End If
ModifyKey = lRetVal
End Function
```

```
Private Function OpenKey(ByRef hKey As Long) As ErrorList

If Len(m_KeyPrefix) = 0 Then
 hKey = m_root
 OpenKey = ERROR_SUCCESS
Else
 OpenKey = RegOpenKeyEx(m_root, m_key, 0, KEY_ALL_ACCESS, hKey)
End If


End Function

Public Function GetAllKeys(ByRef sArray() As String) As ErrorList

On Error GoTo Handler
Dim lRetVal As Long
Dim hKey As Long, lpcSubKeys As Long, lpcMaxSubKeyLen As Long
Dim lpcbMaxClassLen As Long, lpcValues As Long
Dim lpcbMaxValueNameLen As Long, lpcbMaxValueLen As Long
Dim dwIndex As Long, lpcbName As Long
Dim lpName As String, lpClass As String
Dim FTime As FILETIME

lRetVal = OpenKey(hKey)
If lRetVal <> ERROR_SUCCESS Then
 GetAllKeys = lRetVal
 Exit Function
End If

lRetVal = RegQueryInfoKey(hKey, 0&, 0&, 0&, lpcSubKeys, _
 lpcMaxSubKeyLen, lpcbMaxClassLen, lpcValues, _
 lpcbMaxValueNameLen, lpcbMaxValueLen, 0&, FTime)

If lpcSubKeys = 0 Then _
 Err.Raise ERROR_EMPTY_ARRAY

ReDim sArray(lpcSubKeys - 1)

For dwIndex = 0 To lpcSubKeys - 1
 lpName = Space(lpcMaxSubKeyLen + 1)
 lpcbName = lpcMaxSubKeyLen + 1
 lRetVal = RegEnumKeyEx(hKey, dwIndex, lpName, _
  lpcbName, 0&, lpClass, Len(lpClass), FTime)
 sArray(dwIndex) = Left(lpName, lpcbName)
```

```
Next dwIndex

RegCloseKey (hKey)
GetAllKeys = lRetVal
Exit Function

Handler:
If Err.Number = ERROR_EMPTY_ARRAY Then
 Err.Clear
 GetAllKeys = ERROR_EMPTY_ARRAY
Else
 GetAllKeys = lRetVal
End If
RegCloseKey (hKey)
End Function

Public Function GetAllSettings(vArray() As Variant) As ErrorList

On Error GoTo Handler
Dim lRetVal As Long, dwIndex As Long
Dim hKey As Long, lpcSubKeys As Long
Dim lpcbMaxSubKeyLen As Long, lpcbMaxClassLen As Long
Dim lpcValues As Long, lpcbMaxValueNameLen As Long
Dim lpcbMaxValueLen As Long
Dim lpcbValueName As Long, lpcbData As Long
Dim lValue As Long, lpType As Long

Dim lpValueName As String, sClass As String, lpData As String
Dim bValue() As Byte
Dim FTime As FILETIME

If OpenKey(hKey) <> ERROR_SUCCESS Then Exit Function
lRetVal = RegQueryInfoKey(hKey, 0&, 0&, 0&, _
 lpcSubKeys, lpcbMaxSubKeyLen, _
 lpcbMaxClassLen, lpcValues, lpcbMaxValueNameLen, _
 lpcbMaxValueLen, 0&, FTime)

If lpcValues = 0 Then _
 Err.Raise ERROR_EMPTY_ARRAY
ReDim vArray(lpcValues - 1, 1)
 dwIndex = 0
 Do
  lpcbValueName = lpcbMaxValueNameLen + 1
```

```
lpcbData = lpcbMaxValueLen + 1
lpType = 0
lpValueName = Space(lpcbValueName)
If RegEnumValueNull(hKey, dwIndex, 0&, 0&, 0&, _
 lpType, 0&, 0&) _
 = ERROR_NO_MORE_ITEMS Then Exit Do
Select Case lpType
Case REG_SZ:
 lpData = Space(lpcbData)
 lpcbValueName = lpcbMaxValueNameLen + 1
 lRetVal = RegEnumValueString(hKey, dwIndex, _
  lpValueName, lpcbValueName, 0&, lpType, _
  lpData, lpcbData)
 If Left(lpValueName, lpcbValueName) = "" Then
  vArray(dwIndex, 0) = "Default"
 Else
  vArray(dwIndex, 0) = Left(lpValueName, _
   lpcbValueName)
 End If
 If lRetVal = ERROR_SUCCESS Then
  vArray(dwIndex, 1) = Left$(lpData, lpcbData - 1)
 Else
  vArray(dwIndex, 1) = Empty
 End If
Case REG_BINARY:
 ReDim bValue(lpcbData)
 lpcbValueName = lpcbMaxValueNameLen
 lpcbData = lpcbMaxValueLen
 lRetVal = RegEnumValueBinary(hKey, dwIndex, _
   lpValueName, lpcbValueName, 0&, _
   lpType, bValue(0), lpcbData)
 If Left(lpValueName, lpcbValueName) = "" Then
  vArray(dwIndex, 0) = "Default"
 Else
  vArray(dwIndex, 0) = Left(lpValueName, _
   lpcbValueName)
 End If
 If lRetVal = ERROR_SUCCESS Then _
  vArray(dwIndex, 1) = bValue

Case REG_DWORD:
 lpcbValueName = lpcbMaxValueNameLen
 lpcbData = lpcbMaxValueLen
```

```
   lRetVal = RegEnumValueLong(hKey, dwIndex, _
     lpValueName, lpcbValueName, _
     0&, lpType, lValue, lpcbData)
  If Left(lpValueName, lpcbValueName) = "" Then
   vArray(dwIndex, 0) = "Default"
  Else
   vArray(dwIndex, 0) = Left(lpValueName, _
     lpcbValueName)
  End If
  If lRetVal = ERROR_SUCCESS Then _
   vArray(dwIndex, 1) = lValue
 Case Else
  vArray(dwIndex, 0) = "Unsupported Data Type"
  vArray(dwIndex, 1) = "Unsupported Data Type"
 End Select
 dwIndex = dwIndex + 1
Loop

RegCloseKey (hKey)
GetAllSettings = lRetVal
Exit Function

Handler:
If Err.Number = ERROR_EMPTY_ARRAY Then
Err.Clear
GetAllSettings = ERROR_EMPTY_ARRAY
End If
End Function
```

ANNOTATIONS

```
Option Explicit

Private m_key As String
Private m_root As Long
```

The variable *m_root* holds the value of the Registry root that is currently being manipulated. Its data type is a **Long** because, as the next annotation will discuss, the handles to the Registry roots are constants having a Long value.

Only one Registry root at a time can be manipulated. Storing the value of the currently active Registry root in a variable ensures that only one Registry root at a time will be considered "active" by the application.

The variable *m_key* holds the name of and path to the key that is currently being explored. Since this variable is holding a key name and path, its data type is a **String**.

As with the one Registry root, only one subkey of the Registry root at a time can be explored. Storing the value of the currently active subkey in a variable ensures that only one subkey at a time will be considered "active" by the application.

However, while one Registry root has to be chosen to explore the Registry, it is not necessary to choose a subkey. The subkeys and values (if any) of a root key can be viewed. Therefore, it is possible for the value of *m_key* to be an empty string ("").

```
Public Enum RegRoot
  HKEY_CLASSES_ROOT = &H80000000
  HKEY_CURRENT_USER = &H80000001
  HKEY_LOCAL_MACHINE = &H80000002
  HKEY_USERS = &H80000003
  HKEY_PERFORMANCE_DATA = &H80000004
  HKEY_CURRENT_CONFIG = &H80000005
  HKEY_DYN_DATA = &H80000006
End Enum
```

The keyword **Enum** stands for enumeration. The **Enum** statement was introduced in Visual Basic 5.

The **Enum** statement has an *access specifier*, a *name*, and *members*. The **Enum** statement may only be declared at the module level.

In this example, the access specifier is **Public**. It may also be **Private**, but, as discussed below, declaring it **Private** would defeat the purpose here of the **Enum** statement.

In this example, the name of the **Enum** statement is *RegRoot*. As discussed in the annotation to the **Property Get** and **Let Root** procedures, the name of the **Enum** statement is used in a manner similar to a user-defined type.

The members of the **Enum** statement are the values that correspond to the constants for the root keys of the Registry. The values of members of an **Enum** statement are constants. These values, by default, start at 0, and increase by 1 for each succeeding value. However, as in this example, the starting value may be other than 0. Additionally, the succeeding values do not have to increase by 1, and may be any different number within the range of the data type, including a negative number. The default data type of an **Enum** statement is **Long**.

The reason the **Enum** statement is used is that constants in a class module must be **Private**. If it would be helpful to refer to these constant values outside of the class, as with this example, then the constants would have to be declared again outside of the class. This is duplicative.

By contrast, an **Enum** statement may be declared **Public**. Therefore, the constants in the **Enum** statement may be referred to outside of the class without the need again to declare the constants. Making the constant members of the **Enum** statement **Public** does not violate the principle of encapsulation. Since the members are constants, their values cannot be changed from outside of the class.

The **Enum** statement appears in the Object Browser for the application. The name of the **Enum** statement appears in the list view and the members of the **Enum** statement appear in the Contents pane. (See Figure 8-4.)

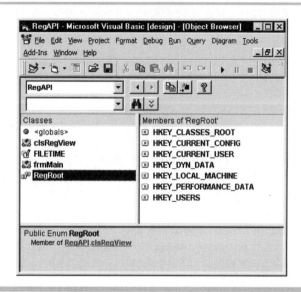

FIGURE 8-4. The RegRoot Enumeration in the Object Browser

```
Public Property Get Root() As RegRoot
 Root = m_root
End Property


Public Property Let Root(ByVal idx As RegRoot)
 If idx < HKEY_CLASSES_ROOT Or idx > HKEY_DYN_DATA _
  Then Exit Property
 m_root = idx
End Property
```

The name of the **Enum** statement also can be used in a manner similar to a user-defined type in a **Property** procedure. The **Property Let** procedure takes a *RegRoot* as a parameter, and the **Property Get** procedure returns a *RegRoot* value.

However, *RegRoot* is not really a data type. Therefore, the *RegRoot* parameter in the **Property Let** procedure will not restrict the parameter to the values, or range of values, in the enumeration. Rather, any long integer may be passed to the **Property Let** procedure. Consequently, validation still is required. Here the parameter of the **Property Let** procedure is validated by checking to see if the parameter is either less than HKEY_CLASSES_ROOT or greater than HKEY_DYN_DATA.

The advantage of using *RegRoot* as a parameter in the **Property Let** procedure and as a return value in the **Property Get** procedure is readability of code. It is clear to someone else viewing your code that the parameter (or return value) is restricted to a certain range of values. This is no small advantage these days when applications are designed by a team of programmers who have to read each other's code. Writing readable code, as well as documenting it, helps establish your reputation among your fellow programmers. Of course, you can also develop a reputation by writing unreadable code, but those types of programmers usually do not last long, either because they are fired or they suffer an even more grisly fate at the hands of their fellow programmers.

```
Public Property Get Key () As String
 Key = m_key
End Property
```

This is a garden-variety **Property Get** procedure. It simply returns the value of *m_key*, the key which is currently being manipulated.

```
Public Function ModifyKey(strKeySuffix As String, _
 flag As Boolean) As ErrorList
```

While this class module has a **Property Get** procedure to retrieve the value of *m_key*, it has no corresponding **Property Let** procedure to change the value of *m_key*. There could have been one. Instead, a conscious design decision was made to use a function to change the value of *m_key*.

A **Property Let** procedure would assign to *m_key* the value of the Property procedure's parameter. However, this wholesale overwriting and replacement of the value of *m_key* is not consistent with the hierarchical nature of the Registry. Moving from one key to another involves either adding suffixes to a current key (for example, Software to Software\VBA and VBA Program Settings) while drilling down into the Registry, or the converse—removing suffixes while moving back up the Registry hierarchy.

For these reasons, this class module does not use a **Property Let** procedure to change the value of *m_key*. Instead, it uses a function that takes two parameters. The first parameter, *strKeySuffix*, is a string which represents the suffix to be added or removed. The second parameter, *flag*, is, as its name suggests, a flag indicating whether the suffix is to be added (True) or removed (False). While this application does not use a List View or Tree View metaphor, this function could be used when the user clicks the plus sign to drill down or the minus sign to move up the hierarchy.

```
Dim strOldKey As String
strOldKey = m_key
```

The value of *m_key* is stored in *strOldKeyPrefix* before the value of *m_key* is changed. The reason is that if the new value of *m_key* is invalid, the former (and valid) value of *m_key* can be restored.

```
If flag Then
 If Len(m_Key) = 0 And Len(strKeySuffix) = 0 Then
  m_key = ""
 ElseIf Len(m_Key) = 0 Then
  m_key = strKeySuffix
 ElseIf Len(strKeySuffix) = 0 Then
  m_key = m_Key
 ElseIf Right(strKeySuffix, 1) = "\" Then
  m_key = m_key& strKeySuffix
 Else
  m_key = m_key& "\" & strKeySuffix
 End If
```

This code adds the suffix, which could be an empty string, to the existing value of *m_key*, which also could be an empty string. It also ensures that the subkey string does not start with a backslash. This becomes important in the next example when a key is created. While Windows 95/98 allow the subkey to begin with a backslash ("\"), Windows NT version 3.5 and later do not.

```
Else

If Len(m_key) >= Len(strKeySuffix) Then _
        m_key = Left(m_Key, Len(m_Key) - Len(strKeySuffix))

End If
```

Conversely, this code subtracts the suffix from the existing value of *m_key*.

```
Dim hkey As Long, lRetVal As Long
lRetVal = RegOpenKeyEx(m_root, m_key, 0, KEY_ALL_ACCESS,hKey)

If OpenKey(hKey) = ERROR_SUCCESS Then
 RegCloseKey (hKey)
Else
 m_key = strOldKey
End If
ModifyKey = lRetVal
End Function
```

The variables *hkey* and *lRetVal* will be parameters to the function used to open the key with its new value. The handle to the opened key (assuming it can be opened) will be assigned in the variable *hkey* and the return value will be assigned to the variable *lRetVal*.

Usually a key is opened to read from or write to it. The purpose here will be data validation. This function should not permanently modify the value of *m_key* without first assuring that its new value will be valid. Accordingly, an attempt is made to open the key with its new value.

If the key can be opened, then the return value of the function **RegOpenKeyEx**, which is discussed in more detail in the annotations below, is the constant ERROR_SUCCESS, which has a value of 0. In that event, the key simply is closed, since the purpose of opening the key was not to read from or write to it, but simply to confirm, by successfully opening it, that it is a valid key.

If the key cannot be opened, then the former and valid value of *m_key*, stored in *strOldKeySuffix*, is assigned back to *m_key*.

```
Private Sub Class_Initialize()
 m_root = HKEY_CURRENT_USER
 m_key = "Software\VB and VBA Program Settings"
End Sub
```

The **Initialize** event occurs when an instance of the class is created. The statements in the **Initialize** event assign default values to the two class variables. The result is that the key to be manipulated is the HKEY_CURRENT_USER\ Software\VB and VBA Program Settings key used by the intrinsic Visual Basic Registry manipulation functions **GetSetting**, **SaveSetting**, **DeleteSetting**, and **GetAllSettings**. However, unlike the intrinsic Visual Basic Registry manipulation functions, this class module can manipulate keys in other sections of the Registry.

```
Public Enum RegData
 REG_NONE = 0&
 REG_EXPAND_SZ = 2&
 REG_SZ = 1&
 REG_BINARY = 3&
 REG_DWORD = 4&
 REG_DWORD_BIG_ENDIAN = 5&
 REG_LINK = 6&
 REG_MULTI_SZ = 7&
 REG_RESOURCE_LIST = 8&
 REG_FULL_RESOURCE_DESCRIPTOR = 9&
End Enum
```

This **Enum** statement lists various data types in the Registry. Information on the data type of value data is needed by several API functions. These data types are summarized in Table 8-8.

```
Public Enum ErrorList
 ERROR_SUCCESS = 0&
 ERROR_FILE_NOT_FOUND = 2&
 ERROR_ACCESS_DENIED = 5&
 ERROR_INVALID_HANDLE = 6&
 ERROR_OUTOFMEMORY = 14&
 ERROR_INVALID_PARAMETER = 87&
 ERROR_BAD_PATHNAME = 161&
 ERROR_MORE_DATA = 234&
 ERROR_NO_MORE_ITEMS = 259&
 ERROR_BADKEY = 1010&
 ERROR_CANTOPEN = 1011&
 ERROR_CANTREAD = 1012&
```

Constant	Data Type
REG_BINARY	Binary.
REG_DWORD	Long.
REG_DWORD_BIG_ENDIAN	Long in "big-endian format" (that is, the most significant byte of a word is the low-order byte).
REG_DWORD_LITTLE_ENDIAN	Long in "little-endian format" (that is, the most significant byte of a word is the high-order byte).
REG_EXPAND_SZ	A null-terminated string containing unexpanded references to environment variables.
REG_LINK	A symbolic link between Registry keys.
REG_MULTI_SZ	An array of null-terminated strings, terminated by two null characters.
REG_NONE	No defined value type.
REG_RESOURCE_LIST	A device-driver resource list.
REG_SZ	A null-terminated string.

TABLE 8-8.   Registry Data Types

```
ERROR_CANTWRITE = 1013&
ERROR_KEYDELETED = 1018&
ERROR_EMPTY_ARRAY = vbObjectError + 512 + 5
End Enum
```

The return value of many of the Registry API functions is an error code. The error code does not necessarily mean that an error occurred. The most common error code (hopefully) is ERROR_SUCCESS, which means success! Table 8-9 lists a number of the more common error codes.

The last member of ErrorList, ERROR_EMPTY_ARRAY, is not listed in Table 8-8. The reason is that it is not an intrinsic error. Rather, it is a user-defined error, that is, an error "created" by the application programmer. ERROR_EMPTY_ARRAY really is not an error in the true sense, that is, an error which if not handled will terminate the application. Rather, it is a condition which the application programmer wishes to treat as if it were an error. Further specifics will be given in the annotation below to **GetAllSettings**.

```
Private Const SYNCHRONIZE = &H100000
Private Const STANDARD_RIGHTS_ALL As Long = &H1F0000
Private Const READ_CONTROL As Long = &H20000
Private Const STANDARD_RIGHTS_READ As Long = (READ_CONTROL)
Private Const STANDARD_RIGHTS_WRITE As Long = (READ_CONTROL)

Private Const KEY_QUERY_VALUE As Long = &H1
```

Value	Meaning
ERROR_SUCCESS	The function was successful.
ERROR_NO_MORE_ITEMS	There are no more keys or values to enumerate.
ERROR_MORE_DATA	The buffer is not large enough to hold the entire value.
ERROR_FILE_NOT_FOUND	The specified key was not found in the Registry database.
ERROR_CANTOPEN ERROR_CANTREAD	Aliases of ERROR_FILE_NOT_FOUND for 16-bit code.
ERROR_ACCESS_DENIED	Attempt to write to a key for which code does not have write access.
ERROR_BADKEY	The subkey string contains an invalid character or the handle identifying the key is invalid.
ERROR_LOCK_FAILED	Registry reentered while blocked by same process.
ERROR_INVALID_PARAMETER	Parameter is required and not specified, an invalid pointer, or otherwise not valid.
ERROR_OUTOFMEMORY	Insufficient memory to open the Registry key or insufficient memory to load the required data from the Registry file.

TABLE 8-9.   Registry Error Codes

```
Private Const KEY_SET_VALUE As Long = &H2
Private Const KEY_CREATE_SUB_KEY As Long = &H4
Private Const KEY_ENUMERATE_SUB_KEYS As Long = &H8
Private Const KEY_NOTIFY As Long = &H10
Private Const KEY_CREATE_LINK As Long = &H20
Private Const KEY_READ As Long = _
 ((STANDARD_RIGHTS_READ Or KEY_QUERY_VALUE Or _
 KEY_ENUMERATE_SUB_KEYS Or KEY_NOTIFY) _
 And (Not SYNCHRONIZE))
Private Const KEY_EXECUTE As Long = _
 ((KEY_READ) And (Not SYNCHRONIZE))
Private Const KEY_WRITE As Long = _
 ((STANDARD_RIGHTS_WRITE Or KEY_SET_VALUE _
 Or KEY_CREATE_SUB_KEY) And (Not SYNCHRONIZE))
Private Const KEY_ALL_ACCESS As Long = _
 ((STANDARD_RIGHTS_ALL Or KEY_QUERY_VALUE Or _
```

```
KEY_SET_VALUE Or KEY_CREATE_SUB_KEY Or _
KEY_ENUMERATE_SUB_KEYS Or KEY_NOTIFY Or _
KEY_CREATE_LINK) And (Not SYNCHRONIZE))
```

These constants concern security attributes for the Registry keys. The system administrator usually would not want all users to have unrestricted access to Registry keys. The security attributes are summarized in Table 8-10.

```
Private Const REG_OPTION_NON_VOLATILE As Long = 0
```

This simply is a constant that will be needed by an API function.

```
Private Type FILETIME
 dwLowDateTime As Long
 dwHighDateTime As Long
End Type
```

This user-defined function parallels the FILETIME structure, to which several of the API functions return a pointer. The FILETIME structure is a 64-bit value representing the number of 100-nanosecond intervals since January 1, 1601. Why 1601? Ask Bill Gates. If you are interested in knowing the number of 100-nanosecond intervals since January 1, 1601, you probably also spend your evenings watching Disk Defragmenter and truly need to get a life (just kidding).

Value	Meaning
KEY_ALL_ACCESS	Combination of KEY_QUERY_VALUE, KEY_ENUMERATE_SUB_KEYS, KEY_NOTIFY, KEY_CREATE_SUB_KEY, KEY_CREATE_LINK, and KEY_SET_VALUE access.
KEY_CREATE_LINK	Permission to create a symbolic link.
KEY_CREATE_SUB_KEY	Permission to create subkeys.
KEY_ENUMERATE_SUB_KEYS	Permission to enumerate subkeys.
KEY_EXECUTE	Permission for read access.
KEY_NOTIFY	Permission for change notification.
KEY_QUERY_VALUE	Permission to query subkey data.
KEY_READ	Combination of KEY_QUERY_VALUE, KEY_ENUMERATE_SUB_KEYS, and KEY_NOTIFY access.
KEY_SET_VALUE	Permission to set subkey data.
KEY_WRITE	Combination of KEY_SET_VALUE and KEY_CREATE_SUB_KEY access.

TABLE 8-10. Security Attributes

Actually, the information contained in the FILETIME structure is used in Windows NT, where the API functions use the members of the FILETIME structure to indicate the last time that the key or any of its value entries was modified. By contrast, this information is not used in Windows 95/98 because that operating system does not keep track of Registry key last write time information. Therefore, in Windows 95/98 the API functions set the members of the FILETIME structure to zero.

```
Private Declare Function RegOpenKeyEx Lib _
 "advapi32.dll" Alias "RegOpenKeyExA" _
 (ByVal hkey As Long, ByVal lpSubKey As String, _
 ByVal ulOptions As Long, ByVal samDesired As Long, _
 phkResult As Long) As Long
```

This Windows API function will be used to open the key to be manipulated. It will be "wrapped" in a user-defined function named **OpenKey** that is discussed in the annotations below. By wrapping a Windows API function in a user-defined function, the programmer prevents the passing of incorrect parameters, which in the case of an API function usually will cause an illegal exception and the resulting crash of the application.

```
Private Declare Function RegCloseKey Lib _
 "advapi32.dll" (ByVal hkey As Long) As Long
```

This function usually is not wrapped in its own user-defined function. First, it is relatively simple to use. **RegCloseKey** takes only one parameter, the handle to the key to be closed. Additionally, it would be unusual for it to be called from outside of the class. Instead, it would be called within the same routine that opened the key. As discussed above, once an opened key is viewed or modified, it should be immediately closed to save system resources.

```
Private Declare Function RegQueryInfoKey Lib _
 "advapi32.dll" Alias "RegQueryInfoKeyA" _
 (ByVal hkey As Long, ByVal lpClass As String, _
 lpcbClass As Long, ByVal lpReserved As Long, _
 lpcSubKeys As Long, lpcbMaxSubKeyLen As Long, _
 lpcbMaxClassLen As Long, lpcValues As Long, _
 lpcbMaxValueNameLen As Long, lpcbMaxValueLen As Long, _
 ByVal lpcbSecurityDescriptor As Long, _
 lftLastWriteTime As FILETIME) As Long
```

The **RegQueryInfoKey** API function retrieves a substantial amount of information about a specified key. This information includes the number of subkeys and the length of the longest subkey name. This information will be used to loop through the subkeys of the key. The information retrieved by the **RegQueryInfoKey** function also includes the names and data of the values of the key and the length of the longest value name and data, respectively.

```
Private Declare Function RegEnumKeyEx Lib _
 "advapi32.dll" Alias "RegEnumKeyExA" _
 (ByVal hkey As Long, ByVal dwIndex As Long, _
 ByVal lpName As String, lpcbName As Long, _
 ByVal lpReserved As Long, ByVal lpClass As String, _
 lpcbClass As Long, lpftLastWriteTime As FILETIME) As Long
```

The **RegEnumKeyEx** API function enumerates subkeys of the specified open Registry key. The function retrieves information about one subkey each time it is called. The second parameter, *dwIndex*, specifies the zero-based index of the subkey. Therefore, this parameter is incremented for each iteration of the loop. A previous call to **RegQueryInfoKey** determined the number of subkeys and therefore the number of iterations. The information provided by this function includes the name of the subkey at the position specified by *dwIndex*.

```
Private Declare Function RegEnumValueNull Lib _
 "advapi32.dll" Alias "RegEnumValueA" _
 (ByVal hkey As Long, ByVal dwIndex As Long, _
 ByVal lpValueName As String, lpcbValueName As Long, _
 ByVal lpReserved As Long, lpType As Long, _
 lpData As Byte, lpcbData As Long) As Long


Private Declare Function RegEnumValueString Lib _
 "advapi32.dll" Alias "RegEnumValueA" _
 (ByVal hkey As Long, ByVal dwIndex As Long, _
 ByVal lpValueName As String, lpcbValueName As Long, _
 ByVal lpReserved As Long, lpType As Long, _
 ByVal lpValue As String, lpcbData As Long) As Long


Private Declare Function RegEnumValueLong Lib _
 "advapi32.dll" Alias "RegEnumValueA" _
 (ByVal hkey As Long, ByVal dwIndex As Long, _
 ByVal lpValueName As String, lpcbValueName As Long, _
 ByVal lpReserved As Long, lpType As Long, _
 lpValue As Long, lpcbData As Long) As Long


Private Declare Function RegEnumValueBinary Lib _
 "advapi32.dll" Alias "RegEnumValueA" _
 (ByVal hkey As Long, ByVal dwIndex As Long, _
 ByVal lpValueName As String, lpcbValueName As Long, _
 ByVal lpReserved As Long, lpType As Long, _
 lpValue As Byte, lpcbData As Long) As Long
```

The **RegEnumValue** API function enumerates the values of the specified open Registry key. The function retrieves information about one value name and data each time it is called. The second parameter, *dwIndex*, specifies the zero-based index of the value. Therefore, this parameter is incremented for each iteration of the loop. A previous call to **RegQueryInfoKey** determined the number of values and therefore the number of iterations.

Four different versions of **RegEnumValue** are declared. The difference between them is the second-to-last parameter, *lpvalue*. That parameter concerns the address of the buffer for the data of a value. Since the data may be of any one of several types, different implementations of **RegEnumValue** are declared for each data type. The use of these implementations will be discussed in the annotation below to **GetAllSettings**.

Care must be taken to declare the *lpReserved* parameter **ByVal**. In certain versions of the Visual Basic API Text Viewer tool, the **ByVal** keyword erroneously was omitted.

```
Private Function OpenKey(ByRef hKey As Long) As ErrorList

If Len(m_KeyPrefix) = 0 Then
 hKey = m_root
 OpenKey = ERROR_SUCCESS
Else
 OpenKey = RegOpenKeyEx(m_root, m_key, 0, KEY_ALL_ACCESS, hKey)
End If


End Function
```

This user-defined function is used to open the specified key. It requires one parameter, the handle to the key to be opened. It does not take as a parameter either the value of the root key or the value of the subkey being manipulated. This prevents the passage of incorrect parameters to the API function **RegOpenKeyEx**. Instead, the API function uses the class variables *m_root* and *m_key*, which as discussed below are private variables. The values of *m_root* and *m_key* only can be changed by the **Root Property** procedure and the **Key** function respectively, both of which have built-in validation routines to ensure that only valid values are written to these class variables.

If the value of *m-key* is an empty string (""), then the return value of **OpenKey** is the value of *m_root*. There is no need to open a key because the root keys of the Registry are always open.

Otherwise, it is necessary to open the key specified by *m_key*. The API function **RegOpenKeyEx** is used. This function takes the parameters specified in Table 8-11.

In this class module, the handle to an open key always will be the value of *m_root*. The reason is that any subkey that is opened for read or write access is closed as soon as the read or write process is completed. This is why **OpenKey** takes *hKey* as a parameter rather than having no parameters and making *hKey* a local variable. By making *hKey* a parameter and having it passed **ByRef**, **OpenKey** can assign to *hKey*

Parameter	Data Type	ByVal or ByRef	Description
hKey	**Long**	**ByVal**	Handle to open key
lpSubKey	**String**	**ByVal**	Address of name of subkey to open
ulOptions	**Long**	**ByVal**	Reserved
samDesired	**Long**	**ByVal**	Security access mask
phkResult	**Long**	**ByRef**	Address of handle to open key

TABLE 8-11. Parameters of **RegOpenKeyEx**

the handle to the key. The statement which called **OpenKey** then can use the value assigned in **OpenKey** to close the key upon the completion of the reading or other manipulation of the key.

Giving the function that calls **OpenKey** a handle to the key also could be accomplished by making *hKey* the return value of **OpenKey**. However, it also is desirable for **OpenKey** to return an error code since it is not a foregone conclusion that the key can be opened. By making *hKey* a paramenter and passing it **ByRef**, we can have our cake (give the function which calls **OpenKey** the handle to the key) and eat it too (return an error code).

The data type of *lpSubKey* is a **String** since the name of and path to the subkey consists of characters. Less obvious is why this parameter is passed **ByVal** rather than **ByRef** when the value of the parameter is an address.

In the C programming language strings are referred to, in Hungarian notation, as LPSTR, which means a pointer to a string that is terminated by a null character (ASCII value of zero). By contrast, in Visual Basic, strings are stored in a different format called BSTR. BSTR strings, like C strings, are null-terminated.

BSTR strings need to be converted to C strings in order for Visual Basic programs to use the Windows API. A programmer reasonably could assume that, since C requires a pointer to a string, Visual Basic should pass strings **ByRef** to Windows API functions. This assumption, while reasonable, is wrong, and would result in the usual illegal exception penalty for passing an API function a bad parameter.

Visual Basic handles the conversion of BSTR strings to C strings by overloading the **ByVal** attribute. Passing a BSTR string **ByVal** does not pass the string by value. Rather, it passes by value a pointer to the string. In other words, passing a BSTR string **ByVal** passes the address of the string. This is the value expected by the API function.

By contrast, passing a BSTR string **ByRef** would pass the address of the pointer to the string. In other words, that which would be passed would be the address of the address of the string. This is not the value expected by the API function, and an illegal exception would result.

The third parameter is reserved, evidently for future use. Its value is always 0&, the "&" type declaration character used since the parameter, though not used, technically has a long value.

The fourth parameter allows unrestricted access.

The fifth parameter will receive the handle to the open key. Therefore, it is passed **ByRef** so its value can be changed. There is no need to explicitly pass it **ByRef**. The **ByRef** attribute is default for the passage of intrinsic data types such as **Long**.

The return value of **OpenKey** is **ErrorList**, the name of the enumeration statement that contains the error codes. This return value enables the statement that calls **OpenKey** to test for errors. If all goes well, the return value will be ERROR_SUCCESS.

```
Public Function GetAllKeys(ByRef sArray() As String) As ErrorList
```

This user-defined function is used to open the specified key. As with **OpenKey**, it takes no parameters for the root key or the subkey to be manipulated. This prevents the passage of incorrect parameters to the API functions that it uses. Instead, **GetAllKeys** uses the class variables *m_root* and *m_key*, which, as discussed in connection with the **OpenKey** subroutine, are protected by validation routines.

GetAllKeys takes one parameter, *sArray*, which is an array of strings. Each element of this array is the name of a subkey. An array is used because there may be more than one subkey. The data type is a **String** because the names of subkeys are strings. This parameter is passed **ByRef** because its value will be assigned by the function.

As with **OpenKey**, the return value is **ErrorList**.

```
On Error GoTo Handler
```

This statement sets up the error handler, which is discussed in the annotations below.

```
Dim lRetVal As Long
Dim hkey As Long, lpcSubKeys As Long, lpcMaxSubKeyLen As Long
Dim lpcbMaxClassLen As Long, lpcValues As Long
Dim lpcbMaxValueNameLen As Long, lpcbMaxValueLen As Long
Dim dwIndex As Long, lpcbName As Long
Dim lpName As String, lpClass As String
```

These variables will be used by API functions. Their use is discussed in the annotation of the calls of those functions.

```
Dim FTime As FILETIME
```

This simply declares a variable of the user-defined type which parallels the FILETIME structure used by several of the API functions. The information provided by the FILETIME structure is not used in this class module, but a variable nevertheless needs to be declared for those instances in which the the FILETIME structure is a parameter.

```
lRetVal = OpenKey(hKey)
If lRetVal <> ERROR_SUCCESS Then
 GetAllKeys = lRetVal
 Exit Function
End If
```

The variable *hKey* is a placeholder for the handle to be retrieved by **OpenKey**. The return value of **OpenKey** is **ErrorList**. If **OpenKey** is not successful, that is, does not return ERROR_SUCCESS, then **GetAllKeys** is assigned the error code and exits. If **OpenKey** is successful, then **OpenKey** assigns to *hKey* the handle of the subkey to be manipulated. This handle then is used to manipulate and finally close the key. This is why *hKey* is passed as a parameter **ByRef** to **OpenKey**.

```
lRetVal = RegQueryInfoKey(hkey, 0&, 0&, 0&, lpcSubKeys, _
 lpcMaxSubKeyLen, lpcbMaxClassLen, lpcValues, _
 lpcbMaxValueNameLen, lpcbMaxValueLen, 0&, FTime)
```

The parameters for **RegQueryInfoKey** are described in Table 8-12.

The only value actually supplied to **RegQueryInfoKey** is the first parameter. That value, the handle to the key to be opened, was returned by the call to **OpenKey**. The remaining parameters are placeholders for values to be retrieved and assigned to them by **RegQueryInfoKey**. The use of those retrieved and assigned values is discussed in the annotations below.

Parameter	Data Type	Description
hKey	**Long**	Handle to key to query
lpClass	**String**	Address of buffer for class string
lpcbClass	**Long**	Address of size of class string buffer
lpReserved	**Long**	Reserved
lpcSubKeys	**Long**	Address of buffer for number of subkeys
lpcbMaxSubKeyLen	**Long**	Address of buffer for longest subkey name length
lpcbMaxClassLen	**Long**	Address of buffer for longest class string length
lpcValues	**Long**	Address of buffer for number of value entries
lpcbMaxValueNameLen	**Long**	Address of buffer for longest value name length
lpcbMaxValueLen	**Long**	Address of buffer for longest value data length
lpcbSecurityDescriptor	**Long**	Address of buffer for security descriptor length
lpftLastWriteTime	FILETIME	Address of buffer for last write time

TABLE 8-12. Parameters for **RegQueryInfoKey**

```
If lpcSubKeys = 0 Then _
 Err.Raise ERROR_EMPTY_ARRAY
```

The variable *lpcSubKeys* is a placeholder that in the call to **RegQueryInfoKey** was assigned the number of subkeys of the key being examined. If there are no subkeys to enumerate, then the error code in **ErrorList** for an empty array (ERROR_EMPTY_ARRAY) is raised. Otherwise the next statement would dimension an array with a lower bound of –1, which would cause an error.

An error is raised by the **Raise** method of the **Err** object. The **Raise** method, quite simply, raises a run-time error which then is handled by the error handler. Only the first parameter of the **Raise** method is mandatory. That parameter is a long integer representing the error to raise. That long integer was assigned to ERROR_EMPTY_ARRAY in the **ErrorList Enum** statement.

You may be wondering why you would want to raise an error when Visual Basic does such a good job generating errors on its own (of course, the errors are not our fault). One reason is that it permits you, as the programmer, to create your own errors, which you can then trap and handle in your error handler just as you could an intrinsic Visual Basic error.

```
ReDim sArray(lpcSubKeys - 1)
```

If there are subkeys, then an array is created to hold the subkey names. The number of elements of the array are the number of subkeys (*lpcSubKeys*) minus one, since the array is zero-based.

The following code involves the **RegEnumKeyEx** API function. The **RegEnumKeyEx** function enumerates subkeys of the specified open Registry key. Its parameters are described in Table 8-13.

```
For dwIndex = 0 To lpcSubKeys - 1
```

Parameter	Data Type	Description
hKey	Long	Handle to key to enumerate
dwIndex	Long	Index of subkey to enumerate
lpName	String	Address of buffer for subkey name
lpcbName	Long	Address for size of subkey buffer
lpReserved	Long	Reserved
lpClass	String	Address of buffer for class string
lpcbClass	Long	Address for size of class buffer
lpftLastWriteTime	FILETIME	Address for time key last written

TABLE 8-13. Parameters of **RegEnumKeyEx**

The **RegEnumKeyEx** function retrieves information about one subkey each time it is called. Therefore it is called in a loop. The number of iterations is the number of subkeys, which is the value of *lpcSubKeys*. However, the index (*dwIndex*) of the subkeys to be enumerated is zero-based, so the loop goes from 0 to *lpcSubKeys* – 1.

```
lpName = Space(lpcMaxSubKeyLen + 1)
```

The *lpName* parameter is a placeholder which receives, through the call to **RegEnumKeyEx**, the subkey name at the specified index. Unlike Visual Basic, in the Windows API sufficient space must be allocated for a parameter of the **String** data type which is to receive a value. The **Space** function returns, depending on how it is called, either a **Variant** or **String** consisting of the specified number of spaces. The number of spaces to reserve should be the length of the longest subkey name plus 1 for the null character appended to the end of strings in C. The length of the longest subkey name is obtained from the *lpcMaxSubKeyLen* parameter of the prior call to **RegQueryInfoKey**.

```
lpcbName = lpcMaxSubKeyLen + 1
```

Similarly, the *lpcbName* parameter of **RegEnumKeyEx** is the number of bytes to reserve for the subkey name at the specified index. The size of this parameter, as was the case with the *lpName* parameter, should be the length of the longest subkey name plus 1 for the null character.

```
lRetVal = RegEnumKeyEx(hkey, dwIndex, lpName, _
    lpcbName, 0&, lpClass, Len(lpClass), FTime)
```

RegEnumKeyEx, like the other Registry API functions discussed in this chapter, returns an error code: ERROR_SUCCESS if successful, the code representing the error otherwise. The variable *lRetVal* will hold the error result.

```
    sArray(dwIndex) = Left(lpName, lpcbName)
Next dwIndex
```

The variable *lpcbName*, upon the return of **RegEnumKeyEx**, holds the number of characters actually loaded into the *lpName* buffer. The **Left** function uses that value to take the leftmost number of characters from *lpName*. Otherwise, the display of the value's name could include a number of empty spaces on the right since the length of the string, before the **Left** function is used, would be the length of the longest value name.

```
RegCloseKey (hKey)
```

RegOpenKeyEx behaves differently in Windows NT than it does in Windows 95/98. In Windows NT **RegOpenKeyEx** always returns a unique handle no matter how many times the same key is opened. By contrast, in Windows 95/98 **RegOpenKeyEx** returns the same handle each time the same key is opened. Windows 95/98 keep a reference count, incrementing it each time the key is opened with **RegOpenKeyEx** and decrementing it each time the key is closed with **RegCloseKey**. The key remains open as long as the reference count is greater than zero.

Because of this difference, if an open key is not closed after its use, and is the subject of another **RegOpenKeyEx** call before it is closed, then the application may run correctly under Windows 95 or 98 but not run correctly or leak Registry handles under Windows NT.

The solution, which is not only simple and direct but also works, is to ensure that there is a corresponding close call for each open call.

```
GetAllKeys = lRetVal
Exit Function
```

These statements execute unless an error has occurred. The error code is returned by **GetAllKeys**. If all has gone well, that error code is ERROR_SUCCESS.

```
Handler:
If Err.Number = ERROR_EMPTY_ARRAY Then
 Err.Clear
 GetAllKeys = ERROR_EMPTY_ARRAY
Else
 GetAllKeys = lRetVal
End If
RegCloseKey (hKey)
End Function
```

If the "error" was an empty array, then that error code was returned by **GetAllKeys**. The ERROR_EMPTY_ARRAY user-defined error is handled by the error handler because of the **Raise** method. In this example the user-defined error is returned to the statement which called **GetAllKeys** to advise that the function call was successful but the array is empty (that is, there are no subkeys). The statement which called **GetAllKeys** then can avoid the errors attendant in attempting to manipulate an empty array.

```
Public Function GetAllSettings(vArray() As Variant) As ErrorList
```

This user-defined function is used to enumerate the values for the specified key. Thus, it is analogous to **GetAllKeys** except that it enumerates values of a key rather than subkeys of a key. As with **GetAllKeys**, **GetAllSettings** takes no parameters for the root key or the subkey to be manipulated. Also as with **GetAllKeys**, **GetAllSettings** has as its sole parameter an array that is passed **ByRef** as its values will be assigned by the function. Also similar to **GetAllKeys**, the return value of **GetAllSettings** is **ErrorList**, which therefore enables the statement that calls **GetAllSettings** to test for errors.

However, there are differences between **GetAllKeys** and **GetAllSettings** in the declaration and handling of their parameter. First, the data type of the parameter in **GetAllSettings** is a **Variant** instead of a **String**. The reason is that the value of the data may not be a **String**. By using the **Variant** data type, all the potential data types can be handled in one function. Additionally, unlike the one-dimensional array in

GetAllKeys, the array in **GetAllSettings** is two-dimensional, since the data as well as the name will be retrieved.

```
On Error GoTo Handler
```

This error handler also will be used primarily to handle the ERROR_EMPTY_ARRAY user-defined error.

```
Dim lRetVal As Long, dwIndex As Long
Dim hkey As Long, lpcSubKeys As Long
Dim lpcbMaxSubKeyLen As Long, lpcbMaxClassLen As Long
Dim lpcValues As Long, lpcbMaxValueNameLen As Long
Dim lpcbMaxValueLen As Long
Dim lpcbValueName As Long, lpcbData As Long
Dim lValue As Long, lpType As Long

Dim lpValueName As String, sClass As String, lpData As String
Dim bValue() As Byte
Dim FTime As FILETIME
```

These variables will be used in the API functions below.

```
lRetVal = OpenKey(hKey)
If lRetVal <> ERROR_SUCCESS Then
 GetAllSettings = lRetVal
 Exit Function
End If
```

These statements are essentially the same as in **GetAllKeys**. The variable *hkey* is a placeholder for the handle to be retrieved by **OpenKey**. The return value of **OpenKey** is **ErrorList**. If **OpenKey** is not successful, that is, does not return ERROR_SUCCESS, then **GetAllSettings** is assigned the error code and exits. If **OpenKey** is successful, then **OpenKey** assigns to *hKey* the handle of the subkey to be manipulated.

```
lRetVal = RegQueryInfoKey(hkey, 0&, 0&, 0&, _
 lpcSubKeys, lpcbMaxSubKeyLen, _
 lpcbMaxClassLen, lpcValues, lpcbMaxValueNameLen, _
 lpcbMaxValueLen, 0&, FTime)

If lpcValues = 0 Then _
 Err.Raise ERROR_EMPTY_ARRAY
```

The logic is essentially the same as in **GetAllSettings**. The variable *lpcValues* is a placeholder that in the call to **RegQueryInfoKey** received the number of values of the key being examined. If there are no values to enumerate, then the error code in

ErrorList for an empty array (ERROR_EMPTY_ARRAY) is raised. Otherwise the following statement would dimension an array with a lower bound of –1, which would cause an error.

```
ReDim vArray(lpcValues - 1, 1)
```

An array is dimensioned. Unlike the one-dimensional array in **GetAllSettings**, this array will have two dimensions, one for the value name, the other for the value data. The number of elements will be the number of values. Since the number of values returned by **RegQueryInfoKey** is one-based but the array is zero-based, the array is dimensioned with *lpcValues* – 1 elements.

The **RegEnumValue** function has the parameters described in Table 8-14.

```
dwIndex = 0
```

The variable *dwIndex* will be the zero-based index of the values being enumerated, so this variable is initialized at zero.

```
Do
  lpcbValueName = lpcbMaxValueNameLen + 1
```

As discussed with **GetAllSettings**, in C, unlike Visual Basic, strings have to be allocated a specific amount of storage space. The variable *lpcbMaxValueNameLen*, returned by **RegQueryKeyInfo**, holds the length of the longest value name. Bacause in C a null character is appended to the end of a string, one is added to *lpcbMaxValueNameLen*. The resulting sum is assigned to *lpcbValueName*, which is used by the **RegEnumValue** function to hold the name of the value at the specified index.

```
lpcbData = lpcbMaxValueLen + 1
```

Parameter	Data Type	Description
hKey	**Long**	Handle to key to query
dwIndex	**Long**	Index of value to query
lpValueName	**String**	Address of buffer for value string
lpcbValueName	**Long**	Address for size of value buffer
lpReserved	**Long**	Reserved
lpType	**Long**	Address of buffer for type code
lpData	**Byte**	Address of buffer for value data
lpcbData	**Long**	Address for size of data buffer

TABLE 8-14.   Parameters for **RegEnumValue**

The variable *lpcbMaxValueLen*, returned by **RegQueryKeyInfo**, holds the length of the longest value data. At this point the data type of that value is unknown. As the data type could be a string, to account for the null character, one is added to *lpcbMaxValueLen*, and the resulting sum is assigned to *lpcbData*, which is used by the **RegEnumValue** function to hold the name of the value at the specified index.

```
lpType = 0
```

The variable *lpType* will hold the type of data at the specified value index. At this point it is assigned the value zero since the type of data has not yet been determined.

```
lpValueName = Space(lpcbValueName)
```

As with **GetAllSettings**, the **Space** function is used to allocate a string of a specific size.

```
If RegEnumValueNull(hkey, dwIndex, 0&, 0&, 0&, _
 lpType, 0&, 0&) _
 = ERROR_NO_MORE_ITEMS Then Exit Do
```

The **RegEnumValueNull** function is called. The purpose is to see if there are any more items to enumerate. If there are none, then the error code returned by **RegEnumValueNull** is ERROR_NO_MORE_ITEMS. In that event, the loop is exited. Otherwise, the loop continues.

The second-to-last parameter, the buffer to receive the value's data, is set to null (0&) because at this point **RegEnumValue** is being used to determine the value's data type. Since the second-to-last parameter is set to null (0&), the last parameter, the length of the buffer to receive the value's data, also may be set to null.

```
Select Case lpType
```

The loop now branches, depending on the data type of the value data. That data type is stored in the *lpType* variable, which was assigned a value in the call to **RegEnumValueNull**.

```
Case REG_SZ:
 lpData = Space(lpcbData)
 lpcbValueName = lpcbMaxValueNameLen + 1
 lRetVal = RegEnumValueString(hkey, dwIndex, _
  lpValueName, lpcbValueName, 0&, lpType, _
  lpData, lpcbData)
```

The first case is if the data type is a **string**.

```
If Left(lpValueName, lpcbValueName) = "" Then
 vArray(dwIndex, 0) = "Default"
Else
 vArray(dwIndex, 0) = Left(lpValueName, lpcbValueName)
End If
```

The call to **RegEnumValueString** assigns to the variable *lpValueName* the name of the value at the specified index. However, the length of that string is the length of the longest value name, which may be much longer than the length of the name of the value at the specified index. Therefore, it is necessary to trim the added spaces on the right side of the string. Otherwise, for example, the name "Data" would be displayed as "Data   ." The empty spaces would not be visible, but as they take up space they could distort the display of the name in, for example, a grid control.

The call to **RegEnumValueString** assigns to the variable *lpcbValueName* the length of the name of the value at the specified index. The **Left** function then is used to extract that number of the leftmost characters of *lpValueName*. The resulting value is assigned to the first dimension of the array, which is the value name.

However, if the value name is Default then the **Left** function will return an empty string (""). In that event the literal string "Default" is explicitly assigned to the first dimension of the array so the display of the value name will not show an empty string.

```
If lRetVal = ERROR_SUCCESS Then
 vArray(dwIndex, 1) = Left$(lpData, lpcbData - 1)
Else
 vArray(dwIndex, 1) = Empty
End If
```

The second element of the array is the value data.

The call to **RegEnumValueString** assigns to the variable *lpData* the data of the value at the specified index. However, the length of that string is the length of the longest value data, which may be much longer than the length of the data of the value at the specified index. Thus, as was done with the value name, the added spaces on the right side of the string need to be trimmed to avoid distortion in the display of the value data.

If the value data is an empty string, then the keyword **Empty** is used to indicate an empty array.

```
Case REG_BINARY:
```

This case addresses binary value data. Binary registy entries often are used to represent flags. Each bit can represent a flag. Thus, 32 flags can be placed in a single **Long** value.

```
ReDim bValue(lpcbData)
```

The variable *bValue* is an array which will hold the number of bytes in the binary value data. Its length is *lpcbData*, the size of the data buffer.

Unlike **Strings**, binary data does not involve null-terminating characters or any other changes to the content of the data.

```
lpcbValueName = lpcbMaxValueNameLen
lpcbData = lpcbMaxValueLen
lRetVal = RegEnumValueBinary(hkey, dwIndex, _
```

```
   lpValueName, lpcbValueName, 0&, lpType, _
   bValue(0), lpcbData)
If Left(lpValueName, lpcbValueName) = "" Then
 vArray(dwIndex, 0) = "Default"
Else
 vArray(dwIndex, 0) = Left(lpValueName, lpcbValueName)
End If
```

This is essentially the same as the corresponding code under the REG_SZ case.

```
If lRetVal = ERROR_SUCCESS Then vArray(dwIndex, 1) = bValue
```

The second dimension of the array, the value data, is assigned the content of the byte array.

```
Case REG_DWORD:
 lpcbValueName = lpcbMaxValueNameLen
 lpcbData = lpcbMaxValueLen
 lRetVal = RegEnumValueLong(hkey, dwIndex, _
   lpValueName, lpcbValueName, 0&, lpType, _
   lValue, lpcbData)
 If Left(lpValueName, lpcbValueName) = "" Then
  vArray(dwIndex, 0) = "Default"
 Else
  vArray(dwIndex, 0) = Left(lpValueName, lpcbValueName)
 End If
```

This also is essentially the same as the corresponding code under the REG_SZ case.

```
If lRetVal = ERROR_SUCCESS Then vArray(dwIndex, 1) = lValue
```

The second dimension of the array, the value data, is assigned the value data retrieved by **RegEnumValue**.

```
Case Else
 vArray(dwIndex, 0) = "Unsupported Data Type"
 vArray(dwIndex, 1) = "Unsupported Data Type"
End Select
```

There are other data types in the Registry as shown by Table 8-8. This class module only addresses the most common ones, so the others simply will display an "Unsupported Data Type" message. However, to the extent you wish to address those other data types, all that needs to be done is to add another case statement with code that, with a few differences, would parallel that above. As for what those differences are, well, we don't want to spoil your fun.

```
 dwIndex = dwIndex + 1
Loop
```

The index of the value being examined is incremented with each iteration of the loop.

```
RegCloseKey (hKey)
GetAllSettings = lRetVal
Exit Function
```

Unless the ERROR_EMPTY_ARRAY error was raised, the error code, hopefully ERROR_SUCCESS, is returned by **GetAllSettings**.

```
Handler:
If Err.Number = ERROR_EMPTY_ARRAY Then
Err.Clear
GetAllSettings = ERROR_EMPTY_ARRAY
End If
End Function
```

The error handler handles the error raised when there is an empty array, that is, when there are no values to enumerate. In this event, that error code is returned by **GetAllSettings**.

Additionally, the **Err** object is cleared by the **Clear** method. The purpose is to ensure that the **Err** object does not retain the ERROR_EMPTY_ARRAY value. In this case the **Clear** method may not be necessary. The **Err** object is cleared when the function exits. However, it is good programming practice to explicitly clear the **Err** object rather than rely on default clearing.

TEST THE CODE

1. Start a new Project, Standard Exe.

2. Insert the class module named **clsRegView**.

3. Insert a form. Accept the default properties. Name it **frmMain**.

4. Place a control array of seven option buttons on the form, preferably inside of a frame. The index numbers and labels of the option buttons are as follows:

Index Number	Label
0	HKEY_CLASSES_ROOT
1	HKEY_CURRENT_USER
2	HKEY_LOCAL_MACHINE
3	HKEY_USERS
4	HKEY_PERFORMANCE_DATA
5	HKEY_CURRENT_CONFIG
6	HKEY_DYN_DATA

5. Place on the form the following additional controls:

Control Type	Control Name	Purpose
MSFlexGrid	MSFlexGrid1	Displays value names and data of a key
ListBox	lstKeys	Lists the subkeys of a given key
TextBox	txtPath	Displays the path of the subkey being manipulated
Label	Label1	Captioned "Current Path." It is associated with the TextBox control.
Command Button	cmdBack	Its caption is "<." Its purpose is to move the subkey being manipulated one up the heirarchy.

The form should appear like Figure 8-5.

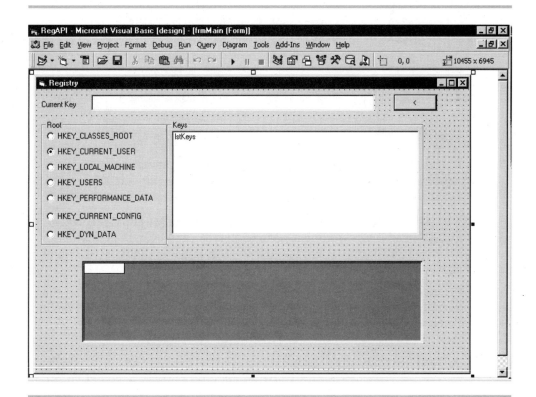

FIGURE 8-5. The Registry Viewer form in Design view

6. Add the following code to the declarations of the form:

```
Option Explicit
Public cReg As clsRegView
```

7. Add the following code to the **Load** event of the form:

```
Private Sub Form_Load()

Set cReg = New clsRegView
MSFlexGrid1.Cols = 2
MSFlexGrid1.ColAlignment(0) = flexAlignLeftCenter
MSFlexGrid1.ColAlignment(1) = flexAlignLeftCenter
MSFlexGrid1.ColWidth(0) = MSFlexGrid1.Width * 0.4
MSFlexGrid1.ColWidth(1) = MSFlexGrid1.Width * 0.6

optRootKeys(cReg.Root - HKEY_CLASSES_ROOT).Value = True
txtPath.Text = cReg.Key

Dim vArray() As String
Dim vValues() As Variant

If cReg.GetAllKeys(vArray()) = ERROR_SUCCESS Then _
 FillKeys vArray()

If cReg.GetAllSettings(vValues()) = ERROR_SUCCESS Then _
 FillValues vValues
End Sub
```

This code hard-codes the number of columns of the **MSFlexGrid** control to 2. Normally, hard-coding is not a good idea. However, in this case the **MSFlexGrid** control displays only the value names and data, so the number of columns always will be 2.

The number of rows is set dynamically since it is not known until run-time how many values will be displayed. This number will be set in the **FillValues** function described below.

The text alignment of both columns is set by the **ColAlignment** property of the **MSFlexGrid** control. Each column is represented by an index, which is zero-based. The value for the **ColAlignment** property is *flexAlignLeftCenter*, an intrinsic constant which means left-aligned horizontally and center-aligned vertically.

The width of both columns is set by the **ColWidth** property of the **MSFlexGrid** control. Once again, each column is represented by an index which is zero-based. The width of the columns is hard-coded at 40% and 60%, respectively, of the total width of the control, the idea being that the length of the name will not be the same as the length of the data.

The width of the columns could be sized dynamically. As discussed in the annotations to **GetAllSettings**, **RegQueryInfoKey** retrieves the length of longest value name and value data respectively. These values could be used to size the relative widths of the two columns. A good idea for the next edition!

The next statement selects the button of the Option button control array that corresponds with the value of the *m_root* class variable. This value is retrieved with the **Property Get Root** procedure of the class.

The text box control's **Text** property is assigned the value of the *m_key* class variable that is retrieved with the **Property Get Key** procedure of the class.

Assuming **GetAllKeys** returns ERROR_SUCCESS, the user-defined function **FillAllKeys**, discussed below, fills the list box with the subkeys of the key being manipulated.

Finally, if **GetAllSettings** returns ERROR_SUCCESS, the user-defined function **FillAllValues**, also discussed below, fills the **MSFlexGrid** control with the value names and data of the key being manipulated.

8. Add the following code to the **Click** event of the Option Button control array:

```
Private Sub optRootKeys_Click(Index As Integer)
MSFlexGrid1.Clear
Dim sArray As String
cReg.Root = HKEY_CLASSES_ROOT + Index
cReg.ModifyKey txtPath.Text, False
If cReg.GetAllKeys(sArray()) <> ERROR_SUCCESS Then Exit Sub
  txtPath.Text = cReg.Key
  FillKeys sArray
End Sub
```

The **MSFlexGrid** control first is cleared so that any values pertaining to the prior key being manipulated do not remain displayed.

The *m_root* class variable then is assigned the value of the option button which was selected. This assignment is accomplished with the **Property Let Root** procedure in the class. The value being assigned is the sum of the index of the option button selected and the HKEY_CLASSES_ROOT constant of the class. Since this constant is a member of an **Enum** statement, it (unlike stand-alone constants) is **Public** and therefore visisble to the form. However, while it is visible to the form, HKEY_CLASSES_ROOT still is a constant and therefore its value cannot be changed in the form. Therefore the principle of encapsulating class values is not violated.

If an option button is selected, then the *m_key* variable should be assigned an empty string, since the key being manipulated will be a root key. The **ModifyKey** function of the class accomplishes this. The current value of *m_key* is passed with a *False* parameter indicating that the first parameter should be "subtracted" from the value of *m_key*. The effect is that the value of *m_key* is subtracted from itself, resulting in an empty string.

If the return value of **GetAllKeys** is ERROR_SUCCESS, then the text box control's **Text** property is assigned the new value of *m_key*. This value is retrieved using the **Property Get Key** procedure. Additionally, the list box is filled with the **FillKeys** procedure discussed below.

9. Add the following code to the **Click** event of the ListBox:

```
Private Sub lstKeys_Click()

Dim vKeys() As String
Dim vValues() As Variant

If Len(txtPath) Then
  txtPath.Text = txtPath.Text & "\" & lstKeys.List(lstKeys.ListIndex)
Else
  txtPath = lstKeys.List(lstKeys.ListIndex)
End If

cReg.ModifyKey lstKeys.List(lstKeys.ListIndex), True
Dim e As ErrorList
e = cReg.GetAllKeys(vKeys())
If e <> ERROR_SUCCESS And e <> ERROR_EMPTY_ARRAY Then Exit Sub
If e = ERROR_SUCCESS Then FillKeys vKeys
If e = ERROR_EMPTY_ARRAY Then lstKeys.Clear

If cReg.GetAllSettings(vValues()) = ERROR_SUCCESS Then _
  FillValues vValues
End Sub
```

The key in the list box which the user clicks is used to update both the text box's **Text** property and the *m_key* class variable. If there already is text in the text box, then a backslash ("\") is appended before the key selected in the list box to delimit the newly selected key. If there is no text in the text box, then a backslash is not needed to delimit and therefore is not appended. Indeed, the backslash should not be appended to the beginning of the subkey name. As mentioned above in the annotation to **ModifyKey**, in Windows NT attempting to create a subkey that begins with a backslash can cause an error.

The **ModifyKey** function of the class is called with the second parameter being *True* to add the newly selected key (the first parameter) to the value of *m_key*.

The variable *e*, which is of the **Enum ErrorList**, is assigned the return value of the class function **GetAllKeys**. If the return value is ERROR_SUCCESS, then **FillKeys** is called with the string array filled by **GetAllKeys**. If the return value is ERROR_EMPTY_ARRAY, then the list box is cleared, as there are no keys to list.

Finally, **GetAllSettings** is called to fill the variant array passed as the first parameter with the value names and data. This array is a variant because the data may be other than a **String**, such as a **Long** or **Byte**. If the return value of **GetAllSettings** is ERROR_SUCCESS, then **FillValues** is called passing the variant array.

10. Add the following code to the command button:

```
Private Sub cmdBack_Click()

Dim intPos As Integer, intCounter As Integer
intPos = 0

For intCounter = 1 To Len(txtPath.Text)
  If Mid(txtPath.Text, intCounter, 1) = "\" _
      Then intPos = intCounter
Next intCounter

If intPos = 0 Then
  cReg.ModifyKey Len(txtPath.Text), False
  txtPath.Text = ""
Else
  cReg.ModifyKey Right(txtPath.Text, _
      Len(txtPath.Text) - intPos + 1), False
  txtPath.Text = Left(txtPath.Text, intPos - 1)
End If

MSFlexGrid1.Clear
Dim sArray() As String
If cReg.GetAllKeys(sArray()) = ERROR_SUCCESS Then _
  FillKeys sArray
End Sub
```

This code permits the user to go back up the hierarchy, just as clicking on the list box permits the user to drill down into the Registry.

The code first checks if a backslash is part of the value of *m_key*. There would not be a backslash if *m_key* is a root key or a first-level subkey. In these cases, **ModifyKey** is called to retain or set (as the case may be) the value of *m_key* as an empty string.

If a backslash is part of the value of *m_key*, then **ModifyKey** is called in conjunction with the **Right** function to subtract from *m_key* the characters to the right of the last backslash.

The **MSFlexGrid** control next is cleared since the values displayed there correspond to the former value of *m_key*.

The **GetAllKeys** function of the class is called, passing as a parameter a **String** array. If the return value is ERROR_SUCCESS then the **FillKeys** function is called, passing the **String** array which, as the result of **GetAllKeys**, holds the value names and data.

11. Add the following procedure to the form module:

```
Private Sub FillKeys(vArray As Variant)
On Error GoTo Handler
Dim i As Long
lstKeys.Clear

If IsArray(sArray) Then
 For i = 0 To UBound(sArray)
  lstKeys.AddItem sArray(i)
 Next
End If
Exit Sub

Handler:
Select Case Err.Number
Case 13:
Resume Next
End Select
End Sub
```

This code fills the list box with the array of key names retrieved by **GetAllKeys**. An error handler is added to protect against a subscript of the array being out of bounds, though the other code should protect against this error.

12. Add the following procedure to the form module:

```
Private Sub FillValues(vArray As Variant)
On Error GoTo Handler
Dim iCurRow As Integer, iCurCol As Integer
MSFlexGrid1.Clear

If IsArray(vArray) Then
 MSFlexGrid1.Rows = UBound(vArray, 1) + 1
 MSFlexGrid1.Cols = 2
```

```
For iCurRow = 0 To UBound(vArray, 1)
 For iCurCol = 0 To 1
  MSFlexGrid1.Col = iCurCol
  MSFlexGrid1.Row = iCurRow
  MSFlexGrid1.Text = vArray(iCurRow, iCurCol)
 Next iCurCol
Next iCurRow
End If
Exit Sub

Handler:
Select Case Err.Number
Case 13:
Exit Sub
End Select
End Sub
```

This code fills the **MSFlexGrid** control with the array of value names and data retrieved by **GetAllSettings**. As with **FillKeys**, an error handler is added to protect against a subscript of the array being out of bounds, though the other code should protect against this error.

Test the code! At startup the form should appear as in Figure 8-6.

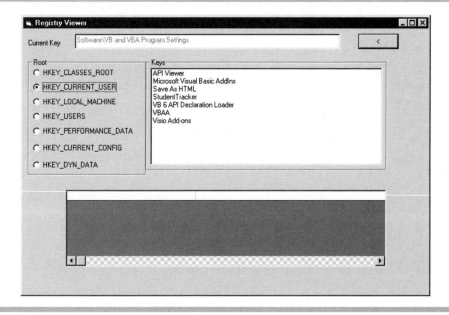

FIGURE 8-6.   The Registry Viewer at startup

Next, drill down into the Registry. On the computer in which this example was prepared, this was done first by clicking "StudentTracker," then by clicking "Directories." (See Figure 8-7.)

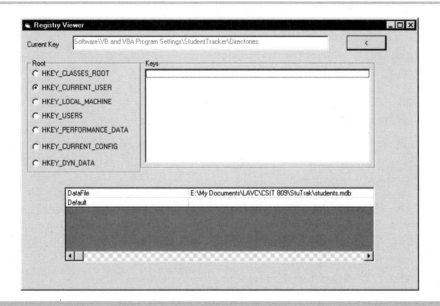

FIGURE 8-7.   Drilling down into the Registry

Finally, using the command button labeled "<", move back up the Registry into the "Software" first-level subkey, which is one level above the "VBA and VBA Program Settings" subkey. (See Figure 8-8.)

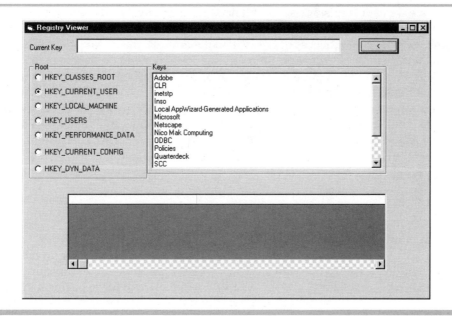

FIGURE 8-8. Moving back up the Registry

RegWrite.vbp

Writing to the Registry

Now it's time for more advanced Registry manipulation. This means writing to the Registry.

Writing to the Registry need not be an example of "Fools rush in where angels fear to tread." However, it is an example of "Don't try this at home, kids—we're trained professionals." No one should be making changes to the Registry without knowing what they are doing. However, we *are* professionals!

While we are professionals, we still need to be careful. As yet another saying goes, "There are old rock climbers, and bold rock climbers, but no old, bold rock climbers." The consequences of failure usually are less drastic for programmers than they are for rock climbers, although this could depend on the propensity for violence of the person whose Registry you have just trashed. Trying to restore a trashed Registry is no picnic.

This example will write *carefully* to the Registry. The only keys and values which will be modified will be those added by the example. Keys and values only will be added in a relatively safe portion of the Registry, the HK_CURRENT_USER/ Software/VBA and VBA Program Settings subkey to which the Visual Basic Registry functions are restricted.

SYNOPSIS OF CODE

This application will open a rich text file (.rtf extension) in a **RichTextBox** control. The path to and name of the file will be stored in the Registry, in the HK_CURRENT_USER/Software/VBA and VBA Program Settings area, under the application name subkey "VBAA." The VBAA subkey will have a value named "Path," under which the path to and name of the file last opened will be stored.

The application first will use the class functions **ModifyKey** and **OpenKey** to attempt to open the key that contains the "Path" value. If the key does not exist, it is created using the class function **CreateKey**, which wraps the API function **RegCreateKeyEx**.

The application next uses the class function **QueryValue**, which wraps **RegQueryValueEx**, to attempt to query the "Path" value. If the value does not exist, it is created using the class function **SetValue**, which wraps the API function **RegSetValueEx**. Different implementations of **RegSetValueEx** are used depending on the data type of the data to be written to the value.

If the path to the file to be opened is not valid, such as if the file had been renamed or moved, then **SetValue** again is used to change the value data to the path and filename chosen by the application user with a common dialog control.

CODE

The italicized code was added to the class module from the RegViewer.vbp project.

```
Option Explicit

Private m_key As String
Private m_root As Long

Public Enum RegRoot
```

```
    HKEY_CLASSES_ROOT = &H80000000
    HKEY_CURRENT_USER = &H80000001
    HKEY_LOCAL_MACHINE = &H80000002
    HKEY_USERS = &H80000003
    HKEY_PERFORMANCE_DATA = &H80000004
    HKEY_CURRENT_CONFIG = &H80000005
    HKEY_DYN_DATA = &H80000006
End Enum


Public Enum RegData
    REG_NONE = 0&
    REG_EXPAND_SZ = 2&
    REG_SZ = 1&
    REG_BINARY = 3&
    REG_DWORD = 4&
    REG_DWORD_BIG_ENDIAN = 5&
    REG_LINK = 6&
    REG_MULTI_SZ = 7&
    REG_RESOURCE_LIST = 8&
    REG_FULL_RESOURCE_DESCRIPTOR = 9&
End Enum


Public Enum ErrorList
    ERROR_SUCCESS = 0&
    ERROR_FILE_NOT_FOUND = 2&
    ERROR_ACCESS_DENIED = 5&
    ERROR_INVALID_HANDLE = 6&
    ERROR_OUTOFMEMORY = 14&
    ERROR_INVALID_PARAMETER = 87&
    ERROR_BAD_PATHNAME = 161&
    ERROR_MORE_DATA = 234&
    ERROR_NO_MORE_ITEMS = 259&
    ERROR_BADKEY = 1010&
    ERROR_CANTOPEN = 1011&
    ERROR_CANTREAD = 1012&
    ERROR_CANTWRITE = 1013&
    ERROR_KEYDELETED = 1018&
    ERROR_EMPTY_ARRAY = vbObjectError + 512 + 5
End Enum


Private Const SYNCHRONIZE = &H100000
Private Const STANDARD_RIGHTS_ALL As Long = &H1F0000
Private Const READ_CONTROL As Long = &H20000
```

```vb
Private Const STANDARD_RIGHTS_READ As Long = (READ_CONTROL)
Private Const STANDARD_RIGHTS_WRITE As Long = (READ_CONTROL)

Private Const KEY_QUERY_VALUE As Long = &H1
Private Const KEY_SET_VALUE As Long = &H2
Private Const KEY_CREATE_SUB_KEY As Long = &H4
Private Const KEY_ENUMERATE_SUB_KEYS As Long = &H8
Private Const KEY_NOTIFY As Long = &H10
Private Const KEY_CREATE_LINK As Long = &H20
Private Const KEY_READ As Long = _
 ((STANDARD_RIGHTS_READ Or KEY_QUERY_VALUE Or _
 KEY_ENUMERATE_SUB_KEYS Or KEY_NOTIFY) _
 And (Not SYNCHRONIZE))
Private Const KEY_EXECUTE As Long = _
 ((KEY_READ) And (Not SYNCHRONIZE))
Private Const KEY_WRITE As Long = _
 ((STANDARD_RIGHTS_WRITE Or KEY_SET_VALUE _
 Or KEY_CREATE_SUB_KEY) And (Not SYNCHRONIZE))
Private Const KEY_ALL_ACCESS As Long = _
 ((STANDARD_RIGHTS_ALL Or KEY_QUERY_VALUE Or _
 KEY_SET_VALUE Or KEY_CREATE_SUB_KEY Or _
 KEY_ENUMERATE_SUB_KEYS Or KEY_NOTIFY Or _
 KEY_CREATE_LINK) And (Not SYNCHRONIZE))

Private Const REG_OPTION_NON_VOLATILE As Long = 0

Private Type FILETIME
 dwLowDateTime As Long
 dwHighDateTime As Long
End Type

Private Declare Function RegOpenKeyEx Lib _
 "advapi32.dll" Alias "RegOpenKeyExA" _
 (ByVal hkey As Long, ByVal lpSubKey As String, _
 ByVal ulOptions As Long, ByVal samDesired As Long, _
 phkResult As Long) As Long

Private Declare Function RegCloseKey Lib _
 "advapi32.dll" (ByVal hkey As Long) As Long

Private Declare Function RegCreateKeyEx Lib _
 "advapi32.dll" Alias "RegCreateKeyExA" _
 (ByVal hKey As Long, ByVal lpSubKey As String, _
```

```
ByVal Reserved As Long, ByVal lpClass As String, _
ByVal dwOptions As Long, ByVal samDesired As Long, _
ByVal lpSecurityAttributes As Long, phkResult As Long, _
lpdwDisposition As Long) As Long

Private Declare Function RegQueryInfoKey Lib _
"advapi32.dll" Alias "RegQueryInfoKeyA" _
(ByVal hkey As Long, ByVal lpClass As String, _
lpcbClass As Long, ByVal lpReserved As Long, _
lpcSubKeys As Long, lpcbMaxSubKeyLen As Long, _
lpcbMaxClassLen As Long, lpcValues As Long, _
lpcbMaxValueNameLen As Long, lpcbMaxValueLen As Long, _
ByVal lpcbSecurityDescriptor As Long, _
lftLastWriteTime As FILETIME) As Long

Private Declare Function RegEnumKeyEx Lib _
"advapi32.dll" Alias "RegEnumKeyExA" _
(ByVal hkey As Long, ByVal dwIndex As Long, _
ByVal lpName As String, lpcbName As Long, _
ByVal lpReserved As Long, ByVal lpClass As String, _
lpcbClass As Long, lpftLastWriteTime As FILETIME) As Long

Private Declare Function RegEnumValueNull Lib _
"advapi32.dll" Alias "RegEnumValueA" _
(ByVal hkey As Long, ByVal dwIndex As Long, _
ByVal lpValueName As String, lpcbValueName As Long, _
ByVal lpReserved As Long, lpType As Long, _
lpData As Byte, lpcbData As Long) As Long

Private Declare Function RegEnumValueString Lib _
"advapi32.dll" Alias "RegEnumValueA" _
(ByVal hkey As Long, ByVal dwIndex As Long, _
ByVal lpValueName As String, lpcbValueName As Long, _
ByVal lpReserved As Long, lpType As Long, _
ByVal lpValue As String, lpcbData As Long) As Long

Private Declare Function RegEnumValueLong Lib _
"advapi32.dll" Alias "RegEnumValueA" _
(ByVal hkey As Long, ByVal dwIndex As Long, _
ByVal lpValueName As String, lpcbValueName As Long, _
ByVal lpReserved As Long, lpType As Long, _
lpValue As Long, lpcbData As Long) As Long
```

```
Private Declare Function RegEnumValueBinary Lib _
 "advapi32.dll" Alias "RegEnumValueA" _
 (ByVal hkey As Long, ByVal dwIndex As Long, _
 ByVal lpValueName As String, lpcbValueName As Long, _
 ByVal lpReserved As Long, lpType As Long, _
 lpValue As Byte, lpcbData As Long) As Long

Private Declare Function RegQueryValueExString Lib _
 "advapi32.dll" Alias "RegQueryValueExA" _
 (ByVal hKey As Long, ByVal lpValueName As _
 String, ByVal lpReserved As Long, lpType As Long, _
 ByVal lpData As String, lpcbData As Long) As Long

Private Declare Function RegQueryValueExLong Lib _
 "advapi32.dll" Alias "RegQueryValueExA" _
 (ByVal hKey As Long, ByVal lpValueName As _
 String, ByVal lpReserved As Long, lpType As Long, _
 lpData As Long, lpcbData As Long) As Long

Private Declare Function RegQueryValueExBinary Lib _
 "advapi32.dll" Alias "RegQueryValueExA" _
 (ByVal hKey As Long, ByVal lpValueName As _
 String, ByVal lpReserved As Long, lpType As Long, _
 lpData As Byte, lpcbData As Long) As Long

Private Declare Function RegQueryValueExNULL Lib _
 "advapi32.dll" Alias "RegQueryValueExA" _
 (ByVal hKey As Long, ByVal lpValueName As _
 String, ByVal lpReserved As Long, lpType As Long, _
 ByVal lpData As Long, lpcbData As Long) As Long

Private Declare Function RegSetValueExString Lib _
 "advapi32.dll" Alias "RegSetValueExA" _
 (ByVal hKey As Long, ByVal lpValueName As String, _
 ByVal Reserved As Long, ByVal dwType As Long, _
 ByVal lpValue As String, ByVal cbData As Long) As Long

Private Declare Function RegSetValueExLong Lib _
 "advapi32.dll" Alias "RegSetValueExA" _
 (ByVal hKey As Long, ByVal lpValueName As String, _
 ByVal Reserved As Long, ByVal dwType As Long, _
 lpValue As Long, ByVal cbData As Long) As Long
```

```
Private Declare Function RegSetValueExBinary Lib _
 "advapi32.dll" Alias "RegSetValueExA" _
 (ByVal hKey As Long, ByVal lpValueName As String, _
 ByVal Reserved As Long, ByVal dwType As Long, _
 lpValue As Byte, ByVal cbData As Long) As Long

Private Sub Class_Initialize()
 m_root = HKEY_CURRENT_USER
 m_key= "Software\VB and VBA Program Settings"
End Sub

Public Property Get Root() As RegRoot
 Root = m_root
End Property

Public Property Let Root(ByVal idx As RegRoot)
 If idx < HKEY_CLASSES_ROOT Or idx > HKEY_DYN_DATA _
   Then Exit Property
 m_root = idx
End Property

Public Property Get Key() As String
 Key = m_key
End Property

Public Function ModifyKey(strKeySuffix As String, _
   flag As Boolean) As ErrorList
Dim strOldKey As String
strOldKey = m_key

If flag Then
 If Len(m_key) = 0 And Len(strKeySuffix) = 0 Then
  m_key = ""
 ElseIf Len(m_key) = 0 Then
   m_key = strKeySuffix
 ElseIf Len(strKeySuffix) = 0 Then
  m_key = m_key
 ElseIf Right(strKeySuffix, 1) = "\" Then
  m_key = m_key & strKeySuffix
 Else
  m_key = m_key & "\" & strKeySuffix
 End If
Else
```

```
    m_key = Left(m_key, Len(m_key) - Len(strKeySuffix))
End If

Dim hKey As Long, lRetVal As Long
lRetVal = RegOpenKeyEx(m_root, m_key, 0, KEY_ALL_ACCESS, hKey)

If OpenKey(hKey) = ERROR_SUCCESS Then
 RegCloseKey (hKey)
Else
 m_key = strOldKey
End If
ModifyKey = lRetVal
End Function


Private Function OpenKey(ByRef hKey As Long) As ErrorList

If Len(m_KeyPrefix) = 0 Then
 hKey = m_root
 OpenKey = ERROR_SUCCESS
Else
 OpenKey = RegOpenKeyEx(m_root, m_key, 0, KEY_ALL_ACCESS, hKey)
End If

End Function


Public Function GetAllKeys(ByRef sArray() As String) As ErrorList

On Error GoTo Handler
Dim lRetVal As Long
Dim hKey As Long, lpcSubKeys As Long, lpcMaxSubKeyLen As Long
Dim lpcbMaxClassLen As Long, lpcValues As Long
Dim lpcbMaxValueNameLen As Long, lpcbMaxValueLen As Long
Dim dwIndex As Long, lpcbName As Long
Dim lpName As String, lpClass As String
Dim FTime As FILETIME

lRetVal = OpenKey(hKey)
If lRetVal <> ERROR_SUCCESS Then
 GetAllKeys = lRetVal
 Exit Function
End If

lRetVal = RegQueryInfoKey(hKey, 0&, 0&, 0&, lpcSubKeys, _
```

```
    lpcMaxSubKeyLen, lpcbMaxClassLen, lpcValues, _
    lpcbMaxValueNameLen, lpcbMaxValueLen, 0&, FTime)

If lpcSubKeys = 0 Then _
    Err.Raise ERROR_EMPTY_ARRAY

ReDim sArray(lpcSubKeys - 1)

For dwIndex = 0 To lpcSubKeys - 1
    lpName = Space(lpcMaxSubKeyLen + 1)
    lpcbName = lpcMaxSubKeyLen + 1
    lRetVal = RegEnumKeyEx(hKey, dwIndex, lpName, _
      lpcbName, 0&, lpClass, Len(lpClass), FTime)
    sArray(dwIndex) = Left(lpName, lpcbName)
Next dwIndex

RegCloseKey (hKey)
GetAllKeys = lRetVal
Exit Function


Handler:
If Err.Number = ERROR_EMPTY_ARRAY Then
    Err.Clear
    GetAllKeys = ERROR_EMPTY_ARRAY
Else
    GetAllKeys = lRetVal
End If
RegCloseKey (hKey)
End Function


Public Function GetAllSettings(vArray() As Variant) As ErrorList

On Error GoTo Handler
Dim lRetVal As Long, dwIndex As Long
Dim hKey As Long, lpcSubKeys As Long
Dim lpcbMaxSubKeyLen As Long, lpcbMaxClassLen As Long
Dim lpcValues As Long, lpcbMaxValueNameLen As Long
Dim lpcbMaxValueLen As Long
Dim lpcbValueName As Long, lpcbData As Long
Dim lValue As Long, lpType As Long


Dim lpValueName As String, sClass As String, lpData As String
Dim bValue() As Byte
```

```
Dim FTime As FILETIME

If OpenKey(hKey) <> ERROR_SUCCESS Then Exit Function
lRetVal = RegQueryInfoKey(hKey, 0&, 0&, 0&, _
 lpcSubKeys, lpcbMaxSubKeyLen, _
 lpcbMaxClassLen, lpcValues, lpcbMaxValueNameLen, _
 lpcbMaxValueLen, 0&, FTime)

If lpcValues = 0 Then _
 Err.Raise ERROR_EMPTY_ARRAY
ReDim vArray(lpcValues - 1, 1)
 dwIndex = 0
 Do
  lpcbValueName = lpcbMaxValueNameLen + 1
  lpcbData = lpcbMaxValueLen + 1
  lpType = 0
  lpValueName = Space(lpcbValueName)
  If RegEnumValueNull(hKey, dwIndex, 0&, 0&, 0&, _
   lpType, 0&, 0&) _
   = ERROR_NO_MORE_ITEMS Then Exit Do
  Select Case lpType
  Case REG_SZ:
   lpData = Space(lpcbData)
   lpcbValueName = lpcbMaxValueNameLen + 1
   lRetVal = RegEnumValueString(hKey, dwIndex, _
    lpValueName, lpcbValueName, 0&, lpType, _
    lpData, lpcbData)
   If Left(lpValueName, lpcbValueName) = "" Then
    vArray(dwIndex, 0) = "Default"
   Else
    vArray(dwIndex, 0) = Left(lpValueName, _
      lpcbValueName)
   End If
   If lRetVal = ERROR_SUCCESS Then
    vArray(dwIndex, 1) = Left$(lpData, _
     lpcbData - 1)
   Else
    vArray(dwIndex, 1) = Empty
   End If
  Case REG_BINARY:
   ReDim bValue(lpcbData)
   lpcbValueName = lpcbMaxValueNameLen
   lpcbData = lpcbMaxValueLen
```

```
     lRetVal = RegEnumValueBinary(hKey, dwIndex, _
      lpValueName, lpcbValueName, 0&, lpType, _
      bValue(0), lpcbData)
     If Left(lpValueName, lpcbValueName) = "" Then
      vArray(dwIndex, 0) = "Default"
     Else
      vArray(dwIndex, 0) = Left(lpValueName, _
       lpcbValueName)
     End If
     If lRetVal = ERROR_SUCCESS Then _
       vArray(dwIndex, 1) = bValue

    Case REG_DWORD:
     lpcbValueName = lpcbMaxValueNameLen
     lpcbData = lpcbMaxValueLen
     lRetVal = RegEnumValueLong(hKey, dwIndex, _
      lpValueName, lpcbValueName, _
      0&, lpType, lValue, lpcbData)
     If Left(lpValueName, lpcbValueName) = "" Then
      vArray(dwIndex, 0) = "Default"
     Else
      vArray(dwIndex, 0) = Left(lpValueName, _
       lpcbValueName)
     End If
     If lRetVal = ERROR_SUCCESS Then _
       vArray(dwIndex, 1) = lValue
    Case Else
     vArray(dwIndex, 0) = "Unsupported Data Type"
     vArray(dwIndex, 1) = "Unsupported Data Type"
    End Select
    dwIndex = dwIndex + 1
  Loop

RegCloseKey (hKey)
GetAllSettings = lRetVal
Exit Function

Handler:
If Err.Number = ERROR_EMPTY_ARRAY Then
Err.Clear
GetAllSettings = ERROR_EMPTY_ARRAY
End If
End Function
```

```
Public Function CreateKey(sKeyName As String) As ErrorList
 Dim hKey as Long
 Dim lRetVal as Long
 lRetVal = RegCreateKeyEx(m_root, sKeyName, 0&, _
  vbNullString, REG_OPTION_NON_VOLATILE, _
  KEY_ALL_ACCESS, 0&, hKey, lRetVal)
 RegCloseKey (hKey)
 CreateKey = lRetVal
End Function

Public Function QueryValue(ByVal strValueName As _
 String, ByRef vValue As Variant) As ErrorList

On Error GoTo QueryValueError
Dim lData As Long, hKey As Long, lType As Long
Dim lValue As Long, lRetVal As Long
Dim sValue As String
Dim bValue() As Byte
lRetVal = OpenKey(hKey)

If lRetVal <> ERROR_SUCCESS Then
 QueryValue = lRetVal
 Exit Function
End If

lRetVal = RegQueryValueExNULL(hKey, strValueName, 0&, _
 lType, 0&, lData)
If lRetVal <> ERROR_SUCCESS Then
 QueryValue = lRetVal
 Exit Function
End If

Select Case lType
 Case REG_SZ:
  sValue = String(lData, 0)
  lRetVal = RegQueryValueExString(hKey, strValueName, _
   0&, lType, sValue, lData)

  If lRetVal = ERROR_SUCCESS Then
   vValue = Left$(sValue, lData - 1)
  Else
   vValue = Empty
```

```
   End If

 Case REG_BINARY:
   ReDim bValue(lData)
   lRetVal = RegQueryValueExBinary(hKey, strValueName, _
    0&, lType, bValue(0), lData)
   If lRetVal = ERROR_SUCCESS Then vValue = bValue

 Case REG_DWORD:
   lRetVal = RegQueryValueExLong(hKey, strValueName, _
    0&, lType, lValue, lData)

   If lRetVal = ERROR_SUCCESS Then vValue = lValue

Case Else
   MsgBox "Data Type Not Supported so ERROR_CANTREAD Returned"
   lRetVal = ERROR_CANTREAD
End Select

QueryValueExit:
QueryValue = lRetVal
Exit Function

QueryValueError:
 Resume QueryValueExit
End Function

Public Function SetValue(sValueName As String, _
 lType As Long, ByRef vValue As Variant) As ErrorList

Dim lValue As Long, hKey As Long
Dim sValue As String
Dim lRetVal As Long
Dim bValue() As Byte
lRetVal = OpenKey(hKey)
If lRetVal <> ERROR_SUCCESS Then
 SetValue = lRetVal
 Exit Function
End If

Select Case lType

 Case REG_SZ
```

```
 sValue = vValue & Chr$(0)
 lRetVal = RegSetValueExString(hKey, sValueName, 0&, _
  lType, sValue, Len(sValue))

 Case REG_BINARY
  bValue = vValue
  lRetVal = RegSetValueExBinary(hKey, sValueName, 0&, _
   lType, bValue(0), LenB(vValue))

 Case REG_DWORD
  lValue = vValue
  lRetVal = RegSetValueExLong(hKey, sValueName, 0&, _
   lType, lValue, 4)

 Case Else
End Select
RegCloseKey (hKey)
SetValue = lRetVal
End Function
```

ANNOTATIONS

```
Private Declare Function RegCreateKeyEx Lib _
 "advapi32.dll" Alias "RegCreateKeyExA" _
 (ByVal hKey As Long, ByVal lpSubKey As String, _
 ByVal Reserved As Long, ByVal lpClass As String, _
 ByVal dwOptions As Long, ByVal samDesired As Long, _
 ByVal lpSecurityAttributes As Long, phkResult As Long, _
 lpdwDisposition As Long) As Long
```

The **RegCreateKeyEx** function creates the subkey specified in the second parameter. If the key already exists in the Registry, the function opens it. The specified subkey must be a subkey of an already open key whose handle is specified in the first parameter.

```
Private Declare Function RegQueryValueExString Lib _
 "advapi32.dll" Alias "RegQueryValueExA" _
 (ByVal hKey As Long, ByVal lpValueName As _
 String, ByVal lpReserved As Long, lpType As Long, _
 ByVal lpData As String, lpcbData As Long) As Long

Private Declare Function RegQueryValueExLong Lib _
 "advapi32.dll" Alias "RegQueryValueExA" _
```

```
(ByVal hKey As Long, ByVal lpValueName As _
String, ByVal lpReserved As Long, lpType As Long, _
lpData As Long, lpcbData As Long) As Long

Private Declare Function RegQueryValueExBinary Lib _
 "advapi32.dll" Alias "RegQueryValueExA" _
 (ByVal hKey As Long, ByVal lpValueName As _
 String, ByVal lpReserved As Long, lpType As Long, _
 lpData As Byte, lpcbData As Long) As Long

Private Declare Function RegQueryValueExNULL Lib _
 "advapi32.dll" Alias "RegQueryValueExA" _
 (ByVal hKey As Long, ByVal lpValueName As _
 String, ByVal lpReserved As Long, lpType As Long, _
 ByVal lpData As Long, lpcbData As Long) As Long
```

The **RegQueryValueEx** function retrieves the type and data for a specified value name associated with an open Registry key. The second to last parameter is a buffer for the value's data. Since that data may be one of several different types, different implementations of **RegQueryValueEx** are declared for these different data types.

```
Private Declare Function RegSetValueExString Lib _
 "advapi32.dll" Alias "RegSetValueExA" _
 (ByVal hKey As Long, ByVal lpValueName As String, _
 ByVal Reserved As Long, ByVal dwType As Long, _
 ByVal lpValue As String, ByVal cbData As Long) As Long

Private Declare Function RegSetValueExLong Lib _
 "advapi32.dll" Alias "RegSetValueExA" _
 (ByVal hKey As Long, ByVal lpValueName As String, _
 ByVal Reserved As Long, ByVal dwType As Long, _
 lpValue As Long, ByVal cbData As Long) As Long

Private Declare Function RegSetValueExBinary Lib _
 "advapi32.dll" Alias "RegSetValueExA" _
 (ByVal hKey As Long, ByVal lpValueName As String, _
 ByVal Reserved As Long, ByVal dwType As Long, _
 lpValue As Byte, ByVal cbData As Long) As Long
```

The **RegSetValueEx** function writes where the **RegQueryValueEx** function reads. The **RegSetValueEx** function sets the type and data for a specified value name associated with an open Registry key. As with the **RegQueryValueEx** function, the second-to-last parameter of the **RegSetValueEx** function is a buffer for the value's data, so since that data may be one of several different types, different implementations of **RegSetValueEx** are declared for these different data types.

```
Public Function CreateKey(sKeyName As String) As ErrorList
 Dim hKey as Long
 Dim lRetVal as Long
 lRetVal = RegCreateKeyEx(m_root, sKeyName, 0&, vbNullString, _
  REG_OPTION_NON_VOLATILE, KEY_ALL_ACCESS, 0&, hKey, lRetVal)
 RegCloseKey (hKey)
 CreateKey = lRetVal
End Function
```

The **CreateKey** function "wraps" the **RegCreateKeyEx** API function. It creates the key whose name is passed in the second parameter, unless that subkey already exists, in which case it opens that subkey. Its return value is the error code that **RegCreateKeyEx** returns.

The parameters of **RegCreateKeyEx** are described in Table 8-15.

As previously mentioned, care must be taken not to have the *lpSubKey* parameter begin with a backslash ("\"). Windows 95/98 allow the subkey to begin with a backslash ("\"), but Windows NT does not. This is why the **KeyPrefix** function starts the subkey without a backslash.

```
Public Function QueryValue(ByVal strValueName As _
 String, ByRef vValue As Variant) As ErrorList
```

This function wraps the **QueryValueEx** API function. Its first parameter is the name of the subkey whose value is being queried. The second parameter is a **Variant** that will contain the name and data pairs of the subkey's values. The data type of this parameter is a **Variant** because the value's data may be one of several data types. The return value, as with the other functions, is an error code.

Parameter	Data Type	Description
hKey	**Long**	Handle to an open key
lpSubKey	**String**	Address of subkey name
Reserved	**Long**	Reserved
lpClass	**String**	Address of class string
dwOptions	**Long**	Special options flag
samDesired	**Long**	Desired security access
lpSecurityAttributes	SECURITY_ATTRIBUTES	Address of key security structure
phkResult	**Long**	Address of buffer for opened handle
lpdwDisposition	**Long**	Address of disposition value buffer

TABLE 8-15.   Parameters of **RegCreateKeyEx**

```
On Error GoTo QueryValueError
```

The purpose of this error handler is to return the error code if the function is unsuccessful in querying the value of the subkey.

```
Dim lData As Long, hKey As Long, lType As Long
Dim lValue As Long, lRetVal As Long
Dim sValue As String
Dim bValue() As Byte
```

These parameters will be used in the API function. The variables *lRetVal*, *sValue*, and *bValue*() will hold the value's data, depending on whether the data type is **Long**, **String**, or **Binary**.

```
lRetVal = OpenKey(hKey)

If lRetVal <> ERROR_SUCCESS Then
 QueryValue = lRetVal
 Exit Function
End If
```

If the subkey cannot be opened, then the function returns the error code and terminates. Otherwise, the subkey whose values are being queried is opened.

```
lRetVal = RegQueryValueExNULL(hKey, strValueName, 0&, _
 lType, 0&, lData)
If lRetVal <> ERROR_SUCCESS Then
 QueryValue = lRetVal
 Exit Function
End If
```

The parameters of **RegQueryValueEx** are described in Table 8-16.

Parameter	Data Type	Description
hKey	**Long**	Handle to key to query
lpValueName	**String**	Address of name of value to query
lpReserved	**Long**	Reserved
lpType	**Long**	Address of buffer for value type
lpData	**Any**	Address of data buffer
lpcbData	**Long**	Address of data buffer size

TABLE 8-16. Parameters of **RegQueryValueEx**

This statement determines if the value can be read. If not, then the function returns the error code and terminates.

If the value can be read, the function fills the *lpType* buffer with the data type of the value's data.

The second-to-last parameter, the buffer for the value's data, is Null (0&). This is done when the value's data is not sought. The value's data is not yet sought because it first is necessary to determine the data type of the value's data. A different implementation of **RegQueryValueEx** will be called, depending on which data type is involved. That data type is determined by *lpType*. This variable is passed to **RegQueryValueEx** by reference and filled with the data type of the value's data.

```
Select Case lType
 Case REG_SZ:
  sValue = String(lData, 0)
  lRetVal = RegQueryValueExString(hKey, strValueName, _
   0&, lType, sValue, lData)

  If lRetVal = ERROR_SUCCESS Then
   vValue = Left$(sValue, lData - 1)
  Else
   vValue = Empty
  End If
```

The call to this implementation of **RegQueryValueEx**, **RegQueryValueExString**, this time has a placeholder, *sValue*, instead of 0& for the second-to-last parameter, as this placeholder will be filled with the value of the data.

Since the value's data type is a **String**, then it is necessary to reserve space for the string *sValue* being passed to the API function. The **String** function creates a string of the size specified in the first parameter padded with the character specifed in the second parameter. The first parameter, *lData*, was the last parameter in the prior call to **RegQueryValueExNull**, which filled that parameter with the length of the data. Thus, *sValue* becomes a string with an *lData* number of zeroes.

If the return value of **RegQueryValueExString** indicates success, then the value of *sValue* will be assigned to the **Variant** *vValue* that had been passed by reference to **QueryKey**. However, first the **Left** function is used to eliminate the null character that the API function appended to *sValue*.

```
 Case REG_BINARY:
  ReDim bValue(lData)
  lRetVal = RegQueryValueExBinary(hKey, strValueName, _
   0&, lType, bValue(0), lData)
  If lRetVal = ERROR_SUCCESS Then vValue = bValue
```

If the value is binary, then the second-to-last parameter is an array of an *lData* number of bytes.

```
Case REG_DWORD:
  lRetVal = RegQueryValueExLong(hKey, strValueName, _
   0&, lType, lValue, lData)


  If lRetVal = ERROR_SUCCESS Then vValue = lValue
```

If the data type of the value is a **Long**, then **RegQueryValueExLong** is called with the second-to-last parameter being a **Long**, again passed by reference.

```
Case Else
  MsgBox "Data Type Not Supported so ERROR_CANTREAD Returned"
  lRetVal = ERROR_CANTREAD
End Select
```

As Table 8-8 reflects, the Registry contains values having data types in addition to the ones supported by this class module. Are these data types not supported because the authors were too lazy to write the code? Of course not! We just don't want to ruin your self-reliance and make you overly dependent on us.

Seriously, the logic of supporting the other data types would be quite similar to the above code. Try it! However, for the moment, these unsupported data types are handled by a message and the return of an error code.

```
QueryValueExit:
QueryValue = lRetVal
Exit Function


QueryValueError:
 Resume QueryValueExit
End Function
```

In case of error, the appropriate error code is returned and the function terminates.

```
Public Function SetValue(sValueName As String, _
 lType As Long, ByRef vValue As Variant) As ErrorList
```

This function wraps the **RegSetValueEx** API function. Its first parameter is the name of the value whose data is being set. The subkey that contains that value already has been opened. The second parameter is the data type of the value. That data type also already has been determined, such as by **QueryKey**. The third parameter is a **Variant** that contains the value to be assigned to the data.

```
Dim lValue As Long, hKey As Long
Dim sValue As String
Dim lRetVal As Long
Dim bValue() As Byte
```

These variables will be used in the API functionn.

```
lRetVal = OpenKey(hKey)
If lRetVal <> ERROR_SUCCESS Then
 SetValue = lRetVal
 Exit Function
End If
```

The function **OpenKey** is used to open the subkey identified by the values of the class variables *m_root* and *m_key*. The variable *hKey* has no assigned value and does not need one as it is being passed by reference to **OpenKey**. If the key cannot be opened, then **SetValue** returns the error code and terminates.

```
Select Case lType

 Case REG_SZ
  sValue = vValue & Chr$(0)
  lRetVal = RegSetValueExString(hKey, sValueName, 0&, _
   lType, sValue, Len(sValue))
```

The **RegSetValueEx** function sets the data and type of a specified value under a Registry key. Its parameters are described in Table 8-17.

Different implementations of **RegSetValueEx** are used for the different data types that are in the Registry. This branch of the **Select Case** statement concerns the **String** data type. Therefore, **RegSetValueExString** is used. This function differs from the

Parameter	Data Type	Description
hKey	**Long**	Handle to key whose value is being set
lpValueName	**String**	Name of value to whose data is being set
lpReserved	**Long**	Reserved; not used so set to zero
dwType	**Long**	The data type
lpData	**Byte**	The first byte of the buffer which contains the data
cbData	**Long**	Length of the *lpData* buffer

TABLE 8-17. Parameters of **RegSetValueEx**

other declared **RegSetValueEx** functions in its second-to-last parameter. That parameter is the string that contains the data to be set.

As with other API functions involving a **String** data type, sufficient space has to be reserved for the string, including the terminating null character. The null character (Chr$(0)) is added to the string. The last parameter of **RegSetValueExString** is the length of that string with the added null character.

```
Case REG_BINARY
  bValue = vValue
  lRetVal = RegSetValueExBinary(hKey, sValueName, 0&, _
   lType, bValue(0), LenB(vValue))
```

This branch of the **Select Case** statement concerns the binary data type. The value being set is passed to the byte array. Unlike the **String** data type, there is no need to add to the length of the byte array. The last parameter of **RegSetValueExBinary**, the length of the byte array, is provided by the **LenB** function, which provides the length in bytes of the byte array.

```
Case REG_DWORD
  lValue = vValue
  lRetVal = RegSetValueExLong(hKey, sValueName, 0&, _
   lType, lValue, 4)
```

This branch of the **Select Case** statement concerns the **Long** data type. The value being set is passed to the **Long** variable *lValue*. The last parameter of **RegSetValueExLong** is 4 because a Long variable has a fixed length of 4 bytes.

```
  Case Else
```

Other data types are not handled.

```
End Select
RegCloseKey (hKey)
SetValue = lRetVal
End Function
```

The opened subkey is closed and the error code, hopefully ERROR_SUCCESS, is returned.

TEST THE CODE

1. Start a new Project, Standard Exe.

2. Insert the code from the class module, which is named **cRegWrite**.

3. Insert a form. Accept the default properties. Name it **frmMain**.

4. Insert the following controls on the form:

Control Type	Control Name	Purpose
RichTextBox	RichTextBox1	Displays .rtf file
Command Button	cmdOpen	Loads .rtf file into RichTextBox
Command Button	cmdClose	Saves and closes .rtf file in RichTextBox
Common Dialog Control	CommonDialog1	Displays a File/Open Dialog in the event .rtf file's name or location has been changed

The form in Design view should appear like Figure 8-9.

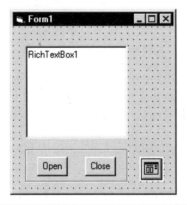

FIGURE 8-9. The form in RegWrite.vbp in Design view

5. The following code should go in the general declarations of the form:

```
Option Explicit
Private Const strKey As String = _
    "Software\VB and VBA Program Settings\VBAA"
Dim strData As String
Dim cReg As clsRegWrite
Private Const BAD_PATH_OR_FILENAME As Long = 75
```

The constant *strKey* points to the "Software\VB and VBA Program Settings\VBAA" section of HKEY_CURRENT_USER. In this example, all Registry values will be written to this portion of the Registry. Therefore, the value of the Registry section is hard-coded.

As previously mentioned, one of the advantages of using the Registry API functions instead of the intrinsic Visual Basic Registry functions is that you are not limited to the "Software\VB and VBA Program Settings" section of HKEY_CURRENT_USER. The reason why this section of the Registry is being used in this example is that, if something goes wrong, little if any damage can be done. This would not be the case with other sections of the Registry.

The term "VBAA" is the application's name, and will be the name of the first-level subkey in the "Software\VB and VBA Program Settings" section.

The variable *cReg* is declared as an instance of the class **cRegWrite**. It will be instantiated in the **Load** event of the form.

The constant BAD_PATH_OR_FILENAME will be used when the file being opened is not at the location indicated in the Registry, usually because the file was moved or renamed.

6. The following code should go in the **Load** event of the form:

```
Private Sub Form_Load()
 ChDrive App.Path
 ChDir App.Path
 Set cReg = New clsRegWrite
End Sub
```

The first two statements simply change the current directory to the subdirectory in which this Visual Basic application is located. These two statements are commonly seen in the startup code, located either in the **Load** event of the startup form or in Sub Main. Otherwise the current directory will be the subdirectory in which the Visual Basic IDE executable is located, a very unlikely and undesirable location for your Visual Basic application.

Changing the current directory to the subdirectory in which this Visual Basic application is located has several advantages. First, it enables you to use relative paths which will be valid wherever the application is located. Second, when a common dialog box is opened, it will open in the desired subdirectory, freeing your application's user from the irritating task of always having to navigate to the desired subdirectory.

The class instance *cReg* was dimensioned in the general declarations of the form. The **Set** statement instantiates *cReg*.

The class instance *cReg* also could have been dimensioned:

   Dim cReg As New clsRegWrite

This alternative also would not have instantiated *cReg*. Rather, *cReg* would not be instantiated until it first used a property or method, which also cannot be done in the general declarations of the form.

The method of instantiating *cReg* in this example is the preferable alternative. The reason is that you, as the programmer, know exactly when *cReg* is instantiated. If instead *cReg* is instantiated when it first uses a property or method, you have to determine where in your code a property or method of *cReg* first will be used. Also, future revisions of your code could change where *cReg* first uses a property or method and thus is instantiated.

It can be important to know exactly when *cReg* is instantiated if you are relying on statements in the **Initialize** event of the class. These statements will run when *cReg* is instantiated, not before and not after.

7. The following code should go in the **Click** event of **cmdOpen**:

```
Private Sub cmdOpen_Click()
On Error GoTo Handler
Dim strFile As String
If cReg.Root <> HKEY_CURRENT_USER Then _
 cReg.Root = HKEY_CURRENT_USER
If cReg.Key <> strKey Then _
 Call cReg.ModifyKey(cReg.Key, False)
 If cReg.ModifyKey(strKey, True) <> ERROR_SUCCESS Then
  If cReg.CreateKey(strKey) = ERROR_SUCCESS Then _
   Call cReg.ModifyKey(strKey, True)
 End If

Dim vResult As Variant
If cReg.QueryValue("Path", vResult) <> ERROR_SUCCESS Then
 vResult = App.Path + "\" + strFile
 Call cReg.SetValue("Path", REG_SZ, vResult)
End If

RichTextBox1.LoadFile vResult, rtfRTF
strData = vResult
Exit Sub
Handler:
Select Case Err.Number
Case BAD_PATH_OR_FILENAME
 CommonDialog1.ShowOpen
 vResult = CommonDialog1.FileName
 Call cReg.SetValue("Path", REG_SZ, vResult)
 Resume
Case Else
 MsgBox "Unrecoverable error"
End Select
End Sub
```

This code opens the text file in the **RichTextBox** control.

The value of the root key is set to HKEY_CURRENT_USER if it is not already that value. Next, for the reasons explained above, the value of the subkey is set to the "Software\VB and VBA Program Settings\VBAA" section. First, the **ModifyKey** class function is called to set the value of *m_key* to a blank string (""). The **Call** statement is used because in this invocation of **ModifyKey** that function's return value, that is, whether the subkey identified by *m_key* can be opened, is not of interest. Since the value of *m_key* simply is a blank string, that which would be opened is a root key, which always is open.

ModifyKey is called again to attempt to set the value of m_key to the "Software\VB and VBA Program Settings\VBAA" subkey. This time we are interested in the return value, because we want to find out if the subkey already exists. If it does not, then it is created using the **CreateKey** class function, and then **ModifyKey** is called once again, this time to set successfully the value of m_key to the "Software\VB and VBA Program Settings\VBAA" subkey.

It is not strictly necessary to determine if the "Software\VB and VBA Program Settings\VBAA" subkey exists. As discussed above, the **RegCreateKeyEx** API function, which is wrapped by the class function **CreateKey**, will open the subkey if it exists, and create and open the subkey if it does not already exist. However, first to check if the subkey exists prevents the inadvertent creation of "extra" subkeys (for example, where the spelling of the value's name may be slightly different).

Next, the **QueryValue** class function is called to determine the data of the value "Path" and assign that data to the variable *vResult*. That data is the path to and filename of the .rtf file to open. If the "Path" subkey does not already exist, then the class function **SetKey** is called to create the subkey and assign a path and filename for the value's data. The call to **SetKey** also assigns the value's data to *vResult*, which is passed by reference to **SetKey**.

An attempt then is made to open the .rtf file using the path and filename in *vResult*. If the file can be opened, the function simply assigns the value of *vResult* to the form-level variable *strData* and ends. However, if the file cannot be opened, then the error handler will come into play. If the error is BAD_PATH_OR_FILENAME, that is, the file path or name is incorrect, then a common dialog control will show in File Open mode. The filename (with path) selected by the application user will be written to the Registry using **SetKey**. With the **Resume** statement, another attempt will be made to open the file, this time with the filename and path chosen by the application user.

8. The following code should go in the **Click** event of **cmdClose**:

```
Private Sub cmdClose_Click()
  RichTextBox1.SaveFile strData, rtfRTF
```

```
  Unload Me
End Sub
```

This code simply saves the file to the filename (and path) represented by *strData*. The second parameter causes the file to be saved in a rich text format.

9. The following code should go in the **Unload** event of the form:

```
Private Sub Form_Unload(Cancel As Integer)
 cmdClose_Click
End Sub
```

This code saves the file (by calling the **Click** event of **cmdClose**) when the form is closed.

Test the code! Try the following steps.

Before starting the application, use the Registry Editor to verify that there is no entry in the Registry for the VBAA application. Open the Registry Editor and navigate to the HK_CURRENT_USER/Software/VBA and VBA Program Settings subkey. (See Figure 8-10.)

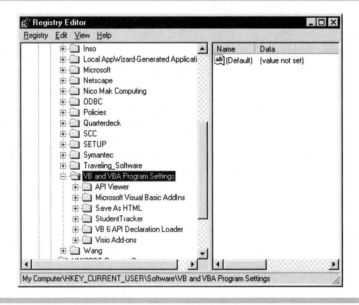

FIGURE 8-10.   No VBAA key at startup

After starting the application, click File | Open. This will open up a common dialog box in File Open mode. Pick an .rtf file. (See Figure 8-11.)

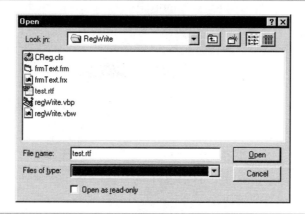

FIGURE 8-11. Choose a file

Using the Registry Editor, verify that clicking the Open button also created a Registry entry for VBAA with a value named "Path" with data being the path to the application. (See Figure 8-12.)

FIGURE 8-12. VBAA key created

Once the Open button of the common dialog control is clicked, then the contents of the test file are loaded into the **RichTextBox** control. (See Figure 8-13.)

FIGURE 8-13. File loaded into **RichTextBox** control

Using the Registry Editor, verify that the data of the Path value has been updated to include the file. (See Figure 8-14.)

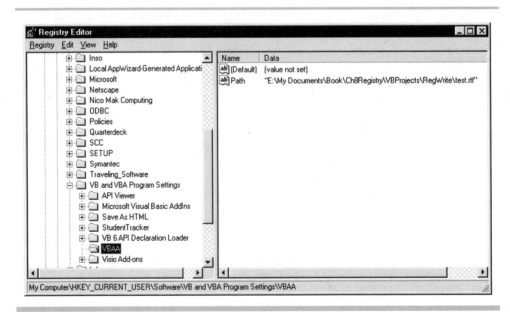

FIGURE 8-14. Data of Path value updated to include filename

Close the application, either by pressing the Close command button or the Close button on the title bar.

Using Windows Explorer, change the name of Test.rtf to Pest.rtf.

Start the application again. Click File | Open. Since you changed the name of the file listed in the Registry, the common dialog box should show in File Open mode. Choose Pest.rtf and open it. Confirm, using the Registry Editor, that the data of the Path value has been updated to change the filename from Test.rtf to Pest.rtf. (See Figure 8-15.)

FIGURE 8-15. Data of Path value changed to new filename

Database Connectivity

V isual Basic 3.0 revolutionized the way the world thought about VB programming. With version 3.0, Microsoft introduced native database features to the language. This gave programmers the ability to work with database objects directly as opposed to having to go through a third-party control and write to that database engine's API (application programming interface) or even write to the ODBC (open database connectivity) API. Writing your applications to use a particular database engine's API proved to be a very effective and efficient method to access data, but as a result, if your organization had to change database management systems (DBMS), chances were you would have to rewrite your application. ODBC offered a way around that by providing a set of APIs that all developers could use, and it was ODBC and the ODBC driver's responsibility to figure out how to talk to the database. As long as there was an ODBC driver available for the DBMS you were using, you'd only have to write your application to access the ODBC API. If an ODBC driver was not available, you'd have to write to that DBMS' API or you'd have to find some other method to access the database through some other middleware product like Intersolv's Q+E data drivers.

With every succeeding version of VB, Microsoft has introduced more robust methods of database connectivity through enhanced object models that provide "wrappers," or layers, over ODBC. First, there was DAO (Data Access Object), which provided a way for VB to access data similar to Microsoft Access. Performance was a bit sluggish as compared to writing against the native ODBC code because DAO was implemented not only as a data access method but also a database engine. This means that along with its ability to perform data access, it also inspected all DML (data manipulation language) and DDL (data definition language) statements to ensure they were correct before letting the statements access the database. Essentially, it worked as a preprocessor for the database. For rapid development, it was a great model to have available to you.

In version 4.0 Enterprise Edition, Microsoft introduced RDO (Remote Data Object), which is only a thin object model layer that resides over ODBC and not a database engine. It also provides objects, methods, and properties very similar to DAO, but performance is greatly enhanced. Shortly after RDO, Microsoft introduced ODBCDirect that allows you to reference ODBC data sources without going through the JET database engine. Instead, ODBCDirect provides a method to use RDO by using DAO features. Essentially, it's a DAO wrapper around RDO. Even though it's a wrapper around a wrapper, you will get slightly better data access performance over DAO through the JET database engine because there is no preprocessing involved.

As Microsoft's data access strategy evolved, their latest object model incarnation was called ADO (ActiveX Data Object). ADO was designed to provide a universal high-level data access method and is a collection of COM (Component Object Model) objects that can retrieve, update, and create records using any OLE DB data provider, rather than using ODBC. OLE DB is the next native driver layer that is to eventually replace ODBC. OLE DB came about because Microsoft discovered that developers weren't just accessing data from a database, but through other sources such as spreadsheets, documents, and electronic mail. These sources are also known as *OLE DB data providers*. Application programs that access data by way of OLE D B interfaces are called *OLE DB data consumers*. Figure 9-1 illustrates the model of OLE DB and its data providers.

Similar to how DAO and RDO are "wrapper" object models for ODBC, ADO is a "wrapper" object model for OLE DB. So does that mean that DAO and RDO are going away? Not right away; but if you're planning to do any new development on both traditional client/server applications or Web-based client/server applications, ADO is the data access object model you should use.

Since ADO requires OLE DB data providers, you might be asking yourself "what does that do with all my existing ODBC drivers?" As usual, Microsoft has thought of everything. There is an OLE DB data provider called "OLE DB for ODBC." This

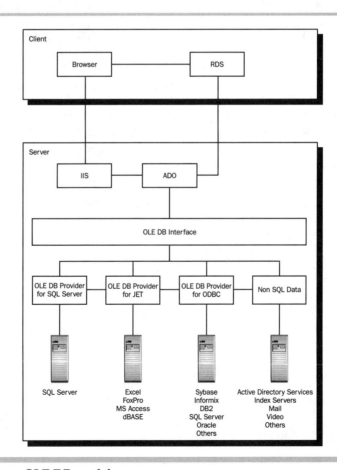

FIGURE 9-1. OLE DB model

allows you to use any ODBC driver with OLE DB. OLE DB comes with data providers for SQL Server and Oracle, as well as others.

If you're concerned that it took you a while to figure out the difference between DAO and RDO, do not worry. Microsoft decided not to throw a completely new object model at you because a lot of the collections, properties, and methods in ADO were taken from both DAO and RDO.

For all the examples, we are going to use the Biblio.mdb that comes with Visual Basic.

Setting Up an ODBC Data Source

In order for any Visual Basic application to access data from a database, you need to establish a connection to it. All three data access methods connect to ODBC data sources in their own way, which we'll go over. But before you can connect to a data source, you need to create one.

Start the ODBC Administrator found in the control panel. It lists all the data source names that are available on your system and it is also the place where you add and maintain them. Figure 9-2 is an example of some data source names already defined. Click on the Add... button to bring up the Add Data Source window. The driver you need will be listed as something like "Microsoft Access Driver." Click on the driver and then click the Finish button. Each driver has a different setup window for a different set of parameters. The Microsoft Access driver's parameters are shown in Figure 9-3. Use Table 9-1 to enter the information to set up the Biblio.mdb database.

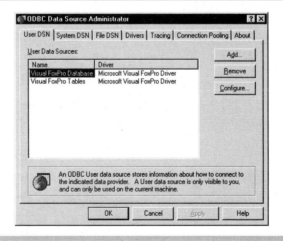

FIGURE 9-2.   ODBC Administrator window

FIGURE 9-3. ODBC Microsoft Access 97 Setup window

Press the Select… button in the Database frame. This will bring up a Select Database window that is used to select the location and the name of the access database you're going to use. Depending on which hard drive you installed VB on, Biblio.mdb can typically be found in the Program Files\Microsoft Visual Studio\ VB98 directory of the drive you installed VB on. Once you've found the database, select OK to close the window, then select OK on the ODBC Administrator to close that window. You're now ready to use this DSN to access Biblio.mdb.

ANNOTATIONS

The DSN that was just created is known as a *User DSN*. There are three types of DSNs: User, System, and File. User and System DSNs are very similar in that they store all the database connectivity information in the Windows Registry of the computer in which the DSN is defined. A System DSN differs from the User DSN

Field	Value
Data Source Name	DsnBIBLIO
Description	Source for the Biblio database

TABLE 9-1. Biblio.mdb Data Source Name Setup Information

in that the database information is made available to anyone accessing the system, whereas the User DSN is only available to the person who is logged on the system. A File DSN connection stores the information in a file that can be read by any application. This makes the project more easily portable between computers because only the file needs to be moved rather than having an installation program set up a User DSN on the target system. As a general rule, Microsoft now recommends that you should always use File DSNs.

The prefix used, dsn, is part of a naming convention so when you enter the DSN in your code, the value won't look like any other value. You will be able to distinguish it as a DSN variable versus any other variable.

dbConnect

Connecting to a Database Through an ODBC Data Source

Once you have defined a DSN, you can now establish a connection to the database defined in the DSN. You can access it using any three of the database access methods, DAO, RDO, or ADO. To do that, you will need to reference the object models by dimensioning variables to an object and using the **CreateObject** method, or simply by referencing the model through VB's Integrated Development Environment. By referencing the object models by using the **CreateObject** method, you are creating the link to the object model using a technique called *late binding*. An example of late binding to ADO would be:

```
Dim ObjTest As Object
Set ObjTest = CreateObject("ADODB.Recordset")
```

The application using the object doesn't need to know detailed information about the object's methods or properties before using it.

By referencing the object through the IDE, you create a direct interface to the object. This is called *early binding*. An example of early binding to ADO is:

```
Dim ObjADO As ADODB.Recordset
Set ObjADO = New ADODB.Recordset
```

This can substantially reduce the time it takes to access the methods and properties of the object because the application knows everything there is to know about the object at design-time. Using the late-binding technique, the application doesn't know anything about the object's methods or properties until the application is executed. Because of this, there is a greater chance of an error because you might reference a property that doesn't exist or use a method improperly and you won't find out until the program is run.

By using early binding, your application references the type or object library of the object you are using. To early-bind to the ADO model, you reference the type or object library through the References windows found under the Project menu. Rather than referencing a variable as *Object* like the code illustrated in late binding, you reference the variable to the object directly. Through early binding, when you work with the *Object* variable, the IDE's List Member drop-down list box displays all the methods and properties that are available to the object. Figure 9-4 shows the List Member filled with methods and properties of the ADO Recordset.

Early binding also is not concerned with localized versions of the software's type and object model it references if you plan to write an application for multiple languages as well as develop using international versions of the Windows environment. For example, your application requires the use of Microsoft Word. If you wrote the application using late-binding techniques, you would be required to use the French version's objects commands; therefore, you would be required to use the **FicheOuvert** method rather than the **FileOpen** method. Early binding, because you've referenced the object library directly, doesn't care what localized version you're using because your application has already "bonded" with the object model of the automation application, regardless of the language.

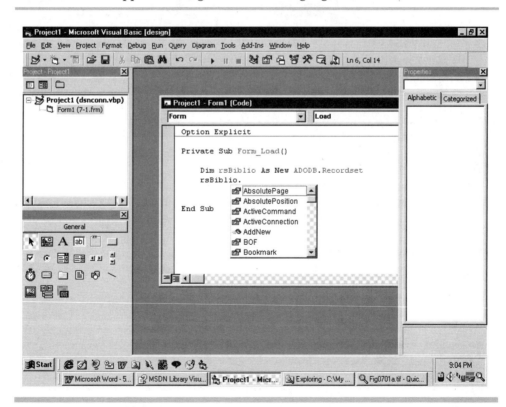

FIGURE 9-4. List Member showing some of the methods and properties of the ADO Recordset object library

For this example, we will be using the early-binding technique to reference the object model listed in Table 9-2. To select the references, select Project | References from the VB main menu.

PROGRAMMER'S NOTE

If you are using VB5, you might not have ADO installed or you might have an early version of the ADO model. You can download the latest ADO components from the Microsoft Web site at ***http://www.microsoft.com/data/downloads.htm****.*

CODE

```
Public Function dbConnect() As Boolean
    Dim oConn As New ADODB.Connection
    On Error GoTo Err_dbConnect
    dbConnect = False
    oConn.Open "dsnBiblio"
    Debug.Print "ADO Connection = " & oConn.ConnectionString
    dbConnect = True
    oConn.Close
    Exit Function
Err_dbConnect:
    MsgBox "Something went wrong!"
    Exit Function
End Function
```

ANNOTATIONS

The function in this exercise is designed to be executed from within a Class module or an ActiveX DLL so that it can be reused. It can also be used within a standard module.

```
Public Function dbConnect() As Boolean
    Dim oConn As New ADODB.Connection
    On Error GoTo Err_dbConnect
    dbConnect = False
```

Reference
Microsoft ActiveX Data Object 2.0 Library

TABLE 9-2.   Reference for ADO

When calling this function, you should expect to receive a Boolean value of either True or False. If the function executes properly, the return value will be True; otherwise it will be False. By default, the return value is set to False. The *oConn* object variable is set to a new instance of the ADO **Connection** object. Figure 9-5 illustrates the ADO Connections object model and its Properties collection. The **On Error** statement is used to capture any errors that occur during this function.

```
oConn.Open "dsnBiblio"
```

The **Open** method is used to establish a connection to an ODBC data source through ADO. In this example, we assigned the connection object variable, *oConn*, to the Biblio DSN. There are four other optional parameters—*ActiveConnection*, *CursorType*, *LockType*, and *Options*—but since they are optional, you don't need to reference them unless you're not going to use their default settings.

```
Debug.Print "ADO Connection = " & oConn.ConnectionString
dbConnect = True
```

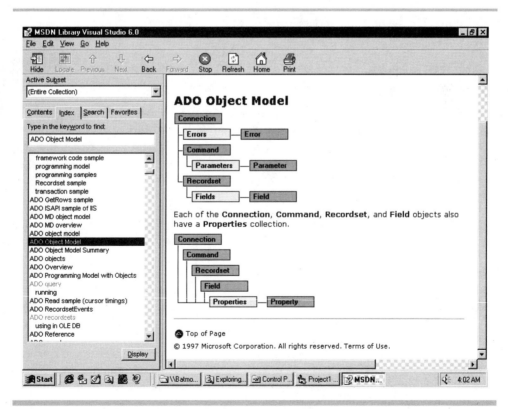

FIGURE 9-5. ADO Connection object model and Properties collection

```
oConn.Close
Exit Function
```

The **Print** method of the **Debug** object is used to display the **ConnectionString** property value. Referenced like this, it displays the information used to establish a connection to the data source. Assuming you get to this point of the function, the return value for **dbConnect** is set to True. The statement that calls this function will know now that the function executed successfully. Otherwise, the return value would still be False, which means that an error occurred. The **Close** method closes all open recordsets and database connections and then you exit the function. If you don't have the **Exit Function** statement, your program will continue on into the error routine.

```
Err_dbConnect:
    MsgBox "Something went wrong!"
    Exit Sub
```

This routine is used to notify the user that an error has occurred within the function. If an error occurred within the function, the **On Error** statement will jump to this routine in the function and execute the **MsgBox** statement and exit the function.

dbDSN-less

Connecting to a Database Through a DSN-less Connection

The most common method to connect to a database is through ODBC using data source name (DSN) connection. With version 4.0 of Visual Basic, you can specify your ODBC driver and server in your connection string using DAO, RDO, and now ADO, which eliminates the need to set up a DSN. This is called a *DSN-less connection* because you don't need to set up a DSN in order to access your ODBC database server or OLE DB provider.

So why should you use DSN-less connections over DSN connections? Why are DSN-less connections important? DSN-less connections are useful if your application is going to be on multiple systems and the server information might change from location to location. By using a DSN-less connection, you can store the data connection information in a file that is read each time the application starts. If the information needs to change, simply change the file information, rather than distributing a new DSN. DSN-less connections are especially useful for web applications because they allow you to move the application from one server to another without re-creating the DSN on the new server.

One might argue that DSN connections are more straightforward than DSN-less connections because if there is a need to change database environments, you change the DSN information via the Control Panel. From an end-user standpoint though, changing ODBC information is not very straightforward; therefore, as the developer, you will need to come up with a way to change the DSN information for

all your users. By using DSN-less connections, you can store the connection
information in a Registry setting or .ini file and when the information changes, you
only need to write a routine that changes the specified information.

CODE

```
Public Function dbDSNLess() As Boolean
    Dim cn As New ADODB.Connection
    Dim sConn As String
    On Error GoTo Err_dbConnect
    dbDSNLess = False
    sConn = "Driver={Microsoft Access Driver (*.mdb)};" _
        & "DBQ=E:\Progra~1\Microso~2\VB98\BIBLIO.MDB;" _
        & "UID=Admin;PWD='';"
    cn.Open sConn
    Debug.Print cn.ConnectionString
    dbDSNLess = True
    Exit Function
Err_dbDSNLess:
    MsgBox "Something went wrong"
    Exit Function
End Function
```

PROGRAMMER'S NOTE

*The **DBQ** parameter in the **sConn** variable is using the directory's short name. Make changes to
accommodate your system because the short names might not be the same on your system. Also, it
might be located on a hard drive other than the "E:" drive.*

ANNOTATIONS

Essentially, this exercise works in a way that is identical to the previous exercise
with the exception of the method of connecting to the database.

```
sConn = "Driver={Microsoft Access Driver (*.mdb)};" _
    & "DBQ=E:\Progra~1\Microso~1\VB98\BIBLIO.MDB;" _
    & "UID=Admin;PWD='';"
cn.Open sConn
```

As you can see, the string variable, *sConn*, is getting assigned the driver name,
database path and name, and user information. The *Driver=* parameter uses the
curly brackets around it. If you wanted to use Microsoft SQL Server, the parameter

would be *{SQL Server}*. An example of a DSN-less connection for Microsoft SQL Server would be:

```
sConn = "Driver={SQL Server}; Server=batcomputer;" _
        & "Database=pubs;UID=SysUser;PWD=Robin; "
```

Notice that you have to specify more information, such as which SQL Server you plan to connect to. Also, you need to specify which database you plan to use and provide a valid User ID and password that has access to the SQL Server and the database you plan to use.

Recset.vbp

Creating a Recordset to Retrieve Data to a Form

Probably the most common task when it comes to data access is retrieving data from a database and placing the data on the form. To do this, ADO—just like DAO and RDO—offers an object called a **Recordset**. Figure 9-6 illustrates the **Recordset** object model and its Properties collection.

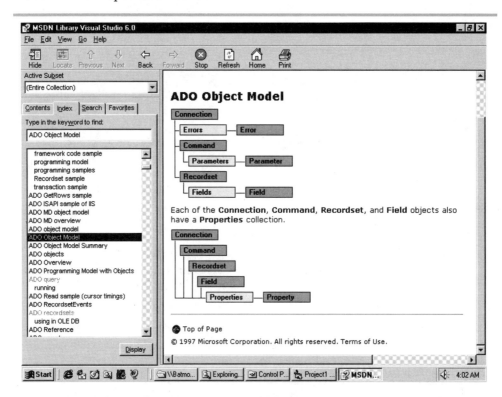

FIGURE 9-6.   ADO Recordset object model and its Properties collection

CODE

```
Private Sub Form_Load()
    Dim sSQL As String
    Dim x As Integer
    sSQL = "SELECT c.Title, a.Author, " _
           & "c.[Year Published] " _
           & "FROM Authors a, " _
           & "[Title Author] b, " _
           & "Titles c " _
           & "WHERE a.Au_ID = b.Au_ID " _
           & "AND c.ISBN = b.ISBN"
    rs.Open sSQL, "dsnBiblio", adOpenDynamic
    If Not rs.EOF Then
        For x = 0 To rs.Fields.Count - 1
            Text1(x).Text = rs(x)
        Next
    End If
End Sub
```

ANNOTATIONS

```
sSQL = "SELECT c.Title, a.Author, " _
       & "c.[Year Published] " _
       & "FROM Authors a, " _
       & "[Title Author] b, " _
       & "Titles c " _
       & "WHERE a.Au_ID = b.Au_ID " _
       & "AND c.ISBN = b.ISBN"
```

By assigning your SQL statement to a variable, it makes it a lot easier to work on than incorporating the SQL statement as part of the **Open** method. The SQL statement in this example is going to retrieve the Title and Year Published from the Titles table and the Author's name from the Authors table. The Title Author table ties together the Titles table and the Authors table to solve for a many-to-many relationship.

```
rs.Open sSQL, "dsnBiblio", adOpenDynamic
```

The **Open** method uses these optional arguments—*Source, ActiveConnection, CursorType, LockType,* and *Options.* The *Source* argument can be any valid **ADO Command** object variable name, SQL statement, stored procedure call, or table name. In this example, we are using a SQL statement. The *ActiveConnection* argument can be a valid **ADO Connection** object variable name (like the DSN connection example) or a string containing *ConnectionString* parameters (like the one used for the DSN-less connection example). In this example, we are using a DSN to connect to the database. The *CursorType* argument is used to determine how the row pointer can navigate through the recordset. By default, it's set to forward-only, which means that the pointer can only go from the beginning to the end of the recordset. In this example, we set the *CursorType* to a dynamic cursor, which allows the pointer to navigate through the recordset dynamically. We're not going to use the last two arguments, *LockType* and *Options. LockType* is used to determine how the recordset should be used for data locking. By default, it is set to read-only, which is adequate for this example. *Options* is an indicator for the data provider to let it know how it should evaluate the *Source* argument if it represents something other than a **Command** object. Figure 9-7 represents how a recordset looks from a flow-charting standpoint.

```
If Not rs.EOF Then
    For x = 0 To rs.Fields.Count - 1
        Text1(x).Text = rs(x)
    Next
End If
```

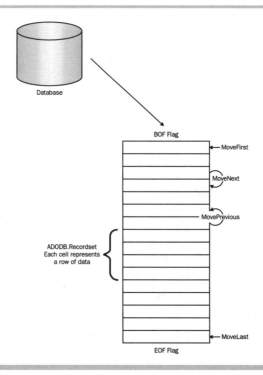

FIGURE 9-7.　How recordsets are processed

The **If...Then** statement is used to determine if data was returned from the **Open** method. If no data was returned, the **BOF** (Beginning-of-File) and **EOF** (End-of-File) flags are set to True. You only need to check either flag; in this example, we're checking the **EOF** flag. If data is returned, then a **For...Next** loop is used to populate the text box array.

TEST THE CODE

1. Start a new project, Standard Exe. The default form may be the startup form. Accept the name Form1 and other default properties.

2. Add the controls shown in Figure 9-8, setting the properties as shown in Table 9-3.

3. Using the Project | References submenu from the VB main menu, select the references shown in Table 9-4. If others are checked that aren't in this table, uncheck them so your project isn't cluttered with DLLs you aren't using.

4. Place the following code in the General Declarations of Form1:

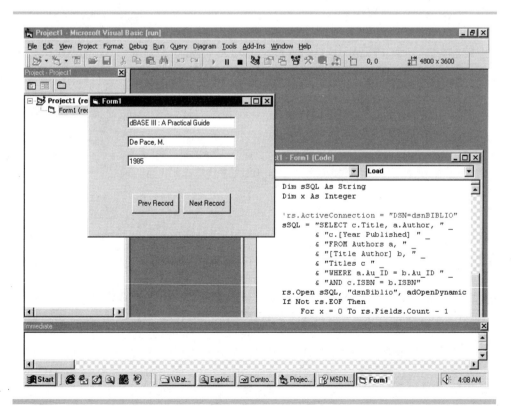

FIGURE 9-8. Viewing the recordset form at run-time

Object	Property	Setting
Form	Name	Form1
TextBox	Name	Text1
	Index	0
TextBox	Name	Text1
	Index	1
TextBox	Name	Text1
	Index	2
CommandButton	Name	CmdPrev
CommandButton	Name	CmdNext

TABLE 9-3.   The Form's Objects and Properties

```
Option Explicit
Dim rs As New ADODB.Recordset
```

The **Option Explicit** statement is used to ensure that all variables are defined before VB will use it. This is very helpful to ensure that you have entered variable names correctly because there is no spell checker in VB. Next, we create a pointer for the variable, *rs*, to the newly created object, **ADODB.Recordset**. By dimensioning the *rs* variable in the General Declarations section, you make it available to the entire form.

5. Place the following code in the **Load** event of the **Form** procedure. This is the same code described at the beginning of this example.

```
Private Sub Form_Load()
    Dim sSQL As String
    Dim x As Integer
    sSQL = "SELECT c.Title, a.Author, " _
            & "c.[Year Published] " _
```

References
Microsoft Visual Basic for Application
Visual Basic Runtime Objects and Procedures
Visual Basic Objects and Procedures
Microsoft ActiveX Data Object 2.0 Library

TABLE 9-4.   References Used in the RecSet Project

```
            & "FROM Authors a, " _
            & "[Title Author] b, " _
            & "Titles c " _
            & "WHERE a.Au_ID = b.Au_ID " _
            & "AND c.ISBN = b.ISBN"
        rs.Open sSQL, "dsnBiblio", adOpenDynamic
        If Not rs.EOF Then
            For x = 0 To rs.Fields.Count - 1
                Text1(x).Text = rs(x)
            Next
        End If
End Sub
```

6. Place the following code in the **Click** event of the **cmdNext** command button. This is the code that will move the recordset pointer to the next record by using the **MoveNext** method. The information will be displayed in the TextBox array. The **On Error** statement is used to detect if an error occurs within this procedure. In the error subroutine, we check to see if the recordset processed all the records. If it has, the **EOF** (End-of-File) flag will be set to True. If True, then set the recordset's pointer to the last record.

```
Private Sub cmdNext_Click()
    Dim x As Integer
    On Error GoTo Err_cmdNext
    rs.MoveNext
    For x = 0 To rs.Fields.Count - 1
        Text1(x).Text = rs(x)
    Next
    Exit Sub
Err_cmdNext:
    If rs.EOF Then
        rs.MoveLast
        Exit Sub
    End If
    Resume
End Sub
```

7. Place the following code in the **Click** event of the **cmdPrev** command button. This is the code that will move the recordset pointer to the next record by using the **MovePrev** method. The information will be displayed in the TextBox array. The **On Error** statement is used to detect if an error occurs within this procedure. In the error subroutine, we check to see if the recordset processed all the records. If it has, the **BOF** (Beginning-of-File) flag will be set to True. If True, then set the recordset's pointer to the first record.

```
Private Sub cmdPrev_Click()
    Dim x As Integer
    On Error GoTo Err_cmdPrev
    rs.MovePrevious
    For x = 0 To rs.Fields.Count - 1
        Text1(x).Text = rs(x)
    Next
    Exit Sub
Err_cmdPrev:
    If rs.BOF Then
        rs.MoveFirst
        Exit Sub
    End If
    Resume
End Sub
```

When you execute this example, your form will contain the first record of the recordset. You can cycle through the rows of the recordset by pressing the command buttons, Previous and Next.

Filllist.vbp

Creating a Recordset to Fill a List Box

There are many times when you want to display information in the form of a list, either in a list box or a drop-down list box. The routine we are about to design is a simple one, designed to display information in a list-based control, such as a list box or combo box.

CODE

```
Public Function FillList(db As String, cntl As Control, _
    sSQL As String) As Boolean

    FillList = False

    Set rs = New ADODB.Recordset

    If TypeOf cntl Is ListBox _
    Or TypeOf cntl Is ComboBox Then

        rs.Open sSQL, db, adOpenDynamic
        If (Not (rs.BOF)) Then
            Dim sAdd As String
            Dim bHasID As Boolean
            Dim i As Integer
```

```
                    'Assume that the first column is meant as ItemData
                    bHasID = ((vbLong = rs.Fields(0).Type) _
                       And (rs.Fields.Count > 1))
                    Do
                          For i = IIf(bHasID, 1, 0) To rs.Fields.Count - 1
                               sAdd = sAdd & CStr(rs(i))
                               If (i < (rs.Fields.Count - 1)) Then _
                                     sAdd = sAdd & vbTab(9)
                          End If
                          Next i

                          cntl.AddItem sAdd
                          sAdd = ""

                          If (bHasID) Then
                               cntl.ItemData(cntl.NewIndex) = rs(0)
                          End If

                          rs.MoveNext
                    Loop Until rs.EOF
                    FillList = True
                    If TypeOf cntl Is ComboBox Then
                          cntl.ListIndex = -1
                    End If
               End If
          End If
          Set rs = Nothing
End Function
```

ANNOTATIONS

This is a function that can be called from any module within your application. As a function, it returns whether or not the function was successful in retrieving the information from the database.

```
Public Function FillList(db As Database, cntl As Control, _
     sSQL As String) As Boolean
```

You will pass three arguments to this function. The *db* argument should be any valid database connection value, valid DSN name, or DSN-less connection string. The *cntl* argument is the name of the control into which the resulting information will be placed. The final argument, *sSQL*, is a string argument that will contain the SQL statement the function is to run.

```
FillList = False
Set rs = New ADODB.Recordset
If TypeOf cntl Is ListBox _
Or TypeOf cntl Is ComboBox Then
```

First, we set the return code of the function to False. If the function works as planned, we will later set the return code of the function to True. The **Set** statement instantiates a new instance of ADO's **Recordset** object. The **If TypeOf** construct is used to determine whether the control passed into the function is a list box or combo box. Because the **DBList** and **DBCombo** controls don't have the **AddItem** method, they can't use this function. If the control matches the list box or combo box type, the function will continue; otherwise, the function would end and return a *False* indicator.

```
rs.Open sSQL, db, adOpenDynamic
```

This statement uses the **Open** method of the **Recordset** object variable to get information from the database using the table name or SQL statement passed in the *SQL* string argument. The *db* argument contains database connection information that describes where the database is located, user ID, and password used to connect to the database.

```
If (Not (rs.BOF)) Then
Dim sAdd As String
Dim bHasID As Boolean
Dim i As Integer
```

The **If...Then** statement checks to make sure that the **BOF** flag is not True. Had the **BOF** flag been True, that would mean that no data was retrieved from the SQL statement.

```
'Assume that the first column is meant as ItemData
bHasID = ((vbLong = rs.Fields(0).Type) _
    And (rs.Fields.Count > 1))
```

Frequently, the first element in a SQL statement is the unique identification value for the row of data, but this is not the information that is displayed on the list. The information displayed is usually the description field for the unique identifier. This set of equations is used to determine if the first column in the SQL statement is the unique identifier. The first equation, **vbLong = rs.Fields(0).Type**, checks the column type of the first element in the Fields collection. The second equation, **rs.Fields.Count > 1**, ensures that more than one column was used in the SQL statement. If both are true, then the variable, *bHasID*, is set to True and the first column's value is going to be placed in the **ItemData** property of the control; otherwise, the value is set to False.

```
Do
For i = IIf(bHasID, 1, 0) To rs.Fields.Count - 1
    sAdd = sAdd & CStr(rs(i))
```

```
        If (i < (rs.Fields.Count - 1)) Then
            sAdd = sAdd & vbTab
        End If
    Next i

    cntl.AddItem sAdd
    sAdd = ""

    If (bHasID) Then
        cntl.ItemData(cntl.NewIndex) = rs(0)
    End If

    rs.MoveNext
    Loop Until rs.EOF
```

The **Do...Loop** statement will execute until the recordset's **EOF** flag gets set to True, which won't happen until all the records are processed. The **IIF** function is used to evaluate the expression, *bHasID*. If the Boolean variable, *bHasID*, is True, then the first lower limit of the **For...Next** statement is set to 1; otherwise, it is set to 0. The upper limit is set by the difference of the **rs.Fields.Count – 1**. The **Count** property of the Fields collection returns the number of columns, or fields, that are used in the recordset. Since members of a collection begin with 0, we need to subtract 1 from the collection so we don't loop through the collection one too many times. If we didn't do that, we would receive a "Subscript out of range" error. Assuming the first column is a unique identifier, the **For...Next** statement would process 1 + *n* number of times. If the first column is not a unique identifier, the **For...Next** statement would process 0 + *n* number of times.

The next section of code is used to retrieve the data from the recordset and add the information to the control. If there are multiple columns retrieved, they are concatenated into the *sAdd* variable and separated by a tab. *vbTab* is equal to **Chr$(9)**. After all the columns of the row have been processed, the *sAdd* string value is added to the control using the **AddItem** method and the *sAdd* string is cleared.

The next **If...Then** statement checks the value of *bHasID*. If it is True, which was established earlier in the code, the first column's value, *rs(0)*, is set to the **ItemData** property. Then the **MoveNext** method moves the pointer to the next row of information.

```
        FillList = True
        If TypeOf cntl Is ComboBox Then
            cntl.ListIndex = -1
        End If
    End If
End If
```

When the code gets to this point, the return code for the **FillList** function is set to True. The following **If...Then** statement is used to set the **ListIndex** property to –1 so the text box portion of the combo box is blank. The procedure that calls the function will then continue.

TEST THE CODE

1. Start a new project, Standard Exe. The default form may be the startup form. Accept the name Form1 and other default properties.

2. Add the controls shown in Figure 9-9, setting the properties as shown in Table 9-5.

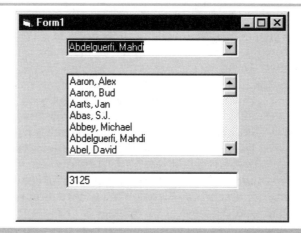

FIGURE 9-9.   Combo box and list box controls filled by the **FillList** function at run-time

Object	Property	Setting
Form	Name	Form1
Combo Box	Name	cboData
	Text	""
List Box	Name	lstData
TextBox	Name	txtDataItem
	Text	""

TABLE 9-5.   The Objects and Properties for the FillList Project

3. Using the Project | References submenu from the VB main menu, select the references shown in Table 9-6. If others are checked that aren't in this table, uncheck them so your project isn't cluttered with DLLs you aren't using.

4. Place the following code in the General Declarations section of Form1:

```
Option Explicit
Dim rs As ADODB.Recordset
```

The **Option Explicit** statement is used to ensure that all variables are defined before VB will use it. This is very helpful to ensure that you have entered variable names correctly because there is no spell checker in VB. Next, we create a reference to the ADO's **Recordset** object assigning it to the *rs* object variable. By dimensioning the *rs* variable in the General Declarations section, you make it available to the entire form.

5. Place the following code in the **Load** event of the **Form** procedure. Two variables are dimensioned that will be used within the procedure. *rc* is used to store the return code from the function and *sSQL* will store the SQL statement passed to the function. The SQL **SELECT** statement is going to retrieve the **au_id** and **Author** from the Authors table from Biblio.mdb and order the information by the **Author**. The **au_id** is a unique identifier and is short for Author ID. Each author in the table is assigned a unique number. **Author** contains both the author's first and last name.

The first function call to **FillList** will fill the combo box, **cboData**, while the second function call will fill the list box, **lstData**. As you can see, by defining a function to fill list-based controls, you don't have to write a lot of code. One function can handle both types of controls.

```
Private Sub Form_Load()
    Dim rc As Integer
    Dim sSQL As String

    sSQL = "SELECT au_id, Author " _
        & "FROM Authors " _
```

References
Microsoft Visual Basic for Application
Visual Basic Runtime Objects and Procedures
Visual Basic Objects and Procedures
Microsoft ActiveX Data Object 2.0 Library

TABLE 9-6. References Used in FillList

```
                & "ORDER BY Author"

        rc = FillList("dsnBIBLIO", cboData, sSQL)
        If Not rc Then
            MsgBox "something went wrong"
         End If

        rc = FillList("dsnBIBLIO", lstData, sSQL)
        If Not rc Then
            MsgBox "something went wrong"
        End If
    End Sub
```

6. Create the **Public** function **FillList** in Form1. This is the same code described at the beginning of this example.

```
Public Function FillList(db As Database, cntl As Control, _
    sSQL As String) As Boolean

    FillList = False
    Set rs = New ADODB.Recordset
    If TypeOf cntl Is ListBox _
    Or TypeOf cntl Is ComboBox Then

        rs.Open sSQL, db, adOpenDynamic
        If (Not (rs.BOF)) Then
            Dim sAdd As String
            Dim bHasID As Boolean
            Dim i As Integer

            'Assume that the first column is meant as ItemData
            bHasID = ((vbLong = rs.Fields(0).Type) _
              And (rs.Fields.Count > 1))
            Do
                For i = IIf(bHasID, 1, 0) To _
                    rs.Fields.Count - 1
                    sAdd = sAdd & CStr(rs(i))
                    If (i < (rs.Fields.Count - 1)) Then
                        sAdd = sAdd & vbTab
                Next i

                cntl.AddItem sAdd
                sAdd = ""

                If (bHasID) Then
```

```
                    cntl.ItemData(cntl.NewIndex) = rs(0)
                End If


                rs.MoveNext
            Loop Until rs.EOF
            FillList = True
            If TypeOf cntl Is ComboBox Then
                cntl.ListIndex = -1
            End If
        End If
    End If
End Function
```

7. Place the following code in the **Click** event of the **cboData** combo box. When the user selects an item from the combo box, the **Click** event will trigger and run this code. The value of the **ItemData** property will be displayed in the **txtDataItem** text box, which is the author's unique ID.

```
Private Sub cboData_Click()
    txtDataItem = cboData.ItemData(cboData.ListIndex)
End Sub
```

8. Place the following code in the **Click** event of the **lstData** list box. When the user selects an item from the list box, the **Click** event will trigger and run this code. The value of the **ItemData** property will be displayed in the **txtDataItem** text box, which is the author's unique ID.

```
Private Sub lstData_Click()
    txtDataItem = lstData.ItemData(lstData.ListIndex)
End Sub
```

When the program loads, it executes the function **FillList** to fill both a combo box and list box control. If an error occurs, a message box will appear to notify the user that something didn't go right. If nothing goes wrong, both controls will be filled with the exact same information. When you select a name from either the combo box or list box, the unique ID is displayed in the text box, **txtDataItem**.

FillGrid.vbp

Creating a Recordset to Fill a Grid

There are times when displaying your information in a group of text boxes, list boxes, or combo boxes just doesn't present itself to be a good user interface design. You want to be able to look at all your information on the screen in a manner where you can see a lot of information at once. Using a grid control is a great way to do this. There are several approaches to using a grid control. One method is to use the data bound grid control, **DBGrid**. Another is to use the **MSFlexGrid** control. Or you can use a third-party grid/spreadsheet control like FarPoint's Spread or Sybase's dbComplete. For this example, we're going to use the **MSFlexGrid** control.

CODE

```vb
Function FillGrid(db as String, cntl As Control, _
    sSQL As String) As Boolean

    FillGrid = False

    If TypeOf cntl Is MSFlexGrid _
    Or TypeOf cntl Is DBGrid Then
        rs.Open sSQL, db
        If (Not (rs.BOF)) Then

            Dim x As Long
            Dim y As Long
            Dim nColumns As Long
            Dim nRows As Long

            nColumns = rs.Fields.Count

            cntl.Cols = nColumns
            cntl.Row = 0
            ' Fill the Column Headers
            For x = 0 To nColumns - 1
                cntl.Col = x
                cntl.Text = rs(x).Name
            Next
            ' Get data
            y = 1
            Do Until rs.EOF
                For x = 0 To nColumns - 1
                    cntl.Col = x
                    cntl.Row = y
                    cntl.Text = rs.Fields(x).Value
                Next
                rs.MoveNext
                y = y + 1
                cntl.Rows = y + 1
            Loop
            FillGrid = True
        End If
    End If

End Function
```

ANNOTATIONS

This function should resemble the **FillList** function described in the last exercise. That's because it uses a lot of the same principles.

```
Function FillGrid(db as String, cntl As Control, _
    sSQL As String) As Boolean
```

You will pass three arguments to this function. The *db* argument should be any valid database connection value, valid DSN name, or DSN-less connection string. The *cntl* argument is the name of the control into which the resulting information will be placed. The final argument, *sSQL*, is a string argument that will contain the SQL statement the function is to run.

```
    FillGrid = False
```

First, we set the return code of the function to False. If the function works as planned, we will later set the return code of the function to True. The **If TypeOf** construct is used to determine whether the control passed into the function is a **MSFlexGrid** or **DBGrid** control. If the control matches either type, the function will continue; otherwise, the function ends and returns a False indicator.

```
    rs.Open sSQL, db
```

The *rs* object variable is assigned to an **ADODB.Recordset** object. It calls the **Open** method of the **Recordset** object and uses the *sSQL* string variable passed at the beginning of the function to retrieve data. The *db* variable is to let the **Open** method know which data source to use.

```
    If (Not (rs.BOF)) Then

        Dim x As Long
        Dim y As Long
        Dim nColumns As Long
        Dim nRows As Long
```

The **If...Then** statement checks to make sure that the **BOF** flag is not True. Had the **BOF** flag been True, that would mean that no data was retrieved from the SQL statement.

```
        nColumns = rs.Fields.Count
```

The *nColumns* variable is used to store the number of columns of data that was requested in the recordset by using the **Fields' Count** property.

```
        cntl.Cols = nColumns
```

Next, the control's property, **Cols**, is set to the number of fields found in the **Count** property.

```
        cntl.Row = 0
```

The **Row** property is used to set a particular row to be active. Often you want column headers to contain the name of the columns retrieved from the database. The row for the column headers is 0, which is why it is being set to 0.

```
For x = 0 To nColumns - 1
    cntl.Col = x
    cntl.Text = rs(x).Name
Next
```

The **For...Next** loop is used to fill the columns with the names of the attributes selected in the SQL statement. For example, if you choose **AU_ID** in the SQL statement, that's what is going to appear in the **rs(x).Name** property. You have some control over that because you can *alias* the column name. By aliasing the column, you change the column header name to something more meaningful than the original column name from the table. You would accomplish this by having your SQL **SELECT** statement look similar to the following:

```
SELECT AU_ID as "Author ID"
```

This will make the **Name** property return "Author ID" instead of "AU_ID."

```
y = 1
```

The *y* variable is used to keep track of how many rows have been processed.

```
Do Until rs.EOF
    For x = 0 To nColumns - 1
        cntl.Col = x
        cntl.Row = y
        cntl.Text = rs.Fields(x).Value
    Next
    rs.MoveNext
    y = y + 1
    cntl.Rows = y + 1
Loop
```

The **Do...Loop** statement will execute until the recordset's **EOF** flag gets set to True, which won't happen until all the records are processed. The **For...Next** statement is used to loop through the columns of the recordset. The upper range of the **For...Next** statement is set to the number of columns in the recordset **Fields** collection minus 1. Because numbering for members of a collection begins with zero, you always code loops starting with the zero member and ending with the value of the **Count** property minus one. For example, if there were three (3) columns, the **Count** property will return 3. But since the **Fields** collection begins with 0, the collection would be processed as follows:

```
rs.Fields(0), rs.Fields(1), rs.Fields(2)
```

We need to subtract 1 from the **Fields** collection so we don't loop through the collection one too many times and result in a "Subscript out of range" error.

Within the **For…Next** statement, the **Col** and **Row** properties are used to place the cursor in a cell in the grid based on the *x* and *y* values. The **Text** property of the active cell is set to the value of the **Fields' Value** property of a given column based on *x*.

After all the columns have been processed, the **MoveNext** method moves the pointer to the next row of information in the recordset. The *y* value is incremented by one and the total number of rows of the grid is increased by one.

```
FillGrid = True
```

When the code gets to this point, the return code for the **FillGrid** function is set to True and the function returns control to the procedure that called the function.

TEST THE CODE

1. Start a new project, Standard Exe. The default form may be the startup form. Accept the name Form1 and other default properties.

2. Add the controls shown in Figure 9-10, setting the properties as shown in Table 9-7.

3. Using the Project | References submenu from the VB main menu, select the references shown in Table 9-8. If others are checked that aren't in this table, uncheck them so your project isn't cluttered with DLLs you aren't using.

PROGRAMMER'S NOTE

You might notice that the Microsoft Data Bound Grid Control doesn't show up in the References list box. That's because the object library for both the Microsoft FlexGrid Control and the Microsoft Data Bound Grid Control are embedded within the controls themselves. Since you selected the Microsoft

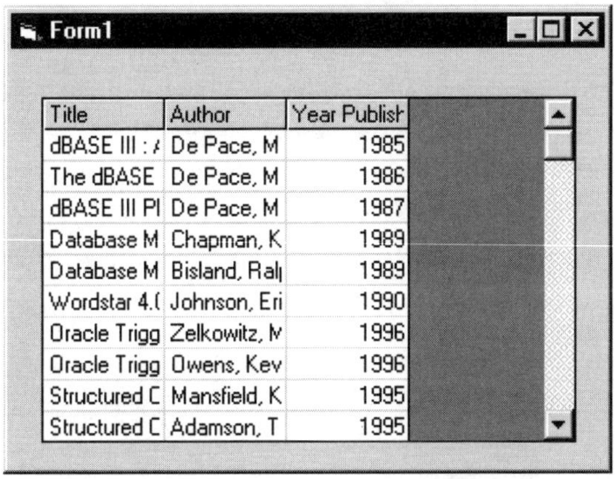

Title	Author	Year Publish
dBASE III : /	De Pace, M	1985
The dBASE	De Pace, M	1986
dBASE III Pl	De Pace, M	1987
Database M	Chapman, K	1989
Database M	Bisland, Ralı	1989
Wordstar 4.(	Johnson, Eri	1990
Oracle Trigg	Zelkowitz, M	1996
Oracle Trigg	Owens, Kev	1996
Structured C	Mansfield, K	1995
Structured C	Adamson, T	1995

FIGURE 9-10. Viewing the data of a recordset in a grid at run-time

Object	Property	Setting
Form	Name	Form1
MSFlexGrid	Name	grdADOData
	AllowUserResizing	1 – flexResizeColumn
	Appearance	0 – flexFlat
	FixCols	0

TABLE 9-7. The Objects and Properties for the FillGrid Project

*FlexGrid Control in step 1, the object library is already marked. To select the reference for the Microsoft Data Bound Grid Control, click on the Browse button to bring up the Add References dialog box. Select **DBGrid32.OCX**, which is usually found in the System32 directory for Windows NT and the System directory for Windows 95/98.*

4. Place the following code in the General Declarations of Form1:

```
Option Explicit
Dim rs As New ADODB.Recordset
```

The **Option Explicit** statement is used to ensure that all variables are defined before VB will use it. This is very helpful to ensure that you have entered variable names correctly because there is no spell checker in VB. Next, we'll create a reference to the ADO's **Recordset** object assigning it to the *rs* object variable. By dimensioning the *rs* variable in the General Declarations section, you make it available to the entire form.

References
Microsoft Visual Basic for Application
Visual Basic Runtime Objects and Procedures
Visual Basic Objects and Procedures
Microsoft ActiveX Data Object 2.0 Library
Microsoft FlexGrid Control
Microsoft Data Bound Grid Control

TABLE 9-8. References Used in FillGrid

5. Place the following code in the **Load** event of the **Form** procedure. Two variables are dimensioned that will be used within the procedure. *rc* is used to store the return code from the function and *sSQL* will store the SQL statement passed to the function. The SQL **SELECT**statement is going to retrieve the first 100 records of book titles and the books' author(s). The event called the function, **FillGrid**, and passes the database connection string, the name of the grid control, **grdADOData**, and the SQL statement stored in *sSQL*. If the return code from the function call is False, a message box will notify the user that something went wrong.

```
Private Sub Form_Load()
    Dim rc As Integer
    Dim sSQL As String

    sSQL = "SELECT top 100 c.Title, a.Author, " _
        & "c.[Year Published] " _
        & "FROM Authors a, " _
        & "[Title Author] b, " _
        & "Titles c " _
        & "WHERE a.Au_ID = b.Au_ID " _
        & "AND c.ISBN = b.ISBN"

    rc = FillGrid("dsnBIBLIO", grdADOData, sSQL)
    If Not rc Then
        MsgBox "something went wrong"
    End If
End Sub
```

6. Create the **Public** function **FillGrid** in Form1. This is the same code described at the beginning of this example.

```
Public Function FillGrid(db as String, cntl As Control, _
    sSQL As String) As Boolean

    FillGrid = False

    If TypeOf cntl Is MSFlexGrid _
    Or TypeOf cntl Is DBGrid Then

        rs.Open sSQL, db
        If (Not (rs.BOF)) Then
            Dim x As Long
            Dim y As Long
            Dim nColumns As Long
            Dim nRows As Long
```

```
            nColumns = rs.Fields.Count

            cnt1.Cols = nColumns
            cnt1.Row = 0
            ' Fill the Column Headers
            For x = 0 To nColumns - 1
                cnt1.Col = x
                cnt1.Text = rs(x).Name
            Next
            ' Get data
            y = 1
            Do Until rs.EOF
                For x = 0 To nColumns - 1
                    cnt1.Col = x
                    cnt1.Row = y
                    cnt1.Text = rs.Fields(x).Value
                Next
                rs.MoveNext
                y = y + 1
                cnt1.Rows = y + 1
            Loop
            FillGrid = True
        End If
    End If

    End Function
```

7. Add this code to the form's **Resize** event. This resizes the grid control, **grdADOData**, when a user changes the size of the form.

```
Private Sub Form_Resize()
    grdADOData.Width = Me.Width - 585
    grdADOData.Height = Me.Height - 945
End Sub
```

When the program loads, it executes the function **FillGrid** to fill the **MSFlexGrid** control. If an error occurs, a message box will appear to notify the user that something didn't go right. If nothing goes wrong, the grid will be filled with the first 100 records of books and their authors. By setting the grid's **AllowUserResizing** to **1 – flexResizeColumn**, we allow the user to change the width of the columns.

In order to make the **FillGrid** function able to fill a **MSFlexGrid** or a **DBGrid**, we needed to reference both objects as specified in step 3. Because we added the **MSFlexGrid** control on the toolbox, the reference to the object is added to the project. If you add the **FillGrid** function to an ActiveX DLL to be used as a reusable component, you will need to make sure that both grid controls are referenced. In

ActiveX DLLs, you only need the object library of the ActiveX control. In order to do that, you'll need to add references to MSFlxGrd.ocx and DBGRID32.ocx.

spp.vbp

Calling a Simple Stored Procedure Using ADO

Stored procedures are very common in database management systems like SQL Server and Oracle. They provide you with another way to separate your data access logic from your application. They also offer you a way to increase your application's database performance because they are compiled SQL programs that reside on the database server. Within a stored procedure, you can perform conditional execution, declare variables, pass parameters, and perform other programming tasks that execute on the server, away from your client's user interface and CPU.

Within a stored procedure, you can program an entire database transaction procedure with business rules. This is advantageous because if any part of the database transaction fails, you can *abend*, or roll back, the transaction and return all values to their original state prior to the transaction's execution. Suppose, for example, that in a hotel reservation system, a customer would like to make a reservation. In a transactional stored procedure, you can develop it so that it will do the following:

◆ Check to make sure the room type the customer wants is available.

◆ Generate a new reservation number.

◆ Save the customer information with the reservation number and room type.

If any portion of the transaction fails for any reason, the stored procedure will return an error and any changes to the database will be reset to how they were before the stored procedure was executed. If this logic was part of the user interface, you would have to program all these steps into your application. By putting them in a stored procedure, the steps are centralized in one place—for logic as well as data access—and this takes the burden of having network traffic going back and forth from the user interface to the database server. Without the stored procedure, there would be minimally three trips from the program to the database and back: one to check the availability of the room type, another to get the reservation number, and another to insert the new record. The program would also have to handle all rollbacks if any portion of the transaction fails.

Enough about stored procedures for now. Let's talk about ADO and how it uses stored procedures. ADO has a lot of flexibility when it comes to executing stored procedures through the use of the ADO **Command** object. Through the use of the **Command** object, you tell ADO everything it needs to know about executing a query or procedure; therefore, the query or procedure usually executes faster and more accurately because the database system doesn't have to figure out any of the parameters. The downside is that in order for the query to execute the way you want it to you must do more coding.

If you don't want to do a lot of coding, you can take the easy route and use the **EXECUTE** statement to run the procedure within your **Recordset** object, but you will need to make sure that the database management system supports the statement. The listing below is an example of how you can execute a stored procedure within the **Recordset** object using the **EXECUTE** statement.

CODE

```vb
Sub ExecSPP()
    Dim sSQL As String
    Dim conn As New ADODB.Connection
    Dim rs As New ADODB.Recordset

    conn.Open "dsn=pubs;uid=sa"
    sSQL = "EXEC byroyalty 30"
    rs.Open sSQL, conn, 0, 1
    While (Not rs.EOF)
        Debug.Print rs(0)
        rs.MoveNext
    Wend
End Sub
```

As you can see, it's fairly straightforward. The **Recordset** object executes the *sSQL* string value, which calls Microsoft SQL Server's **byroyalty** stored procedure in the Pubs sample database. It's a single parameter stored procedure and requires an integer value, which in this example is 30.

A recommended method to execute stored procedures is to use ADO's **Command** object as mentioned earlier. It's a bit more lengthy than using the **EXECUTE** statement, but then again, this method is more reusable.

```vb
Sub CommandSPP()
    Dim cmd As New ADODB.Command
    Dim rs As New ADODB.Recordset
    Dim parm As Parameter

    ' define a command object for the stored procedure
    cmd.ActiveConnection = "DSN=pubs;uid=sa"
    cmd.CommandText = "byroyalty"
    cmd.CommandType = adCmdStoredProc
    ' Set up a new parameter for the stored procedure
    Set parm = cmd.CreateParameter("BookType", adChar, _
        adParamInput, 12, "Business")
```

```
    cmd.Parameters.Append parm
    ' Create a record set by executing the command
    Set rs = cmd.Execute
    While (Not rs.EOF)
        Debug.Print rs(0)
        rs.MoveNext
    Wend

End Sub
```

ANNOTATIONS

Make sure you reference the Microsoft ActiveX Data Object in your project; otherwise you will get a "Compile Error: User-defined type not defined" message.

```
Sub CommandSPP()
    Dim cmd As New ADODB.Command
    Dim rs As New ADODB.Recordset
    Dim prm As Parameter
```

This procedure requires no parameter. If this procedure is part of a business object, though, it should accept parameters; minimally, the arguments should be **Optional** arguments. The variable *cmd* instantiates new instances of the ADO **Command** object. The *rs* variable instantiates new instances of the ADO **Recordset** object. And the *parm* variable is set to the **Parameter** object.

```
    ' define a command object for the stored procedure
    cmd.ActiveConnection = "DSN=pubs;uid=sa"
```

The **ActiveConnection** property is set to the data source name, **pubs**, which connects to the Pubs sample database that comes with Microsoft SQL Server. The user ID used to establish the connection is the system administrator's ID, *sa*. For a DSN-less connection, the **ActiveConnection** property would be set as follows:

```
cmd.ActiveConnection = "driver={sql server};" & _
    "server=batmobile;" & _
    "Database=pubs;uid=sa;pwd=;"
```

As you can see, you need to specify which database driver you wish to use, the server you're connecting to, as well as the database, user ID, and password.

```
    cmd.CommandText = "byroyalty"
```

The **CommandText** property is used to tell ADO which query, stored procedure, or table it is going to use when issuing query instructions to the database provider. In this case, the property is the **byroyalty** stored procedure. It's a good practice to establish your own convention for naming objects in your database. A common practice is to prefix stored procedures with "spp" to distinguish them from server-provided stored procedures. In Microsoft SQL Server, stored procedures and extended stored procedures are prefixed with "sp" and "xp" respectively.

```
cmd.CommandType = adCmdStoredProc
```

The **CommandType** property lets the database provider know what type of **CommandText** has been used. In this exercise, the property is set to **adCmdStoredProc**, which tells the provider that this particular **Command** object is a stored procedure. The list of valid values for the **CommandType** property can be found in Table 9-9.

```
' Set up a new parameter for the stored procedure
Set parm = cmd.CreateParameter("BookType", adChar, adParamInput, _
12, "Business")
```

The **CreateParameter** method is used to create a new **Parameter** object that contains optional parameters that specify a name, data type, direction, size, and value for the object. Any values you use are written to the corresponding **Parameter** properties. Table 9-10 describes the parameters in greater detail.

```
cmd.Parameters.Append parm
```

The **Append** method, which is part of the **Parameters** object, is used to add an object to the collection. In this case, we are adding the **Parameter** object, *parm,* to the **cmd Command** object collection.

```
' Create a record set by executing the command
Set rs = cmd.Execute
```

Now that we've told the provider exactly what stored procedure to use and what parameter is to be used with it, the **Command** object's **Execute** method executes the value stored in the **CommandText** property. As described above, the **CommandText** can contain a query, stored procedure, or a table name. In this example, the stored procedure "byroyalty" is executed. The result of the execution is placed in the *rs* **Recordset** object variable.

Constant	Description
adCmdText	Tells the provider that the **Command** object is a textual string, usually in the form of a query.
adCmdTable	Tells the provider that the **Command** object is a database table.
adCmdStoredProc	Tells the provider that the **Command** object is a stored procedure.
adCmdUnknown	This is the **default** value if no **CommandType** value is specified.

TABLE 9-9.   CommandType Property Value Settings

Optional Parameters	Description
Name	A string value used as the name of the parameter you're creating. In this example, we named it *BookType*. If we leave this parameter blank, then we can't refer to the parameter by name; we would have to reference it by the parameter number.
Type	Specifies the data type used. In this example, we set *Type* to the constant, *adChar*, which means it's a *Char* data type.
Direction	Used to determine if this is an Input, Input/Output, Output, or Return Value parameter. In this example, we set *Direction* to the constant, *adParamInput*, which means it's an Input parameter.
Size	Specifies the size (or length) of the data type. This parameter isn't needed except for variable length data types like *Char* and *VarChar*. In this example, we set the *Size* to 12, because the stored procedure is expecting a *Char* value of up to 12 characters.
Value	The value of the parameter to be used. It is the default value supplied or the actual value passed when a query is run. In this example, we set the *Value* equal to "Business," because we want the stored procedure to use the word "Business" as part of the **Where** clause of the query.

TABLE 9-10. Arguments for the **CreateParameter** Method

```
While (Not rs.EOF)
    Debug.Print rs(0)
    rs.MoveNext
Wend
```

The **While...Wend** statement loops through the **rs Recordset** object until the **EOF** (End-of-File) property is True. The results of the recordset are printed in the **Debug** window.

This exercise illustrates two different ways to execute the same stored procedure. Which way is the correct way to execute a stored procedure is completely up to your organization. From a readability standpoint, the first method discussed, which uses strictly the **Recordset** object, is the most straightforward but you will be sacrificing some performance because the provider needs to figure what type of database command is being executed. Is it a query, table, or stored procedure? Once it figures out it's executing a stored procedure, it needs to determine if the parameter passed is the correct datatype, direction, and so on.

By using the **Command** object, the provider knows exactly what type of execution is being requested and the information needed to execute the procedure is provided because you coded them in. No guesswork on the provider's part is required; therefore, the provider executes exactly what you requested.

Ado_trans.vbp

Using Transactions with ADO

As mentioned in the stored procedure exercise, the use of stored procedures is a great way to control database transaction control. The issue of having stored procedures control transactions is that usually application developers don't have the authority to add or change any item on the database server; the DBA (database administrator) should be the only one who has authority to do anything to the database server. The last thing a DBA wants is a pesky application programmer tinkering around the server. So what's the alternative? Write the transactions in business objects separate from the application and separate from the database server. Now we're dealing with what is known as a "unit of work."

A *unit of work* is a group of different procedures that are used for one transaction. The commonly used example to describe a unit of work is transferring money from one bank account to another. The different procedures validate the bank accounts, debit one account, and credit another account. All three procedures can be used together or a combination of the three can be used as a unit of work. The **Connection** object of ADO is used to help control, or scope, transactions. There are three methods it uses for this. They are **BeginTrans**, **CommitTrans**, and **RollbackTrans**. Essentially, what these methods provide is a way to tell ADO and the database management system to delay full commitment of changes until you tell it to. The **BeginTrans** method begins a new transaction. The **CommitTrans** method, is used to save any changes to the database during the transaction and end the current transaction. It is also used to start a new transaction after the prior one completes. The **RollbackTrans** method is used to cancel any changes made to the database during the transaction and end the current transaction. This method, just like the **CommitTrans** method, can also trigger another transaction after it ends the one it was canceling.

A feature of ADO's transaction methods that's different than its predecessors, DAO and RDO, is that it supports nested transactions, assuming the provider supports it. A nested transaction occurs when you have one transaction (outer) issue another transaction (inner) and the outer transaction doesn't continue until the inner transaction is completed. The outer transaction then completes the transaction based on the return value received from the inner transaction. It's not recommended to use nested transactions within your applications because error trapping might be implemented effectively and you might encounter a "runaway" transaction that fouls up the system. Also, nested transactions are not supported in all database systems. If you must use nested transactions, you should use a transaction monitor like the Component Services. It can support nested transactions even when the database system doesn't. Chapter 15 covers building business components for the Component Services in more detail.

This exercise's project uses the **Connection** object's transaction methods to update the Pubs sample database. Figure 9-11 illustrates this exercise's project just after the **BeginTrans** method has been invoked to move all the authors in the state of California to Washington.

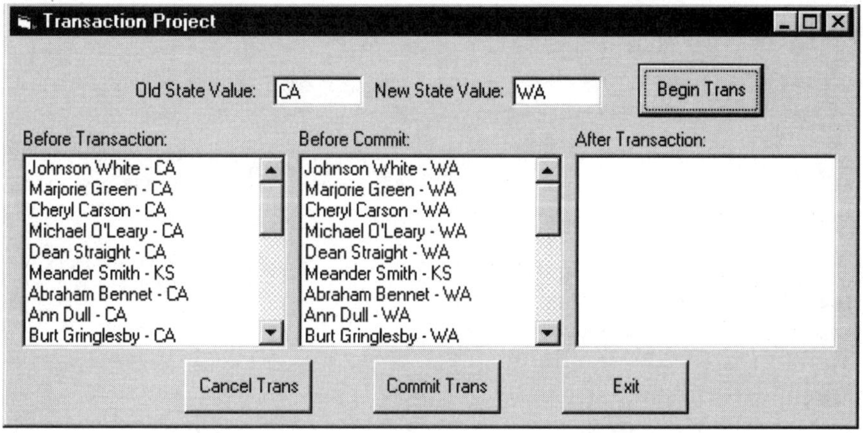

FIGURE 9-11. The project after the **BeginTrans** method has been invoked

CODE

```
Private Sub cmdBeginTrans_Click()

    Dim sSQLUpdate As String
    Dim rs As New ADODB.Recordset

    ' Check for values
    If Len(Trim(txtStateValue(0))) = 0 Or _
        Len(Trim(txtStateValue(1))) = 0 Then Exit Sub

    ' Clear list boxes
    lstBeforeCommit.Clear
    lstAfterTrans.Clear

    sSQLUpdate = "UPDATE authors "
    sSQLUpdate = sSQLUpdate & "SET state = '"
    sSQLUpdate = sSQLUpdate & txtStateValue(1) & "' "
    sSQLUpdate = sSQLUpdate & "WHERE state = '"
    sSQLUpdate = sSQLUpdate & txtStateValue(0) & "'"
```

```vb
    ' Begin trans and perform update
    oConn.BeginTrans
    oConn.Execute sSQLUpdate

    ' Query the update and fill listbox
    rs.Open sSQLQry, oConn
    While (Not rs.EOF)
        lstBeforeCommit.AddItem rs(0)
        rs.MoveNext
    Wend

    ' enable the command buttons
    cmdCancelTrans.Enabled = True
    cmdCommitTrans.Enabled = True

End Sub

Private Sub cmdCancelTrans_Click()

    Dim rs As New ADODB.Recordset

    ' Cancel all changes and end transaction
    oConn.RollbackTrans

    ' Query recordset and fill listbox
    rs.Open sSQLQry, oConn
    While (Not rs.EOF)
        lstAfterTrans.AddItem rs(0)
        rs.MoveNext
    Wend

    ' disable the command buttons
    cmdCancelTrans.Enabled = False
    cmdCommitTrans.Enabled = False

End Sub

Private Sub cmdCommitTrans_Click()

    Dim rs As New ADODB.Recordset

    ' Accept and end the transaction
    oConn.CommitTrans
```

```
    ' Query recordset and fill listbox
    rs.Open sSQLQry, oConn
    While (Not rs.EOF)
        lstAfterTrans.AddItem rs(0)
        rs.MoveNext
    Wend

    ' disable the command buttons
    cmdCancelTrans.Enabled = False
    cmdCommitTrans.Enabled = False

End Sub
```

ANNOTATIONS

The three procedures listed below are used to illustrate the three different
transaction methods. They are invoked through command buttons on the form. A
more detailed explanation will follow in the "Test the Code" section below.

```
Private Sub cmdBeginTrans_Click()

    Dim sSQLUpdate As String
    Dim rs As New ADODB.Recordset

    ' Check for values
    If Len(Trim(txtStateValue(0))) = 0 Or _
        Len(Trim(txtStateValue(1))) = 0 Then Exit Sub
```

The **If...Then** statement verifies that there is data within the two text boxes;
otherwise, the procedure is aborted.

```
    ' Clear list boxes
    lstBeforeCommit.Clear
    lstAfterTrans.Clear
```

The **Clear** method for the list boxes is used to ensure that they are empty.

```
    sSQLUpdate = "UPDATE authors "
    sSQLUpdate = sSQLUpdate & "SET state = '"
    sSQLUpdate = sSQLUpdate & txtStateValue(1) & "' "
    sSQLUpdate = sSQLUpdate & "WHERE state = '"
    sSQLUpdate = sSQLUpdate & txtStateValue(0) & "'"
```

The *sSQLUpdate* string variable contains a SQL **UPDATE** statement to change all
the values in the state column to a new value in the **txtStateValue(1)** text box where
the state equals the value from the **txtStateValue(0)** text box.

```
' Begin trans and perform update
oConn.BeginTrans
```

The **BeginTrans** method is activated, notifying the provider that a transaction has started.

```
oConn.Execute sSQLUpdate
```

The **Execute** method is used to execute the SQL **UPDATE** statement found in the *sSQLUpdate* string variable.

```
' Query the update and fill listbox
rs.Open sSQLQry, oConn
```

The recordset's **Open** method is used to query the Author table using the connection established in the *oConn* connection variable. The *sSQLQry* string variable is a project-wide variable and will be explained in greater detail in the "Test the Code" section.

```
While (Not rs.EOF)
    lstBeforeCommit.AddItem rs(0)
    rs.MoveNext
Wend
```

The **While...Wend** statement loops the recordset until the **EOF** (End-of-File) flag is reached. Each line of the recordset is added to the **lstBeforeCommit** list box.

```
' enable the command buttons
cmdCancelTrans.Enabled = True
cmdCommitTrans.Enabled = True
```

The **Enable** property for two command buttons is set to True so that the transaction can be either accepted or canceled.

The next two procedures are almost identical in nature. Rather than beginning the transaction, the **cmdCancelTrans_Click** procedure contains the **RollbackTrans** method to cancel the transaction while the **cmdCommitTrans_Click** procedure contains the **CommitTrans** method to commit the changes to the database. The differences in both procedures are shown without boldface. In both procedures, after the **CommitTrans** or **RollbackTrans** method is invoked, the result of the database transaction is displayed in a list box.

```
Private Sub cmdCancelTrans_Click()

    Dim rs As New ADODB.Recordset

    ' Cancel all changes and end transaction
    oConn.RollbackTrans

    ' Query recordset and fill listbox
```

```
    rs.Open sSQLQry, oConn
    While (Not rs.EOF)
        lstAfterTrans.AddItem rs(0)
        rs.MoveNext
    Wend

    ' disable the command buttons
    cmdCancelTrans.Enabled = False
    cmdCommitTrans.Enabled = False

End Sub

Private Sub cmdCommitTrans_Click()

    Dim rs As New ADODB.Recordset

    ' Accept and end the transaction
    oConn.CommitTrans

    ' Query recordset and fill listbox
    rs.Open sSQLQry, oConn
    While (Not rs.EOF)
        lstAfterTrans.AddItem rs(0)
        rs.MoveNext
    Wend

    ' disable the command buttons
    cmdCancelTrans.Enabled = False
    cmdCommitTrans.Enabled = False

End Sub
```

TEST THE CODE

1. Start a new project, Standard Exe. The default form may be the startup form. Accept the name Form1 and other default properties.

2. Add the following controls to the form, setting the properties as shown in Table 9-11 and using Figure 9-11 as an example of the positioning.

3. Using the Project | References submenu from the VB main menu, select the references shown in Table 9-12. If others are checked that aren't in this table, uncheck them so your project isn't cluttered with DLLs you aren't using.

Object	Property	Setting
Form	Name	frmMain
Label	Name	lblValue
	Caption	Old State Value:
	Index	0
Label	Name	lblValue
	Caption	New State Value:
	Index	1
TextBox	Name	txtStateValue
	Index	0
	Text	"" (leave blank)
TextBox	Name	txtStateValue
	Index	1
	Text	"" (leave blank)
CommandButton	Name	cmdBeginTrans
	Caption	Begin Trans
Label	Name	lblListTrans
	Caption	Before Transaction:
	Index	0
Label	Name	lblListTrans
	Caption	Before Commit:
	Index	1
Label	Name	lblListTrans
	Caption	After Transaction:
	Index	2
ListBox	Name	lstBeforeTrans
ListBox	Name	lstBeforeCommit
ListBox	Name	lstAfterTrans
CommandButton	Name	cmdCancelTrans

TABLE 9-11. The Objects and Properties for **frmMain** Form

Object	Property	Setting
	Caption	Cancel Trans
CommandButton	Name	cmdCommitTrans
	Caption	Commit Trans
CommandButton	Name	cmdExit
	Caption	Exit

TABLE 9-11. The Objects and Properties for **frmMain** Form (continued)

4. Place the following code in the General Declarations of **frmMain**:

```
Option Explicit
Dim oConn As New ADODB.Connection
Dim sSQLQry As String
```

The **Option Explicit** statement is used to ensure that all variables are defined before VB will use it. This is very helpful to ensure that you have entered variable names correctly because there is no spell checker in VB. Next, we instantiate a new instance of the ADO **Connection** object and assign it to the *oConn* object variable. Then we create a string variable, *sSQLQry*, to contain a query that will be used throughout the project. By dimensioning both *oConn* and *sSQLQry* in the General Declarations section, you make it available to the entire form.

References
Microsoft Visual Basic for Application
Visual Basic Runtime Objects and Procedures
Visual Basic Objects and Procedures
Microsoft ActiveX Data Object 2.0 Library

TABLE 9-12. References Used in the ADO_trans Project

5. Place the following code in the **Load** event of the **Form** procedure. A new instance of the ADO **Recordset** object is created and assigned to *rs*. A query that will get the first and last names of authors and the states they reside in from the Author table is assigned to the *sSQLQry* string variable. A connection is created using a DSN-less connection and is assigned to the *oConn* object variable. Once the connection is made, a recordset is executed using the query in the *sSQLQry* string variable. The **While…Wend** statement loops through the results of the query and displays the contents into the **lstBeforeTrans** list box. Because no transactions other than a read-only query has been performed, the transaction commit and cancel command buttons are disabled. This prevents anyone from pressing them before a transaction has begun.

```
Private Sub Form_Load()
    Dim rs As New ADODB.Recordset

    sSQLQry = "SELECT au_fname + ' ' " & _
        "+ au_lname + ' - ' + state FROM authors"

    oConn.Open "driver={SQL Server};" & _
        "Server=batmobile;database=pubs;" & _
        "uid=sa;"
    rs.Open sSQLQry, oConn
    While (Not rs.EOF)
        lstBeforeTrans.AddItem rs(0)
        rs.MoveNext
    Wend

    cmdCancelTrans.Enabled = False
    cmdCommitTrans.Enabled = False

End Sub
```

6. Place the following code in the **Click** event of the **cmdBeginTrans** command button. The **If…Then** statement validates that information was entered in the two text boxes before proceeding with the procedure. The **Trim** function removes any leading or trailing spaces from the string. The **Len** function returns how many characters are in the text fields of the text boxes. If either one is equal to zero (0), then there is nothing in the text box and the procedure is aborted.

Both the **lstBeforeCommit** and **lstAfterTrans** list boxes are cleared to remove any doubt that a new transaction has started or not. The SQL **UPDATE** query is assigned to the *sSQLUpdate* string variable, where it updates all the state values that equal the text value in the **txtStateValue(0)** text box with the new value specified in the **txtStateValue(1)** text box.

The **BeginTrans** method is invoked to notify the provider that a transaction is beginning. The **Execute** method is used to execute the update query that is defined in the *sSQLUpdate* string variable. After it is executed, a recordset is executed using the query in the *sSQLQry* string variable defined in the **Form_Load** procedure. The **While...Wend** statement loops through the results of the query and displays the contents into the **lstBeforeTrans** list box. Now that a transaction has begun, the transaction commit and cancel command buttons are enabled.

```
Private Sub cmdBeginTrans_Click()

    Dim sSQLUpdate As String
    Dim rs As New ADODB.Recordset

    ' Check for values
    If Len(Trim(txtStateValue(0))) = 0 Or _
        Len(Trim(txtStateValue(1))) = 0 Then Exit Sub

    ' Clear list boxes
    lstBeforeCommit.Clear
    lstAfterTrans.Clear

    sSQLUpdate = "UPDATE authors "
    sSQLUpdate = sSQLUpdate & "SET state = '"
    sSQLUpdate = sSQLUpdate & txtStateValue(1) & "' "
    sSQLUpdate = sSQLUpdate & "WHERE state = '"
    sSQLUpdate = sSQLUpdate & txtStateValue(0) & "'"

    ' Begin trans and perform update
    oConn.BeginTrans
    oConn.Execute sSQLUpdate

    ' Query the update and fill listbox
    rs.Open sSQLQry, oConn
    While (Not rs.EOF)
        lstBeforeCommit.AddItem rs(0)
        rs.MoveNext
    Wend

    ' disable the command buttons
    cmdCancelTrans.Enabled = True
    cmdCommitTrans.Enabled = True

End Sub
```

7. Place the following code in the **Click** event of the **cmdCancelTrans** command button. When this button is pressed, the **RollbackTrans** method is invoked and the transaction that changed the authors' state from the value in **txtStateValue(0)** to **txtStateValue(1)** is canceled. All the changed values are set back to their original information.

   Then a recordset is executed using the query in the *sSQLQry* string variable defined in the **Form_Load** procedure. The **While...Wend** statement loops through the results of the query and displays the contents into the **lstAfterTrans** list box. Since this is the end of a transaction, the transaction commit and cancel command buttons are disabled.

```
Private Sub cmdCancelTrans_Click()

    Dim rs As New ADODB.Recordset

    ' Cancel all changes and end transaction
    oConn.RollbackTrans

    ' Query recordset and fill listbox
    rs.Open sSQLQry, oConn
    While (Not rs.EOF)
        lstAfterTrans.AddItem rs(0)
        rs.MoveNext
    Wend

    ' disable the command buttons
    cmdCancelTrans.Enabled = False
    cmdCommitTrans.Enabled = False

End Sub
```

8. Place the following code in the **Click** event of the **cmdCmmitTrans** command button. When this button is pressed, the **CommitTrans** method is invoked and the transaction that changed the authors' state from the value in **txtStateValue(0)** to **txtStateValue(1)** is permanently updated in the database.

   Then a recordset is executed using the query in the *sSQLQry* string variable defined in the **Form_Load** procedure. The **While...Wend** statement loops through the results of the query and displays the contents into the **lstAfterTrans** list box. Since this is the end of a transaction, the transaction commit and cancel command buttons are disabled.

```
Private Sub cmdCommitTrans_Click()
```

```
Dim rs As New ADODB.Recordset

' Accept and end the transaction
oConn.CommitTrans

' Query recordset and fill listbox
rs.Open sSQLQry, oConn
While (Not rs.EOF)
    lstAfterTrans.AddItem rs(0)
    rs.MoveNext
Wend

' disable the command buttons
cmdCancelTrans.Enabled = False
cmdCommitTrans.Enabled = False

End Sub
```

9. Place the following code in the **Click** event of the **cmdExit** command button.

```
Private Sub cmdExit_Click()
    End
End Sub
```

When the program loads, it executes the authors' first and last names, and the states they reside in are displayed in the **Before Transaction** list box. Both an original State value and new State value need to be provided in order for a transaction to begin. With both values provided, the SQL **UPDATE** statement changes the original State value to the new State value and displays the results in the **Before Commit** list box. This is to show that the change to the database has occurred.

If you like what you see, pressing the **Commit Trans** command button performs the **CommitTrans** method, commits the change to the database, and ends the transaction. If you don't like the data change, press the **Cancel Trans** command button and the **RollbackTrans** method is executed; the information is changed back to its original state prior to the transaction.

Because we're working with transactions, if the program terminates prior to pressing the **Commit Trans** command button, the transaction will be canceled and the data will return to the state it was before the transaction started. The premature termination could occur for many reasons such as power failure, kicking the power cord out of the electrical socket, "blue screen of death," and so on. Using the transaction methods is a great way to ensure that a unit of work is completed and to provide a way for users to change their minds before information is permanently changed.

schema.vbp

Obtaining Database Schema Information

Programming data validation routines into your application is probably one of the most tedious things to do when it comes to software development, especially when the information is going to be stored in a database. You need to take into consideration for each field whether the data is supposed to accept characters and numbers or just numbers. You also need to make sure that the user doesn't enter more characters than the field can hold.

To limit the number of characters entered into a field, you can use the **MaxLength** property in the Text Box control. But that means you have to coordinate each text box's **MaxLength** property with a field in the database. What happens if the length of the field changes or if the data type of the field changes? Then you have to go through your application and make sure that all the text boxes are updated.

With ADO, there is a method called **OpenSchema** that is part of the **Connection** object. This method simply obtains the schema information about a database from the database provider. It is fairly versatile regarding the type of database information it can retrieve. The following example will show how the **OpenSchema** method can get the table information—for example, the table's name and type (such as a base table or view table)—within a specified database. Then a routine is called to get the column attributes, like name, data type, and data size using the ADO **Recordset**'s **Fields** collection. Figure 9-12 shows some of the schema for the Pubs database that comes with SQL Server 6.5 using this exercise's project. The following is a set of procedures for retrieving database schema information.

CODE

```
Public Sub GetSchema()

    Dim rsSchema As ADODB.Recordset
    Set rsSchema = oConn.OpenSchema(adSchemaTables)

    Do Until rsSchema.EOF
        If rsSchema!TABLE_TYPE <> "SYSTEM TABLE" Then
            With lstSchema
                .AddItem "Table name: " & _
                    rsSchema!TABLE_NAME
                .AddItem "Table type: " & _
```

```
                    rsSchema!TABLE_TYPE
            End With
            Call GetFieldInfo(rsSchema!TABLE_NAME)
        End If
        rsSchema.MoveNext
    Loop
    rsSchema.Close


    oConn.Close

End Sub

Public Sub GetFieldInfo(sTableName As String)

    Dim rsFieldInfo As ADODB.Recordset
    Set rsFieldInfo = oConn.Execute(sTableName)

    If Not rsFieldInfo.EOF Then
        Dim x As Integer
        With lstSchema
            For x = 0 To rsFieldInfo.Fields.Count - 1

                .AddItem "Column Name: " & _
                    rsFieldInfo(x).Name
                .AddItem "Column DataType: " & _
                    FieldType(rsFieldInfo(x).Type)
                .AddItem "Column Size: " & _
                    rsFieldInfo(x).DefinedSize
            Next
        End With
        rsFieldInfo.MoveNext
    End If


    rsFieldInfo.Close

End Sub
Public Function FieldType(intType As Integer) As String

    Select Case intType
        Case adChar
            FieldType = "Char"
        Case adVarChar
```

```
            FieldType = "VarChar"
        Case adSmallInt
            FieldType = "SmallInt"
        Case adUnsignedTinyInt
            FieldType = "UnsignedTinyInt"
        Case adDBTimeStamp
            FieldType = "TimeStamp"
        Case adBoolean
            FieldType = "Bit"
        Case Else
            FieldType = intType
    End Select

End Function
```

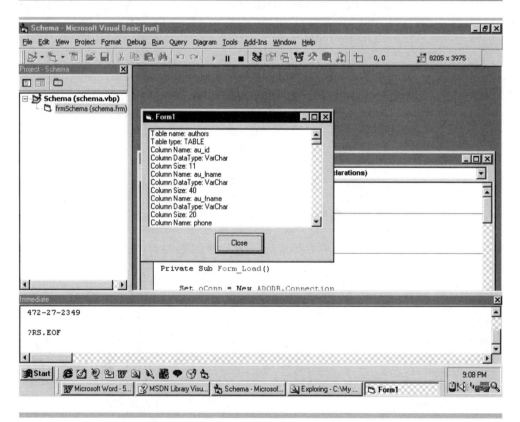

FIGURE 9-12. Some of the schema for the Pubs database

ANNOTATIONS

The combination of three procedures gets the schema from the database.

```
Public Sub GetSchema()

    Dim rsSchema As ADODB.Recordset
    Set rsSchema = oConn.OpenSchema(adSchemaTables)
```

The **OpenSchema** method of the **Connection** object opens the schema of a database and returns the information into the recordset, **rsSchema**. The parameter used in this example, *adSchemaTables*, tells the method to retrieve the *table catalog, table schema, table name,* and *table type.* The table catalog contains the database name and the table schema identifies who the database owner is. The table name is the name of the database table and the table type identifies the type of table it is—base table, view table, or system table. There are over a dozen different parameters to obtain various levels of schema information. For more information, refer to the online documentation under **OpenSchema Method – ADO.**

```
    Do Until rsSchema.EOF
        If rsSchema!TABLE_TYPE <> "SYSTEM TABLE" Then
            With lstSchema
                .AddItem "Table name: " & _
                    rsSchema!TABLE_NAME
                .AddItem "Table type: " & _
                    rsSchema!TABLE_TYPE
            End With
            Call GetFieldInfo(rsSchema!TABLE_NAME)
        End If
        rsSchema.MoveNext
    Loop
```

The **Do…Loop** statement loops through the **rsSchema** recordset until the **EOF** (End-of-File) flag is reached. The **If…Then** statement is used to check if the value in the **Table_Type** column is a system table or some other table type. If the table type is a system table, we skip over the record because we're not interested in system table information in this exercise. All other table types are added to the list box, **lstSchema**, along with the name of the table. Then the procedure calls the **GetFieldInfo** procedure to obtain the column information of each table found within the schema.

```
    rsSchema.Close

    oConn.Close

End Sub
```

After all the information is found, the recordset and connection are closed.

```
Public Sub GetFieldInfo(sTableName As String)

    Dim rsFieldInfo As ADODB.Recordset
    Set rsFieldInfo = oConn.Execute(sTableName)
```

The **GetFieldInfo** procedure expects one parameter to be passed to it. It's the name of the table you wish to seek column information for. The *oConn* connection object variable uses the **Execute** method to open the table specified in the *sTableName* string variable, which was passed to the procedure. The results are stored in the *rsFieldInfo* recordset variable.

```
If Not rsFieldInfo.EOF Then
    Dim x As Integer
    With lstSchema
        For x = 0 To rsFieldInfo.Fields.Count - 1

            .AddItem "Column Name: " & _
                rsFieldInfo(x).Name
            .AddItem "Column DataType: " & _
                FieldType(rsFieldInfo(x).Type)
            .AddItem "Column Size: " & _
                rsFieldInfo(x).DefinedSize
        Next
    End With
    rsFieldInfo.MoveNext
End If                      '
```

The **If...Then** statement checks the recordset's **EOF** (End-of-File) flag. If no information was returned, the flag would be set to True. The **With...End With** command allows us to specify multiple properties for a given object; in this case, we're working with the list box **lstSchema**. The **For...Next** statement will loop through the columns based on the number of columns contained within the recordset. The **Recordset** object contains a number of properties that are polled to get column information. For this exercise, we are retrieving the column name, its data type, and data size. The retrieved information is then added to the **lstSchema** list box.

```
    rsFieldInfo.Close

End Sub
```

After all the information about the specified table is retrieved, the recordset is closed and the procedure is exited.

```
Public Function FieldType(intType As Integer) As String

    Select Case intType
```

```
        Case adChar
            FieldType = "Char"
        Case adVarChar
            FieldType = "VarChar"
        Case adSmallInt
            FieldType = "SmallInt"
        Case adUnsignedTinyInt
            FieldType = "UnsignedTinyInt"
        Case adDBTimeStamp
            FieldType = "TimeStamp"
        Case adBoolean
            FieldType = "Bit"
        Case Else
            FieldType = intType
    End Select

End Function
```

Data types are stored as numeric values, which is fine for a computer but frustrating for the humans who have to interpret what they mean. This function examines the data type's integer value and returns a more meaningful text description of the data type. This is not a complete list of all the data types, only six of the most commonly used data types. If one of the data types defined in the **Select Case** statement isn't found, the numeric value of the data type is returned.

TEST THE CODE

1. Start a new project, Standard Exe. The default form may be the startup form. Accept the name Form1 and other default properties.

2. Add the following controls to the form, setting the properties as shown in Table 9-13 and using Figure 9-12 as an example of the positioning.

3. Using the Project | References submenu from the VB main menu, select the references shown in Table 9-14. If others are checked that aren't in this table, uncheck them so your project isn't cluttered with DLLs you aren't using.

4. Place the following code in the General Declarations of **frmSchema**:

```
Option Explicit
Dim oConn As New ADODB.Connection
Dim sconn As String
```

The **Option Explicit** statement is used to ensure that all variables are defined before VB will use it. This is very helpful to ensure that you have entered variable names correctly because there is no spell checker in VB. The *oConn* object variable is assigned to a new instance of the ADO **Connection** object.

Object	Property	Setting
Form	Name	frmSchema
ListBox	Name	lstSchema
CommandButton	Name	cmdClose
	Caption	Close

TABLE 9-13.   The Objects and Properties for the **Schema** Form

Then we create a string variable, *sConn*, that will be used to contain the database connection information. By dimensioning both *oConn* and *sConn* in the General Declarations section, you make it available to the entire form.

5. Place the following code in the **Load** event of the **Form** procedure. The connection string, *sConn*, is assigned to a DSN-less connection and then the *oConn* object variable opens a connection to the database. Once the database connection is established, the **GetSchema** procedure is executed to get the schema information from the database.

```
Private Sub Form_Load()
    sconn = "driver={SQL Server};server=batmobile;" & _
        "uid=sa;pwd=;database=pubs"
    oConn.Open sconn

    Call GetSchema

    Set oConn = Nothing
End Sub
```

6. Create the following procedure in the **frmSchema** form. This is the same procedure described in the "Annotations" section of this exercise.

References
Microsoft Visual Basic for Application
Visual Basic Runtime Objects and Procedures
Visual Basic Objects and Procedures
Microsoft ActiveX Data Object 2.0 Library

TABLE 9-14.   References Used in the Schema Project

```
Public Sub GetSchema()
    Dim rsSchema As ADODB.Recordset
    Set rsSchema = oConn.OpenSchema(adSchemaTables)

    Do Until rsSchema.EOF
        If rsSchema!TABLE_TYPE <> "SYSTEM TABLE" Then
            With lstSchema
                .AddItem "Table name: " & _
                    rsSchema!TABLE_NAME
                .AddItem "Table type: " & _
                    rsSchema!TABLE_TYPE
            End With
            Call GetFieldInfo(rsSchema!TABLE_NAME)
        End If
        rsSchema.MoveNext
    Loop
    rsSchema.Close

    oConn.Close
End Sub
```

7. Create the following procedure in the **frmSchema** form. This is the same procedure described in the "Annotations" section of this exercise.

```
Public Sub GetFieldInfo(sTableName As String)
    Dim rsFieldInfo As ADODB.Recordset
    Set rsFieldInfo = oConn.Execute(sTableName)

    If Not rsFieldInfo.EOF Then
        Dim x As Integer
        With lstSchema
            For x = 0 To rsFieldInfo.Fields.Count - 1

                .AddItem "Column Name: " & _
                    rsFieldInfo(x).Name
                .AddItem "Column DataType: " & _
                    FieldType(rsFieldInfo(x).Type)
                .AddItem "Column Size: " & _
                    rsFieldInfo(x).DefinedSize

            Next
        End With
        rsFieldInfo.MoveNext
    End If
```

```
        rsFieldInfo.Close
End Sub
```

8. Create the following procedure in the **frmSchema** form. This is the same procedure described in the "Annotations" section of this exercise.

```
Public Function FieldType(intType As Integer) As String
    Select Case intType
        Case adChar
            FieldType = "Char"
        Case adVarChar
            FieldType = "VarChar"
        Case adSmallInt
            FieldType = "SmallInt"
        Case adUnsignedTinyInt
            FieldType = "UnsignedTinyInt"
        Case adDBTimeStamp
            FieldType = "TimeStamp"
        Case adBoolean
            FieldType = "Bit"
        Case Else
            FieldType = intType
    End Select
End Function
```

9. Place the following code in the **Click** event of the **cmdExit** command button.

```
Private Sub cmdClose_Click()
    End
End Sub
```

When the program is executed, the connection to the database is established using the DSN-less connection information. The schema for all the tables within the selected database is retrieved and displayed in the list box, **lstSchema**. This may not seem like anything useful right now, but in a transaction-based system, you can use these routines to get a column's data type and size to determine what type of error checking you want for data entry fields. For example, if you know the database field is 25, you can set the text box's **MaxLength** to 25 or build a business component that uses the value as part of its data validation routine similar to the following:

```
If Len(Trim(txtFname)) > rsFieldInfo(x).DefinedSize Then
    ...
End If
```

You could eliminate a lot of data entry errors this way. Also, by not hard-coding in the value of the data size, if the size changes, you will not have to update the application or business object because the defined size is determined dynamically each time it reads the schema information from the database.

Manipulating Strings

In almost every application, characters and numbers are being processed. A lot of times you might encounter instances where the string value is correct, but it is not displayed properly. This chapter will illustrate some common functions to help you change the way your string values look in order for you to use them in a more effective manner.

You might not find some of these functions useful within a Visual Basic application, but who says that functions written in VB need to be used by VB? The last exercise in this chapter will take you through the steps to place all these functions into an ActiveX DLL. This will allow you to reuse the component within any VBA (Visual Basic for Applications) product like Microsoft Word or Visio, or even within an Active Server Page on the Microsoft Internet Information Server.

CleanQuotes

Prepare Text with Quotes

When it comes to inputting data into a database, one of the most troubling set of characters is the apostrophe (')—also referred to as *tick marks*—and quote marks ("). If you attempt to use either of these characters as part of a string within a SQL statement, the SQL engine will give you an error. This function is used to format those strings so it is safe to use them inside a SQL statement by changing the occurrence of the tick into tick-tick ('') and the occurrence of a single quote mark into double quote marks ("").

PROGRAMMER'S NOTE

*New to VB 6.0 is the **Replace** function. It performs a task similar to the **CleanQuotes** function, except that it replaces an entire substring with another substring a designated number of times. **CleanQuotes** only looks for ticks and quotes. So if you're using VB 6.0, you might use the **Replace** function, but if you're still developing in a version prior to 6.0, you'll have to write the **CleanQuotes** function as it appears in the following example.*

CODE

```
Public Function CleanQuotes(SrcStr As Variant) As String

    ' SrcStr      - Source string
    Dim sSrcStr As String
    Dim RtnStr As String
    Dim x As Long
    Dim sTmpChar As String

    If IsNull(SrcStr) Then
        CleanQuotes = ""
        Exit Function
    End If
```

```
      sSrcStr = CStr(SrcStr)
    ' Check for Ticks or Quotes
    If InStr(1, sSrcStr, "'") > 0 Or _
        InStr(1, sSrcStr, Chr$(34)) > 0 Then
            ' Check the entire string because there may be more
            ' than one tick or quote
        For x = 1 To Len(sSrcStr)
                sTmpChar = Mid(sSrcStr, x, 1)
                If sTmpChar = "'" Then
                    RtnStr = RtnStr & Mid(sSrcStr, x, 1) & "'"
                ElseIf sTmpChar = Chr$(34) Then
                    RtnStr = RtnStr & Mid(sSrcStr, x, 1) & Chr$(34)
                Else
                    RtnStr = RtnStr & Mid(sSrcStr, x, 1)
                End If
        Next
    Else
        RtnStr = sSrcStr
    End If

    CleanQuotes = RtnStr

End Function
```

ANNOTATIONS

```
Public Function CleanQuotes(SrcStr As Variant) As String

    ' SrcStr       - Source string
    Dim sSrcStr As String
    Dim RtnStr As String
    Dim x As Long
    Dim sTmpChar As String
```

The value that is passed to this function will be stored in the *SrcStr* variable. It is assigned as a variant so it can accept any value.

```
    If IsNull(SrcStr) Then
        CleanQuotes = ""
        Exit Function
    End If
```

The **If...Then** statement is used to determine if the value in the *SrcStr* string variable is Null. If it is, then the function will end and the result will be an empty string. It returns an empty string because often a Null value is not allowed in some database columns. Since an empty string is not the same as Null, this is acceptable to the database engine.

```
sSrcStr = CStr(SrcStr)
```

The **CStr** function is used to convert the *SrcStr* variant variable into a string value.

```
' Check for Ticks or Quotes
If InStr(1, sSrcStr, "'") > 0 Or _
    InStr(1, sSrcStr, Chr$(34)) > 0 Then
    ' Check the entire string because there may be more
    ' than one tick or quote
    For x = 1 To Len(sSrcStr)
        sTmpChar = Mid(sSrcStr, x, 1)
        If sTmpChar = "'" Then
            RtnStr = RtnStr & Mid(sSrcStr, x, 1) & "'"
        ElseIf sTmpChar = Chr$(34) Then
            RtnStr = RtnStr & Mid(sSrcStr, x, 1) & Chr$(34)
        Else
            RtnStr = RtnStr & Mid(sSrcStr, x, 1)
        End If
    Next
Else
    RtnStr = sSrcStr
End If
```

This **If...Then** statement is used to determine if a single tick or quote is contained within the string variable, *sSrcStr*. If the string variable does contain one or the other special characters, the entire variable is checked because one never knows if there's more than one tick or quote in the string. The **For...Next** statement is used to loop through the entire length of the source string variable. The **Mid** statement is used so that each character in the source string variable can be checked. If a special character is found, then the next **If...Then** statement is used to determine which special character it is and adds an extra tick or quote accordingly.

```
CleanQuotes = RtnStr
```

Once all the characters in the string variable have been processed, the **CleanQuotes** value is set to the *RtnStr* string variable which was used to build the new string.

CleanURL

Ensure URL Parameters Are Passed Properly

This function might seem a bit out of place in a Visual Basic book, but it is useful for Active Server Pages with Microsoft's Internet Information Server 3.0 and higher. When you pass variables as part of a URL (uniform resource locator) address, you have to pass a parameter that has spaces in it. Microsoft Internet Explorer (MSIE) is smart enough to convert the spaces between words into %20, which is the hexadecimal value for spaces. Netscape Navigator/Communicator, unfortunately, isn't as forgiving and doesn't quite know how to handle parameters with spaces. This function will process a string that is passed to the URL Address field and convert many special characters to their hexadecimal equivalent.

CODE

```
' Purpose: Many special characters like the ampersand (&) and
'          question mark (?) do not translate well on a
'          browser's Address combobox. This return will
'          go through the entire URL line and replace
'          any special characters with their Hexadecimal
'          equivalents.
Public Function CleanURL(sURL As Variant) As String
    Dim sSrcURL As String
    Dim sURLChar As String
    Dim sRtnURL As String
    Dim x As Long

    If IsNull(vURL) Then
        CleanURL = ""
        Exit Function
    End If

    ' Convert the variant to a string
    sSrcURL = CStr(vURL)

    ' Search for special characters
    ' for the length of the address
    For x = 1 To Len(sSrcURL)
        sURLChar = Mid(sSrcURL, x, 1)
```

```
        Select Case sURLChar
        Case "~", "`", "!", "#", "$", "%", "^", "&", "(", ")", _
             "+", "=", "[", "]", "{", "}", "|", ":", ";", _
             ",", "<", ">", "?", """", "'", "/", "\", " "
             ' @, _, -, *, and . have been excluded because
             ' Yahoo and HotBot don't convert them to hex values.
             ' To be consistent with those engines,
             ' they have been removed from the conversion routine
             sRtnURL = sRtnURL & "%" & Hex(Asc(sURLChar))
        Case Else
             sRtnURL = sRtnURL & sURLChar
        End Select
    Next

    CleanURL = sRtnURL

End Function
```

ANNOTATIONS

```
Public Function CleanURL(vURL As Variant) As String
    Dim sSrcURL As String
    Dim sURLChar As String
    Dim sRtnURL As String
    Dim x As Long
```

The value that is passed to this function will be stored in the *vURL* variable. It is assigned as a variant so it can accept any value.

```
    If IsNull(vURL) Then
        CleanURL = ""
        Exit Function
    End If
```

The **If…Then** statement is used to determine if the value of the *vURL* variant variable is Null. If it is, then the function will return an empty string to the calling procedure and exit the function.

```
    ' Convert the variant to a string
    sSrcURL = CStr(vURL)
```

The **CStr** function is used to convert the *vURL* variant variable into a string value.

```
For x = 1 To Len(sSrcURL)
    sURLChar = Mid(sSrcURL, x, 1)
    Select Case sURLChar
        Case "~", "`", "!", "#", "$", "%", "^", "&", "(", ")", _
             "+", "=", "[", "]", "{", "}", "|", ":", ";", _
             ",", "<", ">", "?", """", "'", "/", "\", " "
             ' @, _, -, *, and . have been excluded because
             ' Yahoo and HotBot don't convert them to hex values.
             ' To be consistent with those engines, they have
             ' been removed from the conversion routine
            sRtnURL = sRtnURL & "%" & Hex(Asc(sURLChar))
        Case Else
            sRtnURL = sRtnURL & sURLChar
    End Select
Next
```

The **For...Next** statement will loop through the entire length of the *sSrcURL* string variable. The **Mid$** function is used to check each character within the *sSrcURL* string and stores the character in the *sURLChar* string variable. The **Select Case** statement compares the character in the *sURLChar* variable against most of the punctuation marks and special characters that are known to cause problems with web browsers if they aren't converted to their hexadecimal equivalent. If the *sURLChar* character does need to be converted, the character is turned into its ASCII equivalent using the **ASC** function, then it's converted to hexadecimal using the **Hex** function. The new value is stored in the string variable, *sRtnURL*.

```
CleanURL = sRtnURL
```

Once all the characters have been processed, the *sRtnURL* value is assigned to the **CleanURL** string and returned to the procedure that called it.

Find and Replace a Single Character Within a String

ReplaceChar This function is a spin-off of the last exercise, **CleanURL**. As the name implies, **ReplaceChar** is designed to search for a particular character within a string and replace it with another. This function is only designed to replace one character with another; therefore, it is limited in some of its abilities. It is most useful when used as a component with Microsoft Internet Information Server. As mentioned in the

CleanURL exercise, when passing parameters as part of the URL address with spaces between the words, web browsers don't always handle them properly. **CleanURL** is useful with HTML form pages that are designed to accept any type of input. This function, **ReplaceChar**, is best used on HTML form pages that have limited input. For example, in a library system, you may know that you're looking for a particular author. The user's input is fairly narrow in scope with only a first name, last name, and maybe a middle initial or name. Using the same library system example used for the **CleanURL** function, you would want to use the **ReplaceChar** function in a title or subject search because a book title might be something like "The Cold & the Dark" and the ampersand would need to be translated to hexadecimal.

CODE

```
Function ReplaceChar(SrcStr As Variant, _
    OldChar As String, NewChar As String) As String
    Dim nStart As Integer
    Dim nPos As Integer
    Dim sSrcStr As String

    sSrcStr = CStr(SrcStr)
    ' Find the position of the first occurrence of
    ' OldString in SrcStr
    nStart = InStr(sSrcStr, OldChar)
    nPos = nStart
    While nPos > 0
        ' Do replace
        Mid$(sSrcStr, nPos, 1) = NewChar
        ' Find next occurrence of OldChar
        nPos = InStr(nStart, sSrcStr, OldChar)
        nStart = nPos + 1
    Wend
    ReplaceChar = sSrcStr
End Function
```

ANNOTATIONS

```
Function ReplaceChar(SrcStr As Variant, _
    OldChar As String, NewChar As String) As String
    Dim nStart As Integer
    Dim nPos As Integer
    Dim sSrcStr As String
```

This function is designed to work with three arguments. The first argument, *SrcStr*, is a variant to store the information that is going to be parsed. The second argument, *OldChar*, is the source character that the function is going to look to replace. *NewChar* is a character that is going to replace the *OldChar* character.

```
sSrcStr = CStr(SrcStr)
```

The **CStr** function is used to convert the *SrcStr* variant variable into a string value.

```
' Find the position of the first occurrence of
' OldString in SrcStr
nStart = InStr(sSrcStr, OldChar)
nPos = nStart
```

The **InStr** function will return the numeric position of the character we are looking for with a string value. In this example, the **InStr** function will look for the value in the *OldChar* variable within the *sSrcStr* string variable. The position will be stored in the *nStart* integer variable which will be assigned to the *nPos* integer variable.

```
While nPos > 0
    ' Do replace
    Mid$(sSrcStr, nPos, 1) = NewChar
    ' Find next occurrence of OldChar
    nPos = InStr(nStart, sSrcStr, OldChar)
    nStart = nPos + 1
Wend
```

The **While...Wend** statement is used to loop through the entire string stored in the *sSrcStr* string variable until it finds all the characters in the string that need to be replaced. When it finds them all, then the *nPos* integer variable will be 0.

As the loop is being processed, when a value in the *OldChar* string variable is found, the **Mid$** statement, not to be confused with the **Mid$** *function*, replaces the old character specified in *OldChar* with the new character specified in the *NewChar* string variable back to the *sSrcStr* string variable.

The next occurrence of the *OldChar* string value is searched for within *sSrcStr*. If found, then the position is stored in the *nPos* integer variable, which is then stored in the *nStart* integer variable, but the value is increased by one because you want the search to start right after the position where you found the value. This is because you don't want to start the search where you have already searched.

```
ReplaceChar = sSrcStr
```

Once all the characters in the string variable have been processed, the **ReplaceChar** return value is set with the value in the *sSrcStr* string variable and control is returned to the procedure that called the function.

ReplaceStr

Find and Replace a String

In the previous examples, we have looked at very specific string replacement routines where we replaced one character with another character. This example is a generic string replacement routine so that you can perform a global search and replace on any character or set of characters.

CODE

```
Public Function ReplaceStr(sSrcStr As String, _
    sFind As String, sReplaceWith As String) _
    As String

    Dim nStart As Long
    Dim sStr As String
    Dim nStrLen As String

    nStart = 1

    nStrLen = Len(sReplaceWith)

    While nStart <> 0
        nStart = InStr(nStart, sSrcStr, sFind)
        If nStart > 0 Then
            sSrcStr = Left(sSrcStr, nStart - 1) + _
                sReplaceWith + Mid(sSrcStr, nStart + Len(sFind))
            nStart = nStart + nStrLen
        End If
    Wend

    ReplaceStr = sSrcStr

End Function
```

ANNOTATIONS

```
Public Function ReplaceStr(sSrcStr As String, _
    sFind As String, sReplaceWith As String) _
    As String

    Dim nStart As Long
    Dim sStr As String
    Dim nStrLen As String
```

This function is designed to accept three arguments. The *sSrcStr* string variable contains the string which you wish to search through. The *sFind* string variable contains the substring you wish to look for within the *sSrcStr* string variable. And the *sReplaceWith* string variable is the replacement substring. Unlike the **ReplaceChar** function, it was designed to replace one character and one character only. This function, on the other hand, can replace a substring of any length. For example, you can search for every instance of the letter "d" and replace it with "dee," while with the **ReplaceChar** function you can only replace the "d" with a different single character.

```
nStart = 1
```

When you dimension a variable, it is defined as zero. In this case, we are setting the numeric variable, *nStart*, to 1.

```
nStrLen = Len(sReplaceWith)
```

The length of the replacement string is found using the **Len** function and stored in the numeric variable, *nStrLen*.

```
While nStart <> 0
        nStart = InStr(nStart, sSrcStr, sFind)
        If nStart > 0 Then
            sSrcStr = Left(sSrcStr, nStart - 1) + _
                sReplaceWith + Mid(sSrcStr, nStart + Len(sFind))
        nStart = nStart + nStrLen
        End If
Wend
```

The **While...Wend** statement will loop until the numeric variable, *nStart*, equals 0. That occurs when the substring specified in the *sFind* variable is no longer found.

The **InStr** function is used to obtain the location of the substring in the *sFind* variable. It looks for it within the *sSrcStr* string variable. The function starts looking for the substring depending on the position specified by the *nStart* variable. This number increases based on where the last substring was found.

If the *nStart* value is greater than 0, then the substring that was being sought is replaced. The **Left$** function obtains the first part of the string prior to the *sFind* substring. It is concatenated with the *sReplaceWith* substring. And both substrings are concatenated with the substring based on the **Mid$** function of the *sSrcStr* string, starting from the position of *nStart* plus the length of the *sFind* substring. Confused yet?

Here's an example. The phrase you're working with is "The ball went threw the window." You want to replace the word "threw" with the word "through." As you can see, the lengths of the two words are different. The **InStr** function finds word "threw" starts on the 15th character of the string and stores the number in the *nStart* variable. The **Left$** function returns the substring "The ball went " because it returns the characters starting at the beginning of a string through the *nStart* position minus 1. You subtract 1 from the *nStart* position because you don't want to include the "t" in the word "threw." Then you concatenate the *sReplaceWith* substring, "through," to the substring returned from the **Left$** function. So now the working variable is "The ball went through." The result of the **Mid$** function is concatenated to the product of those two concatenated substrings. The substring returned from the **Mid$** function is the rest of the phrase "the window," because the starting position is the value of *nStart* plus the length of the word "threw," which is 5, so that's 15 plus 5 which is 20. The entire concatenated value is assigned back to the value *sSrcStr*.

After all this takes places, the new *nStart* value is the *nStart* value plus the length of the *sReplaceWith* value.

```
ReplaceStr = sSrcStr
```

When the **While...Wend** statement is completed, the result is assigned to the return value of the function and control is returned to the procedure that called this function.

PROGRAMMER'S NOTE

*New to VB 6.0 is the **Replace** function and the **ReplaceStr** function is almost identical to it, except it has some optional parameters that makes it a bit more flexible. With the VB 6.0 version, there is an argument of how many times the function loops the source string, as well as where the search begins within the string.*

Add Leading Zeros to Numbers

PadStringWZeros

In database development, it's a general rule that you store numbers in a character field, unless you plan to do calculations with the values. That means that all numbers should be stored as Text, Char, or VarChar data type values. The problem with that is that if you want to sort by that column, you won't get the results you're looking for. That's because if a column is defined as *Text, Char, VarChar,* or something similar, the database engine treats the values as a string, even though they contain only numeric values. For example, it's common knowledge that 1 comes before 2 and 10 comes after 2. But to a database engine looking at those values with the numbers stored as character values, the sort order is going to be 1, 10, 2. That's because it looks at the values as characters, not their numeric value, and when a string is sorted on, database engines (as well as spreadsheet programs) look at values left to right while numeric values are looked at from right to left.

This function is designed to help alleviate this problem by adding leading zeros to the number. Assume we have a three-digit field. If you store the numbers as 1, 2, and 10, then perform a database query and sort by those numbers, you're going to get 1, 10, and 2. Since we know that the maximum length of the field is three, we will add as many zeros as it takes to make the value fill all three digits. This means that after the numbers are passed through this exercise's function, the new values would be 001, 002, and 010.

CODE

```
' Purpose: When you add numeric values into a Char/Varchar
'          field, you will get an incorrect sort order when
'          you query the table.
'    e.g.: 3, 30, and 300 will display before 4
'          This function will pad (place leading zeros in front
'          of) the value based on the pad value specified.
'
'          To remove the leading zeros, run the value through
'          the UnpadStringWZero function.
Public Function PadStringWZeros(sSrcStr As String, _
    nPad As Integer) As String

    Dim sWorkingStr As String
    Dim nStrLen As Integer

    nStrLen = Len(sSrcStr)

    If nStrLen < nPad Then
        sWorkingStr = String(nPad, "0")
        Mid(sWorkingStr, ((nPad - nStrLen) + 1), nStrLen) = sSrcStr
        PadStringWZeros = sWorkingStr
    Else
        PadStringWZeros = sSrcStr
    End If

End Function
```

ANNOTATIONS

```
Public Function PadStringWZeros(sSrcStr As String, _
    nPad As Integer) As String

    Dim sWorkingStr As String
    Dim nStrLen As Integer
```

This function is designed to work with two arguments. The first argument, *sSrcStr*, is a string variable to store the information that is going to be padded. The second argument, *nPad*, is the number of digits the padding should consist of. For example, if the database column is a five-digit field, then the *nPad* argument should be 5.

```
' Get the length of the source string
nStrLen = Len(sSrcStr)
```

The **Len** function returns the number of characters contained within the *sSrcStr* variable and stores the value in the *nStrLen* integer variable.

```
If nStrLen < nPad Then
    sWorkingStr = String(nPad, "0")
    Mid(sWorkingStr, ((nPad - nStrLen) + 1), nStrLen) = sSrcStr
    PadStringWZeros = sWorkingStr
Else
    PadStringWZeros = sSrcStr
End If
```

The **If...Then** statement is used to determine if the length of the string in *sSrcStr* is equal to the *nPad* value. If it is, the function returns the value of *sSrcStr* because no leading zeros are needed. Otherwise, the **String** function is used to create a working string variable called *sWorkingStr*, containing a number of repeating zeros based on the *nPad* value. The **Mid$** statement, not to be confused with the **Mid$** *function*, replaces the string of repeating zeros with the value in *sSrcStr*. The **Mid$** statement requires three arguments: working string, starting position, and the string length. The *working string* argument is the string that is going to be manipulated. The *starting position* argument indicates where the string replacement will begin within the *working string* value. In this exercise, the **Mid$** statement takes the *nPad* value, which is the maximum number of characters the string should be and subtracts the length of *sSrcStr* which is stored in the *sStrLen* variable. The *string length* argument indicates how many characters are going to be replaced. In this exercise, the **Mid$** statement uses the value stored in the *sStrLen* variable. The new value, which is stored in the *sWorkingStr* variable, is assigned to the *PadStringWZeros* return value and returned to the procedure that called it.

Remove Leading Zeros for Display Purposes

UnpadStringWZeros

This function provides the reverse effect of the **PadStringWZeros** function. Its purpose is to remove the leading zeros for display purposes, unless of course you like the leading zeros. You won't have the problem of 10 displaying before 2 since the data will be ordered coming from the database. This function only affects the string after the data is retrieved from the database.

CODE

```
' Purpose: This function is to remove the leading zeros
'          from a string so that it displays properly
'          on the source destination.
'    e.g.: 00003 will display as 3
'          00321 will display as 321
Public Function UnpadStringWZeros(sSrcStr As String) As String

    If IsNumeric(sSrcStr) Then
        UnpadStringWZeros = CStr(CDbl(sScrStr))
    Else
        UnpadStringWZeros = sSrcStr
    End If

End Function
```

ANNOTATIONS

```
Public Function UnpadStringWZeros(sSrcStr As String) As String
```

This function is designed to work with one argument, the *sSrcStr* string variable. The procedure that calls this function passes the string that needs to be processed.

```
If IsNumeric(sSrcStr) Then
    UnpadStringWZeros = CStr(CDbl(sSrcStr))
Else
    UnpadStringWZeros = sSrcStr
End If
```

The **If...Then** statement uses the **IsNumeric** function to determine if the *sSrcStr* variable is numeric or not. If it is, then it is first converted to a double data type by using the **CDbl** function. Then it is converted back to a string data type using the **CStr** function. By converting it to a double data type, all the leading zeros are removed because numeric data types don't allow leading zeros. The value is converted back to a string because the value originated as a string.

LeadingCaps

Capitalize the First Character of a Sentence

How many times have you processed information from a database and all the information was entered in all uppercase characters or all lowercase? When you retrieve these records and display them on a report or on the user's screen, the information is difficult to read. This function is designed to convert a string value to all lowercase except for the initial characters of a sentence.

CODE

```
' Purpose:  Converts a string to be all lowercase except for
'           leading characters.
Public Function LeadingCaps(sStr As String) As String

    Dim sChar As String
    Dim x As Integer
    Dim sPhrase As String
    Dim nPos As Integer

    ' Make string all lowercase except 1st char upper
    sPhrase = LCase$(sStr)
    sPhrase = UCase$(Left$(sPhrase, 1)) & Mid$(sPhrase, 2)

    sChar = "."

    nPos = 0
    Do While True
        nPos = CInt(InStr(nPos + 1, sPhrase, ' '))
        If (nPos = 0) Then
            Exit Do
        Else
            sPhrase = Left$(sPhrase, nPos + 1) _
                    & UCase$(Mid$(sPhrase, nPos + 2, 1)) _
                    & Mid$(sPhrase, nPos + 3)
        End If
    Loop

    LeadingCaps = sPhrase
End Function
```

ANNOTATIONS

```
Public Function LeadingCaps(sStr As String) As String

    Dim sChar As String
    Dim x As Integer
    Dim sPhrase As String
    Dim nPos As Integer
```

This function is designed to work with one argument, the *sStr* string variable. The procedure that calls this function passes the string that needs to be processed.

```
' Make string all lowercase except 1st char upper
sPhrase = LCase$(sStr)
sPhrase = UCase$(Left$(sPhrase, 1)) & Mid$(sPhrase, 2)
```

First, the entire *sStr* string value is converted to lowercase by using the **LCase$** function and it is stored in the *sPhrase* string variable. Working with the *sPhrase* string variable, the first character of the string gets converted to uppercase. The first character is converted to uppercase by using the **UCase$** function and the **Left$** function is used to extract the first character from the string. The rest of the string is concatenated with the first character and stored back into the *sPhrase* string variable.

```
sChar = "."
nPos = 0
```

The value assigned to the *sChar* string variable is used as a delimiter value. It is used to tell the function that any character following the delimiter is where the new capital letter is to start. Setting the *nPos* integer variable to 0 is to ensure that the variable is set to.

```
Do While True
        nPos = CInt(InStr(nPos + 1, sPhrase, ' '))
        If (nPos = 0) Then
            Exit Do
        Else
            sPhrase = Left$(sPhrase, nPos + 1) _
                    & UCase$(Mid$(sPhrase, nPos + 2, 1)) _
                    & Mid$(sPhrase, nPos + 3)
        End If
    Loop
```

The **Do...Loop** statement will cycle through the set of logic until *nPos* is equal to 0 again. You are probably wondering why the **Do...Loop** statement is set to loop While True versus using something like Until nPos = 0 or While nPos <> 0. The reason is that since *nPos* is set to 0 before the loop, the condition is already true and the code within the loop would never be processed. If we used the second example, as soon as the *nPos* variable changes to anything other than 0, the condition would be true and the code within the loop would only be executed once. By setting it to True, it will process the enclosed code an infinite number of times. To stop it, we will have to exit the loop programmatically. This is handled within the **If...Then** statement. When the *nPos* variable is zero, which means that the **InStr** function didn't find any more blanks in the string (which means we reached the end of the string), the **Exit Do** statement exits the **Do...Loop** statement.

```
LeadingCaps = sPhrase
```

Once all the characters in the string variable have been processed, the *LeadingCaps* value is set with the *sPhras* string value and control is returned to the procedure that called the function.

Display Currency in Words

MoneyToWords In a lot of financial applications, there are times when you display currency amounts in regular English words; typically, this is used in the printing of checks. This function requires that a numeric value in the form of currency needs to be passed. When you pass the value to the function, you should use the **CCur** function to ensure that the value is a currency value; otherwise, an error will occur.

CODE

```
' Purpose:  Converts a currency amount to a string of English words.
'           Typically to use for check printing.
' Params:   cMoney  (I) The dollar amount.
' Returns:  The English string.
' Note:     Valid up to $999,999,999.00.
Function MoneyToWords(cMoney As Currency) As String
    Dim lRemaining As Long
    Dim sTempStr As String
    Dim nNextNbr As Integer
    Dim sRtnVal As String
    Dim nDigits As Integer
    Dim sSet As String

    lRemaining = Int(cMoney)    'Drops the cents!

    ' Handle cents
    sRtnVal = Format$(100 * (cMoney - lRemaining), "00") & "/100"
    If (lRemaining > 0) Then sRtnVal = "and " & sRtnVal

    ' Prepad zeros so that we can always process full sets of 3
    ' digits
    sTempStr = "000" & lRemaining

    nDigits = 0

    ' Process sets of 3 digits from least to most significant
    Do While (IsNumeric(sTempStr) And Val(sTempStr) > 0)
        nNextNbr = Val(Right$(sTempStr, 2))
        sTempStr = Left(sTempStr, Len(sTempStr) - 2)

        ' Handle tens and units digits this set
        sSet = ""
```

```
        If (nNextNbr > 9 And nNextNbr < 20) Then
            sSet = Choose(nNextNbr - 9, "ten", "eleven", _
                    "twelve", "thirteen", "fourteen", "fifteen", _
                    "sixteen", "seventeen", "eighteen", "nineteen") _
                    & " " & sSet
        ElseIf (nNextNbr > 0) Then
            sSet = Choose(Val(Right(Str(nNextNbr), 1)), _
                    "one ", "two ", "three ", "four ", "five ", _
                    "six ", "seven ", "eight ", "nine ") & sSet
        End If
        If (nNextNbr >= 20) Then
            sSet = Choose(Left$(nNextNbr, 1), "error", _
                    "twenty", "thirty", "forty", "fifty", "sixty", _
                    "seventy", "eighty", "ninety") & " " & sSet
        End If

        ' Handle hundreds digit in this set
        nNextNbr = Val(Right$(sTempStr, 1))
        sTempStr = Left(sTempStr, Len(sTempStr) - 1)
        If (nNextNbr >= 1) Then
            sSet = "hundred " & sSet
            sSet = Choose(nNextNbr, "one", "two", "three", _
                    "four", "five", "six", "seven", "eight", _
                    "nine") & " " & sSet
        End If

        ' Handle set suffix, no suffix if this set was "000"
        If (sSet <> "") Then
            sRtnVal = sSet & Choose(nDigits / 3, "thousand ", _
                    "million ") & sRtnVal
        End If
        nDigits = nDigits + 3
    Loop

    MoneyToWords = sRtnVal

End Function
```

```
Function MoneyToWords(cMoney As Currency) As String
    Dim lRemaining As Long
    Dim sTempStr As String
```

```
Dim nNextNbr As Integer
Dim sRtnVal As String
Dim nDigits As Integer
Dim sSet As String
```

As mentioned at the beginning of this exercise, the value that needs to be passed to the function should be a currency value.

```
lRemaining = Int(cMoney)    'Drops the cents!
```

The **Int** function is used to return the integer portion of the variable, *cMoney*, which means that *lRemaining* will contain only the dollar amounts.

```
' Handle cents
sRtnVal = Format$(100 * (cMoney - lRemaining), "00") & "/100"
```

This statement is going to calculate the cents of the amount of money and display it in hundredths. The **Format** function is used to ensure cents of the fraction will display both digits, even if the first digit is 0.

```
If (lRemaining > 0) Then sRtnVal = "and " & sRtnVal
```

The **If...Then** statement will determine checks to see if there is any remaining value to show cents. If there is, *sRtnVal* is set to "and" plus whatever fraction of 100 *sRtnVal* was set to in the previous line of code.

```
' Prepad zeros so that we can always process full sets of 3 digits
sTempStr = "000" & lRemaining
```

This line pads the remaining value of *lRemaining* to ensure that the value contains at least three digits.

```
nDigits = 0
```

Even though the *nDigits* variable was initialized at the beginning of this function, setting it to 0 ensures that the variable does not contain any value.

```
' Process sets of 3 digits from least to most significant
Do While (IsNumeric(sTempStr) And Val(sTempStr) > 0)
```

The **Do...Loop** statement will process the code within it as long as the *sTempStr* value is a numeric value and the value of it is greater than 0. If either of these conditions is False, then the loop will end and the value of the *sRtnVal* is used by the procedure that called this function. No matter how large the value, this loop processes data three digits at a time and it processes them from right to left, that is, least significant to most significant.

```
nNextNbr = Val(Right$(sTempStr, 2))
sTempStr = Left(sTempStr, Len(sTempStr) - 2)
```

Normally, we read numbers and words left to right. In order for this function to figure out where the hundreds and thousands are found within a number, it needs to look at the *sTempStr* variable right to left (sort of). It looks at the last two digits of the string, which get stored in the *nNextNbr* variable, to determine how the value less than 100 is going to be written out: "twenty," "forty-two," and so on. The remainder of the string gets stored back into the *sTempStr* variable.

```
' Handle tens and units digits this set
sSet = ""
If (nNextNbr > 9 And nNextNbr < 20) Then
    sSet = Choose(nNextNbr - 9, "ten", "eleven", _
            "twelve", "thirteen", "fourteen", "fifteen", _
            "sixteen", "seventeen", "eighteen", "nineteen") _
            & " " & sSet
ElseIf (nNextNbr > 0) Then
    sSet = Choose(Val(Right(Str(nNextNbr), 1)), _
            "one ", "two ", "three ", "four ", "five ", _
            "six ", "seven ", "eight ", "nine ") & sSet
End If
```

The **If...Then** statement is used to determine how the *nNextNbr* variable will be displayed in words. The first half of the **If...Then** statement determines if the *nNextNbr* variable is between 10 and 19 inclusively. The second half of the statement checks to see if the *nNextNbr* variable is between 0 and 9 inclusively.

```
If (nNextNbr >= 20) Then
    sSet = Choose(Left$(nNextNbr, 1), "error", _
            "twenty", "thirty", "forty", "fifty", "sixty", _
            "seventy", "eighty", "ninety") & " " & sSet
End If
```

This **If...Then** statement checks to see if the *nNextNbr* variable is over 20, and if so, by how much. Assuming it is 20 or over, the **Left$** function is used to get the first digit from *nNextNbr*. The **Choose** function returns a value based on a list of choices based on an index value, which in this example is the value returned from the **Left$** function. If the value is 2, the returned value from the **Choose** function will be "twenty." If the value is 4, the returned value will be "forty," and so on. The first choice of "error" is used to ensure proper numbering within the choice index, and if by some strange mishap the value returned from the **Left$** function is 1, the choice index value will return the word "error" to let the user know something went wrong. Once the ten's value is determined, it is concatenated with the string value stored in *sSet*, which was determined in the previous **If...Then** statement.

```
' Handle hundreds digit in this set
nNextNbr = Val(Right$(sTempStr, 1))
sTempStr = Left(sTempStr, Len(sTempStr) - 1)
```

The next half of this function is used to determine how the 100s will be displayed in words. *sTempStr* contains the remaining numbers from the argument variable that was passed to the function. The **Right$** function returns the string's last character and the **Val** function returns the numeric value of that character and stores it into the *nNextNbr* variable. The remaining value is stored in the *sTempStr* variable by using the **Left$** function.

```
If (nNextNbr >= 1) Then
    sSet = "hundred " & sSet
    sSet = Choose(nNextNbr, "one", "two", "three", _
            "four", "five", "six", "seven", "eight", _
            "nine") & " " & sSet
End If
```

This **If...Then** statement is used to determine how many hundreds the *nNextNbr* variable contains. In the previous loop, we determined the tens' and ones' position; therefore, it's only obvious we determine the hundreds' position. The word "hundred" is concatenated to the *sSet* string variable. The **Choose** function is used to find the word that will go in front of the word "hundred" based on the *nNextNbr* number. Just like in the previous **Choose** function, the word that is chosen is based on the value of *nNextNbr*. Then the value is concatenated to the *sSet* string variable.

```
' Handle set suffix, no suffix if this set was "000"
If (sSet <> "") Then
    sRtnVal = sSet & Choose(nDigits / 3, "thousand ", _
                "million ") & sRtnVal
End If
```

The **If...Then** statement is used to determine if the value being worked on is in the hundreds, thousands, or millions. By dividing the *nDigits* value by three, we can determine if the set of three digits belongs in the thousands or millions. Since the **Choose** function's index starts at 1, any dividend value from "nDigits / 3" less than 1 is not a valid index choice; therefore, no value is chosen. The entire product is concatenated with the *sSet* and *sRtnVal* string variables.

```
nDigits = nDigits + 3
Loop
```

Once the three digits are processed, 3 is added to *nDigits* and the process goes back through the loop, assuming the Do condition is still true.

```
MoneyToWords = sRtnVal
```

Once the loop is completed, the *sRtnVal* string value is returned to the **MoneyToWord** function and control is returned to the function that called it.

TextToTag

Prepare Text for the Internet

A lot of department managers want to be able to put data out on their Intranet web sites or out on the Internet. Having a web site data-driven by using server-side scripting like Microsoft Active Server Pages or CGI/Perl to retrieve information from a database is a lot more maintainable then hundreds of static HTML pages. This function is designed to help convert asterisks or underscores into HTML bold and italic tags. It doesn't have to be asterisks and underscores. It can be any character you desire. A lot of people use asterisks as well as underscores to emphasize their point, which is why you might want to choose these characters to search for. The HTML tag to turn bolding on is <B> and to turn it off is </B>. For italic formatting, the HTML tags are <I> and </I>. The characters between the tags will receive the formatting.

This exercise is a bit different from the previous ones because this function is going to call another function. The function **TextToTag** calls the **ReplaceCharWTags** function, which is the real function for this exercise. You can call the **ReplaceCharWTags** function with the parameters yourself, but sometimes it's better to have a function that calls the routines you want to centralize your procedures.

CODE

```
' Purpose: To convert asterisks (*) and underscores (_)
'          to HTML Bold and Italic tags respectively.
Public Function TextToTag(sSrcStr As String) As String

    sSrcStr = ReplaceCharWTags(sSrcStr, "*", "B")
    sSrcStr = ReplaceCharWTags(sSrcStr, "_", "I")
    TextToTag = sSrcStr

End Function
Function ReplaceCharWTags(sSrcStr As String, _
    sFind As String, sReplaceTag As String) _
    As String

    Dim nStart As Long
    Dim sStr As String
    Dim nStrLen As String
    Dim bTagOn As Boolean

    bTagOn = False
    nStart = 1

    nStrLen = Len(sReplaceTag)

    While nStart <> 0
        nStart = InStr(nStart, sSrcStr, sFind)
        If nStart > 0 Then
```

```
        If bTagOn Then
            sSrcStr = Left(sSrcStr, nStart - 1) + _
                "</" & UCase(sReplaceTag) & ">" + _
                Mid(sSrcStr, nStart + Len(sFind))
            nStart = nStart + nStrLen
            bTagOn = False
        Else
            sSrcStr = Left(sSrcStr, nStart - 1) + _
                "<" & UCase(sReplaceTag) & ">" + _
                Mid(sSrcStr, nStart + Len(sFind))
            nStart = nStart + nStrLen
            bTagOn = True
        End If
    End If
Wend

ReplaceCharWTags = sSrcStr

End Function
```

ANNOTATIONS

```
Public Function TextToTag(sSrcStr As String) As String
```

This procedure is set up to accept one argument, the *sSrcStr* string value, which is the string where you want to have special characters converted to HTML tags.

```
    sSrcStr = ReplaceCharWTags(sSrcStr, "*", "B")
```

This statement calls the **ReplaceCharWTags** function to look for asterisks ("*") within *sSrcStr* and replace them with HTML bold tags.

```
    sSrcStr = ReplaceCharWTags(sSrcStr, "_", "I")
```

This statement calls the **ReplaceCharWTags** function to look for the underscore ("_") character within *sSrcStr* and replace it with HTML italic tags.

```
    TextToTag = sSrcStr
```

Once the results from the functions are complete, the *sSrcStr* value is returned to the return value and control is returned to the procedure that called it.

```
Function ReplaceCharWTags(sSrcStr As String, _
    sFind As String, sReplaceTag As String) _
    As String
```

```
Dim nStart As Long
Dim sStr As String
Dim nStrLen As String
Dim bTagOn As Boolean
```

The **ReplaceCharWTag**s function is designed to accept three arguments, similar to the **ReplaceStr** function. The first argument is the *sSrcStr* string variable that contains the entire string that will be searched. The *sFind* string value contains the character that you want to look for. The *sReplaceTag* string variable contains the HTML tag character you want to replace the *sFind* character with. The *bTagOn* Boolean variable is used as a switch variable for determining if the HTML tag has been "turned on" or not. HTML tags come in pairs. The first tag enables the formatting. The second tag disables the formatting.

```
bTagOn = False
nStart = 1
```

The variables *bTagOn* and *nStart* are initialized. *bTagOn* is set to False because no HTML formatting has taken place yet. *nStart* is set to 1; otherwise, it would be set to 0, because when variables are initialized they are set to 0.

```
nStrLen = Len(sReplaceTag)
```

The length of the *sReplaceTag* variable is determined by using the **Len** function and the value is stored in the *nStrLen* variable.

```
While nStart <> 0
    nStart = InStr(nStart, sSrcStr, sFind)
    If nStart > 0 Then
        If bTagOn Then
            sSrcStr = Left(sSrcStr, nStart - 1) + _
                "</" & UCase(sReplaceTag) & ">" + _
                Mid(sSrcStr, nStart + Len(sFind))
            nStart = nStart + nStrLen
            bTagOn = False
        Else
            sSrcStr = Left(sSrcStr, nStart - 1) + _
                "<" & UCase(sReplaceTag) & ">" + _
                Mid(sSrcStr, nStart + Len(sFind))
            nStart = nStart + nStrLen
            bTagOn = True
        End If
    End If
Wend
```

The **While...Wend** statement is used to loop through the procedure until *nStart* equals 0. When it equals 0, that means the character specified in *sFind* no longer is found within the *sSrcStr* string variable.

The **InStr** function is used to determine if the *sFind* value is found within the *sSrcStr* string variable. If so, its location is assigned to the *nStart* variable. The first **If...Then** statement is used to determine if the substring was found. The second **If...Then** statement checks the *bTagOn* switch. If it's True, that means the HTML tag has been enabled, and that the next instance of the *sFind* value should use the "off" tag; otherwise, the HTML tag that should be used is the HTML "on" tag.

If the *bTagOn* value is True, the **Left$** function obtains the first part of the string prior to the *sFind* substring. It is concatenated with "</", the *sReplaceTag* substring, and ">". And both substrings are concatenated with the substring based on the **Mid$** function of the *sSrcStr* string, starting from the position of *nStart* plus the length of the *sFind* substring. This is very similar to the logic used in the **ReplaceStr** function.

If the *bTagOn* value is False, the **Left$** function obtains the first part of the string prior to the *sFind* substring. It is concatenated with "<", the *sReplaceTag* substring, and ">". And both substrings are concatenated with the substring based on the **Mid$** function of the *sSrcStr* string, starting from the position of *nStart* plus the length of the *sFind* substring. Notice the difference between the two statements is that one uses "</" & sReplaceTag & ">", while the other uses "<" & sReplaceTag & ">". The first is the HTML "off" tag and the other is the HTML "on" tag.

After all this takes places, the new *nStart* value is the *nStart* value plus the length of the *sReplaceWith* value.

```
ReplaceCharWTags = sSrcStr
```

When the **While...Wend** statement is completed, the result is assigned to the return value of the function and control is returned to the procedure that called this function.

Placing All the Functions in an ActiveX DLL

All the functions created in this chapter can be used as functions within a standard, class, or form module within a VB application. Most of them can be used as VBScript within an Active Server Page on Microsoft's web server, Internet Information Server. The best way to use these functions is within an ActiveX DLL, which is also known as an *in-process server*. This means that it's an object that can be referenced and used by other applications and the ActiveX DLL resides within the same memory space as the application that called it. For a more thorough description of ActiveX Servers and DLLs, refer to Chapter 12.

CREATE THE ACTIVEX DLL AND TEST IT!

Start a new project, ActiveX DLL. The default class module may be the startup module. Change the name of the Class1 module to **StringUtils**. The other property, **Instancing**, by default is set to 5 – **MultiUse**. *Instancing* refers to how this class is made available to other projects and how it will behave. By setting it to 5, we are making this class object available to other applications. Once one application has access to this object, another instance does not get loaded. All applications use the same instances. Other settings are available and are covered in more depth in Chapter 12.

Add all the code that has been described within this chapter. If you don't wish to go back through the chapter, you can insert the code found on the CD-ROM under Chapter 10's VBAA08 directory. To insert the code, first make sure the Code window has focus. From the Edit menu, select Insert File… and the Insert File dialog box will appear. Go to Chapter 10's directory on the CD-ROM and select the Stringutil.txt file and click OK. This will insert all the code needed for this component.

Select the Project | Project1 Properties… menu item. We are now going to update the project's property information in order to make this component unique. Use the information found in Table 10-1 to fill in the Project1 Properties' dialog box.

1. In order to test this component, we will need to execute it and run another program against it. Run the component by clicking the Start button, then start a new instance of Visual Basic. The new project will be used to test the components.

   In the new instance of VB, select the Standard Exe application. The default form may be the startup form. Accept the name Form1 and other default properties.

Tab	Field Name	Property
General	Project Name	vbaa08
	Project Description	VBAA StringUtils Component
Make	Application Title	vbaa08
	Auto Increment	mark box
Compile	DLL Base Address	&H13000000
Component	Project Compatibility	mark option

TABLE 10-1. The VBAA Project's Properties

Add the controls shown in Figure 10-1, setting the properties as shown in Table 10-2.

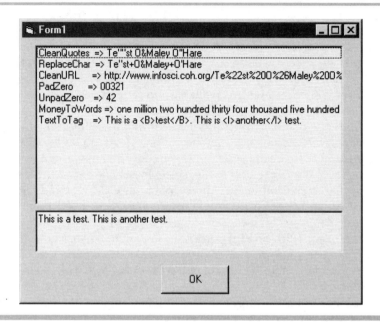

FIGURE 10-1.   The test application at run-time

2.   Using the Project | References menu item from the VB main menu, select the references shown in Table 10-3. If others are checked that are in this table, uncheck them so your project isn't cluttered with DLLs you aren't using.

Object	Property	Setting
Form	Name	Form1
	Height	4980
	Width	6180
ListBox	Name	lstOutput
TextBox	Name	txtOutput
	Text	""
CommandButton	Name	cmdNext
	Caption	OK

TABLE 10-2.   The Form's Objects and Properties

PROGRAMMER'S NOTE

The bottom frame of the References dialog box displays the Location and Language of the object or object library. The Location displays the location of the object or the object library. In this example, the location should be where the Vbaa08.vbp is stored and run from. Had the Vbaa08.vbp been compiled into an ActiveX DLL, the location would be where the DLL is located and the filename would be Vbaa08.dll. The Language should be English if that's the language being used by the system that developed the Vbaa08.vbp.

References
Microsoft Visual Basic for Application
Visual Basic Runtime Objects and Procedures
Visual Basic Objects and Procedures
OLE Automation
VBAA StringUtils Components

TABLE 10-3.   References Used in the TestApp Project

3. Add the following code to the **Load** event procedure of the form. The **Move** method for the form is going to center the form on the screen. The value assigned to *vString* is the string that will be used to test the functions we just designed.

```
Private Sub Form_Load()
    Dim oTest As New vbaa08.StringUtils
    Dim vString As Variant
    Dim vString2 As Variant


    Me.Move ((Screen.Width - Me.Width) / 2), _
        ((Screen.Height - Me.Height) / 2)

    vString = "Te""st O&Maley O'Hare"
    vString2 = "THIS IS A TEST. THIS IS ANOTHER TEST."

    lstOutput.AddItem "CleanQuotes  => " & _
        oTest.CleanQuotes(vString)
    lstOutput.AddItem "ReplaceChar  => " & _
        oTest.ReplaceChar(vString, " ", "+")
    lstOutput.AddItem "CleanURL     => " & _
        "http://www.infosci.coh.org/" & oTest.CleanURL(vString)
    lstOutput.AddItem "PadZero      => " _
        & oTest.PadZero("321", 5)
    lstOutput.AddItem "UnpadZero    => " _
        & oTest.UnpadZero("000042")
    txtOutput.Text = _
        oTest.LeadingCaps(vString2, ".")
    lstOutput.AddItem "MoneyToWords => " & _
        oTest.MoneyToWords(CCur("1234567.89"))
    lstOutput.AddItem "TextToTag    => " _
        & oTest.TextToTag("This is a *test*. " _
        & This is _another_ test.")
End Sub
```

4. Add the following code to the **Click** event procedure of the command button **cmdOK**. When the user triggers this event, the application will end.

```
Private Sub cmdOK_Click()
    End
End Sub
```

5. Click the Start button to compile and run the TestApp project.

As the application loads, the **Form_Load** procedure is executed. The object variable *oTest* is assigned to a new instance of the object **VBAA08.StringUtils**. The **Move** method will center the form on the user's screen. It uses the screen's **Height** and **Width** properties and calculates them against the form's **Height** and **Width** properties for positioning. The values returned by the various functions will be displayed in either the list box **lstOutput** or the text box **txtOutput**. To close the window and end the application, click the OK command button.

Since the VBAA08 component is running in the first instance of the VB, you can step through the code just like any application. This is very useful to help you debug any error that might occur, or just to see how functions work. Figure 10-2 illustrates stepping through the code within the Vbaa08.vbp project.

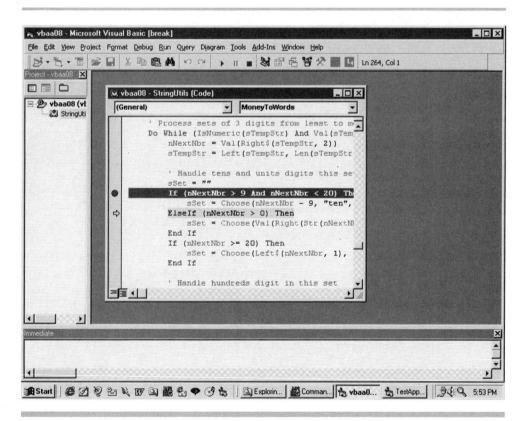

FIGURE 10-2. Stepping through the Vbaa08.vbp while the Testapp.vbp is suspended

To make the VBAA08 project into an ActiveX DLL so that it can be used by other applications and IIS, select the File | Make VBAA08.DLL... menu item. In the Make

Project dialog box, click the OK button just like you would if you were making a VB project into a Standard Exe. That's all it takes. Once you make the project into an ActiveX DLL, it will be assigned a globally unique identifier (GUID) key that is used to identify ActiveX components and their interfaces. For more information about ActiveX components (ActiveX DLL and EXE) and COM, refer to Chapter 12.

Manipulating Drives and Files

When you think about application development, file manipulation never seems to come to mind until you're halfway into the project and you realize that you need to access the file system. With every iteration of VB, Microsoft has added more and more file manipulation features to the development environment. Prior to these added components, you had to access everything through the Win32API. With Visual Studio 6, you can use the **FileSystemObject** class to add file manipulation functionality to your application. To access it in VB, it's a matter of referencing the object model, Microsoft Scripting Runtime, in your project. If you're not running Visual Studio 6.0 (or VB 6.0), but you have the latest version of the Active Scripting Engine on your system, you can still access the object model.

This chapter is slightly different than other chapters in that the exercises described within are designed to be part of an entire collection of functions that are to be encapsulated into an ActiveX DLL, which is explained at the end of the chapter. However, each exercise is a complete function so that you can implement any of the functions into your own application without writing them into the ActiveX DLL. To use them, just place the function in any class module with your application.

Finding Out How Much Disk Space Is Free

AvailableDiskSpace

If you've ever built an application that deals with disk storage, you know it's always a good idea to make sure that there is enough storage space. Windows has two APIs that can be used to obtain this information. They are **GetDiskFreeSpace** and **GetDiskFreeSpaceEx**. They essentially do that same thing, but you will have a problem with the **GetDiskFreeSpace** function if your hard drive is greater than 2GB. This function was originally designed back when hard drives weren't any bigger than 2GB. Now that hard drives on personal computers have the ability to store 16GB and greater, Microsoft created the extended function, **GetDiskFreeSpaceEx**. The only caveat is that this function only works on Windows 95 OSR (OEM Service Release) 2 and greater, Windows 98, or the upcoming Windows 2000 (previously Windows NT 5.0).

CODE

```
Private Declare Function GetDiskFreeSpace _
    Lib "kernel32" Alias "GetDiskFreeSpaceA" _
    (ByVal lpRootPathName As String, _
    lpSectorsPerCluster As Long, _
    lpBytesPerSector As Long, _
    lpNbrOfFreeClusters As Long, _
    lpTotalNbrOfClusters As Long) As Long
Public Function AvailableDiskSpace(DrivePath As String) As Double
    ' Pass the function the drive letter to get the free space of
    Dim Drive As String
```

```
        Dim SectorsPerCluster As Long
        Dim BytesPerSector As Long
        Dim NbrOfFreeClusters As Long
        Dim TotalClusters As Long
        Dim rc As Long

        ' Ensure path is at the root.
        Drive = Left(Trim(DrivePath), 1) & ":\"
        rc = GetDiskFreeSpace(Drive, SectorsPerCluster, BytesPerSector, _
            NbrofFreeClusters, TotalClusters)
        If rc <> 0 Then
            AvailableDiskSpace = SectorsPerCluster * BytesPerSector * _
                NbrofFreeClusters
        Else
            ' Should Call GetLastError here but -1 will do for example
            AvailableDiskSpace = -1
        End If
End Function
```

ANNOTATIONS

A file API, **GetDiskFreeSpace**, allows you to obtain information about the organization of a disk and the amount of free space remaining on the drive.

```
Private Declare Function GetDiskFreeSpace _
    Lib "kernel32" Alias "GetDiskFreeSpaceA" _
    (ByVal lpRootPathName As String, _
    lpSectorsPerCluster As Long, _
    lpBytesPerSector As Long, _
    lpNbrOfFreeClusters As Long, _
    lpTotalNbrOfClusters As Long) As Long
```

lpRootPathName is a string variable for the root path for the disk with the volume name. *lpSectorsPerCluster* is a long variable that stores the value of sectors that are in a cluster. *lpBytesPerSector* is a long variable that stores the value of bytes in a sector. *lpNbrOfFreeClusters* is a long variable that stores the value of free clusters on the disk. *lpTotalNbrOfClusters* is a long variable that stores the number of clusters that are on the disk.

```
Public Function AvailableDiskSpace(DrivePath As String) As Double
```

The function, **AvailableDiskSpace**, is used to allow the API function, **GetDiskFreeSpace**, to be used from any module within an application. The argument *DrivePath* accepts the file path from a procedure that calls it. The value of the argument can be as simple as using App.Path.

```
' Pass the function the drive letter to get the free space of
Dim Drive As String
Dim SectorsPerCluster As Long
Dim BytesPerSector As Long
Dim NbrOfFreeClusters As Long
Dim TotalClusters As Long
Dim rc As Long

' Ensure path is at the root.
Drive = Left(Trim(DrivePath), 1) & ":\"
```

The **Trim** function will remove any leading and trailing spaces from the value in the *DrivePath* argument. The **Left** function gets the first character of the string in the *DrivePath* argument. This is used to strip off the volume name of a drive or any drive path information that might get passed. Then, a colon and backslash (":\") are concatenated to the first character.

```
rc = GetDiskFreeSpace(Drive, SectorsPerCluster, BytesPerSector, _
    NbrOfFreeClusters, TotalClusters)
```

Unlike typical functions where you pass a value to every argument contained within the function, this API function only needs the *lpRootPathName* argument passed to it, which is contained within the *Drive* variable. When the function receives the argument, the other four parameters, *SectorsPerCluster*, *BytesPerSector*, *NbrOfFreeClusters*, and *TotalClusters* are populated based on the drive letter passed.

```
If rc <> 0 Then
    AvailableDiskSpace = SectorsPerCluster * BytesPerSector * _
        NbrOfFreeClusters
Else
    ' Should Call GetLastError here but -1 will do for example
    AvailableDiskSpace = -1
End If
```

A non-zero number means that the **GetDiskFreeSpace** function was successful in retrieving information about the drive. With the information retrieved from the function, multiply the *SectorsPerCluster*, *BytesPerSector*, and *NbrOfFreeClusters* together to calculate the amount of disk space left on the drive specified in the *DrivePath* argument.

In case you were interested in figuring out how much information the drive is capable of handling, multiply the *SectorsPerCluster* and *BytesPerSector*, with the *TotalClusters* value, instead of the *NbrOfFreeClusters*, and the product will be the amount of bytes the drive can hold.

The other function that can be used to retrieve the amount of disk space available on a specified hard drive is the **GetDiskFreeSpaceEx** function. If you use this function on a system that does not support the function, you will receive zeros for the returned values; therefore, we should build in some logic to determine if the system the application is running on supports the function or not. And if it doesn't, use the **GetDiskFreeSpace** function instead. Again, the only systems that support this function are the OEM Service Release of Windows 95, Windows 98, and Windows 2000. The function is as follows:

```
Private Declare Function GetDiskFreeSpaceEx _
    Lib "Kernel32" Alias "GetDiskFreeSpaceExA" _
    (ByVal lpRootPathName As String, _
    lpFreeBytesAvailable As Long, _
    lpTotalNbrOfBytes As Long, _
    lpTotalNbrOfFreeBytes As Long) As Long
```

lpRootPathName is a string variable for the root path for the disk with the volume name. *lpFreeBytesAvailable* is a long variable that stores the value of free space available to the caller. The value returned will usually be zero. *lpTotalNbrOfBytes* is a long variable that stores the value of bytes available on the hard drive. The value will be a negative value, so when you display it, it's best if you use the **Abs** function, which will return a number in absolute values. *lpTotalNbrOfFreeBytes* is a long variable that stores the value of free bytes on the disk.

To update the function, **AvailableDiskSpace** changes it to the following:

```
rc = GetDiskFreeSpaceEx(Drive, FreeBytes, TotalBytes, _
    TotalBytesFree)
If rc <> 0 Then
    AvailableDiskSpace = TotalBytesFree
Else
```

If this function is available to you, determining the amount of free space is a lot easier than using the **GetDiskFreeSpace** function. Also, determining the capacity of the hard drive is very easy because all you need to do is return the absolute value of the *TotalBytes* variable.

FileExists

Finding Out If a File Exists

Whether you're working sequential files for common-delimited information or binary files like a Word document, it's always a good idea to check the status of the file you're planning to access—in particular, to see if the file exists or not. The following function requires the use of a Win32API called **OpenFile**. This API function does more than just check to see if a specified file exists in the file system or not, but for the purpose of this exercise, this is what we're going to be using it for.

CODE

```
Private Declare Function OpenFile Lib "kernel32" _
    (ByVal lpFileName As String, _
    lpReOpenBuff As OFSTRUCT, _
    ByVal wStyle As Long) As Long
Private Type OFSTRUCT
    cBytes As Byte
    fFixedDisk As Byte
    nErrCode As Integer
    Reserved1 As Integer
    Reserved2 As Integer
    szPathName As String * 128
End Type
Public Function FileExists(FileName As String) As Boolean
    Dim rc As Integer
    Dim OpenFileStructure As OFSTRUCT
    Const OF_EXIST = &H4000
    Const FILE_NOT_FOUND = 2
    rc = OpenFile(FileName$, OpenFileStructure, OF_EXIST)
    If OpenFileStructure.nErrCode = FILE_NOT_FOUND Then
        FileExists = False
    Else
        FileExists = True
    End If
End Function
```

ANNOTATIONS

The **OpenFile** function can perform a number of different file operations.

```
Private Declare Function OpenFile Lib "kernel32" _
    (ByVal lpFileName As String, _
    lpReOpenBuff As OFSTRUCT, _
    ByVal wStyle As Long) As Long
```

The *lpFileName* string argument specifies the name of the file to be opened. *lpReOpenBuff* is a user-defined type (UDT) structure that includes information about the file to be interacted with and stores the results of the operation. The *wStyle* long argument specifies which operation the **OpenFile** function is to perform.

```
Private Type OFSTRUCT
    cBytes As Byte
    fFixedDisk As Byte
    nErrCode As Integer
    Reserved1 As Integer
    Reserved2 As Integer
    szPathName As String * 128
End Type
```

The OFSTRUCT structure is used to provide a way to pass information to the function as well as receive information. The *cBytes* parameter sets the length of the structure. By default, it is set to 136. The *fFixedDisk* parameter will store a non-zero value if the file is on the fixed drive. If an error occurs while the function is being executed, it stores the error value in *nErrCode*. *Reserved1* and *Reserved2* are parameters that Microsoft has reserved to be used at a later time. The *szPathName* parameter specifies the full path name of the file.

```
Public Function FileExists(FileName As String) As Boolean
```

The function **FileExists** is used to provide a "wrapper" around the **OpenFile** function. The argument that is passed to the function is a string that can contain the name of a file you are looking for. If you specify the file's directory, like c:\readme.txt, the **OpenFile** function will search for the file in that directory. The function will return the Boolean value True or False depending on whether or not the file was found.

You should be aware of the manner in which the **OpenFile** function searches for a file. Assuming you don't specify the file's drive and path as part of the *FileName* argument, the **OpenFile** function explicitly searches for the specified file in the following order:

♦ The directory in which the application is loaded

♦ The current directory, if it's different than the application directory

♦ The Windows System directory (if Windows 95/98) or the Windows System32 directory (if Windows NT)

♦ The 16-bit Windows System directory, if you're running Windows NT

♦ The Windows directory

♦ Finally, all the directories listed in the PATH environment variable

```
Dim rc As Integer
Dim OpenFileStructure As OFSTRUCT
Const OF_EXIST = &H4000
Const FILE_NOT_FOUND = 2
```

The constant OF_EXIST contains the hexadecimal value that determines if a file exists by attempting to open the file. The constant FILE_NOT_FOUND contains the hexadecimal value for the "File not found" error message. There are over 80 error codes that could be tested for, ranging from "Invalid function" to "Network write fault."

```
rc = OpenFile(FileName$, OpenFileStructure, OF_EXIST)
```

The **OpenFile** function uses the arguments to find the filename specified in the *FileName$* parameter. The OF_EXIST argument tells the **OpenFile** function to try to open the specified file. If the file exists, the function will attempt to open it. If the function can open the file, it will close it and it will return the file handle used when the file was open, but the file handle can't be used for anything else. If the file can't be found, the function will return a negative value. Unlike other return codes, this return code is of no interest to us. We will want to check the **nErrCode** property specified in the OFSTRUCT structure.

```
If OpenFileStructure.nErrCode = FILE_NOT_FOUND Then
    FileExists = False
Else
    FileExists = True
End If
```

The **If...Then** statement is used to check the value of the **nErrCode** property. If the value is 2, which is the value of the FILE_NOT_FOUND constant, the return value of **FileExists** is set to False; otherwise it is set to True.

In Version 6.0 of Visual Basic, you can use the **FileSystemObject**'s method, **FileExists**, to determine if the specified file exists or not. In order to do that, you will need to reference the Microsoft Scripting Runtime class and your code would look like the following:

```
Dim fso As FileSystemObject
Set fso = New FileSystemObject
Debug.Print "fso.FileExists => "; fso.FileExists("c:\readme.txt")
```

The *fso* variable is defined as the **FileSystemObject** class. The **Set fso** method instantiates a new instance of the **FileSystemObject** class. To call the **FileExists** method, simply access it the way you would any other method, by referring to it from the object variable you created; in this case the object variable is *fso*. The last line displays how to call the **FileExists** method to see if the file, readme.txt, exists in the root of the C: drive. If the file exists, the method will return True; otherwise it will return False.

CopyFile

Copying a File

A lot of times when you're working with files, you will want to make a backup of a file before any file manipulation is performed. The following example illustrates how to write a wrapper around Visual Basic's **FileCopy** statement. We're not relying on just the **FileCopy** statement is because there no way to determine if the file was copied properly or not. This simple function can provide feedback to the procedure that calls it, so it can determine if the statement executed properly or not.

CODE

```
Function CopyFile(sSource As String, sDestination As String) _
As Boolean
    On Error GoTo Err_CopyFile
    Dim bOk As Boolean
    bOk = False
    Call FileCopy(sSource, sDestination)
    bOk = True
Exit_CopyFile:
    CopyFile = bOk
    Exit Function
Err_CopyFile:
    Resume Exit_CopyFile
End Function
```

ANNOTATIONS

This is an incredibly simple function. Two arguments are passed to it and the function returns a True or False value depending on whether the function executed the **FileCopy** statement properly or not.

```
Function CopyFile(sSource As String, sDestination As String) _
As Boolean
```

The *sSource* and *sDestination* string arguments should contain the filename of the source file and target file, respectively. The strings should also contain the file's drive and path information. For example, if you wanted to copy a sequential file from one drive's directory to another, the values should look like the following:

```
sSource = "c:\projects\datatrack.txt"
sDestination = "c:\databkup\datatrack.txt"
```

You can also copy the file to the same directory simply by using a different filename.

```
    On Error GoTo Err_CopyFile
```

This **On Error** statement is an important part of the function because if an error occurs during execution of the function, the error-handling routines will be used to provide feedback to the calling procedure that something went wrong during the execution of the **FileCopy** statement.

```
Dim bOk As Boolean
bOk = False
Call FileCopy(sSource, sDestination)
bOk = True
```

Initially, the Boolean value **bOk** is set to False. This is because you want to prove that the function worked. If the **FileCopy** statement does work, **bOk** will be set to True. If an error occurs, the **On Error** statement handles the error and the execution pointer goes to the Err_CopyFile subroutine which immediately exits the function. If the **FileCopy** statement doesn't cause an error, then the Boolean value **bOk** is set to True, proving that the statement worked the way it was supposed to.

```
Exit_CopyFile:
    CopyFile = bOk
    Exit Function
Err_CopyFile:
    Resume Exit_CopyFile
```

The code within the Exit_CopyFile label will get executed either by the Err_CopyFile subroutine or if the **FileCopy** statement executes properly. The **CopyFile** return value will be set to whatever the **bOk** variable is set to. If an error occurs, the point of execution goes to the Err_CopyFile label and the **Resume** statement puts the execution to the Exit_CopyFile label.

In Version 6.0 of Visual Basic, you can use the **FileSystemObject**'s method, **CopyFile**, to copy a file from one area to another. In order to do that, you will need to reference the Microsoft Scripting Runtime class in your project and your code would look like the following:

```
Dim fso As FileSystemObject
Set fso = New FileSystemObject
fso.CopyFile(sSource, sDestination, False)
```

As you can see, the **FileSystemObject**'s **CopyFile** method works almost identically to the **FileCopy** statement, with one exception: You can determine if you want the function to overwrite the destination file if it already exists. This is the third parameter of the **CopyFile** method. By default, the property is set to True; it's an optional argument. If you leave it out, the destination will be overwritten with the new file.

XCopy32

Copying an Entire Directory and Its Subdirectories

There may be times when you will need to copy the entire file directory and its subdirectories from one drive to another. In DOS, you would use the XCopy command to accomplish this. Within VB, you could still use the XCopy command by using the **Shell** statement and executing the XCopy command from within it. But that would be inefficient because you can do the same thing with several VB statements, similar to copying a file.

CODE

```
Public Function XCopy32(SrcDrv As String, SrcDIR As String, _
    DestDrv As String, DestDIR As String, _
    Optional bInc_Subdir As Boolean) As Boolean

    Dim Result As String
    Dim rc as Boolean
    Dim nDirCount As Integer
    Dim x As Integer
    Dim nFileCount As Integer
    Dim Z As Integer
    Dim DIRList() As String
    Dim FileList() As String
    nDirCount = 0
    nFileCount = 0
    XCopy32 = False
    On Error Resume Next
    ChDrive SrcDrv
    If Not Err = 0 Then Exit Function
    ChDir (SrcDrv & "\" & SrcDIR)
    If Not Err = 0 Then Exit Function
    ChDrive DestDrv
    If Not Err = 0 Then Exit Function
    ChDir (DestDrv & "\" & DestDIR)
    If Not Err = 0 Then
        Err = 0
        MkDir (DestDrv & "\" & DestDIR)
        If Not Err = 0 Then Exit Function
    End If
    On Error GoTo 0
    Result = Dir((SrcDrv & "\" & SrcDIR & "\*.*"), vbDirectory)
    Do
        If (Result = "." Or Result = "..") = False Then
            Exit Do
        Else
            Result = Dir()
        End If
    Loop
    Do
        If Result = "" Then Exit Do
        If (GetAttr(SrcDrv & "\" & SrcDIR & "\" & Result)) = _
            vbDirectory Then
            nDirCount = nDirCount + 1
```

```
            ReDim Preserve DIRList(nDirCount)
            DIRList(nDirCount) = Result
        Else
            nFileCount = nFileCount + 1
            ReDim Preserve FileList(nFileCount)
            FileList(nFileCount) = Result
        End If
        Result = Dir()
    Loop
    If bInc_Subdir = True Then
        For x = 1 To nDirCount
            rc = XCopy32(SrcDrv, (SrcDIR & "\" & DIRList(x)), _
                DestDrv, (DestDIR & "\" & DIRList(x))), True)
            If rc = False Then Exit Function
        Next x
    End If
    For Z = 1 To nFileCount
        FileCopy (SrcDrv & "\" & SrcDIR & "\" & FileList(Z)), _
            (DestDrv & "\" & DestDIR & "\" & FileList(Z))
    Next Z
    XCopy32 = True
End Function
```

ANNOTATIONS

```
Public Function XCopy32(SrcDrv As String, SrcDIR As String, _
    DestDrv As String, DestDIR As String, _
    Optional bInc_Subdir As Boolean) As Boolean
```

The *SrcDrv* string argument stores the source of the drive including the colon—for example, "d:". The *SrcDIR* string argument stores the directory name where the source files reside. The *DestDrv* string argument stores the name of the drive to which the files will be copied. It is similar to *SrcDrv* in that the drive letter needs to include the colon. The *DestDIR* string argument stores the name of the directory to which the files will be copied. There is an optional argument that can be used if you wish to include all the subdirectories and their contents within the source to the target directory. This is a standard feature of the XCopy command.

```
Dim Result As String
Dim rc As Boolean
Dim nDirCount As Integer
Dim x As Integer
Dim nFileCount As Integer
```

```
Dim Z As Integer
Dim DIRList() As String
Dim FileList() As String
nDirCount = 0
nFileCount = 0
XCopy32 = False
On Error Resume Next
```

After all the variables used in this function are initialized, the XCopy32 return value is set to False. The **On Error** statement is set so that when an error occurs, the statement that immediately follows the error is executed.

```
ChDrive SrcDrv
If Not Err = 0 Then Exit Function
```

The **ChDrive** statement is used to change the fixed disk specified in the *SrcDrv* variable. If the **ChDrive** statement can't change to the drive specified, than an error will occur. If an error occurs, control returns to the calling procedure and the return value is False.

```
ChDir (SrcDrv & "\" & SrcDIR)
If Not Err = 0 Then Exit Function
```

The **ChDir** statement is used to change the directory to the one specified in the *SrcDrv* and *SrcDIR* variables. If the **ChDir** statement can't change to the directory specified, then an error will occur. If an error occurs, control returns to the calling procedure and the return value is False.

```
ChDrive DestDrv
If Not Err = 0 Then Exit Function
```

The **ChDrive** statement is used to change to the fixed disk specified in the *DestDrv* variable. If the **ChDrive** statement can't change to the drive specified, then an error will occur. If an error occurs, control returns to the calling procedure and the return value is False.

```
ChDir (DestDrv & "\" & DestDIR)
If Not Err = 0 Then
    Err = 0
    MkDir (DestDrv & "\" & DestDIR)
    If Not Err = 0 Then Exit Function
End If
```

The **ChDir** statement is used to change the directory to the one specified in the *DestDrv* and *DestDIR* variables. If the **ChDir** statement can't change to the directory specified, then an error will occur. Unlike the previous usage of the **ChDir** statement, if the error occurs, the target directory is created using the **MkDir** statement. If an error occurs during the creation of the directory, control is returned to the calling procedure and the return value is False.

```
On Error GoTo 0
```

Setting the **On Error** statement to **On Error GoTo 0** disables error handling for this function.

```
Result = Dir((SrcDrv & "\" & SrcDIR & "\*.*"), vbDirectory)
```

The **Dir** function returns a string value representing the name of a file, directory, or folder that matches a given pattern or file attribute. It can also return the volume label of a given drive. The **Dir** function as it is presented in this form retrieves the first entry in the directory specified in the *SrcDrv* and *SrcDIR* variables. This is similar to how the **Input #** statement works with a sequential file.

```
Do
    If (Result = "." Or Result = "..") = False Then
        Exit Do
    Else
        Result = Dir()
    End If
Loop
```

The **Do...Loop** statement will read all the files in the directory that was specified in the previous statement. The **If...Then** statement searches through the specified directory until it gets past the "." and ".." items in the directory. The "." refers to the current directory. The ".." refers to the parent directory. Once it gets past them, the **Do...Loop** statement is exited.

```
Do
    If Result = "" Then Exit Do
    If (GetAttr(SrcDrv & "\" & SrcDIR & "\" & Result)) = _
        vbDirectory Then
        nDirCount = nDirCount + 1
        ReDim Preserve DIRList(nDirCount)
        DIRList(nDirCount) = Result
    Else
        nFileCount = nFileCount + 1
        ReDim Preserve FileList(nFileCount)
        FileList(nFileCount) = Result
    End If
    Result = Dir()
Loop
```

The **Do...Loop** statement is used to process every item found within the specified directory. If the value in the *Result* variable is equal to blank, then the loop will be exited because all the files and directories have been processed.

The **If...Then** statement is used to determine how many directories and files need to be copied to the target drive and directory. The first **If...Then** uses the **GetAttr** function to determine if the *Result* value is a file directory. If it is, the *nDirCount* variable is incremented, the **DIRList** array is redimensioned to the new value, and the *Result* value is placed in the **DIRList** array based on the *nDirCount* value. If the value returned from the **GetAttr** function isn't a file directory, then it must be a file within the directory. The *nFileCount* value is incremented and the **FileList** array is redimensioned to the new value with all its previous elements in the array preserved. Then the *Result* value is placed in the **FileList** array based on the *nFileCount* value.

```
If bInc_Subdir = True Then
    For x = 1 To nDirCount
        rc = XCopy32(SrcDrv, (SrcDIR & "\" & DIRList(x)), _
            DestDrv, (DestDIR & "\" & DIRList(x)), True)
        If rc = False Then Exit Function
    Next x
End If
```

The next **If...Then** statement checks that the **bInc_Subdir** argument is True. If so, then the **XCopy32** function will be processed again based on the *nDirCount* value using a **For...Next** loop.

```
For Z = 1 To nFileCount
    FileCopy (SrcDrv & "\" & SrcDIR & "\" & FileList(Z)), _
        (DestDrv & "\" & DestDIR & "\" & FileList(Z))
Next Z
```

The **For...Next** statement will loop until the *nFileCount* value is reached. The **FileCopy** statement is used to copy the file from the source directory to the target directory.

```
XCopy32 = True
```

Assuming the procedure gets to this point, the **XCopy32** return value is set to True and control is returned to the procedure that called this function.

There is a caveat you should be aware of when you use this function: It will overwrite any existing files in the target directory that have the same name without warning, so you should use caution. You might want to add a feature to check to see if the source file exists in the target area and prompt the user to copy the file or not.

Deleting an Entire Directory and Its Subdirectories

DelTree32

Just as you will need to copy files and directories, you will need to remove files and directories as well. In DOS, there is a command called **DelTree** that will remove all files and their directories specified. Rather than using a **Shell** command, there is a way to perform the same task programmatically using VB statements and functions.

CODE

```
Public Function DelTree32(DrvLtr As String, _
    DeleteDIR As String) As Boolean

    Dim Result As String
    Dim rc As Boolean
    Dim nDirCount As Integer
    Dim x As Integer
    Dim nFileCount As Integer
    Dim Z As Integer
    Dim DIRList() As String
    Dim FileList() As String
    nDirCount = 0
    nFileCount = 0
    DelTree32 = False
    On Error Resume Next
    ChDrive DrvLtr
    If Not Err = 0 Then Exit Function
    ChDir (DrvLtr & "\" & DeleteDIR)
    If Not Err = 0 Then Exit Function
    ChDrive DrvLtr
    RmDir ("\" & DeleteDIR)
    If Err = 0 Then
        On Error GoTo 0
        DelTree32 = True
        Exit Function
    Else
        Result = Dir((DrvLtr & "\" & DeleteDIR & "\*.*"), _
            vbDirectory)
        Do
            If (Result = "." Or Result = "..") = False Then
                Exit Do
            Else
                Result = Dir()
            End If
        Loop
        Do
            If Result = "" Then Exit Do
            If (GetAttr(DrvLtr & "\" & DeleteDIR & "\" _
                & Result)) = vbDirectory Then
                nDirCount = nDirCount + 1
```

```
                    ReDim Preserve DIRList(nDirCount)
                    DIRList(nDirCount) = Result
              Else
                    nFileCount = nFileCount + 1
                    ReDim Preserve FileList(nFileCount)
                    FileList(nFileCount) = Result
              End If
              Result = Dir()
        Loop
        For x = 1 To nDirCount
              rc = DelTree32(DrvLtr, (DeleteDIR & "\" & DIRList(x)))
              If rc = False Then Exit Function
        Next x
        For Z = 1 To nFileCount
              Kill (DrvLtr & "\" & DeleteDIR & "\" & FileList(Z))
        Next Z
        ChDrive DrvLtr
        RmDir ("\" & DeleteDIR)
        DelTree32 = True
        On Error GoTo 0
    End If
End Function
```

ANNOTATIONS

```
Public Function DelTree32(DrvLtr As String, _
    DeleteDIR As String) As Boolean
```

The *DrvLtr* string argument is used to identify the drive letter to be used by the function. The string that is passed should also include the colon—for example, "d:". The *DeleteDIR* string argument identifies the directory name to be deleted. If the function is successful, **DelTree32** will be set to True; otherwise it will be set to False.

```
    Dim Result As String
    Dim rc As Boolean
    Dim nDirCount As Integer
    Dim x As Integer
    Dim nFileCount As Integer
    Dim Z As Integer
    Dim DIRList() As String
    Dim FileList() As String
    nDirCount = 0
    nFileCount = 0
    DelTree32 = False
    On Error Resume Next
```

After all the variables used in this function are initialized, the **DelTree32** return value is set to False. The **On Error** statement is set so that when an error occurs, the statement that immediately follows the error is executed.

```
ChDrive DrvLtr
If Not Err = 0 Then Exit Function
```

The **ChDrive** statement is used to change to the fixed disk specified in the *DrvLtr* variable. If the **ChDrive** statement can't change to the drive specified, then an error will occur. If an error occurs, control returns to the calling procedure and the return value is False.

```
ChDir (DrvLtr & "\" & DeleteDIR)
If Not Err = 0 Then Exit Function
```

The **ChDir** statement is used to change the directory to the one specified in the *DrvLtr* and *DeleteDIR* variables. If the **ChDir** statement can't change to the directory specified, then an error occurs and control is returned to the calling procedure with the return value set to False.

```
ChDrive DrvLtr
RmDir ("\" & DeleteDIR)
If Err = 0 Then
        On Error GoTo 0
        DelTree32 = True
        Exit Function
```

The **ChDrive** statement changes to the drive letter specified in the *DrvLtr* variable. The **RmDir** statement is used to remove the directory specified in the *DeleteDIR* variable. If no error occurs, the **Err** number should be 0 and the return value of **DelTree32** is set to True. Control is then returned to the procedure that called the **DelTree32** function.

```
Else
        Result = Dir((DrvLtr & "\" & DeleteDIR & "\*.*"), _
            vbDirectory)
```

If an error did occur from the use of the **RmDir** statement, the **Dir** function is used to retrieve the first entry in the directory specified in the *DrvLtr* and *DeleteDIR* variables.

```
Do
        If (Result = "." Or Result = "..") = False Then
            Exit Do
        Else
            Result = Dir()
        End If
Loop
```

The **Do...Loop** statement will read all the files in the directory that was specified in the previous statement. The **If...Then** statement searches through the specified directory until it gets past the "." and ".." items in the directory. The "." refers to the current directory. The ".." refers to the parent directory. Once it gets past them, the **Do...Loop** is exited.

```
Do
    If Result = "" Then Exit Do
    If (GetAttr(DrvLtr & "\" & DeleteDIR & "\" _
        & Result)) = vbDirectory Then
        nDirCount = nDirCount + 1
        ReDim Preserve DIRList(nDirCount)
        DIRList(nDirCount) = Result
    Else
        nFileCount = nFileCount + 1
        ReDim Preserve FileList(nFileCount)
        FileList(nFileCount) = Result
    End If
    Result = Dir()
Loop
```

The **Do...Loop** statement is used to process every item found within the specified directory. If the value in the *Result* variable is equal to blank, then the loop will be exited because all the files and directories have been processed.

The **If...Then** statement is used to determine how many directories and files need to be copied to the target drive and directory. The first **If...Then** uses the **GetAttr** function to determine if the *Result* value is a file directory. If it is, the *nDirCount* variable is incremented, the **DIRList** array is redimensioned to the new value, and the *Result* value is placed in the **DIRList** array based on the *nDirCount* value. If the value returned from the **GetAttr** function isn't a file directory, then it must be a file within the directory. The *nFileCount* value is incremented and the **FileList** array is redimensioned to the new value with all its previous elements in the array preserved. Then the *Result* value is placed in the **FileList** array based on the *nFileCount* value.

```
For x = 1 To nDirCount
    rc = DelTree32(DrvLtr, (DeleteDIR & "\" & DIRList(x)))
    If rc = False Then Exit Function
Next x
```

The **For...Next** statement will execute the **DelTree32** function a number of times based on the *nDirCount* value.

```
For Z = 1 To nFileCount
    Kill (DrvLtr & "\" & DeleteDIR & "\" & FileList(Z))
Next Z
```

The **For...Next** statement will execute the **Kill** statement a number of times based on the *nFileCount* value. The **Kill** statement is used to delete files from the storage device.

```
        ChDrive DrvLtr
        RmDir ("\" & DeleteDIR)
        DelTree32 = True
        On Error GoTo 0
    End If
```

The **ChDrive** statement then changes the drive back to the root of the drive specified in the *DrvLtr* variable. The **RmDir** statement is used to remove the directory based on the *DeleteDIR* variable. All the files and directories should have been removed from the base directory specified by the *DeleteDIR* variable; therefore the **RmDir** statement should work without any errors. The **DelTree32** return value is set to True, the function is completed, and the function is returned to the procedure that called the **DelTree** function.

Finding a File's Path Name

GetFilePath

When dealing with files, a lot of times you will need to know the path which a file resides in. This function is designed to do just that.

CODE

```
Public Function GetFilePath(sFile As String) As String
    Dim nLen As Integer
    Dim x As Integer

    nLen = Len(sFile)
    For x = nLen To 1 Step -1
        If Mid(sFile, x, 1) = "\" Then
            GetFilePath = Left(sFile, x)
            Exit For
        End If
    Next
End Function
```

ANNOTATIONS

```
Public Function GetFilePath(sFile As String) As String
```

This function requires that one argument be passed to it. The argument passed to this function is a string variable that contains the entire file information regarding the drive letter it resides on, the path, and the filename.

```
Dim nLen As Integer
Dim x As Integer


nLen = Len(sFile)
```

After initializing the variables that are used within the function, the **Len** function returns the length of the *sFile* string variable.

```
For x = nLen To 1 Step -1
    If Mid(sFile, x, 1) = "\" Then
        GetFilePath = Left(sFile, x)
        Exit For
    End If
Next
```

The **For…Next** statement will loop backwards using the *Step* increment argument. By setting it to –1, the loop will count from the highest value to the lowest value. The **If…Then** statement is used to search for the first instance of a backslash ("\"). The first instance of a backslash within the *sFile* string variable should be just before the name of the file. Once the position has been identified, the **Left** function is used to get the drive and path *sans* the filename, and it is set to the **GetFilePath** return value. The **Exit** statement exits the **For…Next** statement and focus is returned to the procedure that called the function.

In Version 6.0, rather than using the **For…Next** statement, you can use the new string function, **InstrRev**. This function searches from the end of the string to the beginning and returns the position of the string which you searched for. The code would look like the following:

```
GetFilePath = Left(sFile, InStrRev(sFile, "\"))
```

With Version 6.0, you can also use the **FileSystemObject** class's **GetFile** method and **File's ParentDirectory** property. Once you reference the Microsoft Scripting Runtime, the code to use the **GetFile** method and **ParentDirectory** property would look like the following:

```
Dim fso As FileSystemObject
Set fso = New FileSystemObject
Dim f As File
Set f = fso.GetFile(sFile)
GetFilePath = f.ParentFolder
```

First, the *fso* variable is defined as the **FileSystemObject**. The **Set** statement instantiates a new instance of the **FileSystemObject** class. The *f* variable is assigned to the **File** class. The next **Set** statement uses the **GetFile** method to return the corresponding file information into the **File** object. The last statement retrieves the path name using the **ParentFolder** property.

Retrieving the Short Path Name for a File

GetShortFilePath Occasionally, you might have to deal with a function or statement that doesn't work with the long filenames that come with Windows 95/98 or Windows NT. Each file and file path that is greater than the DOS 8.3 format has a corresponding short filename and short file path name. This function provides a wrapper around the Win32API function, **GetShortPathName**.

CODE

```
Public Declare Function GetShortPathName Lib "kernel32" _
    Alias "GetShortPathNameA" (ByVal lpszLongPath As String, _
    ByVal lpszShortPath As String, ByVal cchBuffer As Long) _
    As Long
Public Function GetShortFilePath(sFile As String) As String
    Dim rc As Long
    Dim sPath As String * 256

    rc = GetShortPathName(sFile, sPath, 255)
    If (rc) Then
        GetShortFilePath = Left$(sPath, rc)
    Else
        GetShortFilePath = sFile
    End If

End Function
```

ANNOTATIONS

The **GetShortPathName** function is used to retrieve the short path name for a specified file.

```
Public Declare Function GetShortPathName Lib "kernel32" _
    Alias "GetShortPathNameA" (ByVal lpszLongPath As String, _
    ByVal lpszShortPath As String, ByVal cchBuffer As Long) _
    As Long
```

The *lpszLongPath* string parameter specifies the filename whose short path is to be received. The *lpszShortPath* string parameter is a buffer into which the short path and filename of the file is placed. The *cchBuffer* long parameter is used to store the length of the *lpszShortPath*. The value returned from this function is the number of characters that is loaded in the *lpszShortPath* buffer.

```
Public Function GetShortFilePath(sFile As String) As String
```

This function requires that one argument be passed to it. The argument passed to this function is a string variable that contains the entire file information regarding the drive letter it resides on, its path, and the filename.

```
Dim rc As Long
Dim sPath As String * 256


rc = GetShortPathName(sFile, sPath, 255)
```

After the variables are initialized, the **GetShortPathName** function is executed. It uses the *sFile* parameter to fulfill the *lpszLongPath* parameter.

```
If (rc) Then
    GetShortFilePath = Left$(sPath, rc)
Else
    GetShortFilePath = sFile
End If
```

The **If…Then** statement is used to determine if the return value in the *rc* long variable is positive or negative. If the value returned is positive, the **Left** function will be used to get the short path information from the *sPath* string variable that was populated from the **GetShortPathName** function. If the *rc* value is 0, then the *sFile* value contains a filename with no drive or path information and the value stored in *sFile* is placed in the **GetShortFilePath** return value.

Retrieving the Short Name for a File

GetShortFileName Just as important as it is to get the short path name, you will sometimes need to get the short filename of a file. This function relies on the previous example of the **GetShortFilePath** function.

CODE

```
Public Function GetShortFileName(sFile As String) As String
    Dim nLen As Integer
    Dim x As Integer
    Dim sTempFile As String

    sTempFile = GetShortFilePath(sFile)
    nLen = Len(sTempFile)
    For x = nLen To 1 Step -1
        If Mid(sTempFile, x, 1) = "\" Then
            GetShortFileName = Right(sTempFile, nLen - x)
            Exit For
        End If
    Next
End Function
```

ANNOTATIONS

```
Public Function GetShortFileName(sFile As String) As String
```

This function uses one string argument, *sFile*, which contains file information such as drive letter, path, and filename.

```
Dim nLen As Integer
Dim x As Integer
Dim sTempFile As String

sTempFile = GetShortFilePath(sFile)
```

After the variables used in this function are initialized, the function calls the **GetShortFilePath** function and passes the *sFile* variable to it. It will convert all the long file and path names to their 8.3 equivalents.

```
nLen = Len(sTempFile)
```

The **Len** function returns the length of the *sTempFile*, which helps determine how many times the **For...Next** statement needs to loop through the *sTempFile* string.

```
For x = nLen To 1 Step -1
    If Mid(sTempFile, x, 1) = "\" Then
        GetShortFileName = Right(sTempFile, nLen - x)
        Exit For
    End If
Next
```

The **For...Next** statement will loop backwards using the *Step* increment argument. By setting it to –1, the loop will count from the highest value to the lowest value. The **If...Then** statement is used to search for the first instance of a backslash ("\"). The first instance of a backslash within the *sFile* string variable should be just before the name of the file. Once the position has been identified, the **Right** function is used to get the filename, and it is set to the **GetShortFileName** return value. The **Exit** statement exits the **For...Next** statement and focus is returned to the procedure that called the function.

In Version 6.0, rather than using the **For...Next** statement, you can use the new string function, **InstrRev**. This function searches from the end of the string to the beginning and returns the position of the string which you searched for. The code would look like the following:

```
GetShortFileName = Left(sTempFile, InStrRev(sTempFile, "\"))
```

With Version 6.0, you can also use the **FileSystemObject** class's **GetFile** method and **File**'s **ShortName** property. Once you reference the Microsoft Scripting Runtime, the code to use the **GetFile** method and **ShortName** property would look like the following:

```
Dim fso As FileSystemObject
Set fso = New FileSystemObject
```

```
Dim f As File
Set f = fso.GetFile(sFile)
GetFilePath = f.ShortName
```

First, the *fso* variable is defined as the **FileSystemObject**. The **Set** statement instantiates a new instance of the **FileSystemObject** class. The *f* variable is assigned to the **File** class. The next **Set** statement uses the **GetFile** method to return the corresponding file information into the **File** object. The last statement retrieves the path name using the **ShortName** property.

Placing All the Functions in an ActiveX DLL

Vbaa11.vbp

Testapp.vbp

All the functions created in this chapter can be used either as functions within a standard class or as a form module within a VB application. Most of them can be used as VBScript within an Active Server Page on Microsoft's web server, Internet Information Services. The best way to use these functions is within an ActiveX DLL, which is also known as an in-process server. This means that it's an object that can be referenced and used by other applications and the ActiveX DLL resides within the same memory space as the application that called it. For a more thorough description of ActiveX Servers and DLLs, refer to Chapter 12.

CREATING THE ACTIVEX DLL AND TESTING IT

1. Start a new project, ActiveX DLL. The default class module may be the startup module. Change the name of the Class1 module to **FileUtils**. The other property, **Instancing,** by default is set to **5 – MultiUse.** *Instancing* refers to how this class is made available to other projects and how it will behave. By setting it to 5, we are making this class object available to other applications. Once one application has access to this object, another instance does not get loaded. All applications use the same instances. Other settings are available and are covered in more depth in Chapter 12.

2. Add all the code that has been described within this chapter. If you don't wish to go back through the chapter, you can insert the code found on the CD-ROM under TBD. To insert the code, first make sure the Code window has focus. Select Edit | Insert File and the Insert File dialog window will appear. Go to Chapter 11's directory on the CD-ROM and select the FileUtil.TXT file and click OK. This will insert all the code needed for this component.

3. Select Project | Project1 Properties. We are now going to update the project's property information in order to make this component unique. Use the information found in Table 11-1 to fill in the Project1 Properties' dialog box.

Tab	Field Name	Property
General	Project Name	vbaa09
	Project Description	VBAA StringUtils Component
Make	Application Title	vbaa09
	Auto Increment	mark box
Compile	DLL Base Address	&H1600000
Component	Project Compatibility	mark option

TABLE 11-1.   VBAA Project's Properties

4. In order to test out this component, we will need to execute it and run another program against it. Run the component by clicking the Start button, then start a new instance of Visual Basic. The new project will be used to test the components.

5. In the new instance of VB, select the Standard EXE application. The default form may be the startup form. Accept the name Form1 and other default properties.

6. Add the controls shown in Figure 11-1, setting the properties as shown in Table 11-2.

Object	Property	Setting
Form	Name	Form1
	Height	4980
	Width	6180
ListBox	Name	lstOutput
CommandButton	Name	cmdNext
	Caption	OK

TABLE 11-2.   The Form's Objects and Properties

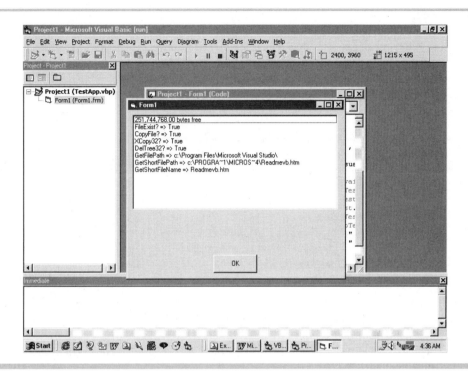

FIGURE 11-1. The test application at runtime

7. Using the Project | References submenu from the VB main menu, select the references shown in Table 11-3. If others are checked that aren't in this table, uncheck them so your project isn't cluttered with DLLs you aren't using.

References
Microsoft Visual Basic for Application
Visual Basic Runtime Objects and Procedures
Visual Basic Objects and Procedures
OLE Automation
VBAA FileUtils Components

TABLE 11-3. References Used in the TestApp Project

PROGRAMMER'S NOTE

The bottom frame of the References dialog box displays the Location and Language of the object or object library. The Location displays the location of the object or the object library. In this example, the location should be where the VBAA11.VBP is stored and run from. Had the VBAA11.VBP been compiled into an ActiveX DLL, the location would be where the DLL is located and the filename would be VBAA11.DLL. The Language should be English if that's the language being used by the system that developed the VBAA11.VBP.

8. Add the following code to the **Load** event procedure of the form. The **Move** method for the form is going to center the form on the screen. The value assigned to *vString* is the string that will be used to test the functions we just designed.

```
Private Sub Form_Load()
    Dim oTest As VBAA11.FileUtils
    Set oTest = New VBAA11.FileUtils
    Dim sFile As String

    Me.Move ((Screen.Width - Me.Width) / 2), _
        ((Screen.Height - Me.Height) / 2)

    sFile = "c:\progra~1\micros~2\readmevb.htm

    lstOutput.AddItem _
FormatNumber(oTest.Availablediskspace(sFile)) _
        & " bytes free"
    lstOutput.AddItem "FileExist? =>   " _
& oTest.FileExists(sFile)
    lstOutput.AddItem "CopyFile? => " & oTest.CopyFile(sFile, _
        "c:\temp\backup.bk!")
    lstOutput.AddItem "XCopy32? => " & oTest.XCopy32("c:", _
        "sandbox", "c:", "sandbox2")
    lstOutput.AddItem "DelTree32? => " & oTest.DelTree32("c:", _
        "sandbox2")
    lstOutput.AddItem "GetFilePath => " _
& oTest.GetFilePath(sFile)
    lstOutput.AddItem "GetShortFilePath => " _
        & oTest.GetShortFilePath(sFile)
    lstOutput.AddItem "GetShortFileName => " _
        & oTest.GetShortFileName(sFile)
End Sub
```

9. Add the following code to the **Click** event procedure of the command button **cmdOK**. When the user triggers this event, the application will end.

```
Private Sub cmdOK_Click()
    End
End Sub
```

10. Click the Start button to compile and run the TestApp project.

As the application loads, the **Form_Load** procedure is executed. The object variable *oTest* is assigned to a new instance of the object **VBAA11.FileUtils**. The **Move** method will center the form on the user's screen. It uses the **Screen**'s Height and Width properties and calculates them against the **Form**'s Height and Width properties for positioning. The values returned by the various functions will be displayed in the list box **lstOutput**. To close the window and end the application, click the OK command button.

Since the **VBAA11** component is running in the first instance of the VB, you can step through the code just like any application. This is very useful for debugging any error that might occur, or just to see how functions work. Figure 11-2 illustrates stepping through the code within the VBAA11.VBP project.

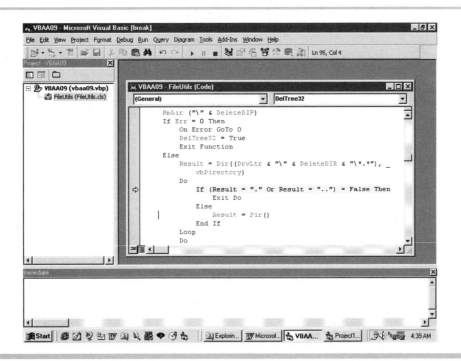

FIGURE 11-2. Stepping through the VBAA11.VBP project while the TestApp.VBP project is suspended

To make the **VBAA11** project into an ActiveX DLL so that it can be used by other applications and IIS, select File | Make VBAA11.DLL. In the Make Project dialog box, select the OK button just like you would if you were making a VB project into a Standard EXE. That's all it takes. Once you make the project into an ActiveX DLL, it will be assigned a globally unique identification (GUID) key that is used to identify ActiveX components and their interfaces. For more information about ActiveX components (ActiveX DLL and EXE) and COM, refer to Chapter 12.

ActiveX Servers

Creating a Splitter Bar ActiveX DLL
    (Split.vbp)

"**M**ay I serve you?" To most people, these words would summon up the image of a waiter or waitress. However, as computer programmers, we are not like most people. These words would remind us of an ActiveX Server. Well, maybe that is a stretch, but the term "server" does have a special meaning, or meanings, to computer professionals.

The server in a client-server network provides network services to the client workstations. The services may permit the workstations to run applications and access databases not on the workstation, use printers not connected to the workstation, and so on. Thus, the server extends the abilities of the workstations to perform tasks.

Just as a network server provides services to client workstations, ActiveX Servers provide services to client applications. A *client application* is an application that uses the services of another software component by creating instances of the other component and calling the other component's properties and methods.

An ActiveX Data Object (ADO), discussed in Chapter 9, is an ActiveX Server used to provide database access to applications. The following code snippet shows how a client application first creates an instance of ADO and then calls methods of ADO to create and then loop through the recordset of a database:

```
Dim conn As Connection
Dim rs As Recordset
Dim strSQL As String
strSQL = "SELECT * FROM tblAuthors"
Set conn = New ADO.Connection
conn.ConnectionString = "DRIVER ={Microsoft Access Driver _
    (*.mdb)};" & DBQ = " & App.Path & vbaaCh12.mdb;"
conn.Open
Set rs = conn.Execute(strSQL)
Do While Not rs.EOF
    Debug.Print rs.Fields("AuthorName").Value
    rs.MoveNext
Loop
```

The client application, in lieu of using ADO, could include classes and other modules that perform the same tasks as ADO. Of course, every one of your client applications that accessed databases would need to include its own copy of this database access code. If the implementation of the database access logic were changed, then that change would have to be made in all of the client applications where you added the database access code.

By contrast, all that is required for the client application to use the ADO is to place a checkmark in the Project | References menu next to Microsoft ActiveX Data Objects 2.0 Library. Additionally, if the implementation of the ActiveX Server was changed, all that would be necessary for the client applications to be able to use the updated code is to upgrade the ActiveX Server file used by the client.

In other words, the ActiveX Server is a "reusable software component." If you have already read Chapter 7 on ActiveX controls, this may seem like "déjà vu all over again." You're correct. ActiveX Servers and ActiveX controls are related. Both are objects based on the Component Object Model (COM). However, there are differences, as will be discussed.

While ADO is a useful and heavily used ActiveX Server, ActiveX Servers can and do perform far more than provide database access. There are ActiveX Servers that perform disparate tasks such as calendaring, charting, graphing and mapping, messaging and other communications, image manipulation, bar coding, credit card authorization, and bestowing eternal life (just seeing if you are paying attention).

Additionally, while Microsoft has created ADO and a number of other ActiveX Servers, Microsoft by no means is the sole source of ActiveX Servers. A number of ISVs specialize in the creation of ActiveX Servers. There also is another important source of ActiveX Servers: you, the programmer. As is the case of ActiveX controls, ActiveX Servers now can be created in the Visual Basic IDE without having to know C or the Windows SDK.

This chapter will show you how to create an ActiveX Server. However, the process of building an ActiveX Server resembles a decision tree far more than a linear path; there are several choices which you have to make. As usually is the case, there is no one "best" choice for all situations. The choices involve tradeoffs. Understanding the advantages and disadvantages of the various alternatives is essential to creating an ActiveX Server which best fits the situation you are addressing.

DLL vs. EXE, or Speed vs. Safety

The first and primary issue you will face in creating an ActiveX Server is whether it will be an ActiveX DLL (dynamic link library) or an ActiveX EXE (executable).

If the ActiveX Server must have the ability to run as a stand-alone application, then it must be an ActiveX EXE. It is not a contradiction for an ActiveX code component to be a "server," which implies its use by a separate client application, and also a stand-alone application in its own right. The authors used an ActiveX Server, Microsoft Word, to write this book. Microsoft Word unquestionably is a stand-alone application and often is used for that purpose. However, Microsoft Word also may be used, for example, as a report writer by client applications.

There also are other issues, such as multithreading and networking, which are beyond the scope of this book. However, the usual decision is the same one you face in driving on an open and unpatrolled stretch of highway: speed vs. safety.

Every application, including your client application, runs in its own process space. An ActiveX DLL is an *in-process* component. Thus, it runs in the same process space as the client. By contrast, an ActiveX EXE is an *out-of-process* component. Thus, it runs in its own process space, separate from the client application's process space.

The bottom line is that an in-process component (that is, an ActiveX DLL) is "faster" than but not as "safe" as an out-of-process component (that is, an ActiveX EXE). The safety issue is relatively easy to define, but speed is a relative concept. The issue is how much faster is an ActiveX DLL than an Active EXE. The answer is: It depends. Actually, the relative difference in speed between an ActiveX DLL and an ActiveX EXE depends on two factors: the number of calls that the client application makes to the ActiveX Server and the amount of time required for the code in the ActiveX Server to execute.

In 32-bit Windows, each process has its own 4GB of addressable memory. Before you panic and go out and buy wheelbarrows full of RAM, you should know that the 4GB of addressable memory is virtual. Nevertheless, each process has the same 4GB range of addressable memory. Additionally, both the start and end values of this range are identical for all processes. However, each process' 4GB of addressable memory is separate. Therefore, an address of (for example) &H1110000 in one process does *not* point to the same location in memory as the address of &H1110000 in another process.

A client application's calls to the methods of an in-process server (that is, an ActiveX DLL) can use the client's stack to pass arguments to the in-process server. This is possible because the client and the in-process server share the same address space. Therefore, the specific location in memory pointed to by the address passed by the client application is the exact same location to the in-process server.

By contrast, a client application's calls to the methods of an out-of-process server (that is, an ActiveX EXE) cannot use the client's stack to pass arguments to the out-of-process server. Since the client application and the out-of-process component are in separate processes, an address of, for example, & H1110000 passed by the client application would refer to a different location in memory to the out-of-process server.

Since the client application's calls to the methods of an out-of-process server cannot use the client's stack to pass arguments to the out-of-process server, an alternative is necessary to pass the method arguments from the client application to the out-of-process server. This alternative of moving method arguments across the boundary between the two processes is called *marshaling*. While a technical discussion of marshaling is beyond the scope of this chapter, the bottom line is that marshaling involves significant overhead. Therefore, calls by a client application which pass arguments to the methods of an ActiveX DLL are faster than the same calls to an ActiveX EXE.

However, it is only partially true that an ActiveX DLL is "faster" than an ActiveX EXE. While communication between a client application and an ActiveX DLL is faster than communication between a client application and an ActiveX EXE, the code within the ActiveX DLL executes no faster than the same code within an ActiveX EXE. Code that executes slowly in an ActiveX EXE, such as a complex manipulation of thousands of records, will not execute any faster in an ActiveX DLL.

Therefore, the speed advantage of the ActiveX DLL becomes significant if the client application makes a relatively large number of calls to the ActiveX Server. However, if the client application makes relatively few calls to the ActiveX Server, and the execution of the code in the ActiveX Server is lengthy or processor-intensive, then the speed advantage of the ActiveX DLL may be relatively insignificant.

The safety issue is less complex. Every application, including a client application, has a *thread* of execution. If that thread stops for any reason, so too will the application.

Just as an in-process component shares its client's process space, it also uses its client's thread of execution. Consequently, the "crash" of an ActiveX DLL will bring the client application a visit from the military (General Protection Fault), the prosecution (Illegal Exception), or the executioner (hanging). If the client application is mission-critical, its crash, depending on your customer's propensity for violence, also could result in your crashing.

By contrast, an out-of-process component has its own thread of execution separate from the client. Therefore, a crash of the ActiveX EXE will not terminate the client application.

Enough theory! Let's build an ActiveX Server.

Split.vbp

Creating a Splitter Bar ActiveX DLL

With each new version of Visual Basic, Microsoft has added more built-in controls. However, one control that still is missing is a splitter bar. The purpose of this highly useful control is to enable users to drag a vertical or horizontal bar across the form to reallocate space between two display areas.

This GUI control is used heavily in Windows applications. For example, Windows Explorer uses a vertical splitter bar to separate the list pane from the contents pane. (See Figure 12-1.) Microsoft Word uses a horizontal splitter bar, which is invoked with the menu command Window | Split. (See Figure 12-2.)

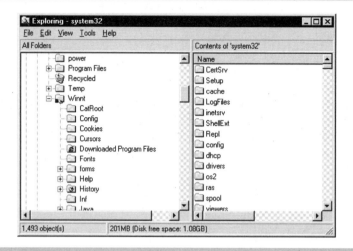

FIGURE 12-1. Vertical split bar in Windows Explorer

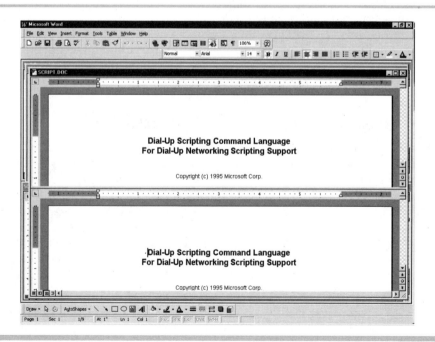

FIGURE 12-2. Horizontal split bar in Microsoft Word

The controls which Microsoft did include in Visual Basic can be added to any application simply by using the Project | References menu command. (See Figure 12-3.) The code components listed under Project | References are not limited to those included by Microsoft or provided by ISVs. These ready-to-add code components may include those that you create.

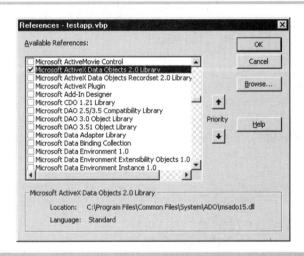

FIGURE 12-3. Using Project | References to include an ADO

This example will create a splitter bar code component which can be incorporated into an application (through Project | References) so your forms may include horizontal and vertical splitter bars. This is relatively easy to do in comparison with the other tasks we have undertaken in this book, and there are many interesting issues to discuss along the way.

The code used in this example originally was written by Michael C. Amundsen and is used with his kind permission, which the authors deeply appreciate. If there are any errors, it would be due to the authors' tweaking, not Mr. Amundsen.

SYNOPSIS OF CODE

The steps to be followed are quite similar to those used in Chapter 7 to create an ActiveX control. This is not surprising because ActiveX DLLs and EXEs are related to ActiveX controls.

The first step is to create the splitter bar code component. This code component is created in a project. The threshold issue is whether the project should be an ActiveX DLL or an ActiveX EXE. If your choice is an ActiveX DLL, you either have a solid grasp of the earlier discussion in this chapter or have read the title of this example.

The first step involves another interesting issue. While we have been using class modules throughout this book, we have not yet had to worry about the properties of these classes. Now we will have to worry. Actually, this will not be an occasion to worry, but rather to learn.

The next step is to create another project to test the component.

Once we have verified that the code component works properly, then the final step is to compile the DLL and test it in the test project.

STEPS TO CREATE THE SPLITTER BAR CODE COMPONENT

1. Create a new project. The type of project is ActiveX DLL. Save the project under the name Split.vbp. When prompted to save the name of the class which is created by default in an ActiveX DLL project, save it as Hsplit.cls.

    Why an ActiveX DLL and not an ActiveX EXE? First, the splitter bar component, by its nature, would not be a stand-alone application. Therefore, it does not need to be an ActiveX EXE. Second, the difference in speed could be meaningful. A call will be made to the ActiveX Server each time the horizontal or vertical splitter bar is moved. Thus, there likely will be numerous calls to the ActiveX Server. By contrast, the code in the ActiveX Server itself should execute quickly.

2. In Project Explorer, right-click Split.vbp and choose Project1 Properties from the context menu to bring up the Project Properties dialog box. Click on the General tab. The Project Type should be ActiveX DLL based on your choice in step 1. The Startup Object should be None as the startup object will be in a separate test project. Change the Project Name to "SplitBar" and the Project Description to "SplitBar Resizing component." (See Figure 12-4.)

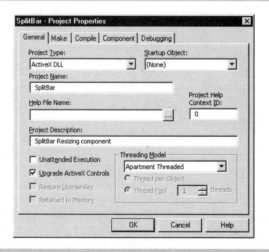

FIGURE 12-4. Project Properties for Split.vbp

ActiveX Servers, like ActiveX controls, do not need a startup object. Usually, an ActiveX Server is started from a call by a client application. An ActiveX Server, like a Standard Exe project, may have a Sub Main procedure as its startup object. If so, the code in that procedure will execute before the code (if any) in the **Initialize** event of the ActiveX Server.

As discussed in Chapter 7 in connection with ActiveX controls, the project name identifies the ActiveX control in the Windows Registry and the Object Browser, and therefore must be a legal identifier. This name is used in the type library, and thus the Object Browser. (See Figure 12-5.)

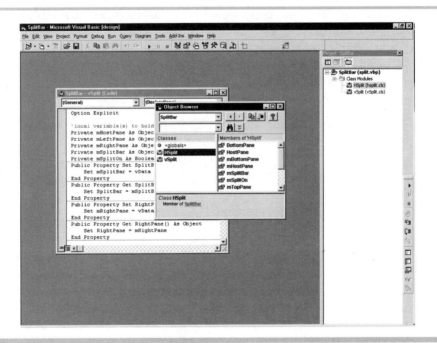

FIGURE 12-5. SplitBar project in Object Browser

Just as the Project Description for an ActiveX control is the text that appears in the Components dialog box, the Project Description for an ActiveX Server appears in the References dialog box. There is no particular naming convention. The name must be unique, but otherwise the choice is yours. The name should be descriptive of the component without, of course, being as long as the Gettysburg Address. One noted commentator's suggestion is to precede the descriptive name with the company name. Since Microsoft does this, the suggestion is probably a good one.

The Help File Name is left blank and the Project Help Context ID is 0 because there is no help for this application (take that whichever way you want). Seriously, a component which is distributed commercially (that is, people pay good money for it) should have a help file. However, this application has no help file, not because the authors are too lazy to create one, but because the subject of creating help files is beyond the scope of this chapter.

Unattended Execution applies if the ActiveX Server project can be run without user interaction. This means that the project will not display a message box or other GUI element to which the user must respond with an action such as by clicking an OK command button. Selecting Unattended Execution permits you, under certain circumstances, to use multithreading. For this example, accept the default setting and leave the Unattended Execution option unchecked.

For the Threading Model setting, accept the default, Apartment Threading. The Visual Basic threading model and multithreading in general are quite complex, and therefore beyond the scope of this book.

The Upgrade ActiveX Controls checkbox should be checked so that Visual Basic will upgrade any obsolete ActiveX controls loaded in the project.

There are other tabs to the Project Properties dialog box. They will be discussed after we have successfully tested the code component and are ready to compile it.

3. Change the name of the class, which by default is named "Class1," to **HSplit**. If you did not do so already in the first step, save the class as Hsplit.cls.

4. In Project Explorer, right-click on **HSplit** and choose Properties from the context menu. Set the **Instancing** property to **MultiUse** using the drop-down list box.

The **Instancing** property has six possible values for ActiveX EXEs, four of which are available for ActiveX DLLs. The default value varies depending on the project type.

♦ **Private** This is the default for class modules in Standard Exe projects. A **Private** class can be accessed only within the component. As a practical matter, it cannot be instantiated from outside of the component (such as from the client application). This limitation would appear to defeat the purpose of an ActiveX Server, which serves the applications that instantiate it. Yet, **Private** classes have a purpose. An ActiveX Server can be made up of more than one class. If a class is a "helper" class, that is, its sole purpose is to render services to other classes within the component, then the OOP principle of encapsulation dictates that it should be **Private**.

♦ **PublicNotCreatable** This is the default for class modules in ActiveX control projects. A **PublicNotCreatable** class can be accessed by applications outside of the component, but can be created only by the component. This property permits the creation of a hierarchy of objects that provide a path through which the inner objects can be accessed. Therefore, this property is used most often for the dependent classes in the object hierarchy.

◆ **SingleUse**   This value is only available for an ActiveX EXE Server. A **SingleUse** class may be created from outside of the component. However, each instantiation of the ActiveX EXE creates another instance of the server running in its own process space. Several instantiations of the ActiveX EXE would create several copies of the server. Numerous instantiations of the server therefore could create a significant amount of overhead.

◆ **MultiUse**   This is the default for class modules in ActiveX DLL and ActiveX EXE projects. A **MultiUse** class also may be created from outside of the component. **MultiUse** means the ActiveX Server can be used multiple times. In other words, all instantiations of an ActiveX EXE run in one instance, or process space. This is more efficient than **SingleUse**. Therefore, why would **SingleUse** ever be used in preference to **MultiUse**? The reason is that if a component, usually the topmost one in an object hierarchy, requires a significant amount of processing time, **SingleUse** ensures the existence of a running component if an object is requested from a class.

◆ **GlobalMultiUse**   This value is similar to **MultiUse**, with one difference. The properties and methods of a **GlobalMultiUse** class can be invoked as if they were simply global functions. In other words, it is not necessary to explicitly create an instance of the class to use its properties and methods. A reference to a property or method of the class automatically will create an instance of the class. This appears convenient, and it is, but referring to a property or method without referring to its class does make your code less readable. Therefore, it generally is used only for components with generic or general-purpose functionality.

◆ **GlobalSingleUse**   This value is similar to **SingleUse** in that it is only available for an ActiveX EXE Server. The one difference with **SingleUse** is that the properties and methods of a **GlobalSingleUse** class can be invoked globally, just as with a **GlobalMultiUse** class.

5. Insert the following code in the **HSplit** class:

```
Option Explicit

Private mHostPane As Object
Private mTopPane As Object
Private mBottomPane As Object
Private mSplitBar As Object
Private mSplitOn As Boolean
```

```
Public Property Set SplitBar(ByVal vData As Object)
    Set mSplitBar = vData
End Property

Public Property Get SplitBar() As Object
    Set SplitBar = mSplitBar
End Property

Public Property Set BottomPane(ByVal vData As Object)
    Set mBottomPane = vData
End Property

Public Property Get BottomPane() As Object
    Set BottomPane = mBottomPane
End Property

Public Property Set TopPane(ByVal vData As Object)
    Set mTopPane = vData
End Property

Public Property Get TopPane() As Object
    Set TopPane = mTopPane
End Property

Public Property Set HostPane(ByVal vData As Object)
    Set mHostPane = vData
End Property

Public Property Get HostPane() As Object
    Set HostPane = mHostPane
End Property

Public Property Let SplitOn(ByVal vData As Boolean)
    mSplitOn = vData
End Property

Public Property Get SplitOn() As Boolean
    SplitOn = mSplitOn
End Property

Public Sub SetPointer(pType As Integer)
    mHostPane.MousePointer = pType
End Sub
```

```
Public Sub ResizePanes(Optional Twips As Single)
    On Error GoTo LocalErr
    If IsMissing(Twips) Then
        Twips = 0
    End If
    With mSplitBar
        .Left = 0
        .Top = .Top + Twips
        .Height = 30
        .Width = mHostPane.ScaleWidth
    End With

    With mTopPane
        .Left = 0
        .Top = 0
        .Width = mHostPane.ScaleWidth
        .Height = mSplitBar.Top
    End With

    With mBottomPane
        .Left = 0
        .Top = mSplitBar.Top + mSplitBar.Height
        .Width = mHostPane.ScaleWidth
        .Height = mHostPane.ScaleHeight - _
            (mTopPane.Height + mSplitBar.Height)
    End With

    Exit Sub
LocalErr:
    ' ignore any errors
End Sub
```

The properties and methods of the **HSplit** class are summarized in Table 12-1.

The **ResizePanes** method deserves further comment. The error handler will catch invalid resize values that might occur if the client attempts to minimize the form or drag the split bar beyond the host-pane boundaries. On an error, the subroutine simply will end. Next, the optional parameter is checked and set to zero, if it wasn't passed. The remainder of the subroutine computes and resizes the controls. First, the value passed into the routine locates the SplitBar control on the host pane. Next, the left-pane control expands to fill

Property or Method	Data Type	Purpose
mHostPane	Object	Holds the other three visual components: mTopPane, mBottomPane, and mSplitBar.
mTopPane	Object	Holds the control which is the top pane.
mBottomPane	Object	Holds the control which is the bottom pane.
mSplitBar	Object	Holds the control which is the split bar.
mSplitOn	Boolean	Keeps track of whether the user has requested the split bar "service." Pressing the mouse button will "turn on" the split bar service. Releasing the mouse button will turn the service off.
SetPointer	Not Applicable	Enables the client application to toggle the mouse pointer from normal to split mode.
ResizePanes	Not Applicable	Keeps track of the position of the SplitBar control and automatically resizes the TopPane and BottomPane controls within the HostPane.

TABLE 12-1. Properties and Methods of the **HSplit** Class

the host pane to the left of the SplitBar control. Finally, the right-pane control expands to fill the host pane to the right of the SplitBar control.

6. Add a class module using the Project | Add Class Module menu command. Name the class **VSplit** and save it as Vsplit.cls.

7. Insert the following code in the **VSplit** class:

```
Option Explicit

Private mHostPane As Object
Private mLeftPane As Object
Private mRightPane As Object
Private mSplitBar As Object
Private mSplitOn As Boolean

Public Property Set SplitBar(ByVal vData As Object)
    Set mSplitBar = vData
End Property
```

```
Public Property Get SplitBar() As Object
    Set SplitBar = mSplitBar
End Property


Public Property Set RightPane(ByVal vData As Object)
    Set mRightPane = vData
End Property


Public Property Get RightPane() As Object
    Set RightPane = mRightPane
End Property


Public Property Set LeftPane(ByVal vData As Object)
    Set mLeftPane = vData
End Property


Public Property Get LeftPane() As Object
    Set LeftPane = mLeftPane
End Property


Public Property Set HostPane(ByVal vData As Object)
    Set mHostPane = vData
End Property


Public Property Get HostPane() As Object
    Set HostPane = mHostPane
End Property


Public Property Let SplitOn(ByVal vData As Boolean)
    mSplitOn = vData
End Property


Public Property Get SplitOn() As Boolean
    SplitOn = mSplitOn
End Property


Public Sub SetPointer(ByVal pType As Integer)
    mHostPane.MousePointer = pType
End Sub
```

```
Public Sub ResizePanes(Optional Twips As Single, _
    Optional ToolbarHeight As Integer _
    Optional StatusBarHeight As Integer)
On Error GoTo LocalErr
    If IsMissing(Twips) Then
        Twips = 0
    End If
    With mSplitBar
        .Top = 0 + ToolbarHeight
        .Left = .Left + Twips
        .Height = mHostPane.ScaleHeight - _
            ToolbarHeight - StatusBarHeight
        .Width = 30
    End With

    With mLeftPane
        .Top = 0 + ToolbarHeight
        .Left = 0
        .Height = mHostPane.ScaleHeight - _
            ToolbarHeight - StatusBarHeight
        .Width = mSplitBar.Left
    End With

    With mRightPane
        .Top = 0 + ToolbarHeight
        .Left = mSplitBar.Left + mSplitBar.Width
        .Height = mHostPane.ScaleHeight - _
            ToolbarHeight - StatusBarHeight
        .Width = mHostPane.ScaleWidth - _
            (mLeftPane.Width + mSplitBar.Width)
    End With

    Exit Sub
LocalErr:
    ' Ignore any errors
End Sub
```

The properties and methods of the **VSplit** class are summarized in Table 12-2.

The **ResizePanes** method is analogous to the one in **HSplit**. The difference is that it takes into account the height of the toolbar and of the status bar. This

Property or Method	Data Type	Purpose
mHostPane	Object	Holds the other three visual components: mLeftPane, mRightPane, and mSplitBar.
mLeftPane	Object	Holds the control which is the left pane.
mRightPane	Object	Holds the control which is the right pane.
mSplitBar	Object	Holds the control which is the split bar.
mSplitOn	Boolean	Keeps track of whether the user has requested the split bar "service." Pressing the mouse button will "turn on" the split bar service. Releasing the mouse button will turn the service off.
SetPointer	Not Applicable	Enables the client application to toggle the mouse pointer from normal to split mode.
ResizePanes	Not Applicable	Keeps track of the position of the SplitBar control and automatically resizes the LeftPane and RightPane controls within the HostPane.

TABLE 12-2. Properties and Methods of the **VSplit** Class

was not necessary in **HSplit** because the toolbar and status bar components affect only height and not width.

8. In Project Explorer, right-click on **VSplit** and choose Properties from the context menu. Set the **Instancing** property to **MultiUse** using the drop-down list box.

9. In the *same instance* of Visual Basic in which the Split.vbp project resides, use the File | Add Project menu command to add a new project, Standard Exe. Save the project as Testapp.vbp and set its name to TestApp. Also, when prompted, save the project group, accepting the default name Group1.vbg. When prompted, save the default form as TestApp.frm and set its name to frmTest. In the project's properties, set the startup object to frmTest.

In the case of an ActiveX DLL, a test project is added and, together with the ActiveX DLL project, comprises a project group. Having the test project and the ActiveX DLL project in the same instance of Visual Basic is possible because the ActiveX DLL runs in the same process as the client application. However, an ActiveX EXE may be tested only from a separate instance of Visual Basic because the ActiveX EXE runs in its own process space. In that case, the test project would have to be created in a second, separate instance of Visual Basic.

10. Add to the form the controls described in Table 12-3.

Name	Control Type	Purpose
txtLeft	TextBox	Left pane
Picture1	PictureBox	Takes up the space of a toolbar
picSplitter	PictureBox	Vertical split bar
txtTop	TextBox	Right top pane
picHSplit	PictureBox	Horizontal split bar
lblBottom	Label	Right bottom pane
picRight	PictureBox	Right pane

TABLE 12-3. Controls of Test Form

In Design view the form should look like Figure 12-6.

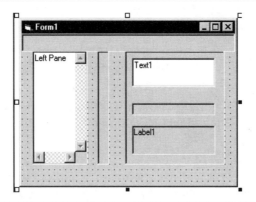

FIGURE 12-6. Test form in Design view

11. Add the following code to the module of the test form:

```
Option Explicit

Dim spVSet As New VSplit
Dim spHSet As New HSplit

Private Sub Form_Initialize()
    Set spVSet.HostPane = Me
    Set spVSet.LeftPane = txtLeft
    Set spVSet.RightPane = picRight
    Set spVSet.SplitBar = picSplitter
    spVSet.SplitOn = False
    Set spHSet.HostPane = picRight
    Set spHSet.TopPane = txtTop
    Set spHSet.BottomPane = lblBottom
    Set spHSet.SplitBar = picHSplit
    spHSet.SplitOn = False
End Sub

Private Sub Form_Resize()
    spVSet.ResizePanes toolbarheight:=Me.Picture1.Height
End Sub

Private Sub lblBottom_MouseMove(Button As Integer, _
    Shift As Integer, X As Single, Y As Single)
    spHSet.SetPointer vbNormal
    spVSet.SetPointer vbNormal
End Sub

Private Sub picHSplit_MouseDown(Button As Integer, _
    Shift As Integer, X As Single, Y As Single)
    spHSet.SetPointer vbSizeNS
    spHSet.SplitOn = True
End Sub

Private Sub picHSplit_MouseMove(Button As Integer, _
    Shift As Integer, X As Single, Y As Single)
    spHSet.SetPointer vbSizeNS
    If spHSet.SplitOn = True Then
```

```
            spHSet.ResizePanes Y
        End If
End Sub

Private Sub picHSplit_MouseUp(Button As Integer, _
    Shift As Integer, X As Single, Y As Single)
    spHSet.SetPointer vbNormal
      If spHSet.SplitOn = True Then
        spHSet.ResizePanes Y
        spHSet.SplitOn = False
      End If
End Sub

Private Sub picRight_Resize()
    spHSet.ResizePanes
End Sub

Private Sub picSplitter_MouseDown(Button As Integer, _
    Shift As Integer, X As Single, Y As Single)
    spVSet.SetPointer vbSizeWE
    spVSet.SplitOn = True
End Sub

Private Sub picSplitter_MouseMove(Button As Integer, _
    Shift As Integer, X As Single, Y As Single)
    spVSet.SetPointer vbSizeWE
    If spVSet.SplitOn = True Then
        spVSet.ResizePanes X, Me.Picture1.Height
    End If
End Sub

Private Sub picSplitter_MouseUp(Button As Integer, _
    Shift As Integer, X As Single, Y As Single)
    spVSet.SetPointer vbNormal
      If spVSet.SplitOn = True Then
        spVSet.ResizePanes X, Me.Picture1.Height
        spVSet.SplitOn = False
      End If
End Sub

Private Sub txtLeft_MouseMove(Button As Integer, _
    Shift As Integer, X As Single, Y As Single)
```

```
    spVSet.SetPointer vbNormal
End Sub

Private Sub txtTop_MouseMove(Button As Integer, _
    Shift As Integer, X As Single, Y As Single)
    spHSet.SetPointer vbNormal
    spVSet.SetPointer vbNormal
End Sub
```

The **HostPane** property of *spVSet*, the instance of the **VSplit** class, is the form (the Me keyword), but the **HostPane** of *spHSet*, the instance of the **HSplit** class, is the **picRight** control. Interestingly, this very same **picRight** control also acts as the right pane for *SpVSet*.

The **Resize** event of the two **HostPanes** occurs each time the form changes in size, and also once when the form is loaded into memory.

Most of the code in the form module concerns mouse events (**MouseMove**, **MouseDown**, and **MouseUp**) for the various controls in the form. Each time the mouse crosses over the **SplitBar** control, its pointer changes from the default arrow to the double-pointed arrow. This is a visual cue to the application user that the control can be dragged. Thus, when the application user presses the mouse button and moves the mouse, the split bar should follow the mouse, and the associated controls (left/right or up/down) should resize to match the relocated **SplitBar** control. Finally, when the user releases the mouse button, the split bar should remain still and the mouse pointer should revert to the standard arrow.

The code in the mouse events that call the **ResizePanes** method passes a parameter. For the **picSplitter** control, the *X* parameter is passed, which tells the **ResizePanes** method how far (left or right) the mouse has moved since the last **Move** event. Since the **picHSplit** control is used to control the horizontal mode, the *Y* parameter is passed instead of the *X* parameter.

Since the right pane control for the vertical split set is the **HostPane** of the horizontal split set, no additional code needs to be added for the **picRight** control.

12. In Project Explorer, right-click TestApp and select Set as Start Up from the context menu.

    TestApp supplies the startup object (its form) and therefore that project needs to be selected as the one from which the project group should be started.

13. In Project Explorer, select TestApp. Using the Project | References menu command, find SplitBar Resizing Component, which is the Project

Description of Split.vbp., and check the box. Note that the location refers to Split.vbp. (See Figure 12-7.)

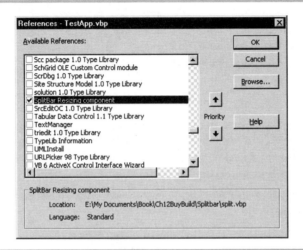

FIGURE 12-7. Split.vbp in references of TestFrm.vbp

At this point the reference is to the ActiveX DLL project file, not a .dll file, because we have not yet compiled the project into the .dll. We will do so once we have verified that the ActiveX DLL project works properly.

14. Run the project group using the Run | Start menu command (or press F5). The test form should show in Run mode, and the splitter bars can be resized with the mouse. (See Figure 12-8.)

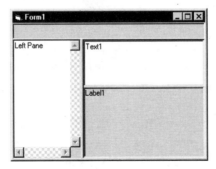

FIGURE 12-8. The test form in Run mode

15. Stop the project using the Run | End menu command, and then stop the Split.vbp project the same way.

    We have confirmed that the ActiveX DLL project works. Therefore, it is time to compile the project into a .dll file. However, before compilation, there are some settings that need to be made.

16. In Project Explorer, right-click on Split.vbp and choose Properties from the context menu. This will bring up the Project Properties dialog box. Click on the Make tab. (See Figure 12-9.) Check the Auto Increment checkbox. This will increment the version number each time the project is compiled, enabling you to keep track of the versions of your project.

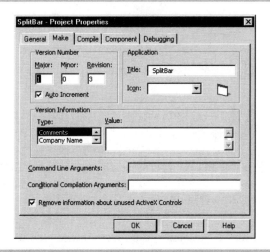

FIGURE 12-9.   The Make tab of the Project Properties dialog box

17. While still in the Project Properties dialog box, click the Compile tab. Accept the default settings for the Compile to Native Code and Optimize for Fast Code options. However, change the DLL Base Address from the default of &H11000000 to &H12a0000. (See Figure 12-10.)

FIGURE 12-10. The Compile tab of the Project Properties dialog box

Native code is faster than P-code because the latter is interpreted code. However, native code tends to be larger. The tradeoff, therefore, is speed versus size. Indeed, P-code often may be the better choice. Often a decision can be made only after compiling and running the component both ways. However, one guideline is that the speed advantage of native code is pronounced when the code is processor-intensive. In this example we have selected native code, but P-code probably would work just as well.

The base address is the memory address into which the ActiveX DLL (or control) will be loaded. The memory range is from 16MB (16,777,216 or &H1000000) to 2GB (2,147,483,648 or &H80000000), inclusively. The address must be a multiple of 64K. Consequently, the last four digits (in hexadecimal) will be 0000.

When Windows loads a DLL, it attempts to load it at the specified address. If the address is available, the DLL loads relatively quickly. However, if another DLL already is using that address, then Windows must relocate the DLL data and code to a new and available location. This is known as *rebasing*. Rebasing is time-consuming and also may complicate Windows' ability to share the DLL code with other applications. Obviously, rebasing is to be avoided.

Visual Basic programmers who did not read this book (or the Visual Basic documentation) often may not bother to change the default DLL base address of &H11000000. Thus, there is a reasonably high probability that the DLL base address of &H11000000 will *not* be available. Thus a different DLL base address is used.

18. While still in the Project Properties dialog box, click the Component tab. Accept the default setting for the Project Compatibility option. (See Figure 12-11.)

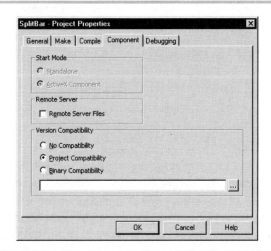

FIGURE 12-11. The Component tab of the Project Properties dialog box

There are three choices for Version Compatibility: No Compatibility, Project Compatibility, and Binary Compatibility. The choices have to do with the component's globally unique identifier (GUID). A GUID is a 16-byte (that's *byte*, not *bit*) number that identifies an object. The number is supposed to be unique, not just in respect to other GUIDs on your computer, but to all GUIDs everywhere. Project compatibility is used in the development stage of projects. Project compatibility allows other instances of the Visual Basic IDE to maintain references to your server even though you are modifying the interfaces of the ActiveX Server, such as by deleting functions or changing function parameters.

Since this is somewhat abstract, an example may be useful. Assume that a client application references an ActiveX Server. The interfaces to the ActiveX Server are changed and then the ActiveX Server is recompiled. With the No Compatibility option, the ActiveX Server's GUID would change and the client's reference to the ActiveX Server no longer would be valid. However, with the Project Compatibility option, the Visual Basic IDE keeps track of changes to the ActiveX Server. Thus, the Visual Basic IDE will synchronize the client application to the changes in the ActiveX Server.

Binary compatibility permits existing compiled client applications to work with a server that has been recompiled with no interface changes. This can be very useful. Assume that a bug was found in the code implementing a function in the server. Fixing the bug would not require any change to the server's interface. However, the server would have to be recompiled. If numerous client applications rely on a server, it would not be a pleasant task to have to recompile and distribute each of these client applications. Recompilation of the client applications is not necessary if the server is binary-compatible.

The reason why binary compatibility is not chosen in this example is that we are still in the development stage and therefore may make changes to the interface of the server.

19. While still in the Project Properties dialog box, click the Debugging tab. Accept the default setting for the "Wait for components to be created" option.

    This tab permits the setting of additional actions to be taken when the Visual Basic IDE goes into Run mode. However, these actions are not used for ActiveX DLLs and EXEs. Rather, they are used in projects that can create ActiveX components such as User Controls, User Documents, and ActiveX Designers (such as DHTML Page Designer and the WebClass Designer). The Debugging tab automates the process of launching these client programs. For example, Visual Basic can start Internet Explorer and display a dummy test page that contains the component.

20. Using the File | Make splitbar.dll menu command, create the DLL.

21. In Project Explorer, right-click Split.vbp and select Remove Project from the context menu. This will display a message box warning that this project is referenced by another project and asking if you're sure you want to remove it. Click Yes.

22. Choose Project | References and make sure that the SplitBar Resizing component refers to the .dll file, not the .vbp file. If necessary, use the Browse button to find the .dll file. (See Figure 12-12.)

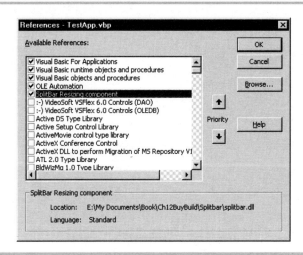

FIGURE 12-12. The test project's reference to DLL

23. Run Testapp.vbp, without Split.vbp. The test form should have the same horizontal and vertical split bar functionality.

Congratulations! You now have successfully created an ActiveX DLL that can be reused in your applications to give your forms split bar functionality.

CHAPTER 13

Automation Using VBA-Compliant Applications

Creating a Summary Page of Microsoft Outlook Information (Outlook.vbp)

Using Microsoft Excel as a Report Writer (Excel.vbp)

Using Automation for a Mail Merge with Microsoft Word (Word.vbp)

O ne of the most common plans for software development is integration. Application integration doesn't have to be solely with other applications written in Visual Basic. It can be with commercial applications developed by companies like Microsoft and Visio. It doesn't have to be with mainstream applications like a word processor or charting tool either. You may have a vertical application specific to your department, like Moss Micro's ActiveSales sales force automation program, or AutoDesk's AutoCAD Design and Drafting software.

In the past, integration with other applications was a very costly process because programs were "closed" environments, meaning that they only talked to programs that were made by the same company. But even then there was no guarantee of integration. Early on, even Microsoft programs were closed systems. It was difficult for one application to work with another one.

With Windows 3.0, Microsoft introduced the concept of Dynamic Data Exchange (DDE). This was their first attempt to allow applications to talk to one another without having to completely understand how each other worked. Later, seeing that the world of software development was becoming more object-oriented, Microsoft and several other ISVs (independent software vendors) created an open design specification that enables applications to communicate with one another in a more integrated fashion. The specification also defined a programming interface to use another application's objects. This design specification is known as OLE (Object Linking and Embedding). The name itself has gone through many revisions but its design has stayed true. It allows users to create compound documents and lets developers create integrated applications, which means that an application can take document information from multiple sources and contain all of it in one document. For example, you can have a Microsoft Word document that contains data calculated from Microsoft Excel, images designed in CorelDRAW, building plans from AutoDesk AutoCAD, and inventory information from Microsoft Access. Prior to OLE, you would have to cut and paste any relevant information and when any information changed, you would have cut and paste again. Through OLE, the information is as up-to-date as the sources because all the information from the other sources are linked to the main document, as shown in this example:

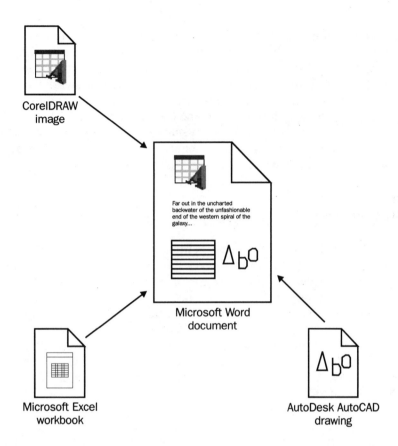

OLE Container Control

In Version 3.0 of VB, Microsoft introduced the OLE Container Control. This is a simple ActiveX control that acts as a placeholder for either linked or embedded OLE objects in your Visual Basic application. You would use this control rather than automation when your user's needs include viewing and manipulating an OLE server's data using the server's own visual interface.

One of the features that the OLE Container Control provides is a method to do *visual editing* from within the placeholder. For example, suppose you have an Excel worksheet embedded in your VB application. Rather than having the user go to Excel to update the information, you can have Excel run from within your application. The user can make changes with all of the features and functionality of Excel without leaving your application. The user will have access to Excel's menus and toolbars as if he or she were in Excel itself. When the user is done editing, the interface is turned back into its placeholder state and Excel is removed from your interface. The use of this control is beyond the scope of this book.

Visual Basic for Applications Edition

In furthering the cause of integration and interoperability, Microsoft CEO Bill Gates announced that Microsoft is going to make the language of Visual Basic the common macro language across all its end-user applications (Word, Access, Excel, and so on). This would make it easier for users to create macros and work with other products because they wouldn't have to learn a new macro language for each application. In the past, you had WordBasic for creating Word macros, Excel had its own scripting language, and Access had AccessBasic. Now that all the products use the same macro language, known as Visual Basic for Applications (VBA), you only have to learn the one language and any different object models the applications use.

Microsoft didn't stop there. In making VBA a standard within its applications, Microsoft makes VBA available to other ISVs so they can integrate VBA into their software solutions and provide interoperability with their VBA applications. You may have seen software packages with the "Powered by Visual Basic Technology" label. Software that has this label has licensed the VBA technology from Microsoft through VBA licensing agents Summit Technology (**http://www.summsoft.com**) or Mystic River Software (**http://www.mysticriver.com**).

Referencing an Object

Before you can use the events, methods, and properties of an object, you must first instantiate, or create an instance, of the object into memory. You do this by first declaring a local object variable to hold a reference to the object; then you assign a reference to the object to the local object variable. There are two methods by which this is done: *early binding* and *late binding*.

Early Binding

Early binding is the most efficient method of accessing an ActiveX component, also referred to as an *object*. This is due to the fact that it directly references the type library of the component before the project is compiled. This gives you, the programmer, access to all the properties, methods, and events of the component, and allows memory to be allocated based on the type library. To provide early binding for a component, you must use the References dialog window to add a reference to the object to your project. Once you have referenced the object to your project within the References dialog window, you can instantiate the object by one of two methods:

```
Dim objBinding As New ObjectName.Class
```

or:

```
Dim objBinding As ObjectName.Class
Set objBinding = New ObjectName.Class
```

Either one is an acceptable method but the latter is the preferred method. The purpose of binding is to instantiate an object and declare it an object variable. By using the first method, you create an instance of the object as soon as the object variable is declared. The problem is that the object is in memory the entire time the host application is running. If the user never chooses the option or function that uses the object, you've wasted quite a number of resources that could have been used by other processes or programs.

The latter method declares the object to an object variable and the **Set** statement instantiates the object when the object is needed. This also provides you with a method of controlling when an object is loaded into memory or not, thus maintaining control over the object and the resources it may use.

Late Binding

In cases where the object you are trying to reference doesn't provide you with a type library, or when you're not sure at design time precisely which object you might need to reference, you can simply declare an object variable as *Object*, rather than the name of the object. An example of an object application without a type library is Microsoft Schedule+ 95. The **CreateObject** function is used to instantiate the object for use. The following code is an example:

```
Dim objBinding As Object
Set objBinding = CreateObject("ObjectName.Class")
```

Visually, you might think there is no difference with the exception of explicitly stating which object you plan to instantiate. In reality, that is the difference. The method of late binding causes your code to execute slower as well as making your development process slower. It executes slower because the application does not "bind" to the object's interface until after it executes. This means that the object's events, methods, or properties aren't available until run-time. It will slow you down during development specifically for the same reason—that the object's events, methods, and properties aren't available to you until run-time. This means that the IDE's IntelliSense Auto List Member/statement completion feature won't assist you in creating your application because it doesn't know anything about the object. Some developers might not like the Auto List Member feature, but without it, when you type any reference to the object, you won't know if you're using a valid event, method, or property until you debug your application.

Object Browser

Each OLE application provides a list of objects, methods, and properties that are available to other developers. This list is known as the object model and it is stored in either an object library (.OLB) or type library (.TLB) file. Visual Basic provides you with a facility that allows you to look at the object model in an hierarchical manner. This facility is called the *Object Browser*. To get to the Object Browser, you can either select the icon on the toolbar, choose the command from the View menu, or press F2 on the keyboard. Shown in Figure 13-1, the Object Browser has several windows to display an object's properties and methods. The left pane displays the object's classes while the right pane displays methods, functions, or properties of a chosen object. The second combo box is a search field. If you're not sure which object has a particular constant, method, property, and so on, you can search for it by simply typing in the value you're looking for and clicking the binoculars. The result will display the library, class, and information you're looking for in the Search Results frame within the Object Browser.

The Object Browser only shows object libraries that are referenced in the project. To add or remove references to object models, you need to use the References dialog window. You get to the References dialog window by selecting References from the Project menu.

COM and DCOM

When dealing with objects, it's important to understand the model on which they are built. The object model which objects are built on is known as COM (Component Object Model). It is a general architecture that lays the foundation upon which OLE

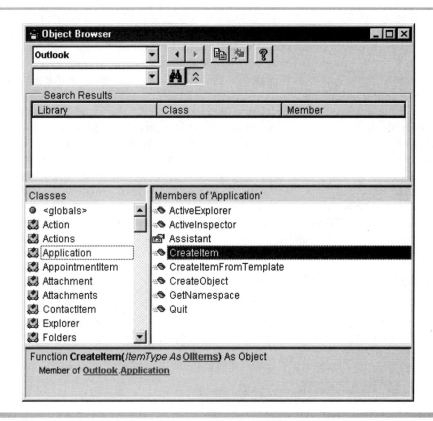

FIGURE 13-1. The Object Browser displaying some elements of Outlook's object model

and ActiveX controls are built. It establishes a common model for interaction among software, like applications, library modules, system software, and more. Therefore, COM can be implemented with almost any kind of software technology using the guideline layout.

COM's fundamental principles are to promote binary components that can be built in any programming language, not just Visual Basic. COM objects can be developed using Java, Delphi, and even Assembler. They can be executed from any location as either in-process, cross-process, or cross-machine, and have no centralized authority. But one thing that a lot of developers miss is that COM is not just about "objects." It's not set out to solve system software problems that arise when hooking up a randomly evolving combination of binary code. It's designed from the perspective that these objects are called components. This is because traditional object concepts are used to solve different sets of requirements in a different problem space. Component services can be called more naturally from object-oriented languages.

As previously mentioned, binary components need to be accessible from any location. Within the COM architecture, this is known as Distributed COM (DCOM). Microsoft totes it as being COM with a longer wire. Its protocol is based on Open Software Foundation (OSF) Distributed Computing Environment (DCE) Remote Procedure Call (RPC) Specifications. For more detailed documentation, you can download a copy at **ftp://ietf.org/intent-drafts/draft-brown-dcom-v1-spec-01.txt**. Microsoft has documented several case studies and has a lot of white papers on DCOM on the Microsoft Developers Network Web site at **http://www.microsoft.com/ msdn**.

Automation Tips

Automation is the process in which you control another application remotely. Because of this, your application's performance and its interaction with the remote application is important. Here are some basic tips to help you optimize your performance.

USE EARLY BINDING WHENEVER POSSIBLE

This was mentioned before, but it's important for you to understand that early binding is the preferred method of working with objects through automation. By early binding the object reference to your project, you can resolve any object collection or method issues at design-time rather than at compile-time. By early binding, the IDE knows more about the object model you working with and any elements of the object will be displayed in the Object Browser. Also, by binding to the object model early, all of the object's constants are accessible to you so you don't have to define them yourself.

Your application's performance will also improve because it doesn't have to resolve any binding issues to the object at run-time because they would have been resolved at design-time.

WHY WRITE WHEN YOU CAN RECORD?

Some developers are hesitant with automation development because they don't feel they know the object model of the automation application well. Fear not! One of the greatest inventions on most applications is called the *Macro Recorder*. You're not too sure what object reference you're supposed to use to open a new document using a specific template in Microsoft Word? No problem! Within Word, start the macro recorder to record the steps as you select File | New and then select a document template you wish to use. To stop the macro recorder, open up the VBA editor and view what you've recorded. Your macro would look something like the following:

```
Documents.Add Template:= _
    "C:\Progra~1\Micros~1\Templa~1\Letter~1\Letter.dot" _
    , NewTemplate:=False
```

As you can see, almost everything is done for you. All you need to do is add a reference to Microsoft Word in your code. Why spend hours trying to figure it out yourself when you have a great assistant like the recorder at your disposal?

USE AS FEW "DOTS" AS POSSIBLE

As you may know, a "dot" in computerese refers to a period between words. The more dots you have within your object reference, the slower automation performance will be because it has to resolve each reference in the hierarchy as it goes. Think of them as speed bumps. The first one you run over really doesn't cause you to slow down that much, but if there are too many in a row, you're going to slow down a lot more. The same is true with dots within your automation routines. The way to reduce the number of object references is by defining each reference to the "upper levels" of the object model to object variables. Then you can use these references to create other objects further down the object hierarchy. For example, to reference all the contact names in Outlook's Contacts folder, you could use the following code:

```
Dim objOutlook As Outlook.Application
Dim oContact As Outlook.ContactItem
Set objOutlook = New Outlook.Application
For Each oContact In _
    objOutlook.NameSpace.GetDefaultFolder(olFolderContacts).Items
    Debug.Print oContact.FullName
Next
```

As you can see, the group element in the **For Each** statement is quite long. If this was someone's name, you would certainly get tongue-tied. In speech, a way to shorten it would be to use pronouns. In automation programming, you simply define certain references at the higher levels. The following code will demonstrate how to shorten the group element, making the code more efficient.

```
Dim objOutlook As Outlook.Application
Dim objNameSpace As Outlook.NameSpace
Dim oContact As Outlook.ContactItem
Set objOutlook = New Outlook.Application
Set objNameSpace = objOutlook.
For Each oContact In _
    objOutlook.NameSpace.GetDefaultFolder(olFolderContacts).Items
    Debug.Print oContact.FullName
Next
```

We've already identified that *objOutlook* is assigned to the **Outlook.Application** object/class reference.

There is no exact measurement on how much time you will save by decreasing the amount of dots.

Creating a Summary Page of Microsoft Outlook Information

Outlook.vbp

Like all Microsoft Office products, Microsoft Outlook has an object model that can be accessed through automation. You might be wondering why would you use automation rather than MAPI (Messaging API), right? MAPI is really only good for sending and receiving messages. If you want to get tasks, calendar events, contact information, and more, Outlook's object model provides connectivity to this information. The advantage of using MAPI is that you don't create an instance of Outlook like you do through automation. However, if you want to do more than just send a message, you will need to use Outlook's object model.

CODE

The following code is used to open and close an instance of Outlook.

```
Option Explicit
Public objOutlook As Object
Public objNamespace As Object
Public mFolder As Object
Public bOutlookRunning As Boolean
Public Const ErrCreatingOutlookObject$ = _
    "Could not create the Microsoft Outlook " _
    & "automation object. Check to make sure " _
    & "that Microsoft Outlook is properly installed."
```

```vba
Public Function OutLook_Open() As Boolean

    On Error Resume Next

    bOutlookRunning = False

    ' Check to see if Excel is already loaded
    Set objOutlook = GetObject(, "Outlook.Application")

    If objOutlook Is Nothing Then
        ' Create a new instance of it
        Set objOutlook = CreateObject("Outlook.Application")

        ' Check to make sure it worked
        If objOutlook Is Nothing Then
            MsgBox ErrCreatingOutlookObject
            GoTo Err_Outlook_Open
        End If

    End If

    Set objNamespace = objOutlook.GetNamespace("MAPI")
    bOutlookRunning = True
    OutLook_Open = True

Exit_Outlook_Open:
    Exit Function

Err_Outlook_Open:
    OutLook_Open = False
    MsgBox "Error: " & Err.Number & " _ " & Err.Description
    GoTo Exit_Outlook_Open
End Function
Public Sub Outlook_Close()

    On Error Resume Next

    If Not objOutlook Is Nothing Then
        objOutlook.Close
    End If

    ' If Outlook was not running before the
    ' app use it, then close it. Otherwise
```

```
    ' leave it open.
    If Not bOutlookRunning Then
        objOutlook.Quit
    End If


    ' Release the application
    Set objOutlook = Nothing

End Sub
```

ANNOTATIONS

```
Option Explicit
Public objOutlook As Object
Public objNamespace As Object
Public mFolder As Object
Public bOutlookRunning As Boolean
Public Const ErrCreatingOutlookObject$ = _
    "Could not create the Microsoft Outlook " _
    & "automation object. Check to make sure " _
    & "that Microsoft Outlook is properly installed."
```

This first section is used to define the object variables needed for the next two functions. The variables are defined as *Object* to show this example using the late-binding technique. If you want to use early binding, you need to reference the Microsoft Outlook 8.0 Type Library object model using the References dialog window.

PROGRAMMER'S NOTE   *Both Outlook 97 and 98 use the same type library.*

If you do this, you would reference the object variables as follows:

```
Public objOutlook As Outlook.Application
Public objNamespace As Outlook.Namespace
Public mFolder As Outlook.Folder
```

The **ErrCreatingOutlookObject$** constant contains an error message that is used if the Outlook object can't be loaded or is installed on the target system.

The following function is designed to determine if Outlook is already loaded. If it is, then a new instance of Outlook doesn't need to be loaded because the automation application will use the existing instance of Outlook. If it is not loaded, then a new instance of Outlook is loaded into memory. If everything within the function works, the function returns True to the procedure that called it.

```
Public Function OutLook_Open() As Boolean

    On Error Resume Next

    bOutlookRunning = False

    ' Check to see if Outlook is already loaded
    Set objOutlook = GetObject(, "Outlook.Application")
```

The **GetObject** method is used to determine if an instance of the application specified is loaded in memory. The argument, *Outlook.Application*, is the class name of an object that consists of the application's name and the object type. In this case, the application name is **Outlook** and the object type which *objOutlook* is looking for is **Application**.

```
    If objOutlook Is Nothing Then
        ' Create a new instance of it
        Set objOutlook = CreateObject("Outlook.Application")
```

If the value of the *objOutlook* object variable is Nothing, that means an instance of the Outlook object is not loaded in memory yet. If this is the case, then the **CreateObject** function attempts to instantiate an instance of Outlook and is assigned to the object variable, *objOutlook*.

```
        ' Check to make sure it worked
        If objOutlook Is Nothing Then
            MsgBox ErrCreatingOutlookObject
            GoTo Err_Outlook_Open
        End If

    End If
```

If the *objOutlook* object variable is still set to Nothing, then that means the application is having problems instantiating Outlook, which usually means that Outlook is not installed on the system. If this is the case, a message box is used to display an error message and then the error subroutine is called.

```
    Set objNamespace = objOutlook.GetNamespace("MAPI")
    bOutlookRunning = True
    OutLook_Open = True
```

If the function gets this far, the *objNamespace* object variable is assigned to the Outlook **NameSpace** object using the **GetNameSpace** object. The *bOutlookRunning* Boolean variable is set to True and the function is also set to True.

```
Exit_Outlook_Open:
    Exit Function
```

```
Err_Outlook_Open:
    OutLook_Open = False
    MsgBox "Error: " & Err.Number & " - " & Err.Description
    GoTo Exit_Outlook_Open
End Function
```

The **Exit_Outlook_Open** subroutine is used to exit the function. If the procedure is directed to go the **Err_Outlook_Open** subroutine, it means that something went wrong during the execution of the function. The function's return value is set to False and a message box displays the error number and description.

This next procedure is used to close the instance of Outlook that was opened by the **Outlook_Open** function.

```
Public Sub Outlook_Close()

    On Error Resume Next

    If Not objOutlook Is Nothing Then
        objOutlook.Close
    End If
```

If the *objOutlook* object variable is not set to Nothing, then it means that an instance of Outlook was opened by the **Outlook_Open** function. If so, then the instance of Outlook that was open is closed.

```
    ' If Outlook was not running before the
    ' app use it, then close it. Otherwise
    ' leave it open.
    If Not bOutlookRunning Then
        objOutlook.Quit
    End If
```

If Outlook was not running before this application used it, the *bOutlookRunning* Boolean value would be False. If Outlook was not running before, then it will be closed; otherwise, the application will remain open. It's not very polite to close Outlook on a user if he or she is still using it.

```
    ' Release the application
    Set objOutlook = Nothing

End Sub
```

Setting the object variable, *objOutlook*, to Nothing releases the object from memory.

TEST THE CODE

Now that we've seen how to open and close Outlook, let's see how you can incorporate some of that knowledge into a program. One of the features of Microsoft

Outlook 98 is a summary page called Outlook Today. This feature provides you with a preview of your day's events, such as appointments for the next few days, outstanding tasks, and how many new e-mail messages you have. Using Visual Basic and automation, you can access Outlook's object model and display similar information with your own application. For Outlook 97 users, this can be handy because the Outlook Today feature is not available to you.

1. Start a new project, Standard Exe. The default form may be the startup form. Before adding any controls to the form, add the Microsoft Windows Common Controls to the project. This project is going to use the **TabStrip** control. Add the controls shown in Figure 13-2, setting the properties as shown in Table 13-1. Once you've finished adding the controls and modifying their properties, save the form as **Outlook.Frm**.

Object	Property	Setting
Form	Name	frmMain
	Caption	Outlook Automation
	Height	4980
	Width	6855
Frame	Name	fraContact
	Caption	Contact Info
ComboBox	Name	cboContacts
TabStrip	Name	tabAddress
	Tab – Index	1
	Tab – Caption	Business
	Tab – Index	2
	Tab – Caption	Home
	Tab – Index	3
	Tab – Caption	Other
TextBox	Name	txtAddress
	Index	0
TextBox	Name	txtAddress
	Index	1
	Visible	False
TextBox	Name	txtAddress
	Index	2

TABLE 13-1. The Form's Objects and Properties

Object	Property	Setting
	Visible	False
Label	Name	lblEMail
	Caption	E-Mail:
TextBox	Name	txtEMail
	Index	0
	Locked	True
TextBox	Name	txtEMail
	Index	1
	Locked	True
	Visible	False
TextBox	Name	txtEMail
	Index	2
	Locked	True
	Visible	False
Frame	Name	fraInBox
	Caption	Inbox Stats
Label	Name	lblUnread
	Caption	Unread Msgs:
TextBox	Name	txtUnread
	Locked	True
Label	Name	lblInbox
	Caption	Msgs in Inbox:
TextBox	Name	txtInbox
	Locked	True
Frame	Name	fraTasks
	Caption	Active Tasks
ListBox	Name	lstTasks
CommandButton	Name	cmdClose
	Caption	Close

TABLE 13-1. The Form's Objects and Properties *(continued)*

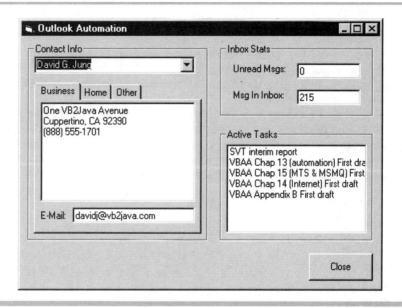

FIGURE 13-2. The Outlook Automation project at run-time

2. Add the following code to the **Load** event procedure of the form. The **Move**
   method for the form is going to center the form on the screen. The **Show**
   method is used to display the form immediately and the **Refresh** method is
   used to refresh the form on the screen. If you just used the **Show** method, the
   background of the form would display on the screen but the areas of the
   frame and other controls wouldn't materialize until after all the information
   is loaded. From a user interface standpoint, this is not acceptable. The
   Refresh method forces Windows to display the entire form before anything
   else happens. The **FillCtrlWithOutlookContacts** procedure is used to fill the
   cboContacts ComboBox with all of the names in Outlook's Contact folder.
   The **GetInboxStats** procedure is used to retrieve either the total number of
   messages in the Inbox folder or the number of unread messages in the Inbox
   folder. The **GetActiveTasks** procedure is used to retrieve all the active tasks
   found in the Task folder and fills the **lstTasks** ListBox.

```
Private Sub Form_Load()
    Me.Move ((Screen.Width - Me.Width) / 2), _
        ((Screen.Height - Me.Height) / 2)
    Me.Show
```

```
      Me.Refresh
      Call FillCtrlWithOutlookContacts(cboContacts)
      txtInbox = GetInboxStats(gInboxMsgs)
      txtUnread = GetInboxStats(gUnreadMsgs)
      Call GetActiveTasks(lstTasks)
  End Sub
```

3. Add the following code to the form's **Unload** procedure. Rather than just using the **End** statement in this procedure, we first need to remove any reference to the OLE application from memory. The code to handle this is in the **Outlook_Close** procedure. After that procedure is performed, then the program is terminated.

```
Private Sub Form_Unload(Cancel As Integer)
    Call Outlook_Close
    End
End Sub
```

4. Add the following code to the **cboContacts'** **Click** event. This procedure calls several functions for several different controls. The **GetContactInfo** and **GetContactEMail** functions will be described in greater detail later in this exercise. In a nutshell, when the user selects a contact name from the **cboContacts** ComboBox, the contact's mailing information and e-mail address are retrieved from the Contact folder and placed in the respective TextBox controls.

```
Private Sub cboContacts_Click()
    txtAddress(0) = GetContactInfo(cboContacts.Text, gBusContact)
    txtEMail(0) = GetContactEMail(cboContacts.Text, gBusContact)
    txtAddress(1) = GetContactInfo(cboContacts.Text, gHomeContact)
    txtEMail(1) = GetContactEMail(cboContacts.Text, gHomeContact)
    txtAddress(2) = GetContactInfo(cboContacts.Text, gOtherContact)
    txtEMail(2) = GetContactEMail(cboContacts.Text, gOtherContact)
End Sub
```

5. Add the following code to the **Click** event procedure of the TabStrip **tabAddress**. This is used to display specific **txtAddress** and **txtEMail** TextBox controls based on which tab was pressed. The two text boxes' **Visible** properties that correspond with the correct tab are set to True while all the other ones are set to False.

```
Private Sub tabAddress_Click()
    Dim i As Integer
    For i = 0 To tabAddress.Tabs.Count - 1
        If i = tabAddress.SelectedItem.Index - 1 Then
            txtAddress(i).Visible = True
            txtEMail(i).Visible = True
```

```
    Else
        txtAddress(i).Visible = False
        txtEMail(i).Visible = False
    End If
Next


End Sub
```

6. Add a **Module** to the project by selecting Add Module from the Project menu. Accept the default properties of the module and save the file as Outlook.bas. In the General Declarations section of the module, add the following code to set up public variables and establish constant variables.

```
Option Explicit
Public objOutlook As Object
Public objNamespace As Object
Public mFolder As Object
Public bOutlookRunning As Boolean
Public Const ErrCreatingOutlookObject$ = _
    "Could not create the Microsoft Outlook " _
    & "automation object. Check to make sure " _
    & "that Microsoft Outlook is properly installed."
Const olFolderCalendar = 9
Const olFolderContacts = 10
Const olFolderDeletedItems = 3
Const olFolderInbox = 6
Const olFolderJournal = 11
Const olFolderNotes = 12
Const olFolderOutBox = 4
Const olFolderSentMail = 5
Const olFolderTasks = 13

Public Const gBusContact = 0
Public Const gHomeContact = 1
Public Const gOtherContact = 2
Public Const gInboxMsgs = 0
Public Const gUnreadMsgs = 1
```

7. Add the **Outlook_Open** function and the **Outlook_Close** procedure to the module. The details of how these procedures work is described earlier in the "Annotations" section.

```
Public Function OutLook_Open() As Boolean

    On Error Resume Next

    bOutlookRunning = False
```

```vb
    ' Check to see if Excel is already loaded
    Set objOutlook = GetObject(, "Outlook.Application")

    If objOutlook Is Nothing Then
        ' Create a new instance of it
        Set objOutlook = CreateObject("Outlook.Application")

        ' Check to make sure it worked
        If objOutlook Is Nothing Then
            MsgBox ErrCreatingOutlookObject
            GoTo Err_Outlook_Open
        End If

    End If

    Set objNamespace = objOutlook.GetNamespace("MAPI")
    bOutlookRunning = True
    OutLook_Open = True

Exit_Outlook_Open:
    Exit Function

Err_Outlook_Open:
    OutLook_Open = False
    MsgBox "Error: " & Err.Number & " " & Err.Description
    GoTo Exit_Outlook_Open
End Function
Public Sub Outlook_Close()

    On Error Resume Next

    If Not objOutlook Is Nothing Then
        objOutlook.Close
    End If

    ' If Outlook was not running before the
    ' app use it, then close it. Otherwise
    ' leave it open.
    If Not bOutlookRunning Then
        objOutlook.Quit
    End If

    ' Release the application
    Set objOutlook = Nothing

End Sub
```

8. Add the **FillCtrlWithOutlookContracts** procedure to the module. The argument variable for this procedure accepts the name of a control. This procedure uses the late-binding technique to interact with Outlook. First the procedure checks to make sure that Outlook can be started. If so, then the object variables are assigned to their hierarchical object reference. If you've used Outlook, you know that everything is stored in folders. The folder that is going to be used for this procedure is the Contact folder; therefore, the *objFolder* object variable is assigned to the Contact folder. The **For...Each** statement is used to loop through the collection of contact names. If the **FullName** property is not blank, then the value is added to the control that was designed in the argument parameter. After all the names in the collection have been processed, the *ListIndex* value of the control is set to –1 so that no item will be selected in the control.

```
Sub FillCtrlWithOutlookContacts(ctrl As Control)

    Dim objFolder As Object
    Dim objAllContacts As Object
    Dim Contact As Object

    Screen.MousePointer = vbHourglass

    If OutLook_Open Then
        ' Set the default Contacts folder
        Set objFolder = _
            objNamespace.GetDefaultFolder(olFolderContacts)
        ' Set objAllContacts = the collection of all contacts
        Set objAllContacts = objFolder.Items
        ' Set the Contact object to ContactItem
        ' Collection of Outlook
        Set Contact = objOutlook.ContactItem
        ' Loop through each contact
        For Each Contact In objAllContacts
            ' Display the Fullname field for the contact
            If Len(Trim(Contact.FullName)) <> 0 Then
                ctrl.AddItem Contact.FullName
            End If
        Next
    End If
    ctrl.ListIndex = -1
    Screen.MousePointer = vbDefault

End Sub
```

9. Add two functions, **GetContactInfo** and **GetContactEMail,** to the module. The purpose of these functions is to get the contact information and e-mail address of a given person. The functions accept two parameters, the

sContactName string variable and the *ContactType* integer variable. The *sContactName* variable contains the name of the person whom we are looking for. The *ContactType* variable is used to denote what type of contact information we should be looking for—business, home, or other. The *objFolder* object variable is assigned to Outlook's Contact folder in order to search for the contact information we are looking for. Depending on the numeric value in the *ContactType* variable, the business, home, or other information will be retrieved from the Contact folder and returned to the procedure that called it.

```
Function GetContactInfo(sContactName As String, _
    ContactType As Integer) As String

    Dim objFolder As Object
    Dim sContact As String

    ' olFolderContacts = Contacts Folder
    Set objFolder = _
      objNamespace.GetDefaultFolder(olFolderContacts)

    With objFolder.Items(sContactName)
        Select Case ContactType
            Case gBusContact
                sContact = .BusinessAddress & vbCrLf
                sContact = sContact & .BusinessTelephoneNumber
            Case gHomeContact
                sContact = .HomeAddress & vbCrLf
                sContact = sContact & .HomeTelephoneNumber
            Case gOtherContact
                sContact = .OtherAddress & vbCrLf
                sContact = sContact & .OtherTelephoneNumber
        End Select
    End With

    GetContactInfo = sContact
    Set objFolder = Nothing

End Function
Function GetContactEMail(ContactName As String, _
    ContactType As String) As String

    Dim objFolder As Object
    Dim sEMail As String

    ' olFolderContacts = Contacts Folder
```

```
Set objFolder = _
  objNamespace.GetDefaultFolder(olFolderContacts)

With objFolder.Items(ContactName)
    Select Case ContactType
        Case gBusContact
            sEMail = .Email1Address
        Case gHomeContact
            sEMail = .Email2Address
        Case gOtherContact
            sEMail = .Email3Address
    End Select
End With

GetContactEMail = sEMail
Set objFolder = Nothing

End Function
```

10. Add the **GetActiveTasks** procedure to the module. This procedure will get all the active tasks from the Tasks folder and display them in the control designated in the procedure argument. In order to determine if the task is still active, the task's property, **Complete**, is checked. If the property is set to True, then the task is complete and it is not added to the control.

```
Sub GetActiveTasks(ctrl As Control)

    Dim objFolder As Object
    Dim objTasks As Object
    Dim sTask As Object

    Set objFolder = _
      objNamespace.GetDefaultFolder(olFolderTasks)

    Set objTasks = objFolder.Items
    ' Loop through each task and
    ' display only incomplete tasks
    For Each sTask In objTasks
        If Not sTask.Complete Then
            ctrl.AddItem sTask.Subject
        End If
    Next

    Set objFolder = Nothing

End Sub
```

11. Add the **GetInboxStats** function to the module. This function will return either the total number of messages in the Inbox folder or the number of unread messages in the Inbox. The *objFolder* folder variable is the Inbox folder. The **Count** property returns the total number of messages in the Inbox folder and the **UnReadItemCount** property returns the total number of unread messages in the Inbox folder.

```
Function GetInboxStats(InboxStats As Integer) As Integer

    Dim objFolder As Object

    Set objFolder = objNamespace.GetDefaultFolder(olFolderInbox)
    Select Case InboxStats
        Case gInboxMsgs
            GetInboxStats = objFolder.Items.Count
        Case gUnreadMsgs
            GetInboxStats = objFolder.UnReadItemCount
    End Select

    Set objFolder = Nothing

End Function
```

Unless you're using Outlook just as an Internet mail client and not using it with a corporate e-mail system, you will be prompted by Outlook to either connect to your e-mail server or work offline. Regardless of how you're using Outlook, when you run the application, an instance of Outlook is loaded in memory but is not visible. It will take about a minute for your application to gather all the contact names, e-mail totals, and active tasks. You can select any name from the Contact Info's ComboBox and the contact's corresponding information will be retrieved and displayed.

This only does a snapshot of the information stored in Outlook. If you wanted the form to update every so often, you can add the **Timer** control to the form, set the interval to 60,000, and put a call to the **GetInboxStats** function for both the total of messages in the Inbox and unread messages. The problem with using the **Timer** control though is that the highest value you can set is 65,535, which is slightly over one minute. Some people might consider that too frequent. A way around using the **Timer** control would be to add a Refresh button that allows the user to refresh the information whenever desired.

Excel.vbp

Using Microsoft Excel as a Report Writer

Occasionally, you might be handed a piece of paper and asked, "We need to get this information for a presentation this afternoon. Can you get it from the database and put it in an Excel spreadsheet for us so we can do our forecasting?" Even if this situation never arises, it's good to know that you can quickly pull information into Excel. Granted, you can do the same task with Microsoft Access, but with automation, you can do more than just a "data dump." You can format the cell sizes, change font sizes, and so on. Anything you can do in Excel, you can do with VB through automation. By using automation, you can turn Excel into a report writer.

Using Excel as a report writer sometimes is more flexible than using a third-party report writer like Crystal Reports because you have complete control over how the information is going to be laid out through automation. With most third-party report writers, you have to predefine the layout of all the information to match your query. If you want to add or remove any information in your query's result set, you will have to change the report layout. By relying on automation and Excel, the layout of your report is an open slate. Once you populate the worksheet with your data, you can format it any way you want.

CODE

The following code is used to open and close an instance of Excel.

```
Option Explicit
Public oExcel As Object
Public bExcelRunning As Boolean
Public Const ErrCreatingExcelObject$ = _
    "Could not create the Microsoft Excel automation object. " _
    & "Check to make sure that Microsoft Excel is properly " _
    & "installed."
Public Function MSExcel_Open(Optional bVisible As Boolean = True)

    On Error Resume Next

    bExcelRunning = False

    ' Check to see if Excel is already loaded
    Set oExcel = GetObject(, "Excel.Application")

    If oExcel Is Nothing Then
        ' Create a new instance of it
        Set oExcel = CreateObject("Excel.Application")

        ' Check to make sure it worked
        If oExcel Is Nothing Then
            MsgBox ErrCreatingExcelObject
            GoTo Err_MSExcel_Open
        End If
    End If
    bExcelRunning = True

    ' Make Excel Visible to the user
```

```
    If bVisible Then
        If Not oExcel.Visible Then
            oExcel.Visible = True
        End If
    End If
    MSExcel_Open = True

Exit_MSExcel_Open:
    Exit Function

Err_MSExcel_Open:
    MSExcel_Open = False
    GoTo Exit_MSExcel_Open
End Function
Public Sub MSExcel_Close()

    On Error Resume Next

    If Not oExcel Is Nothing Then
        If oExcel.workbooks.Count > 0 Then
            oExcel.ActiveWorkbook.Close False
        End If
    End If

    ' If Excel was not running before the
    ' app use it, then close it. Otherwise
    ' leave it open.
    If Not bExcelRunning Then
        oExcel.Quit
    End If

    ' Release the application
    Set oExcel = Nothing

End Sub
```

ANNOTATIONS

```
Option Explicit
Public oExcel As Object
Public bExcelRunning As Boolean
Public Const ErrCreatingExcelObject$ = _
    "Could not create the Microsoft Excel automation object. " _
    & "Check to make sure that Microsoft Excel is properly " _
    & "installed."
```

This first section is used to define the object variables needed for the next two functions. The object variable in this exercise is defined as *Object* to show this example using the late-binding technique. If you wanted to use early binding, you need to reference the Microsoft Excel 8.0 Object Library object model using the References dialog window. If you do this, you would reference the object variables as follows:

```
Public oExcel As Excel.Application
```

The **ErrCreatingExcelObject$** constant contains an error message that is used if the Excel object can't be loaded or is not installed on the target system.

The following function either will retrieve the object handle of Excel if an instance of Excel is already loaded or will open a new instance of it. The reason why it checks to see if Excel is already loaded is so another instance of Excel isn't loaded in memory. Granted, memory is inexpensive and memory management is handled a lot better with Windows 95/98/NT. It's very inconsiderate as a developer to take up your user's resources if you can use the resource that is already available to you.

The optional argument, *bVisible*, is used as a switch either to display Excel or not to display it when the function opens an instance of it. The default value of the switch is set to True; therefore, if you don't provide any value, Excel will be displayed when the instance is loaded.

```
Public Function MSExcel_Open(Optional bVisible As Boolean = True)

    On Error Resume Next

    bExcelRunning = False

    ' Check to see if Excel is already loaded
    Set oExcel = GetObject(, "Excel.Application")
```

The *bExcelRunning* Boolean variable is set to False because we don't know if Excel is running or not. Use the **GetObject** method to determine if an instance of the application specified is loaded in memory. The argument, *Excel.Application*, is the class name of the object that consists of the application's name and the object type.

```
    If oExcel Is Nothing Then
        ' Create a new instance of it
        Set oExcel = CreateObject("Excel.Application")
```

If the value of the *oExcel* object variable is Nothing, that means an instance of Excel is not loaded in memory yet. If this is the case, then the **CreateObject** function attempts to instantiate an instance of Excel and assigns it to the object variable, *oExcel*.

```
        ' Check to make sure it worked
        If oExcel Is Nothing Then
            MsgBox ErrCreatingExcelObject
            GoTo Err_MSExcel_Open
```

```
        End If
    End If
```

If the *oExcel* object variable is still Nothing, then that means the application is having problems instantiating Excel. If it couldn't start Excel, chances are Excel is not installed on the user's system. If this is the case, an error message is displayed and the function goes to an error handling subroutine.

```
    bExcelRunning = True
```

The *bExcelRunning* Boolean value is set to True to signify that Excel is now running. If the function had failed prior to getting to this line of code, the value would have been False.

```
    ' Make Excel Visible to the user
    If bVisible Then
        If Not oExcel.Visible Then
            oExcel.Visible = True
        End If
    End If
```

The **If...Then** statement checks the value of the *bVisible* Boolean variable to determine if Excel should be made visible to the user or not. If Excel was running prior to the VB application, it doesn't matter what the argument was set at because Excel would already be visible.

```
    MSExcel_Open = True
```

The function's return code is set to True.

```
Exit_MSExcel_Open:
    Exit Function


Err_MSExcel_Open:
    MSExcel_Open = False
    GoTo Exit_MSExcel_Open
End Function
```

These two subroutines are to handle exiting the function and error handling within the function. If an error occurred within the function and was directed to come to this subroutine, the function's return code would be set to False and then directed to the exit subroutine.

```
Public Sub MSExcel_Close()

    On Error Resume Next
```

```
If Not oExcel Is Nothing Then
    If oExcel.workbooks.Count > 0 Then
        oExcel.ActiveWorkbook.Close False
    End If
End If
```

The procedure checks the *oExcel* object variable to determine whether Excel is active or not. The user might have closed it before your application gets to this step. If Excel is active, the procedure goes through Excel's **Workbook** collection **Count** property to determine if there are any active workbooks. If there are, the active workbook will be closed without asking if you want to save the workbook. Excel has no way to determine if the active workbook is the one that the automation program opened versus one that was already open in Excel. If the user switched to a different workbook when this procedure is run, this is the workbook that is going to be closed and any changes will not be saved.

```
' If Excel was not running before the
' app use it, then close it. Otherwise
' leave it open.
If Not bExcelRunning Then
    oExcel.Quit
End If
```

To stop the instance of Excel that was loaded through automation, the **Quit** method is invoked on the Excel application object.

```
' Release the application
Set oExcel = Nothing
```

```
End Sub
```

Setting the object variable, *oExcel*, to Nothing releases the object from memory.

TEST THE CODE

As you can see, the process of opening an application through automation is the same from application to application. Once you understand the object model for one application, you can modify the functions to work with other applications.

In the following exercise, we're going to create a project that will return a list of students who are enrolled at a fictitious university called the University of Visual Basic. The application will generate the list of students who are enrolled in a given class and use Microsoft Excel as the report writer.

1. Start a new project, Standard Exe. The default form may be the startup form. Before adding any controls to the form, add the Microsoft ActiveX Data Object 2.0 Library to the project through the References dialog window.

PROGRAMMER'S NOTE   *If you are using VB5, you might not have ADO installed or you might have an early version of the ADO model. You can download the latest ADO components from the Microsoft Web site at* **http://www.microsoft.com/data/downloads.htm**.

2. Add the controls shown in Figure 13-3, setting the properties as shown in Table 13-2. Once you've finished adding the controls and modifying its properties, save the form as **Excel.Frm**. You might think it odd that a text box is going to be used as a status bar. In a way it is, but as you'll see in this exercise, it makes a very effective one without taking up any more custom controls.

Object	Property	Setting
Form	Name	frmMain
	Caption	View Data in Excel
Label	Name	lblClass
	BackStyle	0 - Transparent
	Caption	Class:
ComboBox	Name	cboClass
CommandButton	Name	cmdView
	Caption	View Data
CommandButton	Name	cmdPrint
	Caption	Print Data
CommandButton	Name	cmdExit
	Caption	Exit
TextBox	Name	txtStatus
	BackColor	&H80000004&
	Locked	True

TABLE 13-2.   The Excel Project's Objects and Properties

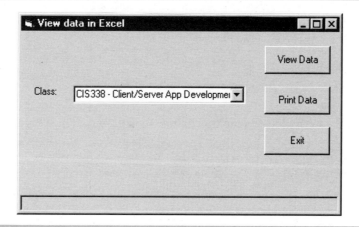

FIGURE 13-3. The Excel project at run-time

3. Add the following variables to the General Declarations section of the form. This establishes two module-wide variables. The *oConn* object variable is used to hold the ADO's Connection information. The *rs* object variable is used to hold the ADO Recordset.

```
Option Explicit
Dim oConn As ADODB.Connection
Dim rs As ADODB.Recordset
```

4. Add the following code to the **Load** event procedure of the form. The **Set** statement instantiates a new instance of the ADO Connection object. The ADO **Open** method is used to open a DSN-less connection to the Microsoft Access database, Chap13.mdb. The **Move** method for the form is going to center the form on the screen. The **LoadClasses** procedure will load the class titles into the **cboClass** combo box.

```
Private Sub Form_Load()

    ' create database connection
    Set oConn = New ADODB.Connection
    oConn.Open "driver={Microsoft Access Driver (*.mdb)};DBQ=" _
        & App.Path & "\chap13.mdb;UID=admin"
```

```
' Center form
Me.Move (Screen.Width - Me.Width) / 2, _
    (Screen.Height - Me.Height) / 2

Call LoadClasses

End Sub
```

5. Add the following code to the form's **Resize** event. This procedure uses the **txtStatus** text box's **Move** method to keep the text box aligned with the form when the form is resized by subtracting the scale height of the form from the height of the text box. It also makes sure that the text box's width is as wide as the form. It's not the most elegant status bar, but it's very functional.

```
Private Sub Form_Resize()
    txtStatus.Move 0, Me.ScaleHeight - txtStatus.Height, _
        Me.ScaleWidth
End Sub
```

6. Add the following code to the form's **Unload** procedure. The procedure will first call the **MSExcel_Close** procedure, which was described in the "Annotations" section of this exercise. Then the ADO Recordset and Connection object variables are set to Nothing to remove their instances from memory.

```
Private Sub Form_Unload(Cancel As Integer)
    Call MSExcel_Close
    Set rs = Nothing
    Set oConn = Nothing
End Sub
```

7. Add the following code to the **cboClass'** **Click** event. The **SendKey** statement in this procedure simulates the keyboard's HOME key being pressed. Seem odd? What you'll find in this exercise is that the class names are longer than the width of the combo box; therefore, when you select a class, only the end of the class name appears in the combo box. By pressing the keyboard's HOME key, the selection goes to the far left of the text and displays the first half of the class name.

```
Private Sub cboClass_Click()
    SendKeys "{home}"
End Sub
```

8. Add the following code to the **cmdView** command button's **Click** event. From the selected text in the **cboClass** combo box, the **GetData** procedure is called and the argument to determine if Excel should be displayed or not is set to True.

```
Private Sub cmdView_Click()

    Screen.MousePointer = vbHourglass

    If Len(Trim(cboClass.Text)) <> 0 Then
        Call GetData(Left(cboClass.Text, 6), True)
    End If

    Screen.MousePointer = vbDefault

End Sub
```

9. Add the following code to the **cmdPrint** command button's **Click** event.
   From the selected text in the **cboClass** combo box, the **GetData** procedure is
   called. After the data has been retrieved and placed into the Excel worksheet,
   the **PrintWorksheet** procedure is called to either print or print preview the
   worksheet. The **MSExcel_Close** procedure is used to close the instance of
   Excel that the procedure used.

```
Private Sub cmdPrint_Click()

    Screen.MousePointer = vbHourglass

    If Len(Trim(cboClass.Text)) <> 0 Then
        Call GetData(Left(cboClass.Text, 6))
        Call PrintWorksheet(Left(cboClass.Text, 6))
        Call MSExcel_Close
    End If

    Screen.MousePointer = vbDefault

End Sub
```

10. Add the following code to the **cmdExit's Click** event. The **Unload** statement
    unloads the specified form from memory, and as this is the only form loaded
    for this project, it also ends the program. The **Unload** statement is used
    instead of the **End** statement because **End** terminates the program
    immediately. The **Unload** statement invokes any code that is in a form's
    Unload event.

```
Private Sub cmdExit_Click()
    Unload Me
End Sub
```

11. Add the **GetData** procedure to the form. This procedure has two arguments,
    one required and one optional. The *sClassNbr* string variable is used to pass

the class number to the query within this procedure. The optional *bVisible* Boolean argument is used to determine if Excel is supposed to be displayed or not. The SQL statement retrieves the enrollment quarter, class name, session number, student ID, and the name of the student based on the *sClassNbr* value passed to the function. Interspersed throughout the procedure, you will find messages assigned to the **txtStatus** text box and the **Refresh** method being invoked. The messages are to provide feedback to the user as to what is happening. Some of the tasks in the procedure might take longer than a user would expect, and by providing feedback you will allay any doubts that the system might have hung or the application has stopped responding. The **Refresh** method forces the form to refresh itself to display the message in the text box. If it wasn't invoked, the message would never be displayed in the text box because the application's focus is directed to the other tasks, such as getting data from the database and interacting with Excel.

As for interacting with Excel, the procedure first checks if Excel is already loaded by using the **MSExcel_Open** function. If there is a problem with Excel, the **MSExcel_Open** function will handle the error messages, and then the procedure is aborted. If the **MSExcel_Open** function comes back as True, the function will add a new workbook to Excel. On the new workbook, a **For...Next** loop is used to process the ADO Recordset to display the column headers in first row of the workbook. The **Do...Loop** method is used to retrieve and display all the information into the recordset and then into the workbook. After all the data has been placed on the workbook, the information is formatted, making the header row text bold and adjusting all the columns' widths to be equal to the longest string value in each column.

```
Private Sub GetData(sClassNbr As String, _
    Optional bVisible As Boolean = False)

    Dim sSQL As String

    sSQL = "SELECT a.Qtr as Quarter, a.ClassNbr as Class, "
    sSQL = sSQL & "a.ClassSessionNbr as Section, "
    sSQL = sSQL & "b.StudentPIN as 'Student ID', "
    sSQL = sSQL & "b.LName + ', ' + b.FName as Student "
    sSQL = sSQL & "FROM tblEnrollment a "
    sSQL = sSQL & "INNER JOIN tblStudent b "
    sSQL = sSQL & "ON a.StudentNbr = b.StudentPIN "
    sSQL = sSQL & "WHERE a.ClassNbr = '" & sClassNbr & "' "
    sSQL = sSQL & "ORDER BY a.Qtr, a.ClassNbr, "
    sSQL = sSQL & "a.ClassSessionNbr, b.LName"

    txtStatus.Text = "Creating connection..."
    Me.Refresh
```

```
txtStatus.Text = "Opening up recordset..."
Me.Refresh
Set rs = New ADODB.Recordset
rs.Open sSQL, oConn

Dim rc As Boolean
Dim x As Integer
Dim y As Integer
x = 1

txtStatus.Text = "Opening Excel..."
Me.Refresh
If MSExcel_Open(False) Then
    With oExcel
        .workbooks.Add
        txtStatus.Text = "Filling worksheet..."
        Me.Refresh

        For x = 0 To rs.Fields.Count - 1
            y = y + 1
            oExcel.ActiveSheet.Cells(1, y).Value = _
                Trim(rs(x).Name)
        Next

        ' Add records to the worksheet
        x = 2

        Do Until rs.EOF
            For y = 1 To rs.Fields.Count
                .ActiveSheet.Cells(x, y).Value = rs(y - 1)
            Next
            rs.MoveNext
            x = x + 1
        Loop
        .Visible = bVisible
    End With
Else
    txtStatus = "Procedure aborted..."
    Me.Refresh
    Exit Sub
End If

txtStatus = "Formatting Worksheet..."
Me.Refresh
```

```
' Format the Worksheet
With oExcel
      .Rows("1:1").Select
      .Selection.Font.Bold = True
      .Rows("2:2").Select
      .ActiveWindow.FreezePanes = True
      .Columns("A:A").EntireColumn.Autofit
      .Columns("B:B").EntireColumn.Autofit
      .Columns("C:C").EntireColumn.Autofit
      .Columns("D:D").EntireColumn.Autofit
      .Columns("E:E").EntireColumn.Autofit
End With

txtStatus.Text = ""
Me.Refresh

End Sub
```

12. Add the following procedure to the form. The **PrintWorksheet** procedure
    accepts one argument, the name of the class that is to be printed. Before
    printing actually occurs, the worksheet is formatted for printing by selecting
    the first row as the "Title Row," which is to be displayed on every printed
    sheet. Also a custom header and footer is assigned to the worksheet. Some
    users of the application might not have a printer attached to their system for
    whatever reason, so the **MsgBox** function is used to ask if the user would like
    to preview the worksheet or print it out. If the user chooses Yes, then Excel's
    PrintPreview function is invoked; otherwise, the worksheet is printed.

```
Private Sub PrintWorksheet(sClassNbr As String)

    Dim rc As Integer
    Dim sMsg As String

    sMsg = "Click ""Yes"" if you want to "
    sMsg = sMsg & "preview rather than print."

    ' format worksheet for printing
    With oExcel.ActiveSheet.PageSetup
        .PrintTitleRows = "$1:$1"
        .PrintTitleColumns = ""
        .LeftHeader = "Class Enroll for &""Arial,Bold""" _
            & sClassNbr
        .CenterFooter = "Page &P of &N"
```

```
            .Zoom = 100
        End With


        rc = MsgBox(sMsg, vbYesNoCancel, App.Title)
        Select Case rc
            Case vbYes
                oExcel.Visible = True
                oExcel.ActiveWorkbook.PrintPreview
                oExcel.Visible = False
            Case vbNo
                oExcel.ActiveWorkbook.PrintOut
        End Select
    End Sub
```

13. Add the following procedure, **LoadClasses**, to the form. The function of this procedure is to obtain the course number and class descriptions from the university database and display them in the combo box on the form. First, the *rs* object variable is assigned to a new instance of the ADO Recordset object. The Recordset's **Open** method opens a query to get the class number and description from the university's class table. It fills the combo box by using the **AddItem** method of the combo box and loops through the recordset collection until the **EOF** (End-of-File) record has been reached. Once the end of the recordset is reached, the recordset is closed because it is no longer needed.

```
Private Sub LoadClasses()

    Dim sSQL As String

    Set rs = New ADODB.Recordset

    sSQL = "select ClassNbr, ClassTitle "
    sSQL = sSQL & "From tblClass "
    sSQL = sSQL & "Order by ClassNbr"
    rs.Open sSQL, oConn
    Do Until rs.EOF
        cboClass.AddItem rs(0) & " - " & rs(1)
        rs.MoveNext
    Loop
    rs.Close
End Sub
```

14. Add a **Module** to the project by selecting the Add Module from the Project menu. The default properties of the module are acceptable and save the file as

Excel.bas. In the General Declarations section of the module, add the following code to set up public variables and establish constant variables.

```
Option Explicit
Public oExcel As Object
Public bExcelRunning As Boolean
Public Const ErrCreatingExcelObject$ = _
    "Could not create the Microsoft Excel automation object. " _
    & "Check to make sure that Microsoft Excel is properly " _
    & "installed."
```

15. Add the **MSExcel_Open** function and the **MSExcel_Close** procedure to the module. The details on what these procedures do and how they work were described earlier in the "Annotations" section.

```
Public Function MSExcel_Open(Optional bVisible As Boolean = True)

    On Error Resume Next

    bExcelRunning = False

    ' Check to see if Excel is already loaded
    Set oExcel = GetObject(, "Excel.Application")

    If oExcel Is Nothing Then
        ' Create a new instance of it
        Set oExcel = CreateObject("Excel.Application")

        ' Check to make sure it worked
        If oExcel Is Nothing Then
            MsgBox ErrCreatingExcelObject
            GoTo Err_MSExcel_Open
        End If
    End If
    bExcelRunning = True

    ' Make Excel Visible to the user
    If bVisible Then
        If Not oExcel.Visible Then
            oExcel.Visible = True
        End If
    End If
    MSExcel_Open = True
```

```
Exit_MSExcel_Open:
    Exit Function

Err_MSExcel_Open:
    MSExcel_Open = False
    GoTo Exit_MSExcel_Open
End Function
Public Sub MSExcel_Close()

    On Error Resume Next

    If Not oExcel Is Nothing Then
        If oExcel.workbooks.Count > 0 Then
            oExcel.ActiveWorkbook.Close False
        End If
    End If

    ' If Excel was not running before the
    ' app use it, then close it. Otherwise
    ' leave it open.
    If Not bExcelRunning Then
        oExcel.Quit
    End If

    ' Release the application
    Set oExcel = Nothing

End Sub
```

Word.vbp

Using Automation for a Mail Merge with Microsoft Word

Microsoft Word has a lot of features as a word processor, and through automation, those features can be made available to your VB application. You can use Word as a report-writing engine, perform mail merges for mass mailings, and take advantage of its spell-checking and grammar-checking abilities.

CODE

The following code is used to open and close an instance of Word, but unlike the previous exercises in this chapter, these routines will use the early-binding technique to attach to Word's object model.

```vb
Option Explicit
Public oWord As Word.Application
Public oWordActiveDoc As Word.Document
Public oWordSel As Word.Selection
Public bWordRunning As Boolean
Public Const ErrCreatingWordObject$ = _
    & "Could not create the Microsoft Word automation object. " _
    & "Check to make sure that Microsoft Word is properly " _
    & "installed."
Public Function MSWord_Open(Optional bVisible As Boolean = True)

    On Error Resume Next

    bWordRunning = False

    ' Check to see if Word is already loaded
    Set oWord = GetObject(, "Word.Application")

    If oWord Is Nothing Then
        ' Create a new instance of it
        Set oWord = New Word.Application

        ' Check to make sure it worked
        If oWord Is Nothing Then
            MsgBox ErrCreatingWordObject
            GoTo Err_MSWord_Open
        End If

    End If
    bWordRunning = True

    ' Make Word Visible to the user
    If bVisible Then
        If Not oWord.Visible Then
            oWord.Visible = True
        End If
    End If
    MSWord_Open = True

Exit_MSWord_Open:
    Exit Function
```

```
Err_MSWord_Open:
    MSWord_Open = False
    GoTo Exit_MSWord_Open
End Function
Public Sub MSWord_Close()

    On Error Resume Next

    If Not oWord Is Nothing Then
        If oWord.Documents.Count > 0 Then
            oWord.ActiveDocument.Close False
        End If
    End If

    ' If Word was not running before the
    ' app use it, then close it. Otherwise
    ' leave it open.
    If Not bWordRunning Then
        oWord.Quit
    End If

    ' Release the application
    Set oWord = Nothing

End Sub
```

ANNOTATIONS

```
Option Explicit
Public oWord As Word.Application
Public oWordActiveDoc As Word.Document
Public oWordSel As Word.Selection
Public bWordRunning As Boolean
Public Const ErrCreatingWordObject$ = _
    & "Could not create the Microsoft Word automation object. " _
    & "Check to make sure that Microsoft Word is properly " _
    & "installed."
```

This first section is used to define the object variables needed for the next two functions. The object variables in this exercise are defined using early binding. This means that each object variable is assigned to the object and class prior to instantiating the OLE Object. By using early binding, you will also need to reference the Microsoft Word 8.0 Object Library object model using the References dialog window. The *oWord* object variable is assigned to Word's **Application** class. The *oWordActiveDoc* object variable is assigned to Word's **Document** class. The *oWordSel* object variable is assigned to Word's **Selection** class.

The **ErrCreatingWordObject$** constant contains an error message that is used if the Word object can't be loaded or it's not installed on the target system.

The following function either retrieves the object handle of Word if an instance of Word is already loaded or opens a new instance of it. The reason why it checks to see if Word is already loaded is so another instance of Word isn't loaded in memory. A lot of developers might think that loading another instance isn't so bad because memory is inexpensive and memory management is handled a lot better with Windows 95/98/NT. But it's very inconsiderate as a developer to take up your user's resources if you can use the resource that is already available to you. The satisfaction of your customers is just as important as getting a functional program delivered. The optional argument, *bVisible*, is used as a switch either to display Word or not to display it when the function opens an instance. The default value of the switch is set to True; therefore, if you don't provide any value, Word will be displayed when the instance is loaded.

```
Public Function MSWord_Open(Optional bVisible As Boolean = True)

    On Error Resume Next

    bWordRunning = False

    ' Check to see if Word is already loaded
    Set oWord = GetObject(, "Word.Application")
```

The *bWordRunning* Boolean variable is set to False because we don't know if Word is running or not. The **GetObject** method is used to determine if an instance of the application specified is loaded in memory. The argument, Word.Application, is the class name of the object that consists of the application's name and the object type.

```
    If oWord Is Nothing Then
        ' Create a new instance of it
        Set oWord = New Word.Application
```

If the value of the *oWord* object variable is Nothing, that means that an instance of Word is not loaded in memory yet. If this is the case, then the **New** method instantiates a new instance of Word and assigns it to the object variable, *oWord*.

```
        ' Check to make sure it worked
        If oWord Is Nothing Then
            MsgBox ErrCreatingWordObject
            GoTo Err_MSWord_Open
        End If

    End If
```

The **If...Then** statement checks the status of the *oWord* object variable. If it's still set to Nothing, it means that the **Set** statement couldn't instantiate Word. When this happens, it means that Word is not installed on the system that your application is running on. The **MsgBox** statement is used to display the error message that something went wrong. Then the procedure goes to an error subroutine within this function.

```
bWordRunning = True
```

The *bWordRunning* Boolean variable is set to True. The variable is global to the application and it denotes that Word was opened by your application.

```
' Make Word Visible to the user
If bVisible Then
    If Not oWord.Visible Then
        oWord.Visible = True
    End If
End If
```

This **If…Then** statement checks the *bVisible* Boolean variable. If the value is set to True, then the application checks Word's **Visible** property. If it's set to False, then the procedure sets the property to True to make Word visible to the user.

```
MSWord_Open = True
```

The return value of **MSWord_Open** is set to True because the application executed without any problems if this line of code is executed.

```
Exit_MSWord_Open:
    Exit Function


Err_MSWord_Open:
    MSWord_Open = False
    GoTo Exit_MSWord_Open
End Function
```

These two subroutines are to handle exiting the function and error handling within the function. If an error occurred within the function and was directed to come to this subroutine, the function's return code would be set to False and then directed to the exit subroutine.

```
Public Sub MSWord_Close()

    On Error Resume Next

    If Not oWord Is Nothing Then
        If oWord.Documents.Count > 0 Then
            oWord.ActiveDocument.Close False
        End If
    End If
```

The procedure checks the *oWord* object variable to determine whether Word is active or not. The user might have closed it before your application gets to this step.

If Word is active, the procedure goes through Word's **Documents** collection **Count** property to determine if there are any active workbooks. If there are, the active document will be closed without asking if you want to save the workbook.

```
' If Word was not running before the
' app use it, then close it. Otherwise
' leave it open.
If Not bWordRunning Then
    oWord.Quit
End If
```

To stop the instance of Word that was loaded through automation, the **Quit** method is invoked on the Word application object.

```
' Release the application
Set oWord = Nothing
```

```
End Sub
```

Setting the object variable, *oWord*, to Nothing releases the object from memory.

TEST THE CODE

Using Microsoft Word as an automation server, you can definitely extend the reporting capabilities of your VB applications. As you may know, Word is very useful for creating mail-merged documents and letters. Word's mail-merge functionality is pretty straightforward because you first define your database, then tie the database fields to your document by placing the database field labels on a document template. With a VB form, a database, and a Word template, you can accomplish the same thing. To accomplish this, you need to use bookmarks in a Word document at specific locations where you wish your data to be placed. When you're done placing the bookmarks through the document, save the document as a Word Template file (.dot).

Bookmarks are placeholders that can be used to move your cursor to any location throughout a document. Once the cursor is placed on the bookmark, the text or area defined as a bookmark is highlighted, which allows the highlighted text to be replaced with any new text.

To create a bookmark in a document, first place your cursor within your document where you want the bookmark to be placed. Then select Bookmark from the Insert menu. The Bookmark dialog window, shown in Figure 13-4, will prompt you for the name you'd like to give the bookmark. Press the Add button to add the bookmark to the document. To view the bookmarks placed in the document, select Options from the Tools menu. On the View tab of the Options dialog window, make sure the Bookmarks checkbox is marked. When the Bookmarks checkbox is marked, brackets ([]) surround all bookmarks in the document. Figure 13-5 shows an example of the Acceptance template document with bookmarks where the student's address and other information is going to be placed.

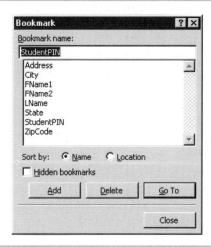

FIGURE 13-4. The Bookmark dialog window displaying the bookmarks within the document

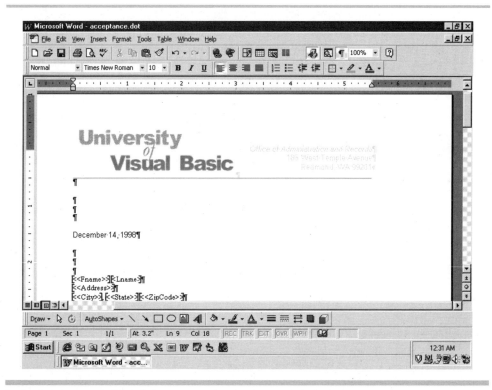

FIGURE 13-5. A Word document displaying its bookmarks

1. In Word, open a new document and save it as a template document named Acceptance.dot. The document is going to be the template of the acceptance letter to the University of Visual Basic. The bookmarks you will make will be placeholders for the students' first and last names, mailing addresses, and student PINs (personal identification numbers).

PROGRAMMER'S NOTE   *On the companion CD under Chapter 13, there is a copy of Acceptance.dot and AcceptanceEx.dot. Acceptance.dot is the template file with the bookmarks already in place. AcceptanceEx.dot contains the message for the letter and fields where the bookmarks should be placed, but the bookmarks haven't been established yet.*

2. Start a new VB project, Standard Exe. The default form may be the startup form. Before adding any controls to the form, add the Microsoft ActiveX Data 2.0 Object Library and the Microsoft Word 8.0 Object Library to the project through the References dialog window. The reference to the Word object library is made so that we can use the early-binding technique when defining our object variables.

PROGRAMMER'S NOTE   *If you are using VB5, you might not have ADO installed or you might have an early version of the ADO model. You can download the latest ADO components from the Microsoft Web site at **http://www.microsoft.com/data/downloads.htm**.*

3. Add the controls shown in Figure 13-6, setting the properties as shown in Table 13-3. Once you've finished adding the controls and modifying its properties, save the form as **Word.Frm**.

Object	Property	Setting
Form	Name	frmMain
	Caption	Student Mailer
ListBox	Name	lstStudents
CommandButton	Name	cmdPrint
	Caption	Print Letter
CommandButton	Name	cmdClose
	Caption	Close
CheckBox	Name	chkAllStudents
	Caption	All Students
Frame	Name	fraLetterType
	Caption	Type of Letter

TABLE 13-3.   The Objects and Properties for the Word Automation Project

Object	Property	Setting
OptionButton	Name	optLetter
	Caption	Intro Letter
	Index	0
	Value	True
OptionButton	Name	optLetter
	Caption	General Announcement
	Index	1
OptionButton	Name	optLetter
	Caption	Donation Letter
	Index	2

TABLE 13-3. The Objects and Properties for the Word Automation Project *(continued)*

4. Add the following variables to the General Declarations section of the form. The *optLetter* integer variable is used to keep track of which type of letter is selected to be printed.

```
Option Explicit
Dim optLetter As Integer
```

5. Add the following code to the **Load** event procedure of the form. The *db* string variable is assigned data connectivity information such as the database access driver, the database location, and the name for a DSN-less connection.

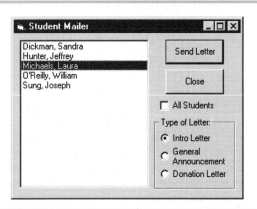

FIGURE 13-6. The Student Mailer form at run-time

The **GetStudentNames** function is used to retrieve students' names from the database. The argument passed to the function is the name of the list control that will be filled with the students' names. If the function returns a negative value, then it means that the function was not successful in retrieving the information from the database and the **MsgBox** statement is used to provide feedback to the user that something is wrong.

```
Private Sub Form_Load()
    Dim rc As Boolean

    db = "driver={Microsoft Access Driver (*.mdb)}; " _
        & "dbq=" & App.Path & "\chap13.mdb"
    rc = GetStudentNames(lstStudents)
    If Not rc Then
        MsgBox "An error occurred while trying get data " _
            & "from the database."
        Unload Me
    End If

End Sub
```

6. Add the following code to the form's **Unload** event. When this event is triggered, it calls the **MSWord_Close** procedure. This procedure closes any instance of Word or any documents that Word used while the VB application was running.

```
Private Sub Form_Unload(Cancel As Integer)
    Call MSWord_Close
End Sub
```

7. Add the following code to the **cmdClose** command button's **Click** event. The **Unload** method will invoke the form's **Unload** event. You don't use the **End** statement because that would terminate the application regardless of the state the automation objects are in. It's always a good practice to close all your connections to any referring object before terminating your application.

```
Private Sub cmdClose_Click()
    Unload Me
End Sub
```

8. Add the following code to the **cmdPrint** command button's **Click** event. The **Select Case** statement checks the value of the *optLetter* integer variable to determine which letter is going to be printed. For this exercise, only the Acceptance Letter is defined. On the companion CD under Chapter 13, you will find the completed project.

```
Private Sub cmdPrint_Click()
    Dim rc As Boolean
    Dim x As Long

    Select Case optLetter
        Case 0
            If chkAllStudents = vbChecked Then
                For x = 0 To lstStudents.ListCount - 1
                    rc = GetStudentInfo(lstStudents.ItemData(x))
                    Debug.Print x & "=" & lstStudents.ItemData(x)
                Next
            Else
                If lstStudents.SelCount = 0 Then Exit Sub
                rc = GetStudentInfo(lstStudents.ItemData _
                                    (lstStudents.ListIndex))
                Debug.Print lstStudents.ItemData _
                            (lstStudents.ListIndex)

            End If
        Case 1
            ' TODO: Add logic to print announcment letter
        Case 2
            ' TODO: Add logic to print Donation letter
    End Select
End Sub
```

9. Add the following code to the *optLetter* option button's **Click** event. The **Index** integer value is assigned to the form-level integer variable, *optLetter*. The **GetStudentNames** function is also invoked to fill the list control, **lstStudents**, with student names.

```
Private Sub optLetter_Click(Index As Integer)
    Dim rc As Boolean

    optLetter = Index
    rc = GetStudentNames(lstStudents, optLetter)
End Sub
```

10. Add a **Module** to the project by selecting Add Module from the Project menu. Accept the default properties of the module and save the file as Word.bas. In the General Declarations section of the module, add the following code to set up public variables and establish constant variables. Since we are using the early-binding technique for defining our objects, we are fully qualifying the object variables. The *oWord* object variable is assigned

to the **Word.Application** object. The *oWordActiveDoc* object variable is
assigned to the **Word.Document** object. This is only defining the variables;
this is not instantiating any instances yet. That will come later.

```
Option Explicit
Public oWord As Word.Application
Public oWordActiveDoc As Word.Document
Public bWordRunning As Boolean
Public Const ErrCreatingWordObject$ = _
    & "Could not create the Microsoft Word automation " _
    & "object. Check to make sure that Microsoft Word is " _
    & "properly installed."
```

11. Add the following function and procedure to the module. The function,
    MSWord_Open, and the procedure, **MSWord_Close**, are the same routines
    described earlier in the "Annotations" section. Refer to that section for a more
    detailed description.

```
Public Function MSWord_Open(Optional bVisible As Boolean = True)

    On Error Resume Next

    bWordRunning = False

    ' Check to see if Word is already loaded
    Set oWord = GetObject(, "Word.Application")

    If oWord Is Nothing Then
        ' Create a new instance of it
        Set oWord = CreateObject("Word.Application")

        ' Check to make sure it worked
        If oWord Is Nothing Then
            MsgBox ErrCreatingWordObject
            GoTo Err_MSWord_Open
        End If

    End If
    bWordRunning = True

    ' Make Word Visible to the user
    If bVisible Then
        If Not oWord.Visible Then
            oWord.Visible = True
        End If
    End If
    MSWord_Open = True
```

```
Exit_MSWord_Open:
    Exit Function

Err_MSWord_Open:
    MSWord_Open = False
    GoTo Exit_MSWord_Open
End Function
Public Sub MSWord_Close()

    On Error Resume Next

    If Not oWord Is Nothing Then
        If oWord.Documents.Count > 0 Then
            oWord.ActiveDocument.Close False
        End If
    End If

    ' If Word was not running before the
    ' app use it, then close it. Otherwise
    ' leave it open.
    If Not bWordRunning Then
        oWord.Quit
    End If

    ' Release the application
    Set oWord = Nothing

End Sub
```

12. Add another standard module to the project and save the file as Word2.bas. This module is going to contain all the other functions used by this application. In the General Declarations section of this module, add the code shown below. The *cn* object variable is used to reference the ADO Connection object. The *rs* object variable is used to reference the ADO Recordset object. The *db* string variable is a public variable that is used to store the database connectivity information.

```
Option Explicit

Dim cn As ADODB.Connection
Dim rs As ADODB.Recordset
Public db As String
```

13. Add the **PadStringWZeros** function to the module. This is the same function defined in Chapter 10 under the section "Adding Leading Zeros to

Numbers." This function is used to pad string values with leading zeros. For a more detailed description on how this function works, refer to Chapter 10.

```
Public Function PadStringWZeros(sSrcStr As String, _
    nPad As Integer) As String

    Dim sWorkingStr As String
    Dim nStrLen As Integer

    nStrLen = Len(sSrcStr)

     If nStrLen < nPad Then
        sWorkingStr = String(nPad, "0")
        Mid(sWorkingStr, ((nPad - nStrLen) + 1), nStrLen) = sSrcStr
        PadStringWZeros = sWorkingStr
     Else
        PadStringWZeros = sSrcStr
     End If

End Function
```

14. Add the **UnpadStringWZeros** function to the module. This is the same function defined in Chapter 10 under the exercise "Removing Leading Zeros for Display Purposes." This function is used to remove any leading zeros from the string value. For a more detailed description on how this function works, please refer to Chapter 10.

```
Public Function UnpadStringWZeros(sSrcStr As String) As String

     If IsNumeric(sSrcStr) Then
        UnpadStringWZeros = CStr(CDbl(sSrcStr))
     Else
        UnpadStringWZeros = sSrcStr
     End If

End Function
```

15. Add the **FillListBox** function to the module. This is the same function defined in Chapter 9 under the exercise "Creating a Recordset to Fill a List Box." This function is designed to take a SQL statement and display the recordset into a list control. The list control the function uses is based on the second argument, *cntl*. For a more detailed description on how this function works, please refer to Chapter 9.

```
Function FillListBox(db As String, cntl As Control, _
    Query As String) As Boolean
```

```
Set cn = New ADODB.Connection
Set rs = New ADODB.Recordset

FillListBox = False


cn.Open db
rs.Open Query, cn

If (Not (rs.BOF)) Then

    cntl.Clear

    Dim sAdd As String
    Dim bHasID As Boolean
    Dim i As Integer

    ' Assume that the first column is meant
    ' as ItemData
    bHasID = (vbLong = rs.Fields(0).Type) _
        Or (rs.Fields.Count > 1)
    Do
        For i = IIf(bHasID, 1, 0) To rs.Fields.Count - 1
            sAdd = sAdd & CStr(rs(i))
            If (i < (rs.Fields.Count - 1)) Then
                sAdd = sAdd & vbTab
            End If
        Next i
        cntl.AddItem sAdd
        sAdd = ""

        If bHasID Then
            cntl.ItemData(cntl.NewIndex) = rs(0)
        End If

        rs.MoveNext
    Loop Until rs.EOF
    FillListBox = True
End If

rs.Close
Set cn = Nothing

End Function
```

16. Add the **GetStudentNames** function to the module. The first argument is the name of the list control which the students' names will be populated with. The second argument is used to determine if all the students in the database are loaded in the list control or just the students who need a university acceptance letter sent to them. If the **OptionIndex** value equals 0, then it means the Intro Letter option button is selected and the SQL statement's **Where** clause will include *WHERE LetterSent = No* as part of the query to retrieve only the records that have the *LetterSent* value equal to No. The SQL statement, as well as the database connectivity information and list control name, is passed to the **FillListBox** function.

```
Function GetStudentNames(cntl As Control, _
    OptionIndex As Integer) As Boolean

    Dim sSQL As String
    Dim rc As Boolean

    sSQL = "SELECT StudentPIN, LName + ', ' + FName "
    sSQL = sSQL & "FROM tblStudent "
    If OptionIndex = 0 Then
        sSQL = sSQL & "WHERE LetterSent = No "
    End If
    sSQL = sSQL & "ORDER BY LNAME"

    rc = FillListBox(db, cntl, sSQL)
    GetStudentNames = rc
End Function
```

17. Add the **GetStudentInfo** function to the module. This function requires one argument to be passed to it. The value is the student's PIN (personal identification number) which is passed as the unique identifier that distinguishes one student from another. There can be multiple students with the same name but each student has a unique PIN. Once the SQL statement is constructed, it is passed to the **GetRow** function. This function performs the actual query from the database.

```
Function GetStudentInfo(StudentPIN As String) As Boolean
    Dim sSQL As String
    Dim rc As Boolean

    sSQL = "SELECT a.StudentPIN, a.FName, a.LName, "
    sSQL = sSQL & "a.Address, "
    sSQL = sSQL & "b.City, b.State, a.ZipCode "
    sSQL = sSQL & "FROM tblStudent a, tblZipCode b "
    sSQL = sSQL & "WHERE a.ZipCode = b.ZipCode "
```

```
sSQL = sSQL & "AND StudentPIN = '"
sSQL = sSQL & PadStringWZeros(StudentPIN, 10) & "'"

rc = GetRow(sSQL)
```

End Function

18. Add the **GetRow** function to the module. This module uses one argument, which is the SQL statement to retrieve the student's mailing information. The first **Set** statement instantiates a new instance of the ADO Connection object to the *cn* object variable. The next **Set** statement instantiates a new instance of the ADO Recordset object to the *rs* object variable. The ADO Connection's **Open** method then creates the connection to the database using the connectivity information stored in the *db* string variable. Once the connection has been made, the ADO Recordset's **Open** method executes the query and the result of the query is stored in the *rs* recordset object variable.

After the **Open** method is executed, the recordset object's **BOF** (Beginning-of-Flag) marker is checked. If the flag is True, that means that no data was returned from the query and the function is aborted; otherwise, the next **If...Then** statement checks the status of Microsoft Word by calling the **MSWord_Open** function. If the **MSWord_Open** function returns True, then the **Do...Loop** statement executes until the recordset's **EOF** (End-of-File) marker is True. Within the loop, the entire recordset is passed to the **GenerateLetter** function that performs the actual mail merge. When all the records have been processed, the connection to the database is closed and removed from memory.

```
Function GetRow(Query As String) As Boolean
    Dim rc As Boolean
    Set cn = New ADODB.Connection
    Set rs = New ADODB.Recordset

    cn.Open db
    rs.Open Query, cn

    If (Not (rs.BOF)) Then
        If MSWord_Open Then
            Do Until rs.EOF
                rc = GenerateLetter(rs)
                rs.MoveNext
            Loop
        End If
    End If
```

```
rs.Close
Set cn = Nothing
```

End Function

19. Add the **GenerateLetter** function to the module. This function performs the mail merge process with the data retrieved from the recordset and the document in Word. The argument passed to this function is the entire ADO Recordset which was retrieved in the **GetRow** function. Using the instance of Word that was established in the **MSWord_Open** function, a new Document object is created using the **Add** method of the **Documents** collection. This is the equivalent of selecting New from the File menu in Word. The new Document object is based on the template file, Acceptance.dot, which was created in step 1.

With the new document created, by using the **Bookmarks** collection to reference each defined bookmark, the information from the ADO Recordset replaces the bookmark placeholder text. Once all the bookmarks have been processed, the Document **PrintOut** method is used to print the letter. The document is then closed without saving the changes and the reference to the **Documents** object is released from memory. Control is then returned to the procedure that called this function.

```
Function GenerateLetter(rs As ADODB.Recordset) As Boolean

    Set oWordActiveDoc = oWord.Documents.Add(Template:= _
        App.Path & "\acceptance.dot", NewTemplate:=False)
    With oWordActiveDoc.Bookmarks
        .Item("fname1").Range.Text = rs.Fields("FName")
        .Item("lname").Range.Text = rs.Fields("LName")
        .Item("address").Range.Text = rs.Fields("address")
        .Item("city").Range.Text = rs.Fields("city")
        .Item("state").Range.Text = rs.Fields("state")
        .Item("zipcode").Range.Text = rs.Fields("zipcode")
        .Item("fname2").Range.Text = rs.Fields("fname")
        .Item("studentpin").Range.Text = _
            UnpadStringWZeros(rs.Fields("studentpin"))
    End With
    oWordActiveDoc.PrintOut
    oWordActiveDoc.Close wdDoNotSaveChanges
    Set oWordActiveDoc = Nothing
End Function
```

To see how this project works, once the application is running, you can either select one name from the **lstStudents** list box and press the Print Letter command button, or mark the All Students checkbox and press the Print Letter command button. If you just select one name, only that student's letter will be printed. If you mark the All Students checkbox, all the students listed in the list box will have a letter printed.

This exercise, as described in this chapter, only explains how to handle the Intro Letter. In the Chapter 13 subdirectory on the companion CD, this project contains the complete project, including the logic for all three letters, and updates the database when an Intro Letter is sent to a student so that he or she doesn't receive duplicate letters.

PART 3

The Internet and Distributed Computing

Internet Components

Integration with Microsoft Transaction
Server and MSMQ

Internet Components

On December 7, 1995, Bill Gates announced that Microsoft intended to develop technologies for the Internet. Since then, Microsoft has introduced many new technologies for end users and developers to publish information to and retrieve information from the World Wide Web. Microsoft has introduced Internet technologies nearly every six months. This chapter will offer background information on some of Microsoft's Internet technology and discuss where Visual Basic fits into its Internet strategy.

Internet Technology Without VB

When the European Laboratory for Particle Physics, better known as CERN, created the World Wide Web technology and made it available as an Internet service to the rest of the Internet community, it changed the way we look at information. People no longer had to use Gopher or WAIS services to retrieve information from the Internet. Hypertext-enabled documents were now available at the click of a mouse button. The World Wide Web, or Web for short, has become the highest-used technology the Internet has to offer, aside from e-mail.

The drawback of the original Web technology was that web documents were static pages with hypertext links to other static pages. Like the early versions of Visual Basic, there was no way to send or retrieve information for a database. Since then, there have been a number of various technological breakthroughs in database connectivity.

IDC/HTX

Microsoft Internet Information Server has become an integral part of Microsoft's Internet strategy. With version 1.0, you were able to interact with a database through Microsoft's Internet Database Connector/HTML Extensions (IDC/HTX) technology rather than using CGI (Common Gateway Interface) scripting. Using the

PROGRAMMER'S NOTE   *This chapter assumes that you have some knowledge of HTML (HyperText Markup Language). If you don't, you can visit Microsoft's SiteBuilder Web site at **http://www.microsoft. com/sitebuilder** or the World Wide Web (W3) Consortium's Web site at **http://www.w3c.org**. Also, in order to run any of the IDC/HTX, ASP, or IIS applications, you will need to have Personal Web Server (Win95/98) or IIS (Windows NT) installed on your system.*

analogy that you must crawl before you can walk, this definitely was Microsoft's first attempt at crawling. CGI and IDC are both methods of server-side scripting. This means that all calculations and data manipulation are processed on the Web server rather than on the client.

Contained within an IDC file is the information needed to connect to a database, execute a SQL statement that queries the database, and output the results onto an HTML document. The database connectivity information that you provide the IDC file is a specific Open Database Connectivity (ODBC) data source name (DSN) defined on the IIS server. Other database connectivity information includes any user-level security information such as user name and password.

An example of the contents of an IDC file is as follows:

```
Datasource:dsnUVB
Template:Current Enrollment.htx
SQLStatement:SELECT tblStudent.FName, tblStudent.LName,
+tblStudent.Address, tblZipcode.City,
+tblZipcode.State, tblStudent.ZipCode
+FROM tblStudent
+INNER JOIN tblZipcode ON tblStudent.ZipCode = tblZipcode.ZipCode
+ORDER BY tblStudent.LName;
Password:futile
Username:billyborg
```

In this example, the IDC file's *Datasource* argument uses the ODBC data source name **dsnUVB**, which is a System ODBC data source. Although you can't tell from the name of the argument, all ODBC data source names for Internet-based applications should be defined as a System DSN. The *Template* argument relates to the HTML Extension file that is used for output. All template files have the file extension .htx. The *SQLStatement* argument contains the SQL query that will be processed against a database. The *Password* and *Username* arguments are used to pass the user-level security information to the server.

The HTX file is a template for the HTML document. It contains field merge codes, denoted by <% %>, that indicate where the values returned by the SQL statement should be inserted. The way the HTX file works is a lot like a mail-merge document using Microsoft Word. The template file used in the IDC example was called Current Enrollment.htx. The following HTML document is really the HTML Extension document for the Current Enrollment.htx file.

```
<HTML>
<HEAD><TITLE>Current Enrollment</TITLE></HEAD>
<BODY>
```

```
<TABLE BORDER=1 BGCOLOR="#FFFFFF" CELLSPACING=0>
<CAPTION><B>Current Enrollment</B></CAPTION>
  <TR><TH>Student Name</TH>
  <TH>Address</TH>
  <TH>City</TH>
  <TH>State</TH>
  <TH>ZipCode</TH></TR>
<%BeginDetail%>
  <TR VALIGN=TOP>
    <TD><%FName%> <%LName%></TD>
    <TD><%Address%></TD>
    <TD><%City%></TD>
    <TD><%State%></TD>
    <TD><%ZipCode%></TD>
  </TR>
<%EndDetail%>
</TABLE></BODY>
</HTML>
```

The first part of the file will look familiar to you if you've done any work with HTML. It basically sets up the HTML document and prepares a table which the data will be displayed in. The field merge codes <%BeginDetail%> and <%EndDetail%> mark the beginning and end of the section where data is returned by the SQL statement. The way these codes work is similar to a loop like:

```
Do While Not rs.EOF
    'TODO: Display records here
Loop
```

Between these two codes, you list the database field names as placeholders for the data returned by the query. If no data is returned from the query, the code between <%BeginDetail%> and <%EndDetail%> is skipped.

When a client makes an HTTP Request for an IDC file on the Web server, the server finds the file on the server and runs it through the Internet Database Connector API, Httpodbc.dll. It generates a new HTML page based on the query contained within the IDC file and uses the HTX file as a template for the output. The newly created HTML file is sent back to the client in the HTTP **Response** command. Figure 14-1 illustrates an IDC/HTX workflow.

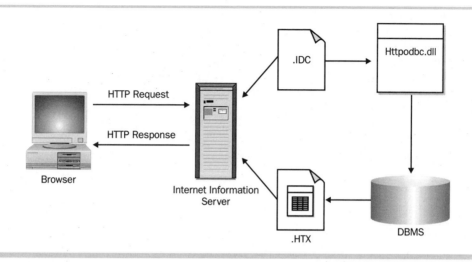

FIGURE 14-1. Workflow of an IDC/HTX request

ACTIVE SERVER PAGES

Not resting on their laurels, Microsoft was soon busy working on the next server-side scripting method that would allow you to access more than just the database information. This new strategy would also allow you to do calculations or information manipulation using ActiveScript technology as well as interact with COM objects on the servers. ActiveScript technology encompasses JavaScript, Perl, and VBScript. ActiveScript technology, combined with ISAPI, sets forth a technology called Active Server Pages (ASP). By accessing COM objects, HTML writers could now access business rules or functions that were normally available to traditional client/server applications. With the introduction of version 3.0 of the Internet Information Server, ASP has become the recommended way for organizations (assuming they're using IIS as their Web server) to make interactive, dynamic Web sites as well as Web-enabled applications. Going back to the earlier analogy, Microsoft is walking at this point.

The HTML tag that denotes an ASP script is <% %>. Any code between these two tags is executed on the server against the Internet Server Application Programming Interface, or ISAPI (pronounced "eye-sappy"), COM object. Figure 14-2 illustrates the request flow process of an ASP page. First, there is an HTTP Request for an ASP to the Web server. Because the page that is requested has the extension .asp, the server processes the request against ISAPI. When all the processing is done, the server sends the resulting HTML page back to the client in the form of an HTTP **Response** command. When the client receives the response, it processes the resulting HTML page just like any other HTML document. Because all the data processing and data manipulation is performed on the server, and the result is an HTML document, when you select View Source from your browser, you only see the resulting HTML—no server-side scripting code is viewable at all. In case you were wondering what would happen if you gave an HTML document the file extension .asp, the result would be that the document would get processed by the ISAPI COM object, and since no scripting tags were found, the HTML document would be sent back through the HTTP **Response** command.

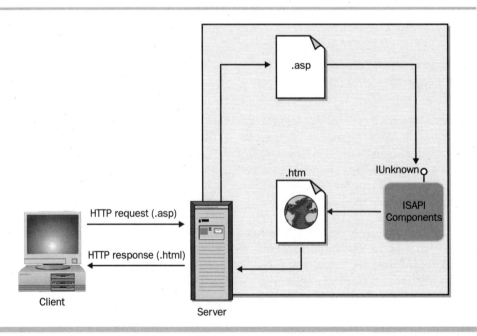

FIGURE 14-2. Workflow of an ASP page

To show an example of how ASP files differ from the IDC/HTX concept, the following code will query the same database information that was performed in the IDC/HTX example.

```
<HTML>
<HEAD>
<TITLE>Current Enrollment</TITLE>
</HEAD>

<BODY>
  <TABLE BORDER=1 BGCOLOR="#FFFFFF" CELLSPACING=0>
  <CAPTION><B>Current Enrollment</B></CAPTION>
    <TR><TH>Student Name</TH>
    <TH>Address</TH>
    <TH>City</TH>
    <TH>State</TH>
    <TH>ZipCode</TH></TR>
<%
  sSQL = "SELECT tblStudent.FName, tblStudent.LName, "
  sSQL = sSQL & "tblStudent.Address, tblZipcode.City, "
  sSQL = sSQL & "tblZipcode.State, tblStudent.ZipCode "
  sSQL = sSQL & "FROM tblStudent "
  sSQL = sSQL & "INNER JOIN tblZipcode ON "
  sSQL = sSQL & "tblStudent.ZipCode = tblZipcode.ZipCode "
  sSQL = sSQL & "ORDER BY tblStudent.LName"

  Set cn = Server.CreateObject("ADODB.Connection")
  cn.Open "data source=dsnUVB;user id=Admin"

  Set rs = cn.Execute(sSQL)

  Do While Not rs.EOF
%>
  <TR VALIGN=TOP>
    <TD><%response.write rs.Fields("FName")%> 
        <%response.write rs.Fields("LName")%></TD>
    <TD><%response.write rs.Fields("Address")%></TD>
    <TD><%response.write rs.Fields("City")%></TD>
    <TD><%response.write rs.Fields("State")%></TD>
    <TD><%response.write rs.Fields("ZipCode")%></TD>
```

```
  </TR>
 <%
  rs.MoveNext
  Loop
%>
</TABLE>

</BODY>
</HTML>
```

As you can see, scripting ASP files to get data from an ODBC data source is a lot like scripting IDC/HTX files, but with two main differences. First, rather than scripting two files you only need to script one file, and second, the data access is using the same data access methods as Visual Basic with ADO. Between the first set of ASP tags, we used the **CreateObject** method to instantiate an instance of ADO's Connection object, then opened a connection to the **dsnUVB** ODBC system data source name. Then we created a recordset using the Connection object's **Execute** method. Just like we would in a VB application, we loop through the recordset as long as the recordset's **EOF** (End-of-File) flag is not True. If the flag is set to True after the recordset object is created, then no data was returned from the query. Similar to the IDC/HTX, we intersperse HTML tags around the ASP tags. The **Response.Write** method returns the data contained within the recordset's *Field* value to the resultant HTML file returned in the HTTP **Response** command back to the client.

VISUAL BASIC AND THE INTERNET

So how does Visual Basic fit into Microsoft's Internet scheme? You could already create COM objects that could be accessed by ASP-based projects. In version 6.0, VB now has the ability to make two different Web-enabled applications. They are IIS applications and DHTML applications.

An IIS (Internet Information Server) application is a Visual Basic application that is accessed and executed from an Internet browser. It uses HTML to present information to the user and compiled Visual Basic code to manage data and perform business processes. An IIS application project can consist of references to HTML and DHTML pages, standard modules, class modules, and WebClass designers. The WebClass designer reference is a special type of object called a *webclass*. A webclass is an object that contains *webitems*, which are HTML pages, MIME-type files, or responses to an HTTP Request, and the code that delivers those webitems to a client's browser. By design, for every WebClass designer, there is one webclass. If you want to add more webclasses to your application, you must add additional designers, as shown in Figure 14-3. The file extension for a designer is .dsr.

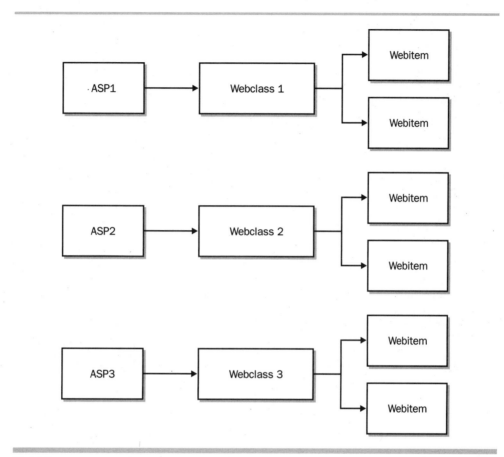

FIGURE 14-3. Architecture of an IIS application

To the casual observer, IIS applications look and feel like Active Server Pages, but unlike ASP files, all the development logic is encapsulated into a VB project rather than a series of ASP files. All your business logic and data access procedures are contained within a single ActiveX DLL that resides on the Web server and interacts with HTML pages. The ActiveX DLL generates a corresponding ASP file that is used to create an instance of the IIS application and the application interacts with the webitems defined for the object.

A DHTML application is the combination of Dynamic HTML and compiled VB code to create a Web-enabled application. DHTML itself is an extension of traditional HTML with enhancements that allow the interface to be changed by the browser without having to request more information from the server each time. This is very useful if you're creating a menu system or outline on your user interface. For example, traditionally if you wanted to display your Web site's menu or table of contents, you would use an outline paradigm. This model allows you to select from main topics, and subtopics or descriptions would appear providing more information. A lot of Webmasters have done this using JavaScript, but each time the user opts to see the subelement, an HTTP **Request** is sent back to the server to gather the requested information and return a new page to the user. Depending on your Internet traffic, this can happen almost instantaneously or it can take minutes. With DHTML, you script all the information in the HTML document with the DHTML extensions at once. When the HTML document is loaded in the browser, the user selects the elements you have designed to display more information and the browser manipulates the document accordingly. The only time a request is sent back to the Web server for more information is when you've scripted it to. A caveat about DHTML applications is that they currently only work with Microsoft Internet Explorer 4.0 and above. To learn more about DHTML itself, you can refer to the Microsoft Web site (**http://www.microsoft.com/dhtml**) or the World Wide Web (W3) Consortium's Web site (**http://www.w3c.org**).

In the earlier analogy we saw Microsoft's Internet technology crawling and walking. With Microsoft's Internet technology introduced in Visual Basic, Microsoft is definitely running! Next step—warp speed!

wcsimple.vbp

An Extremely Simple IIS Application

In every programming book there is always some really simple example that is supposed to provide you with the vision and foresight to completely understand the technology you are about to embark on. This is that example! Well, not really. This example is going to show you how simple it is to create an IIS application with just a little bit of knowledge of HTML.

CODE

The following code will display a "Hello World!" message to your default Web browser.

```
Private Sub WebClass_Start()

    'Write a reply to the user
    With Response
        .Write "<html>"
        .Write "<body>"
        .Write "<h1><font face=""Arial"">Hello World!</font></h1>"
        .Write "<p>IIS Applications Rock!</p>"
        .Write "</body>"
        .Write "</html>"
    End With

End Sub
```

ANNOTATIONS

The procedure **WebClass_Start** is the first procedure to run when an IIS application is executed. It's the equivalent of Form1 or Sub Main within a VB application.

```
With Response
    .Write "<html>"
    .Write "<body>"
    .Write "<h1><font face=""Arial"">Hello World!</font></h1>"
    .Write "<p>IIS Applications Rock!</p>"
    .Write "</body>"
    .Write "</html>"
End With
```

As described in the ASP example, **Response.Write** will return any information to the user within the HTTP **Response** command. In this example, the **With** command is used to help reference properties within the HTTP **Response** object. The result of the series of **Write** statements sends basic HTML codes back through the HTTP **Response** command to create the HTML page illustrated in Figure 14-4, saying "Hello World! IIS Applications Rock!!!"

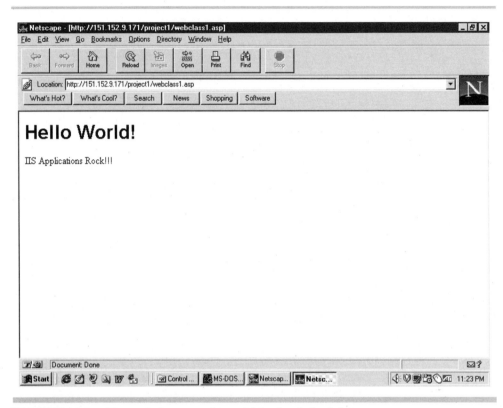

FIGURE 14-4.   The webclass running within the default browser

This is obviously an oversimplified example of what you can do with an IIS application. Honestly, you wouldn't waste your time or system resources creating an application as simple as this one. What this example does provide is an illustration of how an IIS application can be used to create Web sites that are browser-independent. All the code that went into generating this HTML page was created on the server and it doesn't matter what browser it is sending the information to.

An IIS Application with Database Access

uvb_enroll.vbp

Most of the time, when you're developing applications for the Internet, you're probably going to have some data connectivity. In Chapter 13, we worked with a fictitious school called the University of Visual Basic. This example will continue to use that database, but it's okay if you didn't work or read any of the examples in that chapter because the only commonality is the database.

SYNOPSIS OF CODE

Adding database connectivity to an IIS application really isn't any different than adding it to a regular VB application. The only real difference is the method in which the data is displayed. Rather than displaying the information on forms, it is displayed on HTML pages in the form of ASP files. But where do the HTML pages come from? At the beginning of the chapter, we discussed Microsoft's early method of data access using the IDC (Internet Database Connector) and the data we returned on HTX (HTML Extension) files. With IIS applications, HTML Extensions are back, but now they're called HTML Templates. Just like in the IDC/HTX example, HTML Templates are standard HTML files that are created using HTML authoring tools such as Microsoft FrontPage, Microsoft InterDev, and the ever-popular Microsoft Notepad. Unlike HTX files, HTML Templates can be more than just user interface forms for query results. They can be full-fledged user interface pages containing HTML form tags for data input, menu items for Web-based application navigation, and just pages that provide feedback to the user.

Within the WebClass designer, you add HTML Templates to the project the way you would form modules. The difference is that you don't use VB's IDE to create the HTML Template. With the Professional and Enterprise Editions of VB, you can install Microsoft FrontPage Express, which is an HTML WYSIWYG (what you see is what you get) editor that comes with Microsoft FrontPage, for all your HTML Template creation and manipulation. Any HTML editor will do, really. You should use the editor you're most comfortable with.

To better illustrate the components that make up an IIS application, refer to Figure 14-5. An IIS application is composed of some or all of the following elements:

◆ HTML Templates

◆ COM Objects (defined as a transaction in the Microsoft Transaction Server or a stand-alone business object on IIS)

◆ Database connectivity

The information is processed on the server and the HTTP **Response** command that is generated for the client that requested the information displays information on a standard HTML page.

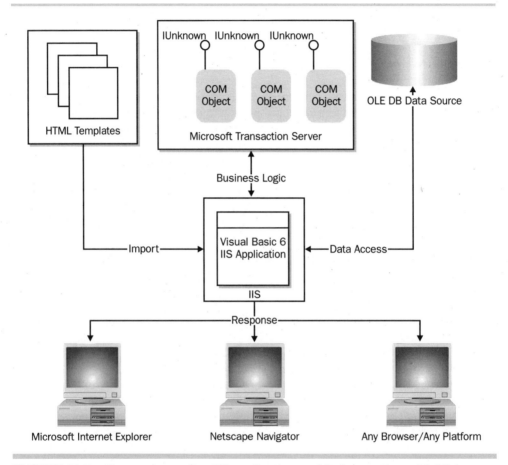

FIGURE 14-5. Components of an IIS application and its interaction with Web clients

BUILD THE PROJECT

1. Start a new project, IIS Application. Select Project1 in the Project window to give it focus in the Properties window and change the name of the project to "UVB_Enroll."

2. Before you can add any HTML Templates or custom webitems to a project, you must first save the project. Select File | Save Project to save both the designer and the project. Save the designer as UVB_Enroll.dsr and the project as UVB_Enroll.vbp.

3. After the project has been saved, double-click on the Designers in the Project window. This will expand the tree and display the IIS application's webclass module, WebClass1. Double-click on WebClass1 to open up the WebClass designer.

4. Add the HTML Templates found on the companion CD in the UVB_Enroll subdirectory of Chapter 14. Click on the Add HTML Template WebItem icon in the WebClass designer's toolbar. In the Open dialog box, go to the directory where the HTML files are located and add the Default.HTML file to the project. When the item is added, it will be named "Template1." Rename the item "Default" and press ENTER. The HTML Template is named "Default" because as in most HTML projects, the first HTML document is named "Default.html." We're just doing this to be consistent.

   You will notice that the HTML page is parsed and that each HTML tag contained within the HTML document is displayed in the right window pane, as illustrated in Figure 14-6. You can create custom events that run when one of the tags is about to be interpreted by the client browser. In the case of HTML forms, data captured in the HTML form fields are passed back to the server.

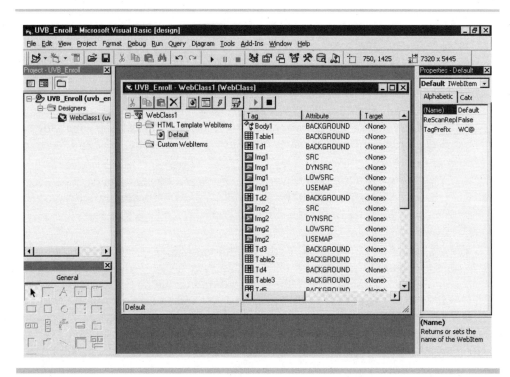

FIGURE 14-6. The HTML Template, Default, and all its HTML tags displayed in the WebClass designer

5. To make this project the first HTML page to be displayed, we will need to add some code to the project. Select "Default" with the right mouse button and select View Code from the context menu. Find the procedure **WebClass_Start** and remove all the code within the procedure, then replace it with the following code:

```
Private Sub WebClass_Start()
        Set NextItem = Default
End Sub
```

It doesn't look like much, but what we just did is tell the IIS application that the next HTML Template to be displayed is the HTML Template webitem "Default."

6. Add the following code to the procedure **Default_Response**. This code will return the HTML Template with the webitem object and return the result to the client's browser.

```
Private Sub Default_Respond()
    Default.WriteTemplate
End Sub
```

7. Return to the WebClass designer and double-click on the form tag item Submit. This will cause a custom event to be created for the Submit button. In the code window, add the following code:

```
Private Sub Default_Submit()

    Dim StudentID As String
    Dim StudentPWD As String

    StudentID = Request.Form.Item("STUDENTID")
    StudentPWD = Request.Form.Item("PASSWORD")

    ' Is Student ID blank?
    If Len(Trim(StudentID)) <> 0 Then
        ' Determine if login is valid
        If StudentLogin(StudentID, StudentPWD) Then
            Set NextItem = Approved
        Else
            Set NextItem = Denied
        End If
    Else
        Set NextItem = Default
    End If

End Sub
```

The **Form.Item** property of the ASPTypeLibrary **Request** object is used to obtain information from an HTML's form item, such as a text or list box. In this procedure, it retrieves the information from the text boxes, StudentID and Password, and stores them into local string variables. The procedure first checks to make sure that the StudentID text box contains a value; otherwise the main page is redisplayed. Assuming the StudentID text box does contain a value, an **If-Then** statement calls the procedure **StudentLogin** to determine if the user entered the correct information.

8. Before we proceed with defining the **StudentLogin** function, we need to add a reference to the Microsoft ActiveX Data Object 2.0 Library and define a few variables that need to be available throughout the project. Add the following code to the General Declarations section of the webclass:

```
Option Explicit
Option Compare Text
Dim StudentFName As String
Dim StudentLName As String
Dim cn As ADODB.Connection
```

9. Create the **StudentLogin** function to determine if the user entered a valid student ID and password. The function accepts two string arguments, one for the student ID and another for the student password. The first thing this function does is determine if there is a connection to the database established by calling the **ConnLive** function. If there is a valid connection, then a query is performed to retrieve the student's name based on the student ID and password entered into the HTML form. If the user entered the correct student ID and password, the student's first and last names will be returned to the recordset and they will be assigned to their appropriate variables. If the recordset returns empty, that means the student information was entered incorrectly and the function will return False as the return code for the called procedure.

```
Function StudentLogin(sStudent As String, _
    sPassword As String) As Boolean
    Dim rs As ADODB.Recordset
    Dim sSQL As String

    If ConnLive() Then

        sSQL = "SELECT fname, lname "
        sSQL = sSQL & "FROM tblStudent "
        sSQL = sSQL & "WHERE studentPIN = '"
        sSQL = sSQL & PadStringWZeros(sStudent, 10)
        sSQL = sSQL & "' AND Password = '" & sPassword & "'"

        Set rs = New ADODB.Recordset
        rs.Open sSQL, cn
```

```
    If Not rs.EOF Then
        StudentFName = rs(0)
        StudentLName = rs(1)
        StudentLogin = True
    Else
        StudentLogin = False
    End If

    rs.Close

End If

End Function
```

10. Add the **ConnLive** function to the module. The function checks for the existence of a valid database connection. If a connection already exists, the function returns True as the return value to the function that called it. Otherwise, it attempts to make a connection to the database using a DSN-less connection method. If the connection attempt still fails, then something is wrong with the database or the method in which the connection is trying to be made.

```
Function ConnLive() As Boolean

    ConnLive = False

    If cn Is Nothing Then
        Set cn = New ADODB.Connection
        cn.Open "driver={Microsoft Access Driver (*.mdb)};" _
            & "dbq=" & App.Path & "\uvb.mdb"
        If cn Is Nothing Then
            MsgBox "Can't make a connection. " _
                & vbCrLf & Err.Description
            Exit Function
        End If
    End If

    ConnLive = True

End Function
```

11. Add the **PadStringWZeros** function to the module. This is same function defined in Chapter 8 under the "Add Leading Zeros to Numbers" section. This function is used to pad string values with leading zeros. For a more detailed description on how this function works, refer to Chapter 8.

```
Public Function PadStringWZeros(sSrcStr As String, _
    nPad As Integer) As String

    Dim sWorkingStr As String
    Dim nStrLen As Integer

    nStrLen = Len(sSrcStr)

      If nStrLen < nPad Then
         sWorkingStr = String(nPad, "0")
         Mid(sWorkingStr, ((nPad - nStrLen) + 1), nStrLen) = sSrcStr
         PadStringWZeros = sWorkingStr
      Else
         PadStringWZeros = sSrcStr
      End If

End Function
```

12. Now that we have all the code in place for the login routine, we need to add a few more HTML Template webitems to the project. Like we did in step 4, go back to the WebClass designer and click on the Add HTML Template WebItem icon in the WebClass designer's toolbar. In the Open dialog box, add the HTML Template webitems listed in Table 14-1.

HMTL Template	Rename to
Denied.HTML	Denied
Approve.HTML	Approved
Curriculum.HTML	Curriculum

TABLE 14-1. HTML Template Webitems to Be Added and Their Webitem Names

13. Add the following code to each **Respond** method for each of the HTML webitem objects we just added to the project:

```
Private Sub Denied_Respond()
    Denied.WriteTemplate
End Sub
Private Sub Approved_Respond()
    Approved.WriteTemplate
End Sub
Private Sub Curriculum_Respond()
    Curriculum.WriteTemplate
End Sub
```

The first time you run the application, it will go through a series of questions that you will need to answer. On the UVB_Enroll – Project Properties dialog box, as shown in Figure 14-7, select OK to accept the defaults. Your default browser will be used to display the application. On the Create Virtual Root dialog box, as shown in Figure 14-8, also choose OK. The name in the dialog box is the name of the virtual root that is created within IIS or Personal Web Server.

FIGURE 14-7. The UVB_Enroll-Project Properties dialog box

FIGURE 14-8.   The Create Virtual Root dialog box

Once the main Default page is loaded, type in the following student ID and password to gain access to the system:

StudentID = 2401
Password = 186232

Once you gain access, the Approved HTML Template will be shown. This HTML page sets up the environment to display information in frames.

Sequencing in IIS Applications

Sequence.vbp

In the previous example, we illustrated how to access an IIS application with a simple login routine that accesses a database for user validity. Savvy Web users will figure out that your security isn't very sophisticated and just bookmark the Web page after the login page so that they don't have to log in each time. As the saying goes, "Your armor is only as strong as the weakest link."

You can't prevent a user from bookmarking any page within your IIS application, but you can add a simple routine at the beginning of each HTML Template that checks a variable which you assign to the **Session** object. Just like in an ASP-based project, the **Session** object is used to maintain information about the current user's session and stores and retrieves state information.

CODE

```
' Has the user already logged in?
If CBool(Session("LoggedIn")) = True Then
    NextItem = Approved
Else
    ' User did not login in from main page
    ' or they had bookmarked the page
```

```
    Session("LoggedIn") = StudentLogin(StudentID, StudentPWD)
    If CBool(Session("LoggedIn")) = True Then
        Set NextItem = Approved
    Else
        Set NextItem = Denied
    End If
End If
```

ANNOTATIONS

The code illustrated here is based on the code found in step 7 of the previous exercise for the **Default_Submit** procedure.

```
If CBool(Session("LoggedIn")) = True Then
    NextItem = Approved
Else
```

This portion of the **If-Then** statement checks to see if the **Session** object property **LoggedIn** is True or False. If the value is True, then the approved HTML Template is assigned to the **NextItem** property; otherwise, the **If-Then** statement continues on to the **Else** portion of this procedure.

```
' User did not login in from main page
' or they had bookmarked the page

    Session("LoggedIn") = StudentLogin(StudentID, StudentPWD)
```

This statement calls the **StudentLogin** function defined in step 9 of the previous exercise. It takes the Student ID and password entered from the main page and checks the student database to determine if the information was entered correctly. If the information is correct, the return value of True is returned and assigned to the **Session** object property, **LoggedIn**.

```
    If CBool(Session("LoggedIn")) = True Then
        Set NextItem = Approved
    Else
        Set NextItem = Denied
    End If
```

This **If-Then** statement is used to reevaluate the **Session** object property, **LoggedIn**. If the **StudentLogin** function returned True, the **Session** object property will be True and the approved HTML webitem is assigned to the **NextItem** property; otherwise, the denied HTML webitem is assigned to the **NextItem** property.

You will add this to the beginning of each HTML Template webitem that is "beyond" the main login screen in order to prevent a user from entering the application through the "backdoor." When you do so, just change

```
        Set NextItem = Approved
```

to whatever HTML Template is supposed to be displayed.

Process Validation with DHTML

dhtml_enroll.vbp

Unlike HTML, DHTML lets you add programs to your Web page that can change all aspects of the page. That's why the "D" stands for "Dynamic." The page can change its layout, validate data, and so on without having to transmit any information back to server. The fundamental concept behind this was the introduction of an *object model* into the Web browser itself. As you might already know from developing in VB, an object model defines and exposes all the features of an object. The object model for DHTML is no different. There is one *big caveat* about the DHTML object model: Not all DHTML object models are created equal, which means that Microsoft's implementation of the DHTML object model is different than Netscape's implementation. This section is going to focus strictly on Microsoft's version of DHTML.

In order to access the object model, you need to write scripts to manipulate the page. Microsoft's Internet Explorer (MSIE) 3.*x* and higher provides two built-in scripting language interpreters, VBScript and JScript. But only version 4.*x* and higher contain the DHTML object model, so unless your organization has standardized on (or has access to) MSIE 4.*x* or greater, you can't take advantage of this technology.

Going back to scripting, in the past most articles, tutorials, books, white papers, and so on only showed scripting DHTML using JScript, which is Microsoft's version of JavaScript. From all accounts, this was because DHTML worked better using JScript than VBScript. With VB able to create DHTML applications, you can now use VBA as your scripting language. If you wrote a DHTML application the old-fashioned way, using your favorite DHTML editor and so on, the source for all your DHTML applications is viewable to anyone who selects View Source in his or her browser. With a DHTML application created in VB, the source the user would see is the HTML used to create the page and a reference to an ActiveX DLL. That's right, VB compiles all the DHTML scripting you write into an ActiveX DLL that gets installed on the client's system, and is removed after the application terminates. Since it's deployed as an ActiveX DLL, you should change the DLL Base Address from &H11000000 to something more useful. Refer to Chapter 12 for more information about the DLL Base Address.

SYNOPSIS OF CODE

The most common usages for DHTML is for creating tree-type sitemaps and menus in outline format, and for dynamically changing graphics and text. One great use for a DHTML is for data validation for a Web-enabled application. In most Windows-based applications, there are field validation routines to ensure that data entry is fairly accurate. An example would be a field validation routine for a social security number field. You would want to ensure that only numbers were entered into the field.

In Web-based applications using HTML and server-side scripting, you would have to wait until the person filled out the entire form before any validation would be completed. You could also use client-side scripting to handle the field validation, but if you wanted to use the same validation routine on more than one form, you would have to copy it onto each form. If the routine changed, the developer would have to go back to each form to make the modification. You can see that there is a high probability of error in this method.

DHTML applications in Visual Basic are a lot like traditional VB applications, only the forms are written in HTML versus form modules. You can write the same type of routines in a DHTML application as you would in a VB application. You write the function or procedure once, and you can use it throughout your application.

In the next section, we are going to build part of a DHTML application for online enrollment into the fictitious University of Visual Basic.

BUILD THE PROJECT

1. Start a new project and select DHTML Application from the New Project dialog box. You will notice that in the Project window, a standard module and a DHTML designer come with each DHTML application. You can add as many DHTML pages as your project needs—it's just like adding form modules. Also, in the Toolbox, you will notice a tab entitled HTML. This contains HTML form controls, text boxes, list boxes, and so on. You can add any ActiveX control you like to the project to enhance your user interface. If you want to add the Microsoft Access Calendar Control so all your users can select from a calendar, you can. Just remember that any control you add to the form will have to be included in your application's CAB file so that it can be installed on the client's system.

2. Select the project name in the Project window to give it focus in the Properties window. Change the name of the project from DHTMLProject to **dhtml_Enroll.**

3. Click the plus (+) sign next to the Designer folder in the Project window. This expands the folder to reveal the default DHTML page that is generated with each new project. Double-click on DHTMLPage1 and it will load the DHTML Designer. Just like a lot of the designers, it has an explorer-type interface with a tree view of your HTML file's tag structure on the left side and an editor on the right.

    When working with a DHTML application, just as with an IIS application, it's probably best to create your HTML file outside of the VB environment. VB doesn't provide the best editing facility nor does it have any HTML validation checkers like some of the dedicated HTML editors such as Microsoft InterDev and Allaire's HomeSite do.

4. In the Properties window, change the ID and Name of DHTMLPage1 to Enroll.

5. On the DHTML Designer window, select the DHTML Page Designer
    Properties button from the toolbar (it's the first button on the second toolbar).
    This displays the Properties page for the DHTML document. Select the Save
    HTML In An External File radio button. Click on the Open button to load an
    existing HTML file for the project. Use the HTML file entitled
    Enrollment.html found in Chapter 14 on the companion CD. Your screen
    should look similar to Figure 14-9. To expand and contract the HTML tag
    hierarchy, click on the plus (+) or minus (–) signs.

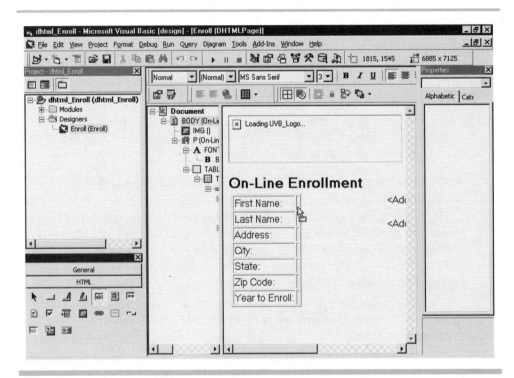

FIGURE 14-9.   The DHTML Page Designer with the external HTML page,
                   Enrollment.html, loaded

6. Now we're going to add all text fields and buttons to the HTML document
    using the controls found under the HTML tab on the Toolbox. We didn't add
    the form tags in the HTML editor for a reason. By adding the controls to the
    HTML document in VB, VB's IDE includes many extended attributes from
    the DHTML object model to the controls. This makes scripting the controls
    much easier. Add the controls and update their properties as found in Table
    14-2. To add the controls to the form, either you can drag the control from the
    Toolbox to where you want it placed, or you can select the tool from the

Toolbox and draw the control on the DHTML document like you would on a form.

Object	Property	Setting
TextField	ID	txtFname
	MaxLength	20
	Name	txtFname
	Size	20
	Value	"" (blank)
TextField	ID	txtLname
	MaxLength	30
	Name	txtLname
	Size	30
	Value	"" (blank)
TextField	ID	txtAddress
	MaxLength	50
	Name	txtAddress
	Size	50
	Value	"" (blank)
TextField	ID	txtCity
	MaxLength	50
	Name	txtCity
	Size	50
	Value	"" (blank)
TextField	ID	txtState
	MaxLength	2
	Name	txtState
	Size	2
	Value	"" (blank)
TextField	ID	txtZipCode
	MaxLength	5
	Name	txtZipCode
	Size	5

TABLE 14-2. Enrollment.html's Objects and Properties

Object	Property	Setting
	Value	"" (blank)
Select	ID	cboYear
	Name	cboYear
	Value	"" (blank)
SubmitButton	ID	btnSave
	Name	btnSave
	Value	Save
ResetButton	ID	btnClear
	Name	btnClear
	Value	Clear

TABLE 14-2.   Enrollment.html's Objects and Properties *(continued)*

7. To add year values to the Select control, click on the ellipse on the Custom field in the Properties window. This will bring up the control's Property Pages, as shown in Figure 14-10. Add the Text and Value entries shown in Table 14-3.

Text	Value
1999	1999
2000	2000
2001	2001
2002	2002

TABLE 14-3.   Text and Value Properties of the cboYear Select Control

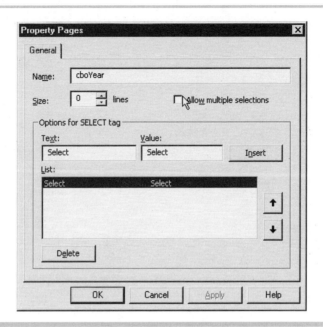

FIGURE 14-10. The Property Pages for the Select control

8. Add the following code to the **OnBlur** event for the **txtFName** textarea
    control. **OnBlur** is the equivalent of the **LostFocus** event of a VB control. The
    code is used to check if there are any numbers in the person's name by
    passing the text value of the control to a function called **ContainNumbers**. If
    the text value does contain numbers, it will return True as the return code
    and a message box will notify the user that there was an error in his or her
    data entry. Then the cursor is returned to the control that had the incorrect
    value. The **Focus** event is the equivalent to VB's **SetFocus** event.

```
Private Sub txtFName_onblur()
    If ContainNumbers(txtFName.Value) Then
        MsgBox "You entered an invalid character in your name"
        txtFName.focus
    End If
End Sub
```

9. Add the following function to either the **modDHTML** standard module or the DHTML's code page. This function checks to see if the passed string argument contains any numbers. If it does, the function returns True; otherwise, it returns False to the procedure that called this function.

```
Public Function ContainNumbers(CheckValue As String) As Boolean
    Dim x As Integer
    Dim nLen As Integer

    ContainNumbers = False

    nLen = Len(CheckValue)
    If nLen = 0 Then
        Exit Function
    End If

    For x = 1 To nLen
        If IsNumeric(Mid(CheckValue, x, 1)) Then
            ContainNumbers = True
            Exit Function
        End If
    Next

End Function
```

10. Add the following code to the **OnBlur** event of the **txtLName** textarea. The code is used to check if there are any numbers in the person's name by passing the text value of the control to a function called **ContainNumbers**. If the text value does contain numbers, it will return True as the return code and a message box will notify the user that there was an error in his or her data entry. Then the cursor is returned to the control that had the incorrect value.

```
Private Sub txtLName_onBlur()
    If ContainNumbers(txtLName.Value) Then
        MsgBox "You entered an invalid character in your name"
        txtLName.focus
    End If
End Sub
```

11. Add the following code to the **OnBlur** event of the **txtState** textarea control. It uses the **ContainNumbers** function to determine if any numbers were entered in this field. It doesn't check for valid state abbreviation. That would be left up to another function. If a state abbreviation does not contain any numbers, the procedure will capitalize both characters by using the **Ucase** statement.

```
Private Sub txtState_onblur()
    If ContainNumbers(txtState.Value) Then
        MsgBox "You entered an invalid character for the State Code."
        txtState.focus
    Else
        txtState.Value = UCase(txtState.Value)
    End If
End Sub
```

12. Add the following code the DHTMLPage's **Load** event. This will make the **txtFName** textarea control the first control to receive focus.

```
Private Sub DHTMLPage_Load()
    txtFName.focus
End Sub
```

Press F5 to start the application. Click OK on the Debugger window. Your default browser, presumably MSIE 4.*x* or greater, is launched and loads the application's page, as shown in Figure 14-11.

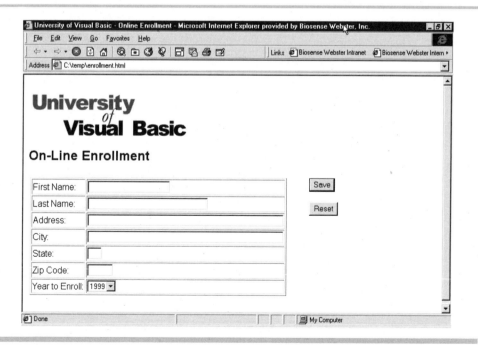

FIGURE 14-11. The University of Visual Basic's On-Line Enrollment form, a DHTML application running in MSIE 4.*x*

To deploy a DHTML application, compile it into an ActiveX DLL. Run the Package and Deployment Wizard to create a CAB file for all the contents of the application just like any other application. You will need to copy any HTML files associated with the project to your Web server because the Package and Deployment Wizard only includes files that are related to the ActiveX DLL itself.

When the user of the application goes to the HTML page of the application, the browser is instructed, through the object model, to check to see if any of the ActiveX DLL and related files are installed on the client's system. The CAB file is then downloaded to the client's system and the items that aren't on the system are extracted from the CAB file and registered on the client's system.

CHAPTER 15

Integration with Microsoft Transaction Server and MSMQ

Creating an MTS Component
(MTSProj.vbp and TestApp.vbp)

Deploying an MTS Component

Using the MTS Component from VB
(TestComp.vbp)

S ince Microsoft has been spreading the word about distributed computing, transaction processing, and message queues, one might think that these are entirely new concepts. The savvy software developer who has been around for a while knows that these concepts aren't new at all. They've been around for years on mainframe and midrange computers systems. But now that more and more companies are relying on local area and wide area networks rather than large mainframe and midrange systems, a lot of the development techniques are finally being addressed by Microsoft.

Distributed computing is not a new concept. To a lot of people, distributed computing means "client/server," where you have a client that makes requests through an application and a server that services the requests. Client/server computing comes on many different levels where the components of the client and server are broken down. Figure 15-1 depicts just some of the various client/server models. Most people can identify with both versions A and B, where the client workstation contains only the user interface or the user interface and business logic for the application. The network server contains both the business logic and database support. This is known as two-tiered client/server computing because the application is distributed on two different environments.

In versions C and D, an additional network server is used to help distribute some of the workload of the application so that separate components can operate independently from one another to complete their various tasks. By moving the business components to their own server, the processes can be completed without interfering with any database processes. For example, in versions A and B, all the business processes are being processed on the same server; therefore, both processes are fighting for both processor time and disk access time. By separating them onto different servers as illustrated in versions C and D, all business processes and database processes have their own processor and disk access. If a business process doesn't need any disk access, it doesn't have to contend with processes that only need database access.

Microsoft has seen the advantage of distributed computing, and through the years they have introduced development models that exemplify this. They first introduced this through the use of automation. As discussed in Chapter 13, we saw how developers could save time by reusing elements of other applications and integrating their processes into another application.

As the model expanded, Microsoft introduced a new model called COM (Component Object Model). This provided the foundation from which all applications with interoperability would be defined.

Windows DNA

With all these components (Visual Basic, automation, and COM) defined, refined, and enhanced, an organization still needs a blueprint to show how all the various components and technology fit together to provide enterprise-wide solutions. Windows DNA provides this blueprint.

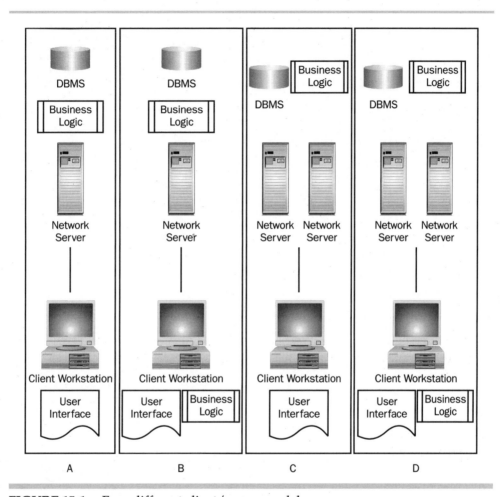

FIGURE 15-1. Four different client/server models

Windows Distributed interNet Applications (DNA) architecture is a framework for building a new generation of computing solutions that brings together the worlds of business computing and the Internet. That's right, this model also includes the Internet. Microsoft realizes that the Internet is more than just a series of computers linked together for providing information; it's a transport mechanism that businesses can use to leverage their technology and customer base. Windows DNA is one of the first application architectures to fully embrace and integrate both the Web and client/server models of application development based on Windows NT. By using the Windows DNA model, developers can build modern, scalable, multitiered business applications based on Windows NT that can be delivered over any network. Figure 15-2 provides a breakdown of the elements that make up the Windows DNA architecture.

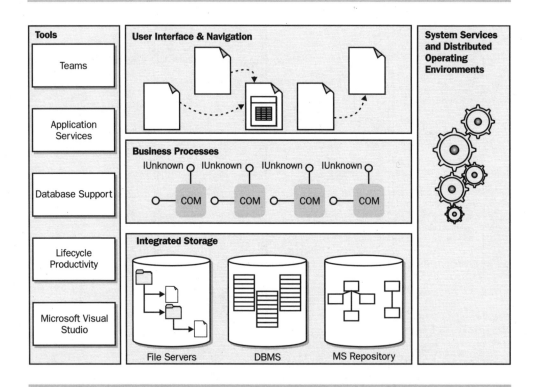

FIGURE 15-2. Windows DNA architecture

Windows DNA unifies the most important application programming models by defining specific points of integration between them. Using scripting and components, it gives developers easy ways of moving between programming models to accomplish their application objectives. For example, an Internet developer can write a script that instantiates an object created with Visual Basic directly into a page for dynamic execution. This script can invoke a control written in C++, which calls a remote line-of-business object written in Java running on a server. And that Java component can exchange information with a DBMS on a database server.

This is just a high-level overview of Windows DNA. For more information, you should visit Microsoft's Web site at **http://www.microsoft.com/dna**.

Transaction Processing

A *transaction* is a collection of database actions that represent a unit of work. A transaction can have many parts, and all parts must succeed in order for the transaction to be valid or it will be rolled back to its original state. *Rollback* is a term in transaction processing that allows any particular transaction to be returned to its original state. In Chapter 9, "Using Transactions with ADO" illustrated how ADO (ActiveX Data Object) can be used for transactions through the use of **BeginTrans,** **CommitTrans,** and **RollbackTrans** methods. Most DBMS environments also provide a way to handle transactions within their stored procedures.

Using ADO, or any of the data access models, is good for a unit of work that consists of one transaction. Using a stored procedure is also a good way to perform transaction processing. But in either case, there doesn't seem to be an easy way to coordinate a nested transaction. For example, in a financial institution, a nested transaction would be transferring money from one account to another. The unit of work for this transaction would be validating that the account does have ample money to transfer, withdrawing the money from one account, and then depositing the withdrawn amount to the new account. If something goes wrong during the middle of the transaction, you need to know how to set all the records back to the way things were before the transaction began. As a developer, you would have to program the proper steps to roll back each transaction within the unit of work in order to roll the transaction back successfully.

Mainframe environments use transaction monitors, such as IBM's CICS, to manage large numbers of simultaneous transactions against a DBMS. The Microsoft Transaction Server (MTS), Microsoft's transaction monitor, is designed for robustness and scalability to the client/server arena. It comes with database support for Microsoft SQL Server and Oracle and will be extended to support DBMS environments in the future.

A transaction should function as a consistent and reliable unit of work for the database system and must pass a so-called "ACID" test to determine that it has the following four key properties:

♦ *Atomic:* All of the work gets done or none of the work gets done.

♦ *Consistent:* The operation being performed is legal and does not endanger the system's integrity.

♦ *Isolated:* The behavior of a transaction is independent of the actions of any other transaction.

♦ *Durable:* Once a transaction has been completed, the work is committed to storage before reporting a success.

Essentially, a transaction forms a binding contract between a client application and the components running on the server. Once the server's components signal the client that a transaction has succeeded, it has effectively guaranteed to the client that it has committed the transaction to storage. Conversely, if the server's components signal the client that the transaction was aborted, the client application assumes that an attempt was made to perform the transaction but failed, and the server will be in a state as if the transaction was never attempted in the first place. Using the analogy of the bank transfer again, what would happen if an error occurred between the process of transferring the money from one account to another? Without a transaction monitor, you would have to know how to roll back each process in order to restore the system to the way it was prior to the beginning of the transaction. With a transaction monitor, the entire unit of work is monitored so that nothing is completely committed to storage until the entire transaction is validated as having been processed correctly. And not only does the transaction monitor oversee that one transaction, it monitors all the transactions that are occurring.

As you can see, transactions greatly simplify the code that you have to write to recover from error conditions. A transaction will either commit in its entirety or roll back in its entirety; therefore, your error-recovery code doesn't have to struggle with undoing partially completed work.

MTS Services

MTS provides your distributed application a number of services that you would normally take into account, but it also allows you to manage the application on a large scale. You will find that MTS is a valuable ally in the development of your distributed applications.

SESSION MANAGEMENT

Maintaining each connection between the client and the server involves establishing some form of session between them. A *session* requires memory resources to store its state and process resources to maintain and update its state. By *state*, we're referring to the server knowing which clients are logged in and connected to at all times. This knowledge is passed on to the applications running on the server, so it can provide data caching and other services to that client as required. If you've done any work with Web-based applications, you've probably discovered that the Internet technology is more or less a stateless environment. This means that each time a user navigates through your Web site, the server doesn't know if you're the same person or if a new person has jumped to the page. By using the session information and cookies, you produce a quasi-state environment.

The cost of maintaining session information is the burden of the server, because there are typically far more clients than there are servers. In a traditional two-tiered client/server environment, you might have a situation where there are x clients that are connected to y server. This means that the total number of connections is x times y. In other words, if you have 10,000 users connecting to 10 servers, the server would need to maintain 100,000 separate sessions to manage.

By adding a transaction monitor like MTS into the fray, you can reduce the amount of sessions required to maintain state throughout your distributed environment. Using the same 10,000 users, if we introduce 10 transaction monitors, each can effectively manage 10% of the total workload; therefore each one maintains 1,000 sessions with its clients. Each transaction monitor must also manage connections to all of the servers; in other words, it also maintains 10 sessions to the servers. The total number of sessions calculates out to 1,000 + 10, or 1,010 sessions, versus the 100,000 separate sessions in our scenario without transaction monitors. By reducing the amount of sessions, we reduce the amount of system resources needed to manage the sessions. This can translate into the system being able to handle more users, which brings us to our next point: server resource management.

SERVER RESOURCE MANAGEMENT

Even by adding transaction monitors into the architecture, it's still possible that we can exceed the threshold of any server. Too many users can exact a toll on both memory and processing time for any given transaction. If you happen to reach beyond the limits of your system, your processor might end up spending too much time juggling all the active sessions instead of dedicating some of its time to processing work that it is supposed to be doing.

In the previous section, we showed you how a transaction monitor can coordinate the activities of one or more servers. More importantly, you can place logic within the transaction monitor that allows for efficient sharing of database connections in a scheme known as *connection pooling*. Connection pooling is not a new concept to the Microsoft development environment. It has been available through DCOM since its introduction in version 4.0 of VB.

MTS ships with a component called the *ODBC resource dispenser*, which automatically pools ODBC connections to ODBC-compliant databases. Pooling can yield significant performance gains, since it eliminates the overhead of constructing and tearing down an ODBC connection each time a user submits work to an ODBC database. Instead, the ODBC resource dispenser maintains a pool of preexisting ODBC connections and assigns incoming work to the next available connection, similar to how a bank assigns incoming customers to the next available teller.

DATA CONTENTION

In distributed database applications, the biggest barrier to scalability is contention for database records. Database manufacturers like Microsoft and Oracle spend hundreds of thousands of man-hours and dollars optimizing their database-locking technology to leverage maximum performance without a database administrator's intervention. But all the burden of database optimization doesn't lie solely on the DBMS. The application developer has a responsibility as well to ensure that he or she isn't providing any more database contention than what is necessary to do the task at hand. In other words, if a developer only needs to return information from a table for a report, it would seem silly for him or her to issue a database lock on the entire table. You might laugh, but it's been known to happen.

The developer can control two elements: (1) the number of database locks held by an application and (2) the amount of time the application holds on to those locks. Redesigning the application code can minimize the number of locks held by the application. Placing code that manipulates the data closer to the database can help minimize the amount of time that an application holds onto a database lock as well.

In a traditional two-tier client/server environment, a lot of the database activity is done through the use of SQL stored procedures. Unfortunately, the language used to implement stored procedures is, on the whole, not based on any object-oriented programming language. Also, database administrators (DBA) usually develop stored procedures since most developers don't have authority to create them on the database server.

MTS objects can be written using virtually any programming language such as VB, C/C++, Delphi, and even Assembler. An MTS object, like any business object, resides on the middle tier of a three-tier client/server environment. These middle-tier components let you centralize the application logic that accesses your databases. More importantly, by centralizing your data access in components that can take advantage of connection pooling and higher-speed connections to the database servers, the total time that database locks are held by these components is minimized. The amount of contention for data in the database services tier is also minimized.

NETWORK ROUND TRIPS

Another factor that can limit the scalability of your application is the total number of network round trips required to do a unit of work on your server. In today's object-oriented client/server applications, we typically perform three atomic operations, each requiring at least one network round trip to perform a given operation. These steps are creating an instance of an object on the server computer, invoking one or more methods on the object, and destroying the object on the server computer.

Since these are middle-tier objects, they are usually acquiring expensive resources to do this work. Typically, these expensive resources are database connections and database locks. For our application to scale, it is essential that we conserve these resources; therefore, application programmers have traditionally created the objects just when they needed to use them and destroyed them immediately thereafter. The implication of this tactic is that we must pay the price of at least three network round trips to invoke a method on a server-side object—create, use, and then destroy.

By requiring three round trips to perform a single logical operation, we introduce yet another potential bottleneck and thus limit the scalability of the application. Additional remote procedure call (RPC) run-time resources are required to handle the overhead of processing three distinct messages where only one does meaningful work. In theory, the operations required to create and destroy the object can be optimized out of existence.

MTS reduces the number of round trips required to perform a single operation to *almost* one. It optimizes the creation and destruction operations out of existence through its use of a *context wrapper* object. The context wrapper object, along with its associated context object, forms an *object run-time environment*, which is conceptually the object that the client application sees.

For MTS to eliminate the need for a client application to create and destroy MTS objects, the client application must follow a completely different set of rules, acquiring a reference to the MTS object as early as possible and releasing it as late as possible. This lets MTS create an instance of the MTS object whenever an incoming procedure call comes in. When the object signals to MTS that it has finished doing what it needed to be doing, MTS destroys it but keeps the context wrapper alive to service the next incoming request. This effectively allows MTS to leverage an object's creation and destruction overhead across the total number of times that you invoke methods on the object.

The MTS network round-trip optimization is called *just-in-time activation*, and the key is the MTS context wrapper object, which implements the methods for the interfaces implemented by the actual object. It is created dynamically at run-time by MTS and is inserted transparently between the client application and the real MTS object. The context wrapper creates an instance of the MTS object at the moment it receives an incoming call from a client application—hence the term *just-in-time* activation.

For MTS to create a context wrapper object for *any* MTS object dynamically, it must know the intimate details of the object's interface. That requires that an MTS object meet a certain set of requirements. This will be discussed in "Creating an MTS Component," later in this chapter.

SECURITY

Programmers who have implemented server-side security have had to deal with a plethora of Windows NT data structures and API functions. To eliminate much of the details that have been associated with security programming, MTS introduced the concept of *role-based security*. To use role-based security, we must group our MTS components into *packages* and assign *roles* to those packages during development. For example, you could create Manager and Teller roles. At deployment time, a Windows NT administrator assigns actual users to the roles defined during development. At run-time, users who have been assigned to particular roles will be allowed or denied access to different pieces of functionality within the MTS package.

Role-based security allows MTS to make security checks automatically. When a client application attempts to make a call into an MTS object, MTS performs a security check on the client. The security check is concerned with *authentication* and *access control*. Authentication involves ensuring that users are who they say they are. MTS takes advantage of Windows NT's existing security infrastructure to perform the authentication. Access control is concerned with whether a user is permitted to perform the operation he or she is requesting. MTS checks whether a user has been assigned to a particular role to determine whether or not the request will succeed.

Message Queues

Essentially, message queuing is application-to-application communication, but unlike e-mail, information that is sent from one application to another is data, not a message, so the terminology might seem misleading. Regardless, the term "message queuing" is an established term in the industry so you can't blame Microsoft for this one. One of the best-known message-queuing applications is IBM's MQ (Message Queue) Series, which probably had an influence on Microsoft's effort to name its own product, the Microsoft Message Queue Server (MSMQ).

To understand message queues, we first need to discuss the types of messaging that can occur. There are essentially two forms of communication pathways: synchronous and asynchronous. In a *synchronous* environment, a sending application has to establish a connection to the receiving application before a message or data is sent. Once the data is sent, the sending application must wait for a response from the receiving application before any further processing can be performed. An analogy of synchronous communication would be a telephone call. In order for any communication to be performed, you need to contact the person you need to communicate with. Once you make the connection, you provide the receiver with information and wait for the receiver to respond before you can do anything else.

In an *asynchronous* environment, the sender makes a request to a receiver application, but rather than waiting for a response, the sender can continue processing information. It's up to the sender to determine when to process a response from the receiver, if it requests to process the response at all. In some cases, a response might not be required. An analogy of asynchronous communication would be an e-mail environment. You can send out dozens of messages to various people. You can do this while online with your network or Internet service provider, or offline while you're traveling on your mobile computer. When the message is sent, you're not concerned with whether the receiver is available or not. There are times when you don't expect an immediate response back from the receiver because some work might have to be done on the receiver's end. You're only concerned about whether or not the message got through.

Message queuing provides a way to implement asynchronous communication into your environment. Requests are sent and responses are received as messages and processed. Messages are stored in a message queue on the sending system before being transmitted to a message queue server. Storing messages in a queue is important for providing disaster recovery. If a transaction sent via a queue is lost or damaged, you can just resubmit the queue from the sending system to continue processing. On a message queue server, there is a service called the *queue manager*, whose purpose is to determine if a message in the queue is supposed to be delivered to an application on its server or forwarded on to a different server. Again using the analogy of e-mail, when you send a message to your e-mail server, it first determines if the message you sent is to be delivered to a user that you identified as a local user or forwarded to a different e-mail server.

We've explained what message queuing is, but why is it important? There are basically five different reasons why message queuing can be advantageous. The first reason is that your organization might have a lot of systems and networks to interact with. We can't always assume that an application is going to be 24/7 (24 hours a day/7 days a week). There are some systems that only process information nightly. In a synchronous environment, if you were processing information against a system that only worked on a nightly basis, you wouldn't get that much work accomplished. By using message queues, you can send your requests to the queue to be processed at a later time and you'd receive an acknowledgment that your request had been processed. Also, as much as we'd like to think that our computers and network environment are bulletproof, the reality is that this isn't always the case. There are going to be times when the network connection is down, a server fails, and so on. With message queues, you can store all transaction requests and process them when the system or network becomes available. With the number of environments becoming distributed, the failure rate of an entire environment multiplies. If a transaction requires interaction with five different systems and the up-time ratio of each system is 95%, you've just increased your probability of a system failure somewhere within the transaction.

The second reason to use message queues is coupled with the first reason: the cost of system failure. As systems multiply, environments become more distributed, and so on, system failure and transaction recovery becomes a cost factor. Imagine how much the Home Shopping Network or stockbrokers would lose if their customers' transactions were lost due to a "hiccup" in the system? Also, when system failures occur, a lot of times human intervention is needed in order to resolve any failure and restart the system.

The third reason why message queues are advantageous is that there is a growing population of mobile users. As the term "mobile" implies, these computer users are probably not connected to their networks at all times; therefore, they need to be able to process information in a disconnected manner in order to get their work completed. An example of a mobile user would be an insurance claims adjuster. If the adjuster needed to be connected at all times in order to process a policy or claim, imagine how long the process would take if he or she had to find a phone line to make a connection, or reached a busy signal, or if the system was down or network traffic was being drained because a department had engaged in a Quake II deathmatch.

The fourth reason for message queuing is to establish workload priorities. If a lot of low-priority transactions, like address changes, are being processed before higher-priority changes, like a transfer of funds from your holdings account to purchase stock in the IPO (initial public offering) of the next hot Internet stock, your consumers will be very upset. In a traditional environment, most transactions are processed in a FIFO (first-in, first-out) manner. In the banking community, this is not always acceptable because a lot of processing, such as payroll and mortgage payments, is now done electronically. For example, you may have direct-deposit with your employer and get paid the same day your mortgage payment is due. In a FIFO environment, the transaction that comes in first gets processed first. That means that if the mortgage payment transaction comes in before your paycheck, you might be overdrawn, which would subject you to late fees, overdraft charges, and so on. By using the message queue priority, you can ensure that all credits to your customers' accounts occur before any debits.

The last reason for using message queuing is when there is a significant concurrency issue. As more and more systems become distributed, the number of users increases, and the number of system connections increases, there is going to be an increased amount of concern that all the transactions occur in a timely and orderly manner. Another concern is that system response time and data availability is available when needed. A message queue can be used as an intermediary buffer for transactions. For example, in the case of trading stocks, there is a high need for systems to be available at all times and that the transactions get committed to the system in real time (or its closest equivalent). If a message queue is used as an intermediary buffer for transactions, if for some reason a server crashes or isn't processing fast enough, any open transactions aren't lost because they haven't been cleared out of the buffer and new transactions can still be accepted. When the server comes back online or when another server is freed up to handle the buffer, the transactions start processing again with no loss of information.

Creating an MTS Component

MTSProj.vbp
TestApp.vbp

Creating an MTS component may sound like a difficult task, but it really isn't any different than developing any other component with VB. There are, however, a few basic requirements that must be met in order for a component to work with MTS.

An MTS component must be created as a 32-bit ActiveX DLL, which means that it must meet the general requirements for COM objects. These requirements are that it must be a self-registering DLL that exports the DLLRegisterServer and DLLUnregisterServer functions, and it must implement the entry points DLLGetClassObject and DLLCanUnloadNow. Additionally, the MTS component must be created through a standard class factory object that implements the IClassFactory interface. Most development tools like Delphi, Visual Basic, Visual J++, and Visual C++ can create ActiveX DLLs that fit these requirements.

MTS also needs to know the function names and parameter types for all interfaces implemented by an MTS component. There are some restrictions with respect to the properties of the interfaces that are implemented by an MTS component. The interface definition information must be provided in some kind of machine-readable form, so that MTS can dynamically create the context wrapper object. The context wrapper object is what external clients see as the actual MTS object. An MTS component's interfaces must be automation-compatible, in which case the MTS object's type library provides the interface definition, or they must be standard-marshaled interfaces that use the fully interpreted marshaler, in which case the proxy/stub DLL provides the interface definition. Marshaling allows interfaces exposed by an object in one process to be used in another process.

This may sound like a lot of steps, but as you'll see in the "Test the Code" section below, it's not as difficult as it may sound.

CODE

```
Public Sub Login(sID As String, sPassword As String, _
    vRecNames As Variant, vRecValues As Variant)

    Dim objContext As ObjectContext
    Set objContext = GetObjectContext()

    On Error GoTo err_Login

    Dim sSelect As String
    Dim sWhere As String

    sSelect = "fname, lname"
    sWhere = "StudentPIN = '" & PadStringWZeros(sID, 10) & "' "
    sWhere = sWhere & "AND Password = '" & sPassword & "' "

    GenericRead "DSN=dsnUVB;UID=admin;PWD=;", "tblStudent", _
        sSelect, sWhere, vRecNames, vRecValues

    objContext.SetComplete
    Exit Sub

err_Login:

    objContext.SetAbort

End Sub
```

ANNOTATIONS

Now you're probably looking at the code and thinking, "How is this any different from what I've normally done?" For the most part, your suspicions are correct. The code listed above is like any other transaction that you've done before, with one exception—it references the MTS **ObjectContext** object model. But let's first explain what this function does.

```
Public Sub Login(sID As String, sPassword As String, _
    vRecNames As Variant, vRecValues As Variant)
```

The **Login** procedure is designed to accept two arguments, the StudentID and the password, and return the column name and value within each column into the two variant arrays, *vRecNames* and *vRecValues*, respectively.

```
Dim objContext As ObjectContext
Set objContext = GetObjectContext()
```

The next two steps in the procedure are the two elements that are going to make this procedure realize that the result of this transaction is going to be handled by MTS. The first line dimensions the *objContext* object variable to the **ObjectContext** object model. The **Set** statement obtains a reference to the **ObjectContext** object model that's associated with the current MTS object. The **ObjectContext** object model provides access to a single MTS object, sometimes referred to as the *root object*. Once the root object has been instantiated, you can create additional objects, also known as *enlisted objects*, which will run within the same context as the root object. By tying these objects together under a single **ObjectContext** object, MTS allows you to manage multiple transactions with multiple data sources through a single object interface. If a transaction fails within any enlisted object, the error is reported back to you via the **ObjectContext** interface. It's this interface that triggers MTS to know that if one part of the transaction fails, the entire transaction fails.

```
On Error GoTo err_Login
```

The **On Error** statement is used to control where the flow of logic goes in case an error occurs within the procedure. The flow of logic is going to go to the **err_Login** label within this procedure.

```
Dim sSelect As String
Dim sWhere As String

sSelect = "fname, lname"
sWhere = "StudentPIN = '" & PadStringWZeros(sID, 10) & "' "
sWhere = sWhere & "AND Password = '" & sPassword & "' "
```

The next two statements assign a SQL statement's SELECT and WHERE clauses that are going to be passed to a generic database access procedure called **GenericRead**. This procedure will be explained in greater detail in the "Test the Code" section of this exercise.

```
GenericRead "DSN=dsnUVB;UID=admin;PWD=;", sSelect, _
    "tblStudent", sSelect, sWhere, vRecNames, vRecValues
```

The **GenericRead** procedure is called to retrieve information based on the passed parameters. In this example, the procedure is using a DSN connection called **dsnUVB** and the login ID is **admin**; no password is needed to access the database.

The procedure is going to attempt to retrieve for the **tblStudent** table the first and last name of the student whose PIN and password equal the value that was originally passed to this procedure. If there is a match, the column names and their values will be stored in the variant arrays, *vRecNames* and *vRecValues*, respectively.

```
objContext.SetComplete
Exit Sub


err_Login:


objContext.SetAbort


End Sub
```

The above procedures are the final steps that make this procedure a MTS transaction. If the procedure executes without an error, the **ObjectContext** object variable, *objContext*, needs to be told that the transaction has completed successfully. Having *objContext* call the **SetComplete** method does this. By doing so, you're telling MTS that the current enlisted object has completed its work and should be deactivated when the currently executing method returns to the client application. For objects that are executing within the scope of a transaction, this is also an indication that the object's transactional updates can be committed to the database server. In case an error occurred within this procedure, the flow of logic will go to the **err_Login** label. Within this subroutine, the *objContext* object variable calls the **SetAbort** method. You call the method within the error handler to ensure that the transaction aborts when the error occurs. If this is the root of the transaction, the MTS aborts the transaction. If this object is part of a unit of work, then the entire unit of work will be aborted, even if the previous components executed successfully.

TEST THE CODE

In the following exercise, we're going to create an MTS component that is part of a login transaction for the fictitious university called University of Visual Basic.

1. Start a new ActiveX DLL project. An ActiveX DLL basically is going to consist of class and standard modules. All Class modules within the project must have their **Instancing** property set to 5 – **MultiUse** in order to work with MTS.

2. In order to reference the MTS object model, we'll need to reference the Microsoft Transaction Server Type Library in the References dialog box. If your development system does not have MTS loaded on it, you can browse your network for the ActiveX DLL, mtxas.dll. Using the Project | References submenu from the VB main menu, select the references shown in Table 15-1. If other references are checked that aren't in this table, unmark them so your project isn't cluttered with DLLs that you aren't using.

References
Microsoft Visual Basic for Applications
Visual Basic Runtime Objects and Procedures
Visual Basic Object and Procedures
OLE Automation
Microsoft Transaction Server Type Library

TABLE 15-1.   References Used in the UVBComp Project

3. Version 6.0 provides a new property to allow you to set the transactional attribute for each class module within your project. The property is **MTSTransactionMode**, and it maps directly to the transaction attributes within MTS. Table 15-2 shows the relationship between the VB property and the MTS transaction attribute. The value of the **MTSTransactionMode** property automatically sets the transaction attribute for the object when the component is added to MTS. For this exercise, set the property to 2.

4. Another requirement that MTS has is that all components built in VB use Apartment threading; therefore, you will need to make sure that Apartment Threaded is selected in the Threading Model frame of the Project Properties dialog box. Select Project | Project1 Properties from the VB main menu. We are now going to update the project's property information in order to make this component unique. Use the information found in Table 15-3 to fill in the Project1 Properties dialog box. For a more detailed explanation as to why the DLL Base Address needs to be changed, refer to Chapter 12.

VB Property	MTS Transaction Attribute
0 – NotAnMTSObject	N/A
1 – NoTransactions	The component does not run within the scope of a transaction.
2 – RequiresTransaction	The component will run within an existing transaction if one already exists. If not, MTS will start a new instance of the component.
3 – UsesTransaction	The component will run within an existing transaction if one exists; otherwise, it will run without a transaction.
4 – RequiresNewTransaction	The component requires a new transaction each time an instance of the component is referenced.

TABLE 15-2.   VB's Properties for **MTSTransactionMode** and Their MTS Transaction Attribute Meanings

Tab	Field Name	Property
General	Project Name	UVBComp
	Project Description	UVB Components
	Threading Model	Apartment Threading
Make	Application Title	Enrollment
	Auto Increment	Mark Box
Compile	DLL Base Address	&H2400000
Component	Project Compatiblity	Mark Option

TABLE 15-3. UVBComp Project's Properties

5. Add the **Login** procedure to the Class1 module. This is the same procedure described earlier in the "Annotations" section of this exercise. Refer to that section for a more detailed description.

```
Public Sub Login(sID As String, sPassword As String, _
    vRecNames As Variant, vRecValues As Variant)

    Dim objContext As ObjectContext
    Set objContext = GetObjectContext()

    On Error GoTo err_Login

    Dim sSelect As String
    Dim sWhere As String

    sSelect = "fname, lname"
    sWhere = "StudentPIN = '" & PadStringWZeros(sID, 10) & "' "
    sWhere = sWhere & "AND Password = '" & sPassword & "' "

    GenericRead "DSN=dsnUVB;UID=admin;PWD=;", sSelect, _
        "tblStudent", sWhere, vRecNames, vRecValues

    objContext.SetComplete
    Exit Sub

err_Login:

    objContext.SetAbort

End Sub
```

6. Change the name of the class module from Class1 to Enrollment and save the
file as Enrollment.cls. Change the name of the project from Project1 to
UVBComp and save the project as UVBComp.vbp.

7. Add a standard module to the project. Change the name of the module from
Module1 to basEnrollment and save the file as Enrollment.bas. This module is
going to contain the procedure and functions to be shared only by the
component. Add the **GenericRead** procedure to the module to handle all the
basic database query operations.

```
Public Sub GenericRead(sDSN As String, sTableCols As String, _
    sTable As String, sWhereClause As String, _
    rgPropNames As Variant, rgPropValues As Variant)

    Dim nFields As Integer
    Dim i As Integer
    Dim sSQL As String
    Dim conn As New ADODB.Connection
    Dim rs As New ADODB.Recordset

    sSQL = "SELECT " & sTableCols
    sSQL = sSQL & " FROM " & sTable
    sSQL = sSQL & " WHERE " & sWhereClause

    conn.Open sDSN
    rs.Open sSQL, conn

    nFields = rs.Fields.Count - 1

    ReDim rgPropNames(nFields)
    ReDim rgPropValues(nFields)

    If Not rs.EOF Then
        ' populate the property bag
        For i = 0 To nFields
            rgPropNames(i) = rs.Fields(i).Name
            rgPropValues(i) = rs(i)
        Next i
    Else
        ' empty result set
        For i = 0 To nFields
            rgPropNames(i) = rs.Fields(i).Name
            rgPropValues(i) = Empty
        Next i
    End If
```

```
    rs.Close
    conn.Close

End Sub
```

8. Add the **PadStringWZeros** function to the module. This is the same function defined in Chapter 10 under the section "Add Leading Zeros to Numbers." This function is used to pad string values with leading zeros. For a more detailed description on how this function works, refer to Chapter 10.

```
Public Function PadStringWZeros(sSrcStr As String, _
    nPad As Integer) As String

    Dim sWorkingStr As String
    Dim nStrLen As Integer

    nStrLen = Len(sSrcStr)

    If nStrLen < nPad Then
        sWorkingStr = String(nPad, "0")
        Mid(sWorkingStr, ((nPad - nStrLen) + 1), nStrLen) = sSrcStr
        PadStringWZeros = sWorkingStr
    Else
        PadStringWZeros = sSrcStr
    End If

End Function
```

9. Add the **UnpadStringWZeros** function to the module. This is the same function defined in Chapter 10 under the exercise, "Remove Leading Zeros For Display Purposes." This function is used to remove any leading zeros from the string value. For a more detailed description on how this function works, please refer to Chapter 10.

```
Public Function UnpadStringWZeros(sSrcStr As String) As String

    If IsNumeric(sSrcStr) Then
        UnpadStringWZeros = CStr(CDbl(sSrcStr))
    Else
        UnpadStringWZeros = sSrcStr
    End If

End Function
```

Now, unlike with non-MTS components, you can't just test this component by creating another application that instantiates the object and uses its methods and properties. In order to make sure that the logic of this component works, you should comment out all the code relating to the **ObjectContext** object model. The lines of code you should comment out are:

```
'    Dim objContext As ObjectContext
'    Set objContext = GetObjectContext()
'
'    On Error GoTo err_Login
'    objContext.SetComplete
'    Exit Sub
'err_Login:
'    objContext.SetAbort
```

10. Once you have commented out the **ObjectContext** object model references, you can then execute the component and run another program against it. When you run the component, you will most likely receive a warning message box, as shown in Figure 15-3. This warning is to remind you that you're attempting to run a component that is designed for MTS and that you are strongly encouraged to set the Version Compatibility option to Binary Compatibility and register the component with the transaction server. Since we are merely testing the component and we haven't compiled it into an ActiveX DLL, select Yes from the dialog box to continue. You can't select the Binary Compatibility option until you've created the ActiveX DLL first.

11. Start a new instance of VB and select a Standard Exe application. The default form may be the startup form. Add the controls shown in Figure 15-4, setting the properties as shown in Table 15-4, then save the project as TestApp.

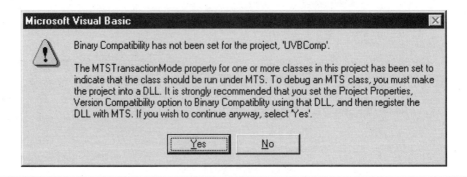

FIGURE 15-3.   Binary Compatibility warning message

FIGURE 15-4. The Logon form at run-time

PROGRAMMER'S NOTE *The location of the UVBLogo.gif file varies depending on whether you copied any of the files from the companion CD to your hard drive or embedded the image right from the CD. Please make the appropriate changes to the file's path.*

Object	Property	Setting
Form	Name	frmLogin
	BorderStyle	3 – Fixed Dialog
	Caption	"" (leave blank)
	ControlBox	False
Image	Name	imgLogo
	BorderStyle	1 – Fixed Single
	Picture	d:\source\chap15\uvbLogo.gif
Label	Name	lblStudentPin
	BackStyle	0 – Transparent
	Caption	Student PIN
Label	Name	lblPassword
	BackStyle	0 – Transparent
	Caption	Password
TextBox	Name	txtUserID
	Text	"" (leave blank)
TextBox	Name	txtPassword
	PasswordChar	"*" (without quotes)

TABLE 15-4. Objects and Properties for the TestApp Project

Object	Property	Setting
	Text	"" (leave blank)
CommandButton	Name	cmdOK
	Caption	OK
	Default	True
CommandButton	Name	cmdCancel
	Caption	Cancel
	Cancel	True

TABLE 15-4.   Objects and Properties for the TestApp Project *(continued)*

12. Using the Project | References submenu from the VB main menu, select the references shown in Table 15-5. If other references are checked that aren't in this table, uncheck them so your project isn't cluttered with DLLs you aren't using.

13. Add the following code to the **Load** event procedure of the form. The **Move** method is going to center the form on the screen.

```
Private Sub Form_Load()
    Move ((Screen.Width - Me.Width) / 2), _
        ((Screen.Height - Me.Height) / 2)
End Sub
```

14. Add the following code to the **Click** event of the command button **cmdOK**. When the user triggers this event, the procedure is first going to check to make sure that the user entered a user ID in the **txtUserID** text box. The **Trim** statement removes any leading or trailing blank spaces from the string. The **Len** function returns the number of characters contained in the **txtUserID** text value. If the value is 0, then the text box is empty and the event is aborted.

References
Microsoft Visual Basic for Applications
Visual Basic Runtime Objects and Procedures
Visual Basic Object and Procedures
OLE Automation
UVB Components

TABLE 15-5.   References Used in the TestApp Project

This procedure uses the UVB Component's **Enrollment** object model and is assigned to the object variable *objEnroll.* The Enrollment **Login** method is called and the value from the **txtUserID** and **txtPassword** text boxes are the passed arguments, along with the variant array variables that will be used as placeholders for any values returned by the query performed in the **Login** method. If the first value in the variant array, *vRecNames,* is empty, that means that the query in the **Login** method executed correctly but no data was returned because the user entered either an incorrect user ID or password. If this happens, an error is raised and the error subroutine is executed notifying the user that a problem was encountered. If data was returned, the user's first and last names are returned in the variant array variables and a message box with his or her name in it greets the user.

```
Private Sub cmdOK_Click()

    If Len(Trim(txtUserID)) = 0 Then Exit Sub

    On Error GoTo err_cmdOK
    Dim objEnroll As New Enrollment
    Dim vRecNames As Variant
    Dim vRecValues As Variant

    Screen.MousePointer = vbHourglass

    objEnroll.Login txtUserID, txtPassword, _
        vRecNames, vRecValues

    If Not IsEmpty(vRecValues(0)) Then
        MsgBox "Greetings, " & vRecValues(0) & " " & vRecValues(1)
    Else
        Err.Raise 1
    End If

Exit_cmdOK:
    Set objEnroll = Nothing
    Screen.MousePointer = vbDefault
    Exit Sub

err_cmdOK:
    MsgBox "Problem encountered!"
    GoTo Exit_cmdOK
End Sub
```

15. Add the following code to the **Click** event of the command button
    cmdCancel. When this event is triggered, the form will unload from memory,
    thus terminating the program.

```
Private Sub cmdCancel_Click()
    Unload Me
End Sub
```

Now you're ready to run the application. When you run the program, the **Logon**
form will load. Once it does, type in the following student ID and password to gain
access to the system:

StudentID = 2401
Password = 186232

Assuming you type the values in correctly, you should receive a message box
with the student's name. In this case, the student's name is Phillip DeCarte. If you
type either the student's ID or password in incorrectly, you will get the message box
notifying you that a problem occurred. Granted, this isn't the sexiest or most
complicated program, but it definitely presents to you a useful sample of how to
access an ActiveX component.

Deploying an MTS Component

You've created your component, you've tested the logic as best you can, and now
you're ready to deploy the component onto your server that hosts MTS. So far, we've
only covered MTS from the standpoint of its purpose and role in the development cycle.

Most of what MTS does happens behind the scenes; the only visible element of MTS is
the MTS Explorer. MTS Explorer runs on the server and provides a way to manage and
deploy MTS packages. A *package* in MTS is a collection of one or more ActiveX DLL
components. Each component can contain one or more classes, which are referred to as
MTS objects. A package can be defined as either a Server Package, which means its
components will be activated in a dedicated server process, or a Library Package, which
means they will be activated in the client's process. Putting these terms into VB
perspective, a Server Package would be equivalent to an out-of-process server and a
Library Package would be equivalent to an in-process server.

The MTS Explorer is available for both Windows 95/98 and Windows NT. You
can install it on your workstation when you install either Personal Web Server or
Internet Information Server from the Windows NT 4.0 Option Pack. As the name
implies, the MTS Explorer uses the Windows Explorer metaphor for its user
interfaces. Figure 15-5 illustrates what the MTS Explorer looks like running on a
Windows 95 workstation and Figure 15-6 shows the MTS Explorer running on a
Windows NT server.

Functionally, both versions do exactly the same thing. They both allow you to package
transaction components into groups for transaction processing. Because Windows
95/98 does not have any integrated security the way that Windows NT does, MTS
Explorer running on Windows 95/98 cannot execute any security validation against

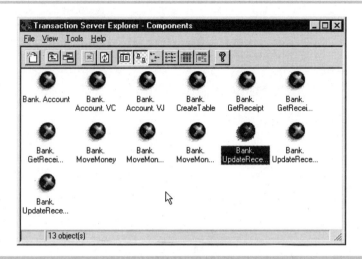

FIGURE 15-5. MTS Explorer on a Windows 95 workstation

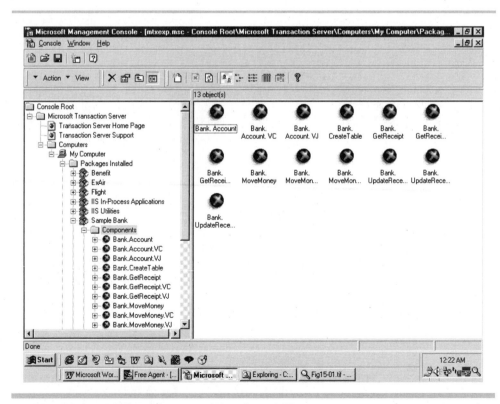

FIGURE 15-6. MTS Explorer on a Windows NT server

defined user roles the way it can on a Windows NT environment. Another difference is that on Windows 95/98, you cannot view the MTS environment in a hierarchical manner like you can on a Windows NT system. Even though there is a menu option to view the object hierarchy, the function simply was never implemented. So in order to navigate through the object hierarchy, double-click on an object to drill down the object model and use the Up One Level toolbar button to move up the hierarchy.

Now before we can use our MTS components in the MTS environment, we must first build and register those components as ActiveX DLLs. When we build an ActiveX DLL from within the VB IDE, our components are automatically registered as COM components. This means that all of the Registry entries that identify our VB class modules as COM components will be automatically created for us. This is why version compatibility is so important: it helps maintain COM registry consistency. This subject is covered in greater depth in Chapter 12. After our components have been registered as COM objects, we need to register them within the MTS run-time environment.

Registering COM components as MTS components is no more difficult than running the MTS Explorer itself. The following steps will illustrate what it takes to register the UVB Component we created in the previous exercise with MTS.

1. Using the component we built in the previous exercise, we must first restore our code to include the reference to the **ObjectContext** object model. Then we compile the component into an ActiveX DLL.

2. In the MTS Explorer, move down the hierarchy of My Computer to Packages Installed. Here you will see all the sample packages that came with MTS when it was installed. Choose Action | New from the MTS toolbar to invoke the Package Wizard. For Windows 95/98 users, choose File | New from the MTS menu bar. On the Package Wizard, select the "Create an empty package" option.

3. On the next dialog window, name the empty package **VBAA** and click the Next button to advance to the next window.

4. If you're running Windows 95/98, the empty package will now be created; however, Windows NT users will be prompted to notify MTS whose account the package should run under, as shown in Figure 15-7. We can have it run either under the account of the user who is currently logged on or use a specific user account. For this exercise, choose the default, Interactive user—the current logged-on user. Click the Finish button to complete the creation of the package.

5. With the creation of the package, we now have a place to put our MTS component. MTS Explorer has two ways of registering MTS components with a package. Either we can use the Component Wizard or we can simply drag and drop the component into the empty package. In either case, we need to drill down the package hierarchy to get to the Components folder. We do that by double-clicking on the VBAA package and double-clicking on the Components folder.

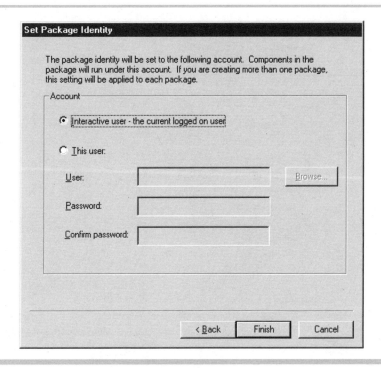

FIGURE 15-7. The Set Package Identity screen

6. Because dragging and dropping is taking the easy way out, let's add the component by using the Component Wizard. Select Action | New | Component from the MTS toolbar. For Windows 95/98 users, select File | New from the MTS menu bar.

7. Select "Import component(s) that are already registered" to install the UVB Component. The reason we selected this option versus "Install new component(s)" is that the latter is for components that aren't already installed and registered on the system. Since we built the UVB Component on the same system as MTS, the component is already registered on the system and we are only concerned with registering it with MTS. By selecting the Import component(s) option, the Choose Components to Import dialog box appears. In Figure 15-8, the dialog box has the Details checkbox marked to expand the view of the components to include the location of the component and its Class ID (or GUID—globally unique identifier). Find the UVB Component as **UVBComp.Enrollment**, select it, and click the Finish button. Voilá! We have now registered the ActiveX component as an MTS component. Figure 15-9 shows the MTS Explorer displaying the **UVBComp.Enrollment** component.

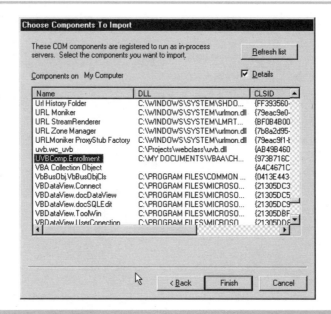

FIGURE 15-8. The Choose Components to Import dialog box displaying ActiveX components installed on the MTS system

FIGURE 15-9. The **UVBComp.Enrollment** component installed in the VBAA package

Using the MTS Component from VB

TestComp.vbp It's not much of a development life cycle but we've come pretty far. The story so far: We've created an ActiveX DLL. We tested the logic to ensure it worked and then compiled it. Then we registered it as an MTS component. Now for a reality check—it worked as an ActiveX DLL, but will it work as a true MTS component? The goal of this exercise is to show that it does work with MTS.

You might be wondering how we can truly see if the component is working with MTS. Oddly enough, the developers at Microsoft had to prove to the marketers at Microsoft the exact same thing. This is where the MTS Explorer becomes more than just a way to manage packages and components. It provides the only visual feedback that an MTS component is actually working, and we'll cover that after we build our application to test the component.

TEST THE CODE

1. The project to test the code is the same project we built in the "Creating an MTS Component" section, TestApp.vbp, which started on step 11. We've reprinted the code below to avoid any confusion and we've also named this project TestComp.vbp.

    Start a new instance of VB and select a Standard Exe application. The default form may be the startup form. Add the controls shown in Figure 15-4 and set their properties as shown in Table 15-4 found earlier in this chapter under the "Creating an MTS Component" section.

2. Using the Project | References submenu from the VB main menu, select the references shown in Table 15-6. If other references are checked that aren't in this table, uncheck them so your project isn't cluttered with DLLs you aren't using.

References
Microsoft Visual Basic for Applications
Visual Basic Runtime Objects and Procedures
Visual Basic Object and Procedures
OLE Automation
UVB Components

TABLE 15-6. References Used in the TestComp Project

3. Add the following code to the **Load** event procedure of the form. The **Move** method is going to center the form on the screen.

```
Private Sub Form_Load()
    Move ((Screen.Width - Me.Width) / 2), _
        ((Screen.Height - Me.Height) / 2)
End Sub
```

4. Add the following code to the **Click** event of the command button **cmdOK**. When the user triggers this event, the procedure is first going to check to make sure that the user entered a user ID in the **txtUserID** text box. The **Trim** statement removes any leading or trailing blank spaces from the string. The **Len** function returns the number of characters contained in the **txtUserID** text value. If the value is 0, then the text box is empty and the event is aborted. This procedure uses the UVB Component's **Enrollment** object model and is assigned to the object variable *objEnroll*. The Enrollment **Login** method is called and the values from the **txtUserID** and **txtPassword** text boxes are the passed arguments, along with the variant array variables that will be used as placeholders for any values returned by the query performed in the **Login** method. If the first value in the variant array, *vRecNames*, is empty, that means that the query in the **Login** method executed correctly but no data was returned because the user entered either an incorrect user ID or password. If this happens, an error is raised and the error subroutine is executed notifying them that a problem was encountered. If data was returned, the user's first and last name is returned in the variant array variables and a message box with his or her name in it greets the user.

```
Private Sub cmdOK_Click()

    If Len(Trim(txtUserID)) = 0 Then Exit Sub

    On Error GoTo err_cmdOK
    Dim objEnroll As New Enrollment
    Dim vRecNames As Variant
    Dim vRecValues As Variant

    Screen.MousePointer = vbHourglass

    objEnroll.Login txtUserID, txtPassword, _
        vRecNames, vRecValues
```

```
        If Not IsEmpty(vRecValues(0)) Then
            MsgBox "Greetings, " & vRecValues(0) & " " & vRecValues(1)
        Else
            Err.Raise 1
        End If


Exit_cmdOK:
        Set objEnroll = Nothing
        Screen.MousePointer = vbDefault
        Exit Sub


err_cmdOK:
        MsgBox "Problem encountered!"
        GoTo Exit_cmdOK
    End Sub
```

5. Add the following code to the **Click** event of the command button **cmdCancel**. When this event is triggered, the form will unload from memory, thus terminating the program.

```
Private Sub cmdCancel_Click()
    Unload Me
End Sub
```

Now for the moment of truth. We are about to see if the component is being executed via MTS or still using the ActiveX DLL without MTS. This is where having the MTS Explorer on the screen at the same time our program is executing comes in handy. Start the TestComp project and minimize all other windows on your desktop except for the application and the MTS Explorer. Make sure that you can see the MTS object in the MTS Explorer screen. Enter the Student ID and password like before, 2401 and 186232, respectively.

When you click the OK button, after a few seconds, if everything goes right, you should see the **UVBComp.Enrollment** object (the image that looks like a marble with an "X" on it) start to roll in place, as shown in Figure 15-10. You might notice that the "X" is slightly higher than it normally is when the MTS object is not instantiated. The marble will stay spinning until you click OK on the message box that is displaying Phillip DeCarte's name. By clicking OK on the message box, the logic within the **Click** event of the command button **cmdOK** sets the instance of the **Enrollment** object to **Nothing**, which releases the application's connection to the object; therefore, MTS releases it from memory because it's no longer needed.

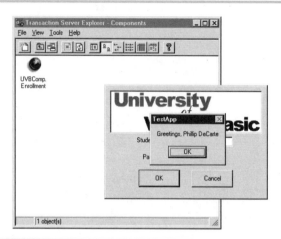

FIGURE 15-10. The TestComp project running in the foreground with MTS Explorer executing the Enrollment Transaction behind the scenes

ACCESSING AN MTS COMPONENT IN A DISTRIBUTED ENVIRONMENT

We've seen how a program can access an MTS component where both the application and MTS are running on the same system. But in a distributed computing environment, this isn't always going to be the case. So how do you resolve this?

Since the MTS component resides on a remote system, we probably won't have access to the type library or object library file for the component. In cases like this, we would use a technique called *late binding*. Late binding is the process of referencing a declaring variable simply as *Object* rather than by the name of the object itself. By doing so, in order to instantiate an object, we would use the **CreateObject** function. The following code is an example of late binding:

```
Dim objBinding As Object
Set objBinding = CreateObject("ObjectName.ClassName")
```

New to version 6.0 is the ability for the **CreateObject** function to specify on which server the object we wish to instantiate is located; therefore in step 4 of the **cmdOK_Click** event, the dimension statement used to instantiate the **Enrollment** object changes from this:

```
Dim objEnroll As New Enrollment
```

to this:

```
Dim objEnroll as Enrollment
Set objEnroll = CreateObject("UVBComp.Enrollment", _
    "Batcomputer")
```

In the above **CreateObject** function, we are still calling the **Enrollment** object, but instead of getting the object from the local system, we are getting it from the server called "Batcomputer." Obviously, the names for your servers are going to vary.

Windows API and Subclassing

T he Windows API was the centerpiece of Part I of this book. Using the Windows API raises the following issues:

- How to identify which Windows API functions to use.

- How to state properly the complex syntax of the Windows API functions.

- How to use Windows API functions in an application targeted for Windows 3.1 in addition to Windows 95/98/NT.

- How to use controls to simplify subclassing.

This appendix will provide the answers to these issues.

Identifying Which Windows API Functions to Use

One way to determine which Windows API functions to use is to buy one of the several reference books on the Windows API. However, computer programmers, used to obtaining information for free on the Net, are notorious freeloaders and may not want to pay for a book (except this one, of course). While we are sure you are not one of these freeloaders, you probably know someone who is, so you can pass along to them the following advice.

The solution is to get help. No, we don't mean reclining on a couch while someone with a thick Viennese accent charging $300 per hour asks you why you hate your mother, and when you reply that you don't hate your mother, responds that he can't help you if you won't cooperate. Instead, the help to which we are referring is the Platform Software Development Kit (SDK) help file. The Platform SDK help file explains the purpose, declaration, and parameters of the Windows API functions.

The Platform SDK help file is in the Microsoft Developer Network (MSDN) Library. The MSDN Library, which comes on two CDs, is included in the Professional and Enterprise versions of version 6 of Visual Basic. The CDs include, in addition to the Platform SDK help file, a wealth of other information. The MSDN Library CDs are in an HTML Help format.

If you do not have the MSDN Library CDs, you still can access the Platform SDK help file online at **msdn.microsoft.com**, and then choose MSDN Library Online. Microsoft does require that you first register to join MSDN. However, it only takes a few minutes to fill out a form. The "membership" is free and without obligation. Besides, this is one "club" that will let anyone in! The Platform SDK help file on MSDN Library Online also is in an HTML Help format.

If you are one of those old-timers who do not like newfangled online help and want your help file to be on your hard drive like in the good old days when, for example, Microsoft actually distributed product documentation with Visual Basic, you can download the help file. However, in one of life's many strange ironies, the download is not from Microsoft, but from Borland! The URL is **ftp://ftp.borland.com/pub/ delphi/techpubs/delphi2/win32.zip**. The help file weighs in at a hefty 7MB, so a fast connection would be helpful.

Obtaining the Correct Syntax for Constants and Declarations

Once you have determined which API functions to use, you next need to declare them correctly, and also include the constants they require. Since these API functions all have 73 parameters (or seem to) with weird names like *dwExStyle*, trying to memorize them is hopeless. Equally hopeless is trying to memorize constants that not only have strange names but also hexadecimal values.

Again, one solution is to buy one of the several reference books on the Windows API. However, there are other alternatives. The simplest is to use the API Viewer add-in in Visual Basic. This tool provides constants and declares which you can copy and paste into your code.

The API Viewer is simple to use. First, you load either a text file (Win32api.txt) or a database file (Win32api.mdb). The database file is faster to access, but on a fast computer there is little meaningful difference in speed between the text and database files. Once the text or database file is loaded, you choose Constants, Declares, or Types from the drop-down list box labeled "API Type." You then type the first few letters of the constant (or declaration or type) you are looking for in the text box labeled, naturally enough, "Type the first few letters of the word you are looking for." As you type, a "smart search" feature similar to the ones used in the Chapter 6 example lists the matches in a list box labeled "Available Items." Select the item you want and click the Add button. This will place the selected item in the list box labeled, for obvious reasons, "Selected Items." You can press the Copy button and then paste the constant or declaration into your code.

However, the information in the API Viewer is not complete. As you may recall from the "Putting Pictures on Your Menu" example in Chapter 4, the constants SM_CXMENUCHECK and SM_CYMENUCHECK could not be found with the API Viewer. The constants, indeed all constants used in the Windows API, are defined by one of the header (.h) files used by C and C++ programs. In the "Putting Pictures on Your Menu" example, we obtained the values of the constants SM_CXMENUCHECK and SM_CYMENUCHECK from the header file *winuser.h*.

The header files used by C and C++ programs should be on your hard drive if you have installed a C or C++ program such as Visual C++. However, some of our readers may not have a C or C++ program on their computers because C and C++ programming is against their religious beliefs (or is too hard). For those readers, there is another alternative. The C header files, which include the C function declarations as well as the constants, are contained in the Platform SDK itself (as opposed to the help file discussed above). The Platform SDK can be downloaded from Microsoft at **msdn.microsoft.com/developer/sdk/bldenv.htm**. The download not only is free, but you also don't even have to register.

Conditional Compilation

This book is about programming for 32-bit operating systems, specifically Windows 95, 98, and NT. Nevertheless, there still are numerous computers that run Windows 3.1, and 32-bit programs will not work on these computers. They require software that will work on a 16-bit operating system.

You have two choices. You can ignore these potential users of your software and hope they go away. If this is your attitude, you have good company: Microsoft. Your other choice is to write your software to support both 16-bit and 32-bit platforms.

If your choice is to support both 16-bit and 32-bit platforms, at the outset you have a minor problem. Versions 5 and 6 of Visual Basic only support 32-bit programs. However, version 4 of Visual Basic does support both platforms. This is why these authors still have their Visual Basic 4 CDs handy!

In supporting both 16-bit and 32-bit platforms, once again you have two choices. One choice is to use Visual Basic 4 to create the 16-bit version and Visual Basic 5 (or 6) to create the 32-bit version of your application. The problem is you will have two separate source codes—16-bit code for Visual Basic 4 and 32-bit code for Visual Basic 5. Having two separate source codes not only increases your maintenance chore but also introduces the risk of inconsistencies between your two code bases.

The other alternative is to use Visual Basic 4 to create both 16- and 32-bit versions of your application in one source code. Indeed, often code that works in a 32-bit platform also will work in a 16-bit platform. For example:

```
Dim num As Integer
Debug.Print num * 2
```

This code works on both platforms because declaring an integer variable or calling **Debug.Print** is exactly the same on both platforms.

However, Windows API functions often must be declared differently depending on the platform. One of the most significant differences is that parameters and return values which are an **Integer** (16-bit) in 16-bit operating systems are **Long** (32-bit) in 32-bit operating systems. For example, the API function **GetScrollRange** function retrieves the current minimum and maximum scroll box (thumb) positions for the specified scroll bar. For Win16 operating systems, the declaration of **GetScrollRange** is:

```
Public Declare Function GetScrollRange Lib "user32" _
    Alias "GetScrollRange" (ByVal hwnd As Integer, _
    ByVal nBar As Integer, lpMinPos As Integer, _
    lpMaxPos As Integer) As Integer
```

By contrast, for Win32 operating systems, the declaration of **GetScrollRange** is:

```
Public Declare Function GetScrollRange Lib "user32" _
   Alias "GetScrollRange" (ByVal hwnd As Long, _
   ByVal nBar As Long, lpMinPos As Long, _
   lpMaxPos As Long) As Long
```

For one source code to work on both platforms, you would have to declare **GetScrollRange** both ways. However, that would cause a compiler error since you cannot declare the same function name twice. The solution to this conundrum is to have the compiler "see" only the declaration that is appropriate for the operating system on which **GetScrollRange** is executing. This is done with *conditional compilation*:

```
#If Win16 Then

Public Declare Function GetScrollRange Lib "user32" _
   Alias "GetScrollRange" (ByVal hwnd As Integer, _
   ByVal nBar As Integer, lpMinPos As Integer, _
   lpMaxPos As Integer) As Integer

#ElseIf Win32 Then
Public Declare Function GetScrollRange Lib "user32" _
   Alias "GetScrollRange" (ByVal hwnd As Long, _
   ByVal nBar As Long, lpMinPos As Long, _
   lpMaxPos As Long) As Long
#Else
   ' Unsupported

#Endif
```

This control structure appears quite similar to the standard If-Else control structure. The constant Win16 refers to a Windows 16-bit operating system, principally Windows 3.1. The constant Win32 refers to a Windows 32-bit operating system—Windows 95, 98, or NT. Thus, you can use one source code to distribute your application to both platforms.

The utility of conditional compilation is not limited to the Windows API. Conditional compilation also can be used to distribute your application to different countries, or to exclude certain code from demonstration versions of your application.

Subclassing

The chapters in Part I explained subclassing. As those examples reflect, subclassing is fraught with danger. No, a mistake will not cause your computer to go up in a mushroom cloud, but your application may crash, and depending on your operating system, the "three-finger salute" (CTRL-ALT-DELETE) may be necessary.

Additionally, debugging a program which uses subclassing is quite difficult since using the Break command often will break your program.

A safer alternative, at least while you are learning subclassing, is to use a subclassing control. These custom controls handle the dangerous aspects of subclassing such as restoring the default Windows procedure. These subclassing controls also permit debugging.

One control, DbgWProc.Dll, is available from Microsoft. Per Microsoft, "The DbgWProc.Dll (Debug Object for AddressOf Subclassing) enables you to debug normally while a subclass is active without adding any unnecessary overhead to your finished product or distributing an extra component." While this is a mouthful, the DbgWProc.Dll control is available from MSDN at the "Controls/Components" page under Visual Basic "Samples and Downloads." The URL is **msdn.microsoft.com/vbasic/downloads/controls.asp**. The price is right—the control is free. However, you do have to register, since the controls are only for licensed users (you are, of course) of Visual Basic.

Another subclassing tool comes with the SpyWorks program. The filename, at least the one the authors have, is Dwsbc32d.ocx. The SpyWorks program is available from Desaware (**www.desaware.com**). Not coincidentally, Desaware's principal, Dan Appleman, is a, if not *the*, guru of Visual Basic Windows API programming. SpyWorks is not free, but of course you get what you pay for.

Index

J

About the CD

Each Visual Basic example from the book is represented on the accompanying CD-ROM. This CD-ROM is ISO-9660 compatible, which means that it will work in practically all CD-ROM drives. Once you access the CD-ROM, you will see all the examples arranged by chapter number and exercise example, as organized in the book. To use any example program from the text, simply copy the files into a new folder on your hard disk.

WARNING: BEFORE OPENING THE DISC PACKAGE, CAREFULLY READ THE TERMS AND CONDITIONS OF THE FOLLOWING COPYRIGHT STATEMENT AND LIMITED CD-ROM WARRANTY.

Copyright Statement

This software is protected by both United States copyright law and international copyright treaty provision. Except as noted in the contents of the CD-ROM, you must treat this software just like a book. However, you may copy it into a computer to be used and you may make archival copies of the software for the sole purpose of backing up the software and protecting your investment from loss. By saying, "just like a book," The McGraw-Hill Companies, Inc. ("Osborne/McGraw-Hill") means, for example, that this software may be used by any number of people and may be freely moved from one computer location to another, so long as there is no possibility of its being used at one location or on one computer while it is being used at another. Just as a book cannot be read by two different people in two different places at the same time, neither can the software be used by two different people in two different places at the same time.

Limited Warranty

Osborne/McGraw-Hill warrants the physical compact disc enclosed herein to be free of defects in materials and workmanship for a period of sixty days from the purchase date. If the CD included in your book has defects in materials or workmanship, please call McGraw-Hill at 1-800-217-0059, 9am to 5pm, Monday through Friday, Eastern Standard Time, and McGraw-Hill will replace the defective disc.

The entire and exclusive liability and remedy for breach of this Limited Warranty shall be limited to replacement of the defective disc, and shall not include or extend to any claim for or right to cover any other damages, including but not limited to, loss of profit, data, or use of the software, or special incidental, or consequential damages or other similar claims, even if Osborne/McGraw-Hill has been specifically advised of the possibility of such damages. In no event will Osborne/McGraw-Hill's liability for any damages to you or any other person ever exceed the lower of the suggested list price or actual price paid for the license to use the software, regardless of any form of the claim.

OSBORNE/McGRAW-HILL SPECIFICALLY DISCLAIMS ALL OTHER WARRANTIES, EXPRESS OR IMPLIED, INCLUDING BUT NOT LIMITED TO, ANY IMPLIED WARRANTY OF MERCHANTABILITY OR FITNESS FOR A PARTICULAR PURPOSE. Specifically, Osborne/McGraw-Hill makes no representation or warranty that the software is fit for any particular purpose, and any implied warranty of merchantability is limited to the sixty-day duration of the Limited Warranty covering the physical disc only (and not the software), and is otherwise expressly and specifically disclaimed.

This limited warranty gives you specific legal rights; you may have others which may vary from state to state. Some states do not allow the exclusion of incidental or consequential damages, or the limitation on how long an implied warranty lasts, so some of the above may not apply to you.

This agreement constitutes the entire agreement between the parties relating to use of the Product. The terms of any purchase order shall have no effect on the terms of this Agreement. Failure of Osborne/McGraw-Hill to insist at any time on strict compliance with this Agreement shall not constitute a waiver of any rights under this Agreement. This Agreement shall be construed and governed in accordance with the laws of New York. If any provision of this Agreement is held to be contrary to law, that provision will be enforced to the maximum extent permissible, and the remaining provisions will remain in force and effect.

NO TECHNICAL SUPPORT IS PROVIDED WITH THIS CD-ROM.